AN ENGLISH-HAWAIIAN
DICTIONARY

AN ENGLISH-HAWAIIAN DICTIONARY

WITH VARIOUS USEFUL TABLES

BY

H. R. HITCHCOCK

Principal of the Lahainaluna Seminary

CHARLES E. TUTTLE CO.: PUBLISHERS
Rutland, Vermont & Tokyo, Japan

Representatives
Continental Europe: BOXERBOOKS, INC., *Zurich*
British Isles: PRENTICE-HALL INTERNATIONAL, INC., *London*
Australasia: PAUL FLESCH & CO., PTY. LTD., *Melbourne*
Canada: m.g. hurtig ltd., *Edmonton*

Published by the Charles E. Tuttle Company, Inc.
of Rutland, Vermont and Tokyo, Japan
with editorial offices at Suido 1-chome, 2-6
Bunkyo-ku, Tokyo, Japan
Copyright in Japan, 1968, by Charles E. Tuttle Co., Inc.

Library of Congress Catalog Card No. 68-13870

PRINTED IN JAPAN

PUBLISHER'S FOREWORD

The first missionaries to Hawaii arrived in 1820, from Boston, bringing with them undaunted spirit, relentless determination, and the *palapala* ("book learning"). Eleven short years later, the first American school west of the Rockies—Lahainaluna Seminary—was established on the island of Maui.

With the influence of outsiders and the close ties with the United States came the importance of speaking English among the indigenous native people. Recognizing this, the Hawaiian government through its Board of Education, authorized educator H. R. Hitchcock of Lahainaluna Seminary to prepare an English-Hawaiian dictionary for use in the public schools. This is the book that Hitchcock took five years to compile and first published in 1887.

Long out of print, the revival of this dictionary is an important contribution to contemporary studies of comparative philology.

PREFACE.

IN the latter part of the year 1882 the subscriber was authorized by the Board of Education to prepare an English-Hawaiian Dictionary for use in the Public Schools. The work has been in progress since that date, and is now placed before the public in its entirety. Its scope has been widened, so as to embrace the wants of the English speaking community in their intercourse with Hawaiians.

Nearly sixteen thousand words have been defined; and over three thousand phrases illustrate the popular use of English and Hawaiian. More than three thousand synonyms give further scope to the Hawaiian in his use of English.

Diacritical marks and marks of accent follow those in Websters's High School Dictionary, from which the vocabulary has been formed. Webster's Unabridged Dictionary has been used as the final authority in the preparation of this work.

Definitions are numbered according to priority of usage.

Hawaiian words are accented, whenever they do not come within the general rules laid down elsewhere for their pronunciation.

The subscriber's grateful acknowledgements are due,

1st. To Revs. A. O. Forbes and L. Lyons for their revision of manuscript.

2nd. To Rev. W. B. Oleson for the Table of Prefixes and Suffixes.

3rd. To Hon. D. Kahaulelio, Police Justice of Lahaina, for valuable critical Hawaiian definitions.

4th. To Hon. A. Fornander for his valuable "Chronological Table of Events in Hawaiian History," continuing down to the year 1854.

5th. To C. M. Hyde, D. D., for the continuation of that Table down to the present time.

6th. And to many others who have expressed marked interest in the progress of this work.

H. R. HITCHCOCK.

LAHAINALUNA

HINTS

TO THE CORRECT PRONUNCIATION OF THE HAWAIIAN LANGUAGE.

1. The Hawaiian is a phonetic language, based upon the European pronunciation of its vowels.

2. The vowels have the following sounds:

A, a, *Italian*, as in **Ärm**; E, e, the sound of **ā** long, as in *obey;* I, i, the sound of long **ē** as in *machine;* O, o, its long sound, as in **ōld;** U, u, has the sound of *oo* in **mōōn.**

3. In pronouncing the digraphs (ai, ao, au, ei, eu, ou,) the stress of voice is given to the first letter; and the second is but lightly touched.

4. Words of two syllables are generally accented on the first. When this is not the case, words used in this book carry the accent mark. Thus: Po-ho is *chalk*, whilst po-ho′ is *loss;* mama means *chewed*, and ma′ma′ means *swift*, or *spry;* pu-a is a *flower* but pu-a′ is a *bundle*, or *herd*, or *flock.*

5. In words of more than two syllables the accent generally falls on the penult. When this is not the case words in this book carry the accent mark; thus, kanaka is a *man*, whilst ka′naka signifies *men.*

6. Reduplicated words follow the accent of their primitives as ku′hiku′hi from ku′hi; ho′loho′lo, from ho′lo; ha′kiha′ki from haki; the penult of the reduplicated word taking the primary accent.

7. The causative, *hoo*, prefixed to a verb does not change its accent, but receives, a secondary accent; thus, hoo′apo′no, hoo′ikai′ka, hoo′alo′halo′ha.

8. The sign of the passive voice, i-a, takes a secondary accent, as huna′, huna′i′a.

9. According to the best usage of the present day the Hawaiian consonants have their unchangeable sounds. Thus——"Ka-lo" is never pronounced *ta-ro* by educated Hawaiians, nor is "Ka-pu" changed by them into *ta-bu.*

10. Words incorporated into the Hawaiian language from the English retain their English consonant sounds. Thus——"Sabbath" becomes *subati* in Hawaiian and is not spelled *kapaki.* "Book" is written *buke* and not *puke;* "Bible" is *Baibala* and not *Paipala.*

SUGGESTIONS TO TEACHERS

This book is intended to assist the Hawaiian pupil to acquire a practical knowledge of the English Language. But if it is placed in the hands of the pupils merely as a book of reference, its mission will not be fulfilled. It is intended to be used as a *text-book in spelling and dictation*, with this advantage in its favor—the pupil can comprehend the meaning of each word as he proceeds. It is also intended to be used in sentence-building.

It is presumed that pupils using this book understand the signifiance of the parts of speech of the English Language, and that they also have a little knowledge of sentence-building.

This being the case, whenever a spelling lesson is assigned to the class, let it be so short that each pupil may become acquainted with the use of each word, by building sentences. Let each word, as it is spelled, be incorporated into a simple sentence, the remaining essential words being furnished by the pupils.

It is not necessary that the alphabetical order of the vocabulary be followed. Let the teacher give the class a list of words to be incorporated into sentences, requiring each pupil to prepare the sentences beforehand. Then, after the class has recited the lesson, and mistakes have been corrected, exercise it in the impromptu construction of sentences, thus forming habits of quick perception.

The idiom of the Hawaiian language requires that the qualifying adjective should *follow* its noun, and, that the predicate of a sentence should *precede* its subject. So the Hawaiian pupil will naturally say *"A horse fine," "runs swiftly the horse fine,"* unless his attention is called to these differences between the idoms of the two languages.

The Chronological Table, at the close of the book, may also be made a very interesting study to the pupil. Assign dates from the table to the class, and let each pupil cluster historical incidents around these dates, drawing them from all available sources. After the class has done its best in this line, let the teacher supplement class effort from his superior sources of information.

KEY TO PRONUNCIATION.

VOWELS.
LONG AND SHORT SOUNDS.

Ā, ā, *long,* as in..Āle, Fāte, Grāy
Ă, ă, *short,* as in...Ădd, Făt, Rănsom
Ē, ē, *long,* as in..Ēve, Mēte, Sēisure
Ĕ, ĕ, *short,* as in..End, Mĕt, Lĕopard
Ī, ī, *long,* as in..Īce, Knīfe, Thrīve
Ĭ, ĭ, *short,* as in...Ĭnch, Skĭn, Trĭbute
Ō, ō, *long,* as in...Ōld, Rōll, Repōse
Ŏ, ŏ, *short,* as in...Ŏdd, Sŏd, Hŏrrid
Ū, ū, *long,* as in..Ūse-ful, Tūbe
Ŭ, ŭ, *short,* as in..Ŭnder, Fŭn, Sŭpper
Ȳ, ȳ, *long,* as in..Flȳ, Simplifȳ
Y̆, y̆, *short,* as in..Hy̆mn, Simply̆

OCCASIONAL SOUNDS.

Â, â, as in...Âir, Fâir, Snâre
Ä, ä, *Italian,* as in..Ärt, Fäther, Scär
A, a, as in...Ask, Grass, Dance
A̤, a̤, *broad,* as in..Awl, Baulk, Talk
A̤, a̤, like short *o,* as in...What, Wander
Ê, ê, like ā, as in..Êre, Thêre, Hêir
Ė, ė, like ā, as in...Eight, Prėy Obėy
Ẽ, ẽ, as in...Vẽr-min, Ẽr-mine
Ị, ị, like ē, as in...Pịque, Machịne
Ï, ï, like ē, as in...Ïrksome, Vïrgin
Ó, ó, like ŭ, as in...Óther, Dóne, Són
O̤, o̤, like long oo, as in...Pro̤ve, Do̤, Mo̤ve
Q̤, q̤, like short oo, as in...Bq̤som, Wq̤man
Ô, ô, like a̤, as in...Ôrder, Fôrm, Stôrm
OO, o͞o, as in...Mo͞on, Fo͞od, Bo͞oty
OO, o͝o, as in...Wo͝ol, Go͝od, Fo͝ot
U, u, as in...Ûrge, Ûrchin
U, u, preceded by *r,* as in...Rule, Rumor
U̇, u̇, like o͝o, as in..Bu̇ll, Pu̇t, Bu̇sh
Oi, oi or Oy, oy, unmarked, as in..Oil, Join, Oyster, Toy
Ou, ou or Ow, ow, unmarked, as in....................................Out, Hound, Owl, Vowel

CONSONANTS.

Ç, ç, *soft,* like *sharp s,* as in...Çēde, Ac-çĕpt′
Ç, ç, *hard,* like *k,* as in..Çall, Çoncur
Ch, ch, (unmarked) as in..Child, Church
Çh, çh, *hard,* like *k,* as in...Çhorus, Eçho
Ċh, ċh, *soft,* like *sh,* as in..Ċhaise, Maċhine
Ḡ, ḡ, (unmarked), *hard,* as in...Ḡun, Tiḡer
Ġ, ġ, *soft,* as in...Ġem, Enġine
S, s, *sharp,* (unmarked), as in...Same, Rust
ṣ, *vocal* or *flat,* like *z,* as in...Haṣ, Amuṣe
Th, th, *sharp,* (unmarked), as in..Thirtieth
Th, th, *vocal* or *flat,* as in..Thither, Thou
X, x, like *gz,* as in..Exact, Example
Ph, ph, (unmarked), like *f,* as in.......................................Philanthropy
Qu, qu, (unmarked), like *kw,* as in....................................Quality
Wh, wh, (unmarked), like *hw,* as in...................................Why, When

ACCENT.

The principal accent is denoted by a heavy mark, (′) and the secondary by a light mark, (‵), as in **Ex-ăm′i-nā′tion,   Im′mor-tăl′i-ty.**

PREFIXES AND SUFFIXES.

PREPARED BY REV. W. B. OLESON,

PRINCIPAL OF THE KAMEHAMEHA SCHOOL.

English prefixes are syllables put before English words to change their meaning. Thus the word 'illegal' is composed of the prefix '*il*' and the recognized English word "*legal*."

But in such words as '*illustrate*,' the '*il*' is not a proper English prefix, but merely an initial syllable.

As a prefix, '*il*' means '*not*;' whilst, as an initial syllable merely, it is not separable from the rest of the word.

In the following tables the definitions are for the various syllables used as prefixes only. Some prefixes are sometimes merely intensive or superfluous, and are largely obsolete; that is, not used. Ex. A-wake, A-rise, Be-dazzle, Be-gird, For-do,

TABLE OF COMMON ENGLISH PREFIXES.

Il- In- Im- Ir- Un- Non- Dis-	as in	Il-lĭb′er-al In′se-cūre′ Im-prŏb′a-ble Ir-rĕs′o-lute Un-trūe′ Nŏn′con-tā′gious Dis-hŏn′est		means not	liberal. secure. probable. resolute. true. contagious. honest.
Dis- De- In- Non- Un-	as in	Dis′bē-liēve′ Dē-năt′u-ral-ize In-jŭs′tice Nŏn-rĕs′i-dence Un-păck′		means opposite to	believe. naturalize. justice. residence. pack.
De- De- En- En- Re- Re- Fore- Miss- A- A-	as in	Dē-crȳ′ Dē-fāme′ En-rāge′ En-fee′ble Rē-frĕsh′ Rē-gāin′ Fōre-tĕll′ Mis-spĕll′ A-sōak′ A-shōre′		means	cry down. to take from fame. to cause rage. to make {feeble. {fresh. gain again. tell before. spell wrong. soak in. on shore.

NOTE A.

Some prefixes are English words and define themselves.

Full- Half- O-ver- O-ver- Out-	as in	Full′grōwn Hǎlf′grōwn O′ver-come′ O′ver-grōwn′ Out′grōwn		denotes	perfection. imperfection. superiority. excess. excess.
Be- Coun-er- For- Sĕlf- With-	as in	Bē-spăt′ter Coun′ter-march For-swear′ Self′love With-stand′		means	over. opposite. from. own. against.

NOTE B.

As initial syllables, the following occur in many **English words, but as** proper English prefixes they **occur but comparatively few times.**

PREFIXES AND SUFFIXES.

Hĕm-i- Dĕm-i- Sĕm-i-	as in	Hĕm′i-sphere Dĕm′i-god Sem-i-cir-cle		means *half.*
Tràns- Hy-per-	as in	Tràns′plänt′ Hy′per-crit′ic-al		means *over.*
Sü′per- Ex-tra-	as in	Su′per-nat′u-ral Ex′tra-ju-di′cial		means *more than.*
Co- Con-	as in	Cō-ē′qual Con-ge′ni-al		means *with.*
An-te- Pre-	as in	An′te-room Pre′ex-ist′		means *before.*
An-ti- Con-tra-	as in	An′ti-sla′very Con′tra-dis-tinc′tion		means *against.*
Sub- In-ter- Post- Ex- Cir-cum-	as in	Sub-of′fi-cer In′ter-is′land Pŏst-nup′tial Ex-gov-er-nor Cir-cum-nav-i-gate	means	*under.* *among.* *after.* *former.* *around.*

English suffixes are syllables placed after English words to change their meaning. The same distinction needs to be made between *suffixes* and *final* syllables as between *prefixes* and *initial* syllables. Thus: "able," is a true suffix in **"văl′u-able,"** but a final syllable merely in the word **"căp′able."** In the latter word it is not separable from it, while in the former word it denotes" having value."

Words ending in 'ness' and 'ship' denote 'quality' or 'being,' as 'goodness,' 'fellow*ship*.' Words ending in 'some' denote 'emphasis,' as lone-*some*.

Words ending in 'ist' denote attachment to a particular calling or profession; as 'journal-*ist*.'

Words ending in 'age, denote the condition of a person or thing; as 'vassal-age.' Several suffixes have nearly the same force in the words in which they are found.

-i-ty -ment -i-on -a-tion -ly -ance	as in	Re-ăl′i-ty Con-tĕnt′ment Con-trăct′ion Rĕf′or-mā′tion Friĕnd′ly Rē-pĕnt′ance	state of being	*real.* *contented.* *contracted.* *re-formed.* *friends.* *repent-ant.*

The following table includes all the commoner suffixes not already noticed.

-like -ish -y	as in	States′man-*like* Child′*ish* Dŭst′y	means	*resembling.*
-er -or	as in	Writ-*er* Ăg′i-tā′tor	means	*one who.*
-al -a-ry	as in	Ĕdu-cā′tion-*al* Dic-tion-*a-ry*	means	*relating to.*
-a-ble -ful -ive -ous	as in	Văl′u-*a-ble* Hōpe′*ful* Of-fĕn′*sive* Dăn′ger-*ous*	means	*having the.* *qualities of.*
-less -a-ble	as in	House′*less* Read-*a-ble*	means	*without.* *that one may.*

ABBREVIATIONS
Used in the Vocabulary.

adj	Adjective	*pl*	Plural
adv	Adverb	*prep*	Preposition
conj	Conjunction	*p. p*	Participle past
f	Feminine	*pron*	Pronoun
interj	Interjection	*Sing*	Singular
m	Masculine	Syn	Synonym
n	Noun	*v*	Verb

AN
English-Hawaiian Dictionary

A art. 1. Kekahi. *A dog ran,* holo kekahi ilio.
2. He. *It is a dog,* he ilio ia.

A-báft', *adv.* Mahope, *abaft the main mast,* Mahope o ke kia nui. Pili i na wahi maluna o ka moku.

A-băn'don, *v.* E haalele loa; e waiho loa'ku. *He abandoned his evil habits.* Waiho loa'ku la oia i kana mau hana ino.

A-băn'doned, *adj.* 1. Haalele loa ia; SYN. forsakened. *The abandoned house,* Ka hale i haalele loa ia.
2. Lilo loa i ka hewa; puni loa i ka hewa. SYN. profligate.

A-bāse', *v.* E hoohaahaa. SYN. degrade; humble; cast down.

A-bāse'ment, *n.* Ka hoohaahaa ana. SYN. degradation.

A-băsh', E hoopilihua; e hoohilahila; e pilihua. SYN. confuse; disconcert; shame. *Peter was abashed when his master looked at him.* Pilihua o Petero i ka nana'na o kona Haku iaia. *Do not confuse me with your talk.* Mai hoopilihua mai ia'u me kou walaau.

A-băt'a-ble, *adj.* Hiki ke hooemiia.

A-bāte', *v.* E emi; e hooemi. SYN. decrease; subside; lessen. *The waters abate,* ke emi nei na wai. *The pain is lessened,* ua hooemiia ka eha.

Ab-brē'vi-āte, *v.* E hoopokole; e hoohapa mai. SYN. abridge. *Abbreviate your speech,* e hoopokole i kau haiolelo.

Ab-bre'vi-ā'tion, *n.* Ka hoopokole ana; ka hoohapa ana mai. SYN. abridgement.

Ăb'di-cāte, *v.* 1. E haalele aku. SYN. vacate. *Abdicate the throne,* e haalele aku i ka noho alii. *Vacate the chair,* e haalele i ka noho
2. E waiho aku. SYN. resign. *To resign the office,* E waiho aku i ka oihana.

Ăb'di-cā'tion, *n.* Ka haalele aku ana; ka waiho aku ana.

Ab-dō'men, *n.* Ka opu; kea hakahaka.

Ab-dŏm'i-nal, *adj.* Pili ana i ke kea hakahaka.

Ab-dŭet', *v.* E kai malu' aku; e kaili. SYN. kidnap. *He abducted the child,* ka-ili aku la oia i ke keiki.

Ab-dŭe'tion, *n.* Ke kai malu' an'aku; ke kaili ana. SYN. kidnapping.

Ab-dŭe'tor, *n.* Ka mea nana e kai malu' aku.

A-bēam', *adv.* Pa aoao mai. *The wind is abeam,* pa aoao mai ka makani.

A-bĕd', *adv.* Maluna o ka moe; ma ka moe.

Ăb'er-rā'tion, *n.* 1. Ke kekee ana.
2. Ka haalele ana i ka pololei.
3. He opulepule o ka noonoo.

A-bĕt', *v.* 1 E kokua ma na mea pono ole. *Do not abet the thief,* mai kokua i ka aihue.
2. E kokua malu'. SYN. connive at. *Do not connive at evil,* mai kokua malu' i ka hewa.

A-bey'-ançe, *n.* Ka hookaulua ana me ka hooko ole. *The work was in abeyance,* ua hookaulua ia ka hana.

Ab-hŏr', *v.* E hoopailua loa. SYN. loathe; abominate. *Abhor evil,* e hoopailua loa i ka hewa.

Ab-hŏr'rençe, *n.* Ka hoopailua loa ana. SYN. loathing; detestation.

Ab-hŏr'rent, *adj.* Ku i ka hoopailua ia. SYN. detestable.

A-bīde', *v.* 1. E noho iki; e hoomoana. SYN. stay. *Abide over night,* e noho a hala ka po.
2. E paa. *I will abide by your decision,* e paa ana au ma kau olelo hooholo.

A-bid'ing-plāçe, *n.* He wahi noho paa. SYN. home.

A-bil'i-ty, *n.* He mana hooko. SYN. capacity.

Ăb'ject, *adj.* 1. Haahaa loa. SYN. mean, vile. *An abject man,* he kanaka haahaa loa.
2. Haukae; Paumaele.
3. *Abject poverty,* ilihune loa.

Ab-jĕct′ly, *adv.* Me ka haukae loa; ma ke ano hoopilimeaai.

Ab-jūre′, *v.* E haalele me ka hoohikiia.

A-blāze′, *adv.* Aa i ke ahi. SYN. on fire.

Ā′ble, *adj.* 1. Makaukau. SYN. capable. *An able man* he kanaka makaukau.
2. Hiki. SYN. can. *Are you able to do this,* hiki anei ia oe ke hana i keia?

Ā′ble-bŏd′ied, *adj.* Kino ikaika; pui-pui.

Ā′bly, *adv.* Me ke akamai; me ka ma-kaukau.

Ab-lū′tion, *n.* 1. Ka holoi ana i ka ma-ka.
2. Ka holoi ana i ke kino okoa.
3. Ka auau ana.

Ab-nŏr′mal, *adj.* Ano e; ku ole i ka rula. SYN. deformed.

A-bŏard′, *adv.* Maluna o ka moku, a o ke kaa paha. *All aboard!* pau mai ma-luna o ka moku, (a o ke kaa paha).

A-bŏde′, *n.* Wahi noho paa. SYN. abid-ing place.

A-bŏl′ish, *v.* E hoopau; e hoonoa. SYN. *Abolish the law,* e hoonoa i ke kanawai.

Ab′o-li′tion, *n.* Ka hoopau ana; ka hoonoa ana. SYN. Abrogation.

A-bŏm′i-na-ble, *adj.* Ino loa; pelapela loa.

A-bŏm′i-nate, *v.* E hoopailua loa. SYN. abhor; detest.

A-bŏm′i-nā′tion, *n.* He mea hoopai-lua; mea pelapela.

Ăb′o-rig′i-nal, *adj.* Mai ka mua mai; maoli. *The aboriginal inhabitants,* na kupa maoli o ka aina.

Ăb′o-rig′-i-nes, *n.* Na kupa maoli o ka aina.

A-bŏr′tion, *n.* Ka hanau e ana. Hee wale.

A-bŏr′tive, *adj.* Makehewa; hoka. *Abortive efforts,* ka hooikaika makehe-wa.

A-bound′, *v.* E paapu.

A-bout′, *prep.* Aneane; kokoke. *He is about to go,* kokoke ia e hele. *About a thousand,* aneane he tausani. SYN. near-ly.

A-bout′, *adv.* 1. Ma kauwahi. SYN. near. *He is about the house,* aia ia ma kauwahi o ka hale.
2. Ma; *I am about my work,* eia au ma ka'u hana.

A-bŏve′, *prep. and adv.* Kiekie ae; ma-luna'e.

A-bŏve′board, *adv.* Ma ke akea; me ka huna' ole; me ka epa ole.

A-bŏve′mĕn′tioned, *adj.* I oleloia ma-luna'e nei.

A-bra′sion, *n.* Ke koli ana a pohole.

A-brĕast′, *adv.* 1. Papa. *Stand abreast,* e ku papa mai.
2. Kupono i kekahi wahi, a mea paha. *Abreast of the harbor,* kupono i ke awa.

A-bridge′, *v.* E hoopokole; e hoohapa mai. SYN. abbreviate.

A-bridge′ment, *n.* Ka hoopokole ana; ka hoohapa ana mai.

A-broad′, *adv.* 1. Laha. *Death is abroad in the land,* laha ka make ma ka aina.
2. I na aina e. *He went abroad,* hele oia i na aina e.

Ăb′ro-gāte, *v.* E hoonoa. SYN. abolish.

Ab-rŭpt′, *adj.* 1. Kalakala. *An abrupt speech,* he olelo kalakala.
2. Ku; *An abrupt precipice,* he pali ku.

Ab-rŭpt′ly, *adv.* 1. Me ke kalakala.
2. Ano pali ku.

Ăb′sçess, *n.* He mai palahee.

Ab-scŏnd′, *v.* E mahuka; e holo malu'.

Ab-scŏnd′er, *n.* He mea mahuka.

Ăb′sençe, *n.* Ke kaawale ana ma kahi e.

Ăb′sent, *adj.* Ma kahi e. *Absent friends,* na hoa'loha ma kahi e.

Ab-sĕnt′, *v.* E hookaawale aku. *Do not absent yourself for a long time,* mai hoo-kaawale aku oe no ka wa loihi.

Ăb′sen-tee′, *n.* Ka mea kaawale aku.

Ăb′so-lūte, *adj.* 1. Loa. *Absolute power,* mana loa. *Absolute perfection,* hemolele loa.
2. Keakea ole ia. *Absolute promise,* olelo paa i keakea ole ia. SYN. uncon-ditional.

Ăb′so-lute-ly, *adv.* 1. Me ke keakea ole ia. *Govern absolutely,* e hoomalu me ke keakea ole ia mai.
2. Maoli. SYN. truly. *It is absolutely so,* pela maoli no; oiaio maoli no.

Ăb′so-lū′tion, *n.* Ke kala ana i ka he-wa. SYN. pardon.

Ab-sŏlve′, *v.* E kala; e kala i ka hewa.

Ab-sŏrb′, *v.* 1. E omo. *The thirsty soil absorbs water,* ke omo nei ka lepo panoa i ka wai. SYN. drink in.
2. Lilo loa. *He is absorbed in his books,* lilo loa oia i kona mau buke.

Ab-sŏrb′ent, *n.* Ka mea e omo ana.
2. Ke kumu i lilo loa ai ka manao.

Ab-sŏrb′ing, *adj.* E hoolilo pau ana i ka noonoo. *An absorbing thought,* he manao e hoolilo pau ana i ka noonoo.

Ab-sŏrp′tion, *n.* 1. Ka omo ana. *The absorption of moisture,* ka omo ana i ka ma-u'.
2. Ka lilo loa ana. *Absorption of mind,* ka lilo loa ana i ka noonoo.

Ab-stāin′, *v.* E hookaawale aku; e hoo-kaaokoa'ku. SYN. refrain; forbear.

Ab-stĕ′mi-oŭs, *adj.* 1. Pakiko.
2. E umi ana i ke kuko.

Ăb′sti-nençe, *n.* Ke kaaokoana'ku.

Ăb′stract, *n.* Moolelo i kaomiia. SYN. epitome.

Ab-stràct′, *v.* 1. E unuhi ae.
2. E kaili aku, SYN. purloin.

Ăb′stract, *adj.* Kuu kaawale; pili ole i kekahi mea. *An abstract number,* he helu ku kaawale, (e laa 10.) *An abstract idea,* he manao kaawale, pili ole i ke-kahi mea i ike maka ia.

Ab-strūse′, *adj.* Pohihihi; maopopo ole.

Ab-sûrd′, *adj.* Lapuwale; ku i ka aka-aka; kaawale loa mai ka oiaio.

Ab-sûrd′i-ty, *n.* He mea lapuwale; he manao lapuwale.

Ab-sûrd′ly, *adv.* Me ke lapuwale.

A-bǔn′dançe, *n.* Ka lawa pono.

A-bǔn′dant, *adj.* Lawa pono; nui wale.

A-būse′, *n.* 1. Ka hana ino. *Abuse of the body,* ka hana ino i ke kino. 2. Ka hoomainoino.

A-būṣe′ (a-būze), *v.* E hoomainoino; e hana ino.

A-bū′sive, *adj.* Hoomainoino; hana ino.

A-bǔt′ment, *n.* 1. Ka pili pu ana. 2. He kahua i kukuluia no ke alahaka.

A-bȳss′, *n.* He wahi kuhoho.

Ac-a-dĕm′ic,) *adj.* Pili i ke kula kie-
Ac-a-dĕm′ic-al,) kie. *An academical education,* ka hoonaaua-oia o ke kula kiekie.

A-cǎd′e-my, *n.* 1. He kula kiekie. 2. He ahahui imi naauao.

Ăc-çēde′, *v.* E ae aku.

Ac-çĕ′ler-āte, *v.* E hoomama; e hoohi-kiwawe; e awiwi. SYN. hasten.

Ăc′çĕnt, *n.* Ke kalele ana o ka leo. *Mark of accent,* he kaha kalele leo.

Ac-çĕnt′, *v.* E kalele leo.

Ac-çĕpt′, *v.* 1. E ae; e lawe. *Accept a report,* e lawe i ka olelo hoike. *Accept a proposition,* e ae i ka manao.

Ac-çĕpt′ançe, *n.* 1. Ka ae ana e lawe. 2. Ka lawe ana. *The acceptance of the report,* ka lawe ana i ka olelo hoike.

Ac-çĕpt′a-ble, *adj.* Oluolu i ka manao, ku i ka makemake.

Ac-çĕpt′a-bly, *adv.* Me ke aponoia, me ka maikai. *It was done acceptably,* ko ia mea me ka maikai.

Ăc′çess, *n.* Ke komo ana aku.

Ăc-çĕss′i-ble, *adj.* 1. Hiki. *Knowledge is accessible to all,* he hiki i ka poe a pau ke loaa i ke ike. 2. Laulea; oluolu. *The teacher is accessible to the scholar,* oluolu ke kumu i ka haumana. SYN. friendly.

Ac-çĕs′so-ry, *n.* He kokua ma ka hoo-haki kanawai; he kokua ma ka hewa. SYN. accomplice.

Ac′çi-dĕnt, *n.* He poino i ulia wale.

Ac′çi-dĕnt′al, *adj.* Ulia wale.

Ac′çi-dĕnt′al-ly, *adv.* Ma ke ano ulia wale. *He was hurt accidentally,* ua eha wale mai no ia.

Ac-claim′,) *n.* Hoo'ho mahalo.
Ac′-ela-mā′tion,)

Ăc-cli′māte, *v.* E hoomaamaa i ke kau o ka aina.

Ac-cliv′i-ty, *n.* Hoopiina mauna.

Ac-cŏm′mo-dāte, *v.* E kokua; e hoo-lako. *He accommodated me with a horse,* ua kokua mai oia i lio no'u. SYN. assist.

Ac-cŏm′mo-da′ting, *adj.* Kokua; olu-olu. *An accommodating man,* he kanaka kokua. SYN. obliging.

Ac-cŏm′mō-dā′tion, *n.* Ke kokua ana; ka hoolako ana.

Ac-cŏm′mo-dā′tionṣ, *n. pl.* Na lako, na pono o ka noho ana. *Poor accommodations,* hemahema na lako o ka noho ana.

Ac-cŏm′pa-ni-ment, *n.* Mea kokua pu. *Instrumental accompaniment,* ke ko-kua pu ana o na mea kani i ka leo.

Ac-cŏm′pa-ny, *v.* E hele pu; e ukali.

Ac-cŏm′pliçe, *n.* He hoa ma ka hewa.

Ac-cŏm-plish, *v.* E hooko. SYN. complete; perform.

Ac-cŏm′plished, *adj.* 1. Hookoia. SYN. completed. 2. Akamai; makaukau ma na mea na-auao.

Ac-cŏm′plish-ment, *n.* Ka hooko ana. SYN. fulfilment. 2. *A full accomplishment,* puni eo.

Ac-cŏrd′, *v.* E ku-like; e lokahi.

Ac-cŏrd′ançe, *n.* Ku-like. *In accordance with his ideas,* ku-like me kona ma-nao.

Ac-cŏrd′ing to, *prep.* Mamuli o. SYN. in accordance with.

Ac-cŏrd′ing-ly, *adv.* Like. SYN. like-wise. *Do accordingly,* e hana like. 2. No laila; no ia mea hoi. SYN. there-fore; for that reason.

Ac-cŏst′, *v.* E kamailio mua aku.

Ac-count′, *n.* 1. He moolelo. SYN. nar-rative. 2. He helu; helu aie. 3. Accounts, na helu. *Public accounts,* na buke helu o ke aupuni.

Ac-count′, *v.* E hoike; e hoike lea. *I cannot account for it,* aole hiki ia'u ke hoike lea no ia mea.

Ac-count′a-bil′i-ty, *n.* 1. Ku i ka hoo-kolokoloia. *Man's accountability to God,* ke ku o ke kanaka i ka hookolokoloia imua o ke Akua. *Man's responsibility to man,* ka pono o ke kanaka i ke ka-naka. 2. Ka ili ana. *The responsibility of the work rests upon him,* ili ka hana maluna ona.

Ac-count′a-ble, *adj.* Ka noho ana ma-lalo o ka hooponopono ana o hai. 2. Hiki ke hoomaopopoia. 3. Kupono ke hoike nona iho. *An id-iot is not responsible,* kupono ole ka hu-po ke hoike nona iho.

Ac-count′ant, *n.* Mea malama buke helu

Ac-cŏu′ter-ments, *n.* 1. Na mea e ka-hiko ai ka lio 2. Na mea e kahiko ai a nani ke kino.

Ac-crĕd′-it, *v.* E hoapono ma ka pala-pala

Ac-crūe′, *v.* E mahuahua mai.

Ac-cū′mu-lāte, *v.* 1. E ho'ahu. SYN. amass. *Accumulate wealth,* ho'ahu wai-wai. 2. E hooiliili; e hooakoakoa. SYN. collect. *Collect stones,* e hooiliili i na po-haku.

Ac-cū'mu-lā'tion, *n.* Ka ho'ahu ana; ka hooiliili ana.

Ac'eu-ra-çy, *n.* Pololei o ka hana, a olelo paha.

Ac'eu-rāte, *adj.* Pololei loa. SYN. exact.

Ac-cûrs'ed, *adj.* Hooinoinoia.

Ac'eu-sā'tion, *n.* Olelo hoohewa.
2. Ka hoopii ana no kekahi hewa.

Ac-cūṣe', *v.* E hoopii no ka hewa; e hoohewa.

Ac-cūṣ'er, *n.* Ka mea nana e hoohewa.

Ac-cūṣ'-tom, *v.* E hoomaamaa; e hoowalea.

Ac-cûṣ'tomed, *adj.* Pakua'. SYN. usual; common. *A common occurrence,* he mea pakua' wale; mea maa wale.

A-çêrb'i-ty, *n.* Awahia; awahia o ka naau.

Ache (āk), *n.* He eha; he hui. SYN. pain.

A-chiëve', *v.* E loaa mamuli o ka hooikaika; e lanakila. *Achieve success,* e ko aku a lanakila.

A-chiëve'ment, *n.* 1. Ka hana i lanakila.
2. Hana nui i hookoia.

A'çid, *n.* He mea awaawa.

Ac-knŏwl'edġe, *v.* 1. E ae i ka pono, a hewa paha. SYN. admit; own. *I acknowledge I was wrong,* ke ae nei au ua hewa wau.
2. E hooia. *He acknowledged the contract,* ua hooia oia i ka olelo ae-like.

Ac-knŏwl'edġe-ment, *n.* 1. Ka ae ana'ku. SYN. admission; confession.
2. Ka hooia ana. *Acknowledgement of the contract,* ka hooia ana i ka palapala ae-like.

Ac'me, *n.* Ka wekiu; ka piko.
2. *Acme of the disease,* ka mahuahua loa mai o ka mai.

A-cōū'stics, *n.* Ka ike e pili ana i ka leo; ke kani; ka haalulu.

Ac-quäint'ançe, *n.* 1. He hoalauna; kanaka ike pono ia.
2. He ike; ka maopopo.

Ac'qui-êsçe', *v.* E apono.
2. E ae i ka manao, a makemake o hai. SYN. submit; yield. *I acquiesce in your decision,* ke ae nei au i kau olelo hooholo.

Ac-quīre', *v.* E loaa. SYN. obtain; get.

Ac'qui-ṣi'tion, *n.* Ka loaa ana; ka mea loaa.

Ac-quīt', *v.* E hookuu hala ole. SYN. *to clear.*

Ac-quīt'tal, *n.* Ka hookuu ana no ka hala ole.

A'ere (ā'ker), *n.* He eka; he 160 roda kuea.

A'ere-aġe, *n.* Ka nui o na eka. SYN. number of acres.

Ae'rid, *adj.* Mulea; awahia; wela. SYN. pungent.

Ae'ri-mō'ni-oŭs, *adj.* Kalae'a; aki.

Ae'ri-mō-ny, *n.* He kalae'a o ka olelo, o ka leo.

Āe'ro-băt, *n.* He kanaka e kea'ka ana me kona kino.

A-erōss', *prep. and adv.* Mai kekahi aoao a i kekahi aoao.
2. *To place one thing across another,* e kau pea i kekahi mea maluna o kekahi.

Áct, *v.* E hana; e hooko.
2. E hoike. *Act the coward,* e hoike iaia iho he maka'u wale.

Áct, *n.* Ka hana.
2. Ka mea i hanaia.
3. He kanawai o ka ahaolelo.

Ae'tion, *n.* 1. He hana.
2. He hoopii imua o ke kanawai.
3. He kaua iwaena o na moku kaua. SYN. naval action.
4. *A man of action, not of words,* he kanaka hooko, aole he kanaka olelo wale.

Ae'tion-a-ble, *adj.* Ku i ka hoopiiia.

Áet'ĭve, *adj.* Mama; miki ma ka hana; makaala. SYN. wide awake.

Ac-tiv'i-ty, *n.* Ka makaala; ka miki ma ka hana. *Mental activity,* ka makaala o ka noonoo.

Áet'or, *n.* 1. He kanaka kea'ka.
2. Ka mea e hana ana.

Áet-ū-al, *adj.* See *Real,*

Áet'u-al-ly, *adv.* SYN. really. *It is actually so,* pela maoli no.

Áet'ū-āte, *v.* 1. E hooeueu; e paipai. SYN. incite; arouse.
2. E hoala. SYN. arouse.

A-eū'men, *n.* Ka makaala o ka noonoo; noeau. SYN. sagacity.

A-cūte', *adj.* 1. Oi. *Acute angle,* huina oi.
2. Eha loa. *Acute pain,* he eha loa.
3. Maalea. SYN. shrewd.
4. Noeau. *An acute reasoner,* he kanaka noonoo noeau.

A-cūte'ly, *adv.* 1. Ehaeha loa.
2. Me ka noeau.

Ad'aġe, *n.* He olelo ao; olelo maa mau. SYN. proverb.

A-dăpt', *v.* E hookupono; e hoopili-pono.

Ad'ap-tā'tion, *n.* Ka pili pono ana; ke kupono ana.

Ádd, *v.* 1. E hoouluulu. *Add numbers,* e hoouluulu i na helu.
2. E kui; e pakui. *Add another room to the house,* e pakui hou mai i keena no ka hale.

Ad-di'tion, *n.* 1. Ka hoouluulu.
2. Ke kui ana; ka pakui ana.

Ad-di'tion-al, *adj.* Hou mai. *Additional expense,* lilo hou mai. *Additional trouble,* pilikia hou mai.

Ad-diet', *v.* E maaa; e walea. *Addicted to strong drink,* maa i ka wai ona.

Ád'dled, *adj.* Howai; huailo. *Addle-pated,* huailo ka noonoo.

Ad-drēss', *v.* E kamailio i kekahi aku. *I address myself to you,* ke kamailio aku nei au ia oe.
2. E kakauinoa ma ka palapala. SYN. direct.

Ad-drĕss′, *n.* 1. He haiolelo. SYN. lecture.
2. Ka inoa i kakauia ma ka palapala, a ukana paha. SYN. superscription.
3. Akamai; makaukau. SYN. dexterity; skill.

A-dĕpt′, *n.* He mea makaukau; mea akamai. *An adept at lying,* he mea makaukau i ka wahahee.

Ăd′e-quāte, *adj.* Lawa pono.

Ad-hēre′, *v.* 1. E kupaa, standfast. *Adhere to the truth,* e kupaa i ka oiaio.
2. E pili paa; e pipili. SYN. stick. *Glue adheres to wood,* pipili ke gelu′ i ka laau.

Ad-hēr′ent, *n.* Mea kupaa. *An adherent of the King,* mea kupaa i ka Moi.

Ad-hēr′ent, *adj.* Pili pu; pili paa. SYN. clinging.

Ad-hē′sive, *adj.* Pipili. SYN. sticky. *Mud is sticky,* pipili ka lepo palolo.

A-dieŭ′, *adv.* He huaolelo e haawi ana i ke aloha kaawale. SYN. goodbye; farewell.

Ad-jā′çent, *adj.* E waiho kokoke ana; pili pu ana. SYN. adjoining.

Ăd′jee-tive, *n.* He hai ano.

Ad-join′ing, *adj.* E pili pu ana.

Ad-joŭrn′, *v.* E hoopanee i ka halawai.
2. *Adjourn sine die,* e hoopau loa i ka halawai.

Ad-joŭrn′ment, *n.* Ka hoopanee ana. *The adjournment of legislature,* ka hoopanee ana i ka ahaolelo.

Ăd′junct, *n.* 1. Hua olelo pili pu.
2. Mea pili pu. *Knowledge is an adjunct to civilization,* he mea pili pu ka ike i ka naauao o ka noho ana.

Ad-jūre′, *v.* E koi mamuli o ka hoohiki.

Ad-jŭst′, *v.* E hooponopono. *Adjust the difficulty,* e hooponopono i ka hihia.

Ăd′ju-tant, *n.* He luna kokua; he hope. *Adjutant-General,* he hope kenela.

Ad-mĭn′is-ter, *v.* 1. E lawelawe. *Administer public affairs,* e lawelawe ma ka oihana aupuni.
2. E haawi. *Administer reproof,* e haawi i ka olelo ao. *Administer relief,* e haawi i ke kokua.
3. E hooponopono. *Administer an estate,* e hooponopono i ka waiwai.
4. *Administer an oath,* e hoohiki.

Ăd-mĭn′is-trā′tion, *n.* 1. Ka lawelawe ana; ka hooko ana.
2. Na poo o ka oihana o ke aupuni. *The present administration,* na poo e lawelawe nei o ke aupuni.

Ad-mĭn′is-tra′tor, *n.* 1. He mea e lawelawe ana ma kekahi oihana aupuni.
2. He luna hooponopono waiwai.

Ăd′mi-ra-ble, *adj.* Ku i ka mahalo nui.

Ăd′mi-ral, *n.* He adimarala; ke ′lii o ke aumoku kaua o ke aupuni.

Ăd′mi-rā′tion, *n.* Ka mahalo nui.

Ad-mīre′, *v.* E mahalo nui; e apono maikai, SYN. esteem.

Ad-mīr′er, *n.* 1. Mea mahalo mai.
2. He ipo. SYN. lover.

Ad-mĭs′si-ble, *adj.* Kupono; kupono ke hookomoia.

Ad-mĭt′, *v.* 1. E hookomo aku. *Admit the bearer,* e hookomo aku i ka mea nana keia i lawe.
2. See *acknowledge. He admits his mistake,* ke ae nei oia i kona-lalau.

Ad-mĭt′tânçe, } 1. Ka ae ana. *Ad-*
Ad-mĭs′sion, } *n. mission of guilt,* ka ae ana ua hewa.
2. Ka hookomo ana. *Admittance to the exhibition,* ka hookomo ana i ka hoikeike.

Ăd-mŏn′ish, *v.* E ao aku; e pa′pa′′ku.

Ăd′mŏ-ni′tion, *n.* He olelo ao; olelo pa′pa′. SYN. reproof; counsel.

A-do′ (a-du), *n.* Pilikia.

A-dŏpt′, *v.* 1. E hookama.
2. E apono. *Adopt the report,* e apono i ka olelo hoike.
3. E apo. *Adopt the truth,* e apo i ka oiaio.

A-dŏp′tion, *n.* 1. Ka hookama ana.
2. Ka apono ana.
3. Ke apo ana. *The adoption of the sentiment,* ke apo ana i ka manao.

A-dŏr′a-ble, *adj.* Ku i ka hoomanaia.

A-dŏre′, *v.* 1. E hoomana; e hoonani.
2. E hoohiwahiwa.

A-dŏr′er, *n.* 1. Ka mea e hoomana ana.
2. Ka mea aloha nui.

A-dŏrn′, *v.* 1. E kahiko a nani.
2. E hoohanohano. *He adorns his profession,* ke hoohanohano nei oia i kana oihana.

A-droit′, *adj.* Makaukau. SYN. expert; skilful.

A-drĭft′, *adj.* Hookuu wale ia. *The boat is adrift,* ua hookuu wale ia ka waapa.

A-dŭlt′, *n.* He kanaka oo; he wahine oo.

A-dŭl′ter-āte, *v.* E kawili pu i ka mea waiwai me ka mea waiwai ole.

Ă-dŭl′ter-y, *n.* He moe kolohe.

Ad-vânçe′, *v.* 1. E nee imua. *Advance in knowledge,* e nee imua ma ka ike.
2. E hookiekie. *Advance in office,* e hookiekie ae ia ma ka oihana.

Ad-vânçe′ment, *n.* 1. Ka nee ana imua.
2. Ka hookiekie ana′e.

Ad-vân′tage, *n.* He pomaikai. SYN. benefit.

Ăd′vân-tā′ģeous, *adj.* Pomaikai. SYN. beneficial.

Ad-vĕnt′ure, *n.* Mea ulia.

Ad-vĕnt′ūr-er, *n.* He kuewa; he aea wale.

Ad-vĕnt′ur-oŭs, *adj.* Aa; nahoa. SYN. bold; daring.

Ăd′vĕrb. *n.* Hainalea.

Ad′ver-sā′ry, *n.* He mea ku-e′; he enemi.

Ad-vĕrse′, *adj.* Ku-e. *An adverse decision,* he olelo hooho lo ku-e′.
2. *In adverse circumstances,* pilikia ka noho′na.

Ad-vĕr'si-ty, *n.* Ke kau o ka poino; ke kau ana mai o na popilikia.

Ăd'ver-tise', *v.* E hoolaha ma ka nupepa; e hoolaha oihana.

Ad-vĕr'tise-ment, *n.* He hoolaha ma ka nupepa.

Ad-viçe', *n,* Olelo ao.

Ad-vis'a-ble, *adj.* Kupono. SYN. expedient; proper.

Ad-vise', *v.* 1. E ao.

2. E kuka' pu.

Ad-vise'ment, *n.* 1. Ke kukala'na.

2. Ka noonoo ana. *The matter is under advisement,* ke noonoo ia nei ia mea.

Ad-vis'or, *n.* Mea ao; mea kuka' pu.

2. He kakaolelo.

Ăd'vo-eate, *v.* E kokua.

Adz, } *n.* Koi kalai.
Adze, }

A-ĕ'ri-al, *adj.* E pili ana i ka lewa. *Aerial flight,* lele ana ma ka lewa.

A̱'er-o-lite, *n.* He pohaku no ka lewa.

A'er-o-na̱ut', *n.* Ka mea e lewa ana ma ka baluna.

A-er-o-na̱ut'ics, *n.* Ka ike no ka hoolewa ana ma ka baluna.

Aes-thĕt'ic, } *adj.* E pili ana i ka
Aes-thĕt'ic-al, } maikai, a i ka nani o ka noho'na.

Aes-thĕt'ics, *n.* Ka ike e pono ai ka maikai, me ka nani o ka noho'na.

A-fär', *adv.* Mamao aku; kaawale loa 'ku; poiuiu.

Ăf'fa-ble, *adj.* Oluolu; laulea. SYN. polite.

Af-fäir', *n.* Hana. *A disgraceful affair,* he hana hilahila.

Ăf'fee-ta'tion, *n.* He ano haakei; ano hookohukohu.

Af-fĕct'ing, *adj.* Manaonao. SYN. pathetic.

Af-fĕc'tion, *n.* 1. He aloha.

2. He mai. *Affection of the heart,* he mai e pili ana i ka puuwai.

Af-fĕc'tion-ate, *adj.* Aloha. *An affectionate disposition,* he ano aloha.

Af-fi'ançe, *v.* E hoopalau. SYN. betroth.

Ăf'fi-dä'vit, *n.* Olelo hoike i kakauia, a i hoohikiia. SYN. deposition.

Af-fil'i-ate, *v.* E launa pu; e hookama.

Af-fin'i-ty, *n.* 1. Pili ma ka mare.

2. Ka pili ana o kekahi mea i kekahi mea.

Af-firm', *v.* 1. E hooia.

2. E hoike pololei. SYN. assert.

Ăf'fir-mä'tion, *n.* 1. He olelo hooia.

2. Ma ke kanawai, he olelo hoike i hoohiki ole ia.

Af-firm'a-tïve, *n.* Ka aoao ae.

Af-fix', *v. t.* 1. E pakui.

2. E kakau mahope. *Affix a signature,* e kakau inoa mahope.

Af-fliet', *v. t.* E hoopilikia; e hoopai; e hooehaeha. SYN. to trouble; to pain.

Af-flie'tion, *n.* He popilikia. SYN. distress.

Ăf'flü-ent, *adj.* Waiwai. SYN. wealthy.

Af-förd', *v.* 1. E haawi. SYN. give. *Afford pleasure,* e haawi i ka hauoli.

2. Hiki. *I cannot afford to buy,* aole hiki ia'u ke kuai. *The student cannot afford to waste his time,* aole hiki i ka haumana ke mauna wale i kona manawa.

Af-fräy', *n.* He haunaele; he hakaka. SYN. tumult quarrel.

Af-frönt', *v.* E hoonaukiuki. SYN. offend.

2. E hookokonoi'e; e hanawale. SYN. insult; provoke.

A-fire', *adv.* A ia i ke ahi. SYN. on fire.

A-flöat', *adv.* Lana ma ka wai.

A-foot', *adv.* Hele wawae.

A-före'said, *adj.* I olelo ia mamua.

A-före'time, *adv.* I ka wa i hala.

A-fräid', *adj.* Maka'u; hopohopo; puiwa.

A-frĕsh', *adv.* Hou. SYN. again.

Ăft, *adv.* Ma ka hope o ka moku.

Ăft'er, *prep. and adv.* Mahope; ihope.

Ăft'er-nöon', *n.* Auina la.

Ăft'er-thought, *n.* Manao i ala mai mahope.

Ăft'er-wards, *adv.* Mahope; i ka wa mahope.

A-gain' (a-gĕn), *adv.* Hou. *Do not do so again,* mai hana hou pela.

2. Eia hou. *Again; if this be true, etc.* Eia hou; ina he oiaio keia, etc.

A-gainst', *prep.* Ku-e'. SYN. versus.

Age, *n.* He au manawa. *The age in which we live,* ke au a kakou e noho nei.

2. Na makahiki o ke ola ana. *What is your age?* ehia ou mau makahiki?

A̱'ged, *adj.* Kahiko; piha na makahiki. SYN. old; venerable.

A̱'gen-çy, *n.* Ka oihana o ke agena.

A̱'gent, *n.* 1. He hope; he agena.

2. He kumu; he mana. *Fire is an agent of heat,* he kumu ke ahi no ka wela.

Ag'grand-ize, *v.* E hoomahuahua. SYN. augment. *Aggrandize power,* e hoomahuahua i ka mana.

Ag'gra-vāte, *v.* 1. E hoonaukiuki; hoouluhua. *He aggravated me,* nana i hoonaukiuki mai ia'u

2. E hoomahuahua ino. *It aggravates the case,* na ia mea e hoomahuahua ino mai.

Ag'gra-vāt'ing, *adj.* 1. Hoonaukiuki. *An aggravating child,* he keiki hoonaukiuki.

2. Hoomahuahua ino.

Ag'gra-vä'tion, *n.* 1. Ka hoomahuahua ino ana.

2. Ke kumu e ukiuki ai.

Ag'gre-gāte, *n.* Ka huina nui. SYN. sum.

Ag-grĕs'sor, *n.* Ka mea i hewa mua.

A-ghäst', *adv.* Pioloke; ilihia. *He stood aghast with fear,* pioloke oia i ka mak'au.

Ag'ile, *adj.* Mama; kaukaulele. SYN. nimble.

A-ġil'i-ty, *n.* Ka mama o ke kino.

Ag'i-tāte, *v.* 1. E hoopuiwa.
2. E hoolulilluli.
3. E hoala. *To agitate the subject*, e hoala i ke kumu noonoo.
4. E hoolalelale.

Ag'-i-ta'tor, *n.* 1. He mea hoolalelale; he mea hoopuiwa.
2. He mea e hoala mau ana i ka naau o kanaka.

A-gö', *adv.* Liuliu i hala. *Long ago*, liuliu loa.

Ag'o-nize, *v.* E kupaka ka naau.

Ag'o-ny, *n.* Eha kukonukonu o ka naau, a o ke kino paha.

A-gree', *v.* 1. E ae like; e kuikahi; e lokahi.
2. E ku like; e kohu like.

A-gree'a-ble, *adj.* 1. Oluolu. *An agreeable breeze*, he makani oluolu; he koaniani.
2. Laulea; launa.

A-gree'ment, *n.* Olelo ae-like; palapala ae-like. SYN. contract.
2. Ke kulike ana; ka hookohu ana.

Ag'ri-cŭl'tur-al, *adj.* E pili ana i ka oihana mahiai. *Agricultural Society*, hui mahiai.

Ag'ri-cŭlt'ure, *n.* Oihana mahiai.

Ag'ri-cŭl'tur-ist, *n.* Kanaka mahiai. SYN. farmer.

A-ground', *adv.* Ili; mau. *The ship is aground*, ua ili ka moku. *The boat is aground*, ua mau ka waapa.

A'gŭe (ä'gu), *n.* Ka mai anu me ka wela.

A-hĕad', *adv. He has gone ahead*, aia oia imua.
2. *Go ahead in your studies*, e nee imua ma kau mau haawina.
3. *To forge ahead*, e nee malie imua. *The ship forged ahead*, nee malie ae la ka moku imua.

Aid, *n.* Kokua. SYN. help; assistance.

Āid'de-camp (äd-de-kong), *n.* He luna lawelawe no ke generala.

Āil, *v.* 1. E omaimai; e nawaliwali.
2. E hoopilikia. *What ails the child?* heaha ka mea e hoopilikia nei i ke keiki? SYN. trouble; disturb.

Āim, *v.* 1. E hoopololei ka nou ana; ke ki-pu' ana.
2. E hookupono i ka manao maluna o kekahi kumu noonoo. *Aim high in the pursuit of knowledge*, e kau aku a kiekie ka manao i ka imi ana i ka naauao.

Āim'less, *adj.* Luana wale ae; nanea wale; noonoo ole. *To live an aimless life*, e noho nanea wale. *To study in an aimless way*, e imi me ke noonoo ole; e imi wale.

Āir, *n.* 1. He ea.
2. Ka leo wahine o ka leo mele. SYN. soprano.
3. *To put on airs*, e hookapukapu; e haanou.

Āir, *v.* 1. E kaulai i ke ea. *Air the bed clothes*, e kaulai na lole moe i ke ea.

2. E wehe i ke ea. *Air the room*, e wehe ke keena i ke ea. SYN. ventilate.

Âir'pump, *n.* He pauma ea e pauma ana i ke ea noloko mai o kekahi mea.

Āir'shaft, *n.* Puka hookomo ea i ka lua eli.

Âir'tight, *adj.* Komo ole ke ea; paa.

Āir'y, *adj.* 1. Hamama i ke ea.
2. Lalelale. SYN. vivacious.

Aisle (ile), *n.* He ala mawaena o na noho o ka luakini, a hale e ae paha.

A-jär', *adv.* Hamama iki; hamama hapa. *The door is ajar*, hamama iki ka puka.

A-kin', *adj.* 1. Pili koko.
2. Ano like.

A-lāc'ri-ty, *n.* Ka mikioi ma ka hana.

A-lärm', *n.* Puiwa; hopohopo; maka'u. SYN. fear.

A-lärm'ing, *adj.* Hooweliweli; hoomaka'u.

A-lärm'clock, *n.* He wati kani hoopuiwa.

A-läs', *interj.* Auwe!

Al-bē'it, *adv.* Oiai nae. SYN. notwithstanding.

Al'bum, *n.* He buke malama i na mea milimili. *Photographic album*, he buke kii helehelena. *Autograph album*, he buke malama kakau lima. *Stamp album*, he buke malama poo leta, me na hoailona pai e ae.

Āl'co-hol, *n.* He wai kulu; he alekoholo; ke kumu o na wai ikaika a pau.

A-lêrt', *adj.* Makaala; hoihoi; miki. SYN. vigilant; prompt. *To be on the alert*, e anehe.

A-lêrt'ness, *n.* Ka noho makaukau; ka makaala.

Äl-ge-brā', *n.* Hoailona helu.

A'li-as, *adv.* Oia hoi; pili i ka lawe ana i ka inoa kapakapa. *Brown alias Smith*, o Baraunu, oia hoi o Kamika.

Āl'i-bi, *n.* Ma kahi e; he olelo no ke kanawai, e hoike ana aia ma kahi e ka mea i hopuia no ke karaima, i ka wa i hana ia ke karaima.

Āl'ien, *n.* He kupa no ka aina e. SYN. foreigner.
2. He malihini.

Āl'ien-āte, *v.* 1. E hoolilo aku i kekahi pono i kuleana na hai.
2. He hoomokuahana i ke aloha.
3. E hoohuli ku-e i ka manao.

A-light', *v.* 1. E lele ilalo; e lehei. *Alight from the horse*, e lehei mai ka lio.
2. E kau. *The bird alights on the branch*, ke kau nei ka manu ma ka lala.

A-lign'ment, *n.* Ka hooponopono ana o ka laina.

A-like', *adv.* Like a like.

Āl'i-mo-ny, *n.* He haawina waiwai na ka wahine mare, ke okiia, a ke hookawaleia paha mai ke kane.

Āl'i-quot, *adj.* Mahele koena ole. *4 is an aliquot part of 12*, o ka 4 he mahele koena ole ia o ka 12.

A-live', *adj.* Ola; e ola ana.

All, *adj.* Pau loa; huina pau. SYN. total; the whole.

Al-lāy′, *v.* E hooemi; e maalili mai. SYN. mitigate.
2. E kena. SYN. quench. *To allay thirst*, e kena i ka make wai.
3. E hoona′; e akakuu. SYN. pacify; appease.

Al-le′ği-ançe, *n.* Ka pono o ka makaainana i kona aupuni.
2. Ka pono a ke kanaka e hana′i.

Al-lēğe′ (al-lej′), *v.* E hai pololei. SYN. affirm.

Al′le-go-ry, *n.* He kaao nanenane. SYN. parable.

Al-lē′vi-āte, *v.* E hoomama. *To alleviate distress*, e hoomama i ka eha kino.

Al′ley, *n.* He alahele ololi iloko o ke kulanakauhale.

Al-li′ançe, *n.* He kuikahi; ke kuikahi ana.
2. He hui. *Evangelical alliance*, hui Euanelio.

Al′li-ga-tor, *n.* He moo nui o na muliwai o America Hema.

Al-low′, *v.* E ae. SYN. permit. *Allow me to go*, e ae ia′u e hele.

Al-low′ançe, *n.* He haawina; he mahele.

Al-lŏy′, *n.* Ka hui ana o na metala ano like ole.

Al-lūde′, *v.* E kuhikuhi. SYN. refer.

Al-lūre′, *v.* E hoowalewale; e onou. SYN. entice.

Al-lūr′ing, *adj.* Hoomalimali. SYN. enticing.

Al-lū′sion, *n.* See *Reference.*

Al-ly′, *n.* He hoa; he kokua.

Al′ma Mā′ter, *n.* Ke kula nui kahi i loaa i ka haumana ka ike.

Al′ma-nac, *n.* 1. He alemenaka, papa kuhikuhi la.
2. He buke hoike ana i na mea e pili ana i ka la, mahina, hoku, etc.
3. *Nautical almanac*, he alemenaka hooholo moku.
4. *Medical almanac*, he alemenaka hoike laau lapaau.

Al-might′y, *adj.* Mana loa. *The Almighty*, Ke Akua Mana Loa.

Al′most′, *adv.* Kokoke; aneane. SYN. very nearly.

Alms, *n.* Na haawina manawalea.

Alms′-house′, *n.* Hale hookipa no ka poe i nele. SYN. poor-house.

Al-ŏft′, *adv.* Iluna. *Look aloft*, e nana iluna. Pili i ka pii ana iluna o ke kia.

A-lōne′, *adj.* Oia hookahi; mehameha.

A-lŏng′, *adv.* 1. *Come along*, e hele mai.
2. *Go along*, e hele pela.

A-lŏng′side′, *adv.* Pili aoao. *Alongside of the wharf*, pili aoao i ka uwapo.

A-loud′, *adv.* Me ka leo moakaka; me ka leo nui.

Al′pha-bet, *n.* Ka papa A.

Al′pha-bĕt′ic-al-ly, *adv.* Hoonohonohoia mamuli o ka papa A.

Al′pine, *adj.* 1. E pili ana i na mauna Alepa.
2. Kiekie, e like me na mauna Alepa. *Alpine hights*, na wahi kiekie o na mauna.

Al-reăd′y, *adv.* I keia manawa no; ano iho nei.

Al′so, *adv. and conj.* No hoi. *Do this also*, e hana nohoi i keia.

Al′tar, *n.* He kuahu; wahi mohai. *Family altar*, ka pule ohana.

Al′ter, *v.* 1. E hoololi; e hoo-ano e. SYN. change.
2. E poa; e kahe i ka laho.

Al-ter-ā′tion, *n.* Ka hoololi ana; ka hoo-ano e ana.

Al′ter-a-tive, *n.* He laau lapaau; e hoo-ano e ana i ke koko.

Al-ter-cā′tion, *n.* Ka hoopaapaa ino ana. SYN. dispute; wrangle.

Al-tĕr′nate-ly, *adv.* Pakahi; ma ke ano kike′.

Al-tĕr′na-tive, *n.* Ka mea i kohoia o na mea elua.

Al-thŏugh′ (al-thō,), *conj.* Ina no paha; oiai.

Al′ti-tūde, *n.* Ke kiekie. SYN. hight or height.

Al′to, *n.* Ka lua o na leo mele kupono i ka wahine; leo aleto.

Al′to-gĕth′er, *adv.* 1. Pau pu; hui like.
2. Pakela loa. *Altogether too much*, oi pakela loa.

A-lŭm′nus, *n. pl. Alumni.* He haumana i puka pono aku mai ke kula nui.

Al′ways, *adv.* I na manawa a pau; mau.

A-măn′u-ĕn′sis, *n.* 1. Ka mea i kakaulima no hai.
2. Ka mea i kakau i ka olelo a hai.

A-măss′, *v.* E hoaahu. SYN. accumulate.

Am′a-teur, *n.* Ka mea e hoomaamaa ana ma kekahi oihana.

A-māz′ing, *adj.* Kupaianaha; lua ole.

Am-băs′sa-dor, *n.* He elele i hoounaia mai kekahi aupuni a i kekahi aupuni aku.

Am′bi-dĕx′ter, *n.* He mea i makaukau like me kona mau lima elua.

Am-big′u-oŭs, *adj.* Moakaka ole; ano lua; loli lua ke ano. *An ambiguous sentence*, he hopuna olelo ano lua. *An ambiguous thought*, he manao lole lua.

Am-bi′tion, *n.* Ke ake o ka naau e lilo i pookela.
2. He manao hooia; manao hookiekie.

Am′ble, *v.* E holo peke. SYN. pace.

Am′bu-lançe, *n.* He kaa halihali no ka poe i eha i ke kaua.

Am′bus-cāde′, *n.* He poe e hoohalua ana i ka enemi; he poipo.

Am′bush, n. He pahele; he wahi hoohalua.

A-mē′li-o-rāte, *v.* 1. E hooakea i ka noho ana. SYN. alleviate. *Ameliorate the condition of the poor*, e hooakea i ka noho-ana o ka poe ilihune.

2. E hooluolu. *Ameliorate pain*, e ho-oluolu i ka eha.

A-mē'na-ble, *adj.* See *Responsible.*

A-mĕnd', *v.* 1. E hoololi. *Amend the constitution*, e hoololi i ke kumukana-wai.
2. E konini; e oiolo; e hoomaka mai e oluolu.
3. E huli mai ka hewa a i ka pono.

A-mĕnd'ment, *n.* Ka hoololi ana.

A-mĕnds', *n.* 1. Ka huikala ana.
2. Ka mea i paniia no kekahi hana ino, a olelo ino paha.

Am'i-a-ble, *adj.* Ku i ke aloha; ano oluolu. SYN. lovely.

Ạm'i-ea-ble, *adj.* Ano launa. SYN. friendly.

A-mid' } *prep.* Iwaena; mawaena. SYN
A-midst } among.

A-miss', *adj.* 1. Ku pono ole.
2. Hele hewa; hu hewa.

Ăm'i-ty, *n.* 1. Ka launa o ka manao. SYN. friendship.
2. Ke aloha hoaluna. SYN. good will. Ka manao maikai.

Am'mu-ni'tion, *n.* Na lako na ke ki pu.

Ăm'nes-ty, *n.* Ke kala ana i ka poe i kipi i ke aupuni.

A-mŏng' } *prep.* SYN. amid.
A-mŏngst' }

Ăm'o-roŭs, *adj.* Kuko wahine. SYN. passionate.

A-mount', *n.* Ka huina.

A-mount', *v.* E lilo. *It amounted to a large sum*, lilo ia i huina nui.

Am-phib'i-oŭs, *adj* Ola like iloko o ka wai a ma ka aina.

Ăm'phi-thē'a-ter, *n.* 1. Hale keaka nui, ano poai, o ka wa kahiko.
2. *Amphitheater of mountains*, na mau-na e poai ana.

Ăm'ple, *adj.* Lawa pono; nui kupono.

Ăm'pli-fi-eā'tion, *n.* Ka hooakea ana; ka hoomahuahua ana. SYN. enlarge-ment.

Ăm'pli-fy, *v.* 1. E hoomahuahua; *am-plify the dimensions*, e hoomahuahua i na palena.
2. E wehewehe hou a nui. *Amplify the analysis*, e wehewehe hou a nui i ka olelo wehewehe.

Ăm'ply, *adv.* Lawa ku pono. SYN. suf-ficiently; bountifully.

Ăm'pu-tāte, *v.* E oki a moku loa.

A-mŭse', *v.* E hoolealea; e hooluolu; e paani pu.

A-mŭse'ment, *n.* He lealea; he paani.

A-mŭs'ing, *adj.* Lea; lealea.

A-năl'o-gy, *n.* Na kumu hoohalike iwaena o na mea ano okoa; ka like a like o kekahi mau mea. *Reason from analogy*, e noonoo ma ka hoohalike.

Anăl'y-sis, *n.* 1. Ka mahele liilii ana o kekahi mea kino a loaa kona mau kumu.
2. Ka wehewehe ana o kekahi manao, nanehai, a ninau pohihihi paha.

Ăn'a-lȳse, *v.* E wehewehe ano.
2. E hookaawale i na huna o kekahi mea kino i loaa i kona mau kumu.

Ăn'areh-y, *n.* 1. Ka malu ole o ka no-ho ana.
2. Ka noho ana kanawai ole.

A-năt'o-my, *n.* Anatomia. He wehe-wehe ano no na mea kino ola.

Ăn'çes-tor, *n.* He kupuna o ka wa kahiko.

An-çĕs'tral, *adj.* No na kupuna mai. *Ancestral home*, ka home o na kupuna.

Ăn'çes-try, *n.* Ke kuauhau. SYN. line-age; birth.

Ăn'chor, *n.* He heleuma.

Ăn'chor-age, *n.* Wahi ku moku.

Ăn'çient, *adj.* Kahiko.

An'çients, *n.* Ka poe o ka wa kahiko.

Ănd, *conj.* 1. A. *And so it is*, a pela no ia.
2. A me. *The dog and cat*, ka ilio a me ka popoki.
3. He hua olelo e hoohui ana i na ma-mala ololo olua. *John went a fishing, and James went to play*, hele o Keoni i ka la-wa-i-a, a hele o Kimo i ka paani.

An-dăn'te, *adj.* Lolohi; malie; pili i ke mele ana.

Ăn'ee-dōte, *n.* He wahi kaao iki.

Ăn'e-mŏm'e-ter, *n.* He mikini ana i ka ikaika o ka makani.

A-new', *adv.* Hou. SYN. again.

Ăn'ġel, *n.* Anela.

Ăn'ger, *n.* Huhu; ukiuki; inaina.

Ăn'ġle, *n.* He huina. *Right angle*, hu-ina kupono. *Acute angle* huina oi. *Ob-tuse angle*, huina peleleu.

Ăn'ġle, *v.* E kamokoi.

Ăn'ġler, *n.* Kanaka kamokoi.

Ăn'gli-çiṣe, *v.* E hoolilo i ano Bereta-nia.

Ăn'ġling, *n.* Ke kamokoi ana.

Ăn'ġling-rod, *n.* He aho kamokoi. SYN. fishing rod.

Ăn'ġling-wôrm, *n.* He koe.

Ăn'ġry, *adj.* Huhu.

Ăn'guish, *n.* Kupaka.

Ăn'gu-lar, *adj.* Mehe huina la.

Ăn'i-mal, *n.* He mea ola, aole nae he uhane kanaka kona; he holoholona.

Ăn'i-mal, *adj.* Holoholona. *Animal instincts*, ka noonoo holoholona. *Ani-mal kingdom*, ka mahele holoholona. *Animal food*, ka ai i o holoholona. *An-imal spirits*, ka hoihoi o na holoholona.

Ăn-i-măl'eule, *n.* Mea ola makalii loa, ike ole ia ka maka maoli.

Ăn'i-māte, *v.* 1. E hookomo ke ola i ke kino.
2. E hooeueu; e hoolalelale. SYN. en-liven; stimulate.

Ăn'i-māte, *adj.* Ola. *Animate bodies*, na kino ola.

Ăn'i-māt'ed, *adj.* 1. Ola. *Animated na-ture*, na mea ola a Ke Akua i hana'i; na mea ola o ke ao nei.
2. Miki; lalelale.

An'i-mā'tion, *n.* Ka eleu; ka hoihoi. *He spoke with animation,* kamailio oia me ka hoihoi.

An'i-mŏs'i-ty, *n.* Ka manao ku-e; manao enemi.

An'i-mŭs, *n.* Ka manao. SYN. mind. *The animus was bad,* ino ka manao.

Ăn'kle, *n.* Ka puupuu wawae.

An'nals, *n.* Ka moolelo. SYN. history; chronicles.

An-nĕx', *v.* E pakui; e hookui. SYN. append; join.

Ăn'nex-ā'tion, *n.* Ka hoohui ana mai; ka hookui mai.

An-ni'hi-lāte, *v.* E hoopau loa; e hoolilo i mea ole loa. SYN. to cause to cease to be.

Ăn'ni-vĕr'sa-ry, *n.* 1. La hoomanao. *Birthday anniversary,* la hoomanao no ka hanau.
2. Ka piha pono o ka makahiki.

An-nounçe', *v.* E kukala; e hoolaha. SYN. proclaim; publish.

An-nounçe'ment, *n.* ke kukala'na; ka hoolaha'na. SYN. proclamation.

An-nŏy', *v.* E hoonaukiuki; e mahaoi; e hoouluhua. SYN. vex; tease; trouble.

An-nŏy'ançe, *n.* He kumu hoonaukiuki; kumu hoouluhua. SYN. disturbance; vexation.

Ăn'nu-al, *n.* 1. He mea kupu ae, a make aku iloko o ka makahiki hookahi.
2. He buke i paiia i kela me keia makahiki.

Ăn'nu-al, *adj.* Kela me keia makahiki.

An-nū'i-ty, *n.* He uku makahiki.

An-nŭl', *v.* E hoopau; e hoonoa. SYN. abolish; nullify; cancel.

Ăn'nu-lar, *adj.* Mehe komo lima la. *Annular space,* ke kowa mawaena o na kaha poepoe elua, i kahaia kekahi iloko ao e kekahi. *Annular eclipse,* ka hoopouli ana o ka la, a koe he malamalama mehe komolima la.

Ăn'o-dȳne, *n.* He laau lapaau hoopau eha.

A-noint', *v.* E hamo i ke kino; e poni.

A-nŏm'a-ly, *n.* He mea mawaho ae o ka loina mau.

A-nŏn'y-moŭs, *adj.* Inoa ole. *Anonymous letter,* he palapala inoa ole.

An-ŏth'er, *adj.* 1. Kekahi mea e; kekahi ae.
2. Mea hou ae.

Ăn'swer (ăn'ser), *v.* 1. E pane; e hai i ka haina.
2. E kupono. *That will answer,* e kupono ana kela.

Ăn'swer, *n.* He haina; he pane ninau.

Ăn'swer-a-ble, *adj.* 1. Hiki ke pane-ia.
2. *You are answerable,* maluna ou ka pilikia. SYN. accountable.

Ănt, *n.* He naonao; he nonanona.

An-tăg'o-nĭst, *n.* 1. He enemi.
2. He hoa paio.

Ant-ăre'tie, *adj.* E moe ana ma ka welau Hema.

Ăn'te-çĕd'ent, *n.* Ka mea e hele ana imua o kekahi mea e ae; ka mua.

Ăn'te-chām'ber, *n.* Ke keena mawaho.

Ăn'te-dāte, *v.* E kakau e mamua.

Ăn'te-di-lū'vi-an, *adj.* Mamua'e o ke Kai-o-kahinalii.

Ăn'te-pe-nŭlt', *n.* Ke kolu o na mamala o kekahi hua olelo.

Ăn-tē'ri-or, *adj.* Mamua. SYN. before.

Ăn'te-rōōm, *n.* He keena mamua o ke keena nui.

Ăn-them, *n.* He leo mele hoolea; i hakuia no na huaolelo o ka Baibala.

Ăn'thra-çite, *n.* Nanahu pohaku.

Ăn'tie, *n.* Paani o na holoholona.

An-tiç'i-pāte, *v.* E manao lana. SYN. expect; hope for.
2. E kau nui ka manao maluna o ka pomaikai i manaoia e hiki mai ana.
3. E noonoo e mamua; e hoomakaukau e mamua. SYN. foresee.

An-tiç'i-pā'tion, *n.* Ka noonoo e mamua; ka hoomakaukau e ana o ka manao. SYN. expectation.

Ăn'ti-dōte, *n.* 1. He huikala.
2. He laau lapaau e huikala ana i na ino i loaa mamuli o na laau make, etc.

An-tip'a-thy, *n.* Naau ku-e'; naau hoowaha'waha'; naau mihimihi.

An-tip'o-dēş, *n.* Ka poe e noho ana ma kela aoao o ka honua.
2. Na wahi ma kela aoao o ka honua.

Ăn'ti-quā'ri-an, *adj.* No ka wa kahiko. *Antiquarian researches,* ka huli ana no na mea o ka wa kahiko.

Ăn'ti-quā'ry, *n.* He kanaka i huli no na mea o ka wa kahiko.

Ăn-tiq'ui-ty, *n.* Ka wa kahiko.
2. Ke kahiko. *The antiquity of the book,* he kahiko o ka buke.

Ăn'ti-quāt'ed, *adj.* No ka wa kahiko.

Ănt'ler, *n.* Ke kiwi o ke dia.

Ăn'vil, *n.* Ka hao kui o ke amara.

Ănx-i'e-ty, *n.* Kupikipiki-o' o ka naau. Pihoihoi o ka naau.

Ănx'ioŭs, *adj.* Hopohopo; pihoihoi.

Ănx'ioŭs-ly, *adv.* Me ka pihoihoi.

Ăn'y (ĕny), *adj.* 1. Kekahi. *Any one of them,* kekahi mea o lakou.
2. *Any place,* ke kau wahi. SYN. any where.

Ăn'y-how, *adv.* Ma kekahi ano.

A-ôr'ta, *n.* Ke aa-lele nui, e pauma ana i ke koko mai ka puuwai a iloko o na aa-koko nui.

A-pāçe', *adv.* Awiwi. SYN. hastily.

A-pārt', *adv.* Kaawale; pakahi. SYN. separately.

Ă-pārt'ment, *n.* He keena. SYN. room.

Ăp'a-thy, *n.* Palaka o ka manao; hoomaloka. SYN. indifference.

Āpe, *v.* E hana e like me ke keko.
2. E hoohalike aku ma ke ano hoopilimeaai.

A-pē'ri-ent, *n.* He laau hoonaha'.

Ap'er-türe, *n.* He puka; he wahi hamama.

Ā'pĕx, *n.* Ka welau; ka wekiu.

A-phē'li-on, *n.* Kahi ma na alapoai o na hoku-hele i mamao loa'ku lakou mai ka La'ku.

Ā'pi-ā'ry, *n.* Wahi malama nalo meli.

Ā-pĭēçe', *adv.* Pakahi.

Ap'o-ġee, *n.* Kahi o ke alahele o ka mahina i kaawale loa'ku oia mai ka honua aku.

A-pŏl'o-ġize, *v.* E haawi i ka olelo hoolaulea.
2. E mihi imua o kekahi. *I apologize for my words,* ke mihi nei au no ka'u mau olelo.

A-pŏl'o-ġy, *n.* He olelo hoolaulea.
2. He olelo mihi. SYN. excuse.

Ăp'o-plĕx'y, *n.* He mai ku hewa.

A-pŏs'ta-tize, *v.* E haalele i ka manaoio a i ka hoomana paha.

A-pŏs'tle, *n.* He luna olelo, kekahi o na haumana he umikumamalua o ka Haku.

A-pŏs'tro-phe, *n.* 1. He kaha (') e hoike ana ua haule kekahi hua olelo.
2. He kamailio pololei aku i kekahi mea iloko o ka haiolelo. *An apostrophe to the ocean,* he kamailio pololei i ka moana.

A-pŏth'e-ea-ry, *n.* Kanaka kaawili a kuai i na laau lapaau.

Ap-pặll', *v.* E hooweliweli; e hooilihia. SYN. terrify.

Ăp'pa-rá'tus, *n.* Na paahana; na lako e pono ai kekahi oihana.

Ap-pär'el, *n.* Ka aahu; na lole komo. SYN. dress; raiment; clothes.

Ap-pär'ent, *adj.* Moakaka. SYN. evident; clear.
2. Moakaka i ka ike maka. SYN. visible.

Ap-pär'ent-ly, *adv.* I ka nana'ku.

Ăp pa-ri'tion, *n.* He uhane; he lapu; he kinowailua. SYN. ghost.

Ap-pëal, *n.* 1. He palapala hoopii mai kekahi aha hookolokolo a i kekahi aha kiekie ae.
2. He olelo nonoi; olelo koi; olelo ao.

Ap-pëal', *v.* 1. E hoopii mai kekahi olelo hooholo.
2. E nonoi; e koi.

Ap-pëar', *v.* 1. E hoea mai. *The ship appears in sight,* ke hoea mai nei ka moku.
2. I ka nana'ku. *It appears he did not go,* i ka nana'ku aole ia i hele.

Ap-pëar'ançe, *n.* 1. Ka nanaina. *The ship presented a beautiful appearance,* nani ka nanaina o ka moku.
2. Ka hiki kino mai. *To put in an appearance,* e hiki kino mai.
3. He hiohiona. *Appearances are against him,* ku-e na hiohiona iaia.

Ap-pëase', *v.* E hoo-na; e hoolaulea; e malili.

Ap-pëased', *adj.* Akakuu. SYN. calmed; quieted. *His hunger was appeased,* akakuu kona pololi.

Ap-pĕl'lant, *n.* Ka mea e hoopii ana imua o ke kanawai.

Ăp'pel-lā'tion, *n.* He inoa. SYN. name; title.

Ap-pĕnd', *v.* E pakui; e hookui. SYN. annex.

Ap-pĕnd'aġe, *n.* Ka mea i pakuiia; ka mea i hookuiia.

Ap-pĕn'dix, *n.* He olelo pakui, ma ka hope o ka buke.

Ăp'pêr-täin', *v.* Pili. SYN. relate to; belong to.

Ăp'pē-tite, *n,* 1. Ono ai. *Without appetite,* kanea; kaea.
2. Ke kuko. *The appetites and passions,* na kuko.

Áp'pe-tiz'er, *n.* Mea hoala i ka ono ai.

Ap-plaud', *v.* E mahalo; e mahalo me ka pai lima.

Ap-plause', *n.* Ka mahalo i hoikeia ma ka pailima, a keehi wawae paha.

Ăp'ple, *n.* 1. He apalu, hua ai.
2. *Apple of the eye,* ka onohi maka.

Ap-pli'ançe, *n.* Ka mea e hiki ai kekahi hana.

Ăp'pli-ea-ble, *adj.* Ku pono; pilipono.

Ăp'pli-eänt, *n.* Ka mea e noi ana. *An applicant for office,* ka mea e noi ana i oihana.

Ăp'pli-eā'tion, *n.* 1. Ka noi ana.
2. Ka pili paa ana i kekahi mea a ko aku la.
3. Ke kupaa ana o ka manao.
4. Ka hoopiliana.

Ap-plȳ', *v.* 1. E hoopili; *he applied the rule,* ua hoopili oia i ka rula.
2. E hoopaa. *Apply your mind to your lessons,* e hoopaa kou manao i kau mau haawina.
3. E hoopii. *He applied to me for work,* hoopii mai oia imua o'u i hana. SYN. ask, noi.

Ap-point', *v.* E hookoho.

Ăp'point-ee', *n.* Ka mea i hookohoia.

Ap-point'ment, *n.* Ka hookoho ana.

Ap-pôr'tion, *v.* E mahele aku.

Ăp'po-site, *adj.* Kupono loa. SYN. very suitable.

Ăp'po-si'tion, *n.* Ke ku ana o kekahi haiinoa no kekahi haiinoa. *Bill, the blacksmith, shod my horse,* na Pila, ke amara, i kapili i na hao o kuu lio.

Ap-präiṣ'al, *n.* Ka hooholo ana no ka waiwai o kekahi mea, mamuli o ke kauoha.

Ap-präiṣe', *v.* E hooholo no ka waiwai o kekahi mea.

Ap-präiṣ'er, *n.* Luna hooholo no ka waiwai o kekahi mea.

Ap-prē'çi-āte, *v.* E hoomaopopo me ka apono.

Ăp'prē-hĕnd', *v.* 1. E hoomaopopo i ke ano. *I apprehend the meaning,* ke hoomaopopo nei au i ke ano.
2. E hopu, ma ke kanawai. *The Sheriff*

apprehends the thief, ke hopu nei ka makai i ka aihue. SYN. arrest.

Ăp'pre-hĕn'sion, *n.* 1. Ka hopu ana. SYN. arrest.

2. Ka hoomaopopo ana. SYN. comprehension. *A man of dull apprehension,* he kanaka hoomaopopo uuku.

3. *Apprehension of mind,* ka hopohopo o ka manao. SYN. doubt; anxiety.

Ăp'pre-hĕn'sive, *adj.* Kanalua; haohao.

Ap-prĕn'tĭçe, *n.* Ka mea i hoopaaia ma ke kanawai, e ao i kekahi oihana hana lima.

Ap-prĕn'tĭçe-ship, *n.* Ka manawa i hoopaaia'i o kekahi no ke ao ana i ka oihana.

Ap-prise', *v.* E hoakaka; e hai aku. SYN. inform.

Ap-prōach', *n,* 1. He ala e kai ana. *The approach to the house,* ke ala e kai ana i ka hale.

2. Ka hookokoke ana; ka hoea ana mai. *The approach of the enemy,* ka hoea ana mai o ka enemi.

Ap-prōach', *v.* E hookokoke; e nee a kokoke.

Ăp'pro-bā'tion, *n.* 1. Ka hoapono; ka apono. *The approbation of the teacher,* ka apono o ke kumukula. SYN. approval.

2. Ka maliu ana.

Ap-prō'pri-ate, *adj.* Kupono. SYN. applicable; suitable.

Ap-prō'pri-āte, *v.* E hookaawale; e hoolaa. *Appropriate a sum of money,* e hookaawale i puu dala. *Appropriate to sacred uses,* e hoolaa.

Ap-prō'pri-ā'tion, *n.* 1. He haawina; *Appropriation bill,* he bila haawina.

2. He puu dala i hookaawaleia no kekahi hana.

Ap-prove', *v.* E apono; e hoapono.

Ap-prŏx'i-māte, *v.* E hookokoke. SYN. approach.

Ap-prŏx'i-mate, *adj.* Ano like; aneane pololei. *An approximate result,* he loaa aneane pololei. SYN. proximate.

Ap-prŏx'i-mā'tion, *n.* Ka hookokoke ana. *An approximation to the truth,* ka hookokoke ana i ka oiaio.

Ap-pûr'te-nançe, *n.* Mea pili. SYN. adjunct; appendage.

Ā'pril, *n.* Aperila. Ka ha o na mahina o ka makahiki.

Ā-pron, *n.* He epana; he pale lole no ke alo, e malama ana i ka maemae o ka aahu.

Ăpt, *adj.* 1. kupono. SYN. fit; suitable. *An apt reply,* he pane kupono.

2. Makaukau. SYN. ready; skillful. *An apt workman,* he kanaka hana makaukau.

3. Maa; walea. SYN. accustomed. *Apt to become careless,* maa i ka hauhili.

Ăpt'i-tūde,\
Ăpt'ness, } *n.* Ke kupono; ka makaukau. SYN. fitness; suitableness.

A-quā'ri-um, *n.* He wahi e malama ai i na mea ola, a me na mea ulu o ka wai.

A-quăt'ĭe, *adj.* 1. O ka wai. *An aquatic fowl,* he manu o ka wai. *Aquatic sports,* na lealea o ka wai.

Ăq'ue-dŭet, *n.* He ha wai; he auwai.

Ăr'ab, *n.* He kamaaina no Arabia.

Ăr'a-bic, *adj.* No Arabia.

Ăr'a-ble, *adj.* Kupono ke mahi.

Ăr'bĭ-tra-ry, *adj.* 1. Mawaho o ke kanawai.

2. Mamuli o ka manao iho. *An arbitrary person,* he kanaka e hooko ana mamuli o kona manao wale iho no.

Ăr'bi-trāte, *v.* E hooholo i ka pono iwaena o na aoao elua; e uwao.

Ăr'bi-trā'tion, *n.* Ka hooholo ana o ka pono iwaena o na aoao elua; ka uwao ana.

Ăr'bi-trā'tor, *n.* Ka mea e hooholo ana no ka pono iwaena o na aoao elua; he uwao.

Ăr'bor, *n.* Wahi malumalu o na laau ulu.

Ăre, *n.* He pio. *An arc of a circle,* he pio o ka poai.

Arch, *adj.* 1. Maalea. SYN. shrewd; mischievous.

2. Kiekie. *Arch-angel,* anela kiekie. *Arch-bishop,* bihopa kiekie.

Arch, *n.* He pio; he pao.

Arch, *v.* E hoopio; e holu.

Ar'chæ-ōl'o-ġy, *n.* Ka ike e pili ana i ka noho ana o na kanaka o ka wa kahiko.

Arch-bĭsh'op, *n.* Bihopa Nui.

Arch-ĕn'e-my, *n.* 1. He enemi nui.

2. Satana; ka diabolo'.

Arch'er, *n.* He mea akamai i ka pana pua.

Arch'er-y, *n.* Ke akamai o ka pana pua.

Ăr-chi-pĕl'a-go, *n.* He pae moku.

Ăr'chi-teet, *n.* He kanaka kukulu hale.

Ăr'chi-tĕet'ūre, *n.* Ke kukulu ana. *Science of architecture,* ka ike no ke kukulu ana.

Ăr'chives, *n.* 1. Na buke moolelo no na oihana aupuni.

2. Ka waihona buke moolelo o ke aupuni.

Arch'ly, *adv.* Me ka maalea. SYN. roguishly; mischievously.

Ăre'tic, *n.* Na wahi o ka honua e hoopuni ana i ka welau akau.

2. *Arc-tic circle,* ka poai anu akau. *Arc-tic weather,* kau anu loa.

Ăr'dent, *adj.* 1. Wela loa. *Ardent heat of the sun,* ka wela loa o ka la.

2. Pumehana. *Ardent love,* aloha pumehana.

Ăr'dent-ly, *adv.* 1. Me ka wela nui.

2. Me ka pumehana loa.

Ăr'dor, *n.* 1. He wela. *The ardor of the sun's rays,* ka wela o na kukuna o ka la.

2. He pumehana, *the ardor of love,* ka pumehana o ke aloha.

3. He iini nui o ka naau. *He studies with ardor,* ke imi nei oia me ka iini nui o ka naau. SYN. eagerness; fervor.

Ar'du-oùs, *adj.* Pilikia; paakiki. SYN. hard; difficult. *An arduous work,* he hana pilikia.

A're-à, *n.* Ili. SYN. surface. *Area of land,* ili o ka aina.

A-rē'na, *n.* Wahi akea, kahi i hookoia'i kela me keia hana akea.

Ar'gūe, *v.* E paio pu; e wehewehe kumu manao. SYN. debate; reason.

Ar'gu-ment, *n.* Ka wehewehe ana.

2. Ke kumu manao; ka paio ana.

Ar'gu-mĕnt'a-tive, *adj.* 1. Pili i ka wehewehe ano.

2. Akamai i ka wehewehe ano. *An argumentative mind,* he naau akamai i ka wehewehe ano.

Ar'id, *adj.* Panoa. SYN. sterile; barren.

A-right', *adv.* Me ka pono; me ka pololei.

A-riṣe', *v.* 1. E ala. *Questions will arise,* e ala mai ana na ninau.

2. E eu.

Ar'is-tŏc'ra-çy, *n.* 1. He aupuni i hoomaluia e na 'lii me ka poe koikoi wale no.

2. Na makaainana koikoi o ka aina.

Ar'is-to-crăt'ic, *adj.* Koikoi; hanohano.

A-rith'me-tic, *n.* Na helu; arimatika. *Mental arithmetic,* helu naau. *Written arithmetic,* helu kakau.

A-rith'me-ti'çian, *n.* Mea i akamai ma na helu.

Ark, *n.* He pahu. *Ark of the covenant,* ka pahu berita.

2. Hale lana. *Noah's Ark,* ka hale lana a Noa.

Arm, *v.* 1. E kahiko i na mea kaua.

2. E hoomakaukau i na lako no ke kaua.

Arm'a-ment, *n.* Na lako no ke kaua.

Arm'chair, *n.* Noho paipai lima.

Arm'ful, *n.* Ka piha lima nui.

Arm'hole, *n.* Ka puka no ka lima.

Arm'i-stiçe, *n.* Ka hoomoe iki ana o ke kaua.

Ar'mor, *n.* Ke kahiko kaua metala.

Ar'mo-ry, *n.* Hale kahiko kaua.

Arm'pit, *n.* Poaeae.

Armṣ, *n.* Na pu, me na pahi kaua o kela a me keia ano.

Armṣ'length, *n.* 1. Hai lima.

2. Kaawale. *To keep at arms length,* e hookaawale aku.

Ar'my, *n.* He puali koa nui.

Ar'my-wôrm, *n.* Ka peelua.

A-rō'ma, *n.* He ala. SYN. fragrance.

Ar'o-măt'ic, *adj.* Aala. SYN. fragrant.

A-round', *prep.* A puni. *All around,* ma na wahi a pau e puni ana.

A-rouṣe', *v.* E hoala; e hooeu'eu'.

Ar-rāign' (ar-rāne), *v.* E hoopii ku-e'.

To arraign a motive, e hoopii ku-e i kekahi manao. *To arraign at the bar of justice,* e hoopii ku-e' imua o ka aha hookolokolo.

Ar-rānge' *v.* E hooponopono; e hoonohonoho pono. SYN. to adjust; to set in order. *Arrange a difficulty,* e hooponopono i ka hihia. *Arrange a room,* e hoonohonoho pono i ke keena.

Ar-rānge'ment, *n.* 1. Ka hoonohonoho ana. *The arrangement of the books,* ka hoonohonoho ana i na buke.

2. Ka hooponopono ana. *The arrangement of the difficulty,* ka hooponopono ana i ka hihia.

3. Ka noomakaukau ana. *The arrangements for a meeting,* ka hoomakaukau ana no ka halawai.

Ar'rant, *adj.* Kaulana no ka ino. SYN. infamous; vile. *An arrant coward,* he maka'u wale i kaulana.

Ar-rāy', *v.* 1. E hoonohonoho i ka hoouka kaua.

2. E kahiko a nani ke kino. SYN. adorn.

Ar-rēarṣ', *n.* 1. Komo i ka aie.

2. Koena aie. SYN. debt.

Ar-rĕst', *v.* 1. E hopu. *Arrest the criminal,* e hopu i ka lawe hala.

2. E keakea; e kau pale. *Arrest his evil course,* e keakea i kona alanui e hele ai i ka ino.

3. E hoopaa. *Arrest the attention,* e hoopaa i ka noonoo.

Ar-riv'al, *n.* 1. Ke ku ana mai. *Arrival of the ship,* ke ku ana mai o ka moku.

2. Ka hiki ana mai. *The arrival of the mail,* ka hiki ana mai o ke eke leta.

3. Ka hoea ana mai, *The arrival in sight,* or *the coming in sight.*

Ar-rive', *v.* E ku mai.

2. E hiki mai.

3. *Arrive in sight,* e hoea mai.

Ar'ro-gánçe, *n.* Hookiekie; haakei. SYN. haughtiness; conceit.

Ar'ro-gāte, *v.* E hookiekie; e hoohaakei.

Ar'rōw, *n.* He pua pana.

Ar'rōw-rōōt, *n.* Pia.

Ar'se-nal, *n.* Hale hooahu no na lako kaua.

Ar'son, *n.* Ka puhi kolohe ana i ka hale, a moku paha, i ke ahi.

Art, *n.* Ka ike akamai no na hana lima. *Mechanical art,* oihana hana lima.

2. *Fine arts,* na oihana haku mele me ka pena kii.

3. *Liberal, or polite arts,* na oihana hoonaauao.

4. Noeau; akamai. SYN. skill.

Ar'tter-y, *n.* Aa lele, e hookahe ana i ke koko iloko o na aa koko.

Ar-tē'ṣian, *adj.* *Artesian well,* he lua wai i wiliia.

Art'ful, *adj.* 1. Noeau. SYN. skillful.

2. Maalea. SYN. cunning.

Är'ti-ele, *n.* He mea. *Any article you please*, aia ka mea au i makemake ai.

2. He hua olelo. *a, an.*

3. He pauku olelo. *Article 1*, Pauku 1.

Ar'ti-fiçe, *v.* 1. He hana epa; hana maalea. SYN. trick; fraud.

2. He hana akamai. SYN. contrivance.

Är-tif'ï-çer, *n.* He kanaka akamai i ka hana lima. SYN. artisan.

Ar'ti-fi'çial, *adj.* 1. Hana ia e ka lima kanaka.

2. Hookamani; oiaio ole. *Artificial smile*, he aka hookamani.

Är-til'ler-ist, *n.* 1. He mea akamai me na pukaua nui.

2. He koa lawelawe pukaua nui.

Är-til'ler-y, *n.* 1. Na pukaua nui me na lako.

2. Ka puali kaua e lawelawe ana me na pukaua nui.

3. Na lako o ka pana me na pua.

Ärt'ist, *n.* 1. He mea akamai ma kekahi o na oihana akamai.

2. He mea pena kii; pai kii.

Är-tis'tie, *adj.* Eleu ma na hana akamai.

Ärt'less, *adj.* Epa ole; maalea ole. Oiaio, me he keiki liilii la.

Ärt'less-ness, *n.* Ke ano oiaio maoli; hookamani ole. SYN. ingenuousness.

As, *adv.* 1. E like me. *Do as I do*, e hana e like me au nei.

2. Penei. *As for instance*, penei paha.

3. Oiai. *As you are tardy you must stop after school*, oiai ua komo hope oe e noho oe mahope o ke kula. SYN. since; for as much.

4. *As if*, mehe mea'la; mehea'la.

As-çend', *v.* 1. E pii; e pii iluna.

2. Pukoo; punohu. *Ascend as smoke*, ke pukoo nei ka uahi.

As-çend'en-çy, *n.* Ka mana. SYN. power; control.

As-çent', *n.* Ka piina; hoopiina.

As'çer-tăin', *v.* E hoomaopopo lea.

As-eribe', *v.* 1. E kapilipili. *Ascribe false motives*, e kapilipili i na manao ino. SYN. impute; attribute.

2. E hoopili; e haawi. *Ascribe power to God*, e hoopili aku ka mana i Ke Akua *Ascriptions of praise*, e haawi i ka hoonani.

Ạ-shämed', *adj.* Hilahila; palaimaka.

Ash'eṣ, *n.* Na lehu ahi.

A-shore', *adv.* Ma kahakai; ua ili. *The ship is ashore*, ua ili ka moku.

2. *To go ashore*, (*from ship or boat*), e lele iuka.

3. *To go ashore*, (*as a boat*), e pae iuka.

Ạsh'y, *adj.* Mehe lehu la.

A'si-at'ie, *adj.* No Asia.

A-side', *adv.* Ma ka aoao; ma kahi ka-awale. *Step aside*, e nee aku ma ka aoao, e nee aku ma kahi kaawale.

As'i--nine, *adj.* Ano kekake; ano nunuha; paakiki.

Ạsk, *v.* 1. E noi. SYN. request.

2. E ninau. SYN. to question.

3. *Ask for information*, e niele; e niele.

4. *Ask continuously*, e ninaninau.

As-kânçe', *adv.* *To look askance*, e awihi na maka.

A-slânt', *adv.* Hi-o'.

Ạ-sleep', *adj.* Hiamoe.

Ạs'pect, *n.* Hiohiona; he nanaina.

As-pĕr'i-ty, *n.* Ano huhu; okalakala. SYN. acrimony.

As-pêrse', *v.* E paokee; e akiaki. SYN. slander; defame.

As-pir'ant, *n.* He hooikaika; mea iini nui. *An aspirant for fame*, he mea hooikaika nui i kaulana.

Ạs'pi-rate, *n.* He leo ha.

Ạs'pi-rä'tion, *n.* 1. Ka ha ana o ka waha.

2. Ka iini o ka naau e holo mua.

As-pir'ing, *adj.* Hooeueu; holomua. SYN. ambitious.

As-pire', *v.* E iini me ka hooikaika pu.

Ạss, *n.* 1. He kakake.

2. He kanaka naaupo, paakiki.

As-säil', *v.* E hakaka'; e ku-e. SYN. attack; assault.

As-säil'ant, *n.* Mea hakaka; mea ku-e.

2. Mea hoomaka e hakaka'.

As-säs'sin, *n.* He kanaka kawa' po.

As-säs'sin-äte, *v.* E kawa' po; e kimo po.

As-sault', *v.* E lima ikaika aku; e hakaka; e pepehi.

2. *Assault and battery*, ka hakaka' meme ka pepehi.

As-säy', *n.* Ka hoomaopopo ana i ka nui o ka metala ma kekahi minerala.

2. Ka hoomaopopo ana i ka nui o ke kala, a gula paha, ma ke dala aupuni.

As-sĕm'ble, *v.* E hooakoakoa.

As-sĕm'bly, *n.* He aha; he anaina. *Legislative Assembly*, ahaolelo kau kanawai. *Religious assembly*, anaina haipule.

As-sĕnt', *v.* E ae, mamuli o kekahi olelo, a hana paha. SYN. consent.

As-sêrt', *v.* E hooia. SYN. affirm.

2. E hai me ke kanalua ole. SYN. aver; declare.

As-sêr'tion, *n.* He olelo hooia; olelo hoomaopopo. SYN. declaration.

2. He olelo wale no. *That is your assertion; prove it.* Kau olelo wale no ia; e hooia mai.

As-sĕss', *v.* E auhau; e helu. *He is assessed for the school tax*, auhauia (heluia) oia no ka auhau kula.

As-sĕss'a-ble, *adj.* Ku pono i ka auhau.

As-sĕss'ment, *n.* Ka helu ana no ka auhau.

As-sĕss'or, *n.* Luna helu no na auhau.

As'sets, *n. pl.* Na pono kino a pau i hiki ke kuaiia no ke dala.

Äs'si-dŭ'i-ty, *n.* Ka hooikaika; ka mikiala. SYN. dilligence.

As-sid'u-oŭs, *adj.* Mikiala; hooikaika. SYN. dilligent.

As-sīgn′, v. 1. E haawi. *I assign this work to you,* ke haawi nei au i keia hana ia oe. *I assign no reason,* aole au e haawi i kumu.
2. *To assign a limit,,* e kau i palena.
3. *To assign a day,* e kuhikuhi i la.
4. *To assign counsel to prisoner,* e hookoho i kokua no ka lawehala.
5. *To assign property,* e waiho i ka waiwai ma ka lima o hai.
6. *To assign a portion,* e mahele i haawina.

Ăs′sign-ee′, n. Ka haku malama waiwai o ka mea i aie, no ka pono o ka poe i aieia.

As-sign′ment, n. Ka waiho ana o ka waiwai o ka mea i aie, no ka pono o ka poe i aieia.

As-sign′or, n. Ka mea nana i waiho i kona waiwai, no ka pono o ka poe nana ia i hooaie.

As-sīm′i-lāte. v. E hoolike; e hoolikelike.

As-sist′, v. E kokua. SYN. aid; help.

As-sist′ançe, n. Kokua. SYN. help.

As-sist′ant, n. He kokoolua: he kokua.

As-sō′çi-ate, n. He hoa; he kokoolua.

As-sō′çi-āte′, v. E launa pu.

As-sō′çi-ā′tion, n. 1. Ka launa pu ana o na noonoo.
2. He aha; ahahui. *Association for the advancement of knowledge,* he ahahui no ka hooholo mua ana o ka ike. SYN. society.

As-sôrt′, v. 1. E hookaawale ma na ano.
2. E ahu, i kela me keia ano.

As-sôrt′ment, n. He ahu o kela me keia mea.

As-suāģe′, v. E hoomalili; e hooemi; e hooluolu. *Assuage grief,* e hooluolu i ka luuluu. SYN. mitigate; alleviate; lessen.

As-sūme′, v. 1. E olelo wale me ka hooia ole.
2. E lawe. *Assume power,* e lawe i ka mana. SYN. take.
3. E hookamani. *Assume a virtue,* e hookamani mamuli o kekahi pono.

As-sūr′ançe, n. 1. Oni paa. *Full assurance of hope,* ka oni paa o ka manao iana.
2. Mahaoi. SYN. impudence.
3. Panai ola. See *insurance.*

As-sūre′, v. 1. E hooia; e hai oiaio.
2. E panai ola. See *insure.*

As-sūr′ed-ly, adv. He oiaio. SYN. certainly.

Ăs′ter-isk, n. He hoailona pai (*).

A-stērn′, adv. *I hope,* o ka moku.

Ăsth′ma, n. Haanou; nae.

Asth-măt′ic, adj. Mai i ka haanou.

As-tŏn′ish, v. E haohao; e puiwa.

As-tŏn′ish-ing, adj. Kupanaha; kamahao. SYN. wonderful.

As-tŏn′ish-ment, n. Haohao o ka manao. SYN. wonder.

A-strāy′, adv. Auwana; hewa. *To go astray,* e hele hewa; e hele auwana.

A-strīde′, adj. Kihelei.

As-trŏl′o-ģer, n. He kilo hoku′.

As-trŏn′o-mer, n. Kanaka ao-hoku′.

As-trŏn′o-my, n. Ao-hoku′.

As-tūte′, adj. Noeau; maalea. SYN. shrewd; sagacious; wily.

A-sŭn′der, adv. Kaawale.

A-sy̆′lum, n. Hale hookipa no ka poe i luuluu i kekahi pilikia. *Insane asylum,* hale hookipa no ka poe pupule.

Ăt, prep. 1. Ma. *At first,* mamua; i kinohou.
2. I. *Look at the child,* e nana i ke keiki.

Ā′the-ist, n. Kanaka hoole akua. SYN. infidel.

Ā′the-ist′ic-al, adj. Hoole akua.

Ath-lēte′, n. Kanaka puipui, kanaka hooikaika kino.

Ath-lĕt′ic, adj. Ikaika; puipui. SYN. lusty; robust. *Athletic sports,* na lealea hooikaika kino.

A-thwạrt′, prep. Mawaena; mai kahi aoao a i kahi aoao. *Athwartships,* mawaena o ka moku, mai kahi aoao a i kahi aoao o ka moku.

Ăt′las, n. He buke palapala aina.

Ăt′mos-phēre. n. Ka lewa; ke ea.

Ăt-mos-phĕr′ic-al, adj. No ka lewa; no ke ea.

A-toll′, n. He mokupuni akoakoa o ke kai, he ane poepoe ma ka loko kai mawaena.

Ăt′om, n. He pula; hu′na.

A-tōne′, v. E kala i ka hala.

A-tōne′ment, n. Ke kalahala.

A-trŏ′çioŭs, adj. Hewa loa; lokoino loa.

A-trŏç′i-ty, n. Ka mainoino nui; lokoino loa.

At-tăch′, v. 1. E hoopili; e hoopaa, *Attach a label,* e hoopili i hoailona. SYN. affix; tie.
2. E pili aloha aku. SYN. enamor.
3. E hopu i ka waiwai, a kino paha, no ka aie. SYN. take.

Ăttaçhe′ (at-ta-shā′), n. He kakau-olelo no ka elele aupuni.

At-tăch′ment, n. 1. Ka hoopaa ana; hoopili ana.
2. Ka pili aloha. SYN. Affection.
3. Palapala hoopaa waiwai.

At-tăck′, v. 1. E hakaka. SYN. assault.
2. E hoouka kaua. SYN. battle.

At-tāin′, v. 1. E loaa, mamuli o ka hooikaika. SYN. arrive at.

At-tāin′a-ble, adj. Hiki ke loaa mamuli o ka hooikaika.

At-tāin′ment, n. Ka loaa mamuli o ka hooikaika.

At-tĕmpt′, n, Ka hoao ana. SYN. trial; effort. *Make an attempt,* e hoao.

At-tĕnd′, v. 1. E hoolohe. SYN. listen; hear.
2. *Attend service,* e hele i ka halawai.
3. E lawelawe. *To attend on the sick,*

e lawelawe no ka poe mai. SYN. wait on.

At-tĕnd′ançe, n. 1. Ka hoolohe ana. SYN. regard. *Attendance on instruction,* ka hoolohe ana i ka naauao.
2. Ka hele mau ana. *Attendance at court,* ka hele mau ana i ka aha hookolokole.
3. Ka lawelawe ana. SYN. waiting upon.

At-tĕnd′ant, n. 1. He mea lawelawe.
2. He mea hele mau. *An attendant at church,* he mea hele mau i ka halawai.

At-tĕn′tion, n. 1. Hoolohe. SYN. heed.
2. *Attention to study,* ka noonoo no ke ao ana.
3. Maliu; hoolaulea. SYN. civility; respect. *Attention to guests,* ka maliu ana i na hoa aina.

At-tĕnt′ive, adj. 1. Hoolohe. *An attentive child,* he keiki hoolohe. SYN. heedful.
2. Maliu; laulea.

At-tĕnt′ive-ly, adj. 1. *Listen attentively,* e haliu pono mai i na pepeiao; e haka pono.

At-tĕn′u-āt-ed, adj. 1. Wiwi; olala. SYN. thin.
2. Lahilahi loa.
3. Makalii loa.

At-tĕst′, v. E olelo hoike. SYN. witness.

Ăt′tie, n. Kauwahi o ka hale malalo pono o ke kaupoko.

At-tire′, n. Na aahu; na lole komo. SYN. garments; raiment· clothes.

Ăt′ti-tŭde, n. 1. Ke ano o ke ku ana, ka noho ana, ka moe ana. *To stand in a lazy attitude,* e ku ma ke ano lomaloma. *To sit in an attitude of attention,* e noho me ka haka pono. *A reclining attitude,* he moe hilinai.
2. *To assume a threatening attitude,* e noho (or ku) ma ke ano hooweliweli.

At-tor′ney, n. He kokua ma ke kanawai; he hope; he loio.

At-trãct′, v. E ume. *The sun attracts the earth,* ume ka La i ka Honua. *To attract attention,* e ume i ka noonoo; or e ume i ka ike o ka maka.

At-trãc′tion, n. 1. Ka ume ana. *Attraction of gravitation,* ka ume ana o ka honua i ke kaumaha.
2. He mea aulii; mea mikioi; he kumu onou.

At-trãct′ive, adj. Aulii; onou. *An attractive woman,* he wahine aulii. *Attractive vice,* na lealea e onou ana.

At-trĭb′ute, v- See *Ascribe.*

Ăt′tri-bŭte, n. He ano; he loina.

Auç′tion, n. Kudala.

Auç′tion-eer′, n. Kanaka kudala.

Au-dā′çioŭs, adj. Nahoa; aa; mahaoi; §yn. bold.

Au-dāç′i-ty, n. Ke ano nahoa; aa wale.

Au′di-ble, adj. Loheia.

Au′di-bly, adv. Maopopo i ka pepeiao.

Au′di-ençe, n. 1. Ka lohe ana. SYN. hearing. *In the audience of the people,* ma ka lohe ana o na kanaka.
2. He anaina. SYN. assembly. *Speak before an audience,* e kamilio imua o ke anaina.

Au′dit, v. E hooia i na helu, a i na buke helu paha.

Au′di-tor, n. 1. Luna hooia helu dala.
2. Ka mea e lohe ana.

Au′ger, n. He wili puka nui.

Aug-ment′, v. E hoomahuahua′e. SYN. increase.

Au′gur, v. E kilokilo; e wanana. SYN. predict; forbode.

Au′gust, n. Ka mahina, Augate.

Au-gŭst′, adj. Hanohano loa.

Äunt, n. Kaikuahine o ka makua; makua ma ka hanau′na.

Au-riç′u-lar, adj. E pili ana i ka pepeiao.

Au-rō′ra, n. Ke alaula.

Au′spi-çes, n. Malu. *Under the auspices of the King,* malalo o ka malu o ka Moi.

Au-spī′çioŭs, adj. Kupono. SYN. propitious. *An auspicious day,* he la kupono.

Au-stĕr′i-ty, n. Ano oolea. SYN. severity.

Au-thĕn′tic, adj. Oiaio, SYN. true; genuine. *An authentic account,* he kaao oiaio.

Au-thĕn′ti-cāte v. E hooia. SYN. prove.

Au′then-tiç′i-ty, n. Ka oiaio maoli. SYN. genuineness.

Au′thor, n. 1. Ke kumu; ka mea i hookumu. *He is the author of the trouble,* ke kumu oia o ka pilikia; or, nana i hookumu i ka pilikia. SYN. source.
2. *The Great Author of life,* ke Kumu Nui o ke ola.
3. Mea haku buke; haku mele, etc.

Au-thor′i-ta-tive, adj. Mana. *An authoritative manner,* he ano mana.

Au-thor′i-ty, n, Ka mana kauoha. SYN. power. *By authority,* ma ke kauoha. *All in authority,* ka poe a pau ia lakou ka mana kauoha.
2. He mea i hilinai ia; he koo. *He is an authority in law,* he mea oia i hilinai ia ma ke kanawai; or, he koo oia ma ke kanawai.

Au′thor-ize, v. E kauoha; e haawi i ka mana.

Au′to-bi-ŏg′ra-phy, n. He moolelo a ke kanaka nona iho.

Au-tŏc′ra-çy, n. Ka mana hookahi.

Au′to-crat, n. Ka mea iaia ka mana hookahi; ka mana a pau.

Au′to-graph, n. Ke kakaulima. SYN. hand-writing; chirography.

Au′tŭmn, n. Kau haule o na lau.

Aux-il′ia-ry, n. 1 He kokoolua. SYN. assistant; ally.

2. *An auxiliary verb*, he haina kokua.

A-vail′, *v.* E kokua. SYN. assist.
Lying will not avail, o ka wahahee he mea kokua ole ia.

A-vails′, *n. pl.* Na loaa. SYN. profits.
The avails of industry, na loaa mamuli o ka hooikaika.

A-vail′a-ble, *adj.* Hiki ke loaa.

Av′a-lanche, *n.* Ke kaa ana. *An avalanche of earth*, ke kaa ana o ka lepo, (ma na pali o kuahiwi).

Av′a-rice, *n.* Puniwaiwai; makee waiwai; alunu.

Av-a-ri′cious, *adj.* Puniwaiwai; alunu.

A-venge′, *v.* E hoopai. SYN. punish; vindicate.

A-ven′ger, *n.* Ka mea hoopai. SYN. vindicator.

Av′e-nue, *n.* 1. He alanui akea iloko o ke kulanakauhale.

A-ver′, *v.* SYN. assert.

Av′er-age, *n.* 1. Averika; ke kaulike.
2. *Adj.* Ike mau ia. *An average amount of rain*, he u-a i ike mau ia. *An average degree of understanding*, he noonoo i ike mau ia. SYN. common.

A-verse′, *v.* Ku-e′ ka manao.

A-ver′sion, *n.* Ke ku-e′ o ka manao. SYN. antipathy; repugnance.

A-vert′, *v.* 1. E hoohuli ku-e′ i na maka.
2. E pale aku. *Avert the danger*, e pale aku i ka popilikia.

A′vi-a-ry, *n.* He hale no na manu o ka lewa.

A-vid′i-ty, *n.* Ka makemake nui. SYN. greediness.

Av′o-ca′tion, *n.* He hana liilii. *The avocations of life*, na hana liilii o keia ola.

A-void′, *v.* E kaaokoa.

A-void′a-ble, *adj.* Hiki ke hookaaokoa ia; hiki ke pale ia.

Av′oir-du-pois′, (**av-er-dū-poiz′**), *a.* *Avoirdupois weight*, ke ana kaumaha no na kino nui.

A-vow′, *v.* E ae hoakaka pono. *He avowed the crime*, ua ae hoakaka mai oia nana i hana i ke karaima. *An avowed intention*, he manao paa i hoakaka pono ia.

A-vow′al, *n.* Ka ae hoakaka ana. SYN. admission. *An avowal of crime*, ka ae hoakaka ana no ke karaima.

A-wait′, *v.* E kakali; e kali. *I await your pleasure*, ke kali nei a′u i kou makemake.

A-wake′, *adj.* Makaala.

A-wake′, *v.* E ala; e makaala.

A-wak′en, *v,* E hooala mai.

A-wak′en-ing, *n.* Ka hooala ana mai.

A-ward′, *n.* He olelo hooholo. SYN. judgement; decision.

A-ware′, *v,* E ike; e maopopo. SYN. know.

A-way′, *adv.* 1. Ma kahi e. *Go away*, e hele ma kahi e.
2. Aku. *Throw it away*, e kiola aku ia mea.

Awe (aw), *n.* Ka ilihia o ka naau; ka weliweli o ka naau.

Aw′ful, *adj.* Weliweli; ilihia; eehia.

A-while′, *adv.* 1. Iki. *Rest awhile*, e hoomaha iki.
2. Liuliu iki. *After a while*, a liuliu iki.

Awk′ward, *adj.* Hemahema; manuea; hauhili. SYN. blundering.

Awl, *n.* He o.

Awn′ing, *n.* He anini; lole pale la.

Axe } *n.* Koi lipi; koi.
Ax }

Ax′i-om, *n.* Akiuma, he oiaio maopopo lea.

Ax′i-o-mát′ie, *adj.* Maopopolea. *Axiomatic truth*, he oiaio maopopolea.

Ax′is, *n.* He iho. *Axis of the earth*, ka iho o ka Honua.

Ax′le, } *n.* Paipaikomo.
Ax′le-tree }

Aye, *adv.* 1. Ae.
2. Wa pau ole. SYN. ever. *For ever and aye*, no ka wa pau ole.

Az′ure, *adj.* Uliuli, e like me na lani.

B

Băb'ble, *v.* E walaau wale; e hauwalaau.

Băb'bler, *n.* Mea walaau wale.

Băbe ⎰ *n.* Keiki kolo; keiki omo waiu.
Bā'by ⎱

Bab-oon', *n.* Keko nui.

Bā'by-hood, *n.* Ka wa keiki kolo.

Bā'by-ish, *adj.* Ano keiki liilii.

Băch'ē-lor, *n.* Kanaka i mare ole.

2. *Bachelor of arts,* he inoa hanohano i haawiia i na haumana i puka pono aku mai ke kula nui.

Băck, *n.* Kua.

Băck, *adv.* Ma ke kua. SYN. behind. *Back of the house,* ma ke kua o ka hale.

2. Mahope ae.

Băck, *v.* 1. E haawe; e waha.

2. E ee maluna. *To back a horse,* e ee maluna o ka lio.

3. E hooemi hope; e emikua.

Băck'bite, *v.* E nuku; e aki.

Băck'bit-er, *n.* Kanaka akiaki.

Băck'bōne, *n.* Iwi kuamoo.

Băck'dōōr, *n.* Ka puka ma ke kua o ka hale.

Băck'side, *n.* Aoao hope.

Băck-slide', *v.* E haalele i ka pono.

Băck-slid'er, *n.* Mea haalele i ka pono.

Băck'ward ⎰ *adv.* 1. I hope ae; emi-
Băck'wards ⎱ kua.

2. Lolohe. *He is backward in his studies,* lolohe oia ma kana imi ana.

Băck-wōōds'man, *n.* He kuaaina; he kaikua.

Bā'eon, *n.* Aoao puaa, i kopiia a kaulaiia i ka uahi.

Băd, *adj.* 1. Ino; hewa.

2. Pupuka. *A bad thing,* he mea pupuka.

Bădge, *n.* He hoailona. SYN. insignia. *A badge of office,* he hoailona o ka oihana. *Insignia of rank,* na hoailona o ke kulana.

Băf'fle, *v.* E hoohoka; e keakea. SYN. balk; frustrate.

Băf'fling, *adj.* Hoolauwili wale. *A baffling wind,* he makani hoolauwili wale.

Băg, *n.* He eke; he hipuu.

Băg'gage, *n.* Ukana pili kino.

Băg'ging, *n.* Lole hana eke.

Bāil, *n.* Bela, ma ke kanawai he dala hoopaa kino.

2. He au bakeke.

Bāil, *v.* 1. E bela; e haawi i bela. *To give bail,* e haawi i ka bela. *To go bail,* e lilo i hope no ka mea i bela ia.

2. E ka i ka liu.

Bāil'a-ble, *adj.* Hiki ke bela ia.

Bāit, *n.* He maunu.

Bāit, *v.* 1. E kau i ka maunu ma ka makau.

2. E hanai ka ai i ka holoholona.

Bāke, *v.* E hoomoa ma ka imu.

Băk'er, *n.* Kanaka puhi palaoa.

Băk'er-y, *n.* Hale puhi palaoa; hale hoomoa mea ai.

Băl'ançe, *n.* 1. He kaupaona kau like.

2. Ke koena i like.

Băl'ançe, *v.* 1. E kaupaona like.

2. E hoohalike. *Balance accounts,* e hoohalike i na aoao elua o ka mooaie.

Băl'ançe-sheet, *n.* He pepa hoike i ka like o na aoao elua o ka mooaie.

Băl'eo-ny, *n.* He lanai uuku.

Băld, *adj.* Ohule; niania; nia.

Băl'der-dăsh, *n.* Olelo lapuwale; ano ole.

Băld'ness, *n.* Ka ohule o ke poo.

Băle, *n.* 1. He ope nui; he puolo nui.

2. He pu-a. *Bale hay,* e pu-a i ka mauu maloo.

Bāle'ful, *adj.* Hoopoino; ino.

Bălk, *v.* 1. E hoohoka. SYN. baffle.

2. E kuemi ihope, e like me ka lio nunuha.

Bălk'y, *adj.* Nuha. *A balky horse,* he lio nuha.

Băll, *n.* 1. He anaina hula.

2. He kini popo.

3. He poka. *Cannon ball,* poka pukuniahi.

4. He popo. *A ball of twine,* he popo kuaina.

Băl'lad, *n.* He mele o ka lahui.

Băl'last, *n.* Ka mea hookaumaha moku, a waapa paha.

Bal-lōōn,' *n.* He baluna; he eke nui i hoopihaia i ke ea mama, i lana pono iloko o ka lewa.

Băl,lot, *n.* He balota; he pepa koho.

Băl'lot, *v.* E koho balota.

Băl'lot-box, *n.* Pahu balota.

Bălm, *n.* 1. Bama; he laau ala.

2. He laau hamo eha.

Băl'sam, *n.* He laau hoola eha.

Băl'us-ter, *n.* He laau liilii o ka pa lanai hale.

Băl'us-trāde', *n.* He pa laau o ka lanai, a alapii paha.

Băm-bōō', *n.* He ohe.

Băm-bōō'zle, *v.* E hoopuniwale. SYN. fool.

Ba-nä'na, *n.* Maia. *Banana skin,* he paaa'. *Peel a banana,* e paaa' i ka maia.

Bănd, *n.* 1. Kaei; apo.

2. He hui; ahahui. SYN. society.

3. Hui puhi ohe.

4. Ili kaa pokakaa.

5. He poe. *A band of robbers*, he poe powa'. *A band of soldiers*, he poe koa.

Band, *v.* E hui no kekahi hana.

Bänd'age, *n.* He wahi' no na eha o ke kino.

Bänd'box, *n.* Pahu papale wahine.

Bän'dit, *n.* He powa. SYN. robber.

Bän'dy, *v.* 1. *Bandy words*, e kamailio aku kamailio mai.

2. E hoolei aku, hoolei mai.

Bäne' *n.* 1. Laau make.

2. Kumu hoopoino. *Bane of existence*, kumu e hoopoino ai ke ola.

Bäne'ful, *adj.* Hoopoino; hoopilikia. SYN. baleful.

Bäng, *n.* 1. He kui.

2. He pani ikaika o ka puka. SYN. slam.

Bän'ish, *v.* E kipaku mai ka one hanau.

Bän'ish-ment, *n.* Ke kipaku ana i ka aina e.

Bän'is-ter, *n.* See *Balluster.*

Bänk, *n.* 1. He kapa. *Bank of a stream*, he kapa kahawai.

2. He ahua. *A bank of earth*, he ahua lepo.

3. He ba'neko; hale malama dala.

Bänk, *v.* 1. E pale me ka lepo.

2. E hoomoe dala ma ka ba'neko.

Bänk'-ae-eount', *n.* Ka mooaie ma ka ba'neko.

Bänk'-bill, *n.* Dala pepa a ka ba'neko.

Bänk'er, *n.* Kanaka lawelawe ma ka oihana ba'neko; kanaka ba'neko.

Bänk'ing-bus'i-ness, *n.* Ka oihana ba'neko.

Bänk'rupt, *n.* He banekarupa; mea i hoka ma kana oihana.

Bänk'rupt-çy, *n.* Ka lilo ana i banekarupa. *To go into bankruptcy*, komo i ka banekarupa.

Bänk'-stoek, *n.* Na mahele o ke kumu paa o ka ba'neko.

Bän'ner, *n.* He hae; he lepa. *Sabbath school banner*, hae kula sabati.

Bän'quet, *n.* He ahaaina hanohano.

Bän'ter, *v.* E hoonaukiuki; e hana wale; e hooaikola. SYN. tease.

Bäp'tism, *n.* Ka bapetiso ana.

Bäp-tize', *v.* E baptiso.

Bär, *n.* 1. He pauku, *A bar of iron*, he pauku hao.

2. Pakaukau kuai waiona.

3. He pa o ka hale hookolokolo. *The prisoner at the bar*, ka lawehala imua o ka pa o ka hale hookolokolo.

4. He pale o ka leo mele.

5. He wahi papau ma ka nuku o ka muliwai, a ma kahi komo o na awa kumoku.

6. He papa loio.

7. He wahi hookolokolo. *Appear before the bar of God*, e ku imua o ke aha hookolokolo o Ke Akua.

8. He pale. *A bar to further progress*, he mea e pale ai ka holo mua.

Bär, *v.* 1. E pani a paa.

2. E kau pale; e keakea.

Bär-bä'ri-an, *n.* Kanaka hihiu; hupo.

Bär'bar-işm, *n.* Ka noho hupo ana; ka noho hihiu ana.

Bär'bar-oüs, *adj.* 1. Hihiu; hupo.

2. Mainoino; lokoino. SYN. cruel.

Bär'ber, *n.* Kanaka ako lauoho.

Bärd, *n.* He mea haku mele. SYN. poet.

Bâre, *adj.* Neo; neoneo; olohelohe. *A bare reef*, he kuaau; koho'la.

Bäre'façed, *adj.* Hilahila ole. SYN. shameless.

Bäre'foot, *adj.* Kamaa ole; wawae olohelohe.

Bäre'häed'ed, *adj.* Papale ole.

Bäre'ly, *adv.* 1. Wale no. *Barely escaped*, pakele wale no. SYN. merely.

Bäre-ness, *n.* Ka nele; ka neoneo; ka olohelohe.

Bär'gain, *n.* Ke kuai ana. *To make a bargain*, e hooholo i ke kuai. *A fair bargain*, he kuai kaulike. *A poor bargain*, he kuai poho'. *A shrewd bargain*, he kuai apiki.

Bär'gain, *v.* E hooholo i ke kuai.

Bärge, *n.* He waapa holoholo lealea.

Bärk, *n.* 1. Ili laau.

2. Aoaoa o ka ilio.

3. He moku kia kolu, nona ka pea nui wale no ma ke kia hope; he kiapa.

Bärk, *v.* 1. E aoaoa.

2. E maihi i ka ili o ka laau.

3. E hoopohole i ka ili.

Bär'ley, *n.* Bale, he ano palaoa.

Bärn, *n.* Hale papaa.

Bär'na-ele, *n.* He unaoa.

Bärn'yard, *n.* Ka pa o ka hale papaa.

Ba-röm'e-ter, *n.* He barometa; mea ana i ke kaumaha o ke ea.

Bär'räeks, *n.* Hale noho no na koa o ke Aupuni.

Bär'rel, *n.* Pahu barela.

Bär'ren, *adj.* 1. Panoa. SYN. sterile. *Barren land*, aina panoa.

2. Koa. *A barren tree*, he laau koa.

Bär'ri-eäde', *n.* He pale kaua.

Bär'ri-er, *n.* He paku; he mea keakea.

Bär'ris-ter, *n.* He loio.

Bär'ter, *v.* E kuai waiwai no ka waiwai; e kuapo.

Bär'y-töne, *n.* Leo pa-ko-li, mawaena o ka leo kane me ke tenore.

Bäse, *n.* 1. Kahua. SYN. foundation.

2. Leo kane o ka leo mele.

3. *Base line*, kaha moe. *Base of a triangle*, aono moe o ka huina kolu.

Bäse, *adj.* 1. Haahaa; haumia. SYN. mean; vile.

2. Pupuka. SYN. worthless.

Bäse'less, *adj.* Kumu ole.

Bäse'ly, *adv.* Ino. *Basely desert*, haalele ino.

Bäse'ment, *n.* Ko lalo loa o ka hale; ke keena malalo.

Băse′ness, *n.* Ka haahaa; ka apiki; ka lapuwale. SYN. turpitude.

Băsh′ful, *adj.* 1. Palaimaka; maka hilahila. SYN. shy; diffident.

2. Oheke. SYN. countrified.

Băsh′ful-ness, *n.* Maka hilahila wale.

Bā′sin, *n.* 1. He pa tini.

2. He poho aina.

3. He loko wai uuku.

Bā′sis, *n.* Kahua; kumu. SYN. foundation.

Băsk, *v.* E lala; e moe nanea i ka la.

Băs′ket, *n.* Hinai; i-e.

Băste, *v.* 1. E omao.

2. E hili me ka laau.

3. E kopi′ i ke kai maluna o ka i-o e pulehu ana.

Băt, *n.* 1. Laau kinipopo.

2. He ope′ape′a.

Bătch, *n.* 1. Ka nui o ka ai i hoomoaia i ka wa hookahi.

2. Na hana i hanaia i ka wa hookahi.

3. Na mea o kela me keia ano i waiho huikauia.

Băth, *n.* He auau.

Băth′-brick, *n.* Pohaku anai pahi.

Băthe, *v.* E auau.

Băth′-house, *n.* Hale auau.

Băth′-room, *n.* Keena auau.

Băth′-tub, *n.* Pahu auau.

Băth′ing-dress, *n.* Lole auau.

Bat-tal′ion, *n.* Puali koa.

Băt′ter, *n.* Palaoa i kawiliia a lahilahi.

Băt′ter-y, *n.* 1. He wahi pa kaua.

2. He huina o na pu nui o ka moku, a o ka pakaua paha.

3. He mikini e hana ana i ka uwila.

4. Ke kui ana. *Assault and battery,* ke kui me ka hakaka′.

Băt′tle, *n.* Hoouka kaua.

Băt′tle-ar-rāy′, *n.* Kulana kaua.

Băwd′y, *adj.* Pelapela; haumia. SYN. obscene.

Băwl, *v.* E uwa; e uwe nui.

Bāy, *n.* 1. He kaikuono.

2. *Sick bay,* he wahi o ka moku manuwa i hookaawaleia no na luina mai.

Bāy′o-net, *n.* He elau.

**Ba-zäar′ } **
Ba-zär′ } *n.* Ka makeke o na aina o ka hikina.

Bē, *v.* He haina kokua. *Be still,* e noho malie.

Beach, *n.* Kahakai one; kaha one.

Bēa′con, *n.* Lama kuhikuhi.

Bēad, *n.* He pupu lei aniani, a metala paha.

Beak, *n.* Nuku manu. SYN. bill.

Bēam, *n.* 1. He kaola. *Beam of wood,* he kaola laau.

2. Ke ana waena o ka moku; ka laula′ o ka moku.

3. Na kaola o ka malamalama, *beam of light.*

Bēam, *v.* E malamalama mai. SYN. shine.

Bēan, *n.* He papapa.

Beâr, *v.* (past. *bore;* p. p. *born.*) E hanau; e hoohua.

Beâr, *v.* (past. *bore;* p. p. *borne.*) 1. E haawe; e koo.

2. E hoomanawanui; e ahonui.

Beâr′a-ble, *adj.* Hiki ke hoomanawanuiia.

Bĕard, *n.* Umiumi.

Bĕard′less, *adj.* Umiumi ole.

Beâr′ing, *n.* 1. Ke ano. SYN. mien; behavior. *His bearing was proud,* haaheo ae la kona ano.

2. Ka hoomaopopo ana kahi o ka moku e holo ana. Ke kukulu o kekahi mea mai ka moku aku

Beâr′ish, *adj.* Me he bea la.

Bĕast, *n.* He holoholona.

Bĕast′ly, *adj.* 1. Kohu holoholona.

2. Haukae; pelapela.

3. Lokoino; mainoino. SYN. brutal.

Bĕat, *v.* 1. E hahau; e pepehi. SYN. thump; pommel; strike.

2. E eo; e lanakila. SYN. vanquish.

3. E pana. *Beat time,* e pana i ka manawa.

4. *Beat to windward,* hoopahua; hoopiipii.

Bĕat′ing, *n.* Ka hahau ana; ka pepehi ana.

Beau (bō), *n.* 1. He kanaka hookahakaha.

2. He hoa kane o ka wahine mare ole.

Beaū′ti-ful, *adj.* Nani; maikai; nonohea; onaona. *A beautiful woman,* he wahine nonohea; kalelei; upalu. SYN. graceful. *Beautifully formed,* auliikolomanu. *A beautiful sight,* he nanaina nani; nanaina maikai.

Beaū′ti-fy, *v.* 1. E kahiko a nani. SYN. adorn.

2. E hoohiehie.

Beaū′ty, *n.* Ka nani; o kela me keia ano; ke kulia. *A beauty,* he kulia; he ui.

Be-cälm′, *v.* E hoolana malie; pohu. *The vessel is becalmed,* ua pohu ka moku

Be-çause, *conj.* 1. No ka mea. *I gave to him because he was needy,* ua manawalea a′u iaia, no ka mea ua nele oia. SYN. inasmuch.

2. Oiai. *You cannot go because you are sick,* aole hiki ia oe ke hele, oiai ua mai oe. SYN. since.

2. No. *We cannot go because of the rain,* Aole hiki ia kakou ke hele, no ka u-a.

Bĕck′on, *v.* E peahi me ka lima.

Be-çôme′ *v.* 1. e ku; kupono; kohupono. SYN. fit.

2. E lilo. *The studious youth will become the wise man,* e lilo ana ke keiki imi i kanaka naauao.

Be-çôm′ing, *adj.* Ku; kupono; kohu pono. *The coat is becoming,* kohu pono ke kuka. SYN. suitable. *Becoming conduct,* ka hana kupono. SYN. appropriate.

Bĕd, *n.* He moe; pela moe; wahi e hiamoe ai.

2. Wahi kanu. *A bed of flowers,* wahi kanu pua.

3. He kowa. *The bed of a river*, ke kowa o ka muliwai.

Be-daub', *v.* E hoohapala; hoohaukae.
SYN. smear.

Bĕd'bug, *n.* Uku lio.

Bĕd'chäm-ber, *n.* Keena moe. SYN. bedroom.

Bĕd'clōtheş, *n.* Na kapa moe.

Be-dĕck', *v.* E kahiko. SYN. trim; ornament.

Bĕd'ding, *n.* Na lako moe.

Bĕd'fel'lōw, *n.* Hoa moe pu.

Bĕd-häng'ings, *n.* Na paku moe.

Be-dim', *v.* E hoopowehiwehi.

Be-dim'med, *adj.* Pinanaea.

Bĕd'quilt, *n.* Kapa apana; kapa uhi owaho o ka moe.

Bĕd'rid-den, *adj.* Moe mau i ka moe, no ka mai.

Bĕd'side, *n.* Aoao o ka moe.

Bĕd'stĕad, *n.* Hikiee moe; he moe.

Bed'time, *n.* Hora moe.

Bee, *n,* Nalo meli.

Beef, *n.* I-o bipi.

Beef'steăk, *n.* I-o bipi koala.

Bee'-hive, *n.* Hale nalo meli.

Beer, *n.* Bia; mea inu.

Bees'wax, *n.* Kukae nalo meli.

Beet, *n.* He uala haole, ulaula; he piki.

Bee'tle, *n.* 1. He hamale laau. SYN. mallet.
2. He elelu'.

Be-fäll', *v.* E loohia mai.

Be-fit', *v.* Kupono. SYN. become.

Be-fit'ting, *adj.* Kupono; kohupono. SYN. becoming; suitable; proper.

Be-fōre', *prep.* 1. Imua o ke alo.
2. *adv.* Mamua.

Be-fōre'hand, *adv.* Mamua'e o ka manawa.

Be-fōre'-mĕn'tioned, *adv.* Haiia mamua.

Be-fōre'time, *adv.* Mamua; i kinohi. SYN. formerly.

Be-friĕnd', *v.* E hookipa; e hoopunahele.

Bĕg, *v.* E koi ikaika; e makilo; e noi wale. *I beg of you to let drink alone*, ke koi ikaika nei au ia oe e kaaokoa aku mai ka wai ona.

Be-gĕt', *v.* E hanau mai.
2. E hoohua mai.

Bĕg'gar, *n.* He noi wale; he makilo; he kamapuka.

Bĕg'gar-ly, *adj.* Nele loa; ilihune loa.

Bĕg'gar-y, *n.* Ka nele o ka noho ana. *Reduced to beggary*, hooliloia a nele loa.

Be-gin', *v.* 1. E hookumu. SYN. originate. *To begin an enterprise*, e hookumu i kekahi oihana.
2. E hoomaka. SYN. commence; enter upon; set about. *To begin a new term of school*, e hoomaka i hapaha hou o ke kula.

Be-gin'ner, *n.* 1. Mea nana e hookumu i kekahi mea. SYN. originator.
2. Ka mea e hoomaka ana.

Be-gin'ning, *n.* 1. Ka hookumu ana. SYN. origin. *In the beginning*, i ka hookumu ana; i kinohi.
2. Ke kumu; ka hoomaka ana; kinohou. *To make a beginning*, e hoomaka.

Be-gōne', *interj.* E hele pela!

Be-guile', *v.* 1. E hoowalewale; e hoohalua. SYN. delude; insnare.
2. E hoonanea. SYN. amuse. E hoohala manawa. *They beguiled the time with stories*, me na kaao lakou i hoonea wale ai.

Be-hälf', *n.* 1. Ka pono a kekahi. SYN. sake. *On your behalf*, or, *for your sake*, no kou pono.
2. No. SYN. for. *He was chosen speaker on behalf of (or for) the multitude*, ua kohoia oia i kakaolelo no ka lehulehu.

Be-häve', *v.* 1. E noho pono, noho malie. *He knows how to behave*, ua ike oia i ka noho pono.
2. E noho a hana. *Do not behave badly*, mai noho a hana kolohe.

Be-häv'ior, *n.* Ka noho ana o ke kanaka; ka hana ana. SYN. conduct; deportment. *Good behavior*, ka noho a hana pono.

Be-hĕad', *v.* E oki ke poo.

Be-hind', *prep.* Mahope; ma ke kua. *Behind the house*, ma ke kua o ka hale; mahope o ka hale.
2. *Adv.* Ihope ae. *He is behind, on the road*, ihope ae nei oia ma ke alanui.

Be-hind'hand, *adv.* Haule ihope; hakalia; lolohi.

Be-hōld', *interj.* Aia hoi! Aia la! SYN. lo!

Be-hōld'er, *n.* He mea ike maka. SYN. spectator.

Be-hoōve', *v.* E kupono.

Be'ing, *n.* Kela mea ola, keia mea ola.

Be-lä'bor, *v.* E hahau ino.

Be-lāt'ed, *adj.* Hoohakaliaia; hoololoheia.

Be-lay', *v.* Bile'; hooki ka huki ana i ke kaula o ka pea.

Be-lāy'ing-pin, *n.* Pine hoopaa kaula pea.

Belch, *v.* E uha'.

Bĕl'fry, *n.* Puoa bele.

Be-lie', *v* E alapahi; e hai hoopunipuni.

Be-lief', *n.* Manaoio.

Be-liev'er, *n.* Ka mea e manaoio ana.

Bĕll, *n.* Bele kani.

Bĕlle, (bel), *n.* He wahine ui; onaona.

Bel-lig'er-ent, *n.* Ka mea e kaua ana.

Bel-lig'er-ent, *adj.* Ano hakaka; ano kaua.

Bĕll'man, *n.* Kanaka hookani bele. SYN. bell ringer.

Bĕl'low, *v.* E uwo, me he bipi la.

Bĕl'lows, *n.* Upa' makani; opu makani.

Bĕl'ly, *n.* Opu.

Bĕl'ly-āche, (āk) *n.* Nahu o ka opu.

Bĕl'ly-band, *n.* Kaula opu; kaei opu.

Be-lŏng′, *v.* 1. Pili ia. *The book belongs to him,* pili iaia ka buke.
2. Na, *or* no. *The book belongs to John,* no Keoni ka buke.

Be-lóv′ed, *adj.* Aloha nui ia; hiwahiwa; halialia. SYN. cherished.

Be-lōw′, *prep. and adv.* Malalo; malalo iho; ilalo ae.

Bĕlt, *n.* Kaei; ili apo; kaula apo, SYN. band.

Be-mŏan′, *v.* E kanikau; e kaniuhu′ SYN. lament; bewail.

Bĕnch, *n.* 1. He noho loihi, kua ole.
2. He papa hana. *Carpenter's bench,* papa hana a ke kamena′.
3. Ka noho hookolokolo.
4. Ka papa lunakanawai.
The Bench and Bar, na lunakanawai me na loio.

Bĕnd, *v.* 1. E pelu. *Bend the back,* e pelu i ke kua.
2. E hoo pelu; e hooholu; e hoopio.
3. E kakiwi; e luhe′. *As withered plants.* SYN. droop.
4. Holuholu; nape; napenape. SYN. to be flexible.
5. E kukuli, *bend the knee.* SYN. bow.
6. E kulou. *Bend the neck or head,* e kulou i ke poo.

Bĕnd, *n.* 1. He pelu; he holu.
2. He hipuu; nipuu. SYN. knot.

Be-nēath′, *prep.* Malalo iho; ilalo ae.

Bĕn′e-dic′tion, *n.* Olelo hoomaikai. SYN. blessing.

Bĕn′e-făc′tion, *n.* Hana hoopomaikai.

Bĕn′e-făc′tor, *n.* Ka mea nana e hoopomaikai; mea hana manawalea; mea kokua.

Be-nĕf′i-çent, *adj.* Manawalea; lokomaikai.

Ben-e-fi′çial, *adj.* Pomaikai.

Ben-e-fi′çi-a-ry, *n.* Ka mea nana ka pomaikai; ka mea i hoopomaikaiia.

Bĕn′e-fit, *n.* He pono; he pomaikai.

Be-nĕv′o-lençe, *n.* Manao lokomaikai. ka imi ana i ko hai pomaikai.

Be-nĕv′o-lent, *adj.* Lokomaikai; manawalea; kokua i ko hai nele.

Be-nign′, (**nin**), *adj.* Oluolu. SYN. kind; generous.

Be-nig′nant, *adj.* Oluolu. SYN. kind; gracious.

Bĕnt, *p. p.* Lakee. SYN. doubled over;
2. pelupelu.

Bĕnt, *n.* Ke ake o ka naau; ka makemake. SYN. inclination; bias.

Be-nŭmb′, *v.* E hoo-maeele.

Be-quēath′, *v.* E hooilina waiwai.

Be-quĕst′, *n.* Waiwai hooilina.

Be-rēave′, *v.* E hoonele. *Me have ye bereaved of my children,* ua hoonele keike mai oukou i′au. *Bereft of his senses,* hooneleia i ka noonoo.

Be-rēave′ment, *n.* 1. Ka hoonele ana.
2. Ke kau ana mai o ka popilikia. SYN. affliction. *Bereaved,* O-a.

Bĕr′ry, *n.* Hua ai liilii; like me ka ohelo.

Bērth, *n.* 1. Kahi i ku ai ka moku ma ka uwapo.
2. He wahi moe maluna o ka moku.
3. He hana; oihana. *He has a good berth,* he oihana maikai kona.

Be-sēech′, *v.* E noi haahaa. SYN. supplicate.

Be-sĕt′, *v.* 1. Hoohei. *Beset with difficulties,* hoohei i na pilikia.
2. E paapu; e hoopuni. *Temptations beset me,* paapu mai na hoowalewale ia′u.

Be-sĕt′ting *sin,* hewa maa mau.
Be-setting sin, hewa maa mau.

Be-sīdes′ } *prep.* 1. Mea e ae; mea
Be-sīde′ } hou ae.
2. Halahu′. *Beside the mark,* halahu ka maka.
3. Nohoi. SYN. also.
4. *To be beside one's self with anger,* e pupuli no ka huhu.

Be-sīēge′, *v.* E hoopuni i ke kaua.

Be-smēar′, *v.* E hoohapala; hoohaukae. SYN. bedaub.

Be-sŏt′ted, *adj.* Haahaa loa; haumia loa.
2. Ona mau.

Be-spēak′, *v.* 1. E olelo e mamua.
2. E hoike e mai.

Bĕst, *adj.* Ka oi o ka maikai.

Bĕs′tial, *adj.* Haahaa; haukae; pelapela. SYN. beastly; vile; carnal.

Be-stir′, *v.* E hooeueu; e makaala; e ala′e.

Be-stōw′, *v.* 1. E haawi aku. *To bestow a blessing,* e haawi i pomaikai. SYN. confer.
2. E hoahu. *I have no place to bestow my goods,* aohe o'u wahi e hoahu ai i ko'u waiwai.

Bĕt, *v.* E pili waiwai. *He won the bet,* Eo oia ma ka piliwaiwai.

Be-tīde′, *v.* E loohia mai.

Be-tīmes′, *adv.* I ka wa kupono.

Be-trāy′, *v.* E kumakaia.

Be-trāy′er, *n.* He mea kumakaia. SYN. traitor.

Be-trŏth′, *v.* E hoopalau.

Be-trŏth′al, *n.* Ka hoopalau ana.

Bĕt′ters, *n.* Ka poe ma ke kulana kiekie ae. SYN. Superiors.

Be-tween′, *prep.* Mawaena o.

Bĕv′el, *n.* He kuea kunihi, no ke kamena′.

Bĕv′er-age, *n.* Mea inu. SYN. drink.

Bĕv′y, *n.* Auna′. *A bevy of birds,* he auna′ manu.

Be-wāil′, *v.* E uwe kanikau; kumakena.

Be-wāre′, *v.* E kiai pono; e makaala. SYN. take care; be cautious.

Be-wil′der, *v.* E hoopilihua: e hoopo hihihi. SYN. puzzle; perplex.

Be-wil′der-ment, *n.* Ka hoopohihihi ana o ka naau; ka hoopilihua ana.

Be-yŏnd′, *prep. and adv.* Ma o aku; i o aku. SYN. over there.

Bib, *n.* He pale-aina na ke keiki.

Bib′ber, *n.* Mea i maa i na waiona.

Bi′ble, *n.* Ka Palapala Hemolele.

Bib′li-cal, *adj.* No ka baibala. *Biblical history*, moolelo o ka baibala.

Bib′li-ŏg′ra-pher, *n.* He kanaka i makaukau ma ka moolelo o na buke i kakauia.

Bib′li-ŏg′ra-phy, *n.* Ka moolelo no ke kakau buke.

Bick′er, *v.* E nuku aku, nuku mai.

Bick′er-ing, *n.* Ka nukunuku ana.

Bid, *v.* 1. E koho, ma ke kuai kudala.

2. E kauoha; e kena′. SYN. order; command.

Bid′der, *n.* Mea nana e koho ma ke kuai kudala.

Bi-ën′ni-al, *adj.* Kela me keia lua makahiki.

Biër, *n.* Manele kupapau.

Big, *adj.* Nui; nunui. SYN. large.

Big′a-mist, *n.* Ka mea e noho ana me na kane mare elua, na wahine mare elua paha.

Big′a-my, *n.* Ka noho mare ana me na kane, a wahine paha, elua.

Big′ot, *n.* He mea pili noonoo ole i kekahi hoomana.

Bile, *n.* Lena.

Bilge, *n.* Kahi palahalaha olalo o ka moku, kahi e ili mua, ke ili ka moku.

Bilge′wä′ter, *n.* Liu o ka moku.

Bill, *n.* 1. He bila. *Bank bill*, bila dala. *Bill of exchange*, bila hooili dala. *Bill of entry*, bila hookomo waiwai i ka aina. *Legislative bill*, he bila kanawai.

2. He palapala. *Bill of divorce*, palapala oki. *Bill of health*, palapala hoike no ke ola. *Bill of lading*, palapala hoike ukana o ka moku. *Bill of mortality*, palapala kuhikuhi i na make. *Bill of rights*, palapala o na pono pili kino o ke kanaka. *Bill of exceptions*, palapala hoike manao ku-e′.

3. Nuku manu. SYN. beak. *A beak*, oia ka nuku o ka manu ai i-o.

Bil′let, *n.* 1. He palapala pokole.

2. Pauku laau.

Bill′iards, *n.* Ka bilioki; pahupahu.

Bill′lings-gāte, *n.* Olelo kuamuamu. SYN. foul language.

Bill′ion, *n.* He biliona; tausani miliona.

Bil′low, *n.* Ale nui o ke kai.

Bil′low-y, *adj.* Aleale.

Bi′mŏnth′ly, *adj.* Kela me keia lua mahina.

Bind, *v.* 1. E pu-a a paa; e nakii; e hikii.

2. E humuhumu. *Bind books*, humuhumu buke.

3. Hoopaa, ma ke kanawai; e paa.

Bind′er, *n.* 1. Mea e paa ai.

2. Mea humuhumu buke.

Bind′er-y, *n.* Hale humuhumu buke.

Bind′ing, *n.* Ka mea e hoopaa ai.

2. Ka humuhumu ana. *The binding*

of the book, ka humuhumu ana o ka buke; ka uhi owaho o ka buke.

Bin′na-cle, *n.* Ka pahu panana maluna o ka moku.

Bi-nŏc′u-lar, *adj.* No na maka elua. *A binocular telescope*, he ohe nana no na maka elua.

Bi-nŏ′mi-al, *adj.* Elua mahele. *A Binomial*, he kuanite hoailona helu, nona na mahele elua (*a+b*).

Bi-ŏg′ra-phy, *n.* Moolelo pili kino i ke kanaka.

Bi-ŏl′o-ġy, *n.* Ka ike e pili ana i ke ola o na mea kino ola.

Bi′ped, *n.* Holoholona wawae elua.

Bird, *n.* He manu o ka lewa. *Bird of prey*, manu ai i-o.

Bird′-cage, *n.* Hale manu.

Bird′-catch′er, *n.* He kawili manu; he kuhea manu.

Bird′s′-eye-view, *n.* Ka nanaina i ikeia mai luna mai; mehe maka o ka manu e nana ana ilalo, oiai oia e lele ana.

Bird′-lime, *n.* Kepau kawili manu.

Bird′s′nest, *n.* Punana manu.

Birth, *n.* Ka hanau ana.

Birth′day, *n.* La hanau.

Birth′place, *n.* One hanau; wahi hanau.

Birth′right, *n.* 1. Ka pono o ka hanau mua.

2. Kela me keia pono e ili mai ana mamuli o ka hanau.

Bis′cuit (bĭs-kĭt), *n.* 1. He paapaa berena.

2. He popo berena liilii palupalu.

Bi-sēct′, *v.* E oki ana ma na apana like elua.

Bi-sēc′tion, *n.* Ka oki ana ma na apana like elua.

Bĭsh′op, *n.* He bihopa.

Bĭsh′op-ric, *n.* Ka huina o na kihapai malalo o ka bihopa hookahi.

Bĭt, *n.* 1. Ka hao o ke kaulawaha.

2. He nao wili, no ka wili umauma.

3. He hunahuna; he hakina; he apana liilii.

Bĭtch, *n.* Ilio wahine.

Bīte, *v.* E nahu; e aki.

Bī′ter, *n.* Mea e nahu ana; e aki ana.

Bĭt′ter, *adj.* 1. Mulea; awahia; mucmue; malailena. SYN. acrid.

2. *A bitter cold day*, he la anuanu loa.

3. Uluhua. *A bitter feeling of resentment*, he manao uluhua, ku-e′.

4. *Bitter poverty*, *bitter want*, ilikole.

Bi-vălve, *n.* He opihi me na pani elua.

Bĭv′ou-ăc (bĭv-wak), *v.* E kiai a hala ka po, (pili i ka puali kaua.)

Bi-week′ly, *adj.* Kela me keia lua hebedoma.

Blăb, *v.* E hai i ka mea huna′; e holoholo olelo.

Blăck, *adj.* Eleele; panopano; nele loa i ka malamalama.

Blăck′board, *n.* Papa eleele.

Blăck'en, v. E hamo a eleele. *Blacken the character*, e hooino i ka inoa maikai.

Biăck'guärd (blag'gard), n. He mea kuamuamu; he waha haumia.

Biăck'lĕad, n. Kepau maloo eleele, pahee.

Blăck'leg, n. He kanaka apuka. SYN. swindler; cheat.

Blăck'ness, n. Eleele; pano.

Blăck'smith, n. Amara; kanaka kui hao.

Blăd'der, n. Opu mimi; koana.

Blăde, n. 1. Lau o ka mauu, huita, me na mea ulu oia ano.
2. Maka. *The blade of the knife*, ka maka o ka pahi.
3. Kahi palahalaha o ka hoe.

Blăm'a-ble, adj. Ku i ka ahewaia. SYN. culpable; faulty.

Blăme, v. E hewa; hoahewa. SYN. censure.

Blăme, n. 1. Ka ahewa i kau ia maluna o kekahi.
2. Ka hewa. *You are to blame*, nau ka hewa.

Blăme'less, adj. Hala ole; hewa ole.

Blăme'wor'thy, adj. See *Blamable*.

Blănd, adj. Oluolu; nahenahe; palanehe; ano waipahe'. SYN. civil; courteous.

Blănd'ish-ment, n. Ano onou; hoomalimali.

Blănk, n. He hakahaka; pepa pai hakahakaia.

Blănk'et, n. Pale lole huluhulu.

Blär'ney, n. Olelo hoomalimali.

Blăs-phême', v. 1. E olelo ino i ka inoa o Ke Akua; o hailiili.
2. E hookae i na mea laa.

Blăs-phĕm'er, n. 1. Ka mea e olelo ino ana no Ke Akua; mea hailiili.
2. Mea hookae ana i na mea laa.

Blăs'phe-my, n. 1. Olelo hailiili; olelo kuamuamu.
2. Ka hookae ana i na mea laa.

Blăst, n. 1. Pa ino mai o ka makani.
2. Ka hooho ana o na pu.
3. Ka hoopa-hu ana.
4. Ka mae ana.

Blăst, v. E hoopa-hu'; e mae; e luhe'.

Blăze, n. Lapalapa ahi.

Blăze, v. E na pono.

Blĕach, v. E hookeokeo.

Blĕak, adj. Oneanea. SYN. desolate; dreary.

Blĕar, adj Piapia.

Blĕar'-eyĕd, adj. Maka piapia; hapopo.

Blĕat, v. E alala', like me ka hipa.

Blĕat
Blĕat'ing } n. Ka alala' o ka hipa.

Bleed, v. E kahe koko.

Blĕm'ish, n. He ki-na'. SYN. defect; flaw.

Blĕnd, v. E kawili pu; e hui pu. SYN. mix.

Blĕss, v. 1. E hoomaikai; hoalohaloha.
2. E hoopomaikai.

Blĕss'ed, adj. Pomaikaî.

Blĕss'ing, n. He pomaikai; hoalohaloha; hoomaikai.

Blight, n. Kakani; ponalo.

Blight, v. 1. E mae; e mimino.
2. E hoohoka. *Blighted hope*, manao lana i hoohokaia.

Blind, adj. Makapo'; makapaa.

Blind'fŏld, v. E uhi ka maka a paa.

Blind'man's-bŭff', n. Ka paani kanaka makapo.

Blind'ness, n. Ka makapo.
2. *Blindness of mind*, Naaupo.

Blink, v. E imo. SYN. wink.

Blink'er, n. He pale maka ma ke kaulawaha o ka lio holo kaa.

Bliss, n. Hauoli piha. SYN. felicity.

Bliss'ful, adj. Piha i ka hauoli.

Blis'ter, n. He oolapu o ka ili.

Blithe, adj. Hoihoi; nakui; olioli. SYN. gay; merry; joyous.

Blōat, v. E hoopehu.

Blŏck, n. 1. He pauku. *A block of wood*, he pauku laau.
2. He palaka hiu, mea huki.
3. *Children's blocks*, mea paani no kamalii.

Blŏck, v. E papani a paa. *Block up the road*, e papani a paa i ke alanui.
3. E keakea. *Block the side walk*, e keakea i ke alanui hele wawae.

Blŏck-āde', v. 2. Ka pani ana a paa o ke awa ku moku e na moku manuwa.
2. Ka pani ana o ke alanui hao i ka hau i hiki ole i na kaa ke hele.

Blŏck'head, n. He poo laau; mea ike ole ma ka imi.

Blŏod, n. Koko.

Blŏod'heat, n. Ka wela o ke koko.

Blŏod'hound, n. Ilio hae kanaka.

Blŏod'less, adj. 1. Koko ole.
2. Hookahe ole i ke koko. *A bloodless victory*, he lanakila hookahe ole i ke koko.

Blŏod're-lā'tion, n. He pili koko.

Blŏod'shĕd, n. Hookahe koko.

Blŏbd'-shŏt, adj. Ula. *Blood-shot eyes*, na maka ulaula.

Blŏod'thirst'y, adj. Puni koko.

Blŏod'vĕs'sel, n. Aa lele; aakoko.

Blŏod'y, adj. Paele i ke koko.

Blŏom, n. Ka ula o ka papalina o ka poe ui.

Blŏom, v. E mohala; e opuu.

Blŏom'ing, adj. Maka onaona.

Blŏs'som, n. He pua i mohala'e. SYN. flower.

Blŏt, n. He paele; he hapala.

Blŏt, v. 1. E paele; e hoohapala.
2. E holoi a nalo. *Blot out iniquity*, e holoi i ka hewa a nalo.

Blŏt'ting-pă'per, n. Pepa hoomaloo inika.

Blŏwse, n. Lole palaka.

Blŏw, v. He haua; he kui.

Blŏw, *v.* 1. E puhi; pa mai; nou.
2. *Blow the nose,* e hooke' ka ihu.
3. E haanou; e kaena. SYN. brag; boast.
4. E paupauaho. SYN. pant.
Blŭb'ber, *n.* Ka momona o ke kohola'.
Blŭb'ber, *v.* E uwe wale.
Blūe, *adj.* Uliuli. *Cerulean blue,* ka uliuli o na lani.
Blūes, *n.* Manao kaumaha; manao luuluu.
Blŭff, *n.* He pali ma kahakai.
Blŭff, *adj.* Okalakala. SYN. gruff.
Blŭn'der, *n.* Lalau; kuhihewa; kapulu. SYN. error; mistake; bull.
Blŭn'der-er, *n.* Kanaka kapulu; hauhili; manuea; lopalaueka.
Blŭn'der-ing, *adj.* Manuea; nahili; hoohemahema; kapulu.
Blŭnt, *adj.* Meumeu; pihi; oi ole; kumumu. SYN. dull.
2. SYN. bluff, *adj.*
Blŭnt'ly, *adv.* Me ka nihaniha.
Blŭr, *n.* He hapala; he kina'.
Blŭrt, *v.* E hai wale aku me ka noonoo ole.
Blŭsh, *v.* E palaimaka; pii ka ula i ka papalina.
Blŭsh'ing, *adj.* Omeomeo.
Blŭs'ter-er, *n.* Kanaka wahapaa; he wahakole; kanaka kehakeha.
Bŏar, *n.* Puaa kane.
Bŏard, *n.* 1. He papa laau.
2. Ka ai, i uku ia. *Good board,* maikai ka ai.
3. He papa. *Board of Education,* Papa Hoonaauao. *Board of Health,* Papa Ola. *Board of Immigration,* Papa Hoopae Lima Hana. *Board of Appeals,* Papa Hoopii Auhau.
4. He oneki moku. *On board,* maluna o ka oneki. *Overboard,* haule mai ka moku a iloko o ke kai.
Bŏard, *v.* E paina mau ma kahi hookahi, me ka uku.
Bŏard'er, *n.* He hoa aina e uku ana.
Bŏard'ing-house, *n.* Hale paina.
Bŏard'ing-school, *n.* Kula hanai.
Bŏast, *v.* E kaena; akena; haanou.
Bŏast'er, *n.* Mea kaena; mea akena.
Bŏat, *n.* 1. Waapa.
2. Kela me keia ano moku. *Steamboat,* mokumanu. *Pilot boat,* moku pailaka. *Fishing boat,* moku lawai-a.
Bŏat'man, *n.* Kanaka hoe waapa.
Bŏat'swain (bō-sn), *n.* Luna malama i na lako moku.
Bŏd'i-ly, *adj.* Pili kino. *Bodily strength,* ikaika o ke kino. *Bodily comforts,* na lako e pono ai ke kino.
Bŏd'y, *n.* Kino.
Bŏd'y-guärd, *n.* Kiai hoomalu kino. *King's body guards,* na koa hoomalu kino o ka Moi.
Bŏd'y-pŏl'i-tie, *n.* Ka Lahui. SYN. nation.
Bŏg, *n.* Nenelu poho; wahi pohopoho'.
Boil, *n.* Mai heehee; he puu.

Boil, *v.* 1. E lapalapa; e baila.
2. *Blood boils with anger,* pii ke kai o ka huhu'.
Boil'er, *n.* 1. He ipu baila wai.
2. Ipu mahu.
Bois'ter-oŭs, *adj.* 1. Uwau'wa; walaau; wahapaa.
2. Mahaoi. SYN. rough. *Boisterous play,* paani mahaoi.
3. He ino nui. *A boisterous sea,* he kai ino nui. *Boisterous weather,* kau makani ino; makani pukiki.
Bŏld, *adj.* Aa; koa; nahoa; wiwo ole.
2. Hueu. *Bold in mischief,* hueu i ke kolohe. SYN. daring.
Bŏld-fāçed', *adj.* Maka hilahila ole; mahaoi. SYN. impudent.
Bŏld'ly, *adv.* Me ka wiwo ole; me ka mak'au ole.
Bŏld'ness, *n.* Ke ano nahoa; aa; mak'au ole.
Bŏl'ster, *n.* Uluna loihi.
Bŏlt, *n.* He makia; hao hoopaa puka; he lou.
Bŏlt, *v.* 1. E mahuka. *The thief bolted,* mahuka aku nei ka aihue.
2. *Bolt the door,* e lou i ka puka.
Bŏlt-ŭp'right, *n.* Ku pololei loa. *Sit bolt upright,* e noho pololei loa. SYN. perpendicular.
Bŏmb, *n.* Poka' pahu'.
Bŏm-bärd', *n.* E kipu me na poka' pahu'.
Bŏm-bärd'ment, *n.* Ke kipu ana i poka' pahu'.
Bŏnd, *n.* 1. He mea liki a paa.
2. Bona; palapala hoopaa i ka olelo ae like.
Bŏnd'age, *n.* Ka noho ana kauwa kuapaa. SYN. slavery.
Bŏnd'māid, *n.* Kauwa wahine kuapaa.
Bŏnd'man, *n.* Kauwa kane.
Bŏnds'man, *n.* He hope ma ka bona.
Bŏnd'-sĕr'vant, *n.* Kauwa kuapaa. SYN. slave.
Bŏne, *n.* Iwi.
Bŏn'fire, *n.* He ahi nui i hoo-aia no ka lealea.
Bŏn-mŏt' (bong-mō), *n.* Olelo akamai.
Bŏn'net, *n.* Papale wahine.
Bŏn'ny, *adj.* Maikai; lea. SYN. blithe.
Bŏ'nus, *n.* He makana wale; makana manuahi.
Bŏ'ny, *adj.* Paapu i na iwi; iwiiwi.
Bŏo'by, *n.* 1. Mea uwe wale.
2. He manu o ke kai.
Bŏŏk, *n.* Buke; palapala i humuhumu-ia.
Bŏŏk'-bīnd'er, *n.* Kanaka humuhumu buke.
Bŏŏk'-cāse, *n.* Pahu waiho buke.
Bŏŏk'-keep'er, *n.* Mea malama buke helu.
Bŏŏk'-keep'ing, *n.* Kakau buke helu.
Bŏŏk'-lĕarn'ing, *n.* Ka ike iloko o na buke.

Book′-märk, *n.* Ka hoailona kuhikuhi wahi iloko o ka buke.

Book′-rack, *n.* Mea paipai buke, i ka wa e waiho hamama ana.

Book′-sel′ler, *n.* Kanaka kuai buke.

Book′store, *n.* Hale kuai buke.

Book′-trade, *n.* Oihana kuai buke.

Book′wórm, *n.* 1. He mu ai buke.

2. Kanaka lilo loa i ka imi buke.

Boom, *n.* 1. Laau nui no ka pea o ka moku.

2. Ka haalulu ana o ka nalu, a o ka pu nui paha i kona kani ana.

Boom, *v.* 1. E nei. SYN. rush

2. E haalulu.

Boor, *n.* He lopa′; he kuaaina. SYN. clown.

Boor′ish, *adj.* Kuaaina; laueka; hoomaniha. SYN. clownish.

Boo′gy, *adj.* Ano ona; ona iki. SYN. tipsy.

Boot, *n.* 1. Kamaa bute.

2. Mea manuahi ma ke kuai ana. *Something to boot,* he manuahi.

Booth, *n.* Hale kamala.

Boot′jaek, *n.* Mea wehe kamaa bute.

Boot′less, *adj.* Waiwai ole; makehewa. SYN. fruitless; vain.

Boot′y, *n.* Waiwai pio: waiwai i haoia. SYN. plunder; pillage.

Bor′der, *n.* Kae; palena; mokuna; lihi.

Bore, *v.* 1. E wili i puka.

2. E hoouluhua.

Bör′row, *v.* E noi i kekahi mea no ka wa pokole.

Bör′row-er, *n.* Mea noi pinepine i ka waiwai o hai no ka manawa iki.

Bo′som, *n.* Ka umauma; ka poli. *Bosom friend,* he pili alo.

Böss, *n.* He haku hana: he luna hana.

Böss, *v.* E hookikina; hoounauna.

Bo-tän′ie-al, *adj.* No ka ike o na mea ulu; no ka botania.

Böt′a-nist, *n.* Kanaka naauao ma ka botania.

Böt′a-nize, *v.* E imi i ke ano o na mea ulu; a me ko lakou waiwai.

Böt′a-nÿ, *n.* Botania; ka ike no na mea ulu, a me ko lakou waiwai.

Bötch, *n.* Hana i hookoia ma ke ano hemahema; kapulu.

Both, *adv.* Na mea elua; laua i elua.

Böth′er, *n.* Mea hoopilikia wale.

Böt′tle, *n.* He omole; huewai.

Böt′tom, *n.* Ko lalo loa; ka papa ku.

Böt′tom-less, *adj.* Palena ole o lalo.

Bou′doir (boo-dwôr), *n.* Keena malu′.

Bough, **(bŏw)** *n.* He lala. SYN. branch.

Boun′çing, *adj.* Puipui. *A bouncing baby,* he bebe puipui.

Bound, *n.* Ka lele mama. SYN. spring.

Bound, *v.* 1. E lelele. *The ball bounds,* lelele ke kinipopo.

2. E kau palena; e hai palena.

3. Hele ana. SYN. destined. *I am bound for Lahaina,* e hele ana au i Lahaina.

Bound′a-ry, *n.* Palena; mokuna; pea.

Bound′less, *adj.* Palena ole; akea loa.

Boun′ti-ful, *adj.* Haawi nui; lokomaikai. SYN. liberal; generous.

Boun′ti-ful-ly, *adv.* Me ka lokomaikai; me ka aua ole.

Boun′ty, *n.* 1. Ka lokomaikai. *Bounty of Providence,* ka lokomaikai a Ke Akua.

2. Ka waiwai i haawi wale ia.

Bou-quet′, (boo-käy), *n.* Puolo pua.

Bŏw, *n.* 1. He kulou.

2. Ka ihu o ka moku.

Bōw, *n.* 1. He pana; kakaka.

2. He pelu; he pio.

Bow′els, *n. pl.* Na naau. *Bowels of the earth,* ka opu o ka honua.

Bow′er, *n.* Hale malumalu

Bowl, *n.* He bola; he apu.

Bowl′der, 1. Pohaku nui poepoe.

2. Puu pohaku nui.

Bow′lēg′ged, *adj.* Wawae onaha.

Bow′line, *n.* Kaula hoopaa pea, i kupono i ka makani.

Bow′sprit, *n.* Laau ihu o ka moku.

Böx, *n.* Pahu.

Böx, *v.* E mokomoko; palepale′.

Böx′er, *n.* Kanaka mokomoko.

Boy, *n.* Kamalii kane; keiki kane.

Boy′hood, *n.* Wa kamalii.

Boy′ish, *adj.* Ano kamalii.

Braçe, *n.* 1. He koo; umii; mea paipai.

2. Wili umauma.

Braçe, *v.* E koo; e paipai.

Braçe′let, *n.* Kupee lima.

Bräck′et, *n.* 1. Kuha apo; [ ]

2. He papa liilii e kau ana ma ka paia o ke keena, i wahi e waiho ai na mea liilii.

3. *Bracket lamp,* kukui no ka paia hale.

Bräck′ish, *adj.* Oliuliu; muemue; hukai; mananalo.

Bräd, *n.* Kui winiwini, poo ole.

Bräg, *v.* E kaena wale. SYN. boast.

Brăg′ga-dô′çio } *n.* Kanaka liki; ka**Brăg′gart** } naka akena wale.

Bräid, *v.* E ulana; e hili.

Bräin, *n.* Ka lolo.

Bräin, *v.* E hoonaha′ i ke poo.

Bräin′less, *adj.* Poo hakahaka; noonoo ole.

Bräke, *n.* Mea hoopaa huila, i ole holo ino ke kaa.

Bräke′man, *n.* Kanaka malama i na *brake* o na kaa alanui hao.

Bräm′ble, *n.* Nahelehele okalakala; he kakalaioa.

Brän, *n.* Ka ihi o ka hua huita.

Bränch, *n.* He lala. SYN. bough. *A branch society,* he lala no ka hui.

Bränch, *v.* E manamana aku.

Bränd, *v.* E kuni; e hoailona.

Bränd, *n.* 1. He hao kuni.

2. He hoailona pai.

Brän′dish, *v.* E oniu aku i mea hooweliweli. SYN. flourish.

Bränd-new, *adj.* Hou loa.

Brăn'dy, *n.* Barani; he wai ona.

Brăss, *n.* Keleawe.

Bra-vá'do, *n.* Olelo akena wale; ka-naka haanou.

Brāve, *adj.* Aa; koa; maka'u ole. SYN. courageous; fearless.

Brāve'ly, *adv.* Koa maoli, me ka wi-wo ole. SYN. fearlessly.

Brạwl, *n.* He hakaka'; he haunaele.

Brạwl'er, *n.* Mea hakaka wale; mea hoohaunaele; hookonokono haunaele.

Brạw'ny, *adj.* Puipui; kino ikaika.

Brāy, *n.* Ka uwe o ke kekake.

Brā'zen, *adj.* 1. Keleawe.
2. Mahaoi.

Brā'zen-fāçed', *adj.* 1. Maka keleawe.
2. Hilahila ole. SYN. barefaced; impudent.

Brēach, *n.* 1. Wahi hiolo; wahi hai. *A breach in the wall,* wahi hiolo o ka pa. SYN. break.
2. Ka uhai ana. *Breach of the peace,* ka uhai ana o ka maluhia.
3. He mokuahana. *A breach in the family,* he mokuahana iwaena o ka ohana.

Brĕad, *n.* Berena; palaoa ai.

Brĕadth, *n.* Laula; akea. SYN. width.

Brēak, *v.* 1. E wahi; wawahi; kuipa-lu. SYN. break down; demolish.
2. E moku; e pai'na, *Break a rope,* e moku ke kaula.
3. E hai; uhai; uhaki. *Break a law,* e uhaki i kekahi kanawai.
4. E kipo'. *Break open a door,* e kipo i ka puka komo.
5. E ulupa'. SYN. dash in pieces.
6. E hoolakalaka. *Break a horse to saddle,* e hoolakalaka ka lio i ka noho.
7. E popoi. *The surf breaks on the shore,* ke popoi nei ka nalu ma kahakai.
8. E haalele; e kaaokoa aku. *Break away from evil companions,* e haalele i na hoalauna ino.
9. E hoopau wale. *The meeting was broken up,* ua hoopau wale ia ka ha-lawai.
10. E haehae. *To break the heart,* e haehae i ka naau.
11. *The day begins to break,* ke wehe nei ke alaula; ke moku nei ka pawa.

Brēak'er, *n.* Kai nalu; poi na nalu.

Brĕak'fast, *n.* Aina kakahiaka.

Brĕak'wa-ter, *n.* He pale kai.

Brĕast, *n.* Ka umauma.

Brĕast, *v.* E ku-e'; e halawai ku-e'; e paio. SYN. stem. *Breast a difficulty,* e paio me ka popilikia.

Brĕast'bŏne, *n.* Iwi umauma.

Brĕast'pin, *n.* He pine no ka poli.

Brĕast'plāte, *n.* Pale kaua no ka umauma.

Brĕast'work, *n.* Pa kaua lepo.

Brĕath, *n.* Ka hanu; ke aho; ke ea.

Brēathe, *v.* E hanu; e ha.

Brēath'ing, *n.* Ka hanu ana; ka ha ana; ke aho.

Brĕath'less, *adj.* Naenae; pauaho; paupauaho. *Breathless haste,* paupana-ho i ka hikiwawe.

Brēech'eṣ, *n.* Lole wawae. SYN. pan-taloons.

Breed, *v.* E hoolaha. *Garbage will breed pestilence,* e hoolaha ana ka opala pilau i ka ma ahulau.
2. E hooulu; e hoala. *Breed dissension,* e hoala i ka mokuahana.

Breed'er, *n.* 1. Mea hoolaha. *A cattle breeder,* mea hoolaha bipi; mea hanai bipi.
2. He kumu hooulu. *A breeder of dissension,* he kumu e hooulu ai ka mo-kuahana.

Breed'ing, *n.* 1. Ka hoolaha ana; ka hanai ana i na holoholona.
2. Ke ano o ka noho ana. *Good breeding,* ano keonimana. SYN. good manners.

Breeze, *n.* He makani oluolu; makani aniani; he ahe. *Beeeze up,* e aniani; e koaniani.

Brĕv'i-ty, *n. See conciseness.*

Brew, *v.* 1. E hana i bia me na wai o ia ano.
2. E ea mai; hoea mai. *That will brew trouble,* e ea mai ana ka pilikia no ia mea.

Brew'er, *n.* Kanaka kawili bia me na wai o ia ano.

Brew'er-y, *n.* Hale hana bia.

Bribe, *n.* Uku kipe'.

Brib'er, *n.* Ka mea e kipe' ana.

Brib'er-y, *n.* Ke kipe ana.

Bribe'tāk'er, *n.* Ka mea e lawe ana i ke kipe'.

Briek, *n.* Pohaku ula; uwinihepa.

Briek'bat, *n.* Apana pohaku ula.

Briek'kiln, (kil), *n.* He umu hoomoa pohaku ula.

Briek'lāy-er, *n.* Kanaka hoomoe po-haku ula.

Briek'māk'er, *n.* Kanaka hana poha-ku ula.

Briek'yärd, *n.* Pa kahi e hanaia'i o na pohaku ula.

Brid'al, *adj.* No ka mare.

Brid'al-pär'ty, *n.* 1. Ka poe e mare ana.
2. Na hoa ukali o ka poe e mare ana.

Brid'al-rōbes', *n.* Na kapa mare.

Bride, *n.* He wahine mare hou:

Bride'-eāke, *n.* Berena ono no ka ma-re ana. SYN. wedding cake.

Bride'grŏŏm, *n.* Kane mare hou.

Brides'-māid, *n.* Hoa kokua o ka wa-hine mare hou.

Bridġe, *n.* 1. Uapo; alahaka.
2. *Bridge of the nose,* ka iwi o ka ihu.

Brī-dle, *n.* Kaula waha.

Brī'dle, *v.* 1. E kau i ke kaula waha.
2. E kaohe. SYN. check; restrain.
3. E hookiekie. SYN. bridle up.

Brī'dle-path, *n.* Alanui lio.

Brief, *adj.* Pokole; haiki. SYN. short.

Brief, n. He palapala hoakaka pokole no ka hihia kanawai.

Brief'ly, adv. Me ka pokole. SYN. concisely.

Brief'less, adj. Hoopii ole. *A briefless lawyer*, he loio me ka hoopii ole; he loio me ka hana ole.

Brier, n. Laau ooi; he kuku; kakalaioa. SYN. bramble.

Brig, n. Moku kialua me na pea kuea ma na kia elua.

Bri-gāde', n. He mau regimana koa i huiia ma ka puali koa hookahi.

Brig'a-dier'-gēn'er-al, n. Ke generala o ka *brigade*.

Brig'and, n. He powa; kanaka hao wale. SYN. robber.

Brig'an-tine', n. Moku kialua me na pea kuea ma ke kia mua wale no.

Bright, adj. 1. Hulali; aiai; lilelile; hinuhinu. SYN. shining; brilliant.
2. Konane; konale. *Bright, as moonlight.*
3. Mikioi; eleu. *A bright child*, he keiki mikioi.

Bril'liant, adj. 1. Alohilohi; olinolino; wakawaka.
2. Mikioi.

Brim, n. Kae. *Brim of the cup*, ke kae o ke kiaha.

Brim'ful, adj. Piha loa; piha a hu.

~~Brim'stone, n. Kukaepele. SYN. sulphur.~~

Brine, n. Kai; wai kai.

Bring, v. E homai; e lawe mai.

Brink, n. Kae. *Brink of the precipice*, kae o ka pali. *Brink of the river*, kae o ka muliwai. *Brink of ruin*, kae o ka poino.

Brisk, adj. 1. Mama; hoihoi; makaala; anehe. SYN. alert; lively.
2. *Business is brisk*, holo ka hana.

Bris'tle, n. Hulu manoanoa ma ke kua o ka puaa.

Brit'ish, adj. No Beritania.

Brit'tle, adj. Uina; hakihaki wale; nahaha'. *Glass is brittle*, he mea nahaha' wale ke aniani.

Brit'tle-ness, n. Ke ano hakihaki wale.

Broach, v. 1. E wehe kinohou no loko mai o ka pahu.
2. E hai mua; e wehe mua i ka manao. *To broach a subject*, e wehe mua i ka manao e pili ana i kekahi kumu.
3. *To broach to*, e huli hewa i ka makani. *The boat broached to*, huli hewa ka waapa i ka makani.

Broad, adj. Laula; akea. SYN. extensive. *Broad shouldered*, kiwaawaa.

Broad'axe, n. Koi kalai.

Broad'cast, adv. Lu lima. *To sow broadcast*, e lu lima'ku i na anoano.

Broad'cloth, n. Lole paina.

Broad'side, n. 1. Ke ki like ana i na pu a pau ma kekahi aoao o ka moku manuwa.
2. Kekahi aoao o ka moku.

3. He palapala hoolaha i paiia ma ka aoao hookahi wale no.

Brogue, n. Olelo kuaaina: puana hemahema ma ka olelo.

Broil, n. He hauwalaau; haunaele; hakaka. SYN. disturbance; turmoil.

Broil, v. E koala; e pulehu.

Bro'ken, adj. Haki. *Broken all to pieces*, haki manunu.

Bro'ken-heärt'ed, adj. Ehaeha ka naau; make loa ka manao; walania.

Bro'ken-wind'ed, adj. Naenae; pauaho.

Bro'ker, n. He agena. SYN. agent.

Bron-chi'tis, n. Mai maloko o ka puu; hanapilo ka leo.

Brood n. Ohana manu.

Brood, v. 1. E hoopunana; e hoomoe hua.
2. E mumule; e nalu.

Brook, n. He kahawai.

Broom, n. He pulumi; he kahili.

Broom'stick, n. Au o ka pulumi.

Broth, n. Supa; kai. SYN. soup.

Broth'er, n. Hoahanau kane. *Older brother*, kaikuaana. *Younger brother*, kaikaina. *Brother of a sister*, kaikunane.

Broth'er-hood, n. Ka noho ana hoahanau.

Broth'er-ly, adj. Hoahanau. *Brother-~~ly love, aloha hoahanau.~~*

Brow, n. 1. Lae. *Eye brow*, kue maka.
2. Kae. SYN. brink.

Brow'beat, v. E hooweliweli; hoomaka'uka'u.

Brown, adj. Hauliuli; haeleele.

Brown-stud'y, n. Poonoonoo. SYN. reverie.

Browse, v. E ai nahelehele, e like me ka bipi, kao. hipa.

Bruise, v. E paopao.

Brunt, n. 1. Hoouka. *The brunt of the battle*, ka hoouka nui o ke kaua.
2. Luhi nui. *The brunt of the work*, ka luhi nui o ka hana.

Brush, n. Pulumi liilii; he balaki.

Brush, v. 1. E kahili; e pulumi.
2. E huli hou i na mea i haule. *Brush up his knowledge of arithmetic*, e huli hou i na mea haule o ke arimatika.
3. E nei awiwi. *Brush past*, e nei awiwi aku.

Brush'wood, n. Nahelehele.

Bru'tal, adj. Lokoino. SYN. cruel.

Bru-täl'i-ty, n. Ka lokoino; mainoino. SYN. cruelty.

Brute, n. 1. He holoholona.
2. He kanaka lokoino.

Bru'tish, adj. Like me ka holoholona; noonoo ole. SYN. stupid; ignorant; unfeeling.

Bub'ble, n. Hu'a o ka wai.

Buck'et, n. Bakeke.

Buck'le, n. Pihipihi.

Buck'le, v. E kaei. *Buckle on the sword*, e kaei i ka pahikaua.

Bud, n. Opuu pua.

Bŭd, *v.* E opuu.
2. *Putting forth of leaves,* liko.
3. *Putting forth of buds,* muo.

Bŭdg′et, *n.* 1. Bila haawina.
2. He puolu. *A budget of news,* puolo nuhou.

Bŭf′fa-lō, *n.* He bufalo: bipi hihiu.

Bŭf-fōon′, *n.* Kanaka kamaniha; mea hehena wale. SYN. clown.

Bŭg, *n.* He uku; mea kolo.

Bŭg′gy, *n.* Kaa lio lealea, e ha **ona** mau huila.

Build, *v.* 1. E kukulu. *Build a house,* e kukulu i hale.
2. E kapili. *Build a vessel,* e kapili moku.

Build′er, *n.* Mea nana e kukulu.

Build′ing, *n.* 1. Ka mea i kukuluia.
2. He hale.

Bŭlk, *n.* Ka nui; ka hapanui.

Bŭlk′head, *n.* He paku laau, a hao paha, iloko o ka moku.

Bŭlk′y, *adj.* Nunui loa.

Bŭll, *n.* Bipi kane.

Bŭll′dog, *n.* Ilio hae bipi.

Bŭl′let, *n.* Poka no ka pu ki poohiwi.

Bŭl′le-tin, *n.* He palapala hoolaha.

Bŭl′le-tin-bōard′, *n.* Papa no na palapala hoolaha.

Bŭl′lion, *n.* Ke kala me ke gula i pai ole ia a lilo i dala.

Bŭl′loek, *n.* Bipi kane opio.

Bŭll′rush, *n,* He naku; akaakai; kaluha.

Bŭlls-eȳe, *n.* 1. He aniani poepoe ma ka aoao o ka moku, mea e lama ai.
2. Ke kiko waenakonu o ka maka e kipu aku ai.

Bŭl′ly, *n.* Kanaka mahaoi; mea hoonaukiuki wale.

Bŭl′wark, *n.* Pale kai o ka moku.

Bŭmp, *n.* He puu.

Bŭmp, *v.* Ku. *He bumped his head,* ku oia i kona lae. SYN. hit.

Bŭmp′kin, *n.* He kuaaina.

Bŭn, *n.* Mea ono liilii; berena ono liilii.

Bŭnch, *n.* 1. Huhui. *Bunch of grapes,* huhui waina.
2. Ahui. *Bunch of Bananas,* ahui maia.
3. He puu.

Bŭn′dle, *n.* 1. Pu-a, *Bundle of wheat,* pua′ huita.
2. He puolo. *A bundle of papers,* he puolo pepa.
3. *Bundle of poi,* pai ai; holoai.
4. Olaolao; laolao, ope.

Bŭn′dle, *v.* E puolo; e pua; e ope; e hoolaolao.

Bŭng, *n.* Ka umoki nui ma ka aoao o ka barela.

Bŭng′hōle, *n.* He puka poepoe ma ka aoao o ka barela.

Bŭng′le, *v.* E kapulu ma ka hana.

Bŭng′ler, *n.* Kanaka i kapulu ma ka hana; mea hawawa ma ka hana.

Bŭng′ling, *adj.* Kapulu; hawawa; hemahema.

Bŭnt′ing, *n.* Lole hana hae.

Bugȳ, (boy), *n.* He mouo.

Bugȳ′an-cy, *n.* Ke ano lana.

Bugȳ′ant, *adj.* Lanalana.

Bŭrr } *n.* Hua o ka puakala; kakalaioa
Bur } kikania.

Bŭr′den, *n.* He haawe kaumaha; he ukana halihali.

Bŭr′den-sŏme, *adj.* Kaumaha; hooluhi.

Bū′reau (bū′rō), *n.* 1. Pahu ume.
2. He mahele nui o ka oihana aupuni. *Bureau of Education,* oihana hoonaauao. *Bureau of Customs,* oihana dute.

Bŭr′glar, *n.* He wawahi hale i ka po me ka manao hewa; mea kipo hale i ka po.

Bŭr′gla-ry, *n.* Ke karaima o ka wawahi hale i ka po.

Bu′ri-al (bĕr′ry-al), *n.* Kanu kupapau. SYN. funeral.

Bur-lĕsque′ (bur-lĕsk′), *adj.* Hooala i ka akaaka; mea e hu ai ka akaaka. SYN. ludicrous.

Bŭr′ly, *adj.* Kino nui ikaika.

Bŭrn, *v.* 1. E a; e hoo-a. *The fire burns,* ke a nei ke ahi.
2. E kuni; e hoowela. *I burnt my finger,* ua hoowela wau i kuu manamana lima.
3. E papaa. *The cake is burnt,* papaa ka berena ono.
4. E puhi i ke ahi; e kuni. *The house was burnt,* ua kuniia ka hale i ke ahi.

Bŭrn, *n.* He palapu ahi.

Bŭrn′er, *n.* Keleawe hoopaa uwiki.

Bŭrn′ing, *adj.* Wewela.

Bŭrn′ing-glass, *n.* Aniani hoo-a ahi, mamuli o na kukuna wela o ka la.

Bŭr′nish, *v.* E hoohulali; e anai a hinuhinu.

Bŭrst, *v.* E pahu′; e poha′.

Bŭr′y (bĕr′ry), *v.* E kanu ma ka lepo.

Bŭr′y-ing-ground′, *n.* Pa kanu kupapau.

Bŭsh, *n.* Laalaau.

Bŭsh′el, *n.* Busela, he ana no na mea maloo.

Bŭs′i-ly (bĭz′i-ly), *adv.* Paa loa i ka hana; lilo loa i ka hana.

Bŭs′i-ness (biz′ness), *n.* Oihana; ka hana i lawelawe ia. SYN. employment; occupation.

Bŭst, *n.* He kii o ke poo me ka umauma wale no.

Bŭs′tle, *v.* E awiwi; e makaala.

Bŭs′y (biz′y), *adj.* Paa i ka hana.

Bŭs′y-bod′y, *n.* He holoholo olelo; e-lepi.

Bŭt, *prep.* 1. Aka. *I called but he had gone,* kahea aku la wau, aka ua hala e oia.
2. Aka hoi; aka nae; eia nae. *I did not see him, but I heard his voice,* aole a'u i ike maka iaia, aka nae ua lohe a'u i kona leo. SYN. nevertheless.
3. Koe nae. *All went but John,* ua hele lakou a pau, koe nae o Keoni.

Butch'er, *n.* Kanaka loli bipi, kao, hipa, etc.

But-end', *n.* Ka welau nui. *The but-end of the log*, ka welau nui o ka pauku laau.

Bŭtt, *n.* He mea i hoohenehene nui ia.
2. He pahu ana me ke poo.
3. He pahu nunui.

Bŭt'ter, *n.* Waiu bata.

Bŭt'ter-flȳ, *n.* Pulelehua.

Bŭt'ter-milk, *n.* Ka waiu o ka waiu bata.

Bŭt'tock, *n.* Okole.

Bŭt'ton, *n.* Pihi lole.

Bŭt'ton, *v.* E pihi.

Bŭt'ton-hōle, *n.* Puka pihi.

Bŭx'om, *adj.* Onaona; ui.

Buȳ (bȳ), *v.* E kuai lilo mai.

Buȳ'er, *n.* Ka mea e loaa ana mamuli o ke kuai.

Bûzz, *v.* Kamumumu.

Bȳ, *prep.* Ma; mahope; ma o. *By-and-by*, mamuli; kokoke.

Bȳ-lạw, *n.* Rula.

Bȳ'path} *n.* He alanui pipa.
Bȳ'way }

Bȳ'stạnd-er, *n.* Mea e ku kokoke ana.

Bȳ'wọrd, *n.* 1. Olelo i wawa wale ia.
2. Kumu hoohenehene; mea i hoowahawahaia.

C

Căb, *n.* Kaa lio me ka uhi oluna. SYN. buggy.

Căb'bage, *n.* Kapiki; mea ai.

Căb'in, *n.* 1. Ke keena mahope o ka moku. 2. He hale pupupu.

Căb'i-net, *n.* 1. Pahu waiho buke; waiho mea milimili.
2. Papa kuhina. *Cabinet council*, aha kuhina.

Căb'i-net-māk'er, *n.* Kamena' hana pahu, noho, papa, me na lako hale e ae.

Că'ble, *n.* 1. Kaula hao heleuma.
2. Kaula nunui no ka moku.
3. *Telegraph cable*, uea telegarapa i hoomoeia malalo o ka moana.

Că'ble, *v.* E hooili i olelo ma ka uia telegarapa moana.

Ca-boose', *n.* Hale kuke oluna o ka moku.

Căche, *(kash)*, *n.* He ahu ai i hunaia.

Căck'le, *v.* E pukaka; e pukoko.

Căe'tus, *n.* Pabipi; panini.

Ca-dăv'er-oŭs, *adj.* Hakea, mehe kupapau la.

Ca-dĕt, *n.* Haumana no ke kula koa.

Că'di, *n.* He lunakanawai ma Tureke.

Căge, *n.* 1. Hale hoopaa holoholona. *A bird cage*, hale manu.

Ca-jōle', *v.* E hoomalimali hoopunipuni.

Cake, *n.* Palaoa ono.

Căl'a-bash, *n.* He umeke. *Water calabash*, hue wai.

Ca-lăm'i-ty, *n.* He popilikia; poino, pilikia nui. SYN. disaster; misfortune.

Căl-eu-lāte, *v.* E helu; e imi ma na helu. SYN. compute; reckon.

Căl'eu-lā'tion, *n.* Ka imi ana ma na helu; ka haina o ka imi ana. SYN. computation.

Căl'eu-lā'tor, *n.* Mea imi helu.

Căl'dron, *n.* Ipu hao nui mea baila.

Căl'en-dar, *n.* He alemenaka. SYN. almanac.

Călf, (käf), *n.* 1. Bipi keiki.
2. Oloolo wawae.

Căl'i-bre, (bur), *n.* 1. Ke ana waena o ka waha o ka pukuniahi me na pu kani e ae.
2. *Mental calibre*, ka ikaika o ka noonoo.

Căl'i-co, *n.* Lole kalikoa.

Căl'is-thĕn'ics, *n.* Hana hoomaamaa, hooikaika kino.

Căl'i-pers, *n.* Upa' ana poepoe.

Călk, *v.* E okomo moku.

Călk'er, *n.* Kanaka okomo moku.

Căll, *v.* 1. E kahea. *Call him*, e kahea iaia.
2. E kapa'ku.
3. E kipa launa.

Căll, *n.* 1. Ka hea ana; leo kahea.
2. Ke kipa launa ana.

Căl-lig'ra-phy, *n.* Ke kakaulima maikai.

Căl'ling, *n.* Oihana i maa ai. SYN. occupation; business; employment.

Căl'loŭs, *adj.* Oolea; maeele; leho.
2. *Callous spots*, leho; leholeho.

Călm, *adj.* Malie; lai; pohu.

Călm, *v.* E hoomalielie; e hoomaalili; e hoonana. SYN. quiet.

Călm'ly, *adv.* Me ka malie; malielie.

Călm'ness, *n.* Ka malu; ka lulu; ka malie. SYN. quietness; tranquility.

Cal-ŏr'ic, *n.* Wela. SYN. heat.

Ca-lŭm'ni-āte, *v.* E hooino wale i ka inoa, e niania; e akiaki. SYN. slander.

Ca-lum'ni-ā'tor, *n.* Kanaka niania; he paokee. SYN. slanderer.

Căl′um-ny, *n.* Alapahi; olelo niania; olelo akiaki. SYN. slander; detraction.

Cälve, *v.* E hanau ka bipi.

Cä′lyx, *n.* Ka wahi′ owaho o ka pua.

Căm′el, *n.* Kamelo.

Cämp, *n.* Wahi hoomoana. *Military camp*, wahi hoomoana o na puali koa.

Căn, *v.* Hiki.
2. *To can fruit*, e hookomo i na hua ai ma na tini.

Căn, *n.* He apu; he pahu metala. *Tin can*, pahu tini.

Ca-năl′, *n.* He auwai.

Ca-nä′ry, Manu kanari.

Căn′çel, *v.* 1. E kapae helu. *Cancel equal factors*, e kapae i na helu hana like.
2. E hoopau. *Cancel an agreement*, e hoopau i ka olelo ae like.

Căn′çel-lä′tion, *n.* Ka hoopau ana; ke kapae ana.

Căn′çer, *n.* He mai aai.

Căn′did, *adj.* Oiaio; epa ole. SYN. frank; truthful.

Căn′di-däte, *n.* 1. Mea e imi ana i kekahi oihana.
2. Mea i manaoia no kekahi oihana.

Căn′did-ly, *adv.* Me ka oiaio. SYN. frankly.

Căn′dle, *n.* Ihoiho; kukui aila.

Căn′dle-stick, *n.* Ihoiho kukui.

Căn′dor, *n.* Ka oiaio; ke kaulike. SYN. truth; fairness; justice.

Căn′dy, *n.* Ko omoomo.

Cäne, *n.* Kookoo. SYN. walking stick.

Cäne′bräke, *n.* Wahi paapu o na ohe.

Ca-nine′, *adj.* Ano ilio.

Căn′nis-ter, *n.* Pahu tini poepoe.

Căn′ni-bal, *n.* Kanaka ai kanaka.

Căn′ni-bal-işm, *n.* Ka ai kanaka.

Căn′non, *n.* Pukuniahi; pu nui.

Căn′non-äde′, *n.* Ke ki ana i na pu nui.

Căn′non-bạll, *n.* Poka′ no ka pu nui. SYN. cannon shot.

Căn′non-iër′, *n.* Mea lawelawe i ka pu nui.

Căn′not, *v.* Aole hiki.

Ca-noe′, (ka-nü′), *n.* Waa maoli.

Căn′o-py, *n.* He uhi maluna′e o ke poo.

Cänt, *v.* E huli iki ma ka aoao.

Căn′ta-loupe, *n.* Huewai tini.

Can-teen′, *n.* Huewai tini.

Căn′ter, *v.* E holo kainepu, e like me ka lio. SYN. gallop.

Căn′vas, *n.* 1. Lole ie; lole hana pea.
2. Na pea o ka moku.

Căn′vass, *v.* 1. E noi. *Canvass for funds*, e noi i dala no kekahi hana.
2. E paipai. *Canvass for votes*, e paipai no ke koho balota.

Căp, *n.* Papale kapu.

Cä′pa-bil′i-ty, *n.* Ka makaukau.

Cä′pa-ble, *adj.* Makaukau; kupono. SYN. able; efficient; competent.

Ca-pä′çioŭs, *adj.* Akea; nunui. *A capacious house*, he hale akea.

Ca-păç′i-ty, *n.* 1. Ke ana piha o kekahi mea.
2. Ke akea o ka noonoo.

Căp′a-pie′, *adv.* Mai ke poo a i na wawae.

Ca-păr′i-son, *n.* Na kahiko no ka lio.

Cäpe, *n.* 1. He lae o ka aina.
2. Kihei liilii no na poohiwi.

Cä′per, *v.* E lelelele; e haa.

Căp′il-la-ry, *adj.* Makalii mehe lauoho la. *Capillary attraction*, ume lauoho.

Căp′i-tal, *n.* 1. Kulanakauhale poo Aupuni.
2. Kumupaa, i hoomoeia ma kekahi hana.

Căp′i-tal-ist, *n.* Ka mea nona ke kumupaa; he kanaka waiwai nui.

Căp′i-tol, *n.* Hale Oihana Aupuni.

Ca-pit′ü-läte, *v.* E haawi iloko o ka lima o ka enemi.

Cä-priçe′, *n.* Manao lolilua; manao kapekepeke. SYN. whim; fancy.

Ca-pri′çioŭs, *adj.* Loli wale; kapekepeke; lolilua. SYN. whimsical; fickle.

Căp-size′, *v.* E kahuli; hookahuli.

Căp′stan, *n.* Pokakaa huki heleuma; huki ukana o ka moku.

Căp′tain, *n.* 1. Kapena moku.
2. Kapena o na koa.

Căp′tain-çy, *n.* Oihana kapena.

Căp′tioŭs, *adj.* Imi hala; keemoa; opukopekope. SYN. peevish; fault-finding.

Căp′tioŭs-ness, *n.* Ka manao imi hala.

Căp′ti-väte, *v.* E lawe pio i ka manao.

Căp′tive, *n.* He pio.

Cap-tiv′i-ty, *n.* Ka noho pio ana.

Căp′tor, *n.* Ka mea nana e lawe pio.

Căp′türe, *n.* Ka lawe pio ana.

Cär, *n.* Kaa alanui hao.

Cär′at, *n.* He ana kaumaha, eha′ huna; he kaupaona no na momi, a no ke gula.

Cär′a-vän, *n.* He huakai hele ma na aina o ka Hikina.

Cär′a-vän′sa-ry, *n.* Hale hookipa ma ka Hikina.

Cär′bine, *n.* He pu pokole ki poohiwi.

Cär′bon, *n.* Ka i-o o ka nanahu, a me na mea a i ke ahi.

Cär-bŏn′ic, *adj.* Pili i ke carbon.

Cär′cass, *n.* Heana; kino make o ka holoholona.

Cärd, *n.* He pepa manoanoa.
2. Pepa paani.
3. Palapala hoolaha pokole, i paila.
4. Pepa inoa. *Visiting card*, pepa inoa no ka makaikai launa ana.
5. He paa laau-kahi no ke kahi ana i ka huluhulu, pulupulu.

Cärd, *v.* E kahi huluhulu, pulupulu.

Cärd′er, *n.* Ka mea e kahi ana.

Cärd′case, *n.* He wahi′ no na pepa liilii.

Cär′di-ac, *adj.* Pili ana i ka puuwai.

Cär′di-nal, *adj.* Ka mea nui; ka mua. *Cardinal points of the compass*, na welelau nui o ka panana. *Cardinal virtues*, na pono nui.

Car'di-nal, *n.* He kahunapule nui o ka ekalesia Roma.

Care, *n.* 1. Manao nui e kaumaha'i.
2. Ka malama ana; ke kiai ana.
3. *Take care*, e akahele; e malama.

Ca-reer', *n.* Ka noho'na i keia ola. SYN course of life.

Ca-reer'ing, *p. p.* E holo mama ana. *The ship is careering over the waves*, ke holo mama nei ka moku maluna o na ale.

Care'ful, *adj.* Akahele; malama pono.

Care'ful-ly, *adv.* Me ke akahele.

Care'less, *adj.* Lalau; kapulu; nahili.

Care'less-ly, *adj.* Me ke akahele ole.

Ca-ress', *v.* E pulike; e milimili aloha.

Ca'ret, *n.* Puumana (∧).

Car'go, *n.* Ka ukana hooili o ka moku. SYN. freight.

Car'i-ca-ture, *n.* Kii hoomakeaka.

Car'i-ca-tur-ist, *n.* Mea kaha kii hoomake aka.

Car'nage, *n.* Ka hookahe koko; ka luku ana. SYN. slaughter; massacre.

Car'nal, *adj.* Pili i ke kino; pili i na kuko o ke kino. SYN. sensual.

Car'nal-ly, *adv.* 1. Ma ke ano kino.
2. Me ke kuko hewa.

Car-niv'o-rous, *adj.* Ai i-o holoholona.

Car'ol, *n.* Leo mele hauoli.

Ca-rot'id, *n.* Kekahi o na aakoko nui elua ma ka a-i.

Ca-rous'al, *n.* Ahaaina uhauha.

Ca-rouse', *v.* 1. E lealea uhauha.
2. E inu pu a ona.

Car'pen-ter, *n.* He kamena'.

Car'pen-try, *n.* Oihana kamena'.

Car'pet, *n.* Moena lole huluhulu.

Car'riage (**car'rij**), *n.* Kaa holoholo lealea.

Car'ri-er, *n.* Mea lawe; mea halihali. *A letter carrier*, he lawe leta.

Car'ri-on, *n.* I-o pilau.

Car'rot, *n.* Karoke; mea ulu.

Car'ry, *v.* 1. E lawe; e hali; e halihali.
2. E amo. *To carry on the shoulder*, e amo.
3. *To carry on the back*, e waha; e haawe.

Cart, *n.* Kaa lawe ukana; kaa kauo.

Cart, *v.* E hali ma ke kaa.

Cart-age, *n.* 1. Ka hali ana ma ke kaa
2. Uku kaa.

Cart'er, *n.* Kanaka hookele kaa ukana.

Car'ti-lage, *n.* Kumukumu; ka pilali iwi o na ami.

Car'tridge, *n.* Wahi' metala e hoopaa pu ana ka pauda me ka poka'.

Car'tridge-box, *n.* He pahu ili liilii waiho poka'.

Cart'-wright, *n.* Kanaka hana kaa.

Carve, *v.* 1. E okioki i-o.
2. E kalai laau, pohaku, etc.

Carv'er, *n.* 1. Mea okioki i-o.
2. Mea kalai laau, pohaku, etc.
3. Pahi nui, oki i-o. SYN. carving knife.

Cas-cade', *n.* Wai kahe; wai lele. SYN. waterfall; cataract.

Case, *n.* He pahu; he wahi'.
2. He hoopii; he hihia.
3. *A case for the doctor*, he mea na ke kauka e lapaau.
4. *A hard case*, he mea paakiki; he kanaka oolea, paakiki.

Case'knife, *n.* Pahi aina.

Cash, *n.* Dala ike maka; dala paa.

Cash, *v.* E uku koke; e uku i ke dala paa.

Cash'book, *n.* Buke helu no na lilo me na loaa ma na dala paa.

Cash-ier', *n.* Ka malama dala o ka ba'neko, a o kekahi hui paha.

Cask, *n.* Pahu barela nui.

Cas'ket, *n.* 1. Pahu liilii waiho momi. SYN. jewel box.
2. Pahu kupapau metala.

Cast, *v.* 1. E kiola; hoolei; e nou. *Cast stones*, e hoolei i na pohaku.
2. E hooheehee metala, no na mea metala.

Cast'a-way', *n.* Mea haaleleia i ka poino.

Caste, *n.* Ke kulana iwaena o kanaka

Cas'ter, *n.* He pokakaa liilii malalo ae o na wawae o na pahuume, etc.

Cas'ti-gate, *v.* E hoopai ma ka hahau ana. SYN. chastise.

Cas'ti-ga'tion, *n.* Ka hoopai hahau ana, a hili ana paha. SYN. chastisement.

Cast'ing, *n.* He mea metala i hanaia ma ka hooheehee mua ana i ka metala.

Cast'ing-vote, *n.* Ka balota e hooholo ana i ka pono iwaena o na aoao elua, ke like a like na balota e ae.

Cas'tle, *n.* Hale nui, kohu pa kaua la.

Cas'tor-oil, *n.* Aila kolii.

Cas'trate, *v.* E poa; e kahe.

Cas'u-al, *adj.* Ulia wale. SYN. accidental.

Cas'u-al-ty, *n.* Mea ulia wale. SYN. accident.

Cat, *n.* Popoki; owao.

Cat'a-comb, *n.* He ana waiho kupapa'u.

Cat'a-lep-sy, *n.* He maule; mai kuhewa.

Cat'a-logue, (log), *n.* Papa kuhikuhi inoa; papa hoike.

Cat'a-logue, *v.* E kakau papa.

Cat'a-mount, *n.* He popoki nui ahiu.
2. He mai iloko o ka maka.

Ca-tarrh', (ka-tär'), *n.* He mai ma ke poo me ke kahe o ka hupe'.

Ca-tas'tro-phe, *n.* He poino nui. SYN. disaster; calamity.

Catch, *v.* 1. E hopu; e hoopaa; e apo. SYN. seize.
2. *Catch a cold*, e loaa i ke kunu.

Catch'er, *n.* Mea nana e hopu.

Catch'ing, *adj.* Lele. *Infectious disease*, mai lele wale. *Contagious disease*, mai lele ma ka pili ana.

Cat'e-chise, (kiz), *v.* E ui; e ninaninau.

Cat'e-chism, (kizm), *n.* He buke ui.

Căt'e-go-ry, *n.* Kulana. Syn. state; condition.

Că'ter, *v.* E hoolako i na mea ai.

Că'ter-er, *n.* Ka mea hoolako i na mea ai.

Căt'er-pĭl'lar, *n.* He peelua.

Că'ter-wạul, *v.* E uwe e like me ka popoki.

Ca-thär'tĭc, *n.* Laau hoonaha'.

Ca-thē'dral, *n.* Luakini bihopa.

Căth'o-lic, *adj.* Akea wale; pili laula.

Căts'pạw, *n.* He mea i hookonokonoia e hana kolohe; he weawea.
2. He onini ma ka ili o ke kai.

Căt'tle, *n.* Na holoholona laka o ke kula.
2. Na bipi.

Căt'tle-range, *n.* He aina kula no na bipi.

Cạu'cŭs, *n.* He halawai ku i ka wa.

Cause, *n.* 1. Kumu. *The cause of all things,* ke kumu o na mea a pau.
2. Hihia ma ke kanawai. Syn. case.

Cause'less, *adv.* Me ke kumu ole.

Cause'way, *n.* Alanui i hookiekieia mawaena o kahi pohopoho.

Cau'ter-ize, *v.* E kuni me ka hao wela; e kuni me ka laau lapaau wela.

Cau'tion, *n.* 1. Ke akahele; ka noonoo pono. Syn. prudence; care.
2. He olelo ao; olelo papa.

Cau'tion, *v.* E ao aku; e papa'ku.

Cau'tioŭs, *adj.* Noonoo; akahele. Syn. prudent.

Cau'tioŭs-ly, *adv.* Me ka noonoo; me ke akahele. Syn. prudently.

Căv'al-cāde', *n.* Huakai hooholo lio.

Căv'a-liĕr', *adj.* 1. Aa; koa; wiwo ole.
2. Haanou; hookano.

Căv'al-ry, *n.* Na koa lio.

Cāve } *n.* He ana iloko o ka honua.
Căv'ern }

Căv'il, *v.* E imi hala; e hoohalahala.

Căv'il-ler, *n.* Ka mea imi hala.

Căv'i-ty, *n.* He hakahaka; wahi po'ho.

Cēase, *v.* E oki; hooki; e hoopau. Syn. desist; forbear.

Cēase'less, *adj.* Pau ole; mau. Syn. incessant.

Çē'dar, *n.* Laau kedera.

Cēde, *v.* E hoolilo ia hai.

Çe-dĭl'la, *n.* He kaha malalo iho o ka huapalapala C (Ç) e hoakaka ana ua pili laia ka leo o S.

Çeil, *v.* E kapili papa ma na aoao a maluna o ke keena.

Çeil'ing, *n.* 1. Ko luna o ke keena.
2. Na papa kapili iloko o ka hale.

Çĕl'e-brāte, *v.* E hookaulana; e hoonani; e kulaia.

Çĕl'e-brāt'ed, *adj.* Kaulana.

Çĕl'e-brā'tion, *n.* Ka hookulaia ana; ka hookaulana ana.

Çe-lĕb'ri-ty, *n.* Ka hanohano; ke kaulana.

Çe-lĕr'i-ty, *n.* Ka mama; ka hikiwawe. Syn. swiftness.

Çe-lĕs'tial, *adj.* 1. No ka lani. *Celestial being,* mea e noho ana ma ka lani.
2. *Celestial Empire,* he inoa no ke aupuni o Kina. *Celestials,* ka poe o Kina.

Çel-i-ba-çy, *adj.* Ka noho ana me ka mare ole.

Çĕll, *n.* 1. Keena liilii. *Prison cell,* keena liilii o ka hale paahao.
2. Na pukapuka o ke kukae nalo meli.
3. Na pukapuka ma na mea ulu.

Çĕl'lar, *n.* Ka lua malalo o ka hale.

Çĕl'lü-lar, *adj.* Pukapuka; paapu i na puka liilii.

Çĕm'ent, *n.* 1. Puna pohaku.
2. He pilali.

Çe-mĕnt', *v.* E hoopili paa aku. E hoopipili.

Çĕm'e-tĕr'y, *n.* Pa ilina kupapau.

Çĕn'ser, *n.* Ipu kuni mea ala.

Çĕn-sō'ri-oŭs, *adj.* Imi hala; hoahewa wale.

Çĕn'sur-a-ble, *adj.* Ku i ka ahewaia.

Çĕn'sure, *n.* Olelo hoahewa. Syn. rebuke.

Çĕn'sus, *n.* Papa helu lahui.

Çĕn'sus-blänk', *n.* Pepa paihakahaka no ka helu lahui.

Çĕn'sus-tāk'er, *n.* Luna helu lahui.

Çĕnt, *n.* Keneta.

Çĕn'taur, *n.* He kupua o ka wa kahiko, nona ke kino i oleloia he hapa kanaka hapa lio.

Çen-tĕn'ni-al, *n.* Ka haneri o na makahiki.

Çĕn'ter, *n.* Ko waenakonu; kikowaena.

Çĕn'ti-ped } *n.* He kanapi.
Çĕn'ti-pe-d }

Çĕn'tral, *adj.* Waena konu.

Çĕn'tral-i-zā'tion, *n.* Ka hoohui ana i kahi hookahi.

Çĕn'tral-ize, *v.* E hoohui i kahi hookahi.

Çen-trĭf'u-gal, *adj.* Ka nee ana mai ke kikowaena aku. *Centrifugal motion,* ka motio mai ke kiko waena'ku.

Çen-trĭf'u-gal, *n.* Mikini hoomaloo ko paa.

Çen-trĭp'e-tal, *adj.* Ka nee ana i ke kiko waena. *Centripetal motion,* ka motio e imi ana i ke kiko waena.

Çen-tü'ri-on, *n.* Luna haneri.

Çĕn'tu-ry, *n.* Haneri makahiki.

Çe-phăl'ic, *adj.* Pili i ke poo.

Çĕr'e-bĕl'lum, *n.* Ka hapa o ka lolo ma ka hope o ke poo.

Çĕr'e-bral, *adj.* Pili i ka lolo.

Çĕr'e-brum, *n.* Ka mahele nui o ka lolo.

Çĕr'e-mō'ni-oŭs, *adj.* Hookahakaha.

Çĕr'e-mō'ny, *n.* He loina; he hana hoonohonoho; hana hookapukapu; hana pili i ka hoomana. *Ceremony of laying the corner stone,* hana hoonohonoho pohaku kumu o ke kihi.

Çĕr'tain, *adj.* Maopopo loa; oiaio loa. Syn. sure.

Çẽr'tain-ly, *adv.* 1. Io. *It will certainly come to pass,* e ko io ana ia mea.
1. Ae no paha. *Please do me a favor?*—*Certainly,* e oluolu oe e kokua iau?—Ae no paha.
3. Pela. *Do you understand?*—*Certainly,* ke hoomaopopo anei oe?—Pela.

Çẽr'tain-ty, *n.* Ka mea maopopo lea.

Çer-tif'i-cate, *n.* Palapala hooia.

Çẽr'ti-fi-er, *n.* Mea nana e hooia.

Çẽr'ti-fy, *v.* E hooia ma ke kakau lima.

Çe-ru'le-an, *adj.* Uliuli, like me ke aouli ana. *Cessation of hostilities,* ka pau ana o ke kaua.

Çes-sa'tion, *n.* Ka pau ana; ka oki ana. *Cessation of hostilities,* ka pau ana o ke kaua.

Çẽs'sion, *n.* Ka hoolilo ana ia hai.

Çhāfe, *v.* 1. E ukiuki; hoonaukiuki. SYN. fret.
2. Maoa. SYN. rub sore.

Çhāff, *n.* He opala.

Çha-grin', *n.* Manao ukiuki. SYN. vexation.

Çhāin, *n.* Kaula apo. *Iron chain,* kaula hao.

Çhāin, *v.* E hoopaa me ke kaula hao.

Çhāir, *n.* 1. He noho maoli.
2. Ka mea e noho ana ma ka noho.
3. He lala o ka oihana hoonaanao. *Chair of Mathematics,* ka oihana ao matimatika.

Çhāir'man, *n.* Luna hoomalu.

Çhaise, *n.* Kaa huila elua, me ka uhi oluna.

Çhāl'dron, *n.* He ana; 36 busela.

Çhąlk, *n.* Po'ho.

Çhāl'lenge, *v.* E aa aku ia hai.

Çhāl'lĕng-er, *n.* Ka mea e aa aku ana.

Çhām'ber, *n.* 1. Keena maluna; keena moe.
2. He ahahui. *Chamber of Commerce,* ahahui kalepa.
3. He aha kauwawai. *Chamber of Deputies,* ahakaukanawai o na luna makaainana.

Çhām'ber-lain, *n.* Luna nui o na keena. *Lord Chamberlain,* luna nui o ka ohana o ka Moi.

Çhām'ber-māid, *n.* Wahine malama keena moe.

Çhāmp, *v.* E nau, e naunau.

Çhām'pi-on, *n.* 1. He kanaka koa.
2. Ka pookela; ka mua.

Çhānçe, *n.* 1. Manawa kupono. SYN. opportunity.
2. Mea ulia wale.

Çhăn'çel-lor, *n.* 1. Ka Lunakanawai kiekie o ke Aupuni.
2. He puuku. *Chancellor of the Exchequer,* ka Puuku o ka Waihona dala.

Çhăn'çel-lor-ship, *n.* Oihana o ke Chancellor.

Çhăn'del-ier, *n.* Manamana huhui kukui.

Çhăn'dler, *n.* *Ship chandler,* he kanaka kuai i na lako moku.

Çhānge, *n.* 1. He loli; he luli; he hoo-ano e.
2. Na hapa dala.

Çhānge, *v.* E loli; e hoololi; hoo-ano e. *Change money,* e hoololi dala; e wawahi dala.

Çhānge'a-ble, *adj.* Loli lua; kaamola; olewa; kapekepe. SYN. fickle.
2. Lauwili. *A changeable wind,* he makani lauwili. SYN. variable.

Çhānge'a-ble-ness, *n.* Ano loli wale.

Çhānge'less, *adj.* Loli ole; oni paa.

Çhăn'nel, *n.* Auwaha; kowa'.

Çhānt, *v.* E oli.

Çhănt'er, *n.* Mea nana e oli.

Çhănt'i-cleer, *n.* Moa kane. SYN. cock.

Çhā'os, *n.* Ka waiho ana huikau; hoo-ponopono ole.

Çha-ŏt'ic, *adj.* Huikau; haunaele.

Çhāp, *n.* Keiki kane; kanaka opio.

Çhāp'el, *n.* Hale halawai hoomana.

Çhăr'ac-ter, *n.* 1. Ke ano o ke kanaka; inoa iwaena o kanaka. SYN. reputation.
2. Ano. SYN. quality. *The character of the enterprise,* ke ano o ka hana.

Çhăr'ac-ter-is'tic, *adj.* Ku i ke ano. *Characteristic of the man,* ku i ke ano o ke kanaka.

Çhăr'ac-ter-ize, *v.* E kuhikuhi ano.

Çhar-āde', *n.* He nanenane hoomai-keike i kekahi hua olelo i hunaia.

Çhăr'coal, *n.* Nanahu wahie.

Çharge, *v.* 1. E kauoha; e haawi i ke kauoha. SYN. exhort.
2. E hoopii no ke karaima. SYN. accuse.
3. E kakau hooaie.
4. E hoopiha i ka pu.
5. E hookui i ke kaua.

Çhārge'a-ble, *adj.* Kupono ke hoopiia kupono ke auhauia.

Çhār'ger, *n.* 1. Lio holo kaua.
2. Pa aina nui.

Çhăr'i-ot, *n.* Kaa holo kaua; kaa kaua.

Çhăr'i-ot-eer', *n.* He hookele kaa kaua.

Çhăr'i-ta-ble, *adj.* Manawalea; loko-maikai. SYN. benevolent.

Çhăr'i-ty, *n.* Aloha; manawalea; lokomaikai. SYN. love; benevolence.

Çhăr'la-tan, *n.* Mea akena wale i kona ike. SYN. quack.

Çhārm, *v.* E hoolealea; hoohoihoi. SYN. please.

Çhārm'ing, *adj.* Nani; nulii.

Çhārt, *n.* 1. Palapala aina holo moana.
2. Palapala hoike.

Çhār'ter, *n.* 1. Palapala hookohu hui, a ke Aupuni.
2. Palapala hoolimalima moku.

Çhāse, *v.* E alualu; e hahai. *The chase,* ka alualu holoholona.

Çhăsm, *n.* Mawae hohonu.

Çhāste, *adj.* Makamae; maemae; pau-maele ole. SYN. pure.

Çhăs'ten, *v.* E hoopai.
2. E hoomaemae.

Çhas-tise', *v.* E hahau; e hili; e hoo-pai. SYN. punish; castigate.

Chăs′tise-ment, *n.* Ka hoopai ana; ka hili ana. Syn. punishment.

Chăs′ti-ty, *n.* Ka haumia ole i na ku-ko o ke kino; maemae o ka manao ma ka noho ana o ke kane a o ka wahine paha.

Chat, *n.* Kamailio hoonanea.

Chăt-eau′ (shat-ō), *n.* Hale noho ha-nohano maloko ka aina.

Chăt′tel, *n.* Waiwai lewa. Syn. per-sonal property.

Chăt′ter, *n.* Walaau wale.

Chăt′ter-box, *n.* Mea walaau wale i na wa a pau.

Chēap, *adj.* Kumukuai haahaa; ma-kepono.

Chēap′ness, *n.* Ka haahaa o ke kumu-kuai; ka makepono.

Chēat, *n.* 1. He mea apuka wale.
2. He hana hoopunipuni; hana apuka.

Chēat, *v.* E hoopunipuni; e hana apu-ka; e epa.

Chēck, *v.* 1. E keakea; e kaohi.
2. E kaha. *Check baggage,* e kaha i ka ukana; e hoailona i ka ukana. *Check off names,* e kaha′ku i na inoa.

Chēck, *n.* 1. He kumu keakea.
2. He kaha; he hoailona.
3. Bila kikoo dala.

Chĕck′er, *v.* Kikokikoi.

Chĕck′er-bōard, *n.* He papa mu.

Chĕck′ers, *n.* Paani papa mu.

Chĕck′māte, *v.* E hoohoka loa.

Chēek, *n.* 1. Papalina.
2. Ano honekoa.

Chēer, *v.* 1. E hoohoihoi; hooeueu; hoolalelale.
2. E hoolana i ka manao.
3. E haawi i ka huro.

Chēer, *n.* 1. Hauoli; lea; hoihoi.
2. He huro.
3. *Good cheer,* na mea ai me na mea inu maikai.

Chēer′ful, *adj.* Hoihoi; oluolu; hauoli.

Chēer′ful-ness, *n.* Ka hauoli o ka na-au; ka oluolu o ka manao.

Chēer′less, *adj.* Kaumaha; luuluu.

Chēese, *n.* Waiu paa.

Chēese′press, *n.* He kaomi no ka waiu paa.

Chĕm′ic-al, *adj.* E pili ana i ke *chem-istry.*

Chē-mīse′ (shē-meez′), *n.* Lole muu-muu.

Chĕm′ist, *n.* He kanaka i akamai ma ke *chemistry.*

Chĕm′is-try, *n.* Ka ike e imi ana i na mole a me na kumu o na mea a pau, a me ka hoohui ana o ia mau mole me na kumu, i loaa na kino o kela me keia ano.

Chĕr′ish, *v.* E malama loa; e hoomili-mili.

Chĕst, *n.* 1. Pahu nui waiho lole, wai-ho mea hana.
2. Ke keapaa; ka umauma.

Chew (chū), *v.* 1. E nau; e mama.
2. *Chew the cud,* e hooluaiuai.

Chī-eān′er-y, *n.* Hana maalea; hana hoohalua; hana epa. Syn. trickery.

Chick ⎱ *n.* Moa keiki.
Chick′en ⎰

Chick′en-heärt′ed, *adj.* Maka′u wale; hopohopo wale. Syn. timid.

Chick′en-pŏx, *n.* Mai puupuu liilii, ano like me ka mai hebera.

Chide, *v.* E papa′ku; e ao aku.

Chīef, *n.* He alii; kiaaina.

Chīef, *adj.* Ka mua; ke poo o ka hana; ka mea nui.

Chīef′ly, *adv.* Ma ka nui.

Chīef′tain, *n.* He kapena; he alakai.

Child, *n.* He keiki; kama; pokii.

Child′birth, *n.* Hanau keiki.

Child′hōod, *n.* Wa keiki.

Child′ish, *adj.* Ano kamalii; noonoo ole.

Child′less, *adj.* Keiki ole.

Child′like, *adj.* Akahai; like me ke keiki.

Chil′dren, *n.* Na kamalii.

Chill, *n.* 1. Haukeke; opili; li.
2. *Chills and fever,* he li me ka wela.

Chill′i-ness, *n.* Anuanu; opili; koe-koe.

Chill′y, *adj.* Koekoe; huihui; opili.

Chime, *n.* He mau bele kani oli pu.

Chim′ney, *n.* Puka uahi.

Chin, *n.* Ka auwae.

Chink, *n.* He owa′; he nakaka.

Chip, *n.* Mamala laau.

Chī-rŏg′ra-phy, *n.* Kakau lima. Syn. handwriting.

Chirp, *v.* E nunulu; e piopio; e ioio.

Chirp′ing, *n.* Ka piopio ana o na ma-nu

Chĭs′el, *n.* He kila.

Chĭt′chat, *n.* Syn. chat.

Chĭv′al-roŭs, *adj.* 1. Ano koa; wiwo ole.
2. Malama pono i na wahine.

Chĭv′al-ry, *n.* 1. Poe koa.
2. Poe laulea, malama pono i na wa-hine.

Chŏck′full, *adj.* Piha loa; piha kui.

Chŏe′o′late, *n.* Mea inu i hanaia mai ke *cocoa.*

Choice, *n.* Ke koho ana; ka wae ana.

Choice, *adj.* Milimili.

Choir (quire), *n.* Aha mele o ka luaki-ni.

Chōke, *v.* 1. (From violence.) E umi. Syn. strangle.
2. (From eating or drinking.) E puua; laowa. Syn. strangle; suffocate.

Chōke′dămp, *n.* Ea ino iloko o na lua me na ana, mea make.

Chŏl′er, *n.* Huhu; inaina. Syn. anger.

Chŏl′e-ra, *n.* Mai kolera.

Chŏl′e-ra-mŏr′bus, *n.* Nahu o ka opu me ka hi a me ka luni pu.

Chŏl′er-ic, *adj.* Hikiwawe i ka huhu. Syn. passionate.

Chōose, *v.* E koho; e wae.

Chōos′er, *n.* Mea koho.

Chŏp, v. 1. E kaka. *Chop up firewood,* e kaka wahie.
2. E kua. *Chop down a tree,* e kua i ka laau; e oki i ka laau.
3. E okioki. *Chop in pieces,* e okioki liilii.

Chŏp, n. Apana i-o, mea koala.

Chŏp′sea, n. Kai kupikipiki-o′; kai ooloku.

Chŏ′ral, adj. Pili i ka aha mele.

Chōre, n. Wahi hana iki. *Chores,* na hana liilii.

Chŏr′is-ter, n. Ke alakai o ka papa himeni.

Chō′rus, n. Leo hui.

Christ, n. Kristo; Ka Mesia.

Christ′en, v. E haawi inoa,, a bapetizo.

Chris′ten-dom, n. Na aupuni kristiano.

Chris′ten-ing, n. Ka bapetizo ana.

Chris′tian, adj. Ano kristiano. *Christian name,* inoa kristiano.

Chris′tian, n. Haumana na Kristo.

Christ-ian′i-ty, n. Ka hoomana kristiano.

Christ′iän-ize, v. E hoohaumana na Kristo.

Christ′-like, adj. Like me Kristo.

Christ′mas, n. La hoomanao no ko Kristo hanau ana.

Chro-mät′ic, adj. 1. E pili ana i na wai hooluu.
2. no ka pa-ko-li.

Chrŏn′ic, adj. Kuluma. *Chronic disease,* mai kuluma.

Chrŏn′i-cle, n. Moolelo o ke Aupuni a Lahui paha. SYN. history.

Chro-nŏl′o-gist, n. He kanaka imi i na helu manawa o na wa i hala.

Chrŏn′o-lŏg′ic-al, adj. Pili i na helu manawa.

Chro-nŏl′o-ġy, n. Ka ike e pili ana no na manawa i hala, me na hana, me ka poe o ia manawa.

Chro-nŏm′e-ter, n. He wati holo pololei loa; wati hooholo moku.

Chŭb′by, adj. Poupou; nepunepu.

Chŭek′le, v. E aka iki iloko iho.

Chŭnk, n. He apana manoanoa.

Chŭrch, n. 1. Hale halawai; hale pule.
2. Ekalesia.
3. He aoao hoomana.

Chŭrch′man, n. Kahuna pule o ka ekalesia Enelani.

Chŭrch-war′den, n. Puuku iloko o ka ekalesia Enelani.

Chŭrch′-yärd, n. Pa hale pule.

Chŭrl, n. Kanaka nainai; nunuha.

Chŭrl′ish, adj. Nainai; hoonunuha.

Chŭrn, n. Pahu kui waiu bata.

Chȳle, (kil), n. Ka wai o ke *chyme.*

Chȳme, (kim), n. Ka ai mahope o ka hoowalela′na iloko o ka opu.

Çi′der, n. Wai o ka hua apala.

Çi-gär′, n. Ki-ka′; owili baka.

Çim′e-ter, n. Pahi kaua pokole.

Çinct′ūre, n. Kaula apo; kaei. SYN. belt; girth.

Çin′der, n. Pula nanahu.

Çin′na-mon, n. Kinamona; laau ala.

Çi′pher, n. 1. Ka hua helu 0; he ole.
2. Kakaulima huna.

Çi′pher, v. E kakau helu; e hana ma na helu.

Çir′cle, n. 1. Poai poepoe.
2. He poe. *Circle of friends,* poe makamaka.

Çir′cle, v. E poai a puni; e kaapuni.

Çir′cuit, n. He kaapuni. *Circuit of Hawaii,* ke kaapuni ana i Hawaii. *Circuit Court,* Aha kaapuni.

Çir-eŭ′i-toŭs, adj. Ma ke ano kaapuni; loloiahili.

Çir′eŭ-lar, adj. Ano poai poepoe.

Çir′eu-lar, n. He palapala hooili laulaha′ku.

Çir′eu-lāte, v. 1. E laha. *The blood circulates through the body,* laha ke koko a puni ke kino.
2. E holo kaapuni.
3. *Circulating medium,* ke dala i laha.

Çir′eu-lā′tion, n. Ka laha ana. *Circulation of blood,* ke kahe ana o ke koko iloko o na aa.

Çir′eum-äm′bi-ent, adj. Lewa ana a puni.

Çir′eum-äm′bu-lāte, v. E poai a puni ma ka hele wawae.

Çir′eum-çise, v. E oki poepoe.

Çir-eŭm′fẽr-ençe, n. Ke ana puni.

Çir′eum-lo-eŭ′tion, n. Kamailio kuawili.

Çir′eum-näv′i-gāte, v. E kaapuni ma ka holo moku.

Çir′eum-näv′i-gā′tion, n. Ke kaapuni ana ma ka moku.

Çir′eum-näv′i-ga-tor, n. Kanaka holo moku a puni ka honua.

Çir′eum-pō′lar, adj. A puni na welau o ka honua.

Çir′eum-seribe, v. E hoohaiki; e kau palena a puni. SYN. limit.

Çir′eum-spëet, adj. Kuoo; kiai. SYN. prudent.

Çir′eum-spëet′ly, adv. Me ke akahele; me ka noonoo. SYN. watchfully; prudently.

Çir′eum-stançe, n. Mea.

Çir′eum-vẽnt′, v. E hoohalua; e hoopunipuni. SYN. to deceive.

Çir′eus, n. Keaka lio.

Çis-äl′pine, adj. Ma ka hema′ku o na mauna Alepe.

Çis′tern, n. Lua wai pao ia.

Çit′a-del, n. He pa kaua o ke kulanakauhale.

Çi-tā′tion, n. 1. He palapala kii.
2. He olelo i unuhiia noloko mai o kekahi olelo. SYN. quotation.

Çite, v. 1. E kena e hele kino mai. SYN. summons.
2. E unuhi olelo. SYN. quote.

Çit′i-zen, n. Makaainana; kupa o ka aina.

Cit'i-zen-ship, *n.* Kulana makaainana.

Cit'ron, *n.* Lemona nui.

Cit'y, *n.* Kulanakauhale nui.

Civ'il, *adj.* 1. Pili i na pono makaaina-na; kiwila. *Civil law,* kanawai kiwila.
2. Ano oluolu; ano keonimana.

Ci-vil'ian, *n.* He makaainana pili ole i ka oihana koa.

Ci-vil'i-ty, *n.* Ke ano oluolu. SYN. po-liteness; courtesy.

Civ'il-i-zā'tion, *n.* Ke ano naauao o ka noho ana.

Civ'il-ize, *v.* E hoonaauao i ka poe na-aupo.

Civ'il-ized, *adj.* Hoonaauaoia.

Civ'il-ly, *adv.* Me ka oluolu.

Clad, *p. p.* Hooaahuia; kahikoia.

Claim, *v.* E koi.

Claim, *n.* He kuleana.

Claim'ant, *n.* 1. Mea nana ke kuleana.
2. Mea e koi ana.

Clam, *n.* He ano opai.

Clam'ber, *v.* E pii kokolo aku.

Clam'my, *adj.* Koo'u; pipili; olikalika.

Clam'or, *n.* Uwa nui.

Clam'or-ous, *adj.* Walaau nui; waha-kole; wahapaa.

Clamp, *n.* He hao upiki.

Clan, *n.* Ka ohana holookoa mai na ku-puna a i na mamo. SYN. tribe.

Clan-des'tine, *adj.* Malu'; hunaia. *Clandestine correspondence,* kakau leta malu'.

Clang, *v.* E kanike'. SYN. ring.

Clang'or, *n.* Ke kanikani o na mea me-tala ke kui kahi i kekahi.

Clank, *n.* Nakeke; leo kani.

Clap, *v.* 1. E pai. *Clap hands,* e pai lima.
2. *Clap of thunder,* he kui hekili.

Clap'board (klāb'burd), *n,* Papa ke-pa.

Clap'per, *n.* 1. He mea kui.
2. *Clapper of bell,* or *tongue of bell,* haku o ka bele.

Clap'trap, *n.* Hana hooakamai wale

Cla'ret, *n.* He waina o Farani.

Clar'i-fi-cā'tion, *n.* Ka hoomaemae ana i na mea wai; ka hooaiai ana.

Clar'i-fy, *v.* E hoomaemae; hooaiai.

Clar'i-net } *n.* He ohe puhi, ano like me ka *flute.*
Clar'i-o-net' }

Clash, *v.* 1. E hookui me ka nakeke.
2. Ku-e' kekahi i kekahi. *Interests clash,* ku-e' kekahi pono i kekahi pono.

Clash'ing, *n.* 1. Ke kui ana. *Clashing of arms,* ke kui ana o na mea kaua.
2. Ke ku-e' ana *The clashing of inter-ests,* ke ku-e' ana iwaena o na pono.

Clasp, *n.* E apo. *The clasp of the hand,* ke apo ana o ka lima.

Clasp, *v.* 1. E apo. *Clasp hands,* e apo lima.
2. E puliki. SYN. embrace.

Clasp'knife, *n.* Pahi pelu.

Class, *n.* He papa; he kulana; na mea a pau o ke ano hookahi.

Clas'si-fi-cā'tion, *n.* Ka hoonoho ana ma na papa; na ano; na kulana.

Clas'si-fỹ, *v.* E hoonohonoho papa; hoonohonoho ano; hoonoho kulana.

Class'māte, *n.* Hoa papa kula.

Clat'ter, *n.* 1. He nakulukulu. *Clat-ter of rain drops,* ka nakulukulu o na paka u-a.
2. Kamumu. *Clatter of shoes,* ke kamu-mu o na kamaa.

Clat'ter-ing, *n.* 1. Ka nakulukulu ana; ke kamumu ana.

Clause, *n.* 1. He pauku olelo. SYN. par-agraph.
2. He mamala o ka hopuna olelo okoa.

Claw, *n.* Maiuu; maiao.

Clay, *n.* Lepo palolo.

Clean, *v.* 1. E hoomaemae.
2. E kaheu. *Clean out weeds.*

Clean, *adj.* Maemae.

Clean'li-ness, *n.* Ka maemae; ke au-lii.

Cleanse, *v.* E huikala; hoomaemae.

Cleans'er, *n.* Ka mea e hoomaemae ana.

Clear, *adj.* 1. Moakaka; maopopo.
2. Huaka; aiai. *Clear water,* wai hu-aka.
3. Laelae. *A clear day,* he la laelae.
4. Kalae. *A clear atmosphere,* he ea kalae

Clear, *v.* 1. E hoopakele; e hookuu. *To clear a prisoner,* e hookuu i ka paahao.
2. E wehe. *To clear up a difficulty,* e wehe i ka hihia.
2. *The weather begins to clear,* ke hoo-maka mai nei ka malie.
4. *Clear out a house,* e hookaawale i ka hale.
5. *Clear out!* e hele pela!

Clear'ance, *n.* He palapala hookuu mo-ku e holo, i haawiia e ka luna dute.

Clear'ing, *n.* 1. Ka hookuu ana; ka wehe ana.
2. He kipuka; aina i hoomakaukauia no ke kanu.

Clear'ly, *adv.* Me ka maopopo; me ka moakaka.

Clear-sight'ed, *adj.* Ike moakaka.

Cleat, *n.* He pine laau hoopaa kaula.

Cleave, *v.* 1. E pili paa aku.
2. E pipili paa.
3. E kaka'; e wawahi me ke koi. SYN. split.

Cleav'er, *n.* Pahi nui oki bipi.

Clef, *n.* He hoailona no ka leo mele.

Cleft, *n.* He owa'; he mauae.

Clem'en-cy, *n.* Ke ahonui; ke aloha; ka oluolu. SYN. mildness; tenderness; kindness.

Clem'ent, *adj.* Oluolu; ahonui. SYN. mild; gentle.

Cler'gy, *n.* Na kahuna pule.

Cler'gy-man, *n.* He kahuna pule.

Cler'i-cal, *adj.* 1. E pili ana i ka oi-hana kahuna pule.
2. Pili i ka oihana kakau olelo, a ku-pakako paha.

Clerk, *n.* 1. Kakauolelo. SYN. secretary.
2. He kupakako. SYN. salesman.

Clerk'ship, *n.* Oihana kakauolelo; oi-hana kupakako.

Clĕv′er, *adj.* Loea; akamai; noeau. SYN. skillful; ingenious.

Clĕv′is, *n.* Ka hao ma ke poo o ka laau kolo o ke kaa, a oopalau paha.

Clew, *n.* 1. Ke kihi o ka pea.
2. He mooa. SYN. trace.

Cli′ent, *n.* Ka mea i hoolimalima i ka loio; ko ka loio mua.

Cliff, *n.* He pali. SYN. precipice.

Cli′mate, *n.* Ke kau o kauwahi.

Cli′max, *n.* Ka piinana a hiki i ka nui loa.

Climb, *v.* E pii iluna, me ka luhi.

Climb′er, *n.* 1. Ka mea e pii ana.
2. Mea ulu hihi.

Clime, *n.* Aina. *Every clime,* na aina a pau.

Clinch, *v.* 1. E puili aku ma ke ano huhu.
2. E pelu a paa ke kui iloko o kekahi mea.

Cling, *v.* SYN. cleave.

Clink, *n.* Ke kani nakeke o na mea metala.

Clink′er, *n.* Ke aa pele.

Clip, *v.* E oki me ka upa′; e oki pokole.

Clip′per, *n.* He moku holo loa.

Clip′ping, *n.* Ka mea i okiia me ka upa′.

Cloak, *n.* He kapa uhi; he koloka.

Cloak, *v.* E uhi; e huna′.

Clŏck, *n.* Wati nui.

Clŏck′work, *n.* Na huila o ka wati.

Clŏd, *n.* Puu lepo.

Clŏd′hŏp-per, *n.* Kanaka lomaloma, hemahema; he kaikua..

Clŏg, *n.* 1. Mea keakea. SYN. hindrance.
2. Kamaa laau; kamaa kaumaha.

Close, *v.* 1. E pani. *Close the door,* e pani ka puka.
2. E hooki; e hoopau. *Close a speech,* e hooki i ka haiolelo.
3. E poi. *Close a book,* e poi i ka buke.
4. E hooholo. *To close with an offer,* e hooholo i ka olelo, a hana paha.

Close, *adj.* 1. Pi; alunu. SYN. stingy.
2. Ane like. *A close vote,* he koho ane like.
3. Paa; komo ole ke ea.
4. Ikiiki. SYN. sultry. *A close, hot day,* he la ikiiki.

Close-fist′ed, *adj.* Lima aua; pi; mau-a. SYN. close.

Close′ly, *adv.* Kokoke loa.

Clŏs′et, *n.* Keena liilii.

Clos′ing, *n.* Ka pau ana. *Closing of school,* ka pau ana o ke kula.
2. Ka pani ana.
3. Ka poi ana, etc.

Clŏth, *n.* Lole.

Clŏthe, *v.* E hookomo lole; e hooaahu. SYN. dress.

Clŏthes, *n.* Lole komo; kapa komo; aahu. SYN. garments.

Clŏth′ier, *n.* Kanaka kuai lole; kanaka hana lole.

Clŏth′ing, *n.* Lole komo; aahu.

Cloud, *n.* He ao.

Cloud, *v.* E hoopouli i na ao; e hoomalumalu.

Cloud′eap′t, *adj.* Uhiia i na ao.

Cloud′less, *adj.* Olino; molaelae.

Cloud′y, *adj.* Malumalu. *A cloudy day,* he la malumalu.

Clŏ′ven-fŏŏt′ed }
Clŏ′ven-hŏŏfed, } *adj.* Wawae holoholona i maheleia.

Clown, *n.* He kuaaina; kanaka hehena.

Clŏwn′ish, *adj.* Kuaaina; ano kamaniha.

Cloy, *v.* E ai a liliha; e kena.

Clŭb, *n.* He newa.

Clŭb′-fŏŏt′ed, *adj.* Wawae muumuu.

Clŭck, *v.* E ko-u′ko-u′.

Clŭmp, *n.* He mau laau e ulu pu ana.

Clŭm′sy, *adj.* Hemahema; hawawa. SYN. awkward.

Clŭs′ter, *n.* He huhui.

Clŭtch, *v.* E apo me ka maiuu.

Clŭt′ter, *n.* Huikau; mea waiho wale ia.

Coach, *n.* He kaa lio nui i uhiia.

Coach′man, *n.* Kanaka hookele kaa lio.

Co′ad-ju′tor, *n.* Hoa hana.

Co-āg′u-lāte, *v.* E hoolilo ka mea wai i mea paa.

Coal, *n.* Nanahu; lanahu.

Co′a-lesçe′, *v.* E hui na kino okoa a liloi kino hookahi. *Salt and water will coalesce,* e lilo ana ka paakai me ka wai i kino hookahi ke hui laua.

Co′a-li′tion, *n.* 1. Ka hui ana. *The coalition of nations,* ka hui ana o na aupuni.
2. Ka hui ana o na mana. *The coalition of forces keeps the world in motion,* o ka hui′na o na mana ka mea e kakaa ai ka honua.

Coal′mine } *n.* Lua eli nanahu.
Coal′pit } Lua puhi nanahu.

Coarse, *adj.* Manoanoa; pakapaka.
2. Ano mahaoi; kamaniha; pawaa; kuaaina.

Coast, *n.* Kahakai.

Coast, *v.* 1. E holo pili aina.
2. E hee hoolua maluna o ka hau.

Coast′er, *n.* Moku holo pili aina.

Coat, *n.* 1. He ku′ka.
2. *A coat of paint,* hookahi hamo ana i ka pena.
2. *Coat of arms,* he hoailona no ke kulana o ke kanaka.

Coat′ing, *n.* Hamo ana. *A coating of paint,* ka hamo ana i ka pena.

Coax, *v.* E hoomalimali; e koi.

Coax′er, *n.* Ka mea koi ikaika me ka hoomalimali.

Cŏb, *n.* 1. Iwi kurina.
2. He wahi lio.

Cŏb′ble, *v.* E kapili hou i na kamaa kahiko.

Cŏb′bler, *n.* Kanaka humuhumu kamaa kahiko.

Cŏb′ble-stŏne, *n.* Pohaku iliili.

Cŏb′web. *n.* Punawelewele.

Cŏck, *n.* Moa kane.
Cŏck, *v.* E hoomakaukau e ki pu.
Cŏck-ade′, *n.* He hipuu lipine **no ka** papale.
Cŏck′fĭght, *n.* He hakaka iwaena o na moa kane.
Cŏck′pĭt, *n.* 1. Wahi e hoohakaka i na moa kane.
2. Lua malalo o ka oneki o ka moku manuwa, kahi e lapaau ai i ka poe i eha i ka hoouka.
Cŏck′roach, *n.* Elelu′.
Cŏck′swain (kŏk-sn) *n.* Luna waapa ma na moku manuwa′.
Cŏ′eoa, *n.* Kumu niu.
Co′eŏa-nut, *n.* Hua niu.
Co-cōon′, *n.* Popo kilika a ka enuhe kilika i hana ai.
Cŏde, *n.* Buke kanawai. *Penal Code,* Buke Kanawai Karaima. *Civil Code,* Buke Kanawai Kivila.
Cŏd′ger, *n.* Kanaka alunu; pi; kanaka kuaaina.
Cŏd′i-çĭl *n.* Olelo pakui i ka palapala hooilina.
Cŏd′i-fi-cā′tion, *n.* Ka hoonohonoho pono ana i na kanawai iloko o ka buke.
Cŏd′i-fȳ, *v.* E hoonohonoho i na kanawai iloko o ka buke.
Cŏd′dle, *v.* E hoomilimili.
Cŏ-ef-fĭ′çient, *n.* He kuaniti hana, ma ka hoaiiona helu.
Co-e′qual, *adj.* Like; like-a-like.
Co-ērçe′, *v.* E kaohi. SYN. compel.
Co-ēr′çion, *n.* Ke kaohi ana. SYN. compulsion.
Co-e′val, *adj.* Ola like; like na makahiki.
Cŏ′ex-ĭst′, *v.* E ola pu.
Cŏ′ex-ĭst′ençe, *n.* Ke ola pu ana.
Cŏ′ex-tĕnd′, *v.* Hoolaulaha like.
Cŏ′ex-tĕn′sĭve, *adj.* Laulaha like.
Cŏf′fee, *n.* He kofe; lau kofe.
Cŏf′fee-house, *n.* Hale inu kofe.
Cŏf′fee-mĭll, *n.* He wili kofe.
Cŏf′fee-pot, *n.* Ipu kofe.
Cŏf′fer, *n.* Pahu waiho dala.
Cŏf′fĭn, *n.* Pahu kupapau.
Cŏg, *n.* Ka niho o ka huila nihoniho.
Co′gen-çy, *n.* Ka mana; ka ikaika; ka mana kaohi. SYN. power; might.
Co′gent, *adj.* Mana; ikaika. SYN. powerful.
Cŏg′i-tāte, *v.* E nalu; e noonoo nui.
Cŏg′i-tā′tion, *n.* Ka nalu ana; ka noonoo nui ana.
Cŏg′nate, *adj.* Pili ma ka hanauna; pili koko.
Cŏg′ni-zançe, *n.* Ike. SYN. knowledge; notice.
Cŏg′-wheel, *n.* Pokakaa nihoniho.
Co-hăb′it, *v.* E noho pu he kane he wahine.
Co-hăb′i-tā′tion, *n.* Ka noho pu ana ma ke ano kane a wahine.
Co-hēre′, *v.* E pili pu. SYN. adhere.
Cō-hē′sion, *n.* Ka pili pu ana.
Co-hē′sive, *adj.* Pili pu.

Çoil, *v.* E owili; hoolapuu′.
Çoil, *n.* He owili.
Çoin, *n.* Dala paa.
Çoin, *v.* E hana i ke dala paa.
Çoin′age, *n.* 1. Ka pai ana i ke dala paa.
2. Kela me keia ano dala paa.
Çō′in-çide′, *v.* 1. E manao like.
2. E kulike. *Our thoughts coincide,* kulike na manao o kaua.
Ço-in′çi-dence, *n.* Ke ko like ana o na mea elua kaawale, i ka wa hookahi.
Çoin′er, *n.* Mea pai dala paa.
Çŏl′an-der, *n.* Ipu tini pukapuka.
Çŏld, *adj.* 1. Anuanu; huihui. *A cold day,* he la anuanu.
2. Nanau. SYN. distant.
Çŏld, *n.* He anu; haukeke; huihui.
Çŏld′ly, *adv.* Naau puanuanu.
Çŏl′ie, *n.* Nahu o ka opu.
Çol-lápse′, *v.* E opaha pu.
Çŏl′lar, *n.* A-i kala; a-i ku.
Çol-lāte′, *v.* E hooiliili a hoonohonoho i na ike e pili ana i kekahi mea.
Çol-lăt′er-al, *adj.* 1. *Collateral security,* waiwai i hoopaaia ma ke ano moraki.
2. Pili aole nae pili pono loa. SYN. indirect.
Çol-lā′tion, *n.* 1. Ka hooiliili ana i na ike e pili ana i kekahi mea.
2. He wahi pai′na.
Çŏl′league, *n.* He kokoolua ma ka oihana.
Çol-lĕet′, *v.* 1. E hooakoakoa; hooahu; hoopuupuu.
2. *Carefully collect small things,* e noii; e nowelo.
3. *To collect one's thoughts,* e noii i ka manao.
Çol-lĕet′ed, *adj.* Pihoihoi ole. SYN. cool; composed.
Çol-lĕe′tion, *n.* 1. Ka hooahu ana; ka hooiliili ana.
2. He ahua.
Çol-lĕet′ive-ly, *adv.* Ma ka huina.
Çol-lĕet′or, *n.* 1. Mea nana e ohi. *Collector of curios,* mea nana e ohi i na mea milimili.
2. Luna ohi. *Collector of Taxes,* Luna ohi Dala Auhau. *Collector of Customs,* Luna ohi Dute. *Collector General of Customs,* Luna Dute Nui.
Çol-lĕet′or-ship, *n.* Oihana Luna ohi
Çŏl′lĕge, *n.* Kula nui.
Çŏl-le′gi-āte, *adj.* Pili ana i ke kula nui. *Collegiate education,* ka hoonaauao ana o ke kula nui.
Çŏll′ier, *n.* 1. Kanaka eli nanahu.
2. Moku hooili nanahu.
Çŏll′ier-y, *n.* Lua eli nanahu. SYN. coal mine.
Çol-li′sion, *n.* Ka hookui ana o kekahi mea i kekahi mea. *Collision of ships,* ka hookui ana o na moku.
Çol-lō′qui-al, *adj.* Pili i ke kamakamailio. SYN. conversational.
Çŏl′lo-quy, *n.* He kamakamailio; he olelo ki-ke′. SYN. dialogue.

Col-lū′ṣion, *n.* Ke kokua malu′ ana i kekahi hana kolohe.

Co′lon, *n.* Kiko kolona (:).

Col′o-nel (kĕr′nel), *n.* Ke poo o ka regimana koa.

Cŏl′o-nel-çy (kĕr′nel-sy), *n.* Ka oihana o ke *Colonel.*

Co-lō′ni-al, *adj.* Pili i na panalaau.

Cŏl′o-nist, *n.* Kamaaina o ka panalaau.

Cŏl′o-ni-zā′tion, *n.* Ka hookumu ana i ka panalaau.

Cŏl′o-nize, *v.* E kukulu i panalaau.

Cŏl-on-āde′, *n.* Lalani kia lanai.

Cŏl′o-ny, *n.* He panalaau; he poe i haalele i ko lakou one hanau e noho loa ma ka aina e.

Cŏl′or, *n.* He wai hooluu; he hooluu.

Cŏl′or-less, *adj.* Aiai; molale; hooluu ole.

Cŏl′orṣ, *n. pl.* He hae; lepa. SYN. flag; ensign; banner.

Co-lŏs′sal, *adj.* Nunui loa. SYN. gigantic.

Cŏlt, *n.* Lio keiki; lio opiopio.

Cŏl′ter, *n.* Ka pahi o ka oo palau.

Cŏlt′ish, *adj.* Ano like me ka lio keiki.

Cŏl′umn, *n.* 1. .He lalani; he kolamu. 2. He kia nui no ka lanai, a hale paha. SYN. pillar.

Cŏmb, *n.* Kahi lauoho.

Cŏm′bat, *n.* Hoouka kaua; hakaka′. SYN. battle; fight.

Cŏm′bat-ant, *n.* Ka mea hakaka′; mea hoouka kaua.

Cŏm′băt-ive, *adj.* Hikiwawe i ka hakaka′; hakaka′ koke.

Cŏmb′er, *n.* Kainalu nui.

Cŏm′bi-nā′tion, *n.* Ka hui ana.

Com-bine′, *v.* E hui pu; hoohui. *Combine together (for a purpose),* e alu pu.

Com-bŭs′ti-ble, *adj.* A i ke ahi.

Com-bŭs′ti-ble, *n.* He mea a wale i ke ahi.

Com-bŭs′tion, *n.* Ka a ana i ke ahi. SYN. burning.

Cóme, *v.* E hele mai; e hookokoke. SYN. approach.

Co-mē′di-an, *n.* Kanaka keaka lealea.

Cŏm′e-dy, *n.* Olelo ki-ke′ lealea.

Cóme′li-ness, *n.* Ka nani; ka maikai o ke kino.

Cóme′ly, *adj.* 1. Onaona; upalu; aulii; puloku. 2. Kupono. SYN. suitable.

Cŏm′et, *n.* Hoku welowelo.

Cŏm′fort, *v.* E hooluolu; e hoona′na′.

Cŏm′fort, *n.* Ka oluolu o ka noho ana; ka maha mai ka eha.

Cŏm′fort-a-ble, *adj.* 1. Oluolu; maha. 2. *Comfortable after eating,* luheana.

Cŏm′fort-er, *n.* Mea nana e hooluolu.

Cŏm′fort-less, *adj.* Maha ole; oluolu ole; pilikia ka noho ana.

Cŏm′ie, *adj.* Hoakaaka.

Cŏm′ie-al, *adj.* Lealea; ku i ka akaakaia.

Cŏm′ing, *n.* Ka hiki ana mai

Cŏm′ing, *adj.* E hiki mai ana. *The coming week,* ka hebedoma e hiki mai ana.

Cŏm′i-ty, *n.* Ka launa o ka noho ana. SYN. friendship.

Cŏm′ma, *n.* Ke koma (,).

Com-mānd′, *n.* He kauoha.

Com-mānd′er, *n.* Ka mea nana e kauoha; he alihi kaua.

Com-mānd′ing, *adj.* 1. Hanohano. *A man of commanding presence,* he kanaka hanohano.
2. Kupono ke kauoha′ku.

Com-mānd′ment, *n.* Kauoha paa; kanawai. SYN. law.

Com-mĕm′o-rāte, *v.* E hana hoomanao. SYN. celebrate.

Com-mĕm′o-rā′tion, *n.* Ka hana hoomanao. SYN. celebration.

Com-mem′o-ra-tive, *adj.* No ka hoomanao ana. SYN. in remembrance of

Com-mĕnçe′, *v.* E hoomaka; e hookumu. SYN. begin.

Com-mĕnçe′ment, *n.* Ka hookumu ana; ka hoomaka ana. SYN. beginning. *Commencement day,* la i haawiia na palapala apono ma ke Kula Nui.

Com-mĕnd′, *v.* E apono; e mahalo. SYN. approve; praise.

Com-mĕnd′a-ble, *adj.* Ku i ka mahalola; ku i ka aponoia. SYN. praiseworthy.

Cŏm′men-dā′tion, *n.* Ka mahalo; ka apono ana. SYN. approval.

Com-mĕn′su-rāte, *adj.* Like; ana like; ku like. SYN. proportional.

Cŏm′ment, *v.* E olelo wehewehe.

Cŏm′men-tā′ry, *n.* Buke wehewehe olelo.

Com′men-tā′tor, *n.* He mea wehewehe olelo.

Cŏm′mĕrçe, *n.* Oihana kalepa. SYN. trade; traffic.

Com-mĕr′çial, *adj.* Pili i ka oihana kalepa.

Com-ming′le, *v.* E hui pu; e kawili pu. SYN. mix.

Cŏm′mi-nū′ted, *adj.* Moka. SYN. broken fine.

Com-miṣ′er-āte, *v.* E menemene. SYN. pity; sympathise.

Com-miṣ′er-ā′tion, *n.* Ke aloha menemene. SYN. sympathy; pity; compassion.

Cŏm′mis-sa-ry, *n.* Ka luna nana ka oihana hoolako ai, me na pono e ae, no na koa. *Commissary department,* ka oihana hoolako i na pono e ola ai na koa.

Com-miṣ′sion, *n.* 1. Palapala hooko ho no ka oihana.
2. Uku no ke kuai ana·i ka waiwai.

Com-miṣ′sion, *v.* 1. E hookoho.
2. E haawi i ka mana; e hooiii mana. SYN. authorize; empower.

Com-miṣ′sion-er, *n.* 1. He elele aupuni; komisina.
2. He Luna Aupuni.

Com-mit′, *v.* 1. E hana. SYN. do; perform. *Commit a crime,* e hana i ke karaima.
2. E hooili. SYN. send. *Commit to prison,* e hooili i ka hale paahao.
3. E waiho; *Commit to one's care,* e waiho malalo o ka malu o mea.
4. E hoopaa. *To commit to memory,* e hoopaa naau.

Com-mit′ment, *n.* 1. Palapala hoopaa.
2. Ka hana ana; ke ko ana.
3. Waiho ana′ku. *The commitment of the cause to the jury,* ka waiho ana′ku o ka hihia imua o ke jury.

Com-mit′tee, *n.* He komite. *A standing committee,* he komite mau. *A select committee,* he komite wae. *Committee of the whole,* komite o ka Hale. *A joint committee,* he komite kuka′.

Com-mō′di-oŭs, *adj.* Akea; oluolu i ka noho ana. *A commodious house,* he hale akea.

Com-mōd′i-ty, *n.* He mea liilii kuai.

Cŏm′mo-dōre, *n.* Luna nui o kekahi au moku.

Cŏm′mon, *adj.* 1. Pili like. *Common divisor,* helu komo pili like. *Common good,* pono pili like.
2. Laulaha. *A common report,* he olelo laulaha; mea i wawa wale ia.
3. *A common sight,* he mea i ike mau ia. *A common man,* he kanaka no ka lehulehu. *Common school,* kula maoli. *Common sense,* noonoo.

Cŏm′mon-ly, *adv.* Mea mau. *Commonly known,* mea ike mau ia. *Commonly reported,* lono akea ia.

Cŏm′mon-plāçe, *adj.* Maa. *Commonplace remark,* olelo maa.

Cŏm′mon-wēalth, *n.* Ke Aupuni.

Com-mō′tion, *n.* He nauwewe.

Com-mūne′, *v.* E kamailio pu; e kuka′ pu.

Com-mū′ni-cant, *n.* Hoahanau; mea ai i ka ahaaina a ka Haku.

Com-mū′ni-ty, *n.* 1. He poe e noho ana ma kauwahi. *The Hawaiian community,* ka poe Hawaii. *Living in the community,* e noho ana mawaena o kekahi poe.
2. *Community of interest,* he pono pili like i kekahi poe.

Cŏm′mu-tā′tion, *n.* Ka loli panai ana. *Commutation of punishment,* ka loli ana o ka hoopai i hoopai e ae.

Com-mūte′, *v.* E hoololi. *To commute a punishment,* e hoololi i ka hoopai, i hoopai e ae.

Com-pāct′, *adj.* Paa; paapu.

Cŏm′pact, *n.* He olelo ae like. SYN. agreement.

Com-păn′ion, *n.* He hoa. SYN. comrade; mate.

Cŏm-păn′ion-a-ble, *adj.* Oluolu; launa; kupono i hoa. SYN. sociable.

Cŏm′pa-ny, *n.* 1. He mau hoa.
2. He mau ohua. *I have company at my house,* he mau ohua ko'u ma ka hale.
3. He hui; he ahahui.
4. He puali. *A great company,* he puali nui.

Cŏm′par-a-ble, *adj.* Hiki ke hoohalikeia.

Com-păr′a-tive, *adj.* 1. Ma ka hoohalike.
2. Iki. *Comparative comfort,* he oluolu iki.

Com-pâre′, *v.* E hoohalike.

Com-pâr′i-son, *n.* Ka hoohalike ana.

Com-pärt′ment, *n.* He mahele.

Cŏm′pass, *n.* 1. He panana. *A ship's compass,* he panana hooholo moku.
2. *Surveyor's compass,* panana ana aina.
3. He kaapuni. *Fetch a compass,* e holo kaapuni.

Cŏm′pass, *v.* 1. E kaapuni; e hoopuni. SYN. surround.
2. E loaa. SYN. obtain; bring about. *To compass a design,* e loaa i ka make make. E ko i ka makemake.

Com-păs′sion, *n. adj.* Aloha menemene. SYN. sympathy; fellow-feeling.

Com-păs′sion-ate, *adj.* Aloha. SYN. sympathizing.

Com-păt′i-ble, *adj.* Kupono. SYN. consistent.

Com-păt′ri-ot, *n.* Hoa makee aupuni.

Com-pel′, *v.* E kaohi. SYN. oblige; necessitate.

Com-pĕn′di-um, *n.* He olelo i hoopokole ia. SYN. abridgement.

Cŏm′pen-sāte, *v.* 1. E pani i ka poho. SYN. recompense.
2. E uku. SYN. remunerate.

Cŏm′pen-sā′tion, *n.* Ka uku ana. SYN. recompense; remuneration.

Com-pete′, *v.* E paio pu no ka lanakila.

Cŏm′pe-tençe } *n.* Ka lawa pono o
Cŏm′pe-ten-çy } ka loaa.

Cŏm′pe-tent, *adj.* Kupono; makaukau. *A competent man,* he kanaka makaukau.

Cŏm′pe-ti′tion, *n.* Ka paio ana no ka lanakila. SYN. emulation.

Com-pet′i-tor, *n.* Hoa paio.

Com-pĕt′i-tive, *adj.* No ka paio lanakila. *A competitive examination* he hoike paio no ka lanakila.

Cŏm′pi-la′tion, *n.* He buke i kakauia ma ka wae ana.

Com-pīle′, *v.* E hoomakaukau i buke ma ka wae ana.

Com-plā′çent, *adj.* Maliu; oluolu.

Com-plāin′, *v.* E ohumu; e hai mau i ka pilikia.

Com-plāint′, *n.* 1. Leo ohumu.
2. He mai, SYN. sickness; disease.
3. He kumu hoopii. *To entertain a complaint,* e waiho aku i kumu hoopii.

Com-plāin′ant, *n.* Mea hoopii. SYN. plaintiff.

Cŏm′plai-çant, *adj.* Oluolu; laulea.

Cŏm'ple-ment, *n.* Ka piha pono ana. *Complement of an angle*, ka huina piha o ka huina kupono.

Com-plète', *adj.* Pau pono; piha pono. ko pono ia. *Complete divisor*, helukomo piha pono. SYN. whole.

Com-plète', *v.* E hooko pono; e paa pono. *The work is completed*, ua hooko pono ia ka hana. SYN. accomplish; fulfill.

Com-plete'ly, *adv.* Pau loa; loa. *Completely exhausted*, naenae loa. *Completely at a loss*, maopopo ole loa.

Com-plē'tion, *n.* Ke ko ana; Ka pau pono ana. SYN. fulfillment; accomplishment.

Com-plěx', *adj.* 1. Pohihihi. 2. *Complex fraction*, hakina huikau.

Com-plěx'ion, *n.* Ka hooluu ana o ka ili o ke kino kanaka. *Light complexion*, ili keokeo. *Dark complexion*, hauliuli.

Com-pli'ant, *adj.* Ae wale aku; kuapelu.

Com'pli-cāte, *v.* E hoohihia; hoohuikau; hoopohihihi.

Cŏm-pli-cā'tion, *n.* Ka hoohuikau ana; ka hoopohihihi ana.

Cŏm'pli-ment, *v.* E olelo hoomalimali; e olelo mahalo.

Cŏm'pli-ment, *n.* E olelo hoomalimali; ano mahalo.

Cŏm'pli-měn'ta-ry, *adj.* Ano hoomalimali; ano mahalo.

Com-plý', *v.* E ae aku i ka hai makemake, a kauoha pela. SYN. assent. *I comply with your wishes*, ke ae nei au i kou makemake.

Com-po'nent, *n.* He hapa o ka mea okoa.

Com-pōse', *v.* 1. E kakau; e haku *To compose a song*, e haku i mele. 2. E hoomaalili; hoomalielie. 3. E kaawili; e hoohui. 4. E kukulu i na kepau hua palapala no ke pai ana.

Com-pos'ed-ly, *adv.* Makaukau; pihoihoi ole.

Com-pos'er, *n.* Mea haku mele, me na mea e ae.

Cŏm'po-sĭ'tion, *n.* 1. He manao i kakau ia.

Com-pos'ĭ-tor, *n.* Mea hoonohonoho i na hua kepau no ka pai palapala.

Cŏm'pound, *n.* He kino hui.

Com-pound', *v.* 1. E hoohui i na mea okoa a lilo i kino hookahi. 2. E kaawili pu. *Compound a preparation*, e kaawili pu i ka laau lapaau. 3. *Compound a felony*, e kala i ke karaima me ka hoopai ole o ke kanawai, no ka pono e loaa mai ana.

Cŏm'pound, *adj.* Ano hui. *Compound fraction*, hakina ano hui.

Cŏm'pre-hĕnd', *v.* E hoomaopopo. SYN. understand.

Cŏm'pre-hĕn'sion, *n.* Ka hoomaopopo ana. SYN. understanding.

Cŏm'pre-hĕn'sive, *adj.* Laulaha; akea. SYN. extensive.

Com-prěss', *v.* E kaomi iho.

Com-prěss'ĭ-bĭl'ĭ-ty, *n.* Ke ano hiki ke kaomiia.

Com-prěs'sion, *n.* Ke kaomi ana.

Com-prĭșc', *v.* E hui. SYN. include; consist of. *The school comprises boys and girls*. E hui ana na keiki kane a me na kaikamahine ma ke kula.

Cŏm'pro-mișe, *v.* E kuikahi; e hooholo ma ka ae like.

Comp-trol'ler, *n.* Luna hooia helu.

Com-pul'sion, *n.* Koina; ke kaohi ana.

Com-pune'tion, *n.* Ka hoopai ana o ka naau. SYN. remorse. *Compunctions of conscience*, ka hoopai ana o ka luna-ike hala.

Cŏm'pu-tā'tion, *n.* Ka helu ana.

Com-pūte', *v.* E helu.

Com-pūt'er, *n.* Mea nana e helu.

Cŏm'rade, *n.* He hoa. SYN. companion.

Cŏn'ceave, *adj.* Poopoo; pio.

Con-çēal', *v.* 1. E huna. SYN. hide; secrete. *Conceal the truth*, e huna i ka oiaio. 2. E pee. *Conceal one's self*, e pee.

Con-çēal'ment, *n.* Ka huna ana. *Place of concealment*, kahi i hunaia ai; kahi i pee ai.

Con-çēde', *v.* E ae i ko hai. SYN. admit; grant; allow.

Con-çeit', *n.* Lanahaakei o ka manao ka hooioi; ka manao nui iaia iho.

Con-çeit'ed, *adj.* Hooioi; hookelakela; akena; haanou. SYN. egotistical; opinionated.

Con-çeiv'a-ble, *adj.* Hiki i ka noonoo ke apo.

Con-çeive', *v.* 1. E hapai keiki. 2. E hooulu i ka noonoo. SYN. devise. 3. E hoomaopopo. SYN. understand; comprehend; suppose.

Con-çen-trāte, *v.* 1. E hooakoakoa ma kahi hookahi. SYN. combine. 2. E kau nui aku. *Concentrate your thoughts*, e kau nui aku i kou noonoo.

Cŏn'çen-trā'tion, *n.* 1. Ka hooakoakoa ana ma kahi hookahi. SYN. combining. 2. Ke kau nui ana. *Concentration of thought*, ke kau nui ana o ka noonoo.

Con-çĕp'tion, *n.* 1. Ka hapai keiki. 2. Ka noonoo o ka naau. SYN. idea; thought. 3. Ka apo ana o ka naau i kela me keia kumu noonoo.

Con-çĕrn', *v.* 1. E pili. *It does not concern me*, aole pili ia mea ia'u, *or* aohe o'u kuleana ma ia mea. 2. Pilihua. SYN. anxious. 3. E komo pu. SYN. engaged in. *He was concerned in the difficulty*, ua komo pu oia iloko o ka hihia.

Con-çĕrn', *n.* 1. Kuleana; pono. SYN. interest. 2. Oihana. SYN. business. 3. Pilihua o ka manao. SYN. anxiety.

Con-çẽrn′ing, *prep.* E pili ana; no; SYN. about; in regard to.

Con-çẽrt′, *v.* E kuka′ pu.

Cŏn′çert, *n.* 1. Aha mele.

2. *Act in concert,* e pualu like ma ka hana. SYN. Act together.

Con-çẽs′sion, *n.* 1. He palapala ae.

2. Ka mea i ae ia.

Conch (kŏnk), *n.* He pupu nui o ke kai.

Con-chŏl′o-ġist, *n.* Kanaka imi no na pupu.

Con-chŏl′o-ġy, *n.* Ka ike e pili ana i na pupu.

Con-çil′i-āte, *v.* E hoolaulea; e hooluolu. SYN. propitiation.

Con-çil′i-ā′tion, *n.* Ka hoolaulea ana; ka hooluolu ana.

Con-çise′, *adj.* Pokole, io nui nae. SYN. terse; succint. *A concise statement,* he haina pokole i-o nui nae.

Con-çise′ly, *adv.* Me ka pokole a me ka i-o nui. SYN. succintly; briefly.

Con-clūde′, *v.* 1. E hooki. SYN. close. *To conclude a speech,* e hooki i ka hai olelo.

2. E hoololo ma ka manao. SYN. infer.

3. E hooholo; *To conclude a treaty,* e hooholo i ke kuikahi.

Con-clū′sion, *n.* 1. Ka hopena; pau ana. SYN. end.

2. Ka mea i hooholoia; SYN. decision; deduction.

Con-elū′sive, *adj.* Lawa pono; hiki ole ke hoole ia. SYN. final. *Conclusive evidence.* Olelo hoike lawa pono.

Con-eŏet′, *v.* E imi; e noonoo. SYN. devise; scheme; plan. *To concoct a lie,* e imi i wahahee.

Cŏn′eŏrd, *n.* Ka manao lokahi.

Con-eŏrd′ançe, *n.* Buke kuhikuhi olelo.

Cŏn′eŏurse, *n.* He anaina nui.

Cŏn′eu-bine, *n.* He haiawahine.

Con-cū′pis-çençe, *n.* Kuko hewa. SYN. lust.

Con-eūr′, *v.* E kokua i ka manao. E apono i ka manao. SYN. approve.

Con-eūr′rençe, *n.* 1. Ke kokua ana; ka apono ana. SYN. approval.

2. Ka halawai pu ana. SYN. union.

3. *Concurrent jurisdiction,* mana like o ka hookolokolo.

Con-eŭs′sion, *n.* Ke kui ana. SYN. shock.

Con-dẽmn′, *v.* E hoahewa i ka hoopai. SYN. sentence.

Cŏn′dẽm-nā′tion, *n.* Ka ahewa ana; ka hoopai ana.

Cŏn′dẽn-sā′tion, *n.* Ke kaomi iho ana i paa.

Con-dẽnse′, *v.* E kaomi iho.

Con-dẽns′er, *n.* He mea e kaomi ana.

Cŏn′de-sçẽnd′, *v.* E maliu mai.

Cŏn′de-sçẽnsion, *n.* Ka maliu ana.

Cŏn′diġn′, (kon-dīn′) *adj.* Kupono. *Condign punishment,* hoopai kupono. SYN. merited.

Cŏn′di-ment, *n.* Inai; mea mikomiko.

Con-di′tion, *n.* 1. Ano. *Condition of life,* ano o ka noho ana. *Condition of the house,* ke ano o ka hale. SYN. state.

2. Loina. *The conditions of the problem,* na loina o ka nanehai.

Con-di′tion-al, *adj.* Mamuli o na loina.

Con-di′tion-al-ly, *adv.* Mamuli o na na loina.

Cŏn-dōle′, *v.* E kaumaha pu; e uwe pu.

Con-dō′lençe, *n.* Ke aloha menemene. SYN. sympathy.

Con-dūçe′, *v.* E kokua. SYN. contribute to. *Industry conduces to happiness,* ke kokua nei ka hooikaika i ka hauoli.

Con-dū-çive, *adj.* E alakai ana i ke ola kino; e kokua ana i ke ola kino.

Cŏn′duet, *n.* Ke ano o ka hana ana; ka noho ana. SYN. behavior.

Con-dŭet′, *v.* E alakai; SYN. lead.

Con-dŭet′or, *n.* 1. He alakai; SYN. director.

2. *A good conductor of heat,* he mea paa pono i ka wela; mea hoolaha pono i ka wela.

2. *A non-conductor of heat,* he mea hoolaha ole i ka wela; hoomohala ole i ka wela.

Cŏn′-duĭt (dĭt), *n.* He hawai; ohe wai: auwai.

Cōne, *n.* Puuoa.

Con-fēe′-tion-er, *n.* Kanaka hana mea ono.

Confēe′-tion-er-y, *n.* Na mea ono i hanaia o kela me keia ano.

Con-fēd′-er-ā′-tion, *n.* Ke kuikahi ana iwaena o na aupuni, e kokua kekahi i kekahi. SYN. alliance; league.

Con-fẽr′, *v.* 1. E haawi. SYN. bestow.

2. E kuka′ pu. SYN. advise.

Cŏn′fẽr-ençe, *n.* 1. Ke kuka′ pu ana.

2. He aha kuka′.

Con-fẽss′, *v.* E hai akaka. SYN. to acknowledge. *To confess a fault,* e hai akaka mai no ka hewa.

Con-fẽs′sion, *n.* Ka hai akaka ana. SYN. avowal. *The confession of guilt,* ka hai akaka ana ua hewa.

Cŏn′fi-dănt′, *n. m.* ⎫
Cŏn′fi-dănte′, *n. f.* ⎬ He punahele.

Con-fide′, *v.* E paulele, e hilinai. SYN. trust; rely.

Cŏn′fi-dençe, *n.* Ka paulele; ka hilinai. SYN. reliance; faith.

Cŏn′fi-dent, *adj.* Manao paulele; manao paa.

Cŏn′fi-dẽn′tial, *adj.* 1. Paulele ia; hilinai ia. SYN. trustworthy.

2. Malu′. *A confidential communication,* he palapala hoike malu′. SYN. secret.

Cŏn′fi-dent-ly, *adv.* Me ke kanalua ole. SYN. positively.

Con-fīne′, *v.* E hoopaa. SYN. restrict. *To confine in a room,* e hoopaa iloko o ke keena.

Cŏn′fine, *n.* Palena; mokuna; pea. Syn. bounds. *The confines of the land*, na pea o ka aina.

Con-fine′ment, *n.* 1. Ka hoopaa ana. 2. Ka wa hanau keiki.

Con-firm′, *v.* 1. E hooia. Syn. verify, *To confirm a statement*, e hooia i ka olelo hoike. 2. E hookupaa. Syn. strengthen. *To confirm in the truth*, e hookupaa ma ka oiaio.

Cŏn′fir-mā′tion, *n.* Ka hooia ana; Ka hookupaa ana.

Cŏn-fis′cate, *v.* E kaili; e lawe ma ke ano hoopai.

Cŏn′fis-cā′tion, *n.* Ka lawe ana o ke aupuni i ka waiwai, ma ke ano hoopai.

Cŏn′fla-grā′tion, *n.* He ahi weliweli; ahi nui.

Con′fliet, *n.* He kaua; hakaka; paio.

Cŏn′flu-ençe, *n.* Ka hui ana o ke kahe. 2. Kahi e hui ai o ke kahe ana.

Con-fŏrm′, *v.* E hookulike; kulike.

Con-fŏrm′i-ty, *n.* Ke kulike; ka hoohalike ana.

Con-found′, *v.* Hookahuli.

Con-frŏnt′, *v.* 1. E ku he alo he alo. 2. E ku-e′.

Con-fūse′, *v.* E hoopihoihoi; hoopuiwa hoopowehiwehi. Syn. distract, disconcert.

Cŏn-fūs′ed-ly, *adv.* pioloke. *Confusedly answered*, pane ia me ka pioloke.

Con-fū′şion, *n.* 1. Ka huikau o ka waiho ana. Syn. disorder. 2. Pioloke o ka naau. Syn. distraction. 3. Haunaele. Syn. tumult. *The meeting broke up in confusion*, hoopauia ka halawai iloko o ka haunaele.

Con-fūte′, *v.* E pale i ka olelo.

Con-gēal′, *v.* E paa i ke anu. Syn. freeze.

Con-gēal′ment, *n.* Ka paa ana o ka mea wai i ke anu. Syn. freezing.

Con-gē′ni-al, *adj.* Kulike ke ano. *Congenial companions*, na hoa pili.

Con-gĕs′tion, *n.* Ka piha kupono ole ana o kauwahi o ke kino i ke koko. *Congestion of the lungs*, ka piha pono ole o ke ake mama i ke koko.

Con-grăt′u-lāte, *v.* E haawi i ka mahalo; e hauoli pu. Syn. felicitate.

Con-grăt′ū-lā′tion, *n.* Ka hoohauoli ana ia hai; ka hauoli pu ana me hai.

Con-grăt′ū-la-tō′ry, *adj.* E haawi ana i ka hauoli.

Cŏn′gre-gāte, *v.* E akoakoa pu. Syn. assemble.

Cŏn′gre-gā′tion, *n.* He anaina pule.

Cŏn′grĕss, *n.* 1. Ka aha kau kanawai o Amerika Huipuia. 2. He anaina kuka′. *A congress of nations*, ka anaina kuka o na lahui.

Con-grĕs′şion-al, *adj.* Pili i ka aha kaukanawai o Amerika Huipuia.

Con′ic, *adj.* Pili i ka puuoa. *Conic sections*, na kaha oki o ka puuoa.

Con-jĕet′ūre, *n.* Manao koho wale. Syn. surmise; guess.

Con-join′, *v.* E hui. Syn. unite.

Con-joint′ly, *adv.* Ma ke ano hui. Syn unitedly.

Cŏn′ju-gal, *adj.* Pili i ka mare. Syn. marital. *Conjugal relations*, na pono o ka mare.

Con-ju-gā′tion, *n.* Aui ana o ka haina.

Con-jūne′tion, *n.* 1. He hua olelo hoohui mamala olelo. 2. Ka pili pu ana. *Conjunction of planets*, ka pili pu ana o na hoku hele, i ka nana′na.

Cŏn′jure, *v.* E kilokilo.

Cŏn′jur-er, *n.* Kanaka kilokilo.

Con-nĕet′, *v.* E hoopili pu; pili pu. Syn. join.

Con-nĕe′tion. 1. Ka pili ana. 2. He pili kino.

Con-nĕe′tive, *n.* Ka mea e hoohui ana i na mea kaawale.

Con-niv′ançe, *n.* Ke kokua malu′ ana i ka mea pono ole. Syn. collusion.

Con-nive′, *v.* E kokua malu′ i ka hewa.

Cŏn′nois-seūr′ (kŏn-nĭs-sūr), *n.* He kanaka akeakamai.

Con-nū′bĭ-al, *adj.* Pili i ka mare; Syn. conjugal.

Con′quer, *v.* E lanakila; e lawe pio.

Cŏn′quer-or, *n.* Ka mea lanakila.

Cŏn′quest, *n.* 1. Ka hoopio ana. 2. Ka mea i lawe pio ia.

Cŏn′săn-guin′i-ty, *n.* Ka pili koko; ka pili hanauna. Syn. relationship.

Cŏn′sçiençe (shens), *n.* Ka lunaikehala.

Cŏn′sçi-ĕn′tioūs, *adj.* Hoolohe i ka ka lunaikehala; akahai.

Cŏn′sçi-ĕn′tious-ly *adv.* Me ka hoolohe i ka ka lunaikehala; me ke akahai.

Cŏn′sçi-ĕn′tious-ness, *n.* Ke ko ana mamuli o ka lunaikehala; ke ko ana me ke akahai.

Cŏn′scioūs, *adj.* Maopopo iloko iho.

Cŏn′scious-ness, *n.* Ka ike; ka ike iloko iho.

Cŏn′se-crāte′, *v.* E hoolaa.

Cŏn′se-crāt′ed, *adj.* Hoolaa ia. Syn. hallowed, sacred.

Cŏn′se-crā′tion, *n.* Ka hoolaa ana.

Con-sēe′u-tive, *adj.* E hahai ana kekahi i kekahi. *Consecutive hours*, na hora e hahai ana kekahi i kekahi.

Con-sĕnt′, *n.* 1. Ka ae ana. Syn. assent. 2. *With one consent*, me ka manao lokahi. Syn. unanimously.

Cŏn′se-quĕnçe, *n.* 1. He hopena. *Poverty is the consequence of idleness*, o ka nele ka hopena o ka molowa. 2. *In consequence of*, no ia kumu; no ia mea. Syn. because of. 3. *A matter of small consequence*, he mea Hiliii loa ia; he mea ole ia. 4. *A man of consequence*, he kanaka koikoi. Syn importance.

Con'-se-quent, *n.* **1.** Ka mahele hope o ka *ratio.*
2. He hopena. SYN. result; effect.
Cŏn'se-quĕn'tial, *adj.* Hookano; hookiekie. SYN. pompous.
Cŏn'se-quent-ly, *adv.* Nolaila, no ia hoi, no ia mea. SYN. therefore; for the reason.
Con-sĕrv'a-tĭve, *adv.* Makee·i ke ano mau, ke ano kahiko.
Con-sĕrv'a-to-ry, *n.* **1.** Hale hooulu i na mea ulu.
Cŏn'sĕrve, *n.* Mea ono i hana ia me na hua ai. SYN. preserve.
Con-sĕrve', *v.* **1.** E hoomoa i na hua ai.
2. E malama i ke ano mau.
Con-sĭd'er, *v.* E noonoo akahele, e poonoo. SYN. reflect.
Con-sĭd'er-a-ble, *adj.* Mahuahua iki.
Con-sĭd'er-ate, *adj.* **1.** Maliu i ka manao o hai. SYN. thoughtful.
2. Akahele ma ka noonoo.
Con-sĭd'er-ā'tion, *n.* **1.** Ka maliu ana. *Consideration for the feelings of others,* ka maliu ana i ko hai manao.
2. He uku. *Work for a consideration,* e hana no ka uku.
Con-sign', *v.* E waiho ma ka lima o hai. *Consign goods for sale,* e waiho i ka waiwai ma ka lima o mea e kuai. SYN. assign.
Cŏn'sign-ee', *n.* Ka mea malama i ka waiwai i hooili ia.
Con-sign'ment, *n.* **1.** Ka hooiliia'na o ka waiwai.
2. Ka waiwai i hooiliia.
Con-sĭst', *v.* E hui. SYN. comprise. *The school consists of foreign and Hawaiian boys,* e hui ana ma ka kula na keiki haole me na keiki Hawaii.
Con-sĭst'en-çy, *n.* Ke ano lauwili ole; ke ano kupaa.
Con-sĭst'ent, *adj.* Lauwili ole; kupaa.
Cŏn'so-lā'tion, *n.* Ka maha o ka naau; ka oluolu ana o ka naau.
Con-sōle', *v.* E hooluolu; hoona; e haawi i ka maha.
Con-sŏl'i-date, *v.* E hooakoakoa i paa; e puili a paa.
Con-sŏl'i-dā'-tion,, *n.* Ka puili ana a paa; ka hoopuupuu ana a paa.
Con-sōl'ing, *adj.* Hooluolu. *A consoling thought,* he manao hooluolu.
Con'so-nance, *n.* **1.** Ke kani like o na leo.
2. Ke kulike ana i ka manao.
Cŏn'so-nant, *adj.* Oluolu; kulike.
Cŏn'so-nant, *n.* Huapalapala leo hui.
Cŏn'sŏrt, *n.* **1.** He hoa mare.
2. He moku e holo pu ana me kekahi moku.
Con-sŏrt', *v.* E hele pu; launa pu. SYN. associate with.
Con-spĭc'u-oŭs, *adj.* Moakaka.; ike lea ia. SYN. plain.

Con-spĭr'a-çy, *n.* **1.** Ke kuka pu ana no ka poino o hai.
2. Ke kipi ana; ohumu kipi.
Con-spĭre', *v.* E ohumu kipi; e kipi.
Cŏn'sta-ble, *n.* He makai; he kaiko.
Cŏn-stăb'u-la-ry, *n.* He papa makai.
Cŏn'stan-çy, *n.* Ke kupaa o ka naau; oni paa o ka naau. SYN. fidelity.
Cŏn'stant, *adj.* **1.** Kupaa; kamau. *A constant friend,* he hoa kupaa.
2. Mau. *A constant stream,* lilo na wai ...he mau.
Cŏn'stant-ly, *adv.* Mau. SYN. invariably.
Cŏn'stĕl-lā'tion, *n.* Huhui hoku paa.
Cŏn'ster-nā'tion, *n.* Ilihia; pilihua; weliweli nui.
Cŏn-sti-pā'tion, *n.* Ka paa o ka hana lepo. SYN. costiveness.
Con-stĭt'u-en-çy, *n.* Ka poe nana e koho; na makaainana koko balota.
Con'sti-tūte, *v.* **1.** E hookoho. *To constitute a member,* e hookoho i lala o ka ahahui.
2. E hoolilo; e lilo. *The people of one country constitute a nation,* lilo na kanaka o ka aina hookahi i lahui.
Cŏn'sti-tū'tion, *n.* **1.** Kumukanawai.
2. Ka hookumu ana.
3. Ke ano mau o ke kino. *A strong constitution,* he ano ikaika, puipui o ke kino.
Cŏn'sti-tū'tion-al, *adj.* **1.** Pili i ke kumukanawai. *Constitutional amendment,* he hooloili o ke kumukanawai.
2. Pili i ke ola kino. *A constitutional difficulty,* he pilikia pili i ke ola kino.
Con-strain', *v.* E koi; e kaohi. SYN. compel.
Con-strāint', *n.* Ke koi'na; ke kaohi ana. SYN. compulsion; restraint.
Con-strŭct', *v.* E kukulu. SYN. build.
Con-strŭc'tion, *n.* **1.** Ke kukulu ana.
2. Ka mea i kukuluia.
3. Ke ano. SYN. meaning.
Con-strŭe', *v.* **1.** E mahele olelo; e unuhi olelo; e wehewehe olelo. SYN. explain; translate.
Cŏn'sul, *n.* He kanikele; luna kiai oihana kalepa o kekahi aupuni me kekahi aupuni e ae.
Cŏn'su-lar, *adj.* Pili i ka oihana o ke kanikele. *Consular certificate,* palapala hooia a ke kanikele.
Cŏn'su-late, *n.* Keena oihana o ke kanikele.
Cŏn'sul-ship, *n.* Oihana kanikele.
Con-sŭlt', *v.* **1** E kuka' pu. SYN. deliberate.
2. E imi. *Consult a book,* e imi iloko o ka buke.
3. *Consult a physician,* e imi i kauka lapaau nana e kokua.
Cŏn'sul-tā'tion, *n.* Ke kuka' ana.
Con-sūme', *v.* **1.** E hoopau; e luku. SYN. destroy.
2. E ai. *To consume food,* e ai i ka ai.

Con-sūm′er, *n.* Ka mea nana e hoopau.

Con′sum-mā′tion, *n.* Ka hopena; ke ko ana. SYN. end; completion.

Con-sŭmp′tion, *n.* 1. Ka mai hokii.
2. Ka hoopau ana. *Consumption of food,* ka hoopau ana i ka ai.

Con-sŭmp′tive, *adj.* Loaa i ka hokii.

Cŏn′tact, *n.* Ka hoopili kino aku.

Con-tā′gion, *n.* Mai lele ma ka pili kino

Con-tā′gioŭs, *adj.* Lele no ka pili ana.

Con-tāin′, *v.* E piha. *A gallon contains four quarts,* piha ke galani i na kuata eha.
2, E loaa. *The book contains instruction,* e loaa ana i ka naauao ma ka buke.

Con-tāin′er, *n.* He apu, he ipu; mea e paa ana.

Con-tăm′i-nāte, *v.* E hoohaumia. SYN. pollute; taint.

Con-tăm′i-nā′tion, *n.* Ka haumia; ka pelapela. SYN. pollution.

Con-tĕmn′, *v.* E hoowaha′waha′. SYN. despise.

Cŏn′tem-plate, v. E noonoo; e manao. SYN. meditate; purpose.

Con′tem-plā′tion, *n.* Ka noonoo ana. SYN. meditation.

Con-tĕm′po-ra-ry, *adj.* Ola like. SYN. cotemporary. *Kamehameha I. and Napoleon were contemporary,* e ola like ana o Napoleona a me Kamehameha I.

Con-tĕmpt′, *n.* Ke ano hoowaha′waha′. *Contempt of court,* ka hoowaha′waha′ i ka aha.

Con-tĕmpt′i-ble, *adj.* Hoowaha′waha′ia; haahaa loa. SYN. mean; vile.

Con-tĕmpt′u-oŭs, *adj.* Ano haakei; hoowaha′waha′. *A contemptuous expression,* he olelo hoowaha′waha′.

Con-tĕnd′, *v.* E aumeume; hakaka; paio pu. SYN. strive.

Con-tend′ing, *adj.* E ku-e′ ana; e hakaka ana. *Contending factions,* na aoao e ku-e′ ana kekahi i kekahi. SYN. opposing.

Con-tĕnt′, *v.* E hoo-na; e hooluolu.

Con-tĕnt′ed, *adj.* Walea; oluolu; luana.

Con-tĕn′tion, *n.* Ka hakaka; ka aumeume; ka hoopaapaa. SYN. strife.

Con-tĕn′tioŭs, *adj.* Hoopaapaa wale; hakaka wale.

Con-tĕnt′ment, } *n.* Hanawalea; oluolu o ka manao.
Con-tĕnt′, }

Cŏn′test, *n.* He hakaka′; he kaua; he paio.

Cŏn-tĕst′, *v.* 1. E ku-e′. *Contest an election,* e ku-e′ i ke kohoia′na.
2. E paio. *Contest a prize,* e paio no ka uku makana.

Con-tig′ū-oŭs, *adj.* E moe pili ana. SYN. adjacent.

Cŏn′ti-nençe, *n.* Ke ano pakiko.

Cŏn′ti-nent, *n.* Mahele aina nui.

Con-ti-nĕnt′al, *adj.* E pili ana i ka mahele aina nui.

Con-tĭn′gen-çy, *n.* Ka mea e loohia mai ana paha.

Con-tĭn′gent, *adj.* E loohia mai ana paha. *Contingent fund,* he puu dala no na lilo e loohia mai ana paha.

Con-tĭn′u-al, *adj.* Mau.

Con-tĭn′u-al-ly, *adv.* Mau; i na manawa a pau.

Con-tĭn′u-ançe, *n.* Ka hoomau ana.

Con-tĭn′ūe, *v.* E hoomau.

Con-tôr′tion, *n.* Ka wili ana; paкaawili ana; kupaka ana.

Cŏn′tour, *n.* Ke ano o ke kii.

Con′tra-band, *adj.* Papaia e ke kanawai. *Contraband goods,* waiwai i papaia e ke kanawai. *Contraband of war,* waiwai i papaia ke kuai ana i ka enemi.

Cŏn′tra-band, *n.* He inoa no na nika o Amerika i ka wa kaua kuloko.

Cŏn′tract, *n.* He palapala ae like.

Con-trăct′, *v.* 1. E hoohaiki. SYN. shrink.
2. E komo aku. *Contract a debt,* e komo i ka aie. SYN. incur.
3. E loaa. *Contract a disease,* e loaa i ka mai. SYN. incur.
4. E hooholo. *To contract, to build a house,* e hooholo e kukulu i hale. SYN. bargain.

Cŏn-trăct′ed, *adj.* 1. Haiki. SYN. narrow.
2. *A contracted mind,* he naau papau o ka noonoo.

Con-trăc′tion, *n.* Ka hoopokole ana.

Con-trăct′or, *n.* Ka mea e paa ana ma ka olelo aelike.

Cŏn′tra-dict′, *v.* E hoopaapaa; e pakike′.

Cŏn′tra-dict′o-ry, *adj.* Pakuikui.

Cŏn′tra-ry, *adj.* 1. Ku-e′. *Contrary to law,* ku-e′ i ke kanawai.
2. Nunuha. SYN. wilful; stubborn.

Cŏn′trast, *n.* Ka like ole; ke ano okoa.

Con-trăst′, *v.* E hooku-e′ ano. *Contrast light with darkness,* e hooku-e′ ka malamalama i ka pouli.

Con-trĭb′ūte, *v.* 1. E kokua. *Contribute a share,* e kokua i ka haawina.
2. E haawi manawalea.

Cŏn′tri-bū′tion, *n.* Ke kokua; ka haawina manawalea.

Con-trĭb′u-tor, *n.* 1. Ka mea e kokua ana. *Newspaper contributor,* ka mea e kokua ana i ka nupepa, ma ke kakau ana.

Con′trite, *adj.* Mihi; walania; akahai. SYN. penitent.

Con-tri′tion, *n.* Ka mihi no ka hewa. SYN. penitence.

Cŏn-triv′ançe, *n.* Ka hua o ka noonoo. SYN. invention. Ka mea e hiki ai.

Con-trive′, *v.* E noonoo a e hana i ka mea e hiki ai. SYN. invent.

Con-triv′er, *n.* He mea i makaukau ma ka noonoo ana a ma ka hana ana i ka mea e pono ai. SYN. inventor.

Con-trōl′, *n.* Mana hoomalu; ka hoomalu ana.

Con-trōl′, E hoomalu. SYN. govern.

Cŏn′tro-vēr′sy, *n.* He hoopaapaa.

Con-tu-mā′çioŭs, *adj.* Nuha; nunuha.
SYN. obstinate; stubborn.

Cŏn′tu-mā-çy, *n.* Paakiki o ka naau;
ano nuha.

Cŏn′tŭ-me-ly, *n.* Olelo hoomaau;
hoomaewaewa. SYN. reproach.

Con-tu′şion, *n.* Palapu.

Co-nŭn′drum, *n.* He olelo huna′.

Cŏn′va-lēs′çençe, ka pohala ana; ka
oluolu ana o ka mai.

Cŏn′va-lēs′çent, *adj.* Pohala; konini;
oioio.

Con-vēne′, *n.* E hooakoakoa.

Con-vēn′iençe, *n.* He mea e pono ai;
mea ku pono.

Con-vēn′-ient, *adj.* He mea hiki. *If
it is convenient to you*, ina he mea hiki
ia oe.

Con-vēn′ient-ly, *adv.* Me ka hiki kupono.

Cŏn-vēn′tion, *n.* He aha; ahahui. *A
convention of teachers*, he ahahui kumukula.

Con-vērge′, *v.* E kai a i ke kikowaena.
Radii converge to a center, kai na kaha hanai a i ke kiko waena.

Con′vēr-sant, *adj.* 1. Makaukau ma
ka ike. *Conversant with a language*,
makaukau ma kekahi olelo. SYN. fa-
miliar.
2. Ike pono. SYN. acquainted.

Cŏn′vēr-sā′tion, *n.* Kamailio.

Cŏn′vēr-sā′tion-al, *adj.* Kamakamailio.

Con-vērse′, *v.* E kamailio pu. SYN.
talk with.

Con-vēr′se′ly, *adv.* Ma ka huli hope.

Con-vēr′şion, *n.* 1. Ka loli ana. *The
conversion of water into ice*, ka loli ana o
ka wai a lilo i hau paa.
2. Ka huli ana o ka naau.

Cŏn′vērt, *n.* Ka mea i hoohuliia kona
naau.

Con-vērt′, *v.* 1. E hoololi. *Convert
water into steam*, e hoololi ka wai a lilo
i mahu.
2. E hoohuli manao.

Con′vēx, *adj.* Poepoe owaho.

Con-vey′, *v.* 1. E lawe; e halihali.
SYN. carry by hand.
2. E hooili; e hoouna. SYN. send by.
3. E hoomaopopo. *Convey the meaning*, e hoomaopopo i ke ano.
4. E hoololi. *Convey property*, e hoolilo waiwai.

Con-vey′ançe, *n.* 1. He mea halihali.
2. Ka halihali ana; ka hooili ana.
3. Ka hoolilo ana i ka waiwai.
4. He palapala hoolilo waiwai.

Con-vey′-anç-er, *n.* Mea kakau palapala hoolilo waiwai.

Con-vey′anç-ing, *n.* Ka oihana hoolilo waiwai paa.

Cŏn′vict, *n.* He paahao; mea i ahe-
waiia no ke karaima.

Con-vict′, *v.* E ahewa. *Convicted of
stealing*, ahewaia no ka aihue.

Con-vic′tion, *n.* 1. Ka ahewa ana;
ka ahewa ana o ka naau no ka hewa.

Con-vince′, *v.* E hoomaopopo i ka
naau. SYN. persuade.

Con-vinc′ing, *adj.* Maopopo lea.

Con-viv′i-al, *adj.* Lealea. SYN. festal.

Con′vo-ca′-tion, *n.* 1. Ka hoakoakoa
ana.
2. He anaina. SYN. assembly.

Con-vōke′, *v.* E kahea; e akoakoa. SYN.
call, summon.

Con-voy′, *v.* E hele pu no ka hoomalu
ana.

Con-vŭlse′, *v.* 1. E hoonaueue. SYN.
shake.
2. Hoohaalulu.
3. *Convulsed with laughter*, pio loa i ka
akaaka.

Con-vŭl′sive, *adj.* Ano haalulu.

Cŏŏk, *v.* E hoomoa; e kuke.

Cŏŏk, *n.* He kuke.

Cŏŏk′y, *n.* Berena ono liilii.

Cōol, *adj.* 1. Oluolu. *A cool day*, he la
oluolu. SYN. pleasant.
2. Pihoihoi ole; makaukau mau. SYN.
collected.

Cōol, *v.* E hoomaalili; e hooluolu.

Cōol′er, *n.* He ipu; e lilo ana ka wai i
huihui.

Cōol′ness, *n.* 1. He anu iki.
2. Ka pihoihoi ole o ka naau.
3. Ka maalili o ke aloha; nanau.

Cōol′ie, *n.* He paahana ma Inia me
Kina.

Cōol′ly, *adv.* 1. Me ka mahaoi. SYN.
impudently.
2. Me ka noonoo pono. SYN. deliber-
ately.

Cōop,, *n.* Hale moa.

Cōop′er, *n.* Kanaka hana pahu; he
kupa.

Cōop′er-age, *n.* Wahi hana pahu.

Cō-ŏp′er-āte, *v.* E kokua pu. SYN.
assist.

Cō-ŏp′er-ā′tion, *n.* Ke kokua pu
ana.

Cō-ŏp′er-ā′tive, *adj.* Kokua hui.

Cō-ŏp′er-ā′tor, *n.* Hoa hana. SYN.
assistant.

Cō-ōr′di-nate, *adj.* Kulana like.

Co-pärt′ner, *n.* He hoa o ka hui.

Co-pärt′ner-ship, *n.* He hui no ka
lawelawe ana i kekahi oihana.

Cōpe, *v.* E ku-e′ lanakila.

Cō′pi-oŭs,, *adj.* Nui; lawa pono. SYN.
abundant; plentiful.

Cō′pi-oŭs-ly, *adv.* Nui. *The rain fell
copiously*, haule nui mai ka u-a. SYN.
abundantly.

Cŏp′per, *n.* Keleawe.

Cŏp′per-plāte′, *n.* Pa keleawe. *A
copperplate engraving*, he kii i kahaiia
ma ka pa keleawe.

Cŏp′per-smith′, *n.* Kanaka hana i na mea keleawe.

Cŏp′ŭ-lāte, *v.* E hui kino ma ke ano kane a wahine.

Cŏp′u-la′tion, *n.* Ka hui kino ana o ke kane me ka wahine.

Cŏp′u-la′tive, *adj.* Hui.

Cŏp′-y, *n.* He hope; mea like.

Cŏp′y, *v.* 1. E kakau kope.
2. E hoohalike. SYN. emulate.

Cŏp′y-book, *n.* Buke kakau kope.

Cŏp′y-ist, *n.* Mea kakau kope.

Cop′y-right, *n.* Ke kuleana iloko o ka buke; he pono a ke aupuni i haawi i ka mea kakau buke.

Co-quĕtte′, *n* (**ko-kĕt**). Wahine ui; puni lealea.

Cŏr-al, *n.* Ako′ako′a; puna.

Cŏr′al-line, *adj.* Pili i ke ako′ako′a. *Coralline formation*, he kahua ako′ako′a.

Cŏrd, *n.* 1. Kaula makalii.
2. He paila. *A cord of wood*, he paila wahie.

Cŏrd, *v.* 1. E nakii. *Cord up the trunk*, e nakii i ka pahu lole.
3. E paila.

Cŏrd′age, *n.* Kaula o kela ano keia ano.

Cŏrd′ial, *n.* He mea e hoohoihoi ai; e hooeueu ai.

Cŏrd′ial, *adj.* Oiaio; pumehana. *Cordial friendship*, aloha pumehana.
2. Hoolnolu; hoolalelale.

Cŏr′di-ăl′i-ty, *n.* Aloha pumehana.

Cŏr′di-al-ly, *adv.* Me ke aloha oiaio.

Cŏre, *n.* Ka pikoi.

Cŏrk, *n.* Umoki laau.

Cŏrk′screw, *n.* Wili umoki.

Corn, *n.* 1. Kurina.
2. Na hua palaoa o na ano a pau.

Cŏrn, *v.* E kopi′ ka i-o i ka paakai. *Corned beef*, bipi i kopiia.

Cŏr-ner, *n.* 1. He kihi. *An outside corner*, he kihi.
2. *An inside corner*, he kuono.

Cŏr′ner-stone′, *n.* Pohaku kihi.

Cŏr′ner-wise, *adv.* Lepe. SYN. diagonal.

Cŏr′nĕt, *n.* Ohe puhi.

Co-rŏl′la, *n.* Ka huina o na lau liilii o ka pua.

Cŏr′ol-la-ry, *n.* Manaopili no ka manaohai.

Cor-o-nā′tion, *n.* Ka poni ana i ka Moi.

Cŏr′o-ner, *n.* He koronera; he luna aupuni; e imi ana no ke kumu make o na kanaka make.

Cŏr′po-ral, *adj.* Pili i ke kino. *Corporal punishment*, hoopai i ke kino.

Cŏr′po-ral, *n.* Kopala; luna koa malalo o ke lukanela.

Cŏr′po-rate, *adj* Huiia mamuli o ke kanawai. *Corporate body*, he hui malalo o ke kanawai.

Cor-pō′re-al, *adj.* Pili i ke kino. *Corporeal existence*, he ola kino.

Cŏrps (kore), *n.* He poe; he papa; *a corps of teachers*, he papa kumu.

Cŏrpse, *n.* He kupapau.

Cŏr′pu-lençe, *n.* Puipui o ke kino.

Cŏr′pu-lent, *adj.* Puipui ; momona kupono ole.

Cor-rēct′, *v.* 1. E hooponopono.
2. E hoopai. SYN. punish.

Cor-rēct′, *adj.* Pono; pololei.

Cor-rēc′tion, *n.* 1. Ka hooponopono ana.
2. Mea hooponopono.
3. Ka hoopai; ka hoopai ana.

Cor-rēct′ly, *adv.* Me ka pololei.

Cor-rēct′ness, *n.* Ka pololei.

Cŏr-rĕs-pŏnd′, *v.* 1. E kulike. SYN. agree.
2. E kakau leta.

Cŏr′res-pŏn′dençe, *n.* Ke kulike ana.
2. Ke kakau leta ana.

Cŏr′res-pŏn′dent, *n.* Hoa kakau leta.

Cŏr′res-pŏnd′ing, *adj.* Kulike. SYN. similar.

Cor-rŏb′ō-rāte, *v.* E hooia i ka hoike a hai.

Cor-rōde′, *v.* E popo. SYN. rust.

Cor-rō′sion, *n.* Ka popo ana o na mea metala.

Cŏr′ru-gāt-ed, *adj.* Mimino.

Cor-rŭpt′, *adj.* 1. Haumia; haukae. SYN. debased; vile.
2. Palaho. SYN. putrid.

Cor-rŭpt′, *v.* E hoohaumia; hoohaukae.

Cor-rŭpt′er, *n.* Mea nana e hoohaumia.

Cor-rŭpt-i-ble, *adj.* Lilo i ka palaho.

Cor-rŭp′tion, 1. Haumia; haukae
2. Palaho.

Cor-rŭpt′ly, *adv.* Me ka haumia; me ka apuka.

Cŏr′set, *n.* Pulike wahine.

Cŏr′tege (kor-tāzh), *n.* Poe ukali.

Coş-mĕt′ic, *n.* Mea poni.

Cŏst, *n.* Kumu lilo.

Cŏst, *v.* E lilo; make.

Cŏs′tive, *adj.* Paa ka hana lepo.

Cŏs′tive-ness, *n.* Ka paa ana o ka hana lepo. SYN. constipation.

Cŏst′ly, *adj.* Nui ka lilo.

Cos′tūme, *n.* Ka aahu.

Cōte, *n.* Hale manu nunu.

Co-tĕm′po-ra-ry, *adj.* E ola like ana i ka hanauna hookahi.

Cŏt′tage, *n.* He hale noho maikai.

Cŏt′ton, *n.* Pulupulu.

Couch, *n.* He punee.

Côugh (kof), *n.* He kunu.

Coun′çil, *n.* Aha kuka′. *Privy council*, aha kuka′ malu′.

Coun′çil-lor, *n.* Hoa no ka aha.

Coun′sel, *n.* Olelo ao. SYN. advice.

Coun′sel-lor, *n.* 1. Kakaolelo. SYN. adviser.
2. He kokua ma ke kanawai; he loio.

Count, *v.* E helu.

Coun′te-nance, *n.* Ka helehelena.

Coun′ter, *n.* Ka papa kuai o na hale kuai.

Coun'ter, adv. Ku-e'. *To go counter to good advice*, e hele ku-e' i ka olelo ao maikai.

Coun'ter-act', v. E keakea.

Coun'ter-băl'ance, v. E paona like ma ka aoao ku-e'.

Coun'ter-feit, adj. 1. Apuka. *Counterfeit money*, dala apuka.

2. Hookamani; oiaio ole.

Coun'ter-feit-er, n. Kanaka apuka dala; apuka ma kekahi mea e.

Coun'ter-mănd', v. E hooloii kauoha.

Coun'ter-pāne, n. Kapa uhi moe.

Coun'ter-părt, n. Ka lua like.

Coun'ter-sign, n. Hua olelo huna', no ka poe koa kiai.

Coun'ter-sign, v. E kakau moa hoike.

Count'ing-house, } n. Keena oihana
Count'ing-room, } kalepa.

Count'less, adj. Kinikini; nuiwale.

Coŭn'tri-fied, adj. Ane kuaaina; oheke

Coŭn'try, n. He paiaina.

Coŭn'try-man, v. He kaikua; kuaaina.

2. *Fellow-countryman*, he hoa makaainana.

Coŭn'try-sēat, n. Wahi noho iloko o ka aina.

Coun'ty, n. Mokuna aina; apana.

Coŭ'ple, n. 1. He mau kokoolua.

2. He paa.

Coŭ'ple, v. E kaulua; e hui palua.

Coŭp-ling, n. Ka hookaulua ana.

Coŭ-pon', n. Palapala hooia no ka uku kuala.

Coŭr'age, n. Ke ano aa; wiwo ole; maka'u ole. SYN. bravery; valor; daring; brave; valiant.

Cour-ā'ģeoŭs, adj. Maka'u ole. SYN. bravely.

Coŭr'ri-er, n. He kanaka kukini; he elele.

Coŭrse, n. 1. He ala. *A chosen course*, he ala i kohoia *A race course*, he ala kukini lio.

2. He au; he wa. *The course of time*, ke au o ka manawa.

3. *Watercourse*, he auwai.

Coŭrs'er, n. He lio kukini; lio heihei.

Coŭrt, n. 1. Ka poe o ke alo moi.

2. He aha hookolokolo.

3. He pahale.

4. *A court of inquiry*, he aha ninaninau.

Coŭrt, v. 1. E hooipoipo; imi i wahine mare.

2. E imi me ka hoomalimali.

Coŭr'te-oŭs, adj. Pihalula; ano oluolu; laulea. SYN. polite.

Coŭr'te-san, n. Wahine hookamakama. SYN. prostitute.

Coŭr'te-sy, n. Ke ano oluolu; keonimana. SYN. politeness.

Coŭr'tier, n. Kanaka e noho ana ma ke alo Moi.

Coŭrt'ly, adj. Hanohano; koikoi. SYN. elegant.

Coŭrt-mär'tial, n. Aha hookolokolo o ka oihana kaua.

Coŭrt'ship, n. Ka hooipoipo ana; ka imi ana i wahine mare.

Coŭrt'-yard, n. He pahale.

Coŭs'in, n. He hoahanau.

Cove, n. He kaikuono liilii.

Cŏv'e-nant, n. 1. He berita.

2. He olelo ae like i kakau ia; palapala ae like. SYN. contract.

Cŏv'e-nant, v. 1. E hoohiki i ka berita.

2. E hoohiki ma ka palapala ae like.

Cŏv'er, v. 1. E uhi. *Cover over*, e uhi.

2. E poi, *to cover with a cover*, e poi.

Cŏv'er, n. 1. He uhi. *A cover of cloth*, 2. He poi; he pani. *A cover of metal or wood*, he poi.

Cŏv'er-ing, n. Mea uhi.

Cŏv'er-let, v. Kapauhi no ka moe.

Cŏv'ert, n. Wahi e pee ai.

Cŏv'ert, adj. Maalea; huna ia. *A covert meaning*, he ano huna. SYN. hidden.

Cŏv'ert-ly, adv. Me ka maalea; ma ke ano malu.

Cŏv'et, v. E kuko hewa; e alunu.

Cŏv'et-oŭs, adj. Alunu; kuko hewa.

Cŏv'et-ous-ness, n. Ke kuko hewa ana i kahai.

Cŏv'ey, n. He pu-a manu liiliii.

Cŏw, n. Bipi wahine.

Cŏw, v. hoopuiwa; hoomak'au.

Cŏw'ard, n. He mea maka'u wale; he holowale; hee wale.

Cŏw'ard-ice, n. Ka maka'u wale.

Cŏw'ard-ly, adj. 1. E holowale; hee wale.

2. Apiki; haahaa. SYN. mean.

Cŏw'er, v. 1. E haalulu no ka maka'u.

2. E kukuli iho no ka weliweli; no kekahi kumu e ae.

Cŏw'herd, n. Kahu bipi.

Cŏw'hide, n. Ili maloo o ka bipi.

Cŏx'comb, n. Kanaka hookeha; hookahakaha.

Cŏy, adj. Palaimaka. SYN. bashful; timid.

Cō'zy, adj. 1. Oluolu; nanea. SYN. snug.

2. *A cozy chat*, he kamakamailio hoonanea.

Crăb, a. He papai.

Crăb'bed, adj. Nainai; nanau.

Crăck, n. He nakaka; owaowa; alualua.

Crăck, v. 1. E kani. *Crack a whip*, e kani ka huipa.

2. E naka.

Crăck'brāined, adj. Pupule. SYN. crazy.

Crăck'er, n. 1. Papaa berena.

2. Mea hoopahupahu'.

Crăck'le, v. E paapaa. *Thorns crackle in the fire*, paapaa na kakalaioa i ke ahi.

Crăck'ling, p. p. Paapaaina.

Crā'dle, n. 1. He moe paipai no ke keiki uuku.

2. Pahi manamana oki palaoa.

Craft, *n.* 1. Oihana hana lima. SYN. trade.
2. He moku liilii.
3. He ano maalea; ano hoohalua. SYN. cunning.
Craft'i-ly, *adv.* Me ka maalea. SYN. cunningly.
Craft'i-ness, *n.* See *Craft*. 3.
Craft'y, *adj.* Maalea.
Crag, *n.* He pali. SYN. Cliff.
Cramp, *n.* Mae'le maee'le.
Cram, *v.* E papaunu; e laiki.
Cra'ni-um, *n.* Iwipoo. SYN. skull.
Crape, *n.* Lole kanikau.
Crash, *v.* E haalulu poha'. *To fall with a crash,* e haule mai me ka haalulu poha'.
Cra'ter, *n.* He luapele.
Cra-vat', *n.* Hainaka' a'i.
Crave, *v.* 1. E iini nui. *To crave food,* e iini nui no ka ai.
2. E noi haahaa. SYN. beseech.
Crav'en, *n.* He makauwale; hee wale. SYN. coward.
Crawl, *v.* E kolo; e kokolo.
Cra'zy, *adj.* Pupu'le; ula'la.
Creak'ing, *n.* Ka uiui ana; ka uwi ana.
Cream, *n.* 1. Kurima waiu'.
2. Ka oi o ka manao maikai.
Crease, *n.* He alualu; he alu.
Cre-ate', *v.* E hookumu; e hana.
Cre-a'tion, *n.* 1. He hana; mea i hanaia. *A creation of the mind,* he mea i hana ia e ka naau.
2. Ke ao nei.
3. Na ao a pau. *Creation's God,* Ke Akua o na Ao a pau.
Cre-a'tor, *n.* Ka Mea nana e hana; nana e hookumu. *The Creator,* Ke Akua.
Crea'ture, *n.* Mea ola.
Cre'dence, *n.* Manaoio. SYN . belief.
Cre-den'tials, *n.* Palapala hoapono.
Cred'i-bil'i-ty, *n.* Ka oiaio. *The credibility of his words,* ka oiaio o kana mau olelo.
Cred'i-ble, *adj.* Hiki ke paulele ia; oiaio. SYN. trustworthy; true.
Cred'it, *n.* 1. He kumu mahalo. *A studious pupil is a credit to his teacher,* o ka haumana imi he kumu mahalo oia i kana kumu.
2. Ka hooaie'. *To give credit,* e hooaie aku.
3. Ka aoao hookaa o na mooaie.
Cred'it, *v.* 1. E lelepau; e hilinai. SYN. trust; believe.
2. E kakau ma ka aoao hookaa.
Cred'it-a-ble, *adj.* Ku i ka mahaloia; maikai. *A creditable performance,* he hana ku i ka mahaloia.
Cred'it-a-bly, *adv.* Me ka aponoia; me ka maikai.
Cred'i-tor, *n.* Mea nana e hooaie; ailihi. [*Obs.*]
Cre-du'li-ty, *n.* Ka paulele kapekepeke.

Cred'u-lous, *adj.* Paulele wale; puni wale.
Creed, *n.* He Berita o ka manaoio.
Creek, *n.* He wahi kaikuono liilii. SYN. cove.
Creep, *v.* E kolo; e kokolo me he keiki la; me he popoki la.
Creep'er, *n.* 1. Mea kolo.
2. Laau hihi.
Creep'ing-thing', *n.* Mea kolo.
Cres'cent, *adj.* E mahuahua ana. *The crescent moon,* mahina hoaka.
Crest'fal'len, *adj.* Hilahila. SYN. ashamed.
Crev'ice, *n.* He alu'alu'a; he owaowa. SYN. crack.
Crew, *n.* Ka poe luina o ka moku.
Crew'el, *n.* Lopi huluhulu hana lihilihi.
Crib, *n.* 1. He moe liilii.
2. *Corn crib,* pahu waiho kurina.
Crib, *v.* E aihue liilii. E kaili.
Crick'et, *n.* 1. Uhini.
2. He paipai wawae.
3. He paani kinipopo.
Cri'er, *n.* Mea kuka'la leo aku.
Crime, *n.* Hewa nui ma ke kanawai; karaima.
Crim'i-nal, *n.* Mea haki kanawai; mea i ahewaia i ke kanawai.
Crim'i-nal-ly, *adv.* Me ka hewa.
Crim'i-nate, *v.* E hoopii no ka hewa; e ahewa.
Crim'son, *adj or n.* Ulaula.
Cringe, *v.* 1. E kuapelu wale.
2. E hoopilimeaai.
Crip'ple, *n.* He oopa; hapakue.
Cri'sis, *n.* He huli ana. SYN. turning point. *The crisis of the disease,* ka huli ana o ka mai; (he ola paha, he make paha.)
Crisp, *adj.* 1. Paapaa; *burned to a crisp,* paapaa i ke ahi.
Cri-te'ri-on, *n.* He ana hoohalike.
Crit'ic, *n.* Mea imi kina; mea imi hewa; kuhikuhi hewa.
Crit'ic-al, *adj.* 1. Pilikia; *the critical period of the disease,* ka wa pilikia o ka mai.
2. Ano hoopololei loa. *A critical analysis,* he wehewehe hoopololei loa.
Crit'i-cise, *v.* 1. E imi hala. SYN. to be censorious.
2. E kuhikuhi hewa. SYN. point out errors.
Crit'i-cism, *n.* Ke kuhikuhi ana i na hewa; na kina.
Croak, *n.* 1. Ka leo o ka manu koraka.
2. E ohumu wale.
Croak'er, *n.* Mea ohumu wale.
Crock'er-y, *n.* Na ipu me na pa i hanaia mai ka palolo. SYN. earthern ware.
Croc'o-dile, *n.* Moo nui.
Cro'ny, *n.* He aikane; hoapili.
Crook, *n.* He mea keekee; wahi keekee.
Crook'ed, *adj.* Keekee.

Crŏp, *n.* Na hua o na mea ulu o ka aina.

Crŏss, *n.* Kea.

Crŏss, *adj* Ukiuki; huhu.

Crŏss, *v.* 1. E alalai; e ku-e′. SYN. obstruct; thwart.
2. E hele mai kahi aoao a i kahi aoao.
3. E kaha aku.

Crŏss′ex-ăm′ine, *v.* E ninau ku-e′.

Crŏss′eÿed, *adj.* Maka ahewa.

Crŏss′grāined′, *adj.* Nanau; opukopekope; nainai. SYN. crabbed.

Crŏss′ing, *n.* Kahi e hele ai a hiki i kela aoao.

Crŏss′ly, *adv.* Me ka ukiuki.

Crŏss-ques′tion, *v.* E ninau pale. SYN. cross-examine.

Crŏss′wise, *adj.* Kau kea.

Crouch, *v.* E kukuli iho; e ku lou.

Croup, *n.* Naeoa′iku′.

Crŏw, *v.* E oo mehe moa kane la.

Crŏw′bar, *n.* Kolopa′; mea une.

Crowd, *n.* He puulu.

Crowd, *v.* E hoo-ke′; e kupiliki. *To crowd together; rush together,* e lulumi.

Crown, *n.* 1. Lei alii; papale alii.
2. Ka piko o ke poo.
3. He apana dala Beritania; elima silina.

Cru′çi-fīx, *n.* He kea. SYN. cross.

Crū-çi-fix′ion, *n.* Ke kaulia′na ma ke kea.

Crū′çi-fÿ, *v.* E kaulia ma ke kea.

Crūde, *adj.* 1. Hemahema; makaukau ole.
2. Maka. *Crude material,* mea maka; na mea i hana ole ia.

Cru′el, *adj.* Mainoino; lokoino.

Cru′el-ly, *adv.* Me ka lokoino.

Cru′el-ty, *n.* Lokoino.

Cruise, *n.* He holo moana; ka holo ana o ka moku.

Cruis′er, *n.* He moku manuwa.

Crŭmb, *n.* Hu′na mea ai. *Crumb of bread,* hu′na berena.

Crŭm′ble, *v.* E helelei liilii.

Crŭp′per, *n.* Kaula huelo.

Crŭsh, *v.* E hoo-pe′; e pe′pe′.

Crŭs′ti-ly, *adv.* Huhu; naaukeemoa.

Crŭs′ty, *adj.* Nainai. SYN. crabbed.

Crŭtch, *n.* Kookoo paipai.

Crÿ, *v.* 1. E uwe; e hookahe waimaka. SYN. shed tears.
2. E kahea.

Crÿs′tal, *n.* 1. Pohaku aiai.
2. Aniani aiai. *Watch crystal,* he aniani no ka wati.

Crÿs′tal, *adj.* Moakaka; aiai; huaka.

Crÿs′tal-i-zā′tion, *n.* Ka lilo ana o kekahi mea i kino aiai.

Cŭb, *n.* Na keiki o kekahi mau holoholona. *Lion's cub,* keiki liona. *Bear's cub,* bea keiki.

Cūbe, *n.* He paailiono.

Cu′bic, *adj.* Paailiono.

Cu′bit, *n.* He kubita.

Cu′cŭm-ber, *n.* Kaukama.

Cŭd′dle, *v.* E moe pili.

Cŭd, *n.* Lualuai.

Cŭd′gel, *n.* He newa. SYN. club.

Cūe, *n.* 2. Laau pahupahu.
2. Kumu hoala manao.

Cŭff, *v.* E pai me ka lima.

Cū′li-na-rÿ, *adj.* Pili i ka oihana kuke. *Culinary utensils,* na mea kuke.

Cŭll, *v.* E ohi; e wae.

Cŭl′mi-nāte, *v.* Hiki i ka wekiu.

Cŭl′pa-ble, *adj.* Hewa; ku i ka hoahewaia. *Culpable ignorance,* naaupo ku i ka hoahewaia; naaupo kumu ole.

Cŭl′pa-bil′i-ty, *n.* Ka hewa. SYN. guilt.

Cŭl′pa-bly, *adv.* Culpatly ignorant, naaupo kumu ole; naaupo i ahewaia.

Cŭl′prit, *n.* Mea hana hewa; mea hana kolohe.

Cŭl′ti-vate, *v.* 1. E mahi. *Cultivate the land,* e mahi i ka aina.
2. *Cultivate a friendship,* e launa pu.
3. *Cultivate the mind,* e hoopiha ka naau i ka ike.

Cŭl ti-vā′tion, *n.* Ka mahi ana.

Cŭl′ti-vā′tor, *n.* 1. Kanaka mahiai.
2. He oo palau liilii mea mahi.

Cŭlt′ūre, *n.* 1. Ka mahi ana.
2. Ka hua o ka naauao.

Cŭm′ber, *v.* E hoopilikia wale; e hookaumaha wale.

Cŭm′ber-sŏme, *adj.* Hoopilikia wale; hookaumaha wale.

Cŭn′ning, *adj.* Maalea. SYN. crafty; artful.

Cŭn′ning-ly, *adv,* Me ka maalea.
2. Me ka mikioi.

Cŭp, *n.* He apu; he kiaha.

Cŭp′board, (kŭb′urd) *n.* Hale pa.

Cu-pid′i-ty, *n.* Puniwaiwai. SYN. avarice.

Cŭr, *n.* Ilio lapuwale.

Cŭr′a-ble, *adj.* Hiki ke lapaauia a ola.

Cŭr′a-tive, *adj.* Hoola. *Curative powers,* na mana hoola.

Cu-rā′tor, *n.* He kahu malama.

Cŭrb, *v.* E uumi.

Cŭrd, *n.* Waiu paa awaawa.

Cŭrd′le, *v.* E paa. *The milk is curdled,* paa ka waiu.

Cūre, *v.* 1. E hoola, mamuli o ka lapaau,
2. E hoopau. *Cure laziness,* e hoopau i ka molowa. SYN. put an end to.

Cū′ri-os′i-ty, *n.* 1. Ke ake nui e ike.
2. He mea ano e; mea milimili.
3. He ano mahaoi.

Cū′ri-oŭs, *adj.* 1. Ake e ike. *I am curious to know,* e ake au e ike.
2. Ano e. *A curious thing,* he mea ano e.
3. Mahaoi. SYN. inquisitive.

Cū′ri-ous-ly, *adv.* 1. Ma ke ano nienicle.
2. Aulii; eleu.

Cŭrl, *v.* E milo. *A curl of hair,* he milo lauoho.

Cŭr'ly, adj. Piipii.
Cŭr-mŭd'geon, n. Kanaka pi; paakiki,
Cŭr'ren-çy, n. 1. He dala ma ke kana-
wai.
2. Ka hoolaha ana.
Cŭr'rent, adj. 1. E hele nei. The cur-
rent year, ka makahiki e hele nei.
2. Lonoia. Current report, ka lono i
lonoia.
Cŭr'rent, n. He au. The current of
time, ke au o ka manawa.
Cŭr'rent-ly, adv. SYN. commonly.
Cŭr'ri-er, n. Kanaka hooluu ili.
Cŭr'ry, v. 1. E hooluu ili holoholona.
2. E kahi i ka hulu o ka lio.
3. Curry favor, e hoolaulea.
Cŭr'ry-comb, n. Kahi no ka lio.
Cûrse, v. E hailiili; e kuamuamu.
Cŭr'so-ry, adj. Pupuahulu.
Cŭr-tâil', v. E hoohaiki; e hoopokole.
Cŭr'tain, n. Paku' lole. Mosquito cur-
tain, paku makika.
Cûrve, n. He pio; kaha pio.
Cûrve, v. E pio; e pelu.
Cŭsh'ion (koosh-un), n. Pela noho;
pela punee.
Cŭs'tard, n. Waiu ono i hoomoaia.
Cus-to'dian, n. Kahu malama.
Cŭs'to-dy, n. 1. Ka hoopaahao ana.
To take into custody, e hoopaahao.
2. Ka malama ana. The custody of
wealth, ka malama ana i ka waiwai.
Cŭs'tom, n. 1. Ka mea maa mau.
2. Ke kuai mau ana ma kahi hookahi.
Custom made, hanaia no ke kuai akea
ana.
Cŭs'toms, n. Ka dute maluna o ka
waiwai. SYN. duties.
Cŭs'tom-â'ry, adj. Maa mau.
Cŭs'tom-er, n. O ka mea kuai. Reg-

ular customer, mea kuai mau ma kekahi hale kuai.
Cŭs'tom-hŏuse', n. Hale dute o ke aupuni.
Cŭt, v. 1. E oki. Cut with a knife, e
oki me ka pahi.
2. E okioki. To cut up in small pieces,
e okioki liilii.
3. E kua. To cut down the tree, e kua i
ka laau.
4. E moku. Cut a finger, e moku i ka
manamana lima.
5. Cut into short pieces, e pohe.
Cu-tâ'ne-oŭs, adj. Pili i ka ili. Cuta-
neous disease, mai ma ka ili.
Cŭ'ti-cle, n. Ka ili lahilahi owaho loa
o ke kino.
Cŭt'lass, n. Pahi kaua palahalaha.
Cŭt'ler, n. Kanaka hana mea oki.
Cŭt'ler-y, n. Na mea oki.
Cŭt'let, n. Apana i-o koala.
Cŭt'throat, n. He kanaka pepehi ka-
naka.
Cŭt'ting, n. He mea i okiia; he okina.
Cŭt'worm, n. He peelua.
Çy'cle, n. He wa; he au o ka manawa.
Çyl'in-der, n. He pauku poepoe.
Çyl-in'dri-cal, adj. Poepoe loihi.
Çym'bal, n. Pa keleawe; hookani ku-
meba'la.
Çyn'ie, n. Kanaka opukopekope; ka-
naka opu ino.
Çyn'ic-al, adj. Opu ino; naaukeemoa.
Çy'press, n. Laau kupero.
Çzär (zär), n. He inoa no ka Emepera
o Rusia.
Çzä-ri'nä (zar-ē'na), n. He inoa no
ka Emepera wahine o Rusia.
Çzär'o-witz (zar-ō-wits), n. He inoa
no ka hooilina Moi o Rusia.

D

Dâft, adj. Pupule; ulala. SYN. insane.
Dag'ger, n. Pahi oi lua.
Da-guërre'o-type, n. He kii i paiia i
ka la ma ke pa keleawe i hoomakaukauia me ka wai dala.
Dâi'ly, adj. Kela me keia la. A daily
newspaper, he nupepa puka la.
Dâin'ti-ly, adv. Me he ono ole la.
Dâin'ty, adj. 1. Ono. A dainty dish,
he ai ono.
2. Aulii; maikai. A dainty dress, he
kapa komo aulii.
3. Ono ole. A dainty child, he keiki
ono ole i ka ai.

Dâi'ry, n. Hale waiho waiu; hana wa-
iu bata, etc.
Dâi'ry-mâid, n. Wahine malama hale
waiu.
Dâle, n. He kahawai uuku.
Dâl'li-ançe, n. Ka hoonanea ana; hoo-
milimili ana.
Dâl'ly, v. E hoonanea; e hoohala ma-
nawa.
Dâm, n. 1. He kumulau.
2. He palewai; paku wai.
Dăm'age, n. Poho; poino. SYN. injury.
Repair damages, e kapili hou i ka mea
poino. Pay damages, uku i ka poho'.

Dăm'aġe, *v.* E hoopoino; e hoopoho'. SYN. injure.

Dăme, *n.* He wahine i mare i ke kane.

Dămn, *v.* 1. E hoahewa; e hoopai mau loa.

Dăm'na-ble, *adj.* Oki loa. SYN. odious.

Dam-nă'tion, *n.* Hoopai mau loa.

Dămp, *adj.* Ma-u' iki; koekoe; kawau; kawakawau. SYN. moist.

Dămp'er, *n.* Pani ea no ke kapuahi hao.

Dămp'ness, *n.* Kawau. SYN. moisture; humidity.

Dăm'sel, *n.* Kaikamahine opio.

Dănçe, *v.* E hula; e haa.

Dănç'er, *v.* Mea hulahula; mea haa.

Dăn'dle, *v.* E hoomilimili.

Dăn'druff, *n.* Kepia.

Dăn'dy, *n.* Kanaka hookahakaha; kanaka hoopulelehua.

Dăn'di-fied, *adj.* Hookahakahaia.

Dăn'ġer, *n.* Pilikia.

Dăn'ġer-oŭs, *adj.* Pilikia; poino. *dangerous place,* he wahi poino.

Dăn'ġle, *v.* E lewa wale.

Dăp'per, *adj.* Uuku, mikioi nae. *A dapper man,* he kanaka uuku, mikioi.

Dăp'ple, *adj.* Kikokiko. SYN. spotted.

Dâre, *v.* E aa; e kuoo.

Dâr'ing, *adj.* Kuoo; aa; maka'u ole. SYN. fearless; brave.

Dărk, *adj.* Poeleele; pouli.

Dărk'en, *v.* 1. E hoopouli; e hoopoeleele. *To darken the room,* e hoopoeleele i ke keena.
2. E poeleele mai; e pouliuli mai.

Dărk'ly, *adv.* Me ka powehiwehi.

Dărk-ness, *n.* Ka poeleele; ka pouli.

Dăr'ling, *adj.* Hiwahiwa; makamae.

Dărn, *v.* E po'ho. *Darn stockings,* e po'ho kakini.

Dărt, *n.* He ihe.

Dărt, *v.* 1. E anapu. *The lightning darts,* ke anapu nei ka uila.
2. E lele mama.

Dăsh, *v.* 1. E paki'. *Dash to the ground,* e paki i ka lepo.
2. E poi; popoi. *Waves dash on the shore,* popoi na nalu ma kahakai.
3. E holo ino. *Dash madly on,* holo ino aku.
4. E kakau hikiwawe. *Dash off a sermon,* e kakau hikiwawe i ka halao.
5. *Dash to pieces,* e wawahi liilii.

Dăsh, *n.* 1. Kaha maha.
2. He kui ana o na kino elua. SYN. crash.
3. He lele hikiwawe; holo hikiwawe. SYN. onset. *To cut a dash,* e hookahakaha.

Dăsh'board, *n.* Ka papa pali omua o ke kaa lio.

Dăsh'er, *n.* Laau kui. *A butter dasher,* laau kui waiu bata.

Dăs'tard, *n.* He maka'u wale; he mea holowale; mea haahaa loa. SYN. poltroon.

Dā'ta, *n. pl.* Na loina i ae like ia.

Dāte, 1. Ka manawa. SYN. time. *The date of the coronation,* ka manawa o ka poni alii ana.
2. He hua lou'lu.

Daub, *v.* E hapala; hoohapala. SYN. smear.

Daub'er, *n.* Ka mea hapala.

Daugh'ter (daw-ter), *n.* Kaikamahine.

Daugh'ter-in-law, *n.* Hunonawahine.

Daunt, *v.* E hoomaka'u; hoopuiwa; hoomake i ka manaolana. SYN. dishearten; dismay.

Daunt'less, *adj.* Kuoo; wiwo ole. SYN. bold; fearless.

Dā'vit, *n.* Manamana hao ma ka aoao o ka moku, mea huki waapa.

Daw'dle, *v.* E hoopau wale i ka manawa; e hoomaunauna manawa.

Dawn, *n.* Ke alaula; ka moku ana o ka pawa. SYN. daybreak.

Dāy, *n.* La.

Dāy'book, *n.* Buke kakau mooaie o ka la.

Dāy'break, *n.* SYN. dayspring; dawn.

Dāy'light, *n.* He ao; malamalama o ka la.

Dāy'star, *n.* Hoku ao. SYN. morning star.

Dăz'zle, *v.* E ohewahewa ka maka i ka malamalama; e olinolino.

Dăz'zling, *adj.* Olehaleha ; wa'kawa'ka; hulili; anapanapa.

Dêa'con, *n.* Puuku ekalesia; diakono.

Dĕad, *adj.* Make loa. *The dead,* ka poe make.

Dĕad'en, *v.* E hoomake; e hoopau. *To deaden pain,* e hoopau i ka eha.

Dĕad'ly, *adj.* 1. Make. *Deadly poison,* laau make.
2. Imi ola. *Deadly enemy,* enemi imi ola.

Dĕaf, *adj.* Kuli; lohe ole.

Dĕaf'en, *v.* E hookuli; kulikuli.

Dĕaf'mûte, *n.* Kanaka a'a', a kuli nohoi.

Dĕaf'ness, *n.* Ke kuli o ka pepeiao.

Dĕal, *n.* He haawina; he mahele.

Dĕal, *v.* 1. E kalepa; e kuai.
2. E hana. *Deal kindly with all,* e hana aloha aku i na mea a pau.

Dĕal'er, *n.* Kanaka kalepa.

Dĕar, *adj.* 1. Hiwahiwa; punahele; makamae.
2. Pii o ke kumukuai.

Dĕar'ly, *adv.* 1. Me ke aloha nui.
2. Me ka nui o ka lilo.

Dĕarth (durth), *n.* Ka wi; ka nele. SYN. scarcity.

Dĕath, *n.* Ka make.

Dĕath'bed, *n.* Ka moe o ka make.

Dĕath'less, *adj.* Make ole; ola mau loa.

Dĕath'war'rant, *n.* Palapala kauoha hoomake.

De-bär', *v.* E pale; e keakea.

De-bāse', v. 1. E hoohaahaa. *To debase one's self*, e hoohaahaa kekahi iaia iho.
2. E hooemi i ka waiwai. *Debase the currency*, e hooemi i ka waiwai o ke dala.

De-bāte', v. E hoopaapaa; e paio.

De-bāt'er, n. Mea hoopaapaa; mea paio olelo.

De-bauch', n. He uhauha; he inu a ona.

De-bauch', v. E hoohaumia; e hoohaukae.

Dēb'au-chee', n. Kanaka ona; kanaka haumia. SYN. drunkard; libertine.

De-bauch'er-y, n; Ka ona; ka haumia; ka uhauha.

De-bil'i-tāte, v. E hoonawaliwali. SYN. enfeeble.

De-bil'i-ty, n. Nawaliwali.

Dēb'it, n. Ka aoao aie. *To debit*, e kakau ma ka aoao aie.

De-brīs' (dā-bree'), n. Lepo opala; opala.

Dēbt (det), n. Aie.

Dēbt'or, n. Kanaka aie.

De-but' (dā-bu'), n. Ka makamua o ka hooikeike ana ma ke keaka, a mamua o ka lehulehu paha.

Dēc'ade, n. He anahulu.

De-cā'dence, n. 1. Ka emi ana. *The decadence of nations*, ka emi ana o na lahui.
2. Ka helelei ana; ka popo ana.

Dēc'a-gon, n. Kii huina umi.

Dēc'a-lōgue, n. Na kanawai he umi o Ke Akua.

De-cămp', v. 1. E haalele i kahi hoomoana.
2. E mahuka. SYN. abscond.

De-cănt', v. E ninini akahele.

De-cān'ter, n. He omole aniani mea inu.

De-căp'i-tāte, v. E oki i ke poo.

De-căp'i-tā'tion, n. Ke oki ana i ke poo.

De-cāy', n. 1. Ka emi ana; ka nawaliwali ana.
2. Ka popo.

De-cāy', v. E popo.

Dē-çeased, *adj.* Make.

De-çeit', n. Epa; hana hoopunipuni, SYN. fraud.

De-çeit'ful, *adj.* Epa; hoopunipuni. SYN. fraudulent.

De-çei've'er, n. Mea hoopunipuni.

De-çem'ber, n. Dekemaba.

Dē'çen-cy, n. Ka mea kupono. SYN. propriety.

Dē'çent, *adj.* Kupono; kohupono; akahai. SYN. fit; proper; becoming.

Dē'çent-ly, *adv.* Me ke kupono. SYN. properly; becomingly.

De-çep'tion, n. SYN. deceit.

De-çept'ĭve, *adj.* 1. SYN. deceitful.
2. Maopopo ole. *A deceptive appearance*, he nanaina maopopo ole.

De-çīde', v. E hooholo manao; e manao paa.

De-çīd'ed, *adj.* 1. Kupaa. *A decided man*, he kanaka kupaa.
2. Hooholoia. *It is decided*, hooholoia. *A decided question*, he ninau i hooholoia.

De-çīd'ed-ly, *adv.* 1. I'o. *Decidedly so*, pela io.
2. Me ka manao paa. *To talk decidedly*, e kamailio me ka manao paa.

Dē'çi-mal, *adj.* Dekimala; pa-umi. *Decimal fraction*, hakina pa-umi.

De-çi'pher, v. E wehewehe i na huaolelo i kakau ia ma ke ano huna'.

De-çi'sion, n. 1. Ke kupaa o ka manao. SYN. firmness.
2. Ka olelo hooholo. SYN. judgement.

De-çis'ĭve, *adj.* Lanakila.

Dēck, v. E kahiko a nani. SYN. adorn.

Dēck, n. Oneki; papa hele o ka moku.

De-clāim', v. E haiolelo.

Dēc'la-mā'tion, n. He haiolelo i hoopaanaau ia.

Dēc'la-rā'tion, n. He hoolaha. SYN. announcement.

De-clāre', v. E hoolaha; e hai. SYN. affirm; announce.

De-clēn'sion, n. 1. Ka hoole ana. SYN. refusal.
2. Ka emi ana. SYN. decrease.

De-clīne', v. E hoole. SYN. refuse.
2. E aui. *The sun is declining*, ke aui nei ka la.
3. E emi; e nawaliwali.

De-clīne', n. Ka emi ana; ka nawaliwali ana. *Decline of strength*, ka emi ana o ka ikaika. *He is on a decline*, ke nawaliwali mai nei oia.

De-clīv'i-ty, n. He kualapa; lapa; he iho'a.

De-cŏc'tion, n. He wai miko ma ka baila ana i kekahi mea.

De'com-pōse', v. E popopo; e palaho.

De-cŏm'po-şi'tion, n. Ka popopo; ka palaho.

Dēc'o-rāte, n. E kahiko a nani. SYN. deck; adorn.

Dēc'o-rā'tion, n. 1. Ke kahiko ana a maikai. SYN. ornamentation.
2. He hoailona o ke kulana hanohano.

Dēc'o-roŭs, *adj.* Kupono; akahai. SYN. becoming; befitting; seemly.

De-cō'rum, n. Ka noho pono ana. SYN. dignity.

De-cŏy', v. E hoohalua; e hoopunihei.

De-cŏy', n. He halua; he pahele.

De-erēase', n. Ka emi ana.

De-erēe', n. Kauoha; kanawai. SYN. edict.

De-erĕp'it, *adj.* Kolopupu; palalauhala.

De-erȳ', v. E hoohalahala. SYN. disparage; depreciate.

Dĕd'i-eāte, *v.* E hoolaa.
Ded-i-eā'tion, *n.* Ka hoolaa ana.
Dĕd'i-eā-to-ry, *adj.* Hoolaa. *Dedicatory services,* na hana hoolaa.
De-dŭçe', *v.* E hoomaopopo mamuli o ka noonoo. SYN. infer.
De-dŭet', *v.* E hoolawe; hookoe; *Deduct from the amount,* e hoolawe mai ka huina. SYN. subtract.
De-dŭe'tion, *n.* 1. Ka hookoe ana.
2. Ka mea i maopopo. *A deduction from reasoning,* he mea i maopopo ma ka noonoo ana.
Deed, *n.* 1. Ka mea i hanaia. SYN. act.
2. Palapala hooliilo waiwai.
Deem, *v.* E manao. SYN. think.
Deep, *adj.* 1. Hohonu; lipolipo. *The deep sea,* kai hohonu. *The deep blue sea,* ke kai lipolipo.
2. Poopoo. *A deep hole,* lua poopoo.
Deep'en, *v.* E eli a hohonu ae.
Deer, *n.* He dia.
De-fāçe', *v.* E hana ino; e hana kolohe. SYN. mar. *To deface a book,* e kolohe i ka buke.
Dĕf'a-mā'tion, *n.* Alapahi; paokee. SYN. slander; calumny.
De-fāme', *v.* E alapahi; e akiaki. SYN. slander; calumniate.
De-fault', *v.* 1. Ke ko ole; ka haule wale ana.
2. Ka hiki kino ole ana imua o ka aha hookolokolo.
De-fault'er, *n.* Kanaka apuka dala.
De-fēat', *v.* E hoopio; hooauhuli; hooauhee. SYN. rout; discomfit.
De-fēet', *n.* He kina'.
De-fēet'ive, *adj.* 1. Kina; hemahema. *Defective work,* hana hemahema.
2. Popo; popopo. *A defective tooth,* he niho popo.
De-fēnd', *v.* E pale i ka ino; e hoomalu. SYN. protect.
De-fēnd'ant, *n.* Ka mea ma ka aoao pale ma ka hookolokolo.
De-fēnd'er, *n.* Ka mea e pale ana i ka ino.
De-fēnse', *n.* 1. He pale; he pakaua.
2. Olelo pale. *Make his defense,* e hai i kana olelo pale.
De-fēnse'less, *adj.* 1. Waiho wale me ka hoomalu ole ia.
2. Lako ole ke koa kaua.
Dé-fēr', *v.* 1. E hoopanee. SYN. postpone.
2. E maliu; e haliu i ka pepelao. *To defer to one,* e maliu aku i kekahi.
Dĕf'er-ençe, *n.* 1. Ka maliu ana. SYN respect.
2. Ka haawi ana i ka mahalo.
De-fi'ançe, *n.* Ke ku-e' akena; ka aa ana.
Dĕ-fi'çien-çy, *n.* Ka nele. *Make good the deficiency,* e hoolako mai i ka nele. SYN. want.
De-fi'çient, *adj.* Nele; lako pono ole. *Deficient in sense,* nele i ka noonoo. SYN. wanting.

Dĕf'i-çit, *n.* Nele. *A deficit in the treasury,* he nele ma ka waihona dala.
De-file', *v.* 1. E hoohaumia; hoohaukae. SYN. corrupt; pollute.
2. E hele lalani aku.
De-file', *n.* 1. He alanui haiki; kahi e hele pakahi ai ka poe hele.
De-fil'er, *n.* Kanaka hoohaumia. SYN. corrupter; polluter.
De-file'ment, *n.* Ka hoohaumia ana. SYN. pollution. Ka mea haumia.
De-fine', *v.* 1. E hoomaopopo. *Define boundaries,* e hoomaopopo i na palena.
2. E wehewehe. *Define a word,* e wehewehe i ka hua olelo.
Dĕf'i-nite, *adj.* Maopopo. SYN exact.
Def'i-nite-ly, *adv.* Maopopo. *Tell me definitely,* e hai maopopo mai ia'u.
Def-i-ni'tion, *n.* Ka wehewehe ana o ka hua olelo.
De-flēet', *v.* E aui ae mai ka pololei.
De-flēe'tion, *n.* Ka aui ana mai ka pololei.
De-fôrmed', *adj.* Hapakue. SYN. crippled.
De-frạud', *v.* E apuka. SYN. cheat.
De-frạud'er, *n.* Kanaka apuka. SYN. defaulter.
De-frāy', *v.* E hookaa. *Defray expenses,* e hookaa i na lilo.
De-fŭnet', *adj.* Make loa. SYN. dead.
De-fȳ', *v.* E aa aku.
De-gĕn'er-a-çy, *n.* Ka hoi ana ihope.
De-gĕn'er-ate, *adj.* Hoi hope. *A degenerate race,* he lahui hoi hope.
Dĕg'ra-dā'tion, *n.* Ka hoohaahaa ana.
De-grāde', *v.* E. hoohaahaa i ke kulana.
De-grād'ed, *adj.* Haahaa loa.
De-grēe', *n.* 1. Ke kulana hanohano i haawiia mai ke kula nui.
Dē'i-fȳ, *v.* E hoo-Akua.
Deign (dāne), *v.* E maliu; e ae.
Dē'i-ty, *n.* Akua. *The Deity,* Ke Akua.
De-jeet'ed, *adj.* 1. Poho' ka manao; pau ke aho; pilihua. SYN. discouraged; cast down.
2. Paumako. SYN. down-hearted; blue.
De-jēe'tion, *n.* Poho' o ka manao; paumako. SYN. sadness; melancholy.
De-lāy', *v.* E hoohakalia. SYN. procrastinate.
De-lāy', *n.* Hakalia; lolohe.
De-lēe'ta-ble, *adj.* Onoono; mikomiko. SYN. delicious.
Dĕl'e-gāte, *v.* E hooili ia hai. *To delegate authority,* e hooiiia hai ka mana.
Dĕl'e-gate, *n.* 1. Ka mea i wae ia; ka me i haawiia ka mana.
2. Lunamakaainana.
Dĕl'e-gā'tion, *n.* Ka poe i kohoia. *The Hilo delegation,* ka poe i kohoia no Hilo. SYN. deputation.
Dĕl'e-tē'ri-oŭs, *adj.* Hoopoino. *Bad air is deleterious to the health,* hoopoino ke ea ino i ke ola.

De-lĭb′er-āte, *v.* E noonoo pono; e poonoo. SYN. consider.

De-lĭb′er-ate-ly, *adv.* Akahele; me ka noonoo.

De-lĭb′er-ā′tion, *n.* 1. Noonoo akahele.

Dĕl′i-eate, *adj.* Palupalu.

De-lĭ′çioŭs, *adj.* Ono loa; mikomiko.

De-light′, *n.* Ka hauoli; ka olioli ka lea.

De-light′ful, *adj.* Hauoli piha; lea maoli.

De-lĭn′e-āte, *v.* 1. E kahakaha. SYN. portray.
2. E hoike lea. *To portray before you,* e hoike lea imua ou.

De-lĭn′e-ā′tion, *n.* 1. Ke kahakaha ana.
2. Ka hoike lea ana.

De-lĭn′e-a-tor, *n.* Mea nana e kahakaha.

De-lĭn′quen-çy, *n.* Ka nele i ka hooko.

De-lĭn′quent, *n.* Mea e ko ole ana i kona mau pono.

De-lĭr′i-oŭs, *adj.* Auwana o ka noonoo; pupule.

De-lĭr-i-um, *n.* Ka auwana hewa o ka noonoo.

De-lĭr′um trē′menş, *n.* Ka mai pupule no ka ona.

De-lĭv′er, *v.* 1. E hoopakele. SYN. save.
2. E haawi iloko o ka lima. *To deliver up to the law,* e haawi iloko o ka lima o ke kanawai.
3. E haawi. *To deliver a speech,* e haawi i haiolelo.

De-lĭv′er-ance, *n.* Ka hoopakele ana. SYN. freedom.

De-lĭv′er-er, *n.* Mea nana e hoopakele.

De-lĭv′er-y, *n.* 1. Ka hoopakele ana.
2. Ka haawi ana. *Delivery of letters,* ka haawi ana i na palapala.

Dĕll, *n.* Kahawai uuku. SYN. dale.

Dĕl′ta, *n.* Aina mawaena o na nuku o ka muliwai.

De-lūde′, *v.* E alakai hewa; e hoopuniwale. SYN. mislead.

Dĕl′uġe, *n.* He wai nui. *The Deluge,* ke Kai-a-kahinalii.

Dĕl′uġe, *v.* 1. E kahe nui.
2. E paapu loa mai. *Deluged with work,* paapu loa mai ka hana.

De-lū′şion, *n.* He mea alakai hewa i ka noonoo; manao kuhi hewa.

De-lū′sive, *adj.* Alakai hewa.

Dĕlve, *v.* E eli me ka oo; me ke kopala.

De-mänd′, *v.* E kaohi; e koi; e kauoha.

Dē′mär-kā′tion, *n.* *Line of demarkation,* palena.

De-mean′or, *n.* Ke ano o ka noho ana. SYN. deportment; behavior.

De-mĕnt-ed, *adj.* Pupule. SYN. crazy.

Dĕm′i-john, *n.* He i-e aniani nui.

De-mŏç′ra-çy, *n.* Lahui; aupuni o ka lahui.

De-mŏl′ish, *v.* E hoohiolo; e kulai; e wawahi.

Dĕm′o-lĭ′tion, *n.* Ka hoohiolo ana; ka wawahi ana.

Dē′mon, *n.* Daimonio.

De-mŏ′ni-ac, *n.* Mea i uluhia i ka daimonio.

Dĕm′on-strāte, *v.* 1. E wehewehe; e hoomoakaka.

Dĕm′on-strā′tion, *n.* 1. Ka wehewehe ana.
2. Ka hoakaka ana. *A public demonstration,* ka hooakaka ana ma ke akea.

Dem′on-strā′tor, *n.* Ka mea nana e wehewehe.

De-mŏr′al-i-zā′tion, *n.* Ka auhuli ana o ka noho kuonoono.

De-mŏr′al-īze, *v.* 1. E hooauhuli i ke kuonoono.
2. E hoopilihua; hoopuiwa.

De-mūr′, *v.* 1. E kanalua; e haohao. SYN. hesitate.
2. E anoni; anoninoni.

De-mūre′, *adj.* Ano noho malie.

Dĕn, *n.* Lua holoholona.

De-ni′al, *n.* He hoole.

Dĕn′i-zen, *n.* He haole i hooku′paia.

De-nŏm′i-nā′tion, *n.* 1. Inoa.
2. Aoao hoomana. SYN. sect.

De-nŏm′i-nā′tor, *n.* Ka mahele o ka hakina. *Common denominator,* mahele pili like. *Least common denominator,* mahele pili like emi loa.

De-nōte′, *v.* E hoike. SYN. indicate; signify.

De-nŏunçe, *v.* E hoopii; e hoahewa.

Dĕnse, *adj.* Paa; paapu. SYN. compact.

Dĕn′si-ty, *n.* Ke ano paa o kekahi mea.

Dĕnt, *n.* He kuma.

Dĕn′tal, *adj.* Pili i ka niho.

Dĕn′ti-frĭçe, *n.* Lepo anae niho.

Dĕn′tist, *n.* Kanaka hana niho.

Dĕn′tist-ry, *n.* Ka oihana hana niho.

De-nūde′, *v.* E hoonele.

De-nȳ′, *v.* E hoole.

De-pärt′, *v.* E hele aku.

De-pärt′ment, *n.* He mahele. *A department of business,* he mahele o ka oihana. *Primary department,* ka mahele kumumua o ka kula.

De-pärt′ūre, *n.* Ka hele an′aku; ka haalele ana.

De-pĕnd′, *v.* 1. E kalele; e hilinai. SYN. rely. *Depend on yourself,* e hilinai oe ia oe iho.
2. E kali. *It depends on the truth of the statement,* ke kali nei kela no ka oiaio o ka haina.

De-pĕnd′ençe, *n.* Ka hilinai; ka paulele. SYN. reliance.

De-pĕnd′ent, *adj.* Hilinai.

De-pict′, *v.* 1. SYN. delineate; portray.
2. E hoike lea mai. *Depict a scene; portray a scene,* e hoike lea mai no kekahi nanaina.

De-plŏr′a-ble, *adj.* Oki loa. *A deplorable state of affairs,* oki loa ka hana. SYN. lamentable.

De-plõre′, v. 1. E kumakena. SYN. lament.
2. E minamina.

De-põ′nent, n. He hoike ma ke kakau ana.

De-põp′u-lāte, v. E hooneoneo ka aina i kanaka.

De-põrt′ment, n. Ke ano o ka noho ana. SYN. behavior.

De-põse′, v. 1. E hoopau; hoohemo; waiho. *Depose from office,* e hoohemo mai ka oihana.
2. E hoohiki ma ka palapala.

De-põs-it′, v. 1. E hoomoe. *Deposit money in the bank,* e hoomoe dala ma ka baneko.
2. E waiho. *Deposit money with you,* e waiho i dala me oe.

Dĕp′o-sĭ′tion, n. 1 Ka hoohemo ana mai ka oihana.
2. Ka olelo hoike i kakauia a hoohikiia. SYN. affidavit.

Dè-põs′i-to-ry, n. He waihona. *A book depository,* he waihona buke.

De-põt′ (de-põ′), n. Hale waiho ukana. *Railroad depot,* hale waiho ukana o ke alanui hao.

De-prāved, adj. Haumia loa; lilo loa i ka hewa. SYN. corrupt.

De-prăv′i-ty, n. Ka haumia; ka hohonu o ka hewa. SYN. corruption.

Dĕp′re-cāte, v. 1. E pule hoopale.
2. E minamina. SYN. regret.

De-prē′çi-āte, v. 1 E hooemi i ka waiwai.
2. E hoowaha′waha′.

Dĕp′re-dā′tion, n. 1. Ka hao ana.
2. Ke komo hewa ana. *Depredations of cattle,* ke komo hewa ana o na bipi.

De-prĕss′, v. 1. E hookaumaha i ka manao.
2. E hooemi; e hoohaahaa.

De-prĕs′sion, n. 1. Kaumaha o ka manao.
2. Wahi poopoo iki.

Dĕp′ri-vā′tion, n. 1. Ka hoonele ana.
2. Ka nele.

De-prive′, v. E hoonele.

Dĕpth, n. Hohonu; poopoo.

Dĕp-u-tā′tion, n. He poe i waeia no kekahi hana. SYN. delegation.

De-pūte′, n. E koho; e wae; e hoonoho i hope.

Dĕp′u-ty, n. He hope. *Deputy Sheriff,* Hope makai nui.

De-rānge′, v. 1. E hoohuikau.
2. E hoolilo i pupule.

De-rānged′, adj. 1. Pupule. SYN. crazy.
2. Hoohuikau.

De-rānge′ment, n. 1. Ka huikau.
2. Ka lilo ana i pupule. SYN. insanity.

Der-e-lic′tion, n. Ka haalele loa. SYN. abandonment.

De-ride′, v. E loiloi; akaaka henehene. SYN. ridicule; taunt.

De-ris′ion, n. Loiloi; henehene. SYN. ridicule.

De-ri′sĭve, adj. Henehene. *Derisive laughter,* akaaka henehene.

Dĕr′i-vā′tion, n. Ka hookumu ana. *Derivation of a word,* ka hookumu ana o ka olelo.

De-rive′, v. 1. E loaa. *Derive benefit,* e loaa i ka pomaikai.
2. Mai. SYN. from. *Hawaiian words derived from the English,* na hua olelo Hawaii mai ka olelo Beritania mai.

De-rŏg′a-to-ry, adj. Kupono ole; ku-e′.

Dĕr′rick, n. Mikini hapai mea kaumaha.

De-sçĕnd′, v. E iho.

De-sçĕnd′ant, n. He mamo.

De-sçĕnt′, n. 1. He iho′na.
2. *Of Hawaiian descent,* no ke kuauhau Hawaii.

De-scribe′, v. E hoike ano; e kuhikuhi.

De-scrip′tion, n. He hoike ano.

De-scrip′tive, adj. Kuhikuhi ano. *A descriptive catalogue,* he papa kuhikuhi ano.

De-serȳ, v. E ike ma kahi mamao aku.

Dĕs′e-crāte, v. E hoohaumia i na mea laa.

Dĕs′e-crā′tion, n. Ka hoohaumia ana i na mea laa. *Desecration of the Sabbath,* ka hoohaumia ana i ka la Sabati.

De-sĕrt′, v. E haalele wale; e mahuka. SYN. abandon; forsake.

De-sĕrt′, n. Ka hua o ka hana. *He will get his deserts,* e loaa ana iaia na hua o kana hana.

Dĕs′ĕrt n,. He waoakua; aina neoneo.

De-sert′er, n. Mea mahuka. *A deserter from the army,* he koa mahuka.

De-sĕr′tion, n. Ka mahuka ana; ka haalele wale ana.

De-sĕrve′, v. E pono ke loaa.

De-sĕrv′ing, adj. Ku pono ke loaa.

De-sĭd′e-rā′tum, n. Ka mea kupono loa.

De-sĭgn′, v. 1. E noonoo e mamua; e manao. SYN. intend.
2. E kaha i kii mea hoike apo.

De-sĭgn′, n. 1. He noonoo; he manao. SYN. intention. *Evil designs,* na noonoo ino.
2. He kii hoike ano.

Dĕs′ig-nāte, v. E kuhikuhi. SYN. point out; indicate.

Dĕs′ig-nā′tion, n. Ke kuhikuhi ana.

De-sĭgn′ed-ly, adv. Me ka noonoo e mamua.

De-sĭgn′er, n. 1. Mea noonoo a kakau i kii o ka mea i manaoia.
2. *A designer of evil,* kanaka i noonoo i ka mea kewa.

De-sĭgn′ing, adj. Maalea. *A designing man,* he kanaka maalea; he kanaka noonoo i na mea hewa.

De-sĭr′a-ble, adj. Ku i ka makemake; kupono.

De-sire′, v. 1. E makemake. SYN. wish.
2. *To desire greatly,* e ake nui; e iini.

De-sīre', *n.* Ka makemake; ke kuko.
2. *Evil desires,* na kuko ino. SYN. evil passions.
De-sīr'oŭs, *adj.* Ake nui; iini. SYN. eager.
De-sīst', *v.* U'oki; e hooki; e hoopau.
Dēsk, *n.* Pahu palapala.
Dēs'o-late, *adj.* Neoneo; mehameha.
Dēs'o-lā'tion, *n.* Ka hooneanea ana.
Dēs-pāir., *n.* Ka pio ana o ka manao lana.
Des-pātça', *v.* 1. E hooko me ka mama. See *dispatch.*
2. E hoou'na.
Dēs'per-ā'do, *n.* He kanaka hehena. SYN. madman.
Dēs'per-ate, *adj.* 1. Poho' loa. *A desperate state of affairs,* poho' loa o ka noho ana.
2. Make ka manaolana. *A desperate man,* he kanaka i make kona manao lana.
3. Aa makehewa. SYN. rash; headlong.
Dēs'per-ā'tion, *n.* Ka poho' loa ana o ka manao. *Driven to desperation,* kaohiia a poho' loa ka manao.
Dēs'pī-ca-ble, *adj.* Pupuka; haahaa loa. SYN. contemptible.
De-spīse', *v.* E hoowaha'waha'; e hoopailua ma ka naau. SYN. disdain.
Dēs-poil', *v.* E hao wale; e pakaha wale; e powa'. SYN. rob.
Dĕ-spŏnd', *v.* E pau ke aho; e make ka manao
De-spŏnd'en-çy, *n.* Ka make o ka manao.
De-spŏnd'ent, *adj.* Manao poho'.
Dēs'pot, *n.* Mea e ko ana me ke kanawai ole; alii lokoino. SYN. tyrant.
Dēs'pot-ism, *n.* Ka mana o ka lima ikaika.
Des-sērt', *n.* Na mea ono i kau hope ia ma ka papa aina, no ka aina awakea.
Dēs'ti-nā'tion, *n.* Wahi e hele ai.
Dēs'ti-nӯ, *n.* Ka hopena. *Mankind have a common destiny,* he hopena like ko kanaka.
Dēs'tine, *v.* 1. E wae; e koho.
2. E hookaawale. *Destined to learn a trade,* hookaawaleia e ao i kekahi oihana.
Dēs'ti-tūte, *adj.* Nele; hune.
Dēs'ti-tū'tion, *n.* Ka nele; ka hune.
De-stroy', *v. t.* E luku; e hoopoino.
De-stroy'er, *n.* Ka mea nana e luku.
De-strŭc'tion, *n.* He make; he poino; he luku.
Dēs'ul-to-ry, *adj.* Kumu ole; lele wale. *A desultory remark,* he olelo kumu ole. *Desultory reading,* heluhelu lele wale i o ianei.
De tăch', *n.* E hookaawale ae; e wehe ia. SYN. separate.
De-tăch'ment, *n.* 1. He mahele. *A detachment of soldiers,* he mahele o ka puali koa.
2. Ka hookaawale ana.

De-tāil', *v.* 1. E kuhikuhi; e koho. *To detail boys to sweep,* e koho i mau keiki e pulumi.
2. E hai liilii mai.
Dē'tails, *n. pl.* Na mea liilii. *To give the details,* e hai mai i na mea liilii.
De-tāin, *v.* E aua; e keakea; e kaohi. *My father detained me,* aua kuu makuakane ia'u.
De-tĕct, *v.* 1. E hoomohala i ka hewa.
2. E hoomohala i ka mea i huna'ia.
De-tēc'tion, *n.* Ka hoomaka'kiu ana.
De-tĕct'ĭve, *n.* He makai hoomaka'kiu.
De-ten'tion, *n.* Ka aua ana; ka hoopaa ana; ke kaohi ana.
De-tĕr', *v.* E kaohi; e keakea. *Deterred from coming,* keakea ia ka hele ana mai. SYN. hinder.
De-tē'ri-o-rāte, *v.* E emi. *To deteriorate in value,* e emi ma ka waiwai. SYN. depreciate.
De-tĕr'mi-nā'tion, *n.* 1. Ka manao paa.
2. Ka hooholo ana. SYN. establishment. *Establishment of boundaries,* ka hooholo ana i na palena aina.
De-tĕr'mine, *v.* 1. E manao paa. SYN. resolve; decide.
De-tĕr'mined, *adj.* Onipaa; wiwo ole. *A determined stand for the truth,* ku onipaa no ka oiaio.
De-tĕst, *v.* E hoopailua ma ka naau. SYN. abhor.
De-tĕst'a-ble, *adj.* Hoopailuaia. SYN. abominable.
Dĕ'tĕs-tā'tion, *n.* Ka hoopailua ma ka naau. SYN. abhorrence.
De-thrōne', *v.* E kipaku mai ka noho alii.
De-trăct', *v.* 1. E hooemi. *Detract from the value of a thing,* e hooemi i ka waiwai o kekahi mea.
2. E hoohaahaa. *Detract from the character,* e hoohaahaa i ke kulana.
De-trăc'tion, *n.* Alapahi; paokee.
Dĕt'ri-ment, *n.* He kumu poho; kumu keakea. *A detriment to progress,* he kumu keakea no ka holo mua.
Dĕt'ri-mĕnt'al, *adj.* Keakea.
Dĕv'as-tāte, *v.* E hoonea; hooneoneo
Dĕv'as-tā'tion, *n.* Ka hoonea ana; ka luku ana.
De-vĕl'op, *v.* E homohaia. *To develop the intellect,* e hoomohala i ka noonoo.
De-vĕl'op-ment, *n.* Ka hoomohala ana.
Dē'vi-āte, *v.* E aui ae; e huli ae.
Dē'vi-ā'tion, *n.* Ka aui ana; ka huli ana.
De-vīçe', *n.* He mea i noonooia. SYN. contrivance.
Dĕv'il, *n.* He diabolo.
Dĕv'il-ish, *adj.* Ano lokoino loa; ano diabolo. SYN. diabolical; fiendish.
Dē'vi-oŭs, *adj.* Pakaawili; kuawili; keekee. SYN. crooked.
De-vīse, *v.* 1. E hana mamuli o ka noonoo.
2. E hooilina waiwai.

Dĕv-is-ee′, *n.* Ka hooilina. SYN. legatee.

De-vis′or, *n.* Ka mea nana e hooilina waiwai.

De-võid′, *adj.* Nele. *Devoid of reason*, nele i ka noonoo.

De-võlve′, *v.* 1. E ili. *It devolves on me*, ke ili nei ia mea maluna o′u. 2. E hooili.

De-võte′, *v.* E hoolilo. *To devote time*, e hoolilo i manawa. *To devote one's self to study*, e hoolilo kekahi iaia iho i ka imi naauao.

De-võt′ed, *adj.* Pili aloha.

De-võ′tion, *n.* 1. Ka hoolaa ana; hoolilo loa ana. SYN. consecration. 2. He aloha nui. SYN. affection. 3. Ka pili aloha ana aku.

De-vour, *v.* 1. E hoonuu. *Devour food*, e hoonuu ai. 2. E luku. *To devour the land*, e luku i ka aina. SYN. devastate.

De-vout, *adj.* Haipule; pono; akahai; SYN. pious; reverent.

Dew, *n.* Hau; kehau.

Dĕx-tĕr′i-ty, *n.* Ke akamai o ka lima. SYN. skill.

Dĕx′ter-oŭs, *adj.* Akamai; noeau ma na hana o ka lima. SYN. skilful; expert.

Di′a-bŏl′ie-al, *ndj.* SYN. devilish.

Di′a-dem, *n.* Lei alii; kaei poo.

Di-aër′e-sis, *n.* He hoailona (··) i kau ia i mea e hookaawale i na leo o kekahi mau hua palapala.

Di′ag-nō′sis, *n.* Ka imi ana no ke ano o ka mai.

Di-āg′o-nal, *n.* Ke kaha hi-o′.

Di-āg′o-nal-ly, *adv.* Lepe; panaiiki.

Di′a-gram, *n.* He kii matematika.

Di′al, *n.* Pa kuhikuhi ho . *Sun dial*, he pa kuhikuhi hora no ka la.

Di′a-lect, *n.* Ke ano o ka olelo ma kau wahi o ka aina, i ano e mai ke kau wahi aku.

Di′a-logue, *n.* He olelo kike′.

Di-ăm′e-ter, *n.* Ana waena.

Dia-mond, *n.* He daimana; he momi.

Di′ăp-er, *n.* He pale no ke keiki.

Di′a-phrăgm (frăm), *n.* 1. He pale mawaena o ka opu. 2. He pale puka iloko o ka ohe na′na′.

Di′ar-rhē′a, *n.* He hi.

Di′a-ry, *n.* Buke kakau la.

Die′tăte, *v.* 1. E hai waha a na hai e kakau. 2. E kauoha; e kaohi. SYN. command. 3. *The dictates of reason*, na kauoha o ka noonoo.

Dic-tā′tion, *n.* 1. Ka hai ana o ka waha. 2. He kauoha.

Dic-tā′tor, *n.* He poo aupuni nana ka mana a pau loa.

Dic-tā′tor-ship, *n.* Ka oihana o ka dictator.

Dic′tion-a′ry, *n.* Buke unuhi huaolelo.

Die, *v.* E make.

Di′et, *n.* Ka ai o ke kanaka. *To diet*, e pakiko ai.

Dif′fer, *v.* 1. E like ole kela me keia. 2. E okoa. *His thought differs from mine*, he okoa kona manao i ko′u.

Dif′fer-ence, *n.* Like ole.

Dif′fer-ent, *adj.* 1. Okoa; ano e. 2. Kela ano keia ano. SYN. various.

Dif′fer-ent-ly, *adv.* Ma ke ano e.

Dif′fi-cult, *adj.* 1. Oolea; paakiki. *A difficult question*, he ninau paakiki. 2. Pilikia. *A difficult place*, he wahi pilikia.

Dif′fi-cŭl-ty, *n.* Pilikia...

Dif′fi-dence, *n.* Ke kanalua o kekahi nona iho; ka hopohopo.

Dif′-fi-dent, *adj.* Hopohopo. SYN. bashful.

Dif′fuse, *v.* E hoolaha; e hohola. SYN. disseminate. *Spread abroad; to diffuse knowledge*, e hohola i ka ike.

Dif-fu′sion, *n.* Ka hoolaha ana; ka hohola ana. SYN. dissemination.

Dig, *v.* E eli; e kohi.

Di-gĕst′, *v.* 1. E hoowali i ka ai iloko o ka opu. 2. E noonoo pono ma ka naau. *To digest a thought*, e noo pono i ka manao; e poonoo.

Di′gest, *n.* ·He huina ɔui o na mea i noonooia. SYN. compendium; summary. *A digest of the laws*, he buke huina nui o na kanawai.

Di-gĕst′i-ble, *adj.* Hiki ke hoowalina.

Di-gĕs′tion, *n.* Ka hoowali ana o ka ai iloko a ka opu.

Dig′it, *n.* 1. He ana; ekolu hapaha o ka iniha. 2. kekahi o na hua helu. 3. He hapa-12 o ka ana waena o ka La, a o ka mahina.

Dig′ni-fied, *adj.* ɔohano; hiehie; ihiihi.

Dig′ni-fȳ *v.* E hoohanohano; e hoohiehie.

Dig′ni-tā′ry, *n.* He kanaka ma ke kulana kiekie; kulana hanohano.

Dig′ni-ty, *n.* He hanohano; hiehie.

Di′graph (di′graf), *n.* Elua huapalapala me hookahi nae leo; e laa, *ea* ma *head*.

Di-gress′, *v.* E auwana; e aui ae. SYN. deviate; wander from. *To digress from the subject*, e auwana aku mai ke kumu manao.

Di-grĕs′sion′ *n.* Ka aui ana; ka huli ana mai ka pololei. SYN. deviation.

Dike, *n.* 1. He auwaha. SYN. ditch. 2. He ahua lepo; paku lepo.

Di-lăp′i-dāt′ed, *adj.* Helelei. SYN. tumble down. *A dilapidated house*, he hale helelei.

Di-lăp′i-dā′tion, *n.* Ka helelei ana o ka mea i kukuluia.

Di-lāte′, *v.* 1. E hoomahuahua olelo. 2. E kaakaa i ka maka.

Dil′ā-to-ry, *adj.* Lolohi; loiele; hakalia.

Di-lĕm′ma, *n.* Na pilikia elua. *To be in a dilemma*, e ku mawaena o na pilikia elua.

Dil′i-ġenᶜe, *n.* 1. Ka makaala; ka hooikaika.

2. Kaa lawe ohua ma Farani.

Dil′i-ġent, *adj.* Hooikaika; makaala.

Dil′i-ġent-ly, *adv.* Me ka hooikaika.

Di-lūte′, *v.* 1. E kakale′; e kaawili a lahilahi. SYN. to thin.

2. E kaawili me ka wai, i emi ka ikaika.

Di-lūt′ed, *adj.* Kakale′. *Thin poi*, poi kakale′.

2. Kaawiliia i emi ka ikaika.

Dim, *adj.* Powehiwehi; molehulehu.

Dim, *v.* E hoopowehiwehi.

Dime, *n.* He dime; he kenikeni.

Di-mĕn′sionᵴ, *n. pl.* Ke ana owaho o kekahi kino. SYN. size.

Di-min′ish, *v.* E hooemi; e kanahae. SYN. decrease; lessen.

Dim′i-nu′tion, *n.* Ka emi ana. SYN. decrease.

Di-min′u-tive, *adj.* Poupou; a′a′; liilii.

Dim′ly, *adv.* Powehiwehi; akaka ole.

Dim′ple, *n.* Mino.

Din, *n.*He nakeke: nakulukulu; kamumu. SYN. clangor.

Dine, *v.* 1. E ai i ka aina awakea.

2. E haawi i ka aina awakea.

Din′ġy, *adj.* Paele; ekaeka.

Din′ner, *n.* Aina awakea; ka aina nui o ka la.

Di′o-ġese, *n.* Ke kihapai o ka bihopa.

Dip, *v.* 1. E kioe. *Dip up water*, e kioe wai.

2. E hoo-u′. *Dip into water*, e hoo-u′ iloko o ka wai.

3. E hoo-o′. *To place in water*, e hoo-o′ iloko o ka wai.

4. E komo. *To dip the oar into the water*, e komo ka hoe iloko o ka wai.

5. *To dip the colors*, e huki ilalo a iluna i ka hae, ma ke ano e hoohanohano.

Diph-the′ri-á, *n.* He mai weliweli o ka puu.

Diph′thong, *n.* Leo hui o na leo kumu elua.

Di-plō′ma, *n.* 1. Palapala hoohanohano.

2. Palapala apono, mai ke kula nui mai.

Di-plō′ma-ᶜy, *n.* Ke kuka′ ana mawaena o na aupuni; oihana kuka′ aupuni.

Dip′lo-măt′ie, *adj.* No ke kuka′ ana o na aupuni.

Di-plō′ma-tist, *n.* Kanaka akamai ma ka oihana kuka′ me na aupuni.

Dip′per, *n.* Ka apu kioe.

Dire, *adj.* Weliweli. SYN. dreadful.

Di-rĕct′, *adj.* Moe pololei. *The direct road*, ke alanui moe pololei.

Di-rĕct, *v.* E kuhikuhi; e hoopololei.

Di-rĕc′tion, *n.* 1. Ka moe ana. *An eastern direction*, e moe ana i ka hikina.

2. Ka hooponopono ana. *To take the direction of affairs*, e hapai i ka hooponopono ana o na hana.

3. Loina; kuhikuhi ana. *According to directions*, e like me ke kuhikuhi ana.

Di-rĕct′ly, *adv.* A no′ SYN. immediately. *To go directly*, e hele a no′.

Di-rĕct′or, *n.* Luna hooponopono.

Di-rĕc′to-ry, *n.* 1. Buke kuhikuhi i kela me keia mea.

2. He poe luna hooponopono.

Dirġe, *n.* Kanikau.

Dirk, *n.* He pahi hou aku.

Dirt, *n.* Lepo.

Dirt′y, *n.* Lepo; paele; paumaele.

Dis′a-bĭl′i-ty, *n.* Ka hiki ole.

Dis-ā′ble, *v.* E hoonele i ka hiki.

Dis′a-bûġe′, *v.* E hoopololei i ke kuhihewa.

Dis′ad-vän′taġe, *n.* 1. Mea pomaikai ole.

2. *To take at a disadvantage*, e loaa iloko o ka pilikia.

Dis′af-fĕct′ed, *adj.* Ohumu wale; ano kipi.

Dis′a-gree′, *v.* 1. Kulike ole ka manao.

2. Kupono ole. *The food disagrees with him*, kupono ole ka ai iaia.

Dis′a-gree′a-ble, *adj.* Kohu ole; oluolu ole. *Disagreeable day*, he la oluolu ole.

2. Malailena. SYN. unpalatable.

Dis′a-gree′ment, *n.* 1. Ka lokahi ole; ka mokuahana.

2. Ke kupono ole.

Dis′al-low′, *v.* E. ae ole; e hoole.

Dis′ap-pĕar′, *v.* E nalo aku.

Dis′ap-pĕar′anᶜe, *n.* Ka nalo ana′ku.

Dis′ap-point′, *v.* E hoohoka i ka manao.

Dis′ap-point′ment, *v* Ka hoka o ka manao.

Dis-ăp′pro-bā′tion, *n.* Ka manao apono ole.

Dis-ap-prŏv′al, *n.* Ka apono ole; ka ahewa ana.

Dis′ap-prŏve′, *v.* E hoahewa.

Dis-ạrm′, *v.* E hoonele i na mea e eha ai.

2. E waiho i na mea kaua.

Dis′ar-ränġe′, *v.* E waiho huikau; e hoohuikau i ka hoonoho ana. SYN. displace.

Dis′ar-ränġe′ment, *n.* Ka huikau o ka waiho ana.

Dis-ăs′ter, *n.* Popilikia; poino. SYN. calamity.

Dis-as′trous *adj.* Poino.

Dis′a-vow′, *n.* E hoole pale; ka hoole; e ae ole. SYN. disallow. *He disavows the theft*, ke hoole pale nei oia i ka aihue ana.

Dis-bănd′, *v.* E hookuu loa. *To disband an army*, e hookuu loa i ka puali koa.

Dis-bûrse′, *v.* E mahele aku; e haawi. SYN. distribute; dispense. *To disburse charities*, e mahele aku i na manawalea.

Dis-bûrse'ment, *n.* Ka mahele an'aku.
Dis-cärd', *v.* 1. E haalele loa. *To discard strong drink,* e haalele loa i ka wai ona.
2. E kiola aku. *To discard bad fruit,* e kiola aku i na hua ai palaho'.
Dis-çêrn', *v.* E hoomaopopo; e noonoo pono. SYN. discriminate.
Dis-çêrn'ing, *adj.* Noonoo pono. SYN. discriminating; sagacious.
Dis-çêrn'ment, *n.* Noonoo; ka noonoo kaupaona like. SYN. judgement; sagacity.
Dis-chärge', *v.* E hookuu loa. *To discharge a workman,* e hookuu loa i ka paahana.
2. E hoolei ukuna. *To discharge a ship,* e hoolei i ka ukana o ka moku.
3. E ki pu. SYN. fire; shoot.
4. E hookaa. *To discharge a debt,* e hookaa i ka aie.
5. E hooko. *To discharge a duty,* e hooko i kekahi pono. SYN. fulfil.
6. E hookahe. *To discharge water,* e hookahe wai.
Dis-çi'ple, *n.* He haumana. SYN. follower.
Dis'çi-plin-ā'ri-an, *n.* Mea hoomalu pono.
Dis'çi-pline, *n.* Ka malu pono.
Dis-çlāim', *v.* E hoole; e hoole me ka haalele.
Dis-çlōse', *v.* E hoike akea; e wehe ae. SYN. reveal.
Dis-çól'or, *v.* E hoo-ano e i ka wai hooluu.
Dis-çôm'fort, *n.* Ka inea o ka noho ana; ka haiki o ka noho'na.
Dis'çom-mōde', *v.* E hoopilikia.
Dis'çom-pōse', *v.* E hoopihoihoi; e hoohopohopo.
Dis'çon-çêrt', *v.* E hoopilihua; hoopihoihoi.
Dis'çon-nëct', *v.* E hookaawale; e hoohemo; e kala.
Dis-çŏn'so-late, *adj.* Mehameha ma ka naau; kaumaha; maha ole ma ka naau.
Dis'çon-tënt'ed, *adj.* Maha ole; ohumu wale.
Dis'çon-tĭn'ūe, *v.* E kapai ae; e hoopau.
Dis'çord, *n.* Huahua'; hakaka; aumeume. SYN. dissention; strife.
Dis'çount, *n.* Uku hooemi.
Dis-çoun'te-nânçe, *v.* E maliu ole; e hoohewa. SYN. disapprove.
Dis-çoûr'age, *v.* E hoomake manao; e paupauaho; e manaka'.
Dis-çoûr'age-ment, *n.* Ka manaka'; paupauaho; ka make o ka manao.
Dis'çourse, *n.* He kamailio; he haiolelo.
Dis-çoûr'te-oŭs, *adj.* Niha; keemoa; nainai. SYN. uncivil.
Dis-çŏv'er, *v.* E ike mua; e loaa mamuli o ka noonoo.
Dis-çŏv'er-êr, *n.* Ka mea ike mua.
Dis-çŏv'er-y, *n.* Ka ike mua ana.

Dis-erēd'it, *n.* 1. Hilahila. *Idleness is a discredit,* he mea hilahila ka molowa. SYN. disgrace.
2. Manaoio ole.
Dis-erēd'it-a-ble, *adj.* 1. Ku ole i ka oiaio.
2. Kupono ole. *Discreditable companions,* na hoa kupono ole.
Dis-creet', *adj.* Noeau; noonoo; akahele. SYN. cautious.
Dis-erēp'an-çy, *n.* Ka like ole o na olelo elua.
Dis-crē'tion, *n.* Noonoo akahele. SYN. prudence.
Dis-erim'i-nāte, *v.* E noonoo pono no kela me keia. SYN. discern; distinguish.
Dis-crim'i-nā'tion, *n.* Ka noonoo kaupaona like. SYN. discernment.
Dis-eŭss', *v.* E noonoo pu. SYN. debate.
Dis-eus'sion, *n.* Ka noonoo pu ana; he paio.
Dis-dāin', *n.* Haaheo; hookano. SYN. arrogance.
Dis-ęase', *n.* Mai.
Dis'em-bärk', *v.* E hoopae'; e lele iuka.
Dis'en-cŭm'ber, *v.* E kiola i ke kaumaha; e kala i ke kumu keakea.
Dis'en-gāge', *v.* E kala i ka hihia; e wehe i ka hihia. SYN. extricate.
Dis'en-gāged', *adj.* 1. Kaawale. *The house is disengaged,* ua kaawale ka hale. SYN. vacant.
2. Kaawale; hana ole. SYN. at leisure.
Dis-en-tän'gle, *v.* E wehe i ka hihia.
Dis-fā'vor, *n.* Maliu ole; ku-e' ka manao.
Dis-fĭg'ūre, *v.* E hoinoino. SYN. mar.
Dis-frän'chise, *v.* E lawe i na pono makaainana.
Dis-grāçe', *n.* Hilahila; inoa ino. SYN. shame; ignominy.
Dis-grāçe'ful, *adj.* Hilahila maoli; haukae loa. SYN. shameful; ignominious.
Dis-guise', *v.* E hooaano; e hoo-ano e.
Dis-gŭst', *n.* Hoopailua o ka manao.
Dis-gŭst'-ing, *adj.* Pelapela loa; haumia loa.
Dish, *n.* He pa. *To dish up,* e hao ka ai iloko o ke pa.
Dis-heärt'en, *v.* E hoomake manao. SYN. discourage.
Dis-heärt'en-ing, *adj.* Hoomake manao.
Dis-hŏn'est, *adj.* Epa; hoopono ole; apiki.
Dis-hŏn'es-ty, *n.* Hana kupono ole; hana apiki.
Dis-hŏn'or, *v.* 1. E hoino.
2. E hoole. *To dishonor a bill,* e hoole i ka bila dala.
Dis-hŏn'or-a-ble, *adj.* Kupono ole i ka inoa maikai; haahaa; apiki.
Dish'-wä'ter, *n.* Wai holoi pa.
Dis-in'cli-nā'tion, *n.* Huli ku-e' o ka manao.

Dis'in-fĕct', v. E hoomaemae i ke ea ino.

Dis'in-fĕc'tion, n. Ka hoomaemae ana i ke ea ino.

Dis'in-ġĕn'u-oŭs, adj. Nele i ka oiaio; apiki. SYN. deceitful; artful.

Dis'in-hĕr'it, v. E kapai mai ka hooilina ana.

Dis-in'te-grāt'ed, p. p. Hooliloia a ae-ae.

Dis'in-tĕr', v. E huai.

Dis-in'ter-est-ed, adj. Ewaewa ole; kaulike o ka noonoo.

Dis'in-tĕr'ment, n. Ka huai ana o ke kupapau.

Disk, n. He ili palahalaha poepoe. Sun's disk, ka ili o ka La.

Dis-like', v. E makemake ole.

Dis'lō-cate, v. E hemo i ka iwi mai kona ami. SYN. displace.

Dis'lo-cā'tion, n. Ka hemo ana o ka iwi mai kona ami.

Dis-lŏdġe', v. E hookuke mai kahi noho.

Dis-lŏy'al, adj. Manao kipi; ku-e' aupuni.

Dis'mal, adj. 1. Pouliuli. A dismal day, he la pouliuli.
2. Kaumaha. A dismal countenance, he helehelena kaumaha.

Dis-mǎn'tle, v. E hoonele i na lako. Dismantle a ship, e hoonele ka moku i na lako.

Dis-mǎst'ed, adj. Lilo na kia.

Dis-mǎy', n. Pilihua; puiwa nui.

Dis-miss', v. E hookuu.

Dis-miss'al / n. Ka hookuu ana.
Dis-mis'sion \

Dis-mount', v. E lele ilalo. Dismount from a horse, e lele ilalo mai ka lio.

Dis'o-bē'di-ençe, n. Hookuli; hoolohe ole.

Dis'o-bē'di-ent, adj. Konia; hookuli; kue' i ke kauoha.

Dis'o-bey', v. E hookuli; hoolohe ole.

Dis'ŏ-blĭġ'ing, adj. Oluolu ole; kokua ole; nanau.

Dis-ŏr'der, n. 1. Huikau; haunaele.
2. He mai.

Dis-ŏr'der-ly, adj. 1. Kuonoono ole.
2. Hoohaunaele. SYN. lawless.

Dis-ŏr'gan-ized, adj. Hooauhuli ia; hoohuikau ia.

Dis-ŏwn', v. E hoole loa. To disown an action, e hoole loa i kekahi hana. SYN. disclaim.

Dis-pǎr'aġe, v. E manao liilii aku; e ano hoahewa. SYN. depreciate.

Dis-pǎr'i-ty, n. Ka like ole iwaena o na mea elua.

Dis-pǎs'sion-āte, adj. Me ka huhu ole; noonoo ponoia.

Dis-pătch', v. 1. E hookikina. To dispatch a messenger, e hookikina i ka elele.
2. E pepehi a make. SYN. slay; kill.

Dis-pătch', n. 1. Hikiwawe; wikiwiki. With dispatch, me ka hikiwawe.

2. Palapala i hooiliia me ka awiwi Telegraphic dispatch, he palapala telegarapa.

Dis-pĕl', v. E hoopuehu. To dispel doubt, e hoopuehu i ka manao kana lua.

Dis-pĕn'sa-ry, n. Wahi e haawi i na laau lapaau.

Dis'pen-sā'tion, n. 1. He haawina A dispensation of Providence, he haawina no ke Akua mai.
2. He oihana. The Christian dispensa tion, ka oihana Euanelio.

Dis-pĕnse', v. 1. E haawi; e mahele aku. SYN. disburse. Dispense charities e haawi i na manawalea.
2. E hoole. To dispense with one's ser vices, e hoole i ke kokua ia mai o ke kahi.

Dis-pĕns'er, n. Ka mea e haawi ana A dispenser of charities, ka mea e haaw ana i na manawalea.

Dis-pĕrse', v. E hooauhee; e hoopu ehu. SYN. scatter.

Dis-pĕr'sion, n. Ka hoopuehu ana.

Dis-pir'it-ed, adj. Make ka manao SYN. discouraged.

Dis-plāçe', v. 1. E hoonee; e kapai ae.

Dis-plāçe'ment, n. Ka hoonee ana; ke kapai ana.

Dis-plǎy', v. 1. E hoikeike. To dis play goods, e hoikeike i na waiwai.
2. E hoike. To display courage, e hoike i ka manao wiwo ole. Syn. show.

Dis-please', v. E hoonaukiuki.

Dis-plěaş'ure, n. He ukiuki; huhu inaina.

Dis-pŏrt', v. E hoolealea; e paani lea lea.

Dis-pōs'al, n. Ka hoolilo ana.

Dis-pōse', v. 1. E hoolilo aku. To dispose of wealth, e hoolilo aku i ka wai wai.
2. E maliu mai. Disposed to take ad vice, maliu mai i ka olelo ao.

Dis-pōsed', adj. Huli ia ka manao Disposed to grant a request, huli ia ka manao e ae aku i ka noi.

Dis'po-si'tion, n. 1. Ano. A mild dis position, he ano oluolu.
2. Ka hoolilo ana. SYN. disposal.
3. Ka hoonohonoho ana. The disposi tion of things in a room, ka hoonohonoho ana o na mea iloko o ke keena.

Dis'pos-sĕss', v. E hoohemo ae.

Dis-prove', v. E hooia i ka wahahee kekahi mea; e hoike i ka oiaio ole kekahi aoao. SYN. confute.

Dis'pu-ta-ble, adj. Hiki ke hoopaa paa ia.

Dis'pu-tant, n. Mea e hoopaapaa ana.

Dis'pu-tā'tioŭs, adj. Ake nui i ka hoo paapaa.

Dis-pūte', v. E hoopaapaa.

Dis-quǎl'i-fi-cā'tion, n. Ke kumu i kupono ole ai.

Dis-quǎl'i-fied, adj. Kupono ole; ho ole ia no kekahi kumu.

Dis-quäl′i-fy, *v.* E hoole. *Theft disqualifies a man for public office*, o ka aihue ka mea e hoole ai i ke kanaka no ka oihana aupuni.

Dis′re-gärd′, *v.* E hoolohe ole; e hoomae′ae′a.

Dis-rĕl′ish, *n.* Ka makemake ole.

Dis-rèp′u-ta-ble, *adj* Kaulana ino.

Dis′re-pūte′, *n.* Ke kaulana no ka ino.

Dis′re-spĕet′, *n.* Hoowaha′waha′.

Dis′re-spĕet′ful, *adj.* Ano hoowaha′-waha′.

Dis-röbe′, *v.* E wehe i ka lole. SYN. unrobe; undress.

Dis-sät′is-fäc′tion, *n.* Ke ko ole o ka makemake.

Dis-sät′is-fied, *adj.* Oluolu ole; ko ole o ka makemake.

Dis-sĕet′, *v.* E okioki liilii.

Dis-sĕe′tion, *n.* Ka okioki liilii ana.

Dis-sĕm′ble, *v.* E hookamani.

Dis-sĕm′bler, *n.* Mea hookamani. SYN. hypocrite.

Dis-sĕm′i-nāte, *v.* E lulu; e hoolaha. *Disseminate knowledge*, e hoolaha i ka ike. SYN. sow.

Dis-sĕm′i-nä′tor, *n.* Ka mea nana e hoolaha.

Dis-sĕn′sion, *n.* Huahua′; mokuahana. SYN. contention.

Dis-sĕnt′, *v.* E manao ku-e′.

Dis′ser-tä′tion, *n.* He haiao. SYN. discourse.

Dis-sĭm′i-lar, *adj.* Like ole. SYN. unlike.

Dis-sĭm′u-lä′tion, *n.* Hookamani. SYN. hypocrisy.

Dĭs′si-pāte, *v.* 1. E hoopuehu. SYN. dispel; scatter.

2. E uhauha. SYN. squander.

Dĭs′si-pāt′ed, *adj.* Uhauha; ona; haukae. SYN. dissolute.

Dis-si-pä′tion, *n.* 1. Ka hoopuehu ana.

2. Ka uhauha ana.

Dĭs′so-lute, *adj.* Uhauha; haukae.

Dis-so-lū′tion, *n.* 1. Ka hopena o ka make.

2. Ka hooheehee ana; ka hoopau ana.

Dĭs-sŏlve′, *v.* 1. E hooheehee i ka wai.

2. E hoopau. *To dissolve a partnership*, e hoopau i ka hui.

Dĭs-sŏlv′ent, *n* Ka mea e hooheehee ai.

Dĭs-suäde′, *v.* E pa′pa′ ′ku.

Dĭs-suä′sion, *n.* Ka pa′pa′ ′na.

Dĭs-sÿl′la-ble, *n.* He hua olelo me na mamala elua.

Dĭs′tançe, *n.* Ka mamao.

Dĭs′tant, *adj.* 1. Ma o loa.

2. *Distant in manner*, kapukapulani.

Dis-täste′ful, *adj.* 1. Ono ole; malailena.

2. Ku ole i ka makemake. SYN. nauseous.

Dis-tĕm′per, *n.* 1. He ano mai. SYN. disease.

2. He ano pena i hoomakaukau ia no ka pena kii; a pena hale paha.

Dis-tĕnd′, *v.* E hoo-pehu; e pehu.

Dis-till′, *v.* 1. E hookulu; e kahe liilii. SYN. drop; flow gently.

2. E puhi wai ona.

Dis′til-lä′tion, *n.* 1. Ke kulu ana. Ka puhi ana i ka wai ona.

Dis-til′ler, *n.* Mea puhi wai ona.

Dis-til′ler-y, *n.* Kahi e hanaia′i o ka wai ona.

Dis-tinet′, *adj.* 1. Kaawale; okoa loa. SYN separate.

2. Moakaka. SYN. clear.

Dis-tine′tion, *n.* Ano okoa.

2. Kaulana. *A man of distinction*, kanaka kaulana. See *distinguished*.

Dis-tinet′ly, *adv.* Moakaka; maopopolea; SYN. clearly.

Dis-tin′guish, *v.* 1. E hoomaopopo. SYN. discriminate.

2. E hookaulana. *To distinguish one's self*, e hookaulana kekahi iaia iho.

Dis-tin′guished (gwisht), *adj.* Kaulana. SYN. renowned.

Dis-tôrt′, *v.* E hoolauwili; e pakaawili.

Dis-trăet′, *v.* 1. E kaili i ka noonoo. *Distract the mind from the lesson*, e kaili i ka noonoo mai ka haawina.

2. E hoopilihua.

Dis-trăe′tion, *n.* Ke kaili o ka noonoo.

2. Pilihua.

Dis-trĕss′, *v.* E hooehaeha. SYN. pain.

Dis-trĕss′, *n.* 1. Eha. SYN. pain.

2. Pilikia; popilikia. SYN. difficulty; peril; danger. *A ship in distress*, he moku iloko o ka popilikia.

Dis-trĕss′ing, *n.* Eha; pilikia.

Dis-trib′ute, *v.* E mahele; e puunaue. SYN. disburse.

Dis′tri-bü′tion, *n.* Ka mahele an′aku.

Dis′trict, *n.* Apana. *District of Kona*, apana o Kona.

Dis-trŭst′, *v.* E haoheo; e kanalua. SYN. suspect. E kuipehi.

Dis-trŭst′, *n.* Kuipehi; haohao.

Dis-trŭst′ful, *adj.* Piha i ke kanalua; SYN. suspicious.

Dis-tûrb, *v.* 1. E hoopilikia wale.

2. E hoohaunaele. *Disturb the peace*, e hooauhuli i ka maluhia.

Dis-tûrb′ançe, *n.* Haunaele.

Dis-tûrb′er, *n.* 1. Mea hookonokono hakaka.

2. Mea hoopilikia wale.

Dĭs′ü-nīte′, *v.* E hookaawale i na mea i hoohuila.

Dĭs-üse′, *n.* Ka waiho wale ana o kekahi mea.

Ditch, *n.* Auwai; auwaha.

Dit′to, *n.* Ia mea hookahi no. SYN. the same.

Dit′ty, *n.* Mele pa-ko-li.

Di-ûr′nal, *adj.* I kela me keia la. SYN. daily.

Dive, *v.* E luu i ka wai. *Dive headlong*, e luu kimo; e kuhoopoo.

Di′ver, *n.* Mea luu i ka wai.

Di-vĕr'ġe', v. E manamana; e ka ana.
Di-vĕr'ġence, n. Ke ka ana; ka mana-mana ana.
Di'vers, adj. Kekahi mau. SYN. several.
Di-vĕrse', adj. Ano e; okoa. SYN. different.
Di-vĕr'si-fȳ, v. E hooano e.
Di-vĕr'ṣion, n. Lealea. SYN. amusement.
Di-vĕrs'i-ty, n. Like ole.
Di-vĕrt', v. 1. E aui ae. SYN. turn aside.
  2. E hoolealea.
  3. E alakai aku i ka manao mai kekahi noonoo a i kekahi aku.
Di-vĕrt'ing, adj. Lealea. SYN. amusing.
Di-vĕst', v. 1. E hoonele. Divest of property, e hoonele i ka waiwai. SYN. dispossess.
  2. E wehe ae; e hoohemo.
Di-vide', v. E mahele; e puunaue.
Di-vide', n. He kualapa mawaena o na muliwai elua. SYN. watershed.
Div'i-dend, n. 1. Kumu puunaue.
  2. Puu dala maheleia.
Di-vid'ers, n. Upa ana.
Di-vine', adj. Ano Akua. A divine, he kahunapule.
Di-vin'i-ty, n. Ke Akua.
  2. Hoike Akua. SYN. theology.
Di-vis'i-ble, adj. Hike ke maheleia.
Di-vis'ion, n. 1. Puunaue; mahele. A division of property, he mahele o ka waiwai.
  2. Mokuahana. A division in the family, he mokuahana ma ka ohana.
Di-vis'or, n. Helu komo. Common divisor, helu komo pili like. Greatest common divisor, helu komo pili like oi loa.
Di-vŏrce', n. E oki mare.
Di-vŭlġe', v. E kuailo.
Diz'zi-ness, n. Kaihi; poniuniu.
Diz'zy, adj. Kaihi; poniuniu.
Dǫ (dū), v. 1. E hana; e hooko. SYN. perform.
  2. He haina e kokua ana i na haina e ae. Did you see? ua ike anei oe?
  3. How do you do? pehea oe?
Dǒ'çile, adj. Hoolohe; akahai. SYN. tractable.
Do-çil'i-ty, n. Ke ano hoolohe; akahai.
Dog-mät'ie, adj. 1. Mamuli o ka loina.
  2. Paakiki ma kona manao iho; haanou.
Dǒck, n. 1. Wahi e hookomo moku, i kapili hou ia.
  2. Wahi e kui ai o ka lawehala iloko o ke keena hookolokolo.
Dǒck, v. 1. E hoopokole; e poko.
  2. E hooemi. To dock the wages, e hooemi i ka uku.
Dǒck'et, n. Ka papa o na hihia imua o ka aha hookolokolo.

Dǒck'yärd, n. Wahi e hooahu ai i na lako no na moku aupuni.
Dŏe'tor, n. 1. Kahuna lapaau; kauka.
  2. Doctor of Divinity, he kahuna akamai ma na mea o ka Baibala.
Dŏe'trine, n. 1. Ka mea i aoia.
  2. Christian doctrine, na loina kristiano.
Dŏe'u-ment, n. Palapala hoike.
Do-dee'a-gon, n. Kii matematika; hu-ina 12.
Dŏdġe, v. E aloalo'; hooalo.
Dŏff, v. E wehe. To doff a hat, e wehe i ka papale.
Dŏg, n. Ilio.
Dŏg, v. E hahai; e alualu.
Dŏg'ged, adj. Nunuha; opukopekope; nainai. SYN. sullen; morose.
Dŏg'ma, n. He loina.
Dŏg'trot, n. Ka holo mau o ka ilio.
Dǫ'ings, n. pl. Na hana. The day's doings, na hana o ka la.
Dōle'ful, adj. Kaumaha ma ka manao; piha i ke kaumaha.
Dŏll, n. He be'be' kii.
Dŏl'lar, n. He dala; 100 keneta.
Dŏl'or-oŭs, adj. Ehaeha; kaumaha.
Dŏl'phin, n. He i-a nui, nani.
Dŏ'main, n. Aina. The King's domain, ka aina a ka Moi i hoomalu ai. SYN. dominion.
Do-mĕs'tie, adj. 1. Pili i ka ohana. Domestic duties, na pono ohana.
  2. Kuloko. Domestic news, nuhou kuloko.
Do-mĕs'tie, n. He ohua no ka ohana.
Do-mĕs'ti-eāte, v. E hoolakalaka.
Dŏm'i-çile, n. Wahi noho mau; home.
Dŏm'i-neer', v. E hookickie maluna'e o kekahi; e kauoha hookickie.
Do-min'ion, n. Ka mana; ke aupuni.
Dŏ'nāte, v. E makana aku, e haawi wale. SYN. give; present.
Do-nä'tion, n. Makana; kokua; manawalea. SYN. gift; present.
Do-nee', n. Ka mea e loaa ana i ka makana.
Dŏn'key, n. Kekake; hoki.
Dŏ'nor, n. Ka mea e makana ana.
Dŏom, n. Ka hoopai.
Dŏoms'day, n. La hoopai. Ka la hookolokolo nui. SYN judgment day.
Dŏor, n Puka komo.
Dŏor'-keep'er, n. Kiai puka.
Dŏr'mant, adj. E waiho moe ana. Dormant passions, na kuko e waiho moe ana.
Dŏr'mer-win'dow, v He puka makani ma ke kaupako o ka hale.
Dŏr'mi-tō-ry, n. He hale moe; keena moe.
Dōse, n. He mahele laau inu.
Dōse, v. E hoohainu i ka laau.
Dŏt, n. Kiko.
Dŏ'taġe, n. Wa palalauhala.
Dŏ'tard, n. He palalauhala.
Doŭb'le, adj. Pa-lua; papalua.
Doŭb'le-deal'ing, n. Hana paewaewa.

Doūbt′, *v.* 1. E kanalua. SYN. uncertain.

2. Anoni; anoninoni. SYN. *suspense as to result;* hesitation.

Dŏubt′ful, *adj.* Kanalua; anoninoni.

Dŏubt′less, *adv.* Me ke kanalua ole.

Dōugh (dō), *n.* Berena maka.

Dough′ty (dow-ty), *adj.* Koa; kaulana no ka ikaika.

Douse, (dowse), *v.* E lu kino iloko o ka wai.

Dōve (dŭv,) *n.* Manu nunu.

Dōve′cŏt, *n.* Hale manu nunu.

Dōve′tāil, *v* E oleole papa.

Dow′er, *n.* Ka mahele waiwai o ka wahine mare, a wahine kane make paha.

Down′, *prep.* Lalo; ilalo.

Down′east, *adj.* Kaumaha ka manao. SYN. down-hearted.

Dow′dy, *n.* Wahine i pono ole kona kapa komo.

Down′fall, *n.* Ka haule ana; ka poino.

Down-heärt′ed, *adj.* Kaumaha ma ka manao; paumako.

Down′hill, *adj.* Iho′na; makai.

Down′right, *adj.* Maopopo lea.

Dŏwn′ward, *adj* 1. Iho ana. *The downward path,* ke alanui e iho ana.

2. I lalo.

Dox-ŏl′o-ġy, *n.* Himeni hoomaikai.

Dōze, *v.* Kulihiamoe; kuluhiamoe.

Dŏz-en, *adj.* He kakini, na mea okoa he 12.

Drāft, *n.* 1. Palapala kikoo dala.

2. Ka pa ana o ka makani mawaena o na puka elua.

3. Ke kakau ana; he kope.

4. Ka wae ana. *Draft for the army,* **ka** wae ana i poe koa no ka puali koa.

Drăg, *n.* E kauo.

Drăg, *v.* He hao kahi lepo; he papa kauo pohaku, lepo, etc.

Drāin, *n.* 1. He auwaha e hookahe aku ai i ka wai mai ka aina.

2. Ka hookahe aku ana.

Drāin′aġe, *n.* Ka wai i hookaheia aku.

Drāke, *n.* Manu kaka′ kane.

Drăm, *n.* 1. He ana kaumaha.

2. Hookahi inu ana o ka wai ona.

Drä′mä, *n.* Olelo kike′ no ke keaka.

Drăm′a-tist, *n.* Kanaka kakau olelo kike′ no ke keaka.

Drāpe, *v.* E hoouhi i ke kapa.

Drāp′er-y, *n.* Kapa uhi.

Drāught (draft,) *n.* 1. Hookahi inu ana.

2. Ka hohonu o ke komo ana o ka moku i ka wai.

3. Uulu i-a iloko o ka upena.

Drāughts′man, *n.* Kanaka kahakaha kii; kanaka kakau kope.

Draw, *v.* 1. E huki; e kauo.

2. E kakau kii.

3. E ume. SYN. attract.

Draw′back, *n.* 1. Kumu keakea. SYN. hindrance.

2. Ka auhau dute i hoihoiia.

3. He poino; he poho.

Draw′bridġe, *n.* Alahaka i hukiia iluna.

Draw′er, *n.* He holowaa no ka pahu; no ka papa paha.

Draw′ing, *n.* 1. He kii i kahaia.

2. Ka hookahe ana. *Drawing off oil from a barrel,* e hookahe ana i ka aila mai ka barela.

3. Ka ume ana. SYN. attraction.

Draw′ing-knife, *n.* Pahi paauma.

Draw′ing-room, *n.* Keena hookipa. See *parlor.*

Drawl, *n.* Leo kauo.

Drawn, *adj.* Paiwale, hula. *A drawn battle,* he hoouka kaua paiwale.

Drāy′man, *n.* Kahu kaa ukana.

Drēad, *n.* Weliweli; eehia.

Drēad′ful, *adj.* Weliweli; eehia.

Drēam′, *n.* He moe; he moeuhane.

Drēam′er, *n.* Mea moeuhane.

Drēar′y, *adj.* Neanea; oneanea.

Drĕgs, *n.* Maku.

Drĕnch, *v.* Pulu; hoopulu.

Drĕss, *v.* 1. E hookomo lole. SYN. clothe.

2. E hoomaakaukau. SYN. prepare. *To dress food,* e hoomakaukau i ai.

3. E wahi′ SYN. bind up. *To dress a wound,* e wahi′ i ka eha.

4. *To dress a line of soldiers,* e hoopololei i ka lalani koa.

Drĕss, *n.* 1. Lole komo. SYN. clothes.

2. Holoku′.

3. He uhi no kela me keia mea. SYN. covering.

Drĕss′ing, *n.* 1. Ka laau i kau ia maluna o ka eha.

2. He mea kipulu aina.

3. Mea i hookomoia. SYN. stuffing.

Drĕs′sing-room, *n.* Keena hookomo lole.

Drift, *v.* E lana wale io ia nei.

Drift, *n.* He piha wale. *A snow drift,* piha wale mai o ka hau.

Drift′wood, *n.* Pihea′.

Drill, *n.* 1. Wili puka liilii.

2. Paikau. SYN. military drill.

Drink, *v.* E inu.

Drip, *v.* E kulu.

Drive, *v.* 1. E hoo-a′. *Drive cattle,* e hoo-a bipi.

2. E hooeueu, hookikina. *To drive work,* e hooeueu i ka hana.

3. *To drive a hard bargain,* e hoopaakiki ma ke kuai ana.

4. *Drive with the wind,* e kaalelewa. *Wind driven clouds,* na ao kaalelewa.

Driv′er, *n.* 1. Kanaka hookele kaa.

2. Kanaka hoo-a′ holoholona.

3. Kanaka hookikina.

4. Kanaka hooeueu.

Driz′zle, *n.* Noe; kilihau.

Drŏll, *adj.* Ku i ka aka SYN. funny.

Drŏm′e-dā′ry, *n.* Kamelo puu hookahi.

Drōne, *n.* 1. Nalo meli kane.

2. He makahiamoe; he mea loma wale.

Drōop. *v.* Loha; mae; luhe′.

Drŏp, n. 1. He kulu. *A drop of water,* he kulu wai.

2. Paka. *A drop of rain,* he **paka** u-a.

Drŏp, v. E haule; e hoohaule.

Drŏp'sy, n. Mai pehu.

Drŏss, n. Opala o ka metala i hooheeheeia.

Drŏuth, n. 1. Ka paa ana o ka u-a

2. Ka maloo ana o ka aina; ka wi.

Drŏve, n. Pu-a holoholona.

Drŏv'er, n. Kanaka hoo-a holoholona.

Drŏwn, v. E make i ka wai; e lumai.

Drŏw'sy, adj. Makahiamoe.

Drŭb'bing, n. 1. Ka hahau ana me ka laau.

2. Ke kui ana me ka puu lima.

Drŭdge, n. He kauwa kuapaa.

Drŭdg'er-y, n. Hana inea; hana luhi.

Drŭg, n. 1. Laau mea lapaau.

2. Kela me keia waiwai i lohi ma ka lilo ana. *A drug in the market,* he waiwai i hiki ole ke hooliloia ma ka makeke.

Drŭg'gist, n. Kanaka kuai laau lapaau.

Drŭm, n. Pahu kani.

Drŭm'mer, n. 1. Mea hookani pahu.

2. He piele waiwai.

Drŭm'stick, n. Laau hookani pahu.

Drŭnk, adj Ona. SYN. intoxicated.

Drŭnk'ard, n. Kanaka ona mau.

Drŭnk'en, adj. Ona.

Drŭnk'en-ness, n. Ka ona.

Drȳ, adj 1. Maloo. *Dry clothes,* lole maloo.

2. Koele; koeleele. *Dry ground,* aina koele.

3. Panoa. SYN. barren.

4. Makewai. SYN. thirsty.

Drȳ, v. E hoomaloo.

Drȳ'gŏŏds, n. Na lole kuai o kela me keia ano.

Drȳ'ness, n. Ke ano maloo; ano koele.

Drȳ'shod, adj. Pulu ole o ka wawae.

Dū'al, adj. Pa-lua.

Dū'bi-oŭs, adj. Maopopo ole. SYN. doubtful.

Dŭch'ess, n. Ka wahine mare o ke *Duke.*

Dŭck, n. He kaka'; he koloa.

Dŭck, v. E luu iloko o ka wai.

Dŭck'ing, n. Ka luu ana iloko o ka wai.

Dŭc'tile, adj. Hiki ke hooloihi ia.

Dŭds, n. Lole komo kahiko.

Dūe, adj. Aie; kupono. *Due time,* wa kupono.

Dū'el, n. Hakaka' o na mea elua.

Dū'el-ist, n. Kanaka maa i ka hakaka' me ka hoa.

Dū-ĕt', n. Mele me na leo elua.

Dūke, n. He 'lii kiekie ma Europa.

Dūke'dom, n. Ke kulana o ke *Duke,* a me kona aina.

Dŭl'cet, adj. Nahenahe.

Dŭll, adj. 1. Oi ole; pihipihi; kumumu.

2. Loiele. SYN. slow; stupid.

Dŭl'lard, n. He mea kolo o ka ike; he lolo ma ka naau.

Dū'ly, adv. Pono. *Came duly to hand,* hiki pono mai i ka lima.

Dŭmb, adj. Aa; mumule.

Dŭmp'y, adj. Poupou.

Dŭn, adj. Ahinahina.

Dŭn, n. Ke koi 'na no ka aie.

Dŭnce, n. He haumana imi ole; loiele.

Dŭng, n. Kukae.

Dŭn'geon, n. Hale pouli.

Dū'o-dē'num, n. Ka mua o na naau liilii.

Dūpe, n. Mea hoopunihei wale ia.

Dū'pli-cāte, n. Lua like, he kope.

Dū-plic'i-ty, n. Ano epa; wahahee. SYN. deceit; lying.

Dū'ra-bĭl'i-ty, n. Ano paa; ano mau.

Dū'ra-ble, adj. Paa; mau.

Dūr'ance, n Ka hoopaahao ana. SYN. duress; imprisonment.

Du-rā'tion, n. Ka mau o ka manawa.

Dū'ress, n. Ka hoopaaia'na o ke kino.

Dūr'ing, prep. Oiai; i ka wa.

Dŭsk, n. Liula'; molehulehu. SYN. twilight.

Dŭsk'y, adj. 1. Moolehulehu. SYN. shady.

2. Haulluli.

Dŭst, n. Lepo aeae.

Dŭst, v. E kahili i ka lepo.

Dŭs'ter, n. 1. Kahili no ka lepo.

2. He kuka pale lepo.

Dŭst'y, adj Lepo; paapu i ka lepo.

Dū'ti-a-ble, adj. Ku i ka auhau dute.

Dū'ti-ful, adj. Hoolohe. SYN. obedient.

Dū'ty, n. 1. Pono.

2. He dute waiwai; auhau waiwai.

Dwärf, n. He keko; kanaka a-a; kanaka poupou.

Dwĕll, v. E noho mau. SYN. reside; live.

Dwĕl'ler, n. Kamaaina.

Dwĕll'ing, n. Wahi noho. SYN. habitation; residence.

Dwīn'dle, v. 1. E mae. SYN. droop.

2. E emi liilii.

Dȳe (dī), v. E hooluu lole; e kupena.

Dȳe'ing, n. Ka hooluu ana i ka lole.

Dȳ'er, n. Kanaka kupena lole; kanaka hooluu lole.

Dȳ-năm'ics, n. Ka mana e nee aku ai.

Dȳ'nas-ty, n. Kuauhau Moi, o ka ohana hookahi.

Dȳs'en-tĕr'y, n. Mai hi koko.

Dȳs-pĕp'sia, n. Mai o ka opu hoowale ai.

Dȳs-pĕp'tic, adj. Wale ole o ka ai maloko o ka opu.

E

Each, *adj.* Pakahi. *Each one of you,* oukou pakahi.
Ea'ger, *adj.* Ake nui; iini.
Eag'er-ly, *adv.* Me ka iini nui.
Ea'gle, *n.* Aeto.
Ear, *n.* 1. Pepeiao.
2. Huhui. *An ear of corn,* he huhui kurina.
Ear'ly, *adv.* Me ka makaala; me ka wiki e.
Earn, (urn), *v.* E loaa mamuli o ka hana.
Earn'est, *adj.* Ikaika ma ka manao.
Earn'est-ly, *adv.* Me ka manao ikaika.
Earn'ings, *n.* Na loaa mamuli o ka hana.
Ear'ring, *n.* Komo pepeiao.
Ear'shot, *n.* Ka lohe o ka pepeiao *Within earshot,* ma ka lohe o ka pepeiao.
Earth, *n.* 1. Ka Honua Nei.
2. Lepo. *Fall to the earth,* haule i ka lepo, or, haule i ka honua.
Earth'en, *adj.* Hanaia mai ka lepo palolo.
Earth'quake, *n.* He olai; nauwewe.
Ease (ēz), *n.* 1. Maha; olu. SYN. comfort.
2. Ano hiki wale no.
3. Ano palaka.
Eas'i-ly, *adv.* Hiki wale no.
East, *n.* Hikina.
East'er, *n.* Ka la hoomanao no ko Kristo ala hou ana.
East'er-ly, *adv.* or *adj.* I ka hikina'ku; moe aku i ka hikina.
East'ern, *adj.* No ka hikina.
East'ward, *adv.* I ka hikina' ku.
Eas'y, *adj.* 1. Hiki wale; moakaka.
2. Maha; pohala.
Eat, *v.* E ai; e pai'na.
Eat'a-ble, *adj.* Kupono ke ai
Eaves, *n.* Na umalu o ka hale.
Eaves'drŏp'per, *n.* He mea hakilo.
Eaves'drŏp'ping, *n.* Ka hakilo ana.
Ebb, *n.* Ka emi ana. *Ebb of the tide,* ka emi ana o ke kai.
Eb'on-y, *n.* Laau paa, eleele.
Eb'ul-li'tion, *n.* 1. Ka lapalapa ana. o ka wai.
2. Ka hooe ana. *Ebullition of temper,* ka hooe ana o ka huhu.
Ec-cen'tric, *adj.* 1. Ka aui ana mai ke kiko waena.
2. Ano e; like ole me kanaka e.
Ec'cen-tri'ci-ty, *n.* Ke ano like ole me ko kanaka e.
Ec-cle'si-ăs'tic, *n.* Kahunapule.

Ec-cle'şi-ăs'tic-al, *adj.* Pili i ka Ekalesia.
Ech'o (ĕk'o), *n.* He kupinai; e-ko.
E-clät' (ĕk-lä), *n.* Ka mahalo nui; ke kaulana.
E-clipse', *n.* He pouli o ka La, ka mahina.
E-clip'tic, *n.* Ke ala heie o ka La.
E-co-nŏm'ic-al, *adj.* Malama pono; u'hau'ha ole.
E-eŏn'o-mist, *n.* Kanaka malama pono.
E-eŏn'o-mişe, *v.* E malama pono. *Economise time,* e malama pono i ka manawa; e kalai pono.
E-eŏn'o-my, *n.* 1. Ka malama pono; ke kalai pono ana. *Political economy,* kalai aina.
2. Na rula me na loina no kela me keia mea. *The economy of nature,* na rula me na loina o ke ao nei.
Ĕc'sta-sy, *n.* Hauoli piha.
Ĕdġe, *n.* 1. Kae. SYN. brim or brink. *Edge of a precipice,* ke kae o ka pali.
2. Kumu. *edge of a tool,* kumu o ka mea paahana.
3. Lihi. *Edge of cloth,* lihi lole. *Edge of forest,* lihi o ka ulu laau. SYN. border
4. Niao. *Edge of board,* niao papa.
Ĕdġed, (ejd). *adj.* Me ke kumu; oi.
Ĕdġ'ing, *n.* Lihilihi lole
Ĕdġe' tool', *n.* Mea oi
Ĕdġe-wişe, *adv.* Kunihi; lihi.
Ĕd'i-ble, *adj.* SYN eatable.
E'dict, *n.* Kanawai i hoolahaia. SYN. decree.
Ĕd'i-fi-eā'tion, *n.* Ka hoonaauao ana.
Ĕd'i-fiee, *n.* Hale nunui.
Ĕd'i-fy, *v.* E hoonaauao.
Ĕd'it, *v.* E hooponopono nupepa, a buke paha.
E-di'tion, *n.* Ka nui o na nupepa, a buke paha i paiia i ka wa hookahi.
Ĕd'i-tor, *n.* Luna hooponopono nupepa a buke paha.
Ĕd'i-to'ri-al, *n.* Manao hoopuka a ka luna hooponopono.
Ĕd'i-tŏr-ship', *n* Oihana hooponopono nupepa.
Ĕd'u-eāte, *v.* E hoonaauao; e ao. SYN. instruct, teach.
Ĕd'u-eā'tion, *n.* Ka hoonaauao ana; ke ao ana. SYN. instruction.
Ĕd'u-eā'tion-al, *adj.* Pili i ka hoonaauao.
Ĕd'ū-ea'tor, *n.* Kumu ao. SYN. instructor; teacher.
Eel, *n.* He puhi.

Ĕf-fā̱çe′, v. 1. E holoi. SYN. erase. *To efface a mark,* e holoi i ke kaha.
2. E anai. SYN. blot out; obliterate.
Ef-fĕct′, n. 1. Ka hua o ka hana. *Cause and effect,* ka kumu me kona hua.
2. Ka hua o ka olelo. *Words without effect,* na huaolelo hua ole.
3. Ano. *He spoke to that effect,* kamailio oia ma ia ano.
4. E ko. *To effect a purpose,* e ko i ka makemake.
Ef-fĕcts′, n. pl. Na waiwai lewa o kela me keia ano. SYN. goods; chattels.
Ef-fĕct′u-al, adj. Ko pono.
Ef-fĕm′i-nāte, adj. Hookohukohu wahine la.
Ĕf′fĕr-vĕs̱çe′, v. E pipili; e huahuai.
Ĕf′fi-cā′çioŭs, adj. Mana. SYN. effectual; powerful.
Ĕf′fi-ca-çy, n. Ka mana o ke ko ana. SYN. power.
Ĕf′fi-ġy, n. He kii o ke kanaka.
Ĕf′flu-ent, n. He kahawai e kahe aku ana mai ka lokowai; a kahawai e ae paha.
Ĕf-flū′vi-um, n. He hauna.
Ĕf′fort, n. He hoao. SYN. attempt; endeavor. *To make an effort,* e hoao.
Ĕf-frŏnt′er-y, n. Ano mahaoi; ano pakike′.
Ef-fūl′ġençe, n. Alohilohi.
Ef-fū′sion, n. Ka hookahe ana. *Effusion of blood,* ka hookahe ana o ke koko.
Ĕgg, n. He hua, *Hen′s egg,* hua moa.
Ē′go-tism, n. Ano haanou; kaena wale.
Ē′go-tist, n. Kanaka kaena wale.
E-grē′ġioŭs, adj. Launa ole. *An egregious mistake,* he kuhihewa launa ole.
Ē′gress, n. Ka puka ana iwaho.
Eight (āte), adj. Ewalu.
Eigh-teen′, adj. Umikumamawalu.
Eight′fold′, adj. Pa-walu.
Eighth, adj. 1. Ka walu. *The eighth day,* ka walu o na la.
2. Hapa-walu. *One eighth,* hookahi hapawalu.
Eight′y, adj. Kanawalu.
Eith′er (ē-ther or ī-ther), adj. Kekahi o na mea elua.
E-jĕct′, v. E hookuke; e kiolaiwaho.
E-jĕct′ment, n. Ka hookuke ana. *Writ of ejectment,* palapala hookuke.
Ēke, v. E hoomahuahua; e hooloihi. *Eke out a living,* e hoomahuahua i na loaa.
E-lăb′o-rate, adj. Aulii. SYN. perfected.
E-lăb′o-rāte, v. E hana me ka noonoo; E hana me ke akahele. SYN. to take pains.
E-lăb′o-rate-ly, adj. Me ke akahele o ka hana; me ka aulii; me ka mikioi.
E-lăb′o-rā′tion, n. Ka mikioi ana ma ka hana.
E-lăpse′, v. E hala. *Several days must elapse,* e hala ana ekahi mau la.
E-lăs′tic, adj. Holuholu; linalina.

E-lāte′, v. E hoohoihoi; hooeueu.
Ēl′bōw, n. Kuekue lima.
Ĕl′bōw, v. E hookuekue; e hoo-ke′.
Ĕl′der, adj. Kahiko ae. *Elder brother,* kaikuaana. *An Elder,* he lunakahiko.
Ĕld′est, adj. Ka oi o ke kahiko. *Eldest son,* ka makahiapo.
E-lĕct′, v. E koho; e wae.
E-lĕct′, n. Poe i kohoia.
E-lĕc′tion, n. Ke koho ana.
E-lĕc′tion-eer′, v. 1. E hooholo balota.
2. E paipai balota.
E-lĕct′or, n. Kanaka koho.
E-lĕc′trie, } adj. Pili i ka uila.
E-lĕc′tri-cal, }
E-lĕc-tri′çian, n. Kanaka lawelawe uila.
E-lĕc-tric′i-ty, n. Uila.
El-e-gançe, n. Ka nani. *Elegance of attire,* nani o ka aahu.
Ĕl′e-gant, adj. Nani; nonohe.
Ĕl′e-gant-ly, adv. A nani. *Dress elegantly,* e aahu a nani
Ĕl′e-ġy, n. He mele kanikau.
Ĕl′e-ment, n. 1. He mole; he kumu.
2. *Elements,* na mea hookumu.
Ĕl′e-mĕnt′a-ry, adj. Kumu mua
Ĕl′e-phant, n. Elepani.
El′e-vate, v E hapai iluna; e hookiekie ae.
El′e-vā′tion, n. 1. Kahi kiekie.
2. Ka hookiekie ana.
El′e-vā′tor, n. 1. Ka mea e hapai ana.
2. Ka mea e hookiekie ana.
3. He pahu nui e pii ana, a e iho ana.
E-lĕv′en, adj. Umikumamakahi.
E-lĕv′enth, adj. 1. Ka umikumamakahi.
2. He hapa—11.
E-lic′it, v. E loaa mamuli o ka ninaninau ana. SYN. bring to light.
Ĕl′i-ġi-bil′i-ty, n. Ke kupono. *Eligibility to office,* ke kupono no ka oihana.
Ĕl′i-ġi-ble, adj. Kupono.
E-lim′i-nāte, v. E kapai.
E-lim′i-nā′tion, n. Ke kapai ana.
E-liṣ′ion, n. Ka oki ana; ke kapai ana. SYN. cutting off from.
Ĕl-lipse′, n. Poai-loihi.
Ĕl′o-cū′tion, n. 1. Ke kamailio; ka haiolelo.
2. Ka puana pono ana.
Ĕl′o-cū′tion-ist, n. Kanaka akamai ma ka heluhelu ana.
E-lón′gate, n. E panainai; e pakuikui.
E-lōpe′, v. E mahuka pu; e holo malu′.
E-lōpe′ment, n· Ka holo malu′ ana, o ke kane me ka wahine.
Ĕl′o-quençe, n. Ke akamai ma ka hai olelo.
Ĕl′o-quent, adj. Akamai ma ka olelo.
Ĕl′o-quent′ly, adv. Me ke akamai o ka olelo.
Ĕlse, pron. E ae. *some one else,* kekahi mea e ae.
Ĕlse, adv. I ole. SYN. otherwise.
Ĕlse′whĕre, adv. Ma kahi e.

E-lū′çi-date, *v.* E hoomoakaka; e we-hewehe. SYN. explain; make clear.

E-lū′çi-dā′tion, *n.* Ka hoomaopopo ana; ka wehewehe ana. SYN. explanation.

E-lūde′, *v.* E haliu aku; e aloalo′. SYN. avoid; shun.

E-mā′çi-āt′ed, *adj.* Panauea; wiwi.

Em′a-nāte, *v.* E puka no loko mai. SYN. proceed from.

Em-a-nā′tion, *n.* Ka mea i puka mai.

E-mān′çi-pāte, *v.* E hookuu. SYN. set free. E kala.

E-mān′çi-pā′tion, *n.* Ka hookuu ana. SYN. liberation. Ke kala ana.

E-mān′çi-pa′tor, *n.* Ka mea nana e hookuu. SYN. liberator.

Em-bálm′, *v.* E ialoa.

Em-bánk′ment, *n.* He kapa; he paku.

Em-bär′go, *n.* Palapala hoopaa moku, i holo ole.

Em-bärk′, *v.* Ee moku. SYN. go aboard.

Em′bär-kā′tion, *n.* Ka ee ana i ka moku. SYN. going aboard.

Em-bär′rass-ing, *adj.* Mea e hooulu-hua. SYN. confusing.

Em-bär′rass-ment, *n.* 1. Ka pihoihoi. 2. Pilikia. *Pecuniary embarrassment,* ka pilikia no ke dala ole.

Em′bas-sy, *n.* He poe elele aupuni.

Em-bël′lish, *v.* E hoonani. *Embellished with engravings,* hoonaniia me na kii.

Em′bers, *n.* Nanahu euaena. SYN. live coals.

Em-bēz′zle, *v.* E apuka dala.

Em-bēz′zle-ment, *n.* Ka apuka ana i ke dala.

Em-bēz′zler, *n.* Mea apuka dala. SYN. defaulter.

Em′blem, *n.* He hoailona; he ouli. SYN. symbol; sign.

Em′blèm-āt′ic, *adj.* E hoailona ana.

Em-bŏd′y, *v.* E hoohui. *To embody thought,* e hoohui manao.

Em-bōld′en, *v.* E hoo-a′-a′.

Em-brāçe′, *v.* E hii; e puliki.

Em′bro-cā′tion, *n.* Laau hamo.

Em-broid′er, *v.* E hoonionio; e hana lihilihi.

Em-broid′er-y, *n.* Lihilihi lole.

Em-brŏil′, *v.* E hoohaunaele; e hoala i ka hakaka.

Em′bry-o, *v.* Ka mole; ka makamua.

Em′er-ald, *n.* Pohaku momi; emerala.

E-mērġe′, *v.* E puka mai.

E-mēr′ġen-çy, *n.* Pilikia ulia wale mai; pilikia kuhewa.

Em′ēr-y, *n.* Lepo metala, mea anai.

E-mèt′ic, *n.* Laau hoo-luai.

Em′i-grant, *n.* Mea haalele aina ha-nau a noho ma ka aina e.

Em′i-grāte, *v.* E haalele aina hanau.

Em-i-grā′tion, *n.* Ka haalele aina.

Em′i-nençe, *n.* 1. Kahi kiekie. *On an eminence,* ma kahi kiekie. 2. Kulana kiekie. *Rise to eminence,* e pii i ke kulana kiekie.

Ém′i-nent, *adj.* Kiekie; kaulana. SYN. distinguished; celebrated.

Em′is-sa-ry, *n.* He kiu. SYN. spy.

E-mit′, *v.* 1. E hoopuka. *Emit a sound,* e hoopuka i leo. 2. E mohala; e moani. *To emit fragrance,* e moani.

E-mŏl′u-ment, *n.* Ka loaa; ka puka. *Emoluments of office,* na loaa o ka oihana.

E-mō′tion, *n.* 1. Pihoihoi. SYN. agitation. 2. Manao. SYN. feeling. *A joyful emotion,* he manao hauoli.

Ém′per-or, *n.* He Emepero.

Em′pha-sis, *n.* Ke kalele ana o ka leo.

Em′phä-size, *t.* E kalele leo. 2. E hoomaopopo lea.

Em-phăt′ic, *adj.* Loa. *An emphatic denial,* he hoole loa. 2. Koikoi; ano nui. *An emphatic thought,* he manao koikoi.

Em-phăt′ic-al-ly, *adv.* 1. Io; maoli. *Emphatically so,* pela io no; *or,* pela maoli no. 2. Me ka leo koikoi.

Ém′pire, *n.* 1. Aupuni o ka Emepero. 2. Ka mana nui.

Em-ploy′, *v.* 1. E lawelawe. SYN. use. 2. E hoolimalima. SYN. hire. 3. E hoohana; hoonauna. SYN. work.

Em-ploy′, *n.* Hana. *To be in the employ of one,* e noho ma ka hana o ke-kahi.

Em-ploy′er, *n.* Haku hana.

Em-ploy′ment, *n.* Hana; oihana. SYN. business; occupation.

Em-pow′er, *v.* E kau mana aku. SYN. authorize.

Em′press, *n.* Emepera wahine.

Emp′ti-ness, *n.* Ka nele; ka waiho kaawale ana.

Emp′ty, *adj.* Nele; hakahaka; kaawale. *An empty house,* he hale kaawale. *An empty head,* he poo hakahaka; *or,* he poo nele i ka ike.

Emp′ty, *v.* E ninini: e kiola aku.

Em′u-lāte, *v.* E hooikaika i like.

Em′u-lā′tion, *n.* Ka hooikaika ana i like. SYN. competition.

Ém′u-loŭs, *adj.* Ake nui e like.

En-ā′ble, *v.* E kokua. SYN. assist.

En-āct′, *v.* E hooholo i kanawai.

En-āct′ment, *n.* 1. He kanawai i hoo-holoia. SYN. act. 2. Ka hooholo ana i ke kanawai.

En-cãmp′ment, *n.* Wahi e hoomoana ai. SYN. camp.

En-chāin′, *v.* E hoopaa. *To enchain the attention,* e hoopaa i ka manao.

En-chànt′, *v.* 1. E hoohalua i ka ma-nao. 2. E hoohoihoi. SYN. delight. 3. E hana kilokilo. SYN. bewitch.

En-çir′cle, *v.* E hoopuni; e poai a puni.

En-core′ (ong-kōr′), *n.* E kahea e hana hou.

En-coŭn′ter, *v.* E halawai he alo he alo.

En-cŏur′aġe, v. E hoolana manao; e hoohoihoi.

En-cŏur′aġe-ment, n. Ka hooikaika ana i ka manao.

En-cŏur′aġ-ing, adj. Hoihoi; hoohoihoi.

En-crŏach′, v. E komo hewa. SYN. intrude.

En-crŏach′ment, n. Ke komo hewa ana. SYN. intrusion.

En-cŭm′ber, v. E hookaumaha; e hoohihia; hoopilikia. SYN. overload; embarrass.

En-cŭm′brançe, n. 1. He haawe kaumaha.

2. He aie′. An encumbered estate, he waiwai i hookaumahaia i ka aie′.

Én′çy-clo-pĕ′di-a, n. Buke hoike pokole no kela me keia mea.

Énd, n. Ka hopena. The end of all things, ka hopena o na mea a pau.

2. Ka piko. End of a rope, ka piko o ke kaula.

3. Ke kala. End of a house, ke kala o ka hale. SYN. gable.

4. Welau. End of a board, ka welau o ka papa. Ends of the earth, na welau o ka honua.

Énd, v. E hoopau; e hoo-oki.

En-dân′ġer, v. E hoopilikia.

En-dear′, v. E halialia ke aloha; e hoonui i ke aloha; e paiauma. Endearing affection, aloha paiauma.

En-dear′ment, n. Hana hoomilimili; hana hoala aloha.

En-deav′or, n. Ka hoao ana. SYN. effort; attempt.

Énd′ing, n. Ka pau ana.

Énd′less, adj. Pau ole; mau loa.

En-dôrse′, v. 1. E apono.

2. E kakau inoa ma ke kua o ka bila dala.

3. E kakau kokua i ka inoa ma ko hai bila aie′.

En-dŏw′, v. E hoolako. To endow a school, e hoolako ke kula i ke dala.

En-dŏw′ment, n. Ka hoolako ana.

En-dûr′ançe, n. Hoomanawanui; ahonui.

En-dûre′, v. 1. E hoomanawanui; e ahonui.

2. E mau. Endure for ever, e mau a mau loa.

Énd′ways,
Énd′wise, } adv. Ma ka welau.

Én′e-my, n. He enemi.

Én′er-ġĕt′ic, adj. Makaala; noke. SYN. active; vigorous.

Én′er-ġy, n. Ikaika o ka manao; kuoo; kamaehu. SYN. vigor; spirit.

E-nêr′văte, v. E hoonawaliwali; hoopalupalu. SYN. enfeeble.

Én′er-vă′tion, n. Ka hoonawaliwali ana. SYN. enfeeblement.

En-fôrçe′, v. E hooko′.

En-frän′chiṣe, v. E haawi i na pono makaainana.

En-gāġe′, v. 1. E kauoha. SYN. speak for.

2. E hoolimalima. SYN. hire.

3. E ae paa. SYN. agree.

4. E paa i ka hana. SYN. employ. Engaged in business, paa ma ka oihana; komo ma ka oihana.

5. E hoouka kaua.

En-gāġed′, adj. 1. Lilo. SYN. spoken for.

2. Hoopalau. SYN. betrothed; espoused.

3. Paa i ka hana. SYN. busy.

En-gāġe′ment, n. 1. Olelo paa. SYN. agreement.

2. Ka hoopalau ana. SYN. betrothal.

3. Hoouka kaua. SYN. combat; battle.

En-gāġ′ing, adj. Aulii; kohu. SYN. attractive.

Én′ġine, n. Enikini; mikini; mea kokua i ka hana o ka lima.

Én′ġin-eer′, n. 1. Kanaka malama enikini.

2. Civil engineer, kanaka ana aina; ana alanui, etc.

En′ġlish, adj. Beritania. English language, olelo Beritania.

En-grāve′, v. E kahakaha.

En-grāv′er, n. Mea kahakaha kii.

En-grāv′ing, n. 1. Ke kahakaha ana.

2. Kii i kahaia.

En-grŏss′, v, 1. E kakau poepoe.

2. E hoopaa. To engross the attention, e hoopaa loa i ka noonoo.

3. Lilo loa. The work engrosses all his time, lilo loa kona manawa i ka hana.

En-grŏss′ment, n. 1. Ke kakau poepoe.

2. Ka lilo loa ana o ka manao; a manawa paha.

En-hánçe′, v. E hoonui ae. SYN. increase.

E-nig′ma, n. Olelo nane. SYN. puzzle.

Én-jŏin′, v. 1. E kauoha; e koi.

2. E papa mamuli o ke kanawai.

En-jŏy′, v. E hoihoi; e lealea; e olioli.

En-jŏy′ment, n. He lealea; he olioli; he hauoli.

En-lârġe′, v. 1. E hoomahuahua; e hookea.

2. E hoonui olelo. Enlarge upon a subject, e hoonui olelo ma ke kumu manao.

En-light′en, v. E hoonaauao; hoo-malamalama. SYN. instruct.

En-light′en-ment, n. Ka hoonaauao ana.

En-list′, v. 1. E kakau inoa no kekahi oihana.

2. E hoala. To enlist the sympathy, e hoala i ka manao kokua.

En-list′ment, n. Ke komo ana. Enlistment in the cause of education, ke komo ana ma ka oihana hoonaauao.

En-liv′en, v. E hoo-hoihoi; hoo-eu-eu; hoo-lalelale.

Én′mi-ty, n. Ke ku-e′; enemi ma ka noho ana.

En-nō′ble, v. E hoohanohano.

E-nŏr′mi-ty, *n.* Ka ino loa; ka hohonu o ka ino. SYN. depravity.

E-nŏr′moŭs, *adj.* Nui loa; weliweli ka nui. SYN. immense.

E-noŭgh′ (e-nŭf), *adj.* Lawa. SYN. sufficient.

En-quire′, *v.* E ninau aku. SYN. inquire.

En-ráge′, *v.* E hoopiha i ka inaina.

En-rich′, *v.* 1. E hoolako. SYN. to make rich.
2. E kipulu. SYN. fertilize.

En-rŏll′, *v.* E kakau inoa ma ka papa inoa.

En-rŏll′ment, *n.* Ke kakau ana o ka inoa ma ka papa inoa.

En′sign, *n.* 1. Ka mea nana e lawe i ka hae.
2. He hae.

En-slāve′, *v.* E hookauwa kuapaa.

En-slāve′ment, *n.* Ka hookauwa ana.

En-sūe′, *v.* E hahai. *Evil will ensue,* e hahai auanei ka ino.

En-tān′gle, *v.* E hoohihia.

En′ter, *v.* 1. E hookomo. *To enter an account,* e hookomo i ka inoa ma ka buke helu.
2. *To enter a business,* e komo aku ma ka oihana.
3. *To enter an action,* e hoopii. SYN. sue.

En′ter-prïse, *n.* Hana nui. SYN. undertaking.

En′ter-prïs′ing, *adj.* Aa i ka hapai ana i ka hana nui.

En′ter-tāin′, *v.* 1. E hookipa. *Entertain strangers,* e hookipa i na malihini.
2. E hoo-oluolu; e hoo-hoihoi.

En′ter-tāin′er, *n.* Mea hookipa.

En′ter-tāin′ment, *n.* Ke kipa ana.

En-thū′si-ȧsm, *n.* Ka hoihoi o ka manao; ke ano hoolalelale.

En-thū′si-ȧst′ic, *adj.* Piha i ka hoihoi.

En-tïçe′, *v.* E hoowalewale; e onou.

En-tïçe′ment, *n.* Ka hoowalewale; ka onou ana. SYN. seduction.

En-tï′çer, *n.* Mea nana e hoowalewale; mea onou. SYN. seducer.

En-tïre′, *adj.* Holookoa; pauloa.

En-tïre′ly, *adv.* Loa. *Entirely finished,* pau loa i ka hana ia. SYN. completely. *Entirely subdued,* laka loa.

En-tï′tle, *v.* E hoo-kuleana.

En-tŏmb′ (tōom), *v.* E hookomo ma ka ilina.

En′to-mŏl′o-ġist, *n.* Kanaka ike no na mea kolo.

En′to-mŏl′o-ġy, *n.* Ka ike no na mea kolo.

En′trāils, *n.* Na naau liilii.

En′trȧnçe, *n.* 1. Ke komo ana.
2. Kahi e komo ai.

En-trȧnçe′, *v.* E hoohoihoi; hoohauoli. SYN. enrapture.

En-trȧp′, *v.* E hoohalua; e upiki. SYN. decoy.

En-trēat′, *v.* E koi; e noi haahaa. SYN. supplicate; petition.

En-trēat′y, *n.* Ka noi haahaa. SYN. supplication.

En′try, *n.* Ka entrance.

E-nū′mer āte, *v.* E helu pakaki.

E-nū′mer-ā′tion, *n.* Ka helu ana.

E-nŭn′çi-āte, *v.* E hai maopopo mai.

En-vĕl′op, *v.* 1. E hoopaapu. *Enveloped in smoke,* hoopaapuia i ka u-ahi.
2. E wahi′ i kekahi mea. SYN. wrap up.

Ĕn′vel-ōpe, *n.* 1. Wahi leta.
2. Wahi′. SYN. wrap.

Ĕn′vi-ous, *adj.* Hoo-huo′i; huahuwa′; keke′ue.

En-vi′rons, *n.* Na wahi e hoopuni ana i ke kulanakauhale.

Ĕn′voy, *n.* He elele kiekie o ke aupuni. SYN. ambassador.

Ĕn′vy, *v.* Huahuwa′; lili.

Ĕp′au-let, *n.* Lei poohiwi.

E-phēm′e-ral, *adj.* Hee wale; pau ko-ke. SYN. fleeting.

Ĕp′i-cūre, *n.* Kanaka manao nui i na mea ai me na mea inu.

Ep-i-dĕm′ic, *n.* He mai laha.

Ep-i-dĕr′mis, *n.* Ka ili. SYN. skin.

Ep-i-glŏt′tis, *n.* He uhi no ka puka e alakai ana i ke ake mama.

Ĕp′i-lep-sy, *n.* Mai lo′lo′.

E-pïs′co-pa-çy, *n.* Ka oihana bihopa.

E-pïs′co-pal, *adj.* Pili i ka ekalesia bihopa.

E-pïs′tle, *n.* Palapala. SYN. letter.

Ĕp′i-taph, *n.* He olelo i kahaia ma ka pohaku ilina.

Ĕp′i-thet, *n.* Hua olelo hoike pono i ke ano.

Ĕp′och (ĕp′ok), *n.* He wa kaulana.

Ēq′ua-ble, *adj.* Kaulike; kupono.

E′quäl, *n.* Mea like. *An equal,* he hoa ma ke kulana like.

E-quäl′i-ty, *n.* Ka like.

E′qual-ly, *adv.* Like a like.

E′qua-nim′i-ty, *n.* Oluolu o ka manao.

E-quā′tion, *n.* He kaulike; ke kau like ana o na kuaniti elua.

E-quā′tor, *n.* Poai waena honua.

E′qua-tō′ri-al, *adj.* Pili i ka poai waena.

E-quĕs′tri-an, *n.* Mea hooholo lio.

E′qŭi-ȧn′gu-lar, *adj.* Huina-like.

E′qui-dïs′tant, *adj.* Kaawale like.

E′qui-lăt′er-al, *adj.* Aoao like.

E′qui-lïb′ri-um, *n.* Kaumaha like.

E′quine, *adj.* Pili i ka lio.

E′qui-nŏc′tial, *adj.* or *n.* Ka poai waena o ke aouli; a hiki ka la ilaila ua li-ki ke ao me ka po ma na wahi a pau.

E′qui-nox, *n.* Ka wa i like a like ke ao me ka po ma na wahi a pau.

E-quïp′, *v.* E hoolako a makaukau.

Ĕq′ui-paġe (ĕk′wi-pej), *n.* 1. Na ukali o kela me keia ano.
2. Na kahiko o kela me keia ano.

E-quïp′ment, *n.* Na lako hoomakaukau.

E′qui-poise, *n.* Ke kaupaona like. Syn. equilibrium.

Éq′ui-ta-ble, *adj.* Kaulike; kupono. Syn. fair; just.

Éq′ui-ty, *n.* Ke kaulike; ka hoopono.

E-quiv′a-lent, *n.* Ka mea waiwai like.

E-quiv′o-cal, *adj.* Epa-epa; wahahee.

E-quiv′o-cate, *v.* E olelo epa; e hoopunipuni.

E′rä, *n.* He au; he wa. *The Christian era,* ke au Kristiano.

E-rad′i-cate, *v.* 1. E anai. Syn. erase. 2. E uhuki; e hehu ae. Syn. extirpate.

E-rãse′, *v.* E holoi. Syn. efface; obliterate. *To erase a writing,* e holoi i ka mea i kakauia.

E-rä′sion, } *n.* Ka holoi ana o ka mea
E-rä′sure, } i kahaia a kakauia paha.

Ere (âr), *prep.* and *adv.* Mamua; mamua′e.

E-rĕct′, *adj.* Ku pololei; kupono. Syn. perpendicular.

E-rĕct′, *v.* 1. E kukulu. 2. E hoo-ku′ pololei.

E-rĕc′tion, *n.* 1. Ke kukulu ana. 2. Ka mea i kukuluia.

Ére′lŏng′, *adv.* Aole liuliu.

Érr, *v.* E kuhihewa; e lalau.

Er′rand, *n.* He kumu hoounauna. *To send on an errand,* e hoounauna.

Er-rä′tic, *adj.* Keekee; kuawili.

Er-rä′tum, *n.* Hewa ma ka pai ana.

Er-rō′ne-oŭs, *adj.* Hewa; kuhihewa.

Er′ror, *n.* 1. Hewa. Syn. evil; sin. 2. Kuhihewa; lalau. Syn. mistake.

Er′u-dite, *adj.* Naauao. Syn. learned.

Er-u-di′tion, *n.* Ka naauao; ka ike. Syn. learning.

E-rŭp′tion, *n.* 1. He puupuu ma ke kino. 2. Ka pahu′ ana o ka pele.

Ér′y-sip′e-las, *n.* He mai ulaula kolo; ano laina.

Es-cãpe′, *v.* E holo a pakele; e hee aku. *Way of escape,* kahi e pakele ai.

Es-chéat′, *v.* E hoi hou i ka haku aina; a i ke aupuni paha.

Es-chew′, *v.* E haalele; e kaaokoa′ku. *Eschew evil,* e haalele i ka hewa. Syn. forsake; avoid.

Es-côrt′, *v.* 1. E huakai hoohanohano. 2. E ukali i mea malama.

Ês′cort, *n.* 1. He huakai hoohanohano. 2. He poe koa; mea malama.

És′cri-toir (es-cri-twär), *n.* Pahu kakau palapala. Syn. writing desk; secretary.

És′cu-lent, *n.* Mea kupono ke ai.

E-sŏph′a-gŭs, *n.* Ka puu. Syn. gullet.

Es-pē′cial-ly, *adv.* Oiaio hoi.

Ês′pi-on-age, *n.* Ka hoomaka′kiu.

Es′pla-nâde′, *n.* Wahi kaawale iloko o ke kulanakauhale.

Es-pŏus′al, *n.* Ka hoopalau ana.

Es-pŏuse′, *v.* 1. E hoopalau. Syn. betroth. 2. E kokua mamuli o kekahi mea.

Es-sãy′ *v.* E hoao. Syn. endeavor *Essay to go,* e hoao e hele.

És′say, *n.* He kumumanao i hakuia.

És′say-ist, *n.* Mea haku manao.

Es′sence, *n.* 1. He wai ala. 2. Ka i′o; ke ano nui. Syn. meaning.

Es-sĕn′tial, *adj.* Kupono loa. Syn. necessary.

Es-tăb′lish, *v.* 1. E hoonohonoho. *Establish boundaries,* e hoonohonoho palena aina. Syn. settle. 2. E hookumu; hookahua. *Establish schools,* e hookumu i na kula. 3. E hookupaa. *Establish principles,* e hookupaa i na loina.

Es-tăb′lish-ment, *n.* 1. Ka hoonohonoho ana. 2. Hale oihana. *A printing establishment,* he hale pai palapala.

Es-tãte′ *n.* 1. Waiwai. Syn. property. *Real estate,* waiwai paa. *Personal estate,* waiwai lewa. 2. Kulana. Syn. rank. *High estate,* kulana kiekie. 3. Kekahi o na mana o ke aupuni.

Es-teem′, *v.* E mahalo nui.

Ês′ti-ma-ble, *adj.* Mahaloia.

Ês′ti-mãte, *v.* E noonoo no ka nui o kekahi mea.

Ês′ti-mã′tion, *n.* 1. Ka noonoo ana. Syn. computation. 2. Ka mahalo. *A high estimation,* he mahalo nui.

Es-trãnge′, *v.* E hoohuli ku-e′. Syn. alienate.

Es-trãnge′ment, *n.* Ka hoohuli ku-e′ ana o ka manao. Syn. alienation.

Ês-trãy′, *n.* He holoholona hele hewa

E-tēr′nal, *adj.* Mai kinohi a mau loa aku. *The Eternal,* Ke Akua Mau Loa.

E-tēr′ni-ty, *n.* Ke Ao pau ole.

Éth′ics, *n.* Ka ike e pili ana i ka hoike uhane.

Eth-nŏl′o-ġy, *n.* Ka olelo e pili ana i kela me keia lahui, ma kona ano.

Êt′i-quette (ĕt′i-kĕt) *n.* Na rula no ka launa pono ana.

Êt′y-mŏl′o-ġist, *n.* Kanaka imi i ke ano o na hua olelo.

Êt′y-mŏl′o-ġy, *n.* Ka ike i imi i ke kumu o kela me keia hua olelo.

Eü′lo-ġize, *v.* E mahalo nui ma ka olelo.

Eü′lo-ġy, *n.* He haiolelo e haawi ana i ka mahalo. Syn. encomium.

Eü′pho-ny, *n.* Ke kani pono o ka leo ma ka puana leo.

Eü′ro-pē′an, *adj.* No Europa.

E-vãc′u-ãte, *v.* 1. E haalele. Syn. quit; vacate. 2. E hoonaha′ laau lapaau.

E-vãc′u-ã′tion, *n.* 1. Ka haalele ana. 2. Ka hoonaha′ ana. 3. Hana lepo.

E-vãde, *n.* E alo ae; e huli ae. Syn. avoid; elude.

Ĕv'a-nĕs'çent, *adj.* Pau wale; lele koke; hee wale; mahani. *The thought has escaped me,* mahani aku nei ka manao.

Ĕv'an-gĕl'ie-al, *adj.* Kulike me ka euanelio. SYN. orthodox.

E-vän'gel-ĭst, *n.* He haiolelo.

E-vän'gel-ize, *a.* E hoohuli mamuli o ka euanelio.

E-väp'o-rāte, *v.* E omo wai i ka wela.

E-väp'o-rā'tion, *n.* Ka omo ana o ka wai i ka wela.

E-vās'ive, *adj.* Lauwili; pololei ole. *An evasive answer,* he haina lauwili.

Ēve, *n.* Ahiahi. SYN. evening.

Ē'ven, *adj.* 1. Laumania. *An even surface,* ili laumania.
   2. Kau-like. *An even number,* helu kau-like.
   3. (*Adv.*) *Even so,* pela i'o no.

Ĕv'en-ing, *n.* Ka na-po' ana o ka la; ke ahiahi; ka liula'.

Ē'ven-ly, *adv.* Like a like. *To divide evenly,* e mahele like a like.

E-vĕnt', *n.* 1. He hana nui; he ouli.
   2. Ka mea i koia.

E-vent'ful, *adj.* Paapu i na hana nui.

Ē'ven-tide, *n.* SYN. evening.

Ĕv'er, *adv.* 1. Kekahi wa.
   2. Mau. *Forever and ever,* mau, a mau; ia ao aku. ia ao aku.

Ĕv'er-glāde, *n.* Aina i uhiia i ka wai a me ke mauu.

Ĕv'er-green, *n.* Laau uliuli mau.

Ĕv'er-lāst'ing, *adj.* Mau loa. SYN. eternal.

Ĕv'er-y, *adj.* Pau loa. *Each and every one,* pau loa, kela me keia.

Ĕv'er-y-whêre, *adv.* Ma na wahi a pau; huli moku.

E-vĭet', *v.* E kipaku. SYN. eject.

E-vĭe'tion, *n.* Ke kipaku ana. SYN. ejection.

Ĕv'i-dençe, *n.* Olelo hoike. SYN. testimony.

Ĕv'i-dent, *adj.* Moakaka; maopopo lea.

Ĕv'i-dent-ly, *adv.* Maopopo lea.

E'vil, *n.* 1. He ino. SYN. sin; hewa.
   2. Poino. SYN. disaster.

E-vinçe', *v.* E hoike. SYN. show. *To evince determination,* e hoike i ka manao paa.

E-vōke', *a.* 1. E kahea. *To evoke assistance,* e kahea i kokua. SYN. call forth.
   2. E hoike. *To evoke the powers of the mind,* e hoike mai i na mana o ka noonoo.

Ĕv'o-lū'tion, *n.* Ka hoomohala ana, mai ke kumu mai.

E-vōlve', *v.* E hoomohala no loko mai; e unuhi ae no loko mai.

Ewe (yū), *n.* Hipa wahine.

Ew'er (yūer,) *n.* Pika wai.

Ex̱-ăct', *adj.* Like loa. SYN. precise.

Ex̱-ăet', *v.* E koi. *Exact tribute,* e koi i ka auhau.

Ex̱-ăet'ing, *adj.* Paakiki; oolea. *An exacting man,* he kanaka paakiki.

Ex̱-ăe'tion, *n.* 1. Ke koi ana me ka mana o ke kanawai.
   2. Ka mea i koi ia.

Ex̱-ăet'ly, *adv.* 1. Pela i'o. *Exactly so,* pela i'o no. SYN. precisely.
   2. Like loa.

Ex̱-ăg'ger-āte, *v.* E hoonui ae; e haanui.

Ex̱-ăg'ger-āt-ed, *adj.* Oi ae i ko ka oiaio.

Ex̱-ăg'ger-ā'tion, *n.* Ka hoonui ana mamua o ka mea oiaio; ka haanui ana.

Ex̱-ălt', *v.* 1. E hookiekie ae. *Righteousness exalteth a nation,* hookiekie ae la ka pono i ka lahui.
   2. E hoano. SYN. laud; praise.

Ex̱'al-tā'tion, *n.* 1. Ka hookiekie ana.
   2. Ka hoano ana.

Ex̱-ălt'ed, *adj.* 1. Kiekie. SYN. high.
   2. Hookiekieia'e. SYN. elevated.

Ex̱-ăm'i-nā'tion, *n.* 1. Ka imi ana; ka huli ana. SYN. investigation.
   2. He hoike. *A school examination,* he hoike kula.

Ex̱-ăm'ine, *v.* 1. E mili. SYN. look into carefully.
   2. Ninaninau. *Examine a witness,* e ninaninau i ka hoike.
   3. E hoike. *Examine a school,* e hoike kula.

Ex̱-ăm'in-er, *n.* Mea nana e mili; nana e hoike, etc.

Ex̱-ăm'ple, *n.* 1. He ninau hoomaamaa.
   2. He kumu hoohalike. SYN. pattern.

Ex̱-ăs'per-āte, *v.* E hoonaukiuki.

Ex̱-ăs'per-ā'tion, *n.* Ka ukiuki ino.

Ĕx'ca-vāte, *v.* Ekohi; e eli. SYN. dig.

Ĕx'ea-vā'tion, *n.* Ka lua i eliia.

Ex-çeed' *v.* E oi aku; e pakela'ku. SYN. surpass; transcend.

Ex-çeed'ing-ly, *adv.* Loa. *Exceedingly small,* makalii loa. *Exceedingly great,* nunui loa.

Ex-çel', *v.* E kela. SYN. surpass; exceed.

Ĕx'çel-lençe, *n.* Ka maikai oi.

Ĕx'çel-len-çy, *n.* Inoa hanohano no ke kiaaina, a kuhina aupuni paha.

Ĕx'çel-lent, *adj.* Maikai oi; kilohana.

Ex-çĕpt', *v.* 1. E hoohalahala; e ku-e' i ka olelo. SYN. object.
   2. E hookoe. SYN. exclude.

Ex-çĕpt', *prep.* 1. Koe. SYN. not including.
   2. Ke ole. SYN. unless.

Ex-çĕpt'ing, *prep.* Koe; koe nae.

Ex-çĕp'tion, *n.* 1. Ke ku-e' ana i ka olelo.
   2. Ka mea pili ole; ka mea i koe.

Ex-çĕp'tion-a-ble, *adj.* Kupono ole; ku i ka hoohalahala ia.

Ex-çĕss', *n.* 1. Ka mea kaulele; ka oi.
   2. Ka u'ha-u'ha. SYN. dissipation.

Ex-çĕs'sive, *adj.* Kaulele; oi pakela.

Ex-chānge', *v.* E haawi panai; e panai.

Ex-chānge', *n.* Kahi e kuka'ai o ka poe kalepa. *Merchants' exchange,* hui kuka' o ka poe kalepa.

Ex-cheq'uer (eks-chĕk-er), *n.* Waihona dala o ke aupuni.

Ex'cise, *n.* Ka dute waiwai. SYN. duty.

Ex-cit'a-ble, *adj.* Pihoihoi wale; puiwa; kapalili wale ka houpo.

Ex-cite', *v.* 1. E hoohoihoi; e hoopihoihoi.

2. E hooeueu; e hoolalelale. SYN. incite.

3. E hoala. *Excite a disturbance*, e hoala i ka haunaele.

Ex-cit'ing, *p. a.* Hoopihoihoi; hoopilihua. *Exciting times*, wa hoopilihuaai ka manao.

Ex-cite'ment, *n.* 1. Ka pihoihoi.

2. Ka hoihoi o ka naau.

3. Uluao'a; haunaele. SYN. disturbance.

Ex-claim', *v.* E kahea nui; e hoo'ho.

Ex'cla-ma'tion, *n.* He kahea nui; he hoo'ho leo.

Ex'cla-ma'tion point, *n.* Kiko puiwa (!).

Ex-clam'a-to-ry, *adj.* Ano hoo'ho; ano puiwa o ka leo.

Ex-clude', *v.* E pani aku; e pale aku iwaho. SYN. debar.

Ex-clu'sive, *adj.* 1. Helu ole ia. SYN. excepting.

2. Ihiihi; noho kaawale; launa ole.

Ex-clu'sive-ly, *adv.* Wale no. *Yours exclusively*, nou wale no.

Ex'com-mu'ni-cate, *v.* E oki aku.

Ex-cres'cence, *n.* He puu ulu wale mai.

Ex-cru'ci-at-ing, *adj.* Mahuahua loa o ka eha.

Ex-cul'pate, *v.* E kaaokoa i ka hewa. SYN. exonerate.

Ex-cur'sion, *n.* Ka hele makaikai i kau wahi.

Ex-cus'a-ble, *adj.* Kupono ke kalaia.

Ex-cuse, (ex-kūz'), *v.* E kala.

Ex-cuse' (ex-kūs'), *n.* He olelo apono. SYN. apology.

Ex'e-cra-ble, *adj.* Ino loa. SYN. detestable.

Ex'e-crate, *v.* E hooino; e olelo ino. SYN. curse.

Ex'e-cute, *v.* 1. E hooko'. SYN. perform.

2. E hoomake, mamuli o ke kanawai.

Ex'e-cu'tion, *n.* 1. Ka hooko' ana. SYN. performance.

2. Ka hoomake ana.

Ex'e-cu'tion-er, *n.* Kanaka hoomake mamuli o ke kanawai.

Ex-ec'u-tive, *n* Mana, a poe paha, hooko kanawai.

Ex-ec'u-tor, *n.* Kahu hooko kauoha no ka waiwai hooilina.

Ex-ec'u-trix, *n.* Kahu wahine hooko' kauoha.

Ex-em'pla-ry, *adj.* Kupono ke hoohalike ia.

Ex-em'pli-fy, *v.* E hoikeike hoomaamaa.

Ex-empt', *adj.* Hookuuia. *Exempt from taxation*, hookuuia mai ka auhau.

Ex-empt', *v.* E hookuu; e hookaawale.

Ex-emp'tion, *n.* Ka hookuu ana. *Exemption from taxes*, ka hookuu ana mai na auhau.

Ex'er-cise, *n.* 1. Ka hooikaika kino.

2. He haawina hoomaamaa.

Ex'er-cise, *v.* 1. E hooikaika kino.

2. E hoohana. SYN. employ; use.

Ex-ĕrt', *v.* 1. E hoo-eu'eu; hoolalelale.

2. E hooikaika. SYN. put forth effort.

Ex-ēr'tion, *n.* Ka hooikaika ana. SYN. effort. *Great exertion*, ka hooikaika nui.

Ex-hale', *v.* E moani; e mohala. SYN. emit.

Ex-haust', *v.* 1. E hoopau. SYN. spend.

2. E paupauaho. SYN. weary.

3. E hoomaluhiluhi loa. SYN. tire out.

Ex-haus'tion, *n.* 1. Ka paupauaho.

2. Maluhiluhi; naenae. SYN. weariness.

3. Ka hoopau loa ana.

Ex-haust'less, *adv.* Pau ole. SYN. unlimited.

Ex-hib'it, *v.* E hoike; e hoikeike. SYN. show; display. *To exhibit goods*, e hoikeike i na waiwai.

Ex'hi-bi'tion, *n.* 1. He hoikeike. *International exhibition*, he hoikeike o na lahui nui.

2. He hoike hai olelo. *A school exhibition*, hoike haiolelo no ke kula.

Ex-hil'a-rate, *v.* E hoo-eu'eu'; hoohoihoi. SYN. cheer; enliven.

Ex-hil'a-ra'tion, *n.* Ka hoihoi o ka manao. SYN. animation.

Ex-hort', *v.* E paipai; e kauleo. SYN. counsel.

Ex'hor-ta'tion, *n.* Olelo paipai.

Ex-hort'er, *n.* Mea paipai.

Ex-hume', *v.* E huai. SYN. disinter.

Ex'i-gen-cy, *n.* Pilikia kuhewa; pili kia ku i ka wa. SYN. necessity.

Ex-ile, *n.* He kuewa.

Ex-on'er-ate, *v.* E kaaokoa i ka hewa. SYN. exculpate.

Ex-ŏr'bi-tant, *adj.* Kaulele; pakela loa. SYN. excessive.

Ex-ŏr'cise, *v.* E mahiki.

Ex-ŏt'ic, *n.* Mea ulu malihini ma ka aina.

Ex-pand', *v.* 1. E hoomohala. SYN. bloom.

2. E moana. SYN. spread out.

Ex-panse', *n.* Ke akea. *The expanse of the heavens*, ke akea o na lani.

Ex-pan'sion, *n.* 1. Ka mohala ana.

2. Ka hooakea ana.

Ex-pa'ti-ate, *v.* E hooakea i ka olelo; e kamailio akea.

Ex-pa'tri-ate, *v.* E wailana. SYN. banish.

Ex-pect', *v.* E kakali.

Ex'pec-ta'tion, *n.* 1. Ke kali ana o ka manao.

2. Makemake. SYN. desire.

Ex-pec'to-rant, *n.* Laau kunu.

Ex-pec'to-rate, *v.* E kuha.

Ex-pē'di-en-çy, *n.* Ke kupono. SYN. desirableness.

Ex-pē'di-ent, *adj.* Kupono. SYN. desirable.

Ex'pe-dite, *v.* E hoohikiwawe. SYN. hasten; accelerate.

Ex'pe-di'tion, *n.* 1. Ka hikiwawe; ka wikiwiki.

2. He hana nui.

Ex'pe-di'tioŭs, *adj.* Hikiwawe; wikiwiki.

Ex-pĕl', *v.* E hookuke; e kipaku.

Ex-pĕnd', *v.* E hoolilo. SYN. spend.

Ex-pĕnd'i-ture, *n.* Ka hoolilo ana.

Ex-pĕnse', *n.* Lilo. SYN. cost.

Ex-pĕn'sive, *adj* .Nui o ka lilo; kumu kuai nui.

Ex-pē'ri-ençe, *n.* Ka ike i loaa mamuli o ka hana; he ike iho.

Ex-pē'ri-ençed, *adj.* Makaukau mamuli o ka ike iho. *An experienced man,* he kanaka i ike nona iho.

Ex-pĕr'i-ment, *n.* Hana hoao.

Ex-pĕrt', *adj.* Noeau; akamai. SYN. skilful; handy.

Ex'pi-āte, *v.* E huikala. SYN. atone.

Ex'pi-ā'tion, *n.* Ka huikala ana. SYN. atonement.

Ex-pire', *v.* 1. E make. SYN. die.

2. E pio. SYN. go out. *The fire expires,* ke pio nei ke ahi.

3. Pau. *The time expires,* ke pau nei ka manawa.

Ex-plāin', *v.* E wehewehe; e kuailo. SYN. expound.

Ex'pla-nā'tion, *n.* Ka wehewehe ana.

Ex-plăn'a-to-ry, *adj.* Hoakaka ana; wehewehe ana.

Ex'pli-ca-ble, *adj.* Hiki ke wehewehe. SYN. explainable.

Ex-pliç'it, *adj.* Moakaka. SYN. plain; clear.

Ex-plōde', *a.* E pahu'; e poha'. SYN. burst.

Ex'ploit, *n.* Hana hookaulana.

Ex'plo-rā'tion, *n.* Ka imi ana i na wahi, me na mea i ike ole ia.

Ex-plōre', *v.* E makaikai i na mea, me na wahi hou.

Ex-plō'sion, *n.* Ka pahu' ana; ka poha' ana. SYN. bursting.

Ex-pō'nent, *n.* 1. Hoailona kuhikuhi mana, x=x, mana elua.

2. Hoailona hoike. SYN. index. *An exponent of the mind,* he hoailona hoike manao.

Ex-pōrt', *v.* E hooili waiwai i na aina e.

Ex'pōr-tā'tion, *n.* Ka hooili ana i ka waiwai.

Ex-pōrt'er, *n.* Mea hooili waiwai i ka hi e.

Ex'pōrts, *n.* Na waiwai o ka aina i hooiliia'ku.

Ex-pōse', *v.* 1. E hoike akea. *Expose falsehood,* e hoike akea i ka wahahee.

2. E waiho wale. *Exposed to the rain,* waiho wale ia i ka u'-a.

Ex-po-ṣi'tion, *n.* 1. Ka wehewehe ana. SYN. expounding; interpretation.

2. Ka hoikeike ana. SYN. exhibition.

Ex-pŏṣ'i-tor, *n.* He wehewehe olelo. SYN. expounder.

Ex-pŏst'u-lāte, *v.* E papa' ikaika. SYN. remonstrate.

Ex-pŏṣ'ure, *n.* 1. Ka hoike akea ana.

2. Ka waiho wale ana. *Exposure to the sun,* ka waiho wale ana i ka la.

Ex-pound', *v.* E wehewehe. SYN. explain.

Ex-press', *v.* 1. E hoakaka; e hai aku. SYN. utter; declare; intimate.

2. E hoike. SYN. indicate; signify.

Ex-press', *adj.* 1. Ano hookahi. *The express image of his father,* ke ano hookahi no me kona makua kane.

2. *Express purpose,* ia kumu hookahi no.

Ex-press', *n.* 1. *Express messenger,* he kanaka kukini.

2. *Express company,* he hui e hoohikiwawe i ka hooili ana i ka ukana.

3. Kaa halihali ohua.

Ex-prĕs'sion, *n.* 1. He olelo. SYN. phrase.

2. Ka hoakaka ana. SYN. intimating.

3. Ke ano. *A pleasing expression of countenance,* ke ano oluolu o ka helehelena.

Ex-press'ive, *adj.* 1. Ano nui. *An expressive phrase,* he olelo ano nui, olelo hohonu.

Ex-press'ly, *adv.* 1. Pololei loa. *He told me so expressly,* hai pololei loa mai oia ia'u pela.

2. Wale no. *Expressly for you,* nou wale no.

Ex-pŭl'sion, *n.* Ka hookuke ana; ke kipaku ana.

Ex-pŭnge', *v.* E kapai; e holoi aku. *Expunge from the laws,* e kapai mai na kanawai.

Ex-quiṣ'ite, *adj.* Eleu; aulii; nani.

Ex-tănt', *adj.* E noho nei; e waiho nei. *Extant writings,* na palapala e waiho nei.

Ex-tĕm'po-re, *adv.* Noonoo ole ia mamua; ku i ka wa. *An extempore speech,* haiolelo ku i ka wa. SYN. off hand.

Ex-tem'po-riṣe, *v.* E haku wale i ka olelo.

Ex-tĕnd', *v.* 1. E hoo-akea; hoo-moana; e hoopalahalaha. *Extend his dominion,* e hoo-akea i kona aupuni.

2. E kikoo; e o mai. SYN. stretch forth.

3. E hooloihi. SYN. lengthen. *Extend the time,* e hooloihi i ka manawa.

4. E hoolaha. SYN. publish. *To extend notice,* e hoolaha i ka olelo hoolaha.

5. E hohola; e uhola. SYN. stretch. *Extend the awning,* e hohola i ke anini. *Extend help,* e haawi i ke kokua; or, e kokua.

Ex-tĕn'sive, *adj.* 1. Laulaha; akea; moana. SYN. broad; expansive.

2. Nui. *Extensive preparations*, hoomakaukau nui. *Extensive fire*, he ahi nui.
Ex-tĕn′sive-ly, *adv.* Laulaha; akea.
Ex-tĕnt′, *n.* 1. Ke akea. SYN. expanse.
2. Palena. *The extent of the law*, ka palena o ke kanawai. SYN. bounds.
Ex-tĕn′u-āte, *v.* E pale i ka hewa. SYN. palliate.
Ex-tĕ′ri-or, *n.* Ko waho. SYN. outside.
Ex-tĕr′mi-nāte, *v.* E luku loa; e hoopio loa. SYN. extirpate.
Ex-tĕr′nal, *adj.* No waho; mawaho. SYN. outside.
Ex-tĕr′nal-ly, *adv.* Ma ko waho.
Ex-tĕr′nal̦s, *n.* Na nanaina o waho.
Ex-tinet′, *adj.* Pio; nalo; nalowale. *An extinct crater*, he luapele i pio.
Ex-tine′tion, *n.* Ka pio ana; ka nalo ana. *The extinction of the race*, ka pio ana o ka lahui.
Ex tin′guish, *v.* 1. E hoopio. *Extinguish the race*, e hoopio i ka lahui. *Extinguish the fire*, e hoopio i ke ahi.
2. E kinai.
Ex-tir′pāte, *v.* 1. E uhuki loa. *Extirpate weeds*, e uhuki loa i na nahelehele. SYN. eradicate; exterminate.
2. E hoopau loa.
Ex-tŏl′, *v.* E hoolea; e hoonani. SYN. praise.
Ex-tŏrt′, *v.* 1. E alunu. *Extort money*, e alunu dala; e pakaha.
2. E kaohi. *To extort a confession*, e kaohi i olelo ae.
Ex-tŏr′tion-er, *n.* Kanaka alunu.
Ex′traet, *n.* 1. He mahele o ka olelo.
2. Ka i′-o̧o kekahi mea.
Ex-trăet′, *v.* E unuhi ae; e wehe ae.
Ex-trăe′tion, *n.* 1. Ka unuhi ana; ka wehe ana.
2. He kuauhau; he kumu. *Of Hawaiian extraction*, no ke kumu Hawaii.
Ex′tra-di′tion, *n.* Ka hoihoi kuikahi ana o na lawehala iwaena o na aupuni.
Ex′tra-ŏr′di-nā-ry, *adj.* Kupaianaha.

Ex-trăv′a-gaṇçe, *n.* U′hau′ha waiwai. SYN. prodigality.
Ex-trăv′a-gant, *adj.* 1. U′hau′ha wale ka waiwai.
2. Oiaio ole. SYN. exaggerated.
Ex-trême′, *n.* 1. Ka mua me ka ha o na kuaniti o ke kau-kolu.
2. Ka welau; ka hope loa.
Ex-trême′, *adj.* 1. *Extreme punishment*, ka hoopai nui loa.
2. *Extreme measures*, na hana oolea loa.
Ex-trême′ly, *adv.* Loa. *Extremely slow*, lohi loa.
Ex-trĕm′i-ty, *n.* 1. Ka hope loa; ka welau.
2. *The extremity of pain*, ka nui loa ana o ka hui.
Ĕx′tr′-eāte, *v.* E hoohemo mai ka pilikia.
Ex-ū′ber-ançe, *n.* Ka piha oi. *Exuberance of joy*, ka piha oi o ka hauoli.
Ex-ū′bĕr-ant, *adj.* Piha oi. *Exuberant joy*, hauoli piha.
Ex-ūde′, *v.* E kulu mai; e kahe mai.
Ex-ŭlt′, *v.* E hauoli; e olioli. SYN. rejoice.
Ex′ul-tā′tion, *n.* Hauoli nui. SYN. joy.
Ēye (i), *n.* Maka.
Ēye′bal̦l, *n.* Onohi maka.
Ēye′brŏw, *n.* Kuekue maka.
Ēye′glass, *n.* Maka aniani; aniani maka.
Ēye′lid, } *n.* Lihilihi maka.
Ēye′lash, }
Ēye′lĕss, *adj.* Maka ole.
Ēye′sĕrv′ant, *n.* Kauwahoomaka′kiu.
Ēye′sĕrv′içe, Hana hoomaka′kiu.
Ēye′sight, *n.* Ka ike o ka maka.
Ēye′sore, *n.* Mea ehai ka maka.
Ēye′tŏŏth′, *n.* Ka niho malalo pono o ka maka.
Ēye′wä′ter, *n.* Wai hamo maka.
Ēye-wĭt′ness, *n.* Mea ike maka; he ike maka.

F

Fā′ble, *n.* Olelo nane; e hoike ana no kekahi kumu oiaio.
Făb′riç, *n.* 1. Mea i hana ia, like me ka hale, uapo, etc.
2. Mea i hana ia, like me ka lole.
Făb′ri-eāte, *a.* 1. E hana lima. SYN. manufacture.
2. E kukulu. *Fabricate a lie*, e kukulu i wahahee.
Făb′u-loùs, *adj.* Oiaio ole.

Fāçe, *n.* 1. Helehelena; maka.
2. Alo. SYN. front. *Face of a building*, ke alo o ka hale.
Fāçe, *v.* E ku he alo he alo.
2. E alo. *Face opposition*, e alo i ke ku-e′ ia mai.
Fa-çē′tioùs, *adj.* Lealea.
Fa-çĭl′-i-tāte, *v.* E hoowiwi; e hoohikiwawe. SYN. expedite.

Fa-çil'i-ty, *n.* Hikiwale; hikiwawe. Syn. ease.

Fac-sim'i-le, *n.* Ka lua like.

Fact, *n.* He oiaio; mea i hookoia.

Fac'tor, *n.* 1. Helu hana.

2. He agena; he hope.

Fac'to-ry, *n.* Hale oihana hana lima. Syn. manufactory.

Fac-tō'tum, *n.* Kauwa lawelawe akea. Syn. manufactory.

Fac'ul-ty, *n.* 1. Ka mana. Syn. power. *Faculty of speech*, ka mana e kamailio.

2. He poe kumuao o ke kula nui.

Fāde, *v.* 1. E mae; e luhe'; e loha Syn. droop; wilt.

2. E akeakea. Syn. bleach.

Fād'ed, *adj.* Ahiahia. Syn. bleached.

Fād'ing, *adj.* Mae; luhe'.

Fāg, *v.* 1. E hooluhi wale.

2. *Completely fagged out*, maluhiluhi loa.

Fāg'end, *n.* Koena waiwai ole.

Fāg'ot, *n.* Laolao laau.

Fāil, *v.* 1. E haule. *To fail in a lesson*, e haule ma ka haawina.

2. E poho. *To fail in business*, e poho ma ka oihana.

3. E nawaliwali. *To fail in health*, e nawaliwali ma ke ola kino.

Fāil'ure, *n.* 1. Ka haule ana.

2. Poho ma ka oihana.

3. Ka nawaliwali o ke kino.

Fāint, *adj.* Naenae; nawaliwali.

Fāint, *v.* E ma-u'le.

Fāint'-heārt'ed, *adj.* Puiwa wale; ma-ka'u wale. Syn. timid.

Fāint'ly, *adv.* 1. Nawaliwali. *Speak faintly*, kamailio nawaliwali.

2. Powehiwehi. *See faintly*, e ike po-wehiwehi.

Fāir, *adj.* 1. Pono; kaulike.

2. Onaona; upalu. *A fair woman*, he wahine onaona.

3. Maikai. *Fair weather*, wa maikai.

Fāir, *n.* He fea. Syn. exhibition.

Fāir'ly, *adv.* Me ke kaulike; me ka pololei.

Fāir'ness, *n.* 1. Ka pono; ke kaulike.

2. Ka maikai o ke kino, a helehelena paha.

Fāir'y, *n.* He kupua.

Fāith, *n.* He paulele; manaoio.

Fāith'ful, *adj.* Kupaa; oiaio. Syn. steadfast.

Fāith'ful-ly, *adv.* Me ka oiaio.

Fāith'less, *adj.* 1. Manaoio ole; hoo-maloka.

2. Ano kumakaia.

Fall, *v.* 1. E haule. Syn. drop.

2. E hina ilalo. Syn. tumble down (of men or animals).

3. E hiolo. Syn. tumble (of buildings).

Fall, *n.* 1. Ka haule ana; hiolo ana; hina ana.

2. Wailele. Syn. waterfall.

3. Kau haule lau. Syn. Autumn.

Fal-lā'çioûs, *adj.* Wahahee; oiaio ole.

Fāl'la-çy, *n.* Ka wahahee; ka oiaio ole. Syn. falsity.

Fāl'li-ble, *adj.* Hikiwawe i ka lalau; ke kuihee.

Fall'ing-stär, *n.* Hoku lele. Syn. shooting-star; meteor.

Fāl'low, *adj.* Mahakea.

Fạlse, *adj.* Wahahee.

Fạlse'hood, *n.* He wahahee; he hoo-punipuni.

Fạl'si-ty, *v.* E hoopunipuni. *To falsify accounts*, e kakau hoopunipuni i na helu.

Fạl'ter, *v.* E haalulu; e kulanalana. Syn. tremble; hesitate.

Fạl'ter-ing, *adj.* Kulanalana. Syn. hesitating.

2. Haalulu, *faltering accents*, leo haa-lulu.

Fāme, *n.* Ka lono; ke kaulana. Syn. celebrity; renown.

Fāmed, *adj.* Kaulana. Syn. renown; celebrated.

Fa-mil'iar, *adj.* Maa; walea; ike lea ia.

Fa-mil'iar-ise, *v.* E hoomaamaa; e walea.

Fa-mil-iar'i-ty, *n.* Ano maa; walea.

Fa-mil'iar-ly, *adv.* Me ka walea.

Fām'i-ly, *n.* Ohana; mamo.

Fām'ine, *n.* Wi.

Fām'ish, *v.* E make i ka pololi. Syn. starve.

Fā'moûs, *adj.* Kaulana.

Fān, *n.* He peahi.

Fa-nāt'ic, *n.* Kanaka manaoio me ka noonoo ole.

Fān'çy, *n.* Manao ulia wale.

Fān'çy, *v.* E manao wale. Syn. im-agine.

Fāng, *n.* Niho holoholona.

Fär, *adj.* Mamao; ma-o' loa.

Fārçe, *n.* Hana hoo-akaaka.

Fāre, *n.* Uku moku; uku kaa.

2. He ai. Syn. food. *Good fare*, ai maikai.

Fāre'well, *interjec.* Aloha; no ke kaa-wale ana. Syn. good-by.

Färm, *n.* He mahina ai.

Färm, *v.* E mahi-ai.

Färm'er, *n.* Kanaka mahi ai.

Färm'ing, *n.* Ka mahi ana i ka aina.

Fär'ri-er, *n.* 1. Kanaka kapili wawae hao.

2. Kanaka lapaau lio.

Fär'ther, } *adv,* Mao aku.

Für'ther, }

Fär'thing, *n.* He palekini.

Fäs'çi-nāte, *v.* E hoohoihoi i ka ma-nao. Syn. captivate.

Fāsh'ion, *n.* Ka mea i hoomahuiia.

2. 2. Ke ano mau.

Fāsh'ion, *v.* E hana. Syn. make.

Fāsh'ion-a-ble, *adj.* Hoomahuiia.

Fāst, *v.* E hooke' ai.

Fāst, *adj.* 1. Paa. Syn. tight.

2. Ma'ma'. Syn. swift.

3. Uhauha. Syn. dissipated.

Fāst'day, *n.* La hooke' ai.

Fāst'en, *v.* 1. E hoopaa; e makia; e kakia. *Fasten slightly*, maulihilihi.

Fàst'en-ing, n. Mea hoopaa; he ma-
kia.
Fas-tïd'i-oŭs, adj. Palawaiki; aulii
Fàt, n. Kelekele; aila holoholona.
Fàt, adj. Momona; puipui.
Fā'tal, adj. Make. SYN. deadly. Fa-
tal sickness, mai make.
Fā'tal-ly, adv. E make ai. Injured fa-
tally, eha e make ai.
Fāte, n. Hopena.
Fä'ther, n. Makuakane To father, e
hookama.
Fä'ther-länd, n. Aina makua.
Fä'ther-less, adj. Makuakane ole.
Fä'ther-ly, adv. Me he makuakane la.
SYN. paternal.
Fàth'om, n. Anana.
Fàth'om, v. E ana i ka hohonu.
Fàth'om-less, adj. 1. Hohonu palena
ole.
2. Lipolipo. The fathomless ocean, ka
moana lipolipo.
Fa-tigue' (fateeg'), n. Luhi; maloe-
loe; maluhiluhi.
2. Mao'pao'pa. SYN. fatigue through
walking.
Fät'ten, v. E hanai i momona.
Fau'cĕt, n. Mea ukuhi wai.
Fault, n. 1. Hewa.
2. Kina'. SYN. blemish.
Fault'less, adj. 1. Hewa ole. SYN.
perfect.
2. Kina' ole. SYN. unblemished.
Fault'y, adj. Hewa; pono ole.
Fau'na, n. Na mea ola a pau o ka aina.
Fā'vor, n. 1. Lokomaikai. SYN. kindness.
2. He kokua. To do a favor, e kokua
lokomaikai.
Fā'vor, v. 1. E kokua lokomaikai.
2. E maliu.
Fā'vor-a-ble, adj. 1. Kupono. A
favorable wind, he makani pa pono mai.
2. Maliu; oluolu. Favorable to the cause,
maliu i ka aoao; or, oluolu i ka aoao.
Fā'vor-a-bly, adv. Apono. To think
favorably of a thing, e manao apono aku
i kekahi mea.
Fā'vor-ite, n. He milimili; he puna-
hele.
Fā'vor-it-ïsm, n. Ewaewa o ka hana.
Fàwn, v. E hoopilimeaai.
Fear, n. Maka'u; puiwa; weliweli.
Fear, v. E maka'u; e puiwa. SYN.
dread.
Fear'ful, adj. 1. Puiwa; maka'u. SYN.
afraid.
2. Weliweli; eehia. SYN. dreadful;
terrible.
Fear'less, adj. Maka'u ole; wiwo ole;
SYN. bold.
Fear'less-ly, adv. Makoa me ka ma-
ka'u ole.
Fear'less-ness, n. Ke ano wiwo ole.
SYN. boldness.
Feas-i-ble, adj. Hiki ke hookoia; hiki
wale no. SYN. practicable.
Fēast, n. Ahaaina.

Fēast, v. 1. E ai a nui.
2. E kukulu i ahaaina.
Fēat, n. He hana kupaianaha.
Fēath'er, n. Hulu manu.
Fēat'üre, n. 1. Helehelena.
2. Hiohiona.
Fĕb'ri-fŭġe, n. Laau lapaau mai wela.
Fĕb'rū-a-ry, n. Feberuari.
Fĕd'er-al, adj. Hui. Federal government, aupuni hui.
Fee, n. 1. Na koina o ke kanawai.
2. Uku o ka loio.
Fee'ble, adj. Nawaliwali; palupalu.
Fee'ble-ness, n. 1. Ka palupalu.
2. Ka nawaliwali.
Feed, v. E hanai.
Feed, n. Ai na na holoholona.
Feel, v. 1. E ha'ha'. SYN. touch
2. E manaonao. SYN. pity; sympa-
thize.
3. SYN. to be. To feel happy; or to be
happy, e olioli; ua oluolu.
4. SYN. think. How do you feel about
it; or, what do you think about it, pehea
kou manao no ia mea?
Feel'ing, n. 1. Ka ha'ha' ana. SYN.
touch.
2. Manao. An angry feeling, he manao
huhu.
3. Ka hoomaopopo ana. SYN. sense.
A feeling of pain; or, a sense of pain, ka
hoomaopopo ana i ka eha.
Feel'ing-ly, adv. Me ka hoomaopopo.
2. Menemene.
Fee-sim'ple, adj. Alodio. Fee simple
title, he palapala alodio.
Feign (fāne), v. 1. Aano.
2. Hoomala-e'. SYN. to put on appearances.
3. E ake. Feign to eat. e ake e ai.
desire.
Feint, n. Hana hookamani.
Fe-liç'i-tāte, v. E haawi i ka hauoli.
SYN. congratulate. To offer congratula-
tions, e haawi i ka hauoli.
Fe-liç'i-toŭs, adj. Kupono loa. Hau
happy. A felicitous expression, he olelo
kupono loa.
Fe-liç'i-ty, n. Ka hauoli nui. SYN.
bliss.
Fē'line, n. ano popoki.
Fĕll, v. 1. E kua. SYN. cut down.
Fell a tree, e kua i ka laau.
2. E kulai. SYN. knock down.
Fĕll, adj. Lokoino; mainoino. SYN.
cruel.
Fĕl'lōw, n. He hoa; he kokoolua.
Fĕl'lōw-crēa'turo, n. Hoa kana'ka.
Fĕl'lōw-feel'ing, n. Launa o ka ma-
nao.
Fĕl'lōw-ship, n. Ka launa ana. SYN.
society; intercourse.
Fĕl'ly, n. Laau po-ai o ka huila kaa.
Fĕl'on, n. 1. Kanaka i hoahewaia i ke
karaima nui.
2 He puha' ma ka lima.
Fĕl'o-ny, n. Karaima nui. SYN. fel-
oni.

Fē-māle, *n.* and *adj.* Wahine.

Fēm′i-nine, *adj.* Ano wahine.

Fē′mur, *n.* Iwi u-ha′.

Fēnçe, *n.* He pa laau.

Fēnçe, *v.* E ka′ka′pahi.

Fēnç′ing, *n.* 1. Na lako kukulu pa.
2. Kakapahi.

Fēnd, *v.* E pale aku. SYN. ward off.

Fēnd′er, *n.* He hao hoopaa ahi iloko o ke kapuahi.

Fēr′ment, *n.* 1. He haunaele; uluao′a.
2. Ka hu ana.

Fer-mĕnt′, *v.* 1. E hoo-hu′ae.
2. E hoo-awaawa.
3. Ka lilo ana i awaawa.

Fērn, *n.* He laau i ikeia kona mau ano-ano malalo iho o na lau; e like me ka palapalai; ke amauu; ka iwaiwa.

Fe-ro′çioŭs, *adj.* Ahiu; hae; kuna-hihi.

Fe-rŏç′i-ty, *n.* Ke ano hae; ano ahiu.

Fēr′ret, *v.* E imi a hookuke. SYN. search out.

Fēr′ry, *n.* Waa halihali ma na muli-wai me na kowa haiki.

Fēr′ry-boat, *n.* Waapa halihali.

Fēr′ry-man, *n.* Kanaka malama waapa halihali.

Fēr′tile, *adj.* 1. Momona; hua nui. *Fertile soil,* lepo momona.
2. Makaukau. SYN. ready. *Fertile in expedients,* makaukau ma na ano o ka hana ana.

Fēr′til-ize, *v.* E kipulu; e hoomomona.

Fer-til′i-ty, *n.* 1. Ka momona. *Fertility of the soil,* ka momona o ka lepo.
2. Lako; makaukau. *Fertility of resource,* lako o ka noonoo; or, makaukau ma ka noonoo.

Fēr′ule, *n.* 1. Laau pai lima.
2. He komo metala no ke kookoo o ka mamalu.

Fēr′vent, *adj.* 1. Enaena. *Fervent heat,* wela enaena. SYN. intense.
2. pumehana, *Fervent love,* aloha pumehana. SYN. ardent.

Fēr′vent-ly, *adv.* Me ka ikaika o ka manao. SYN. ardently.

Fēr′vor, *n.* 1. Ikaika. *The fervor of heat,* ka ikaika o ka wela. SYN. ardor.
2. Iini o ka naau.

Fēs′tal, *adj.* Hauoli; lea; olioli. SYN. festive; gay; joyful.

Fēs′ter, *v.* E hookahe i ka palaheehee.

Fēs′ti-val, *n.* Anaina hauoli; manawa lealea.

Fes-tiv′i-ty, *n.* Lealea hoolauna.

Fes-tōōn′, *n.* He lei no ke keena.

Fes-tōōn′, *v.* E kahiko ke keena i na lei.

Fĕtch, *v.* E homai; e ki a e lawe mai. SYN. bring.

Fête (fāte), *n.* See *festival.*

Fet′id, *adj.* Pilau; hauna. SYN. stinking.

Fĕt′lock, *n.* Ka lauoho loloa ma ke kuekue wawae hope o ka lio.

Fĕt′ter, *v.* E hoopilikia; e hoohaiki. SYN. impose restraint.

Feŭd, *n.* He hoomauhala.

Fē′ver, *n.* Mai wela; fiva.

Fē′ver-ish, *adj.* 1. Wela iki.
2. pihoihoi. SYN. nervous.

Few (fū), *adj.* Kakaikahi; kawalawala.

Fi′at, *n.* Kauoha paa.

Fīb, *n.* Olelo hoopunipuni.

Fī′ber, *n.* He maawe. *Fiber of wood,* nao.

Fick′le, *adj.* Lolilua; olewa; muhee; lauwili. SYN. changeable.

Fick′le-ness, *n.* Manao kapckepeke.

Fic′tion, *n.* 1. He kaao. SYN. fable; novel.
2. Mea oiaio ole.

Fic-ti′tioŭs, *adj.* 1. Oiaio ole.
2. Kapakapa. *Fictitious name,* inoa kapakapa.

Fid′dle, *n.* Pila hookani. SYN. violin.

Fid′dler, *n.* Mea hookani pila pahu.

Fi-dĕl′i-ty, *n.* Ke ano ku paa. SYN. faithfulness; integrity.

Fid′get, *v.* E onioni.

Fid′get-y, *adj.* Onioni.

Field, *n.* 1. He mala. *A field of grain,* he mala huita.
2. Aina kula. *The open field,* ke kula.
3. Akea. *Field of vision,* ke akea o ka ike o ka maka. SYN. range.
4. Wahi. *A field for enterprise,* he wahi no ka hooikaika.

Field′-book, *n.* He buke kakau no ke ana aina.

Field′-mär′shal, *n.* Alihikaua nui o ka puali koa nui.

Field′-ŏff′i-çer, *n.* He mekia; lukanela; kenela kaua.

Fiĕnd, *n.* He diablo; uhane ino.

Fiĕrce, *adj.* Ahiu; hae. SYN. ferocious.

Fiĕrçe′ness, *n.* 1. Ka wela o ka huhu.
2. Ano hae; ahiu. SYN. ferocity.

Fi′er-y, *adj.* Wela; enaena.
2. *Fiery tempered,* hikiwawe o ka huhu.

Fife,, *n.* Ohe puhi uuku.

Fif-teen′, *adj.* Umikumamalima.

Fifth, *adj.* 1. Ka lima; ka mahele elima.
2. He hapa-lima.

Fif′ti-eth, *adj.* Ke kanalima o. *The fiftieth year,* ke kanalima o na makahiki.
2. He hapa-kanalima.

Fif′ty, *adj.* Kanalima.

Fig, *n.* Fiku.

Fight, *n.* 1. He hakaka′. SYN. brawl.
2. He hoouka kaua. SYN. battle.

Fight, *v.* E hakaka; e kaua.

Fight′er, *n.* Kanaka hakaka; kanaka kaua.

Fig′ūr-a-tīve, *adj.* Hoohalike. SYN. typical.

Fig′ū-ra-tive-ly, *adv.* Ma ka nane ana; ma ka hoohalike ana.

Fig′ūre, *n.* 1. He kino. SYN. shape.
2. He hiohiona. SYN. appearance.
3. Kii.
4. Hua helu.

FIGURE 88 FIT

Fig'ūre, v. 1. E kakau helu. SYN. cypher.
2. E kaulaua. SYN. to be distinguished.
Fil'a-ment, n. He maawe makalii loa.
Filch, v. E aihue. SYN. steal; pilfer.
File, n. 1. He apuapu.
2. He lalani. *A file of soldiers,* he lalani koa.
3. He puolo pepa.
File, v. 1. E hookala me ka apuapu.
2. E huakai lalani.
3. E hookomo pu ma ka puolo pepa.
4. E waiho kekahi palapala imua o ka aha hookolokolo.
Fil'ial, adj. Pili i ka pono a na keiki i na makua. *Filial obedience,* ka hoolohe o na keiki i na makua.
Fil'ings, n. Na hunahuna hookala.
Fill, v. E hoopiha.
Fil'li-bŭs'ter, n. He powa; kanaka hoala haunaele.
Fil'ly, n. Lio wahine opiopio.
Film, v. He ili lahilahi.
Fil'ter, n. He mea kanana wai.
Fil'ter, v. E hoo-kulu hoomaemae i ka wai.
Filth, n. He mea pilau; opala pilau.
Filth'y, adj. Paele; penopeno; haukae.
Fil-tra'tion, n. 1. Ke kulu ana.
2. Ka hoomaemae ana i ka wai.
Fin, n. Pekekeu. *Back fin,* kuala. *Side fin,* pewapewa;
Fin'a-ble, adj. Ku i ka uku hoopai.
Fi'nal, adj. Hope loa. SYN. ultimate.
Fi'nal-ly, adv. I ka hope loa. SYN. ultimately.
Fi'nance, n. Ka oihana malama dala.
Fi'nanc-es, n. Na loaa o ke aupuni. SYN. revenue.
Fi-nan'cial, adj. Pili i ka oihana dala. *Financial difficulty,* pilikia o ka waihona; nele o ka waihona.
Fi'nan-cie'r, n. Kanaka akamai ma ka oihana waiwai.
Find, v. 1. E loaa mamuli o ka imi.
2. Ike. SYN. see. *I find I cannot come,* maopopo i'au aole au e hiki ana.
Fine, n. Uku hoopai.
Fine, adj. 1. Makalii, nawele. *Fine thread,* lopi nawele.
2. Aeae. *Fine dust,* lepo aeae.
3. Nani; aulii; maikai.
Fine, v. E kau i ka uku hoopai.
Fine'ly, adv. Nani; aulii; maikai.
Fine'ness, n. Ka makalii; ka aeae.
Fin'er-y, n. Na kahiko e nani ai ke kino.
Fi-nĕsse', n. Ano maalea.
Fin'ger, n. Manamana lima.
Fr'nis, n. Ka pau ana; ka hopena. SYN. end.
Fin'ish, v. 1. E hoopau pono. SYN. complete.
2. E hooko. SYN. perform.
Fin'ish, n. Hana hoohinuhinu; hana e hoo-nani ai.
Fin'ished, adj. 1. Hoopau pono ia. *A*

finished piece of work, he hana i hoopau pono ia.
2. *A finished education,* hoonaauao nui ia.
3. Maikai loa. *A finished composition,* he haku manao maikai loa.
Fin'ish-ing touch'es, n. Na hana liilii i koe.
Fi'nite, adj. Kau palena ia. *The finite mind,* ka noonoo i kau palena ia.
Fire, n. Ahi. *To prepare a fire,* e kukulu i ahi. *To kindle a fire,* e hooa' i ke ahi. *To extinguish a fire,* e kinai i ke ahi. *To take fire,* e a i ke ahi.
Fire, v. 1. E hoo-a' i ke ahi.
2. E ki. *Fire a gun,* e ki pu.
3. E hoo-ala i ka huhu.
Fire'ärms, n. Na pu ki o kela me keia ano.
Fire'brand, n. Momoku ahi; moku ahi.
Fire-ĕn'ġine, n. Enikini kinai ahi.
Fire'man, n. 1. Kanaka kinai ahi.
2. Kanaka puhi ahi o ka enikini.
Fire'plaçe, n. Kapuahi.
Fire'plug, n. Ohe wai kinai ahi.
Fire'proof, adj. Pau ole i ke ahi.
Fire'side, n. Ke kapuahi o ka ohana.
Fire-ward'en, n. Luna kiai ahi.
Fire'-wood, n. Wahie.
Fire'works, n. Na ahi kaolele.
Firm, adj. 1. Paa. SYN. compact; stable.
2. Kupaa; oni paa. SYN. constant; resolute.
Firm, n. He hui kalepa.
Fir'ma-ment, n. Ka lanipaa; ka papalani; ke aouli. SYN. heavens; sky.
Firm'ly, adv. 1. Me ka paa. SYN. solidly.
2. Me ka wiwo ole; me ka lauwili ole. SYN. resolutely.
First, adj. 1. Ka mua; ka makamua.
2. Ka pookela. SYN. chief.
First'born, n. Ka makahiapo; ka hanau mua.
First'fruits, v. Na hua mua.
First'räte, adj. Keu maoli; maikai loa.
Fis'cal, adj. Pili i ka waihona waiwai o ke aupuni. *Fiscal year,* makahiki haawina dala'.
Fish, n. He i'-a.
Fish, v. 1. E lawa-i'-a.
2. *Fish with rod and line,* e kamokoi.
Fish'er-man, n. Kanaka lawa-i'-a.
Fish'er-y, n. 1. Oihana lawa-i'-a.
2. He wahi lawa-i'-a.
Fish'hook, n. He makau.
Fish'mŏng'er, n. Kanaka kuai i'-a.
Fish'y, adj. 1. Kohu i'-a la.
2. Wahahee paha.
Fis'sūre, n. He mawae; he owa'. SYN. cleft.
Fist, n. Puulima.
Fist'i-cuffs, n. Ke kui ana me na puu lima.
Fit, n. 1. He mai.
2. Ka pilipono. *A perfect fit,* he aahu pili pono loa i ke kino puliki.

Fit, *v.* 1. E hoo-ku-ku lole.
2. E hoo-kupono.
Fit'ness, *n.* Ke kupono. SYN. adaptation; propriety.
Fit'ting, *adj.* Kupono. SYN. proper; adapted.
Five, *adj.* Elima.
Five-fold', *adj.* Pa-lima.
Fix, *v.* 1. E hoopaa. SYN. fasten.
2. E hooholo. SYN. settle; determine. *To fix boundaries,* e hooholo i na palena aina.
3. E kapili hou. SYN. mend.
4. E hookupaa. SYN. establish.
Fix, *n.* He pilikia. SYN. dilemma; predicament.
Fix'ture, *n.* He mea paa.
Fiz'zle, *v.* E hoka.
Fiz'zle, *n.* 1, He hoka.
2. He kanapi o ka pauda.
Flăb'by, *adj.* Alualu; peheu. SYN. flaccid.
Flăg, *v.* E onawaliwali; e hoopalaleha.
Flăg, *n.* He lepa; he hae.
Flăg-el-late, *v.* E hili me ke kaula.
Flăg-ŏf'fi-çer, *n.* Ke kapena nui o ke aumoku manuwa'.
Flăg'on, *n.* He hue no ka wai ona.
Flă'grant, *adj.* Hewa loa.
Flăg'ship, *n.* Ka moku o ke ademirala.
Flăg'staff, *n.* Kia hae; pahu hae.
Flăg'stone, *n.* Pohaku nui, palahalaha.
Flāme, *n.* Lapalapa ahi.
Flăm'ing, *adj.* 1. Ka lapalapa ana.
2. Wakawaka. SYN. glittering. *Flaming sword,* pahi kaua wakawaka.
Flănge, *n.* Ke kae o ka huila kaa ahi.
Flănk, *n.* Aoao. *To march by flank,* e huakai pili aoao.
Flăn'nel, *n.* Lole hulu hipa.
Flăp, *v,* 1. E upoi; e kapalili. *To flap the wings,* e upoi i na eheu.
2. E welowelo; e kilepalepa. *To flap as a flag or sail.*
Flāre, *v.* E ana'pa.
Flăsh, *v.* 1. E anapu; e huila.
2. E kanapi. *Flash in the pan.*
Flăsh'y, *adj.* 1. Anapanapa.
2. Hookahakaha wale.
Flăsk, *n.* He hue nuku loloa.
Flăt, *adj.* 1. Palahalaha; malaelae; omalio.
2. Palanai. *A flat dish,* he pa palanai. SYN. shallow.
Flăt'ten, *v.* E hoo-pe'pe'; hoopalahalaha.
Flăt'ter, *v.* E hoomalimali.
Flăt'ter-er, *n.* Mea hoomalimali.
Flăt'ter-y, *n.* He hoomalimali.
Flăunt, *v* E hookeha; e haanou.
Flā'vor, *n.* Ka miko.
Flăw, *n.* 1. He kina.
2. He puahiohio. *flaw of wind,* he puahiohio.
Flăx, *n.* Laau olona'; laau lilina.
Flāy, *v.* E lole. SYN. skin.

Flēa, *n.* Uku lele.
Flee, *v.* E holo hee; e auhee; e mahuka.
Fleeçe, *n.* Hulu o ka hipa.
Fleeçe, *v.* E pakaha.
Fleet, *adj.* Mama; ki'ki'. SYN. swift.
Fleet, *n.* He aumoku; ulumoku.
Fleet'ing, *adj.* Hee ana; pau wale; mau ole. SYN. swiftly passing.
Flēsh, *n.* 1. I'-o.
2. Ka'naka. *All flesh,* kanaka a pau. SYN. All mankind.
Flĕsh'-brush, *n.* Hulu balaki mea holoi kino.
Flĕsh-eŏl'or, *n.* Ka hooluu o ka i-'o.
Flĕsh'ly, *adj.* Pili i na mea o ke kino. SYN. carnal.
Flĕsh'y, *adj.* Puipui. SYN. corpulent.
Flĕx'i-ble, *adj.* 1. Napenape; holuholu; pa'he
2. Ie. *Flexible as cloth.*
Flĕx'i-bĭl'i-ty, *n.* Ano holuholu; pahe.
Flick'er, *v.* Pi'-pi' *The light flickers,* ke pipi nei ke kukui.
Flight, *n.* 1. Ka lele ana. *Flight of birds,* ka lele ana o na manu.
2. Ka hee ana. *Flight of the enemy,* ka hee ana o ka enemi.
3. *A flight of stairs,* he ala anuu.
4. *To put to flight,* e hooauhee.
Flight'y, *adj.* Opulepule; lele wale o ka noonoo.
Flĭm'sy, *adj.* Palupalu; lahilahi.
Flinch, *v.* E ku-emi ihope no ka ma-ka'u; e wiwo.
Fling, *v.* E hoolei.
Flint, *n.* Pohaku paea.
Flĭp'pant, *adj.* Walaau wale.
Flirt, *n.* He wahine hoomahie.
Flir-tā'tion, *n.* Ka hoomahie ana.
Flōat, *v.* 1. E lana.
2. *To float ashore,* e hoo-pae'.
Flŏck, *n.* 1. He pu-a'. *Flock of sheep,* pu-a' hipa.
2. Auna'. *A flock of birds,* he auna' manu.
Flŏck, *v.* *To flock together,* e akoakoa pu.
Flŏe, *n.* He moku hau-paa, palahalaha.
Flŏg, *v.* E hahau ikaika.
Flŏg'ging, *v.* He hahau nui.
Flŏod, *n.* Wai manini; wai kahe nui.
Flŏod'gāte, *n.* Puka pani no ka wai.
Flŏor, *n.* Papahele.
Flŏor'ing, *n.* Na papa kapili papa hele.
Flŏp, *v.* E lele; e huli. *To flop over,* e huli ma kela aoao.
Flō'ra, *n.* Na mea ulu maoli o ka aina.
Flō'ral, *adj.* Pili i na pua. *A floral offering,* he makana o na pua.
Flŏr'id, *adj.* 1. Hauliuli. *A florid complexion* hauliuli ka ili.
2. Nane.
Flō'rist, *n.* Kanaka mahi pua.
Flŏt'sam, *n.* Waiwai e lana wale ana ma ke kai.
Flounçe, *v.* Kupaka; e onioni.
Flounçe, *n.* Lepa aahu.
Flour, *n.* Palaoa.
Flouŕ'ish, *v.* 1. E ulu ae.

Floŭr'ish-ing, adj. 1. Puka. *A flourishing business*, he oihana puka.
2. Kuonoono. SYN. thriving.

Flŏw, v. 1. E kahe
2. *Flow slowly*, laumiki
3. *Flow as a current*, e miha; e miki.

Flow'er, n. He pua.

Flow'er-ing sea'son, n. Kau mohala pua.

Flow'er-y, adj. Me he pua la.

Flŏw'ing, adj. Kahe; miha.

Flŭe'tu- āte, v. Iluna, ilalo; kulanalana.

Flŭe, n. Puka u-ahi.

Flŭ'ent, adj. Maiele; noili; palolo; makaukau ma ka olelo.

Flŭ'ent-ly, adv. Me ka pahee o ka leo.

Flŭ'id, n. Kela me keia ano wai.

Flŭ'id, adj. Hehee'; kahe me he wai la.

Flŭke, n. 1. Ka manamana o ka heleuma.
2. Ka hiu o ke kohola'.

Flūme, n. He ha wai. *To flume*, e hookomo ma ka ha.

Flŭr'ry, n. Pioloke; pilihua.

Flŭsh, n. Omeomeo. *Flushed with anger*, ku ka heu

Flŭs'tered, adj Pihoihoi; pu'pu'ahu lu. SYN. confused; agitated.

Flŭte, n. Ohe puhi.

Flŭt'ist, n. Kanaka puhi ohe.

Flŭt'ter, v. E kapalili; e welowelo.

Flŭt'ter, n. He kapalili o ka houpo.

Flȳ, v. 1. E lele; e hoolele.
2. E hee; e auhee. SYN flee.
3. E holo mama. SYN. run swiftly.
4. E kaalelewa *Flying clouds*, na ao kaalelewa

Flȳ, n. 1. He nalo.
2. He kaa ma'ma'.

Flȳ'leaf, n. He aoao o ka buke i pai ole ia

Flȳ'wheel, n. Ka pokakaa nui o ka mikini.

Fōal, n. Lio keiki.

Fŏam, n. Hu'wahu'wa; hu'a. *The foaming sea*, kai ahulu.

Fō'eal, adj. Pili i ke kiko hui o na kukuna malamalama.

Fō'eus, n. Ke kiko kahi e hui ai na kukuna malamalama.

Fō'eus, v. E hooponopono i ke aniani i ike pono.

Fŏd'der, n. Ai holoholona. SYN. feed.

Fōe, n. He enemi. SYN. adversary.

Fŏg, n. He o-hu.

Fŏg'gy, adj Paapu i ka o-hu.

Fō'gy, n. Kanaka hahai i ke ano o ka wa kahiko.

Foi'ble, v. He kina o ka manao.

Foil, v. E hoka; e hoohoka. SYN. frustrate.

Fōld, n. 1. He opi; he pelu.
2. He pa. *Sheep fold*, pa-hipa. *Fourfold*, pa-ha'.

Fōld, v. E opiopi; e pelu ae.

Fōld'er, n. Mea opiopi.

Fō'li-age, n. Na lau o na laau.

Fō'li-o, n. Hookahi opi o ke kalana.

Fŏlk, } n. Poe. *Our folks*, ko kakou
Fŏlks, } poe; ko makou poe.

Fŏl'lŏw, v. E haihai mahope; e ukali.
2. *It follows therefore*, nolaila ua aka'-ka.
3. *In the following manner*, penei. SYN. thus.

Fŏl'lŏw-er, n. 1. He haumana. SYN. disciple.
2. He mea ukali.

Fŏl'ly, n. He lapuwale; he naaupo.

Fo-mĕnt', v. E hookonokono. SYN. incite; instigate.

Fo-mĕn-tā'tion, n. He mea hamo eha.

Fo-mĕnt'er, n. He mea hoala hakaka'; hoala mokuahana, etc.

Fŏnd, adj. 1. Makemake; ake.
2. Ono. *Fond of food*, ono i ka ai.
3. Aloha.

Fŏn'dle, v. E hooaumoe; e hiipoi; e hoomilimili.

Fŏnd'ly, adv. Me ke aloha pumehana. SYN. lovingly.

Fōod, n. Ai. SYN. provisions.

Fŏol, n. He ai-a'; he kanaka lapuwale.

Fŏol, v. E epa; e hoopuniwale.

Fŏol'här'dy, adj. Aa wale.

Fŏol'ish, adj. Naaupo; lapuwale.

Fŏol'ish-ness, n. Naaupo. SYN. folly.

Fŏols'eap, n. Kalana nunui.

Fŏŏt, n. He wawae.
2. He kapuai; 12 iniha.
3. Kumu. Syn. base. *Foot of a mountain*, kumu o ka mauna.

Fŏŏt, v. 1. E hehi; e hele wawae.
2. E hookaa. SYN. pay. *To foot a bill*, e hookaa i ka bila.
3. E hoouluulu. SYN. run up; add. *Foot up an amount*, e hoouluulu i ka huina.

Fŏŏt'ball, n. Kinipopo kee'hi wawae.

Fŏŏt'fall, n. Ka hehi ana o ka wawae.

Fŏŏt'hŏld, n. Wahi e ku ai ka wawae.

Fŏŏt'păth, n. Alanui hele wawae.

Fŏŏt'print, n. He meheu.

Fŏŏt'stĕp, n. Kapuai wawae.

Fŏŏt'stŏol, n. Kehina wawae.

Fŏp, n. Kanaka hoopuahi. SYN. coxcomb.

Fŏp'pish, adv. Hookelakela wale; hookahakaha.

Fŏr, prep. No; na; *conj.* no ka mea. SYN. because.

Fŏr'āge, n. Ai i hoomakaukau ia no na holoholona.

Fŏr'as-mŭch', adv. Oiai. SYN. since.

For-beâr', v. 1. E hoo'ki. SYN. cease.
2. E ahonui; e hoomanawanui. SYN. have patience.

For-beâr'ance, n. Ahonui; hoomanawanui.

For-bid', v. E pa'pa' aku. E hoole.

For-bid'ding, adj. Inoino; kohu ole.

Fŏrçe, n. Ikaika; mana.

Fŏrçe, v. 1. E kaohi maoli.
2. E lima ikaika aku.

Fŏrçe'meat, n. I'o i kuiia a wale.

Fôr′ceps, *v.* U-pa′ upiki o ke kauka.
Fôr′ci-ble, *adj.* 1. Mana; ikaika
  2. Koikoi. *A forcible thought,* he manao koikoi.
Fôr′ci-bly, *adv.* 1. Me ka lima ikaika.
  2. *The thought strikes me forcibly,* ku ikaika mai ka manao ia′u.
Fôrd, *n.* Wahi hele wawae o ka muliwai; ke kahawai.
Fôrd′a-ble, *adj.* Hiki ke hele wawae ia.
Fôre′arm, *v.* E lolii.
Fôre′cas-tle (fō-kas′l), *n.* Wahi noho o na luina moku.
Fôre′close′, *v.* E hooko i ka palapala moraki.
Fôre′fâth′er, *n.* He kupuna o ka wa kahiko.
Fôre′fin′ger, *n.* Manamanalima mua.
Fôre′frônt, *n.* Ke alo; imua loa. SYN. van.
Fôre-gŏ′, *v.* E haalele aku. *A foregone conclusion,* olelo hooholo e mamua.
Fôre′ground, *n.* Ke alo o ke kii.
Fôre′hand′ed, *adj.* Lako; kuonoono. SYN. well off.
Fôre′head (for′ed), *n.* Ka lae.
Fôr′eign (for′in), *adj.* Haole; no na aina e.
Fôr′eign-er, *n.* He haole; kanaka no na aina e mai.
Fôre-knŏw′, *v.* E ike e mamua.
Fôre-knŏwl′edge, *n.* Ka ike e no na mea e hiki mai ana.
Fôre′lock, *n.* Hili lauoho ma ka lae.
Fôre′man, *n.* He luna hana.
Fôre′mŏst, *adj.* 1. Ka mua loa.
  2. *The foremost boy in school,* ke keiki pookela o ke kula.
Fôre′noon, *n.* Mamua iho o ke awakea.
Fôre′or-dâin′, *v.* E wae e mamua.
Fôre′pärt, *n.* Ka hapa omua.
Fôre′rŭn-ner, *n.* He elele i hoouna mua ia.
Fôre-see′, *v.* E ike e mamua.
Fôre-shŏwn′, *p. p.* Hoike e ia.
Fôre′sight, *n.* Ka ike e hoomakaukau e ana mamua.
Fôr′est, *n.* He ulu laau.
Fôre-stâll′, *v.* See *anticipate.* E makaala e mamua.
Fôre′tâste, *n.* E wanana. SYN. predict.
Fôre′thought, *n.* Ka noonoo e mamua.
Fôr-ĕv′er, *adv.* Mau loa; no ke ao pau ole; mau a mau.
Fôre-wärn′, *v.* E ao e mamua.
Fôr′feit, *v.* 1. E uku hoopai.
  2. E hoonele i kekahi pono.
Fôrge, *n.* Ke kapuahi no ke amara.
Fôrge, *v.* 1. E kui hao.
  2. E apuka. SYN. counterfeit.
  3. E neenee iki imua. *The ship forges ahead,* ke neenee iki nei ka moku imua.
Fôrg′er-y, *n.* Apuka.
For-gĕt′, *v.* E poina; e hoo-poina.
For-gĕt′ful, *adj.* Poina wale.
For-give′, *v.* E kala; e huikala. SYN. pardon.
For-give′ness, *n.* Ke kala ana.

For-giv′ing, *adj.* Manao kala.
Fôrk, *n.* 1. He o.
  2. Kahi e manamana ai. *The fork of a river,* kahi e manamana ai ka muliwai; or, he manamana o ka muliwai.
Fôrk′ed, *adj.* Manamana.
For-lôrn′, *adj.* Oki loa; mehameha; neoneo.
Fôrm, *n.* 1. Kii; kino. SYN. figure; body.
  2. *In some form or other,* ma kekahi ano.
Fôrm, *v.* 1. E lilo. SYN. become. *It forms a part,* lilo ia i hapa.
  2. E kukulu i hui.
Fôrm′al, *adj.* Ku i na rula; like me na loina. SYN. precise
For-mâl′i-ty, *n.* Ke ko ana mamuli o na loina.
For-mâ′tion, *n.* Ka hana ana; ke kukulu ana.
Fôr′mer, *adj.* 1. Mua. *The former,* ka mua.
  2. Mamua. *Former times,* na wa mamua.
Fôr′mer-ly, *adv.* Mamua; i ka wa mamua.
Fôr′mi-da-ble, *adj.* Weliweli. *A formidable obstacle,* he kumu keakea weliweli.
Fôr′mu-lâ, *n.* He loina.
Fôr′ni-eâ′tion, *n.* Hookamakama.
For-sâke′, *v* E haalele. SYN. abandon.
For-sâk′en, *adj.* Haaleleia.
For-sôôth, *adv.* He oiaio. SYN. in truth; indeed.
For-sweâr′ *v.* 1. E haalele me ka ho-hiki. SYN abjure.
  2. E hoohiki wahahee.
Fôrt, *n* Pa-kaua; papu′. SYN. fortress; fortification.
Fôrte, *n.* Ka hana i pookela ai kekahi. *Mathematics are his forte,* pookela oia ma na helu.
Fôrth-eŏm′ing, *adj.* Hoea mai ana; kokoke mai ana.
Fôrth′wĭth′, *adv.* A no; koke. SYN. now; immediately.
Fôr′ti-fŷ, *v.* 1. E kukulu i pa-kaua.
  2. E hooikaika; hookupaa. SYN. strengthen.
Fôr′ti-tûde, *n.* Ke kupaa o ka manao; hoomanawanui. SYN. endurance; firmness.
Fôrt′nĭght, *n.* Elua hebedoma.
Fôrt′u-nâte, *adj.* Pomaikai.
Fôrt′ûne, *n.* 1. Waiwai nui; lako nui.
  2. *Good fortune,* pomaikai.
  3. *Bad fortune,* poino.
Fôrt′une-tĕl′ler, *n.* Mea kilokilo.
Fôr′ty, *adj.* Kanaha′; he kaau.
Fôr′ward, *adj.* Mahaoi; hoo-a-a-no.
  2. I mua.
Fŏs′sil, *n.* He mea ulu, a he kino holoholona paha, i hooliloia i pohaku, a i eliia noloko mai o ka honua.
Fŏs′ter, *v.* 1. E hanai. SYN. nourish.
  2. Ehii. SYN. cherish.
  3. E malama. SYN. to promote; care for.

Fŏs'ter-child', *n.* Keiki hanai.
Fŏs'ter-pā'rent, *n.* Makua hanai.
Foul, *adj.* 1. Haumia; pelapela.
2. Kolohe. SYN. villainous.
Foun-dā'tion, *n.* He kumu; he kahua.
Foun'der, *n.* 1. Ka mea nana e hookumu.
2. Kanaka hoo-hee' metala.
Found'er, *v.* E piholo; e palemo. SYN. sink.
Found'ry, *n.* Wahi hoo-hee' metala. *An iron foundry*, wahi hoo-hee' hao.
Found'ling, *n.* Keiki i haaleleia e na makua.
Fount,
Fount'ain, } *n.* Wai puai.
Fount'ain-hĕad', *n.* He poowai. SYN. source.
Foŭr, *adj.* E ha'; he kauna.
Foŭr'fōld, *adj.* Pa-ha'.
Foŭr'fōōt'ed, *adj.* Wawae e-ha'.
Foŭr'scōre, *adj.* Kanawalu; eha' iwakalua.
Foŭr'squāre, *adj.* Huina-ha-like.
Foŭrth, *adj.* 1. Ka ha. 2. He hapaha'.
Fowl, *n.* He manu.
Fowl'er, *n.* Kanaka ki manu; kanaka kawilimanu.
Fŏwl'ing-piēçe, *n.* Pu-ki-manu.
Fŏx, *n.* He alopeke.
Fra'eas, *n.* Hakaka'. SYN. fight; quarrel.
Frăc'tion, *n.* He hakina; he hapa. *Common fraction*, hakina maoli. *Proper fraction*, hakina pili. *Complex fraction*, hakina ano huikau. *Compound fraction*, hakina o ka hakina. *Improper fraction*, hakina kuokoa.
Frăc'tioŭs, *adj.* Hookuli; nunuha. SYN. stubborn; obstinate.
Frăc'tūre, *n.* He haki. SYN. break.
Frăg'īle, *adj.* Hakiwale; palupalu. frail; brittle.
Frăg'ment. 1. Apana. *A fragment of cloth*, he apana lole.
2. He huna. *A fragment of food*, he huna ai.
3. Lihi iki.
Frā'granee, *n.* He ala.
Frā'grant, *adj.* Aala; ala. *Too fragrant*, alapakui.
Frāil, *adj.* 1. Nawaliwali; palupalu.
2. Ae wale i ka hewa.
Frāil'ty, *n.* 1. Ano nawaliwali; palupalu.
2. Ka manao ae wale i ka hewa.
Frāme, *v.* E kapili; e kukulu. *Frame a law*, e kukulu i kanawai.
Frāme, *n.* He mea hoopaa. *A picture frame*, he laau hoopaa kii; *or*, mea hoopaa kii.
Frāme'-work, *n.* Na iwi. *Frame work of a house*, na iwi o ka hale.
Frănk, *adj.* Ano huna'ole; oiaio. SYN. honest; candid.
Frănk'ly, *adv.* Me ka oiaio maoli. SYN. honestly; candidly.

Frăn'tic, *adj.* Pioloke loa; uluhua loa.
Fra-tēr'nal, *adj.* Hoahanau. SYN. brotherly. *Fraternal love*, aloha hoahanau.
Fra-tēr'ni-ty, *n.* Hui hoahanau. SYN. brotherhood.
Frā'ter-nīze, *v.* E hui ma ke ano hoahanau.
Frăt'ri-çide, *n.* Mea pepehi hoahanau.
Frąud, *n.* Hana apuka; hana epa.
Frąud'ū-lent, *adj.* Apuka; epa.
Frąught (frawt), *adj.* Paapu. *Fraught with danger*, paapu i na popilikia. SYN. full.
Frāy, *v.* E weluwelu.
Frēak, *n.* Manao ulu wale.
Frēck'le, *n.* Kiko ma ke kino.
Free, *adj.* 1. Kuokoa. *A free man*, kanaka kuokoa.
2. Mama; holo. *A free horse*, he lio holo.
3. *A free wind*, makani mahope mai.
Free, *v.* 1. E hookuu.
2. *To free the mind*, e hai pau loa i ka manao.
3. *To be free and easy*, e luana; e hoonanea.
Free'-bôrn, *adj.* Kupa.
Free'dóm, *n.* Kuokoa; ku i ka wa.
Free'hōld, *n.* Aina alodio; aina kuleana.
Free'hōld-er, *n.* Haku kuleana.
Free'ly, *adv.* Me ka aua ole.
Free'-schōōl, *n.* Kula uku ole.
Free-think'er, *n.* He aia'; he hoomaloka; he hoomalau.
Free-will', *n.* Ka mana e hooko mamuli o ka makemake. *Of his own free will*, mamuli o kona makemake iho.
Freeze, *v.* E make i ke anu.
2. E paa i ke anu. SYN. congeal.
Freight, *n.* Ukana moku.
Freight, *v.* E hoopiha moku; e hooili ukana maluna o ka moku.
Freight'-list, *n.* Papa nelu ukana.
Frēnch, *adj.* Farani. *French language*, olelo Farani.
Fre-quēnt', *v.* 1. E makaikai pinepine;
2. E hele mau.
Frē'quent, *adj.* Pinepine. SYN. common.
Fre-quēnt'er, *n.* Mea makaikai pinepine; mea hele mau.
Frē'quent-ly, *adv.* Pinepine. SYN. often.
Frēsh, *adj.* 1. Hou. *Fresh goods*, na waiwai hou. SYN. new.
2. Maka. SYN. raw.
3. Ikaika. *Feel fresh*, e ikaika hou. SYN. strong.
4. Huihui. *Fresh water*, wai huihui. SYN. cold.
Frĕsh'et, *n.* He wai manini; wai nui.
Frĕsh'ly, *adv.* Hou.
2. Oluolu. *The wind blew freshly*, pa oluolu mai ka makani.
Frĕsh'man, *n.* Haumana o ka papa komo o ke kula nui.

Frĕt, v. E ne; e ohumu wale.

Frĕt'ful, } adj. Ne; na ole. A fretful
Frĕt'ting, } child, he keiki ne. SYN. peevish.

Fri'a-ble, adj. Hakihaki wale; pai'na wale. SYN. brittle.

Fric'tion, n. Ka anai ana.

Fri'day, n. Po-alima.

Friĕnd, n. Hoa'loha; hoalauna.

Friĕnd'less, adj. Hoalauna ole; mehameha.

Friĕnd'ly, adj. Oluolu; launa.

Friĕnd'ship, n. Aloha hoalauna.

Frig'ate, n. Moku manuwa nui.

Fright, n. Puiwa. SYN. alarm; terror.

Fright'en, v. E hoopuiwa. SYN. scare.

Fright'ful, adj. Eehia; weliweli.

Frig'id, adj. 1. Auuanu. SYN. cold.
2. Frigid zone, kaei anu.

Frig'id-ly, adj. Puanuanu. SYN. coldly.

Fringe, n. Lihilihi lole.

Frisk, v. E lelelele; e haa.

Frisk'y, adj. Lelelele, me he hipa keiki la.

Frit'ter, v. To fritter away the time, e hoohala wale i ka manawa.

Fri-vōl'i-ty, n. He lealea noonoo ole.

Friv'o-loŭs, adj. Lealea noonoo ole.

Frō, adv. I-o'. To and fro, i-o' ia nei.

Frŏck, n. Lole palaka. A frock coat, puapuamoa.

Frŏg, n. He ra'na.

Frŏl'ic, n. He paani lealea. SYN. sport.

Frŏl'ie-some, adj. Lealea i ka paani.

Frŏm, prep. Mai. From Honolulu, mai Honolulu mai. From Honolulu to Hilo, mai Honolulu aku i Hilo.

Frŏnt, n. 1. Ke alo.
2. Imua.

Frŏnt'age, n. Ke alo o ka pa, a hale paha.

Frŏn-tier, n. Mokuna aina; pea. SYN. boundary.

Frŏnt'is-pieçe, n. Ke kii ma ka aoao mua loa o ka buke.

Frŏst, n. Kehau anu.

Frŏth, n. Hu'a; huwa.

Frō'ward, adj. Haakei.

Frown, n. He hookue maka.

Frown, v. E hoomaku'e.

Fru'gal, adj. 1. Pakiko. SYN. economical.
2. Uuku o ka lilo.

Fruit, n. 1. Hua.
2. Hua ai.

Fruit'ful, adj. Hua nui; momona. SYN. fertile.

Fruit'ful-ness, n. 1. Ka hua nui ana mai. SYN. productiveness.
2. Ka momona o ka lepo. SYN. fertility.

Fru-i'tion, n. Ke ko ana.

Fruit'less, vdj. 1. Hua ole. A fruitless tree, he laau hua ole.
2. Ke ko; makehewa. A fruitless effort, he hoao makehewa.

Fruit'tree, n. Laau hua.

Frŭs'trāte, v. E hoohoka. SYN. defeat.

Frŭs'tum, n. He okina o ke kino paa. Frustum of a cone, he okina o ka puoa

Frȳ, v. E parai.

Frȳ'ing-pan, n. Pa-parai.

Fu'el, n. 1. Wahie no ke ahi.
2. Kela mea, keia mea i a i ke ahi.

Fū'ġi-tive, n. He kuewa; kanaka auwana; kanaka mahuka.

Fŭl'erum, n. He unu; he koo.

Fŭl-fill', v. E hooko'. SYN. accomplish.

Fŭl-fill'ment, n. Ka hooko' ana. SYN. accomplishment.

Fŭll, adj. Piha.

Fŭll'ness, n. Ka piha ana.

Fŭll'y, adj. Lea. Fully understand, maopopo lea.

Fŭm'ble, v. E ha'ha' wale aku.

Fūmeṣ, n. pl. 1. Uahi. SYN. smoke.
i. Ka mahu o na mea baila; ke ala o na mea e a ana.

Fū'mi-gāte, v. E hoopuhi i ka u-ahi.

Fū'mi-gā'tion, n. Ka hoopuhi ana i ka u-ahi.

Fŭn, n. Paani lealea.

Fŭne'tion, v. Hana.

Fŭne'tion-a-ry, n. Luna oihana.

Fŭnd, n. He waihona.

Fŭn'da-mĕnt'al, adj. Kumu. Fundamental principle, he loina hookumu.

Fū'ner-al, n. Halawai hoolewa kupapau.

Fu-nē're-al, adj. Ano kanikau.

Fŭn'gus, n. Pepeiao laau.

Fŭn'nel, n. 1. Puka u-ahi no ka enikini. SYN. smoke stack.
2. Puka hookomo ea i ka opu o ka moku.
3. Tini ukuhi wai.

Fŭn'ny, adj. Lealea; mea akaaka.

Fŭr, n. Hulu palupalu, like me ko ka popoki.

Fŭr'bish, v. E anai; e hoohinuhinu. SYN. scour.

Fū'ri-oŭs, adj. 1. Weliweli o ka huhu.
2. Ikaika loa; pukiki. A furious wind, makani pukiki.

Fŭrl, v. E opiopi. E opiopi i ka pea.

Fŭr'long, n. He setadia; hapawalu o ka mile.

Fŭr'lough (fŭr'lō), n. Palapala hookuu koa no ka wa pokole.

Fŭr'naçe, n. 1. Kapuahi hooheehee metala.
2. Kapuahi hoomehana.

Fŭr'nish, v. E hoolako. SYN. supply.

Fŭr'ni-tūre, n. Na lako. Household furniture, na lako hale.

Fŭr'row, n. Auwaha o ke o'palau.

Fŭr'ther, adv. Oi ae; ma o aku.

Fŭr'ther, v. E kokua. SYN. assist; promote. To further the undertaking, e kokua mamuli o ka hana.

Fŭr'ther-ançe, n. Koʌua; koo. In furtherance of the object, i kokua no ka manao.

Fŭr'ther-mōre, adv. Eia hou. SYN. moreover.

Fûrth′est, adj. Ma-o′ loa.
Fûr′tive, adv. Maalea; malu′; ano ai-hue.
Fü′ry, n. 1. Huhu weliweli; inaina lua ole.
2. Ke ano o ka ikaika ino. *The fury of the tempest*, ka ikaika ino o ka makani.
Fûrz′y, adj. Heu. *Furzy cane*, ko heu.
Fûse, n. He kaula pauda; mea hoopahu′.
Füse (füze) v. E hooheehee i ka wela.
Fü′si-ble, adj. Hiki ke hooheeheeia.

Füs′ion, n. 1. Ka hooheehee ana i ka wela.
2. Ka lilo ana o na aoao ku-e elua a oi paha, i aoao hookahi; ka lokahi ana.
Füss, n. Hauwalaau.
Füs′sy, adj. Ano hoopilikia wale.
Fü′tile, adj. Makehewa; waiwai ole. SYN. useless; vain.
Fu-til′i-ty, n. Ke ano makehewa. SYN. uselessness.
Fü′ture, }
Fu-tü′ri-ty,} n. Ko mua aku: ka wa mahope.
Fÿ! *interj.* Ka! kaha′ha′!

G

Gäb′ble, v. E walaau wale, me he mau keko la. SYN. jabber.
Ga′ble, n. Hakala o ka hale.
Gâd, v. E holoholo wale.
Gâd′a-bout, n. He mea holoholo wale; he a′ea wale.
Gäg, E o-a.
Gäg, n. Laau hoopaa waha.
Gäin, n. 1. Waiwai puka.
2. Pomaikai.
Gäin, v. 1. E puka.
2. To gain a point, e ko i ka makemake
Gäin′less, adj. Poho′; waiwai ole. SYN. losing.
Gäin′say, v. E pale i ka olelo; e hoole i ka olelo.
Gäit, n. Ke ano o ka hele ana. *A slow gait*, ka hele lolohi ana.
Gäit′er, n. He ano kamaa.
Gä′la-dây, n. La hauoli.
Gäle, n. Makani nui.
Gäll, n. Ke au.
Gäll, v. 1. E hoopohole i ka ili. SYN. chafe.
2. E hoonaukiuki.
Gal-lânt′, v. E kokua pono i ka wahine.
Gäl′lant, adj. Koa; maka′u ole. SYN. brave; courageous.
Gäl′lant-ry, n. 1. Ke ano koa.
2. Ke kokua pono ana i na wahine.
Gäl′ler-y, n. 1. Wahi noho oluna.
2. Keena hoikeike kii.
3. *Photographic gallery*, hale pai kii.
Gäl′ley, n. Hale kuke oluna o ka moku.
Gäl′lic, adj. No Farani. SYN. french.
Gal′li-nip′per, n. He makika nui.
Gäl′lon, n. He galani.
Gäl′lop, v. Ka holo loa ana o ka lio.
Gäl′lows, n. Amana.
Gäl′van-ism, n. He mana ano like me ka uila.
Gäm′ble, v. E pili waiwai.
Gäm′bler, n. Kanaka pili waiwai.

Gäm′bol, v. E lelelele; e haa. SYN. frisk.
Gäme, n. 1. He paani.
2. Na holoholona i ki-pu ia.
Gäme′ster, n. Kanaka pili waiwai. SYN. gambler.
Gäm′mon, n. 1. He hoka. SYN. humbug.
Gäm′ut, n. Na leo ewalu o ka pa-ko-li. SYN. scale.
Gän′der, n. Manu ne′ne′ kane.
Gäng, n. He poe. *A gang of laborers*, he poe paahana.
Gän-grêne′, n. Ka palaho o kau wahi o ke kino.
Gäng′way, n. Kahi e komo aku ai o ka moku.
Gäol (jail), n. Hale paahao. SYN. jail.
Gäol′er (jail′er), n. Luna hale paahao. SYN. jailer.
Gäp, n. 1. Wahi helelei o ka pa.
2. Wahi haahaa mawaena o na kuahiwi.
Gäpe, v. E hamama waha. SYN. yawn.
Gärb, n. Aahu.
Gärb′âge, n. Opala holoholona; opala.
Gär′ble, v. E kalai ino i ka olelo.
Gär′den, n. He kihapai.
Gär′den-er, n. Kahu malama kihapai.
Gär′gle, v. E o′lao′la ma ka puu.
Gär′land, n. Lei. SYN. wreath.
Gär′ment, n. Lole komo.
Gär′ner, n. Hale papaa. SYN. barn.
Gär′ner, v. E hooiliili ma ka hale papaa.
Gär′net, n. Pohaku momi ulaula.
Gär′nish, v. E kahiko a maikai. SYN. decorate; adorn.
Gär′nish-ee′, v. E hoopaa waiwai o ka mea ai-e.
Gär′ret, n. Ke keena oluna loa o ka hale. SYN. attic.
Gär′ri-son, n. Na koa o ka pa-kaua.

Gar-rōte′, *v.* E uumi.

Gär′ru-loŭs, *adj.* Walaau wale.

Gär′ter, *n.* Lipine hoopaa kakini.

Gäs, *n.* Ea mama.

Gäs′e-ous, *adj.* Pili i ke ea mama.

Gäsh, *n.* Wahi moku ma ke kino.

Gäs′light, *n.* Ka malamalama o ke ea mama.

Gas-ŏm′e-ter, *n.* Wahi e hooahu ai o ke ea mama.

Gäsp, *v.* E hanupaa. E mauliawa.

Gäs′trie, *adj.* Pili i ka opu hoowale ai.

Gäs′trie Jŭiçe, *n.* Wai hoowale ai o ka opu.

Gāte, *n.* Puka pa.

Gāte′way, *n.* Kahi e komo ai.

Gäth′er, *v.* 1. E hooakoakoa. SYN. assemble.

　2. E hooiliili. SYN. collect things.

　3. E hoouluulu. SYN. collect animals together.

　4. E ohi. SYN. gather fruit.

　5. E hooahu. SYN. hoard.

Gäth′er-er, *n.* Mea nana e hoiliili, etc.

Gäth′er-ing, *n.* 1. He anaina. SYN. assembly.

　2. Ka mea i ohi ia; hooiliiliia, etc.

　3. He puu ma ke kino.

Gaud′y, *adj.* Hoohiehie pono ole.

Gäuge (gāj), *n.* Mea ana pahu barela.

Gäug′er, *n.* Kanaka ana pahu.

Gäunt, *adj.* Wiwi; olala.

Gäunt′let, *n.* Pale lima loloa.

Gäuze, *n.* Lole lahilahi loa.

Gäwk′y, *adj.* Kuaaina; hemahema.

Gāy, *adj.* 1. Lealea; olioli. SYN. merry.

　2. Nani; maikai loa. SYN. fine.

Gāy′e-ty, *n.* Lealea. SYN. merriment.

Gāy′ly, **Gāi′ly,** } *adv.* Me ka lealea; me ka nani.

Gāze, *v.* E haka pono ka maka.

Ga-zĕlle′, *n.* He dia.

Ga-zĕtte′, *n.* He nupepa no na mea e hoolaha. *Official Gazette,* ka pepa hoolaha ma ke kauoha o ke aupuni.

Gäz′et-eer′, *n.* He buke e hoike ana no na wahi a pau o ka honua.

Gäz′ing-stoek, *n.* Kanaka i hoohene-heneia e ka lehulehu.

Gēar, *n.* Na lako o kela me keia ano.

Gĕld′ing, *n.* Lio i poa ia.

Gĕm, *n.* He momi.

Gĕn′der, *n.* 1. *Masculine gender,* ano kane.

　2. *Feminine gender,* ano wahine.

　3. *Neuter gender,* ano ku okoa.

　4. *Common gender,* ano pili like.

Gĕn′e-a-lŏg′ie-al, *adj.* Kuauhau.

Gĕn′e-äl′o-gist, *n.* Kanaka imi kuauhau.

Gĕn′e-äl′o-gy, *v.* Ke kuauhau.

Gĕn′er-al, *adj.* Pili i na mea a pau; akea. *General good,* pomaikai o ka lehulehu. *General meaning,* ke ano nui. *General intelligence,* ike akea. *General sickness,* mai laulaha.

Gĕn′er-al, *n.* Generala.

Gĕn′er-äl′i-ty, *n.* 1. Ka hapa nui. SYN. majority.

　2. *Generalities,* na mea ano nui.

Gĕn′er-äl-ize, *v.* E hoomaopopo ma ke ano nui.

Gĕn′er-al-ly, *adv* 1. Ma ke ano mau.

　2. *Generally so,* pela i ka hapa nui o ka manawa.

　3. *Generally useful,* makaukau ma kela me keia mea.

　4. *Generally understood,* hoomaopopo ia e ka hapa nui.

Gĕn′er-al-ship, *n.* Ke kulana, ke akamai o ka generala.

Gĕn′er-āte, *v.* E hoohua mai.

Gĕn′er-ā′tion, *n.* 1. Ka hoohua ana mai.

　2. He hanauna. *Third generation,* ku-akahi.

Gĕn′er-ā-tor, *n.* Mea e hoohua ana.

Ge-nĕr′ie, *adj.* Pili i ka papa; ke kulana; ke ano like, ka hanauna.

Gĕn′er-ŏs′i-ty, *n.* Ano lokomaikai; manawalea. SYN. liberality.

Gĕn′er-oŭs, *adj.* Lokomaikai; manawalea. SYN. liberal.

Gĕn′e-sis, *n.* Ka hookumu ana.

Gĕ′ni-al, *adj.* Oluolu; launa; laulea.

Gĕ′ni-äl′i-ty, *n.* Ke ano launa; ano oluolu.

Gĕ′ni-äl-ly, *adv.* Me ka oluolu.

Gĕn′ius, *n.* 1. Ke akamai maoli o ka noonoo.

　2. Mea akamai maoli.

Gen-teel′, *adj.* Ano mikioi; aulii.

Gĕn′tile, *n.* Kanaka no na aina e, wahi o ka poe Judaio.

Gen-til′i-ty, *n.* Ke ano mikioi; ano aulii.

Gĕn′tle, *adj.* 1. Laka. SYN. tame.

　2. Oluolu. SYN. mild; quiet.

　3. Akahai. SYN. meek.

Gĕn′tle-man, *n.* Kanaka hoopono; he keonimana.

Gĕn′tle-man-ly, *adj.* Hoopono; keonimana.

Gĕn′tle-ness, *n.* Laka; oluolu; akahai.

Gĕn′tle-wọm′an, *n.* Wahine hoopono; noho pono; he lede.

Gĕn′tly, *adv.* Me ka oluolu; me ka akahai.

Gĕn′try, *n.* Poe naauao; poe pihalula.

Gĕn′u-ine, *adj.* Oiaio; oia maoli no.

Gē′nus, *n.* He papa o na mea ano like.

Gĕ′o-grăph′ie, **Gĕ′o-grăph′ie-al,** } *adj.* No ka hoike honua.

Gē-ŏg′ra-phy, *n.* Hoike honua.

Gĕ′o-lŏg′ie-al, *adj.* Pili i ke ano o ka honua.

Gē-ŏl′o-gist, *n.* Kanaka huli i ke ano o ka honua.

Gē-ŏl′o-gy, *n.* He hoike no ke ano o ka honua; no ka hana′na o ka honua.

Gĕ′o-mĕt′rie-al, *adj* Pili i ka ana honua.

Gĕ-ŏm′e-tri′çian, *n.* Kanaka huli ana honua.

Gĕ-ŏm′e-try, *n.* Ana honua.

Ġĕrm, n. He mole; he kumu.

Ġĕr-māne′, adj. Pili; pili pono. SYN. fitting; appropriate.

Ġĕr′mi-nate, v. E kupu. SYN. sprout.

Ġĕr′mi-nā′tion, n. Ke kupu ana.

Ges-tic′ū-lāte, v. E kikoo i ka lima, ma ke kamailio ana.

Ges-tic′ū-lā′tion, n. Ke kikoo ana me ka lima.

Ġest′ūre, n. Kikoo lima.

Ġĕt, v. 1. E loaa. SYN. obtain.
2. Get off, e lele ilalo.
3. To get away safely, e pakele.
4. To get under weigh, e hoomaka e holo.

Gew′gaw, n. Mea milimili waiwai ole.

Ghast′ly (gäst′ly), adj. Hakeakea, me he make la.

Ghost (gōst), n. Uhane lapu.

Ġi′ant, n. Kanaka nui loa.

Ġi′ant-ess, n. Wahine nui loa.

Ġib′ber, v. E namunamu. SYN. jabber.

Ġib′ber-ish, n. He olelo namunamu wale.

Ġib-bet, n. Amana. SYN. gallows.

Ġib′boŭs, adj. Ano poepoe. A gibbous moon, ka mahina e piha ana. SYN. convex.

Ġibe, n. Loiloi; henehene. SYN. sneer.

Ġib′lets, n. Ka puuwai me ke ake o na manu.

Ġid′di-ness, n. 1. Poniuniu.
2. Lealea kupono ole o ka naau.

Ġid′dy, adj. 1. Poniuniu.
2. Lealea kupono ole.

Ġift, n. 1. He makana. SYN. present.
2. He ike. SYN. talent; quality.

Ġift′ed adj. Piha i ke akamai; piha i ka naauao. SYN. talented.

Ġig, n. He kaa lio me na huila elua.

Ġi-gän′tic, adj. Nunui loa.

Ġig′gle, v. E akaaka naaupo. SYN. titter.

Ġĭld. v. 1. E hamo me ke gula lahilahi loa.
2. E hoomalamalama, me he alaula la.

Ġill, n. He gila, hapa-ha o ke paina.

Ġill, n. Api; mahamaha.

Ġilt, adj. Hamoia i ke gula.

Ġim′let, n. Wili puka uuku.

Ġin, n. 1. He waiona. gini.
2. He upiki. SYN. trap.
3. Mikini wehe i ka anoano o ka pulupulu.

Ġin′ger, n. Awapuhi.

Ġin′ger-brēad, n. Berena ono i hoomiko pu ia ka awapuhi.

Ġin′ger-ly, adv. Me ke akahele. SYN. cautiously.

Ġing′ham, n. Ginamu.

Ġird, v. E kaei; e haawele; e kahai.

Ġird′er, n. He kaola.

Ġir′dle, n. Kaei.

Ġirl, n. Kaikamahine.

Ġirl′hoŏd, n. Ka wa kaikamahine.

Ġirl′ish, adj. Ku i ke kaikamahine.

Girth, n. 1. He kaula opu.
2. Ke anapuni o kekahi mea.

Ġist, n. Ka i′o o kekahi olelo, a hana paha.

Give, v. E haawi; e manawalea.
2. Give heed, e hoolohe.
3. Give up, e haalele; e paupauaho.
4. Given to reflection, planning or devising, paumaalea; pauakamai.

Ġiv′er, n. Ka mea nana e haawi.

Ġlā′çiĕr, n. Muliwai hau paa o kuahiwi, ma na aina anu, e nee malie loa ana a iloko o na awawa.

Ġlăd, adj. Olioli; hauoli. SYN. delighted; gratified.

Ġlăd′den, v. E hoohauoli.

Ġlăde, n. He kipuka ma ka ulu laau.

Ġlăd′ly, adv. Me ka hauoli.

Ġlăd′ness, n. Hauoli. SYN. joy.

Ġlănçe, n. Ka leha ana o ka maka.

Ġlănd, n. He i-o palupalu, me he huahuakai la; nana ka hana e hookawale i na wai iloko o ke kino.

Ġlâre, n. Malamalama olinolino.

Ġlâre, v. 1. E hulili.
2. E nana me ka maka huhu.

Ġlâss, n. Aniani.

Ġlâss′y, adj. Me he aniani la. A glassy sea, he kai malino.

Ġlāze, v. E hookomo aniani ma ka puka aniani.

Ġlā′zier, n. Kanaka hookomo aniani.

Ġlēam, n. Kukuna malamalama; he ui′uiki. SYN. glimmer.

Ġlēan, v. 1. E ohi i na hua helelei.
2. E noi′i. SYN. collect information secretly.

Ġlēan′er, n. Mea ohi.

Ġlee, n. 1. He olioli; he oli.
2. He leo mele hoolealea.

Ġlee′ful, adj. Piha i ka oli. SYN. merry.

Ġlĕn, n. He awawa uuku. SYN. dell.

Ġlib, adj. Pahee. A glib tongue, he alelo pahee.

Ġlib′ly, adv. Pahee. To talk glibly, e kamailio pahee.

Ġlide, v. 1. E kokolo; mehe nahesa la.
2. E holo niau; mehe kaa ahi la.

Ġlim′mer, n. Uiuiki.

Ġlimpse, n. He ike aweawea; he awiha.

Ġlis′ten, v. E oa′oaka.

Ġlit′ter, v. E wakawaka; e hulili.

Ġlōbe, n. He kino poepoe. SYN. sphere.

Ġlŏb′u-lar, adj. Poepoe. SYN. spherical.

Ġlŏb-ule, n. He kulu. SYN. drop.

Ġloōm, n. Pouli; powehiwehi. Gloom of a forest, lipo waonahele.

Ġloōm-i-ly, adv. 1. Me ka pouliuli.
2. Me ka ehaeha o ka naau.

Ġloōm′y, adj. 1. Pouliuli. SYN. dark. A gloomy day, he la pouliuli.
2. Nunuha; mumule. SYN. sullen.

Ġlō′ri-fi-eā′tion, n. Ka hoonani ana.

Ġlō′ri-fỹ, v. E hoonani.

Ġlō′ri-oŭs, adj. Nani; kamahao.

Glŏ-ry, *n.* Nani; kamahao.

Glŏss. *n* He hinuhinu; he ili pahoehoe.

Glŏs′sy, *adj.* Hinuhinu; pahoehoe.

Glŏve (glŭv), *n.* Pale lima.

Glŏw, *v.* 1. E hooenaena; enaena. *The fire glows,* enaena ke ahi.
2. Omeomeo; ulaula.

Glŏw′ing, *adj.* 1. Enaena. *A glowing fire,* he ahi enaena.
2. Hooeueu; hoolalelale. *A glowing account,* he olelo hooeueu. SYN. inspiriting.

Glūe, *n.* Gelu′; mea pipili.

Glūe, *v.* E hoopipili me ke gelu′.

Glŭm, *adj.* Keemoa; nunuha.

Glŭt, *v.* 1. E hoolawa a lawa loa. *To glut the market,* e hoolawa i kekahi mea a koe, i hiki ole ke kuai.

Glū′ten, *n.* Ka mea pipili iloko o ka palaoa.

Glū′tin-oŭs, *adj.* Pipili. SYN. sticky.

Glŭt′ton, *n.* 1. He wahau′hau′ha. SYN. gormandizer.
2. Kanaka hoonuu ai.

Glŭt-ton-oŭs, *adj.* Hoonuu; uhauha.

Glŭt′ton-y̆, *n.* Hoonuu ai; uhauha.

Gnärled (närld), *adj.* Paapu i na lala. *A gnarled board,* he papa i paapu i na lala.

Gnăsh (năsh), *v.* E uwi ka niho.

Gnăt (nat), *n.* Nalo aki.

Gnăw (naw) *v.* E nalinali; e nau.

Gŏ, *v.* 1. E hele. *Go a-foot,* e hele wawae.
2. E holo. *Go on horseback,* e holo maluna o ka lio.
3. *Go in,* e komo iloko. *Go out,* e puka iwaho.

Gŏal, *n.* 1. Kahi i manaoia e kukini.
2. Ka hopena i manaoia.

Gŏad, *n.* 1. Laau hookikina.
2. Kumu hooeueu.

Gŏad, *v.* E hookikina; e hooeueu.

Gŏat, *n.* He kao.

Gŏat-ee′, *n.* Ka umiumi, koho kao la, o ka auwae.

Gŏat′hĕrd *n.* Kahu hanai kao.

Gŏb, *n.* He puu; he oolopu ai.

Gŏb′ble, *v.* E hoonuu ai; e ai wikiwiki.

Gŏb′bler, *n.* Pelehu′ kane.

Gŏb′let, *n.* Kiaha inu.

Gŏd *n.* 1. Ke Akua; Jehova.
2. He akua.

Gŏd′dess, *n.* Akua wahine.

Gŏd′head, *n.* Ke Akua Kahi-Kolu.

Gŏd′less, *adj.* Nele i ke Akua ole; aia′.

Gŏd′like, *adj.* Ano like me ko Ke Akua.

Gŏd′li-ness, *n.* Ke ano Ke Akua; ke ano hemolele.

Gŏd′ly, *adj.* Haipule; hemolele; pono.

Gŏd′send, *n.* 1. Pomaikai mai Ke Akua mai; pomaikai i ulia mai. SYN. unexpected piece of good fortune.

Gŏg′gles, *n.* Aniani palemaka.

Gŏ-ing, *n.* Ka hele ana.

Gŏi′tre, *n.* Puu alaala ma ka a-i.

Gŏld, *n.* He gula.

Gŏld′en, *adj.* Gula; like me ke gula.

Gŏld′leaf, *n.* Gula i kuiia a lahilahi loa.

Gŏld′smith, *n.* Kanaka hana mea gula.

Gŏn′do-la, *n.* He waa holo lealea ma Venice.

Gŏn′do-llĕr, *n.* Kanaka hoe *gondola.*

Gŏng, *n.* Pa metala palahalaha, poepoe, mea kani; ke bele hookani o ka poe pake′.

Gŏŏd, *adj.* 1. Maikai; pono. SYN. righteous.
2. Kina′ ole; paa. SYN. without flaw.
3. Pololei. SYN. correct.

Gŏŏd-by̆′, *n.* Aloha hookaawale. SYN. adieu.

Gŏŏd′ly, *adv.* 1. Mahuahua. *A goodly number of persons,* he poe mahuahua no.
2. Aulii; mikioi. *A goodly appearance,* he nanaina aulii.

Gŏŏd′ness, *n.* Ke ano maikai; ka pono.

Gŏŏds̱, *n.* Na waiwai liilii o kela me keia ano. *Dry-goods,* na lole kuai o na ano a pau.

Gŏŏd-will′, *n.* Manao lokomaikai; manao oluolu.

Gŏŏse, *n.* Manu ne′ne′.

Gŏŏse′flesh, (on account of cold). Anuhenuhea.

Gŏre, *n.* 1. Koko i hookahe ia.
2. Apana huinakolu o ka lole, a aina paha.

Gŏre, *v.* E hou aku me ke kiwi.

Gŏr′di-an Knŏt, *n.* He pilikia pohihihi. *To cut the Gordian knot,* e hoopau i ka pilikia me ka lima ikaika. SYN. inextricable difficulty.

Gŏrg̱e, *n.* 1. Ka pu a-i.
2. Wahi kuhoho iwaena o na kuahiwi.

Gŏr′g̱eoŭs, *adj.* Nani loa; kamahao.

Go-ril′la, *n.* Keko kanaka o Aferika.

Gŏr′mand-ize, *v.* E no′u.

Gŏr′mand′iz-er, *n.* He wa′hauhau′ha.

Gŏ′ry, *adj.* Paele i ke koko.

Gŏs′ling, *n.* Manu nene opiopio.

Gŏs′pel, *n.* Euanelio.

Gŏs′sip, *n.* Holoholo olelo; lonolonoa′.

Gouge, *n.* Kila o-o′ma.

Gouge, *v.* 1. E poalo. *Gouge out the eye,* e poalo i ka maka.
2. E kalai me ke kila oo′ma.

Gŏurd, *n.* Ipu awa.

Gout, *n.* Ka mai pehu o na ami.

Gŏv′ern, *v* E hoomalu i kanaka.

Gŏv′ern-ess, *n.* 1. Kahu wahine no na keiki o ka ohana.
2. Kiaaina wahine.

Gŏv′ern-ment, *n.* Aupuni.

Gŏv′ern-mĕnt′al, *adj.* No ke aupuni.

Gŏv′ern-or, *v.* 1. Kiaaina.
2. Kahu hoomalu.
3. Mikini hooponopono ana i ka enikini mahu.

Gown, *n.* He holoku′.

Grăb, *v.* E kaili ino; e apo ino aku.

Grāçe, *n.* 1. Lokomaikai. SYN. kindness.
2. Nani. SYN. beauty.
Grāçe'ful, *adj.* 1. Lokomaikai
2. Nani; aulii; upalu; eleu.
Grāçe'ful-ly, *adv.* 1. Me ka lokomaikai.
2. Me ka mikioi.
Grā'çioŭs, *adj.* Lokomaikai.
Grā'çioŭs-ly, *adv.* Me ka oluolu.
Grāde, *n.* 1. He kulana; he papa.
2. Ka moe ana o ke alanui. *Level grade,* moe iliwai.
Grāde, *v.* 1. E hoonoho kulana; e hoonoho papa.
2. E hoomoe i alanui.
Grăd'ū-al, *adj.* 1. Malie. *A gradual ascent*, he pii'na malie.
2. Liilii. *Gradual diminution*, he hooemi liilii.
Grăd'ū-al-ly, *adv.* Ma ka noii; me ka malie.
Grăd'u-āte, *v.* 1. E loaa ka palapala apono mai ke kula nui mai.
2. E kaha i na degere maluna o kekahi mea.
Grăd'u-ā'tion, *n.* Ka hookuu ana me ka palapala apono.
Grăft, *n.* He opuu i pakuia i kehahi laau e ae.
Grāin, *n.* 1. Na hua palaoa o na ano a pau.
2. He huna. *A grain of sand*, he huna one.
Grāin, *v.* E pena kohu hooluu laau la.
Grăm'i-nĭv'o-roŭs, *adj.* E ai ana i ke mauu; ai mauu.
Grăm'mar, *n.* Hoike olelo.
Gram-mā'rian, *n.* Kanaka makaukau ma ka hoike olelo.
Gram-măt'ie-al-ly, *adv.* Like me na rula o ka hoike olelo.
Grăn'a-ry, *n.* Waihona no na hua palaoa.
Grănd, *adj.* Nani; kamahao.
Grănd-chĭld, *n.* He moopuna.
Grănd'eur, *n.* Ka nani; ke kamahao.
Grănd'fāth'er,} *n.* Kupuna kane.
Grănd'sire,}
Grănd-jū'ry, *n.* Ke jure nui, e imi e ana i na hihia karaima, mamua o ka hookolokolo ana.
Grănd'mŏth'er, *n.* Kupuna wahine.
Grănt, *n.* He haawina o kela me keia ano waiwai.
Grănt, *v.* E ae; e haawi.
Grănt-eeʼ, *n.* Ka mea e loaa ana.
Grănt'or, *n.* Ka mea nana e haawi.
Grăn'u-lāte, *v.* E hoolilo kekahi mau mea wai i mau huna paa. *Granulate cane juice*, e hoolilo ka wai o ke ko i mau huna ko paa.
Grāpe, *n.* 1. Hua waina.
2. Poka' nui i hoopihaia i na poka' liilii.
Grāpe'vīne, *n.* Kumu waina.
Grăph'ie, *adj.* Moakaka ke kakau ana.

Grăph'īte, *n.* Kepau mea hana penikila.
Grăp'ple, *v.* 1. E aumeume.
2. E apo aku.
Grăsp, *v.* E apo.
Grăsp, *n.* 1. He apo lima.
2. *The grasp of thought*, ke apo ana i ka manao.
Grăsp'ing, *adj.* Alunu; puniwaiwai.
Grăss, *n.* Mauu; weuweu.
Grăss'hop-per, *n.* He uhini.
Grăss'y, *adj.* Uliuli i ke mauu; uhiia i ke mauu.
Grāte, *v.* 1. E olo; e kolikoli.
2. E oe; oeoe.
Grāte, *n.* Hao manamana o ke kapuahi.
Grāte'ful, *adj.* 1. Aloha aku no ke kokuaia mai. SYN. thankful.
2. Oluolu. SYN. pleasant.
Grāte'ful-ly, *adv.* 1. Me ke aloha no na pono i loaa mai.
2. Me ka oluolu. SYN. pleasantly.
Grāt'er, *n.* Mea olo; mea kolikoli.
Grăt'i-fi-cā'tion, *n.* 1. Ka oluolu o ka manao. SYN. satisfaction.
2. Ke ko ana o ka makemake.
Grăt'i-fȳ, *v.* 1. E hooluolu; e hoolaulea.
2. E ko i ka makemake.
Grāt'ing, *n.* Hao manamana.
Grāt'ing, *adj.* Oeoe.
Grăt'is, *adv.* Makana wale.
Grăt'i-tūde, *n.* Ke aloha no ke kokuaia mai. SYN. thankfulness.
Gra-tū'i-toŭs, *adj.* Manawalea; uku ole. *Gratuitous aid*, kokua manawalea.
Gra-tū'i-toŭs-ly, *adv.* Manawalea wale.
Gra'tū'i-ty, *n.* He makana. SYN. gift.
Grāve, *n.* Lua kupapau.
Grāve, *adj.* Koikoi. *A grave thought*, he manao koikoi.
Grāve, *v.* E kahakaha.
Grăv'el, *n.* Iliili.
Grāve'ly, *adv.* Me ke koikoi o ka manao.
Grăv'er, *n.* Mea kahakaha.
Grāve'-stōne, *n.* Pohaku hoomanao, no ka ilina.
Grāve'-yard, *n.* Pa kupapau; ilina.
Grăv'i-tāte, *v.* E ume kaumaha.
Grăv'i-tā'tion, *n.* Ka ume kaumaha.
Grăv'i-ty, *n.* 1. Ke kaumaha; ke koikoi.
2. Ke koikoi o ka manao.
Grā'vy, *n.* Kai o na i'o i hoomoaia.
Grāy,} *adj.* Ahinahina; hina.
Grey}
Grāy'bĕard, *n.* Kanaka poohina.
Grāze, *v.* E ai mauu.
2. E aneane pili; e pohole iki.
Grā'zier, *n.* Kanaka hanai holoholona.
Grēase, *n.* Aila hamo.
Grēase, *v.* E hamo i ka aila.
Grēas'y, *adj.* Paele i ka aila hamo.
2. *A greasy fluid*, kai likoliko.
Greăt, *adj.* Nui; hanohano.

Great'ly, *adv.* Nui loa; loa. *Greatly beloved,* aloha nui loa ia.

Great'ness, *n.* Ke ano nui; ka hanohano.

Grē'çian, *n.* No Helene.

Greed'i-ly, *adv.* Me ke alunu.

Greed'i-ness, *n.* Alunu; he uha wale.

Greed'y, *adj.* Alunu; uha wale.

Green, *adj.* 1. Omaomao; uliuli.
2. Maka. SYN. unripe.

Green-grō'çer, *n.* Kanaka kuai mea ai maka.

Green'horn, *n.* Kanaka hemahema; kanaka hawa'wa'.

Green'house, *n.* Hale hoo-ulu mea ulu.

Greens, *n. pl.* Na ai i like me ka luau, ha'ha', limu etc.

Green'sward, *n.* Mauu uliuli.

Greet, *v.* E aloha aku; SYN. salute.

Greet'ing, *n.* Ke aloha i ka halawai pu ana. SYN. salutation.

Gre-gā'ri-oŭs. *adj.* Ano launa; maa i ka hele pu ma na pua'.

Grey-hound, *n.* He ilio nunui, wawae loloa.

Grid'dle, *n.* Pa parai palaoa.

Grid'iron, *n.* Hao manamana.

Grief, *n.* Kaumaha; ehaeha; uhu'

Griēv'ançe, *n.* Kumu kaumaha; kumu pilikia.

Grieve, *v.* E uwe; e kaniuhu'

Griēv'oŭs, *adj.* Kaumaha; ehaeha.

Grī-mace', *n.* Haikaika. SYN. grin.

Grim, *adj.* Keemoa; kuemaka.

Grim'ly, *adv.* Keemoa.

Grin, *n.* Haikaika.

Grind, *v.* E hookala. SYN. sharpen.
2. E wili. *Grind sugar cane,* e wili ko.
3. E hookaumaha. SYN. oppress.

Grind'er, *n.* Niho nui.

Grind'stone, *n.* Hoana kaa.

Grip, *v.* E apo ikaika. SYN. grasp.

Gripe, *n.* Nahu; umii'.
2. *Gripe of poverty,* ka lokomo o ka nele.

Gris'tle, *n.* Kumukumu. SYN. cartilage.

Grist, *n.* Na hua palaoa i wiliia.

Grist'mill, *n.* He wili palaoa.

Grit, *n.* 1. He o'ne.
2. He hoomanawanui; manao kupaa. SYN. spunk.

Griz'zly, *adj.* Hina. *Grizzly hair,* hina ka lauoho.

Grōan, *v.* E uhu'; e nu.

Grōan'ing, *n.* Ka uhu ana o ka leo.

Grō'çer, *n.* Kanaka kuai i na mea ai.

Grō'çer-ies, *n. pl.* Kela me keia ano mea ai.

Grō'çer-ӯ, *n.* Hale kuai o na mea ai.

Grŏg, *n.* Wai ona i kawili pu ia me ka wai.

Grŏg'shop, *n.* Hale kuai wai ona.

Groin, *n.* Puhaka.

Groom, *n.* 1. Kane akahi no a mare. SYN. bridegroom.
2. Kahu malama lio.

Groove, *n.* He ho'le.

Grōpe, *v.* E haha aku me he makapo la.

Grōss, *n.* 12 Kakini.

Grōss, *adj.* 1. Nunui pono ole.
2. Haumia; pelapela.

Grōss'ness, *n.* 1. Ka nui kupono ole.
2. Ka haumia; ka pelapela.

Grōss'ly, *adv.* I kana ole, launa ole. *Grossly ignorant,* naaupo launa ole.

Grŏt, } *n.* He ana.
Grŏt'to, }

Gro-tēsque, *adj.* Ku i ka akaaka. SYN. fantastic.

Ground, *n.* Lepo; honua.
2. Kahua. SYN. foundation.

Ground, *v.* Ili; mau. *The boat has grounded,* ua ili ka waapa.

Ground-floor, *n.* Ka papa hele o lalo loa o ka hale.

Ground'less, *adj.* Kumu ole; kahua ole. *Groundless fear,* maka'u kumu ole, *or,* maka'u wale.

Ground'plan, *n.* Kii o ke kahua-hale.

Ground'plot, *n.* Kahua o ka hale.

Ground'rent, *n.* Uku hoolimalima no ke kahua hale.

Ground'work, *n.* Ka hana hoo-kahua.
2. *Groundwork of knowledge,* na kumu mua o ka ike.

Group, *n.* He pu-a. SYN. collection.
2. Huhui. SYN. cluster. *A cluster of stars,* he huhui ho-ku'

Grōve, *n.* He wahi ululaau uuku.

Grŏv'el, *v.* 1. E kokolo maluna o ka honua.
2. E hoohaahaa a i ka lepo.

Grŏv'el-er, *n.* Mea haahaa loa; mea kolo ma ka lepo.

Grōw, *v.* 1. E kupu; e ulu ae; e hoo-ulu.
2. E lilo. SYN. become. *Grow rich,* or *become rich,* e lilo i waiwai.

Growl, *v.* E uwo; e keke.

Grōwth, *n.* Ka ulu ana; ka mahuahua ana.

Grŭb, *n.* 1. He enuhe.
2. Ai.

Grŭdge, *v.* E aua.

Grŭdge, *n.* He hoomauhala.

Grŭ'el, *n.* He pudina lahilahi.

Grŭff, *adj.* Kalakala; nihaniha.

Grŭff-ly, *adv.* Me ke kalakala o ka leo.

Grŭm'ble, *v.* 1. E ohumu.
2. *Grumble to one's self,* e kinaunau.

Grŭnt, *v.* E nu'; e u'hu me he puaa la.

Guã'no, *n.* Kukae manu.

Guãr'an-tee', *v.* E hooia.

Guãr'an-tee', *n.* He hookiki no ka pono o kekahi mea.

Guārd, *v.* E kiai; e kuoo.

Guārd'i-an, *n.* He kahu ma ke kanawai

Guãr'di-an-ship, *n.* Oihana kahu.

Guārd'room, *n.* Keena o na koa kiai.

Guā'va, *n.* He hua puawa.

Gŭ'ber-na-tō'ri-al, *adj.* Pili i ka oihana kiaaina.

Guĕss, *v.* E koho wale.

Guĕst, *n.* Hoaaina; mea i hookipaia.

Guĕst'-cham-ber,) *n.* Keena hookipa.
Guĕst'-room, }
Guid'ance, *n.* Ke alakai ana.
Guide, *n.* He alakai.
Guide'post, *n.* Kia kuhikuhi.
Guile, *n.* Epa: maalea. SYN. craft.
Guile'less, *adj.* Akaka; oiaio; epa ole. SYN. honest.
Guil'lo-tine, *n.* Mikini oki poo.
Guilt, *n.* Hewa; hala.
Guilt'i-ly, *adv.* Me ka hewa.
Guilt'i-ness, *n.* Hewa.
Guilt'less, *adj.* Hala ole; hewa ole.
Guilt'y, *adj.* Hewa.
Guin'ea (gin'y) *n.* Apana dala gula o Beritania; 21 silina.
Guise, *n.* Ano o ko waho. SYN. external appearance.
Gulf, *n.* Kaikuono.
Gŭll, *n.* 1. He manu o ke kai.
2. Mea puni wale.
Gŭl'let, *n.* Ka puu. SYN. esophagus.
Gŭl'ly, *n.* He auwaha.
Gŭlp, *v.* E moni me ka pono ole.
Gŭm, *n.* He pilali.
Gŭm'boil, *n.* He puu ma kahi o na niho.
Gŭm'my, *adj.* Pipili. SYN. sticky.
Gŭmp'tion, *n.* Noeau; akamai.
Gŭn, *n.* He pu ki.
Gŭn'boat, *n.* He waapa manuwa' me ka pu nui.
Gŭn'ner, *n.* Kanaka lawelawe pu.
Gŭn'ner-y, *n.* Ka ike no ke ki pu.
Gŭn'pow-der, *n.* Pauda ki pu.

Gŭn'shot, *n.* 1. Poka'; lu.
2. Ka loihi kahi e lele ai ka poka'.
3. *Gunshot wound*, eha i ka poka'.
Gŭn'smith *n.* Kanaka hana pu.
Gŭn'stock, *n.* Ke kumu o ka pu.
Gŭn'wale (gŭn'nel) *n.* Ka papa kae o ka waapa.
Gŭr'gle, *v.* 1. E omo; e like me ka wai e piha ana i ka omole; e olaola.
2. E kakahe walaau. *The gurgling brook*, kahawai kakahe walaau.
Gŭsh. *v.* E kahe ino mai.
Gŭst, *v.* Makani puahiohio.
Gŭst'y. *adj.* Pukiki. *A gusty wind*, he makani pukiki.
Gŭt, *n.* Naau liilii.
Gŭt'tà-pêr'chà, *n.* He pilali ano like me ka laholio.
Gŭt'ter, *n.* Kio lepo.
Gŭt'ter-al, *adj.* Pili i ke kania-i. *A gutteral sound*, leo no loko ae o ke kania-i.
Guȳ, *n.* Kaula e koo ana i kekahi mea.
Gŭz'zle, *v.* E pakela inu.
Gym-nā'ṣi-um, *n.* 1. Wahi hooikaika kino.
2. He kula kiekie.
Gȳm'nast, *n.* Kanaka hooikaika kino.
Gȳm-nās'tic, *adj.* Pili i ka hooikaika kino.
Gȳm-nās'tics, *n. pl.* Ka hooikaika kino.
Gȳp'sy, *n.* Kekahi o na mamo kuewa wale o Europa.
Gȳ-rā'tion, *n.* Ka nee poai ana.

H

Hā'be-as Côr'pus, *n.* Palapala hookuu kino.
Ha-bil'i-ment, *n.* Aahu. SYN. clothing.
Hăb'it, *n.* 1. Hana maa. SYN. custom.
2. Aahu. SYN. dress.
Hăb'it-a-ble, *adj.* Hiki ke noho ia.
Hăb'i-tā'tion, *n.* Wahi noho mau. SYN. abode; dwelling.
Ha-bit'ū-al, *adj.* Maa; walea. SYN. customary.
Ha-bit'ū-al-ly, *adv.* Mau.
Ha-bit'ū-āte, *v.* E hoomaamaa. SYN. accustom.
Hăck, *n.* Kaa lio holoholo.
Hăck, *v.* E oki hemahema.
Hăck'neyed, *adj.* Kahiko. *A hackneyed subject*, kumu manao kahiko. SYN. old.
Hăft, *n.* He au pahi.
Hăg, *n.* He luwahine pupuka ino.
Hăg'gard, *adj.* Haikea; onawaliwali.

Hăg'gle, *v.* E hoohalahala no ke kumukuai.
Hăg'gler, *n.* Kanaka hoohalahala mau no ke kumu kuai.
Hăil, *n.* Hua hekili.
Hăil, *v.* 1. E haule mai he hua hekili.
2. E kahea leo nui,
3. E haawi i ke aloha.
Hăil'stone, *n.* SYN. hail.
Hăil'storm, *n.* Ka haule ino ana o ka hua hekili.
Hăir, *n.* Lauoho.
Hăir'brĕadth, *adj.* Mahunehune. SYN. narrow. *An hairbreadth escape*, he pakele mahunehune.
2. Kokoke loa. SYN. very nearly.
Hăir'brŭsh, *n.* Hulu kahi lauoho.
Hăir'clŏth, *n.* Lole hanaia i ka lauoho.
Hăir'less, *adj.* Ohule; lauoho ole.
Hăir'y, *adj.* Paapu i ka lauoho; huluhulu.

Häl′cy-on, *adj.* Malia; malino. SYN. calm; peaceful.

Häle, *adj.* Ikaika; puipui.

Hälf; *n.* He hapalua.

Hälf′cäste, *n.* He hapahaole.

Hälf′pay, *n.* Uku hapa.

Hälf′wit-ted, *adj.* Ano lolo ma ka noonoo.

Hall, *n.* 1. Keena komo o ka hale.
 2. Keena nui no na halawai.
 3. Hale nui.
 4. *Halls of justice*, na keena hookolokolo.

Hä′le-lū′jah, *interj.* Aleluia!

Hal-loo′, *interj.* E o! leo kahea.

Häl′lōw, *v.* E hoano.

Hal-lū′ci-nä′tion, *n.* He hihio o ka naau.

Hä′lo, *n.* Pona′hana′ha; Lua hoana; luakalai.

Halt, *v.* 1. E ku, e noho iki. SYN. stop.
 2. E holo ku-ku. SYN. limp.

Hal′ter, *n.* 1. Kaula punuku.
 2. Kaula kaawe. SYN. noose.

Hälve, *v.* E mahele hapalua.

Hälves, **(halvz)** *n. pl.* Na hapalua

Häl′yard, *n.* Kaula huki pea; kaula huki hae.

Häm, *n.* Puaa hama.

Hämes, *n.* Na hao e hoopaa ana i na kaula huki kaa lio, i ka a-i o ka lio.

Häm′let, *n.* Kauhale uuku. SYN. small village.

Häm′mer, *n.* Hamale.

Häm′mer, *v.* E kui me ka hamale.

Häm′mock, *n.* Moe e lewa ana.

Häm′per, *n.* He i-e nunui, mea lawe ai.

Häm′per, *v.* E hoopilikia; e keakea. SYN. encumber; embarrass.

Händ, *n.* Lima.

Händ, *v.* E haawi lima. *Hand over the book*, e haawi lima mai i ka buke.

Händ′bill, *n.* Olelo hoolaha i paiia.

Händ′book, *n.* Buke liilii, o kela me keia ike, i makaukau ma ka lima.

Händ′euff, *n.* Kupee lima; upiki lima.

Händ′ful, *n.* Piha lima.

Händ′i-craft, *n.* Oihana hana lima.

Händ′i-ly, *adv.* Me ka mikioi.

Händ′i-work, *n.* Ka hana o ka lima.

Händ′ker-chief, *n.* Hainaka′.

Hän′dle, *n.* 1. He au.
 2. *Hoe*, or *o-o handle*, kano.

Hän′dle, *v.* 1. E lawelawe· SYN. use.
 2. E lalau lima. *To handle baggage*, E lalau lima aku i ka ukana.
 3. E mili; e milimili. SYN. *handle carefully for examination*, or *from curiosity*.

Händ′mäid, ⎫
Händ′mäid′en,⎬ *n.* Kauwa wahine.

Händ′saw, *n.* Pahi-olo lalau lima.

Händ′sŏme, *adj.* Upalu; onaona; maikai.

Händ′sŏme-ly, *adv.* Me ka nani; me ka maikai; me ka eleu.

Händ′writ′ing, *n.* Ke kakau lima.

Händ′y, *adj.* Makaukau. *A handy man*, he kanaka makaukau. SYN. ready.

Häng, *v.* 1. E li. *To hang on the gallows*, e li ma ka amana.
 2. E kaawe. SYN. to hang one's self.
 3. E kau; e kaulai. *Hang up to dry*, E kaulai i maloo.
 4. *To hang on the cross*, e kaulia ma ke kea.

Häng′er-on′, *n.* 1. Kanaka hoopilimeaai.
 2. He a′ea wale.

Häng′ings, *n.* Na paku lole o kela me keia ano.

Häng′man, *n.* Kanaka li kanaka.

Hänk, *n.* He mau owili lopi i owili pu ia.

Hänk′er, *v.* E kuko nui.

Hänk′-er-ing, *n.* Ke kuko nui ana.

Häp′häz′ard, *n.* Mea ulia wale. SYN. chance.

Häp′pen, *v.* 1. Loohia. SYN. occur.
 2. Wale. *To happen on a person*, e loaa wale i kekahi.

Häp′pi-ly, *adv.* Oluolu. *To live happily together*, e noho oluolu pu.
 2. Pomaikai. SYN. fortunately.

Häp′pi-ness, *n.* Ka oluolu o ka manao.

Häp′py, *adj.* Oluolu.

Här′ass, *v.* E hoopilikia; e hoonaukiuki; hoouluhua.

Här′bin-ger, *n.* He ouli.

Här′bor, *n.* Awa ku moku.

Här′bor, *v.* 1. E hookipa. *Harbor evil designs*, e hookipa i na noonoo ino.
 2. *Harbor ill will*, e hoomauhala.

Härd, *adj.* 1. Paa; paakiki.
 2. Oolea. *A hard man*, he kanaka oolea.
 3. Pilikia. *Hard times*, na wa pilikia.

Härd′en, *v.* E hoopaakiki; e hoo-olea; e hookai-i.

Härd′ened, *adj.* Paakiki. *A hardened sinner*, he kanaka ino paakiki.

Härd-heärt′ed, *adj.* Lokoino; paakiki o ka naau. SYN. cruel.

Härd′i-hood, *n.* Ka aa i na mea kupono ole. SYN. effrontery.

Härd′ly, *adv.* 1, Me ka oolea. SYN. harshly.
 2. Aole kupono loa. *Hardly true*, aole kupono loa i ka oiaio.

Härd′ness, *n.* Ke ano paakiki; ano paa; ano oolea.

Härd′ship, 1. He popilikia.
 2. Haawe kaumaha.

Härd′wâre, *n.* Na mea hao o kela me keia ano.

Härd-y, *adj.* Uaua; ui.

Häre, *n.* He rabita nui.

Häre′brāined, *adj.* Noonoo ole; aa wale.

Hä′rem, *n.* Ohana wahine ma ka aina hikina.

Härk, *interj.* Hamau! SYN. listen.

Här′lot, *n.* Wahine hookamakama.

Härm, *n.* Poino; pilikia.

Härm′less, *adj.* Poino ole; hooeha ole.

Har-mŏn′ics, *n.* Ka ike e pili ana i na leo mele.

Har-mö'ni-oŭs, *adj.* 1. Kani like.
2. Lokahi.
Har-mö'ni-oŭs-ly, *adv.* Me ka lokahi.
Här'mo-nize, *v.* E lokahi pu.
Här'mo-ny, *n.* 1. Ke ano nahenahe o ka leo.
2. Ka lokahi ana.
Här'ness, *n.* Lei kauo no ka lio.
Här'ness, *n.* E hoa i ka lei.
Härp, Lira hookani.
Härp'er, *n.* Mea hookani lira.
Här-pöon', *n.* Mea o kohola'.
Här-pöon'er, *n.* Kanaka o i'-a
Här'röw, *n.* He hapuku no ka aina; he mea kahi aina.
Här'röw, *v.* 1. E hapuku i ka aina i palau mua ia; e kahi i ka aina.
2. E hoopilihua; hoouluhua. SYN. lacerate.
Härsh, *adj.* 1. Niha; kamaniha. SYN. harsh in manner.
2. Aaka; kalakala. SYN. harsh in voice.
Härsh'ly, *adv.* Nihaniha; kalakala.
Här'vest, *a.* Ka wa ohi.
Här'vest, *v.* E ohi.
Häsh, *n.* Haki; he i-o a me ka uala i okiokiia a liilii, a kawili puia.
Häste, } *v.* 1. E awiwi; e hikiwawe.
Häs'ten, } 2. E hoohikiwawe.
Häs'ti-ly, *adv.* 1. Me ka awiwi. SYN. quickly.
2. Me ka pupuahulu; me ka noonoo pono ole. SYN. without consideration.
Häs'ty, *adj.* Pupuahulu. *Hasty words,* na huaolelo i noonoo ole ia. SYN. inconsiderate, noonoo ole ia.
Hat, *n.* Papale.
Hatch, *v.* E kiko i na hua.
Hatched, *p. p.* Laukoa.
Hatch'et, *n.* Koi liilii.
Hätch'wäy, *n.* Kahi e hookomo ai ka ukana.
Häte, *v.* E inaina; e hoopailua.
Häte'ful, *adj.* Hoopailuaia.
Hä'tred, *n.* Inaina; huahua'.
Hät'ter, *n.* Kanaka hana papale.
Haugh'ti-ly, *adv.* Me ka haakei; me ka hookiekie.
Haugh'ty, *adj.* Haakei; hookiekie.
Haul, *v.* E huki. SYN. pull.
Häunch, *n.* Uha'.
Häunt, *v.* 1. E loaa mau ma kauwahi.
2. E uluhia i ka lapu; ka daimonio.
3. Ala mau mai. *The thought haunts me,* ala mau mai ka noonoo iloko o'u.
Have, *v.* 1. E loaa. SYN. possess.
2. He haina kokua i na haina e ae; e hoike ana no ka wa i hala.
Hä'ven, *n.* He puuhonua; wahi e malu ai. SYN. shelter; refuge.
Häv'oe, *n.* Poino; luku. SYN. destruction.
Hä-wai'ian, *n.* Kamaaina no Hawaii.
Hąw'şer, *n.* Kaula nui hoopaa moku i ka uapo; a e hookolo moku paha.

Hąwşe'höle, *n.* Puka ma ka ihu o ka moku, no ke kaula hao o ka heleuma.
Häy, *n.* Mauu maloo.
Häy'ing-time, *n.* Wa hana mauu maloo.
Häy'stack, *n.* Ahua mauu maloo.
Häz'ard, *v.* E aa i ka poino; e komo ma kahi o ka poino.
Häz'ard-oŭs, *adj.* Paapu i ka poino. SYN. perilous.
Häze, *n.* Poluhiluhi; molehulehu.
Häz'y, *adj.* Moakaka ole; powehiwehi.
Hē, *pron.* Ia; oia.
Hēad, *n.* Poo.
Hēad, *v.* 1. E ku poo; e ku mua. SYN. lead.
2. E keakea; e pale. SYN. head off.
Hēad'äche (äke), *n.* Nalulu; nipoa.
Hēad'dress, *n.* Ke kahiko no ke poo.
Hēad'first, *adj.* Ki'mo'.
Hēad'land, *n.* Lae kiekie. SYN. promontory.
Hēad'long, *adj.* Noonoo ole e mamua. SYN. rash; inconsiderate.
Hēad'quär'ters, *n.* Kahi e noho ai o ke poo o kekahi oihana.
Hēad'stąll, *n.* Kaula punuku.
Hēad'strong, *adj.* Ai oolea. SYN. stiffnecked.
Hēad-wäy, *n.* Ka nee ana imua. *To make headway,* e nee imua.
Hēad'wind', *n.* Makani pa mamua mai.
Hēad'work'man, *n.* Luna hana. SYN. foreman.
Hēad'y, *adj.* 1. Paakiki ma ka manao; a-i oolea; nunuha. SYN. selfwilled; ungovernable.
2. Ona. SYN. intoxicating.
3. Huhu koke; inaina koke. SYN. violent; rash.
Hēal, *v.* E ola pono ka eha; e hoola i ka eha.
Hēalth, *n.* Ka ola pono o ke kino, a o ka naau paha.
Hēalth'ful, *adj.* Ku i ke ola o ke kino.
Hēalth'i-ness, *n.* Ke kupono i ke ola kino.
Hēalth'y, *adj.* Mai ole; ui; ola pono; puipui.
Hēap, *n.* He ahua; he puu.
Hēap, *v.* E hoo-ahu.
Hēar, *v.* E lohe; e hoolohe.
Hēar'er, *n.* Mea e lohe ana.
Hēar'ing, *n.* Ka lohe ana.
Hēärk'en (härk-en), *v.* E hoolohe; e haliu mai ka pepeiao.
Hēarse, *n.* Kaa halihali kupapau.
Hēar'say, *n.* Lono; lonolono-a'. SYN. rumor; report.
Hēärt, *n.* Puuwai; naau.
Hēärt'äche, *n.* 1. Eha ma ka puuwai.
2. Luuluu o ka naau.
Hēärt'bŭrn, *n.* Umaumanaha'; hahoa
Hēärt'felt, *adj.* Pumehana. *Heartfelt thanks,* aloha pumehana.
Hēärth. *n.* Kapuahi.

Heärt′i-ly, *adv* 1. Me ka naau apau; me ka ikaika. SYN. vigorously.
2. Nui. *Eat heartily,* ai a nui. SYN. freely.

Heärt′less, *adj.* Menemene ole; aloha ole; opukopekope.

Heärt′rend′ing, *adj.* Kupaka; walania.

Heärt′sick, *adj.* Poho′ ka manao. SYN. disheartened.

Heärt′y, *adj.* 1. Oiaio. SYN. true.
2. Puipui. SYN. strong; healthy.
3. Manao ikaika.

Heat, *n.* Wela.

Hëa′then, *n.* He pegana.

Hëa′then-ish, *adj.* Pegana.

Hëa′then-ism, *n.* Ka noho ana o ka pegana.

Heave, *v.* 1. E hoolei SYN. throw.
2. Naenae. SYN. pant.

Hëav′en, *n.* Lani. *Heavens,* na aouli.

Hëav′en-ly, *adj.* Lani. SYN. celestial.

Hëav′i-ly, *adv.* 1. Kaumaha. *Heavily in debt,* kaumaha i ka aie.
2. Nui loa. *Rain heavily,* u′-a nui loa.

Hëav′i-ness, *v.* Ke kaumaha.
2. Luuluu.

Hëav′y, *adj.* Kaumaha; koikoi.

Hë′brew, *v.* He ludaio.

Hëc′tor, *v.* E hoonaukiuki. SYN. bully; tease.

Hëdge, *n.* Pa laau e ulu ana.

Hëdge, *v.* 1. E hoopuni i ka pa.
2. E hoopuni. SYN. surround.

Heed, *v.* E hoolohe; e malama.

Heed′less, *adj.* Hoolohe ole; malama ole. SYN. careless.

Heed′less-ly, *adv.* Me ka hoolohe ole. SYN. carelessly.

Heed′less-ness, *n.* Ke ano malama ole; hoolohe ole. SYN. carelessness.

Heel, *n.* Kuekue wawae.

Hëft, *n.* Kaumaha. SYN. weight.

He-gi′rä, *n.* Ka hee ana o Mahometa mai Mecca aku, July 16, A. D. 622.

Hëif′er, *n.* Bipi wahine opio.

Height, } *n.* Kiekie. *Grand mountain*
Hight, } *n.* *hight,* kilakila.

Height′en, } *v.* E hoomahuahua.
Highten, } *v.* E hookiekie ae.

Hein′oŭs, *adj.* Hewa loa. SYN. atrocious.

Hëir (är), *n.* Hooilina.

Hëir′ess, *n.* Hooilina wahine.

Hëir′loom, *v.* Waiwai i hooilinaia mai kahi hanauna a i kahi hanauna.

Hëir′ship, *n.* Ke kulana hooilina.

Hë′li-o-trope, *n.* 1. He pua.
2. He mea e hoopaa ana i na kukuna malamalama o ka la, a e hoolei ana ia lakou ma kahi i makemakeia.

Hëll, *n.* Gehena; ka luaahi.

Hël′lish, *adj.* Kohu luaahi la; hewa lua ole.

Hëlm, *n.* Hoeuli. SYN. rudder.

Hëlm′et, *n.* Mahiole.

Hëlp, *v.* E kokua. SYN. assist; aid.

Hëlp′er, *n.* He mea kokua; kokoolua. SYN. assistant.

Hëlp′ful, *adj.* Makaukau i ke kokua; kokua.

Hëlp′less, *adj.* Hiki ole ke kokua iaia iho; Hiki ole ke kokua.

Hëlp′less-ness, *n.* Ka hiki ole ole ana. SYN. inability.

Hëlp′meet, *n.* 1. Kokoolua. SYN. assistant.
2. Wahine mare. SYN. wife.

Hël′ter-skël′ter, *adv.* Huikau.

Hëlve, *n.* Au koi.

Hëm, *n.* Lepa.

Hëm, *v.* E humu pelu.

Hëm′i-sphëre, *n.* Hapa poepoe.

Hëm′or-rhäge (raj), *n.* Luai koko.

Hëmp, *n.* He olona′ ma na aina haole.

Hën, *n.* Moa wahine.

Hënçe, *adv.* 1. Mai nei aku.
2. Nolaila; no ia mea. SYN. therefore.

Hënçe-förth′, } *adv.* Mai keia wa
Hënçe-for′ward, } aku.

Hëp′ta-gön, *n.* Huina-lehulehu-aoao-ehiku.

Hër, *pron.* Kona; paniinoa no ka wahine.

Hër′ald, *v-* E kukala e mamua.

Hër′ald, *n.* He elele.

Hërb (ûrb), *n-* Mea ulu palupalu.

Hër-bä′çeoŭs, *adj.* Ano palupalu.

Hërb′age, *n.* 1. Na mea ulu palupalu.
2. He mauu.

Hër-bä′ri-ŭm, *n.* Buke malama lau, me na mea ulu.

Her-biv′o-roŭs, *adj.* Ai i na mea ulu.

Her-eü-le-an, *adj.* Ka ikaika o Hercules, ke akua o ka ikaika o ka poe Helene; nolaila, he ikaika lua ole.

Hërd, *n.* He pu-a holoholona nunui. *A herd of cattle,* he pu-a bipi.

Hërd, *v.* E ho-akoakoa mau i na holoholona; e hoo-pu-a.

Hërdş′man, *n.* Kanaka hoo-pu-a holoholona.

Hëre, *adv.* Eia; maanei; nei.

Hëre′ä-boŭts′, *adv.* Ma kauwahi o nei.

Hëre-äft′er, *adv.* Mai keia mua aku; mahope aku.

Hëre-by′ *adv.* Ma keia, mamuli o keia.

He-rëd′i-ta-ry, *adj.* Kuu-na′.

Hëre-in′, *adv.* Ma keia; maloko o keia. *Herein specified,* i hoikeia maloko o keia, *or* maloko ae nei.

Hëre-up-ön′, *adv.* No keia mea; mamuli o keia mea.

Hër-e-sy, *n.* Kuhihewa o ka manaoio.

Hër′e-tic, *n.* He kanaka kue ma ka manaoio; heretiko.

Hëre′to-före, *adv.* Mamua iho nei.

Hëre-with′, *adv.* Me keia.

Hër′it-age, *n.* Waiwai hooilina. SYN. inheritance.

Her-mäph′ro-dite, *n.* He mahu′.

Her-mët′ie-al-ly, *adv.* Paa loa; komo ole ke ea.

Hër′mit, *n.* Kanaka noho mehameha.

Hër′mit-äge, *n.* Wahi noho mehameha.

Hē′ro, *n.* Kanaka aa nui i na pilikia; kanaka koa.

He-rō′ic, *adj.* Koa; aa nui; wiwo ole.

Hēr′o-ine, *n.* He wahine koa.

Hēr′o-ism, *n.* Ke ano koa.

Her-sēlf′, *pron.* Oia iho; iaia iho, (pili i ka wahine).

Hēs′i-tan-çy, *n.* 1. Kanalua; kuipehi. SYN. doubt; uncertainty.
2. Uu o ka leo. SYN. hesitancy of speech.

Hēs′i-tāte, *v.* 1. E kanalua; e kulanalana. SYN. falter; waver.
2. E uu. SYN. stammer.

Hēs′i-tā′tion, *n.* SYN. hesitancy.

Hēt′er-o-dox, *adj.* Kulike ole i ke kulana i kukuluia.

Hew (hū), *v.* 1. E kalai. SYN. shape.
2. E kua. SYN. hew down.
3. Okioki. SYN. hew in pieces.

Hew′er, *n.* Kanaka kalai; kanaka kualaau.

Hēx′a-gon, *n.* Huina-lehulehu–aoao-eono.

Hi-ā′tus, *n.* 1. He kowa kaawale.
2. He manao i nalowale.

Hic′cough (hĭc′up), *n.* Mauliawa.

Hid, } *p. p.* Hunaia.
Hid′den,

Hide, *v.* 1. E huna′. SYN. conceal; secrete.
2. E pee. SYN. hide one's self.

Hide, n. Ili holoholona nui.

Hide and seek, *n.* Haupeepee; peepee-akua.

Hid′e-oŭs, *adj.* Weliweli ka ino o ka nanaina.

High, *adj.* 1. Kiekie.
2. Leoleo; leolani. SYN. tall; lofty. *A tall mast,* he kia leoleo, *or* leolani.
3. Ikaika. *A high wind,* he makani ikaika.
4. *A high surf,* he okaikai.
5. *High words,* na huaolelo hoonauki-uki.

High′land, *n.* Aina kuahiwi.

High′land-er, *n.* Kanaka i noho ma kuahiwi.

High′ly, *adv.* Nui. *To praise highly,* e mahalo nui aku.

High-mind′ed, *adj.* 1. Naau hoopono. SYN. honorable.
2. Hookiekie. SYN. proud.

High′ness, *n.* 1. Ke kiekie. SYN. altitude.
2. Inoa hanohano. *His highness,* ka mea kiekie.

High′-priēst, *n.* Kahuna Nui.

High′-prin′çi-pled, *adj.* Kupaa ma ka pono.

High-soŭnd′ing, *adj.* Hoo-haaheo.

High-spir′it-ed, *adj.* 1. Haaheo; pi-hoihoi; puiwa.
2. Koa.

High′way, *n.* 1. He alanui i hele mau ia.
2. Alanui aupuni.

High-wāy′man, *n.* He powa′. SYN. robber.

Hi-lär′i-ty, *n.* Lealea; hauoli. SYN. gaiety; mirth; laughter.

Hill, *n.* 1. He puu.
2. Pue. *A hill of potatoes,* he pue uala.

Hill′y, *adj.* Apuupuu.

Hilt, *n.* Au o ka pahikaua.

Him-sēlf′, *pron. m.* Oia iho.

Hind′er, *adj.* Ko hope.

Hin′der, *v.* E keakea; hoololohi; e hoohakalia. SYN. retard; check.

Hin′der-ançe } *n.* Kumu keakea. SYN.
Hin′drançe } obstacle; obstruction.

Hind′er-most } *adj.* Hope loa.
Hind′most }

Hin-doo′, *n.* Kamaaina no Inia.

Hinģe, *n.* Ami puka.

Hint, *v.* E kuhikuhi iki.

Hip, *n.* Kikala; papa kole.

Hire, *n.* Uku hoolimalima. SYN. wages.

Hire′ling, *n.* Kauwa i hoolimalimaia.

Hiss, *v.* E pio.

His-tō′ri-an, *n.* Kanaka kakau moolelo o ka wa kahiko.

His-tōr′ic } *adj.* Pili i ka wa kahiko
His-tōr′ic-al } me kona moolelo.

His′to-ry, *n.* Moolelo o ka wa i hala.

His′tri-ōn′ic, *adj.* Pili i ke keaka. SYN. theatrical.

Hit, *v.* E ku; e ki aku, a ku.

Hitch, *v.* 1. E hikii.
2. E anee. SYN. hitch along.

Hith′er, adv.

Hith′er-to′, *adv.* A hiki i keia wa. SYN. heretofore.

Hith′er-wärd, *adv.* Ia nei ae; ia nei mai.

Hive, *n.* Hale nalo meli.

Hive, *v.* E hookomo i na nalo meli iloko o ka hale nalo meli.

Hōar } *adj.* Hina. *Hoary head,* poo-
Hōar′y } hina.

Hōard, *v.* E hooahu. SYN. amass.

Hōarse, *adj.* Leo ha; hanupilo.

Hōarse′ly, *adv.* Papala.

Hōax, *n.* He hana epa, i mea paani.

Hŏb′ble, *v.* E hele opa′. SYN. limp.

Hŏb′by, *n.* He kumu i noonoo nui ia, aole nae i maopopo kona waiwai.

Hŏb′by-horse, *n.* Lio laau, mea paani no kamalii.

Hŏd, *n.* Pahu halihali puna, a pohaku ula paha.

Hŏdģe′-pŏdģe } *adj.* Huikau.
Hŏtch′-pŏtch }

Hōe, *n.* He ho; o-o kope.

Hŏg, *n.* Puaa nui.

Hŏg′gish, *adj.* Ano puaa; alunu; aua.

Hŏgs′hēad, *n.* Poo; 63 galani.

Hoi′den, *n.* He kaikamahine mahaoi.

Hoist, *v.* E huki iluna.

Hōld, *v.* E apo a paa; e hoopaa.

Hōld, *n.* 1. Ka lua waiho ukana o ka moku.
2. Ke apo ana a paa.
3. He kuleana. SYN. claim.

Hōle, *n.* He puka; he lua.

Hōle′y, *adj.* Pukapuka; huhu′ku.

Hŏl′i-day, *n.* La kulaia.

Hō'li-ness, *n.* Ano hemolele; maka-mae. SYN. purity.

Hŏl'lŏw, *adj.* 1. Hakahaka.

2. Oiaio ole; hookamani. SYN. vain; false.

Hŏl'lŏw, *n.* He wahi po'ho iki. *The hollow of the hand,* ka po'ho lima.

Hŏl'lŏw-cheeked', *adj.* Homa.

Hŏl'lŏw-heärt'ed, *adj.* Hookamani. SYN. insincere.

Hŏl'ster, *n.* Eke pu panapana no ka noho lio.

Hō'ly, *adj.* Hemolele; ihiihi; hoano.

Hō'ly-dāy, *n.* La hemolele; la hoano.

Hŏm'age, *n.* 1. Mahalo. SYN. praise; respect.

2. Hoano. SYN. worship; reverence.

Home, *n.* Wahi noho o ka ohana; ho'-me.

Home'less, *adj.* Ohana ole; ho'me ole; kuewa.

Home'ly, *adj.* 1. Pili i ka ho'me.

2. Eleku'; eleeleku'; pou'hu.

Home'-made, *adj.* Hanaia ma ka ohana; hanaia ma ka ho'me.

Hō'me-ŏp'a-thȳ, *n.* He ano lapaau, ma ka haawi liilii ana i ka laau.

Home'sick, *adj.* Manaonao i ka ho'me i haaleleia.

Home'stead, *n.* Ke kuleana o ka ho'me.

Home'wärd, *adv.* I o ka ho'me la.

Hŏm-i-cīd'al, *adj.* Pepehi kanaka. *Homicidal intent,* manao pepehi kanaka.

Hŏm'i-cīde, *n.* 1. Mea pepehi kanaka.

2. Ka pepehi kanaka. *Justifiable homicide,* pepehi kanaka aponoia.

Hŏm'i-lȳ, *n.* Haiolelo haipule.

Hŏm'i-ny, *n.* Kurina, i kuiia.

Hō-mo-gē'ne-oŭs, *adj.* Kulike loa; ano like.

Hōne, *n.* Pohaku hookala. SYN. whetstone.

Hŏn'est (ŏn'est), *adj.* Hoopono; oiaio. SYN. true.

Hŏn'est-ly, *adv.* Me ka hoopono; me ka oiaio. SYN. truly.

Hŏn'est-y, *n.* Ke ano oiaio; ano hoopono. SYN. truth.

Hŏn'ey, *n.* Meli. *Honey comb,* pilali meli.

Hŏn'eyed (hŭn'nid), *adj.* Malimali. SYN. flattering.

Hŏn'ey-cŏmb, *n.* Pilali meli.

Hŏn'ey-mōŏn, *n.* Ka mahina mua o ka noho mare ana.

Hŏn'or, *n.* 1. Ke ano hoopono. *A man of honor,* he kanaka hoopono.

2. Hanohano. *His Honor,* ka mea hanohano.

3. *I have the honor,* ili ia'u ka hanohano.

Hŏn'or (ŏn'or), *v.* 1. E haawi i ka hanohano; e hoo-hanohano.

2. E malama. SYN. obey.

Hŏn'or-a-ble, *adj.* Ku i ka hoopono; ku i ka oiaio.

2. Hanohano.

Hŏn'or-a-bly, *adv.* 1. Me ka aponoia. *Honorably discharged,* hookuuia me ka apono.

2. Me ka hoopono.

Hŏn'or-ā'ry, *adj.* Hanohano. *Honorary member,* lala hanohano; *or,* hoa hanohano.

Hoŏd, *n.* Kapa uhi poo.

Hoŏd'wink, *v.* E hoopunihei. SYN. deceive.

Hoŏf, *n.* Kapuai holoholona.

Hoŏk, *n.* He lou; kilou.

Hoŏp, *n.* He apo.

Hoŏp'ing-cough (kof), *n.* Kunu kalea.

Hoŏt, *n.* Ka leo o ka puueo.

2. Leo hoohenehene.

Hŏp, *v.* E lelelele ma ka wawae hookahi.

2. E lehelehei, me he manu la.

Hōpe, *n.* Manaolana.

Hope'ful, *adj.* Piha i ka manaolana; lana ka manao.

Hope'ful-ly, *adv.* Me ka lana o ka manao.

Hope'less, *adj.* Make ka manaolana; pioloke.

Hope'less-ly, *adv.* Me ka pioloke o ka naau; me ka lana ole o ka manao.

Hŏp'per, *n.* Pahu hoopaa hua no ka wili.

Hŏrde, *n.* He mamo auwana wale.

Hŏr-ī'zon, *n.* Ka huina auli; alihi-lani.

Hor'i-zŏn'tal, *adj.* Moe iliwai.

Hŏrn, *n.* 1. He hao; he kiwi.

2. Ohe puhi keleawe.

Hŏr'net, *n.* Nalo aki.

Hŏr'ri-ble, *adj.* Echia; weliweli ka ino. SYN. dreadful.

Hŏr'ri-bly, *adv.* Weliweli ino. SYN. dreadfully.

Hŏr'rid, *adj.* Weliweli ino; ilihia. SYN. shocking.

Hŏr'ror, *n.* Eehia; weliweli.

Hŏrse, *n.* Lio.

Hŏrse'back, *n.* Maluna o ka lio.

Hŏrse'-breäk-er, *n.* Kanaka hoolaka-laka lio.

Hŏrse'-jock'ey, *n.* Kanaka kuai lio.

Hŏrse'-läugh, *n.* Akaaka ino. SYN. boisterous laugh.

Hŏrse'man, *n.* Kanaka hooholo lio.

Hŏrse'man-ship, *n.* Ka ike no ka hooholo lio.

Hŏrse'-pow'er, *n.* Mana lio; he mana i ana ia mamuli o ka ikaika o ka lio hookahi.

Hŏrse'-race, *n.* Heihei lio.

Hŏrse'shoe, *n.* Kamaa lio.

Hŏrse'-thief, *n.* Kanaka aihue lio.

Hŏrse'whip, *n.* Laau hili lio.

Hŏr'ti-cŭlt'ure, *n.* Ka mahi ana i na pua.

Hŏr'ti-cŭlt'ur-ist, *n.* Mea mahi pua.

Hō-sän'na, *n.* Leo hoolea i Ke Akua.

Hōse, *n.* 1. Kakini wawae.

2. He ili wai; ohe ili wai.

Hō'sier, *n.* Kanaka kuai kakini.

Hŏ′ṣier-y, n. Na kakini wawae o kela me keia ano.
Hŏs′pit-a-ble, adj. Ano kipa.
Hŏs′pi-tal, n. Halemai.
Hŏs′pi-tăl′i-ty, n. Ke kipa ana. To offer hospitality, e kipa; e hookipa.
Host, n. 1. He puali nui.
　2. Ka mea nana e hookipa; hakuhale.
Hŏs′tage, n. Mea i hoopaaia ma ke ano panai.
Hŏst′ess, n. Wahine hookipa; ka wahine poo o ka hale.
Hŏs′tile, adj. 1. Enemi. A hostile land, he aina enemi.
　2. Ku-e′; opu ino. SYN. unfriendly.
Hŏs-til′i-ty, n. Ka ano ku-e′; ano enemi.
Hŏs-til′i-ties, n. Kaua.
Hŏs′tler, n. Kahu lio.
Hŏt, adj. 1. Wela. A hot day, he la wela.
　2. Enaena. A hot fire, he ahi enaena.
Hŏ-tĕl′ n. Hotele; hale hookipa.
Hŏt-head′ed, adj. Hikiwawe i ka huhu.
Hŏt′house, n. Hale mahana; wahi e hoo-ulu ai i na mea ulu ma na aina anu.
Hound, n. Ilio hahai holoholona.
Hour, n. Hora; mahele manawa.
Hour′glass, n. Aniani kuhikuhi hora.
Hour′ly, adv. Kela me keia hora.
House, a. Hale.
House (howz), v. E hookomo ma ka malu o ka hale.
House′break′er, n. Kanaka wawahi hale. SYN. burglar.
House′break′ing, n. Wawahi hale. SYN. burglary.
House′hold, n. Na ohua o ka hale.
House′hold-er, n. Ka ona o ka hale; ke poo o ka ohana.
House′keep-er, n Kahu malama hale.
House′keep-ing, n. Oihana malama hale.
House′maid, n. Wahine hooponopono hale.
House′wife, n. 1. Haku wahine o ka ohana.
　2. He eke i hoolakoia i na mea humuhumu.
House′wife-ry, n. Oihana malama hale.
Hŏv′el, n. Hale pupupu.
Hŏv′er, v. 1. E upaipai i na eheu.
　2. E lahai; lalahai.
How, adv. Pehea; ma ke ano hea.
How-be′it, adv. Aka nae. SYN. nevertheless; yet.
Howl, v. E aoaoa.
Hŭb, n. Ka laau waenakonu o ka huila. SYN. nave.
Hŭb′bub, n. Haunaele; hauwalaau.
Hŭd′dle, v. E puuluulu.
Hŭff, n. Huhu; ukiuki. SYN. fit of anger.
Hue, n. 1. Hooluu. SYN. color.
　2. Wawa nui. SYN. clamor.

Hŭg, v. 1. E hii; e puliki.
　2. Hug a shore, e holo pili aina.
Huge, adj. Nunui loa.
Hŭlk, n. Kino popopo o ka moku kahiko.
Hŭll, n. 1. Oka palaoa.
　2. Kino o ka moku hou.
Hăm, v. E hamumu.
Hŭ′man, adj. Ano kanaka.
Hŭ-mane′, adj. Menemene; lokomaikai.
Hŭ-māne′ly, adv. Me ka menemene.
Hŭ-măn′i-ty, n. 1. Ka′naka o ke ao nei.
　2. Ke ano kana′ka.
Hŭ′man-ize, v. E hoolakalaka; hoonaauao. SYN. civilize.
Hŭ′man-kind′, n. Ka′naka.
Hŭm′ble, adj. Haahaa; akahai.
Hŭm′bly, adv. Haahaa.
Hŭm′bug, n. Mea hoka wale.
Hŭ′mid, adj. Kawau. SYN. damp.
Hŭ-mid′i-ty, n. Ke ano mau′; ano koekoe.
Hŭ-mil′i-āte, v. E hoohaahaa; hoohilahila.
Hŭ-mil′i-ā′tion, n. Ka hoohaahaa ana.
Hŭ-mil′i-ty, n. Ke ano akahai; ano haahaa.
Hŭ′mor, v. E hoolaulea; e ae i ka makemake.
Hŭ′mor-oŭs, adj. Ku i ka aka.
Hŭmp, n. He puu. SYN. hunch.
Hŭmp′back, } n. Kuapuu.
Hŭnch′back, }
Hŭn′dred, adj. Haneri.
Hŭn′drĕdth, n. Ka hapa haneri; ka haneri.
Hŭn′ger, n. Pololi.
Hŭn′ger, v. 1. E pololi.
　2. Iini nui; ake nui.
Hŭn′gry, adj. Pololi.
Hŭnt, v. 1. E hahai holoholona.
　2. E imi. SYN. search.
Hŭnt′er, n. Kanaka hahai holoholona.
Hŭrl, v. 1. E kiola ikaika; e nou ino.
　2. Hurl to the ground, e kulai ilalo.
Hŭr′ly-bŭr′ly, n. Haunaele. SYN. hubbub.
Hŭr-räh′! interj. Huro!
Hŭr′ri-cane, n. Makani pukiki.
Hŭr′ry, 1. v. E awiwi; e lalelale.
　2. E hookikina.
Hŭrt, n. Eha; poino. SYN. injury; harm.
Hŭrt′ful, adj. Hooeha; poino. SYN. injurious.
Hŭṣ′band, n. Kane mare.
Hŭṣ′band, v. E malama pono. SYN. economise.
Hŭṣ′band-man, n. Kanaka mahiai. SYN. farmer; cultivator of the soil.
Hŭsh, v. 1. E na; e hoomalielie.
　2. Kulikuli. SYN. hush up.
Hŭsh′mŏn′ey, n. Dala ki-pe′. SYN. bribe.
Hŭsk, n. Aa; ihi.
Hŭsk, v. E ihi; e maihi.

Hŭsk′y, *adj.* Papala. SYN. hoarse.
Hŭt, *n.* Hale pupupu. SYN. hovel.
Hȳ′brid, *n.* He mahu′.
Hȳ′drant, *n.* Kiowai.
Hȳ-drau′lics, *n.* Lala o ka ike e pili ana i ka nee ana o na wai.
Hȳ′dro-gen, *n.* He ea mama. Kekahi o na kumu o ka wai.
Hȳ-drŏg′ra-pher, *n.* Kanaka kaha kii o na kai, kaikuono, muliwai, etc.
Hȳ-drŏg′ra-phy, *n.* Ke kakau kii o na kai, etc.
Hȳ-drŏm′e-ter, *n.* Mea ana wai, ana i kona kaumaha, etc.
Hȳ-drŏp′a-thist, *n.* Mea lapaau me ka wai wale no.
Hȳ-drŏp′ä-thy, *n.* Ka lapaau ana me ka wai.
Hȳ′dro-phō′bi-a, *n.* Maka′u i ka wai; he mai weliweli loa iwaina o na ilio ma na aina anu.
Hȳ-drō-stät′ies, *n.* Ka lala o ka ike e hoakaka ana no na wai.

Hȳ′gi-ëne, *n.* Ka ike e pili ana i ke ola maikai o ke kino.
Hȳ-grŏm′e-ter, *n.* Mikini e ana ana i ka ma-u′ o ke ea.
Hȳ-mē′ne-al, *adj.* Pili i ka mare. SYN. marital.
Hȳmn, *n.* Himeni.
Hȳ′phen, *n.* Kiko moe (-).
Hȳ′po-chŏn′dri-a, *n.* Ka luuluu mau o ka naau.
Hȳ-pŏc′ri-sy, *n.* Ka hookamani.
Hyp′o-crite, *n.* He hookamani.
Hyp′o-crit′i-cal, *adj.* Hookamani.
Hȳ-pŏt′e-nūse, *n.* Aoao hi-o′ o ka huina-kolu kupono.
Hȳ-pŏth′e-eäte, *v.* E panai waiwai no ka aie′.
Hȳ-pŏth′e-sis, *n.* Kumu manao kahua.
Hȳs′sop, *n.* Husopa; mea ala.
Hȳs-tĕr′ies, *n.* He ano mai pihoihoi, pili i na wahine; he akaaka, a he uwe.

I

I pers. pron. Au; owau.

Ice, *n.* Hau paa.
Ice′bĕrg, he moku hau paa; e lana ana ma ke kai.
Ice′créam, *n.* Waiu i paa i ka hau.
Ice′house, *n.* Hale hooahu hau paa.
Ice′man, *n.* Kanaka kuai hau paa.
Ich′thy-ŏl′o-gist, *n.* Kanaka ike no na i-′a.
Ich′thy-ŏl′o-gy, *n.* Ka ike e pili ana i na i′-a.
I′ci-cle, *n.* He kulu hau paa.
I-eŏn′o-elást, *n.* 1. Mea wawahi kii hoomana.
2. Mea hoike akea i na ano wahahee.
I′cy, *adj.* He hau la ke anu.
I-de′a, *n.* Manao. SYN. notion; thought.
I-de′al, *adj.* Manao wale ia. SYN. imaginary.
I-dĕn′ti-eal, *adj.* 1. Like loa.
2. Oia maoli no.
I-dĕn′ti-fi-eä′tion, *n.* Ka hooia ike maka.
I-dĕn′ti-fy, *v.* E hooia ma ka ike maka.
I-dĕn′ti-ty, *n.* Ka like loa; oia no.
Id′i-o-cy, *n.* Ka lolo o ka naau.
Id′i-om, *n.* Ke ano maoli o kekahi o-lelo.
Id′i-o-mät′ie, *adj.* Pili pono i kekahi olelo. *Idiomatic Hawaiian*, olelo maoli o ko Hawaii poe.
Id′i-ot, *n.* He lolo; he hupo.
Id-i-ŏt′ie, *adj.* Lolo; hupo.

I′dle, *adj.* Noho wale; hana ole.
I′dle, *v.* E noho wale; e hoopalaleha; e liloa.
I′dle-ness, *n.* Ka noho wale; hana ole.
I′dler, *n.* Mea noho wale; kanaka hoopalaleha.
I′dly, *adv.* Me ka noho wale.
I′dol, *n.* He akua kii.
I-dŏl′a-ter, *n.* Mea hoomanakii.
I-dŏl′a-troŭs, *adj.* Hoomanakii.
I-dŏl′a-try, *n.* Ka hoomanakii.
I′dŏl-ize, *v.* E aloha kupono ole.
If, *conj.* Ina paha. SYN. suppose.
Ig′nite, *v.* E hoo-a′; e kuni. SYN. kindle; light.
Ig-nō′ble, *adj.* Haahaa. SYN. mean; base
Ig′no-min′i-oŭs, *adj.* Hilahila. SYN. disgraceful.
Ig′no-min′y, *n.* Hilahila; hoowahawaha. SYN. disgrace; reproach.
Ig′no-rā′mus, *n.* Mea ike ole; mea naaupo. SYN. blockhead.
Ig′no-rance, *n.* Naaupo; ike ole.
Ig′no-rant, *adj.* Naaupo; ike ole.
Ig′no-rant-ly, *adv.* Me ka ike ole; me ka naaupo.
Ig-nōre′, *v.* E ike ole aku; e nana ole aku.
Ill, *adj.* 1. Nawaliwali; mai; SYN. sick.
2. *Adv.* Ino. SYN. badly.
Ill, *n.* He poino; he popilikia. *Ills that flesh is heir to*, na popilikia e kau ana maluna o kanaka.

Ill′brĕd, adj. Ao pono ole ia; kuaaina.
Ill′breed′ing, n. Ka ao pono ole ia.
Il-le′gal, adj. Ku ole i ke kanawai.
 SYN. unlawful.
Il′le-găl′i-ty, n. Ke kulike ole i ke
 kanawai. SYN. unlawfulness.
Il-le′gal-ly, adv. Me ke kanawai ole.
 SYN. unlawfully.
Il-lĕg′i-ble, adj. Hiki ole ke heluhe-
 luia.
Il-lĕg′i-bly, adv. Me ka maopopo ole.
Il′le-ģit′i-mate, adj. Mawaho ae o ke
 kanawai.
Ill-fā′vored, adj. Pupuka; ino. SYN.
 ugly.
Il-lib′er-al, adj. Pi; aua. SYN. stingy.
Il-liç′it, adj. Kanawai ole.
Il-lim′it-a-ble, adj. Palena ole. SYN.
 boundless.
Il-lit′er-ate, adj. Makaukau ole ma
 ka ike o na buke.
Ill-nā′tur-ed, adj. Naaukeemoa; nai-
 nai. SYN. morose; cross.
Ill′ness, n. Mai; nawaliwali. SYN sick-
 ness.
Il-lŏg′ie-al, adj. Aole noonoo pono ia.
Ill′starred, adj. Poino mau; pilikia
 SYN. always unfortunate.
Ill-tĕm′pered, adj. SYN. ill natured.
Il-lū′mi-nate, v. E hoomalamalama.
Il-lū′mi-nā′tion, n. Ka hoomalama-
 lama ana.
Il-lū′sion, n. 1. He kuhihewa.
 2. He hihio o ka naau.
Il-lū′sive, adj. Alakai hewa.
Il-lŭs′trāte, v. 1. E hoonani me na
 kii. SYN. adorn.
 2. E hoomaopopo ma ka hoohalikelike.
Il′lŭs-trā′tion, n. 1. He kii nupepa;
 kii buke.
 2. Ka hoohalike. SYN. comparison.
Il-lŭs′tri-oŭs, adj. Kaulana. SYN. dis-
 tinguished; eminent.
Ill′will, n. Manao ku-e; manao enemi.
Im′aģe, n. Kii. Graven image, kii ka-
 laiia. Molten image, kii hooheehee ia.
Im-aģ′in-a-ble, adj. Hiki ke noonooia.
Im-aģ′i-na-ry, n. Manao wale ia.
Im-aģ′i-nā′tion, n. Noonoo ulu wale.
Im-aģ′ine, v. E manao wale.
Im′be-çile, v. Lola; lolo.
Im-bibe′, v. E omo.
Im-brūe′, v. 1. E hoo-u′.
 2. E paumaele; hands imbrued with
 blood, na lima paumaele i ke koko.
Im′i-tate, v. E hoomahui.
Im-i-tā′tion, n. He mea like; ka hoo-
 halike ana.
Im′i-tā′tor, n. Mea hoomahui; mea
 hana like.
Im-măe′u-late, adj. Makamae; kina′
 ole.
Im′ma-tē′ri-al, adj. 1. Pili ole. SYN.
 irrelevant.
 2. Mea ole. SYN. matters not.
 3. Pili i ka uhane; kino ole.
Im′ma-tūre′, adj. O ole; maka.

Im-mĕaş′ur-a-ble, adj. Hiki ole ke
 ana ia; manuunuu.
Im-mē′di-āte, adj. Koke; hakalia ole.
Im-mē′di-ate-ly, adv. A no; I keia
 wa koke.
Im′me-mō′ri-al, adj. Wa ike ole ia i
 hala.
Im-mĕnse′, adj. Nui palena ole.
Im-mĕnse′ly, adv. Palena ole. SYN.
 boundlessly.
Im-mĕn′si-ty, n. Ke ao palena ole.
Im-mĕrse′, adj. 1. E lu i ka wai.
 2. Immersed in thought, lilo loa i ka
 noonoo.
Im-mĕr′şion, n. Ka lu i ka wai.
Im′mi-grant, n. Kanaka hoo-pae aina
 mai na aina haole.
Im′mi-grāte, v. E hoo pae aina mai
 na aina haole. Board of Immigration,
 papa hoopae lima hana.
Im′mi-grā′tion, n. Hoopae aina mai
 na aina e mai.
Im′mi-nent, adj. E kau weliweli ana.
 Imminent danger, popilikia e kau weli-
 weli mai ana. SYN. impending; threat-
 ening.
Im′mo-bil′i-ty, n. Onipaa. SYN. fix-
 edness.
Im-mŏd′er-ate, adj. Kela loa i ka
 mea kupono. SYN. excessive.
Im-mŏd′est, adj. Hilahila ole.
Im′mo-late, v. E mohai. SYN. sacri-
 fice.
Im-mŏr′al, adj. Ku-e′ i ka pono; hewa;
 ino.
Im′mo-răl′i-ty, n. Hana ku-e′ i ka po-
 no; hana haukae; hewa.
Im-mŏr′tal, adj. Make ole; ola mau.
Im′mŏr-tăl′i-ty, n. Ke ola mau loa.
Im-mŏr′tal-ize, v. E hoomau aku.
 Immortalize a name, e hoomau aku i ka
 inoa.
Im-mŏv′a-ble, adj. Onipaa; ku paa.
Im-mū′ni-ty, n Ka pakele ana. Immu-
 nity from punishment, ka pakele ana
 mai ka hoopai.
Im-mūre′, v. E hoopaa iloko o ka hale
 paahao.
Im-mū′ta-bil′i-ty, n. Ka loli ole; ka
 oni ole, SYN. unchangeableness.
Im-mū′ta-ble, adj. Loli ole; onipaa.
 SYN. unchangeable.
Im-pâir, v. E hooemi i ka maikai.
Im-pän′el, v. E koho i jure.
Im-pärt′, v. 1. E haawi. SYN. to give.
 2. E mahele; e puunaue. SYN. to
 part with.
 3. E hoolaha; e hai. Impart knowledge,
 e hai aku i ka ike.
Im-pär′tial, adj. Ewaewa ole; kaulike.
 SYN. just.
Im-pär′tiăl′i-ty, n. Ewawa ole; kau-
 like. SYN. justice
Im-pär′tiăl-ly, adv. Me ke kaulike;
 ewaewa ole.
Im-păss′a-ble, adj. Hiki ole ke hele ia.
Im-pä′tiençe, n. Paupauaho o ka ma-
 nao.

Im-pā′tient, *adj.* Paupauaho wale; ahonui ole.

Im-pā′tient-ly, *adv.* Me ke ahonui ole.

Im-pēach′, *v.* E hoopii; e hoopii no ka pono ole o ka hana.

Im-pēach′a-ble, *adj.* Ku i ka hoopii ia.

Im-pēach′ment, *n.* 1. Ka hoopii ana no ka hewa o ka hana.
2. Ka hoahewa ana.

Im′pe-cūn′i-oŭs, *adj.* Dala ole. SYN. poor; penniless.

Im-pēde′, *v.* E keakea; hoopilikia; hoohihia. SYN. hinder; obstruct.

Im-pĕd′i-ment, *n.* Kumu keakea; kumu hihia. SYN. hindrance; obstruction.

Im-pĕnd′, *v.* E kau maluna a′e. *Punishment impends over the guilty,* e kau ana ka hoopai maluna′e o ka poe hewa.

Im-pĕnd′ing, *adj.* E kau mai ana. *Impending punishment,* ka hoopai e kau mai ana.

Im-pĕn′e-tra-bĭl′i-ty, *n.* Hiki ole ke komoia; paapu loa.

Im-pĕn′e-tra-ble, *adj.* Paapu loa; hiki ole ke komoia; hiki ole ke hoomaopopoia.

Im-pĕn′i-tençe, *n.* Mihi ole; paakiki o ka naau.

Im-pĕn′i-tent, *adj.* Mihi ole; paakiki.

Im-pĕr′a-tive, *adj.* Kaohiia; hiki ole ke hoole ia.

Im′per-çĕpt′i-ble, *adj.* Maopopo ole i ka ike o ka maka.

Im-pĕr′feet, *adj.* Hemolele ole; hemahema; kina′.

Im′per-fĕe′tion, *n.* Kina′: he hemahema.

Im-pĕr′feet-ly, *adv.* Me ka hemahema; makaukau ole.

Im-pē′ri-al, *adj.* Pili i ka Emepero.

Im-pĕr′il, *v.* E hoopilikia. SYN. endanger.

Im-pē′ri-oŭs, *adj.* Hoohaakei; hookiekie. SYN. haughty; arrogant.

Im-pĕr′ish-a-ble, *adj.* Popo ole; mau.

Im-pĕr′me-a-ble, *adj.* Hiki ole i ka wai ke komo. SYN. impervious.

Im-pĕr′ti-nent, *adj.* Pakike′; mahaoi.

Im-pĕr′tur-a-ble, *adj.* Pihoihoi ole.

Im-pĕr′vi-oŭs, *adj.* *See* impermeable.

Im-pĕt′ū-ŏs′i-ty, *n.* 1. Ka hikiwawe noonoo ole. SYN. violence.
2. Ka pa ikaika mai ana.
3. Ka nee awiwi ana. *The impetuosity of the current,* ka nee awiwi ana o ke au.

Im-pĕt′ū-oŭs, *adj.* 1. Hikiwawe noonoo ole.
2. Paa ikaika; pukiki.
3. Nee awiwi.

Im′pe-tus, *n.* Ka nee ana imua.

Im-pī′e-ty, *n.* Manao aia′; hoomaloka.

Im-pinǧe′, *v.* E ku. SYN. hit.

Im′pi-oŭs, *adj,* Haililii; kuamuamu.

Im-plā′ea-ble, *adj.* Makona; laulea ole.

Im-plănt′, *v.* E kanu iloko; e hookomo.

Im′ple-ment, *n.* Mea hana lima; mea lawelawe. SYN. tool; utensil.

Im-pli′eate, *v.* E hoahewa pu; e komo like ma ka hihia.

Im′pli-çā′tion, *n.* 2. Hihia like; hewa like.
2. Mea i manaoia, aole nae i olelo ia. SYN. inference.

Im-pliç′it, *adj.* Kanalua ole. *Implicit obedience,* hoolohe kanalua ole.

Im-pliç′it-ly, *adv.* Me ke kanalua ole; me ke kapekepeke ole.

Im-plōre′, *v.* E noi haahaa. SYN. beseech.

Im-plȳ′, *v.* E hoike; SYN. mean; signify.

Im′pō-lite′, *adj.* Nihaniha.

Im′po-lite′ness, *n.* Ano nihaniha; pihalula ole.

Im-pŏl′i-tie, *adj.* Ku pono ole. SYN. unwise; imprudent; inexpedient.

Im-pŏrt′, *v.* E hookomo waiwai i ka aina.

Im′pŏrt, *n.* 1. Waiwai i hookomoia i ka aina.
2. Ano. SYN. purport; meaning.
3. Ano nui. SYN. importance.

Im-pŏr′tançe, *n.* Ke ano koikoi; hanohano.

Im-pŏr′tant, *adj.* Ano nui; waiwai nui.

Im′por-tā′tion, *n.* 1. Ka hookomo waiwai i ka aina.
2. Ka waiwai i hookomo ia i ka aina. *Recent importations,* na waiwai hou i hookomoia.

Im-pŏrt′er, *n.* Mea hookomo waiwai.

Im-pŏrt′ū-nāte, *adj.*E noi ikaika a noi mau.

Im′pŏr-tūne′, *v.* E koi ikaika a e koi mau.

Im′pŏr-tū′ni-ty, *n.* He noi mau.

Im-pōse′, *v.* 1. E kau. SYN. put on.
2. E punihei; e epa; e hana apiki.

Im-pōs′ing, *adj.* Kamahao.

Im′po-si′tion, *n.* 1. Ke kau ana. SYN. laying on. *Imposition of hands,* ke kau ana o na lima.
2. Ka hana apiki; hana epa.

Im-pŏs′si-bĭl′i-ty, *n.* Mea hiki ole. *Waste time on impossibilities,* e hoopau manawa wale ma na mea hiki ole.

Im-pŏs′si-ble, *adv.* Ole loa e hiki.

Im′pŏst, *n.* He dute waiwai. SYN. duty.

Im-pŏs′tor, *n.* He hookamani; kanaka epa.

Im-pŏst′ure, *n.* Wahahee. SYN. deception; lying.

Im′po-tençe, *n.* Ikaika ole; ano lolo.

Im′po-tent, *adj.* Lolo.

Im-pŏv′er-ish, *v.* 1. E hooilihune.
2. E hoolilo i panoa; e hoopanoa.

Im-prāe′ti-ea-bĭl′i-ty, *n.* Ke hiki ole o ka hooko′.

Im-prāe′ti-ea-ble, *adj.* Hiki ole.

Im′pre-eā′tion, *n.* Olelo haililii. SYN. curse.

Im-prĕg′na-ble, *adj.* Hiki ole ke hoopio ia. SYN. invincible.

Im-prĕg′nàte, *v.* E miko; e hoo-u.

Im-prĕss′, *v.* 1. E pai paa aku. *Impress on the mind,* e pai paa aku ma ka naau. 2. E ku i ka manao. *To impress favorably,* e kupono i ka manao.

Im′press, *n.* He hoailona pai; hoailona.

Im-prĕss′si-ble, *adj.* Lauwili. *An impressible youth,* he ui lauwili wale.

Im-prĕs′sion, *n.* 1. Ka pai ana me na hua kepau. 2. Ke ku ana i ka manao. *A good impression,* kupono i ka manao.

Im-prĕs′sive, *adj.* Koikoi. *An impressive speech,* he haiolelo koikoi.

Im-print′, *v.* 1. E pai. *To imprint on the mind,* e pai paa loa ma ka naau.

Im-pris′on, *v.* E hoo-paahao.

Im-pris′on-ment, *n.* Ka hoopaahao ana.

Im-prŏb′a-ble, *adj.* 1. Paha. *It is improbable,* aole paha pela. *It is not improbable,* aole no he paha. 2. Aole oiaio paha. *An improbable story,* he olelo oiaio ole paha.

Im-prŏmp′tu, *adv.* Ku i ka wa; noonoo ole ia mamua. SYN. off hand; extempore.

Im-prŏp′er, *adj.* Kupono ole; kohu ole. SYN. unbecoming.

Im-prŏp′er-ly, *adv.* Me ke kupono ole.

Im′pro-pri′e-ty, *a* Ke ano kupono ole.

Im-prŏve, *v.* 1. E holo mua. 2. E hoopaa pono. *Improve the time,* e hoopaa pono i ka manawa. 3. E apo. *Improve the opportunity,* e apo i ka wa kupono. SYN. seize. 4. E kela aku i ka maikai.

Im-prŏve′ment, *n.* 1. Ka hoo-oi ana. 2. Ka hana hou ana a maikai ae. 3. *Improvements,* na hana hou i mea e maikai ai.

Im-prŏv′i-dent, *adj.* Hoomaunauna; uhauha; malama ole. SYN. wasteful.

Im′pro-vise′, *v.* E haku wale mai.

Im-prū′dence, *n.* Ka noonoo ole i mea e pono ai. SYN. indiscretion.

Im-prū′dent, *adj.* Noonoo pono ole. SYN. indiscreet.

Im-prū′dent-ly, *adv.* Me ka noonoo ole. SYN. indiscreetly.

Im′pu-dent, *adj.* Hilahila ole; honekoa.

Im′pulse, *n.* 1. *Impulse of the moment,* mamuli o ka manao ulu wale mai; manao pukiki. 2. He manao ulu wale mai. *Governed by impulse rather than by reason,* e hooko ana mamuli o ka manao ulu wale, aole mamuli o ka noonoo.

Im-pŭl′sive, *adj.* *An impulsive man,* he kanaka e hooko ana mamuli o ka manao ulu wale mai; pukiki.

Im-pū′ni-ty, *n.* Ka hoopai ole; ka pakele i ka hoopai.

Im-pūre′, *adj.* Maemae ole; paumaele; pelapela.

Im-pu′ri-ty, *n.* Ka maemae ole; ka haukae.

Im′pu-tā′tion, *n.* Ka hoopili ana; ka hooili ana. *Imputation of evil,* ka hoopili ana o ka hewa.

Im-pūte′, *v.* E hoopili; e hooili. SYN. charge.

In, *prep.* 1. Iloko. *In the house,* iloko o ka hale. 2. Maloko. 3. Ma. *In the place of,* ma kahi o.

In′a-bil′i-ty, *n.* Ka hiki ole.

In′ac-cĕss′i-ble, *adj.* Hiki ole ke hookokoke aku.

In-ăc′eu-ra-çy, *n.* Ka pololei ole.

In-ăc′eu-rāte, *adj.* Pololei ole.

In-ăc′tion, *n.* Ka noho ana hana ole.

In-ăc′tive, *adj.* Noho wale; hana ole; nanea; loma.

In-ăd′e-qua-çy, *n.* Ka lawa pono ole.

In-ăd′e-quate, *adj.* Lawa pono ole.

In′ad-mis′si-ble, *adj.* Hiki ole ke hookomo ia; hiki ole ke lawe ia. *Inadmissible evidence,* olele hoike i hiki ole ke lawe ia.

In′ad-vĕrt′ence, *n.* Ka palaka o ka manao. SYN. forgetfulness.

In′ad-vĕrt′ent-ly, *adv.* Me ka palaka; akahele ole.

In-ăl′ien-a-ble, *adj.* Pili paa loa; hiki ole ke hooilo ia aku.

In-ăn′i-mate, *adj.* Nele i ke ola; make. SYN. inappropriate.

In-ăp′pli-ea-ble, *adj* Pili ole. SYN. unsuitable.

In′ap-prō′pri-ate, *adj.* Ku pono ole. SYN. unsuitable.

In-ăpt′, *adj.* Makaukau ole; ku ole. *An inapt expression,* he olelo ku ole. SYN. unsuitable.

In′ar-tie′u-late, *adj.* Maopopo ole o ka leo.

In′as-much′, *adv.* Oiai. SYN. since.

In′at-tĕn′tion, *a.* Ka hoolohe ole.

In′at-tĕn′tive, *adj.* Hoolohe ole.

In-au′di-ble, *adj.* Lohe ole ia.

In-au′di-bly, *adv.* Me ka lohe ole ia.

In-au′gu-ral, *adj.* Hookumu. *Inaugural address,* haiolelo hookumu.

In-au′gu-rāte, *v.* 1. E hookomo i ka o:-hana. 2. E hoomaka; hookumu. SYN. to begin.

In-au′gu-rā′tion, *n.* Ka hookomo ana i kekahi ma ka oihana.

In′au-spi′çioŭs, *adj.* Kupono ole na ouli.

In′bŏrn, *adj.* Noho ana iloko. *Inborn passions,* na kuko e noho ana iloko.

In-eăl′eu-la-ble, *adj.* Hiki ole ke helulia; manomano.

In′ean-tā′tion, *n.* Pule hoomanamana; pule anaana.

In-eā′pa-ble, *adj.* Maukaukau ole; hemahema.

In′ea-păç′i-tāte, *v.* E hoonele i ka hiki.

In'ca-pāç'i-ty, *n.* Ka nele o ka hiki.
In-eār'çer-āte, *v.* E hoo-paahao. SYN. imprison.
In-eār'çer-ā'tion, *n.* Ka hoopaahao ana.
In-eār'nāte, *adj.* E noho ana ma ke kino. *The incarnate Son of God*, o ke Keiki a Ke Akua e noho ana ma ke kino.
In-cạu'tious, *adj.* Akahele ole. SYN. heedless.
In-çĕn'di-a-rĭsm, *n.* Ka puhi kolohe ana i ke ahi.
In-çĕn'di-a-ry, *n.* Mea puhi kolohe i ke ahi.
In'çense, *n.* Ala kuni.
In-cense', *v.* E hoohuhu; hoonaukiuki.
In-çĕn'tive, *n.* Kumu hoo-hoihoi; kumu hoolalelale.
In-çĕp'tion, *n.* Ka hoomaka ana. SYN. beginning.
In-çĕs'sant, *adj.* Mau; hoo'ki ole. SYN. unceasing.
In-çĕs'sant-ly, *adv.* Me ka hoo'ki ole. SYN. unceasingly.
In'çest, *n.* Ka moekolohe me ka hoa hanau.
In-çĕst'u-oŭs, *adj.* Moekolohe pili koko.
Inch, *u.* Iniha.
In'ci-dençe, *n.* Ka haule ana o ke kukūna malamalama maluna o kekahi ili.
In'çi-dent, *n.* Mea e pili ana.
In'çi-dĕnt'al, *adj.* E pili ana. *Incidental expenses*, na lilo e pili ana.
In'çi-dĕnt'als, *n.* Na lilo o kela me keia ano e pili ana.
In-çin'er'āte, *v.* E kuni i ke ahi a lilo i lehu. SYN. burn to ashes.
In-çĭp'i-ent *adj.* Ka hoomaka ana; ka makamua. *Incipient light of day*, ka hoomaka ana o ka malamalama.
In-çĭs-ion, *n.* He oki iloko o ke kino. SYN. cut; gash.
In-çite', *v.* 1. E hookonokono.
2. E hooeueu; hoolalelale.
In-çite'ment, *n.* Kumu hooeueu. SYN. incentive.
In'çi-vil'i-ty, *n.* Ke ano mahaoi. SYN. disrespect.
In-clĕm'ent, *adj.* Ino; oluolu ole. SYN. boisterous; stormy. *Inclement weather*, waino.
In'eli-nā'tion, *n.* 1. Ka hi-o' ana.
2. Ka hilinai ana o ka naau. SYN. disposition
In-cline', *v.* 1. E hi-o'.
2. E hilinai.
In-clōse', *v.* 1. E hoopuni. SYN. surround.
2. E hookomo. SYN. to put within.
In-clōs'ure, *n.* 1. Wahi i hoopuniia.
2. Mea i hookomoia.
In-clūde', *v.* E helu pu.
In-çlū'sive, *adj.* Helu pu ia.
In-cŏg-ni-to, *adv.* Hooaano.
In'eo-hē'rent, *adj.* Namunamu wale; pili ole.

In'cō-hē'rent-ly, *adv.* Namunamu wale.
In'com-bŭs'ti-ble, *adj.* Pau ole i ke ahi.
In'eŏme, *n.* Na loaa, SYN. revenue. *Annual income*, na loaa makahiki.
In'eom-mōde', *v.* E hoopilikia; e hoohaiki i ka pono o ka noho ana. SYN. inconvenience.
In-cŏm'par-a-ble, *adj.* Lua ole.
In'com-pāt'i-ble, *adj.* Ku like ole. SYN. inconsistent.
In-cŏm'pe-tençe, } *n.* Hiki ole. SYN.
In-cŏm'pe-ten-cy, } inability.
In-cŏm'pe-tent, *adj.* Hiki ole; hemahema. SYN. unable.
In'eom-plēte', *adj.* Paa hapa; paa pono ole. SYN. unfinished.
In-cŏm'pre-hĕn'si-ble, *adj.* Hiki ole i ka naau ke apo aku. SYN. inconceivable.
In'con-çĕiv'a-ble, *adj.* Mawaho ae o ka noonoo.
In'con-clū'sĭve, *adj.* Maopopo ole ka oiaio.
In'con-grū'i-ty, *n.* Ke kulike ole. SYN. impropriety.
In-cŏn'gru-oŭs, *adj.* Kulike ole. SYN. inappropriate.
In'con-sĭd'er-a-ble, *adj.* Mea uuku wale no; mea ole; aole noonoo ia.
In-cŏn-sĭd'er-āte, *adj.* Noonoo ole. SYN. thoughtless; heedless.
In'con-sĭst'ent, *adj.* Ewaewa; kulike ole.
In'con-sŏl'a-ble, *adj.* Na ole; hiki ole ke hooluolu ia.
In-cŏn'stan-çy, *n.* Lauwili wale. SYN. fickleness.
In-cŏn'stant, *adj.* Muhee; palai-e; kapekepeke; lauwili. SYN. changeable; fickle.
In'con-tĕst'i-ble, *adj.* Hiki ole ke ku-e' ia; paa. SYN. unquestionable.
In-cŏn'ti-nent, *adj.* Makaleho; umi ole ke kuko. SYN. unchaste.
In-cŏn'tro-vērt'i-ble, *adj.* Paa loa; hiki ole ke hoohuli ia. *An incontrovertible argument*, he olelo paa loa; he manao i hiki ole ke hoohuliia.
In'con-vēn'iençe, *n.* Mea hoopilikia.
In'cŏn-vēn'ient, *adj.* Kupono ole. *An inconvenient time*, wa kupono ole.
In-cŏr'po-rāte, *v.* E hui, a lilo i kino hookahi.
In'cor-rēct', *adj.* Pololei ole; hewa. SYN. inaccurate.
In'cor-rēct'ly, *adv.* Hewa; me ka pololei ole; kuhapa.
In-cŏr'rĭg-i-ble, *adj.* Paakiki ma ka naau; hiki ole ke hoohuli ia.
In'cor-rŭpt'i-ble, *adj.* 1. Mae ole. SYN. unfading; not corruptible.
2. Hoopono; ewaewa ole. SYN. inflexibly just; not to be bribed.
In-erēase', *v.* 1. E hoomahuahua; e nui ae.

2. Kawowo; kaioio. Syn. germinate rapidly.

In'erease, n. Ka hua; ka nui ana mai; ka mahuahua ana.

In-crĕd′i-bil′i-ty, n. Oiaio ole; hala ka palena o ka manaoio.

In-crĕd′i-ble, adj. Hiki ole ke manaoioia. Syn. not to be believed; beyond belief.

In're-dū′li-ty, n. Manaoio ole; hoomalau; hoomaloka. Syn. unbelief.

In-erĕd′ū-loŭs, adj. Hoomaloka; manaoio ole. Syn. unbelieving.

In-crŭst′, v. E papaa. Incrusted with mud, papaa i ka lepo.

In'erŭs-tā′tion, n. Ka papaa ana i ke-kahi mea.

In′eu-bāte, v. E hoomoe hua.

In′eu-bŭs, n. 1. He moe hewa. Syn. nightmare.

2. Kela me keia mea e hookaumaha'i.

In-cŭl′eate, v. E ao. Syn. teach.

In-cŭl′pate, v. E hoopii pu no ka hewa.

In-cŭm′ben-çy, n. Ka noho ana ma ka oihana.

In-cŭm′bent, n. Ka mea e noho ana ma ka oihana.

In-cŭm′bent, adj. He mea pono.

In-cŭm′brançe, n. He kumu keakea; haawe kaumaha. Syn. burden.

In-cŭr′, v. E halawai. Incur displeasure, e halawai me ka huhu. Incur peril, e halawai me ka popilikia.

In-cŭr′a-ble, adj. 1. Ola ole. An incurable disease, he mai ola ole.

2. Pau ole. Incurable laziness, molowa pau ole.

In-cur′sion, a. Ke komo ana. Incursion of the enemy, ke komo ana o ka enemi. Syn. invasion.

In-dĕbt′ed, adj. Aie.

In-dĕbt′ed-ness, n. Ka aie.

In-dē′çen-çy, n. Ano hilahila ole; ano haumia; ano haukae. Syn. immodest.

In-dē′çent, adj. Haumia; pelapela.

In-dē′çent-ly, adv. Ma ke ano haukae.

In′de-çis′ion, n. Lolilua o ka manao.

In-dēe′o-roŭs, adl. Kupono ole, hilahila. Syn. unbecoming.

In-deed′, adv. Pela i'-o. Syn. verily.

In′de-făt′i-ga-ble, adj. Paupauaho ole; hoomanawanui. Syn. unwearied.

In′de-fĕn′si-ble, adj. Hiki ole ke kokuaia. A bad cause is indefensible, hiki ole ke kokuaia ka aoao ino.

In′de-fin′a-ble, adj. Hiki ole ke hoomaopopoia.

In-dĕf′i-nite, adv. 1. Maopopo ole; hoakaka ole ia.

2. Loa. Indefinite postponement, hoopanee loa ia.

In-dĕl′i-ble, adj. Paa loa; hiki ole ke holoi ia.

In-dĕl′i-eate, adj; Hilahila. Syn. indecent.

In-dĕm′ni-fy, v. E pani i ka poho'. Syn. reimburse.

In-dĕnt′, v. E kumumu.

In′den-tā′tion, n. He kumumu.

In-dĕnt′ūre, n. Olelo ae-like i kakau ia.

In-dĕnt′ūre, v. E hoopaa ma ka olelo ae-like.

In′de-pĕn′dençe, n. Ke kuokoa o ka noho′na.

In′de-pĕnd′ent, adj. Kuokoa.

In′de-serib′a-ble, adj. Hiki ole ke hai ia.

In′de-strŭet′i-ble, adj. Hiki ole ke lukuia; hiki ole ke hoopoino ia.

In′dex, 1. Lima kuhi (☞).

2. Papa kuhikuhi.

3. He hoailona. Syn. indication; sign.

In′di-an, n. He inikini.

In′dia-rŭb′ber, n. Laho lio; mea holoi kaha.

In′di-eāte, v. E kuhikuhi. Syn. show; point out.

In′di-ça′tion, n. 1. He hoailona. Syn. sign.

2. He ouli. Syn. omen.

In′di-eā′tor, n. Mea kuhikuhi.

In-dict′ (in-dite), v. E hoopii ma ka palapala hopu.

In-dict′a-ble (indite-able), adj. Ku i ka hoopiia.

In-dict′ment, n. Palapala hopu.

In-dif′fer-en-çe, n. Ka palaleha; hoomaloka; manao ole aku.

In-dif′fer-ent, adj. Hoomaloka; molowa ma ka naau; palaleha.

In′di-gençe, n. He ilihune; nele. Syn. poverty.

In-dig′e-noŭs, adj. Kamaaina i ka lepo o ka aina.

In′di-gent, adj. Ilihune; ilikole; nele. Syn. poor; destitute.

In′di-gĕst′i-ble, adj. Wali ole ke ai ia.

In′di-ges′tion, n. Ka wali ole o ka ai iloko o ka opu'.

In-dig′nant, adj. Ukiuki; huhu. Syn. angry.

In′dig-nā′tion, n. Huhu hoowaha′waha'.

In-dig′ni-ty, n. He hana hoowaha′waha'.

In′di-reet′, adj. 1. Pili pono ole.

2. Lauwili.

In′dis-creet′, adj. Noonoo pono ole ia. Syn. injudicious; imprudent.

In′dis-crē′tion, n. Ka noonoo pono ole. Syn. imprudence.

In′dis-erim′i-nate, adj. Huikau; koho pono ole; noonoo ole ia.

In′dis-pĕn′sa-ble, adj. Hiki ole ke hoonele ia; pili pono loa.

In′dis-pōsed′, adj. 1. Nawaliwali iki; omaimai.

2. Makemake ole. Indisposed to help, makemake ole ke kokua.

In-dis′po-si′tion, n. 1. Ka nawaliwali iki o ke kino.

2. Ka makemake ole o ka manao.

In′dis-pūt′a-ble, adj. Hiki ole ke hoole ia. Syn. unquestionable.

In'dis-tinct', adj. 1. Powehiwehi. SYN. obscure. Indistinct vision, ike powehiwehi.

2. Nonoa'; koliuliu; laulahea. Indistinct as to sound.

In-dite', v. 1. E haku. SYN. compose; write.

2. E haku, a na hai e kakau. SYN. dictate.

In'di-vid'ū-al, n. 1. Mea hookahi; mea.

2. adj. Pakahi.

In'di-vid'ū-al-ize, v. E kuhikuhi pakahi.

In'di-vid'ū-al-ly, adv. Pakahi. SYN. singly.

In'di-vis'i-ble, adj. Hiki ole ke maheleia.

In'do-lençe, n. Ke ano lomaloma; luana; noho wale. SYN. sloth.

In'do-lent, adj. Luana wale; molowa. SYN. slothful.

In-dŏm'i-ta-ble, adj. Pio ole; lanakila. SYN. unconquerable.

In-dŏrse', v. 1. E kakau inoa ma ke kua o ka bila dala.

2. E apono ma ke kakau lima.

3. E kakau i ke ano oloko o kekahi palapala ma kona kua.

In-dŏrs'er, n. Ka mea kakau inoa ma kekahi pepa, ma ke ano apono.

In-dŏrse'ment, n. 1. Ke kau ana o ka inoa ma kekahi pepa, ma ke ano apono.

2. Ka apono ana.

In-dū'bi-ta-ble, adj. Kanalua ole ia; maopopo lea.

In-dūçe', v. E koi, e kono. SYN. lead on; urge.

In-dūçe'ment, n. Kumu e koi ai.

In-dŭct', v. E hookomo. Induct to office, e hookomo ma ka oihana.

In-dŭlge', v. E ae mamuli o ka makemake; e oluolu. Syn. gratify.

In-dŭl'gençe, n. Ke ko ana i ka makemake. SYN. gratification.

In-dŭl'gent, adj. Oluolu; ae wale i ka makemake.

In-dŭs'tri-oŭs, adj. Hooikaika; makaala; hana mau. SYN. diligent.

In'dus-try, n. 1. He hooikaika; he hana mau.

2. He oihana hanalima.

In-dwĕll'ing, adj. E noho ana maloko. Indwelling sin, ka hewa e noho ana maloko o ka naau.

In-ē'bri-āte, n. Kanaka ona. SYN. drunkard.

In'ē-brī'e-ty, n. Ka ona. SYN. drunkenness.

In-ĕf'fa-ble, adj. Hiki ole ke haiia! nani loa; kamahao. The ineffable joys of heaven, na hauoli o ka lani i hiki ole ke haiia.

In'ef-fáçe'a-ble, adj. Hiki ole ke hololoia; paa loa.

In'ef-fĕc'tu-al, adj. Makehewa; ko ole. SYN. vain; useless.

In-ĕf'fi-ca-çy, } n. Ka lawa ole; mana ole.
In'ef-fi'çien-cy, }
In'ef-fi'çient, adj. Hemahema; hawawa.

In-ĕl'e-gant, adj. Maikai ole; kohu ole.

In-ĕl'i-ġi-ble, adj. Kupono ole. Ineligible to office, kupono ole ke kohoia no ka oihana.

In'e-quăl'i-ty, n. Ka like ole.

In-ērt', adj. 1. Loma; molowa. SYN. inactive; sluggish.

2. Oni ole; make. SYN. lifeless.

In-ēr'tia, n. Ke ano o kela me keia kino e moe malie ina e nee ole ana, a ina hoi e nee ana e hoomau kona nee ana.

In-ĕs'ti-ma-ble, adj. 1. Hiki ole ke ana ia.

2. Makamae. Inestimable privilege, he pono makamae.

3. Lua ole. Inestimable worth, waiwai lua ole.

In-ĕv'i-ta-ble, adj. Hiki ole ke pale ia; maopopo loa.

In-ĕv'i-ta-bly, adv. Me ka maopopo loa; mau. Punishment inevitably follows sin, e hahai mau ana ka hoopai i ka hana hewa.

In' ĕx-eūş'a-ble, adj. Hiki ole ke kala ia.

In'ex-hąust'i-ble, adj. Pau ole; mau.

In-ĕx'or-a-ble, adj. Maliu ole; hiki ole ke pale ia. SYN. inevitable.

In'ex-pē'di-ent, adj. Kupono ole.

In-ĕx-pē'ri-ençed, adj. Walea ole; maa ole; akahiakahi.

In-ĕx'pli-ca-ble, adj. Hiki ole ke wehewehe ia; pohihihi.

In'ex-press'i-ble, adv. Hiki ole ke hai ia.

In'ex-tĭn'guish-a-ble, adj. Hiki ole ke kinaiia. SYN. unquenchable.

In-ĕx'tri-ca-ble, adv. Hiki ole ke wehe ia. Inextricable tangle, hihia hiki ole ke wehe ia.

In-făl'li-bil'i-ty, n. Kuhihewa ole; pono loa.

In-făl'li-ble, adj. Hiki ole ke kuhihewa.

In-făl'li-bly, adj. 1. Me ke kuhihewa ole.

2. Mau. SYN. invariably.

In'fa-moŭs, adj. Kaulana ino.

In'fa-my, n. Ke kaulana no ke ino.

In'fan-çy, n. 1. Ka wa kolo.

2. Ka wa hookumu; ka hoomaka ana. SYN. beginning.

3. Ka wa oo ole ma ke kanawai. SYN. minority.

In'fant, n. 1. Keike ai waiu. SYN. babe.

2. Keike oo ole ma ke kanawai. SYN. minor.

In-făn'ti-çide, n. Umi keike.

In'fant-ile, adj. Ano keiki kolo.

In'fant-ry, n. Poe koa hele wawae; koa kani wawae.

In-făt'ū-āt'ed, adj. Punilea.

In-făt'u-ā'tion, *n.* Ka punilea i kekahi mea.

In-fēc'tion, *n.* 1. Ka lele ana o ka mai. 2. Mai lele.

In-fěc'tioŭs, *adj.* Lele. *Infectious disease,* mai lele.

In'fē-lĭç'i-ty, *n.* Oluolu ole. SYN. unhappiness.

In-fěr', *v.* E ohi i ka manao.

In'fer-ençe, *n.* He manao ohi,

In-fē'ri-ŏr, *adj.* Haahaa iho; emi iho.

In-fē'ri-ŏr'i-ty, *n.* Ka haahaa iho; ka emi iho.

In-fĕr'nal, *adj.* No Gehena. *Infernal regions,* Gehena.

In-fěst', *v.* E paapuu ino mai.

In'fi-del, *n.* He aia'; hoomaloka. SYN. atheist.

In'fi-dĕl'i-ty, *n.* Hoomaloka; hoomalau. 2. Kolohe me hai o ka poe mare.

In'fi-nite, *adj.* Palena ole; aohe kumu, aohe welau.

In-fin'i-ty, *n.* Ke akea palena ole; ke ao palena ole.

In-firm', *adj.* Nawaliwali; palupalu; omaimai.

In-firm'a-ry, *n.* He hale mai. SYN. hospital.

In-firm'i-ty, *n.* He nawaliwali; kumu palupalu.

In-flāme', *v.* 1. E hoowela; ho-a'. *Inflame the passions,* e ho-a' i na kuko. 2. E pehu. SYN. swell.

In-flăm'a-ble, *adj.* Pau wale i ke ahi. SYN. combustible.

In'flam-mā'tion, *n.* He pehu; he wela ma ke kino.

In-flāte', *v.* 1. E hoopiha i ka makani. 2. *Inflated with pride,* piha i ka haaheo.

In-flěct', *v.* E kalele leo.

In-flěc'tion, *n.* Ke kalele ana i ka leo.

In-flěx'i-ble, *adj.* Pelu ole; kupaa. SYN. unbending.

In-flĭet', *v.* E kau aku. SYN. impose. *Inflict punishment,* e kau i ka hoopai.

In-flĭc'tion, *n.* 1. Hoopai. SYN. punishment. 2. Ke kau ana i ka hoopai.

In'flu-ençe, *n.* Mana hoohuli manao; mana koi manao.

In'flu-ençe, *v.* E kaohi i ka manao; e hoohuli i ka manao.

In'flu-ĕn'tial, *adj.* Koikoi; ikaika ma ka hoohuli manao; hilinai nui ia.

In'flu-ĕn'za, *n.* He wela, a anu; he kunu, a nalulu.

In'flux, *n.* 1. Ke kahe ana iloko. 2. Ke komo ana mai. *Influx of strangers,* ke komo ana mai o na malihini.

In-form', *v.* 1. E hai. SYN. tell. 2. E imi; e hoomaopopo. SYN. acquaint. 3. *A well informed man,* he kanaka i makaukau ma kela me keia ike.

In-form'al, *adj.* 1. Hookiekie ole; launa oluolu. 2. Kupono ole i na rula.

In'for-măl'i-ty, *n.* Ke ku like ole me na rula.

In-fôrm'ant } *n.* 1. Mea nana e hai.
In-fôrm'er } *n.* 2. He kiu. SYN. spy.

In'for-mā'tion, *n.* 1. Ike. SYN. knowl- edge. *General information,* ike akea. 2. Nu hou. SYN. news.

In-frăe'tion, *n.* Ka haki ana. *Infraction of the law,* ka haki ana o ke kanawai.

In-frē'quent, *adj.* Kakaikahi. SYN. seldom.

In-fringe', *v.* 1. E haki. *Infringe on the contract,* e haki i ka olelo ae-like. 2. E komo hewa. SYN. trespass. *Infringe on the rights of others,* e komo hewa ma na pono a hai.

In-fringe'ment, *n.* 1. Ka haki ana. 2. Ke komo hewa ana.

In-fūse', *v.* 1. E hoo-u'. SYN. steep. 2. E hookomo. SYN. instill. *Infuse hope,* e hookomo i ka manaolana.

In-fu'sion, *n.* 1. He wai i hoo-u ia me kekahi mea. 2. Ka hookomo ana. SYN. instilling.

In-gĕn'i-oŭs, *adj.* Noeau; akamai. SYN. skilful.

In'ge-nū'i-ty, *n.* Loea; hailea; aka- mai. SYN. skill.

In-gĕn'ū-oŭs, *adj.* Oiaio. SYN. truthful; frank.

In-glō'ri-oŭs, *adj.* Haahaa; hanohano ole; hilahila. SYN. ignominious.

In'gō-ing, *adj.* Ke komo ana iloko.

In'got, *n.* Auka' metala. *An ingot of gold,* he auka gula.

In'grāte, *n.* Mea aloha ole; mea loko- ino.

In-grāt'i-tūde, *n.* He lokoino.

In-grē'di-ent, *n.* Kekahi mea o ke kino hui.

In'gress, *n.* 1. Kahi e komo ai. SYN. entrance. 2. Ke komo ana.

In-gŭlf', *v.* E palemo. SYN. overhelm.

In-hăb'it, *v.* E noho. SYN. live.

In-hăb'it-ant, *n.* Kamaaina.

In'ha-lā'tion, *n.* 1. Ka hanu ana; ka upa' ana o ke ake mama.

In-hāle', *v.* E hanu; e omo i ke ea. SYN. breathe.

In'har-mō'ni-oŭs, *adj.* 1. Lokahi ole. SYN. discordant. 2. Kani like ole.

In-hē'rent, *adj.* Mau maloko. SYN. innate; inborn. 2. Hanau pu ia.

In-hěr'it, *v.* E loaa ma ka hooilina.

In-hěr'it-ançe, *n.* Waiwai hooilina.

In-hěr'it-or, *n.* He hooilina.

In-hĭb'it, *n.* E pa'pa'. SYN. prohibit.

In-hŏs'pi-ta-ble, *adj.* Kipa ole; kee- moa.

In-hū'man, *adj.* Lokoino; mainoino. SYN. cruel.

In'hu-măn'i-ty, *n.* Ano mainoino. SYN. cruelty.

In-im'i-cal, *adj.* Ku-e'; mihimihi. SYN. hostile; opposed to.
In-im'it-a-ble, *adj.* Aole o kona like; lua ole; pookela.
In-iq-ui-toŭs, *adj.* Hewa. SYN. wicked; nefarious.
In-iq'ui-ty, *n.* Hewa; ino. SYN. wickedness; crime.
In-i'tial, *n.* 1. Hua mua.
2. Ka mua. *Initial letter,* ka hua palapala mua o ka huaolelo.
In-i'ti-āte, *v.* 1. E ao ma na kumu mua.
2. E hookumu. SYN. begin.
In-i'ti-ā'tion, *n.* 1. Ka ao mua ana.
2. Ke komo mua ana.
3. Ka hookumu ana. SYN. beginning.
In-i'ti-a-tive (ish'i), *adj.* or *n.* Hookumu. *To take the initiative,* e hookumu.
In-jĕct', *v.* E hahano; e pakelo
In-jĕc'tion, *n.* He pakelo.
In'ju-di'çioŭs, *adj.* Noonoo pono ole ia. SYN. unwise; indiscreet.
In-jŭne'tion, *n.* Kauoha; olelo pa'pa'; SYN. command.
In'jure, *v.* E hooeha; hoopoino.
In-jŭ'ri-oŭs, *adj.* Poino; ehaeha; mea e eha ai. SYN. hurtful.
In'ju-ry, *n.* He poino; he eha.
In-jŭs'tiçe, *n.* He hana paewaewa.
Ink, *n.* Inika.
Ĭnk'ling, *n.* He wahi ike iki.
Ĭnk'stănd, *n.* Ipu inika.
In'land, *adj.* Maloko o ka aina; iuka
Ĭn'let, *n.* 1. He kowa'.
2. He muliwai e kahe ana iloko o ka loko.
In'māte, *n.* He ohua hale.
Ĭnn, *n.* Hale hookipa.
In-nāte', SYN. inherent.
In'ner-mōst, *adj.* Maloko loa.
In'no-çençe, } *n.* Hala ole; maemae o
In'no-çen-çy,} ka naau.
In'no-çent, *adj.* 1. Hewa ole; hala ole.
2. Makamae. *An innocent child,* he keiki makamae.
In-nŏc'ū-oŭs, *adj.* Ehaeha ole; poino ole. SYN. harmless.
Ĭn'no-vā'tion, *n.* 1. Ke ano hou i ku-e i ke ano kahiko.
2. Ka hoala ana i ka mea hou.
Ĭn'no-vā'tor, *n.* Ka mea e hoala ana i na mea hou.
Ĭn'nu-ĕn'do, *n.* Olelo kapilipili. SYN. insinuation.
In-nū'mer-a-ble, *adj.* Manomano; kinikini; lehulehu.
In'nu-tri'çioŭs, *adj.* Pono ole ke ai.
In-ŏc'ū-lāte, *v.* E o palaheehee no kekahi mai.
Ĭn'of-fĕn'sive, *adj.* Hewa ole; noho pono.
Ĭn'of-fi'çial, *adj.* Aole mamuli o ke kauoha. SYN. unofficial.
In-ŏp'por-tūne', *adj.* Ku ole i ka manawa. SYN. unseasonable.

Ĭn-ôr'di-nate, *adj.* Oi i ka mea ku pono; kela i ka mea kupono. SYN immoderate.
Ĭn'or-gán'ic, *adj.* Nele i ke kino ola.
Ĭn'quest, *n.* He nieniele mamuli o ke kanawai.
In-quire', *v.* 1. E imi. SYN. seek after.
2. E ninau. SYN. ask.
In-quir'er, *n.* Mea imi. SYN. searcher; seeker.
Ĭn'qui-ry, *n.* I. He ninau. SYN. question.
2. Ka imi ana. SYN. search.
In-quiş'i-tive, *adj.* 1. Nieniele wale.
2. Lilo loa i ka imi; ano kiu.
In-quiş'i-tive-ness, *n.* Ke ano nieniele wale; ano kiu.
Ĭn'road, *n.* Ke komo ino ana; komo nui ana. SYN. encroachment.
Ĭn'sa-lū'bri-ty, *n.* Ano omaimai o ke kau o ka aina. SYN. unhealthiness.
In-sāne', *adj.* Pupule. SYN. crazy; demented.
In-sän'i-ty, *n.* Pupule.
In-sā'ti-a-ble, *adj.* 1. Lawa ole.
2. Maona ole.
In-seribe', *v.* 1. E kakau.
2. E kaha.
In-serip'tion, *n.* Na hua i kakauia.
In-serū'ta-ble, *adj.* Hiki ole ke hoomaopopoia. SYN. unsearchable.
Ĭn'seet, *n.* Mea kolo liilii.
Ĭn'sĕe-tiv'o-roŭs, *adj.* Ai i na mea kolo.
Ĭn'se-eure', *adj.* Paa ole; malu ole; kaulei.
Ĭn'se-eūre'ly, *adv.* Me ka paa ole; paa hemahema.
Ĭn'se-eūr'i-ty, *n.* Ka malu ole; ka paa ole.
In-sĕn'sate, *adj.* Nele i ka ike; naaupo.
In-sĕn'si-ble, *adj.* 1. Maule; ike ole.
2. Hoomaloka; maliu ole.
In-sĕn'si-bly, *adj.* Noii; ma ka liilii. SYN. little by little.
In-sĕp'a-ra-ble, *adj.* Pili paa loa.
In-sĕp'a-ra-bly, *adv.* Pili paa.
In-sĕrt', *v.* E hookomo.
In-sĕr'tion, *n.* 1. Ka hookomo ana.
2. He ano lole lihilihi.
In-sīde', *adv.* Iloko. *n.* Ko loko..
In-sid-i-oŭs, *adj.* 1. Maalea. SYN. sly.
2. Loohia mai me ka ike ole ia.
Ĭn'sight, *n.* Ka ike maopopo o ka naau.
In-sig'ni-â, *n. pl.* Na hoailoua. *Insignia of rank,* na hoailona o ke kulana.
n'sig-nif'i-eant, *adj.* Eleku; eeleku; mea waiwai ole. SYN. unimportant; trivial.
In'sin-çēre', *adj.* Hookamani; oiaio ole. SYN. false.
In'sin-çēr'i-ty, *n.* He hookamani ; he oiaio ole.
In-sin'u-āte, *v.* E kapilipili ino; e kuhikuhi ino.
In-sin'u-ā'tion, *n.* Olelo kuhi wale.

In-sĭp′id, *adj.* Hukahukai; muka; anea; ono ole.

In-sĭst′, *v.* E koi ikaika.

In-snáre′, *v.* E hoohalua; hoopahele.

Ĭn′so-lent, *adj.* Mahaoi; pakike′.

In-sŏl′ū-ble, *adj.* Hui ole me ka wai.

In-sŏl′ven-çy, *n.* Ke komohia ana i ka aie. SYN. bankruptcy.

In-sŏl′vent, *adj.* Komohia iloko o ka aie.

In-sŏm′ni-a, *n.* Ke ano hiaa; hiki ole ke hiamoe. SYN. sleeplessness.

Ĭn′so-mŭch′, *adv.* No ia hoi; nolaila hoi.

Ĭn-spēct′, *v.* E nana hooponopono. SYN. examine.

In-spēc′tion, *n.* Ka nana hooponopono.

In-spēct′or, *n.* Luna nana hooponopono.
　2. *Inspector General of schools,* Kahu Kula Nui.

Ĭn′spi-rā′tion, *n.* 1. Ka hanu ana; omo ana i ke ea.
　2. Noonoo mai a Ke Akua mai.

In-spire′, *v.* 1. E hooeueu; hoolalelele.
　2. Aoia e ka Uhane Hemolele.

Ĭn′sta-bĭl′i-ty, *n.* Ke ano loli wale! ano muhee.

In-stạll′, *v.* 1. E hookomo ma ka oihana.
　2. E hoolaa no ka oihana.
　3. E waiho ma kahi i hoomakaukauia.

In-stạll′ment, *n.* 1. He mahele. SYN. part.
　2. Loaa hou. *A fresh installment of goods,* ka loaa hou ana mai o na waiwai.
　3. *On the instalment plan,* ma ke ano hookaa hapa.

Ĭn′stạnçe, *n.* He mea hoohalike; i nane.

Ĭn′stạnçe, *v.* E nane; e laa.

Ĭn′stạnt, *n.* He sekona; manawa pokole loa.

Ĭn′stạnt, *adj.* Koke. *Instant obedience,* hoolohe koke.

Ĭn′stăn-tā-ne-oŭs, *adj.* Manawa ole; emo ole; kuhewa.

In-stăn′ter, *adv.* A no. SYN. immediately.

Ĭn′stạnt-ly, *adv.* Emo ole; manawa ole.

In-stĕad′, *adv.* Ma kahi. *John instead of James,* o Keoni ma kahi o Kimo.

Ĭn′step, *n.* Ka paipai wawae.

Ĭn′sti-gāte, *v.* E hookonokono; e paipai. SYN. urge.

Ĭn′sti-gā′tor, *n.* Mea hookonokono; mea paipai.

In-stĭll′, *v.* E hookomo. SYN. infuse.

Ĭn′stinct, *n.* Noonoo ulu wale.

In-stĭnct′ive-ly, *adv.* 1. Mamuli o ka noonoo ulu wale.
　2. Me ka manao ole e mamua.

Ĭn′sti-tūte, *v.* E hookumu; e hoomaka. begin,

Ĭn′sti-tūte, } *n.* Mea i hookumuia.
Ĭn′sti-tū′tion,} *Institution of learning,* he kula o ka naauao. SYN. establishment.

In-strŭct′, *v.* E ao; e hoonaauao. SYN. teach.

In-strŭc′tion, *n.* 1. Ka naauao.
　2. Ka hoonaauao ana.

In-strŭct′ive, *adj.* Naauao; waiwai no ka naau; koikoi.

In-strŭct′or, *n.* Kumu ao. SYN. teacher.

In-strŭct′ress, *n.* Kumu wahine.

Ĭn′stru-ment, *n.* 1. Mea hana hoopaa lima.
　2. *Instrument of music,* mea hookani.
　3. He agena. SYN. agent.

Ĭn′stru-mĕnt′al, *adj.* 1. Pili i na mea kani. *Instrumental music,* ka leo o na mea kani.
　2. Mamuli o. *He was instrumental of much good,* nui ka pono i loaa mai mamuli ona; or, oia ke kumu o na pono he nui. SYN. the means of.

Ĭn′sub-ôr′di-nate, *adj.* 1. Hoolohe ole.
　2. Hoohaunaele; ano kipi. SYN. rebellious.

Ĭn′sub-ôr′di-nā′tion, *n.* Ke ano hookuli; ano kipi; ano hoohaunaele.

In-sŭf′fer-a-ble, *adj.* 1. Hiki ole ke hoomanawanuiia.
　2. *Launa ole. Insufferable pain,* eha launa ole.

In-sŭf′fer-a-bly, *adv.* Launa ole. *Insufferably painful,* eha launa ole. *Insufferably stupid,* naaupo launa ole.

Ĭn′sŭf-fĭ′çien-çy, *n.* Ka lawa pono ole; nele.

Ĭn′sŭf-fĭ′çient, *adj.* Lawa pono ole.

Ĭn′su-lar, *adj.* Hoopuniia i ka wai.

Ĭn′su-lāt′ed, *p. p.* Waiho kaawale ia; ku kaawale.

Ĭn-sŭlt′, *v.* E hanawale; e hookokonoi′ e.

In-sŭlt′ing, *adj.* Hanawale.

In-sū′per-a-ble, *adj.* Hiki ole ke hoopauia. *An insuperable objection,* he pilikia i hiki ole ke hoopauia. SYN. insurmountable.

Ĭn′sŭp-pôrt′a-ble, *adj.* SYN. insufferable.

In-sūr′ançe, *n.* Ka panai dala. *Life insurance,* panai ola.

In-sûre′, *v.* E panai dala.

In-sûr′gent, *adj.* Kipi.

Ĭn′sûr-rēc′tion, *n.* He kipi aupuni. SYN. rebellion.

In-tăn′gi-ble, *adj.* Maopopo ole i ka ike.

Ĭn′te-ger, *n.* Mea okoa; helu okoa.

In-tĕg′ri-ty, *n.* Ano hoopono; ano oiaio. SYN. honesty; truthfulness.

In-tĕg′u-ment, *n.* Ili. SYN. skin.

Ĭn′tĕl-leet, *n.* Ka noonoo; ka uhane. SYN. mind; soul.

Ĭn′tĕl-lēct′u-al, *adj.* Noonoo; naauao. *An intellectual countenance,* he helehelena noonoo,

In-tĕl'li-gent, *adj.* 1. Noonoo; naauao; ike.
2. Aoia. *An intelligent animal*, he holoholona i aoia; he holoholona ike.
In-tĕl'li-gent'ly, *adv.* Me ka noonoo;
poonoo.
In-tĕl'li-gi-ble, *adj.* Maopopo; akaka.
SYN. plain.
In-tĕl'li-gi-bly, *adv.* Me ka moakaka;
me ka maopopo.
In'tĕm'per-ançe, *n.* 1. Ka ona. SYN.
drunkenness.
2. Uhauha; pakiko ole.
In-tĕm'per-ate, *adj.* Ona; pakela inu
waina.
2. Uhauha.
3. Huhu; noonoo oleia. SYN. hasty.
Intemperate words, na hua olelo i noo-
noo ole ia.
In-tĕnd', *v.* E manao. SYN. purpose.
In-tĕnd'ed, *n.* Mea i hoopalaula. SYN.
betrothed.
In-tĕnse', *adj.* Nui loa. *Intense heat*,
wela nui loa.
In-tĕnse'ly, *adv.* Ikaika loa; nui loa.
To suffer intensely, e ehaeha nui loa.
In-tĕn'si-fy, *v.* E hoomahuahua mai.
Intensify the evil, e hoomahuahua mai i
ka ino.
In-tĕnt', *adj.* Lilo loa; hoomaihaiha. *In-
tent upon learning*, lilo loa i ka imi na-
auao.
In-tĕnt', } *n.* Manao; manao e ma-
In-tĕn'tion, } mua.
In-tĕn'tion-al-ly, *adv.* Me ka manao
e mamua. SYN. purposely.
In-tĕnt'ly, *adv.* Me ka lilo loa o ka ma-
nao; me ka paa o ka manao. SYN.
earnestly.
2. *Listen intently*, e hoolohe pono.
In-tĕr', *v.* E kanu.
In'ter-cēde', *v.* E uwao.
In'ter-çĕpt', *v.* E hopu; e kaili e.
In'ter-çĕs'sor, *n.* Mea uwao. SYN.
mediator.
In'ter-change', *v.* E panai like; e haawi aku e haawi mai.
In'ter-change'a-ble, *adj.* Kupono ke
panai ia.
In'ter-com-mūn'i- cā'tion, *n.* Ka la-
una aku launa mai.
In'ter-coûrse, *n.* Ka launa ana.
In'ter-dïet', *v.* E pa'pa' aku. SYN.
forbid.
In'ter-est, *n.* 1. Uku kuala; uku pa-
nee.
2. Ka lilo o ka manao.
3. Kuleana. SYN. claim.
In'ter-est, *v.* 1. E hooala i ka manao.
2. E kokua. SYN. assist.
In'ter-ĕst-ed, *adj.* Komo kuleana. *An
interested party*, he poe i komo kuleana
ma kekahi hihia.
In'ter-est-ing, *adj.* SYN. pleasing.
In'ter-fēre', *v.* 1. E komo kuleana ole.
SYN. intermeddle.

2. E komo mawaena. *Interfere to pre-
vent a quarrel*, e komo mawaena i ole ai
e hakaka'.
In'ter-fĕr'ençe, *n.* Ke komo ana kuleana ole.
In'ter-jĕe'tion, *n.* He huaolelo hoopuiwa; hoomaka'u, etc.
In'ter-im, *v.* Kowa manawa. SYN.
mean time.
In-tē'ri-or, *n.* 1. Ko loko. *Interior of
the earth*, ko loko o ka honua. SYN inside.
2. Iloko. *Interior of the country*, iloko
o ka aina.
3. Kuloko. *Interior affairs*, na oihana
kuloko.
4. *Minister of the Interior*, Kuhina Kalai Aina.
In'ter-lāçe', *v.* E ulana; owili pu.
In'ter-lïne', *v.* E kakau mawaena o na
lalani i kakauia.
In'ter-lïn'e-ā'tion, *n.* Ke kakau ana
mawaena.
In'ter-lüde, *n.* 1. He hookani pila pokole mawaena o na pauku o ke mele.
2. He keaka iki.
In'ter-lŏp'er, *n.* Mea komo wale ma
ko hai pono. SYN. intruder.
In'ter-mär'riage, *n.* Ka mare ana ma-
waena o kekahi mau ohana.
In'ter-mĕd'dle, *v.* SYN. interfere.
In'ter-mĕd'dler, *n.* Mea hookeakea
wale i ko hai pono.
In-ter-mē'di-ate, *adj.* Moe ana ma-
waena.
In-tĕr'ment, *n.* Ke kanu ana. SYN.
burying.
In-tĕr'mi-na-ble, *adj.* Hopena ole.
SYN. without end.
In'ter-min'gle, *v.* 1. E launa pu.
SYN. asociate.
2. E kawili pu; e huipu.
In'ter-mis'sion, *n.* Wa hoomaha; wa
kaawale.
In'ter-mit'tent, *adj.* Kaulele.
In-tĕr'nal, *adj.* Kuloko; iloko.
In'ter-nä'tion-al, *adj.* Mawaena o na
aupuni.
In-tĕr'po-lā'tion, *n.* He olelo i hoo-
komo hewa ia.
In'ter-pōse', *v.* SYN. interfere.
2. E waiho mai. *Interpose obstacles*, e
waiho mai i mau kumu keakea.
In-tĕr'pret, *v.* 1. E mahele olelo.
2. E hoike ano.
In-tĕr'pret-er, *n.* He mahele olelo;
mea wehewehe ano.
In'ter-rĕg'num, *n.* Ka manawa i waiho kaawale ia o ka noho alii.
In-tĕr'ro-gäte, *v.* E ninaninau. SYN.
question.
In-tĕr'ro-gā'tion, *n.* Ninau. *Inter-
rogation point*, kiko ninau. SYN. question.
In'ter-rŏg'a-tïve, *adj.* Ninau. *Inter-
rogative pronoun*, paniinoa ninau.

In'ter-rŭpt', v. 1. E keakea. *Interrupt conversation*, e hookeakea i ke kamailio.
2. E hoopilikia wale. *Interrupt the work*, e hoopilikia i ka hana.
In'ter-rŭp'tion, n. Ke keakea ana; ka hoopilikia wale.
In'ter-sēct', v. E oki kekahi i kekahi.
In'ter-sēc'tion, n. Ka oki like ana. *Point of intersection*, kiko oki.
In'ter-spērse', v. 1. E hoohelelei i-o' ianei.
2. E hookau liilii; e hookomo liilii io' ia nei.
In'ter-stīçe, n. Kowa kaawale mawaena. SYN. empty space between.
In'ter-twine', v. E owili pu; e hili.
In'ter-val, n. He wa; kowa manawa.
In'ter-vēne', v. 1. E komo mawaena; SYN. interfere.
2. E hala mawaena. SYN. come between.
In'ter-vēn'tion, n. 1. Ke komo ana mawaena. SYN. interposition.
2. E komo aku ma ke ano kokua.
In'ter-view, v. E halawai pu.
In-tēs'tate, adj. Kauoha ole. *Died intestate*, ua make kauoha ole.
In-tēs'tine, adj. Kuloko. *Intestine difficulties*, na pilikia kuloko. SYN. internal; domestic.
In-tēs'tines, n. Na naau liilii.
In'ti-ma-çy, n. Ka launa loa ana.
In'ti-māte, v. E kuhikuhi. SYN. point out.
In'ti-mate, adj. Launa loa.
In'ti-mate-ly, adv. Pono loa. *Intimately acquainted*, ike pono loa.
2. Launa nui. *Intimately acquainted with one*, launa nui me kekahi.
In'ti-mā'tion, n. Ke kuhikuhi ana.; ka hai ana; hoakaka ana.
In-tim'i-dāte, v. E hoomaka'u; hoopuiwa. SYN. frighten; cause to fear.
In-tim'i-dā'tion, n. Ka hoopuiwa ana.
In'to, *prep.* Iloko.
In-tŏl'er-a-ble, adj. Hiki ole ke hoomanawanui ia. SYN. insufferable.
In-tŏl'er-ant, adj. Ae ole i ka manao o hai.
In'to-nā'tion, n. Ke kani ana o ka leo.
In-tōne', v. E kauo leo.
In-tŏx'i-eate, v. E hoolilo i ona. SYN. to make drunk.
In-tŏx'i-eā'tion, n. Ka ona. SYN. drunkenness.
In-trǎet'a-ble, adj. Nunuha; hoolohe ole; paakiki. SYN. obstinate; unruly.
In-trẽnch'ment, n. 1. Pa kaua. SYN. field works.
2. Ke komo hewa ana ma ka pono o hai.
In-trĕp'id, adj. Aa; maka'u ole; wiwo ole. SYN. bold; fearless.
In'tre-pid'i-ty, n. Ke ano koa; maka'u ole. SYN. valor; courage.

In'tri-eate, adj. Pohihihi; lauwili.
In-trīgue' (in-treeg), n. Hana hoopunihei.
In-trīgu'er, n. Kanaka hana maalea.
In-trin'sie, adj. I'-o; maoli. *Intrinsic worth*, waiwai maoli. *Intrinsic goodness*, pono i-o. SYN. real; genuine.
In'tro-dûçe', v. 1. E hookomo. *Introduce a bill*, e hookomo i bila kanawai. SYN. bring in.
2. E hoike. SYN. acquaint.
In'tro-dûç'er, n. Ka mea nana e hookomo; mea nana e hoikeike.
In'tro-dûç'tion, n. 1. Ka hookomo ana.
2. Olelo mua.
3. Hoike malihini.
In'tro-spēe'tion, n. Ka huli ana e nana iloko.
In-trûde', v. E komo hewa; e komo wale me ka ae ole ia.
In-trû'sion, n. Ke komo hewa ana.
In-trû'sive, adj. E mahaoi i ke komowale.
In-trûst', v. E waiho. *To intrust property to the care of any one*, e waiho i ka waiwai ma ka lima o kekahi.
In'tu-i'tion, n. Ka ike wale; ka ike i noonoo ole ia e mamua.
In-tū'i-tive, adv. I noonoo ole ia. *Intuitive perception*, ka ike i noonoo ole ia mamua; ka ike iloko iho, aole no waho mai.
In-ûn'date, v. E halana; e manini.
In-ûre', v. E hoomaamaa.
In-vāde', v. E komo hewa; e komo kaua.
In-vād'er, n. Mea komo hewa; mea komo kaua.
In'va-lid, n. Mea nawaliwali; mea omaimai.
In-văl'id, adj. Mana ole; waiwai ole.
In-văl'ū-a-ble, adj. Makamae.
In-vā'ri-a-ble, adj. Loli ole; mau.
In-vā'ri-a-bly, adj. Invariably so, pela mau.
In-vā'sion, n. Ke komo ino ana; ke komo kaua ana.
In-vēe'tive, v. Olelo hooino.
In-veigh' (in-vāy'), v. E olelo hooino.
In-vēi'gle (in-vē'gl), v. E hoohalua; hoowalewale. SYN. entice.
In-vĕnt', v. 1. E loaa mamuli o ka noonoo ana.
2. E noonoo a hana.
In-vĕn'tion, n. He hana hou. He mea i hanaia mamuli o ka noonoo.
In-vĕnt'ive, adj. Imi mea hou; poonoo.
In-vĕnt'or, n. Kanaka poonoo.
In'ven-tō'ry, n. Papa helu waiwai.
In-vērse'ly, adv. Ma ka hoololi ana.
In-vērt', v. E hoololi; hookahuli.
In-vĕst', v. 1. E hoomoe dala.
2. E hoopuni. SYN. surround.
3. E kahiko. SYN. clothe.
In-vĕs'ti-gāte, v. I. E imi a maopopo.
2. E ninaninau.

In-věs'ti-gā'tion, *n.* Ka imi hooma-opopo.
In-věs'ti-gā'tor, *n.* Mea imi a loaa i ka oiaio.
In-věst'ment, *v.* Ka hoomoe dala.
2. Ka hoopuni ana.
3. Ka hookahiko ana. SYN. clothing.
In-vět'ĕr-ate, *adj.* 1. Maa loa. SYN. confirmed. *Inveterate habit,* hana maa loa.
2. Mau. SYN. long established. *Inveterate enemy,* he enemi mau.
In-vid'i-oŭs, *adj.* E kono ana i ka lili.
In-vig'o-rāte, *v.* E hooikaika. SYN. strengthen.
2. E hooeueu; hoolalelale.
In-vin'çi-ble, *adj.* Pio ole. SYN. unconquerable.
In-vi'o-la-ble, *adj.* 1. Hiki ole ke haki.
2. Kupaa. *Inviolable truth,* oiaio kupaa.
In-vi'o-lāte, *adj.* Kina' ole; makamae.
In-vis'i-ble, *adj.* Ike maka ole ia.
In'vi-tā'tion, *n.* Ke kono ana; ke kauoha ana. *Invitation to a feast,* he kauoha no ka ahaaina.
In-vīte,' *v.* E kono; e kauoha.
In-vit'ing, *adj.* Aulii; mikioi; eleu.
In'voiçe, *n.* 1. Bila kumu lilo no kela me keia waiwai.
2. Bila waiwai.
In-vōke', *v.* E pule. SYN. supplicate.
In-vŏl'un-tā'ri-ly, *adv.* Wale; me ke kokua ole o ka makemake.
In-vŏl'un-tā'ry, *adj.* Wale. *Involuntary acts,* na hana i hana wale ia.
In'vo-lū'tion, *n.* Ka hoonui mana.
In-vŏlve', *v.* 1. Komo hia; owili pu. *War involves misery,* komo hia ka popilikia me ke kaua.
2. Hihia; maopopo ole. *Raise to a power,* e imi i na mana o na kuanite.
In-vūl'ner-a-ble, *v.* Hiki ole ke hooeha ia.
In'wărd, *adj.* Oloko. *Adv.* iloko.
In'wărds, *n.* Na naau liilii. SYN. intestines.
I-ō'ta, *n.* Lihi iki. SYN. jot; tittle.
I-rás'çi-ble, *adj.* Huhu wale. SYN. irritable.
Ire, *n.* Huhu; inaina. SYN. wrath; anger.
Ir'i-dĕs'çent, *adj.* E like me ka waianuenue.
Irk'some, *adj.* Luhi.
I'ron (i'urn), *n.* Hao.
I'ron-clăd, *n.* He moku manuwa hao.
I-rŏn'Ī-çal, *adj.* Henehene; loiloi.
I'ron-mŏng'er, *n.* Kanaka kuai mea hao.
I'ron-y, *n.* Olelo henehene.
Ir-rā'di-āte, *v.* E hoomalamalama.
Ir-rā'tion-al, *adj.* Ku ole i ka noonoo. SYN. unreasonable.
Ir're-clāim'a-ble, *adj.* 1. Lilo loa.
2. Loaa ole hou.
3. Hiki ole ke hoihoiia ka poho'.

Ir-rĕc'on-çil'a-ble, *adj.* 1. Hiki ole ke hoolaulea ia. SYN. implacable.
2. Hiki ole ke hookulike ia. SYN. incompatible.
Ir're-cóv'er-a-ble, *adj.* 1. Hiki ole ke loaa hou; lilo loa.
2. Ola ole. *Irrecoverable disease,* mai ola ole.
Ir-ref'rā-ga-ble, *adj.* Hiki ole ke hoole ia; hiki ole ke pani ia. SYN. unanswerable.
Ir-reg'u-lar, *adj.* 1. Pololei ole.
2. Kupono ole. *Irregular habits,* na hana kupono ole.
3. Ano e; like ole me ka mea mau.
Ir-reg'u-lăr'i-ty, *n.* 1. Ka mea mawaho ae o ka mea mau.
2. Ka mea kupono ole.
Ir-rĕl'e-vant, *adj.* Pili ole. SYN. not applicable.
Ir're-lī'ģioŭs, *adj.* Hoomaloka; aia'.
Ir-rĕp-a-ra-ble, *adj.* 1. Hiki ole ke paniia.
2. Hiki ole ke hana hou ia.
Ir're-prĕs'i-ble, *adj.* Hiki ole ke umi ia.
Ir're-prōach'a-ble, *adj.* Kina' ole; hewa ole.
Ir're-sĭst'i-ble, *adj.* Hiki ole ke pale ia.
Ir-res'o-lūte, *adj.* Lauwili; kapekepeke.
Ir-res'o-lū'tion, *n.* Ke kapekepeke o ka manao.
Ir-re-spĕct'ive, *adj.* Manao ole aku. SYN. regardless. *Irrespective of consequences,* me ka manao ole aku i ka hopena.
Ir' re-spŏn'sĭ-ble, *adj.* Ku ole i ka hookolokoloia.
Ir're-triĕv'able, *adj.* SYN. irreclaimable.
Ir-rĕv'er-ençe, *n.* Ka hoowahawaha i na mea laa; hoohenehene.
Ir're-vĕrs'i-ble, *adj.* Hiki ole ke hooloili; paa.
Ir'rĕv'o-ca-ble, *adj.* SYN. irreversible.
Ir'ri-gāte, *v.* E ka wai; e hookahe wai. SYN. water.
Ir'ri-gā'tion, *n.* Ka hookahe ana i ka wai. SYN. watering.
Ir'ri-ta-ble, *adj.* Ukiuki wale. SYN. cross.
Ir'ri-tāte, *v.* 1. E hoonaukiuki. SYN. vex.
2. E hoopehu. *Irritate a wound,* e hoopehu i ka mai.
Ir'ri-tā'tion, *v.* 1. Ukiuki.
2. Ka hoopehu ana.
Ir-rŭp'tion, *n.* He komo ino. SYN. invasion; inroad.
Is'lam-ism, *n.* Hoomana Mahometa. SYN. Mahometanism.
Is'land (i-land), *n.* Mokupuni.
Isle (īle), } *n.* Mokupuni liilii.
Is-let (i-let), }

Ĭs′o-lāte, v. E hookaawale; e hoonoho mehameha.

Ĭs′o-lā′tion, n. Ke ano mehameha; ano neoneo.

Ī-sŏs′çe-lēṣ, adj. Elua aoao like. Isosceles triangle, huina-kolu aoao-lua like.

I′so-thēr′mal, adj. Wela like.

Iṣ′ra-el-ite, n. He mamo na Iseraela.

Ĭs′sue, v. E puka mai.

Ĭs′sue, n. 1. Na keiki pono i; na mamo.

2. Ka hopena. SYN. result.

Ĭsth′mus, n. Aina puali.

Ĭt, pron. Ia; ia mea.

Ī-tăl′ian, adj. No Italia.

Ĭ-tăl′i-çīse, v. E pai hua Italia.

Ĭtch, n. Kakio; meau.

Ĭtch′ v. E maneo.

Ī′tĕm, n. Itamu; huna olelo.

I-tĭn′er-ant, n. Kanaka helewale; he kuewa. SYN. journeyman.

It-sĕlf′, pron. Ia mea no. For itself, no na iho.

Ī′vo-ry, n. Nihopalaoa.

J

Jăb′ber, v. E walaau wale; e namunamu.

Jăck′ass, n. Kekake kane.

Jăck′boots, n. Kamaa bute loihi.

Jăck′et, n. He pili lakeke.

Jăck′knife, n. Pahi pelu.

Jăck′o′lăn′tern, n. Ahi koli.

Jăck′plāne, n. Koi kahi pokole.

Jăck′screw, n. He wili nui, mea hapai.

Jăg′ged, adj. Kumumu.

Jāil, n. Hale paahao. SYN. prison

Jāil′bird, n. He paahao.

Jāil′er, n. Luna hale paahao.

Jăm, n. 1. He hua ai maka i baila pu ia me ke ko.

2. Ke kupiliki ana.

Jăm, v. 1. E hoopepe.

2. E kupiliki.

Jămb, n. Kikihi; lapauila.

Jăn′gle, n. He walaau uluaoa.

Jăn′i-tor, n. He kiai puka.

Jăn′u-a-ry, n. Januari.

Jär, n. He ipu pohaku; ipu lepo.

2. He naueue; houluliluli.

3. He mokuahana. Family jars, na mokuahana iwaena o ka ohana.

Jär, v. 1. E hoonaueue; e houluliluli.

2. E hookue′i ka manao. SYN. clash.

Jär′gon, n. Walaau maopopo ole; namunamu wale.

Jäunt, n. He hele makaikai. SYN. excursion.

Jäv′e-lin, n. Ihe au pokole.

Jaw, n. Iwi a.

Jaw, v. E nuku; e olelo huhu.

Jĕal′oŭs, adj. Lili; kekeue.

Jĕal′oŭs-y, n. Hoohuoi; lili; huwa.

Jeer, v. E loiloi; e hoohenehene.

Je-hō′vah, n. Iehova; Ke Akua.

Jĕl′ly, n. Ka wai o na hua ai i bailaia me ke ko paa.

Jĕop′ard-īze, v. E hoopilikia. SYN. hazard; imperil.

Jĕop′ard-y, n. Pilikia.

Jĕrk, n. E huki ino.

Jĕst, n. He hana hoomake aka; he olelo akaaka.

Jĕt, n. 1. Pohaku eleele; hinuhinu.

2. Ka puai ana.

Jew, n. He Hebera.

Jew′el, n. He momi.

Jew′el-er, n. Mea hana a kuai i na momi.

Jew′el-ry, n. Na momi o kela me keia ano.

Jew′ess, n. Wahine Hebera.

Jew′ish, adj. Hebera.

Jews′harp, n. Ukeke.

Jĭb, n. Pea ihu.

Jĭb-bōom′, n. Ka laau o ka pea ihu.

Jĭn′gle, v. 1. E nakeke; e kanikani.

2. E hookani.

Jŏb, n. He pauku hana; he uku pau. Job work, hana ukupau.

Jŏck′ey, n 1. Kanaka malama a kuai lio.

2. Kanaka kukini lio.

Jo-cōse′, adj. Ku i ka aka. SYN. laughable.

Jŏc′ŭnd, adj. Lealea. SYN. merry.

Jŏg, v. 1. E hoo-ke′; e hookuekue. SYN. jostle.

2. E maalo malie aku.

Join, v. 1. E hui; e hoohui.

2. E pakui; e hookui.

Join′er, n. He kamena′; mea hookui papa.

Joint, n. 1. Kahi i hookuiia.

2. He pona. Joint of sugar cane, pona ko.

3. Ami. Joints of the body, na ami o ke kino.

Joint-ĭn′ter-est, n. Kuleana like.

Joint'stŏck, *n.* Waiwai pili like.

Jŏint'üre, *n.* Waiwai i hoopaaia no ka wahine mare.

Jŏist, *n.* Auka laau.

Jŏke, *n.* Olelo akaaka. SYN. jest.

Jŏl'ly, *adj.* Lealea.

Jŏlt, *n.* E hooluliluli.

Jŏs'tle, *v.* SYN. jolt.

Jŏt down. E kakau iho. SYN. make a note of.

Joûr'nal, *n.* 1. Moolelo o na hana o ka la.
2. Kahi i kaa ai na pokakaa.
3. He nupepa-

Joûr'nal-ism, *n.* Oihana kakau nupepa.

Joûr'nal-ist, *n.* Mea hooponopono nupepa.

Joûr'nal-ize, *n.* 1. E kakau ma ka buke helu.
2. E kakau nupepa.

Joûr'ney, *n.* Huakai hele la.

Joûr'ney-man, *n.* Kanaka hoolimalima la.

Jŏ'vi-al, *adj.* SYN. jolly.

Joy, *n.* Hauoli; oli; olioli.

Joy'ful, *adj.* Olioli; lealea; piha i ka hauoli.

Joy'ful-ly, *adv.* Me ka hauoli.

Joy'ful-ness, *n.* Ke ano hauoli.

Joy'less, *adj.* Nele i ka hauoli; luuluu. SYN. cheerless.

Joy'oŭs, *adj.* SYN. joyful.

Jū'bi-lant, *adj.* SYN. joyful.

Jū'bi-lee, *n.* Iubile.

Jŭdġe, *n.* 1. Lunakanawai.
2. Luna nana. *Judge of elections,* luna nana koho balota.
3. Mea akamai i ke koho.

Jŭdġe, *v.* 1. E hookolokolo.
2. E hoohola i ka pono.

Jŭdġe'ment, *n.* 1. Ka olelo hoohola a ka lunakanawai.
2. Noonoo; poonoo.
3. *Day of judgement,* la hookolokolo.

Ju-dī'çial, *adj.* E pili i ka ahahookolokolo; pili i ka lunakanawai, a kanawai paha. *Judicial opinion,* manao o ka lunakanawai.

Ju-dī'çi-a-ry, *n.* Ka papa lunakanawai.

Ju-dī'çioŭs, *adj.* Noonoo pono; kaupaonā pono. SYN. prudent; discreet.

Ju-dī'çioŭs-ly, *adv.* Me ka noonoo pono. SYN. wisely.

Jŭg, *n.* Omole pohaku.

Jŭg'gler, *n.* Kanaka kilokilo; kanaka hana akamai.

Jŭg'gler-y, *n.* Na hana kilokilo.

Jŭ'gu-lar, *adj.* No ka puu o ka a-i.

Jūiçe (jūs), *n.* Ka wai o na hua ai.

Ju-īy', *n.* Iulai.

Jŭmp, *v.* E lele. *Jump up and down,* e lelele; lelelele.

Jŭne'tion, *n.* Kahi i hui ai; ka huina. *Railroad junction,* huina o na alanui hao.

Jūne, *n.* Iune, ka ono o na mahina.

Jŭn'gle, *n.* Waonahele.

Jūn'ior, *adj.* 1. Opio ae.
2. Papa ekolu o ke kula nui.

Jū'pi-ter, *n.* 1. Iupita, ke akua nui o ko Helene poe mamua.
2. Ka inoa o kekahi o na hoku hele.

Jū'ris-dic'tion, *n.* Ka mana o ka ahahookolokolo.

Jū'ris-prū'dence, *n.* Ka ike e pili ana i na kanawai.

Jū'rist, *n.* Mea ike ma na kanawai; he loio naauao ma kana oihana.

Jū'ror,
Jū'ry-man } *n.* Lala o ke jure.

Jū'ry, *n.* He jure.

Jū'ry-mast, *n.* Kia moku, ku i ka wa pilikia.

Jŭst, *adj.* Kaulike; hoopono.

Jŭst, *adv.* Akahi no a. *Just arrived,* a kahi no a hiki mai.

Jŭst'içe, *n.* 1. Ke kaulike; ka hoopono.
2. Lunakanawai. *Chief Justice,* Lunakanawai Kiekie.
3. *Police Justice,* Lunakanawai Hoomalu.

Jŭs-ti-fi'a-ble, *adj.* Aponoia.

Jŭs'ti-fi-cā'tion, *n.* Ka apono ana.

Jŭst'ti-fy, *v.* E apono; e hoapono.

Jŭst'ly, *adv.* Pono; me ka hoopono.

Jŭst'ness, *n.* Ka pono. *The justness of his case,* ka pono o kona aoao.

Jŭt, *v.* E ohuku. SYN. project.

Jū've-nile, *n.* He poe opio. SYN. youth.

Jū've-nile, *adj.* Opiopio. SYN. young.

K

Kĕdġe, *n.* He heleuma liilii.

Keel, *n.* Iwikaele.

Keen, *adj.* 1. Oi. SYN. sharp.
2. Akamai; noeau. *A keen reply*, he pane akamai.

Keen'ly, *adv.* Me ka ehaeha nui.

Keep, *v.* 1. E malama. SYN. preserve.
2. *Keep on*, e hoomau. *Keep out of*, e hookaaokoa. *Keep still*, e noho malie.

Keep'er, *n.* Mea nana e malama; mea nana e kiai. *Door keeper*, he kiai puka.

Keep'ing, *a.* Ka malama ana.

Keep'sāke, *n.* He pa'a lo'ha; paumaunoonoo.

Kĕġ, *n.* Barela liilii.

Kĕn, *n.* Ka nanaina o ka maka.

Kĕn-nel, *n.* Hale ilio.

Kĕr'chief, *n.* Hainaka'.

Kĕr'nel, *n.* 1. Hua kurina; hua palaoa.
2. Ka i-o o na hua paakiki.
3. Ewai. SYN. lump in the flesh.

Kĕt'tle, *n.* Ipu hao baila wai. *Tea kettle*, ipu tī.

Kĕt'tle-drŭm, *n.* Pahu kani liilii keleawe.

Kĕy, *n.* 1. Ki puka.
2. Papa kuhikuhi haina.
3. Leo kumu o ka leo mele.

Kĕy'nōte, *n.* Leo hookumu mele.

Kĕy'stōne, *n.* Ka pohaku iwaenakonu o ka pio; pohaku hoopaa.

Kick, *v.* E peku; e keehi.

Kid, *n.* Kao keiki.

Kid'nap, *v.* E kaili kanaka.

Kid'nāp-er, *n.* Mea kaili kanaka.

Kid'ney, *n.* Ka puupaa.

Kill, *v.* E pepehi a make. SYN. slay; murder.

Kiln (kil), *n.* He imu. *Lime kiln*, imu hoomoa puna.

Kiln'dry (kil'dry), *v.* E hoomaloo ma ka imu.

Kin, *n.* Hoahanau; pilikoko. SYN. relative.

Kind, *adj.* Oluolu; lokomaikai. SYN. benevolent.

Kind, *n.* Ano. SYN. sort.

Kin'dle, *v.* E a; hoo-a'; e kuni.

Kind'ly, *adv.* Me ka oluolu.

Kind'ness, *n.* Ka lokomaikai; ka oluolu. SYN. benevolence.

Kin'dred, *n.* Poe hoahanau; poe pili koko.

King, *n.* Moi'.

King'dom, *n.* Aupuni moi'.

King'ly, *adv.* Ma ke ano moi'.

King'pōst, *n.* He pou e koo ana i ke kaupoku hale.

Kings-e'vil, *n.* Ka mai alaala. SYN. scrofula.

Kink, *n.* He wahi kekee; wahi hihia. *Kink in a chain*, he wahi hihia ma ke kaula hao.

Kins'fōlks, *n.* Poe hoahanau; poe makamaka.

Kins'man, *n.* Hoahanau kane.

Kins'wo-man, *n.* Hoahanau wahine.

Kiss, *n.* He honi waha.

Kit, *n.* 1. He pahu poepoe liilii.
2. He pahu waiho mea hana.

Kitch'en, *n.* Keena hoomakaukau ai.

Kite, *n.* Lupe.

Kit'tĕn, *n.* Popoki keiki.

Knăck (năk), *n.* Ano mikioi; ano makaukau. SYN. skill.

Knăp'sack (năp), *n.* Eke lawe ukana o ke koa.

Knāve (nāv), *n.* Kanaka apuka.

Knāv'er-y (nāv'er-y), *n.* Hana apuka.

Knāv'ish (nāv'ish), *adj.* Apuka.

Knēad (need), *v.* E lomilomi. *Knead dough*, e lomilomi palaoa.

Knee (nee), *n.* Ke kuli.

Kneel (neel), *v.* E kukuli; e kulou.

Knee'-pan (nee'-pan), *n.* Iwi kuli.

Knĕll (nĕl), *n.* Bele kanikau.

Kniek'-knăck (nik'-năk), *n.* Kela me keia mea paani a kamalii.

Knife (nif), *n.* Pahi.

Knight (nit), *n.* Inoa o kekahi kulana hanohano; naita.

Knight'hŏŏd, *n.* Ke kulana o ka naita.

Knīt (nīt), *v.* 1. E hana lihilihi; hana kakini.
2. *Knit the eyebrows*, e hookuekue maka.
3. E hui; e kui.

Knit'ting-need'le, *n.* Kui hana kakini.

Knŏb (nŏb), *n.* Poka'. *Door knob*, poka' puka.

Knŏck (nŏk), *v.* 1. E kikeke; e olou.
2. E kui; e kulai. *Knock down*, e kulai.

Knŏck'er, *n.* Hamale kikeke.

Knŏt (nŏt), *n.* He nipuu; hipuu. *Hymeneal knot*, berita mare.

Knŏt'ted } *adj.* 1. Paapu i na hipuu.
Knŏt'y } 2. Pohihihi. *A knotty point in law*, he mea pohihihi ma ke kanawai.

Knŏut (nowt), *n.* Laau hili weliweli o ke aupuni Rusia.

Knōw (nō), *v.* E ike ma ka naau; e hoomaopopo.

Knōw'a-ble, *adj.* Hiki ke hoomaopopoia.

Knōwl'edġe (nŏl'ej), *v.* Ike.

Knŭck'le (nŭk'l), *n.* Puupuu lima.

Kō'ran, *n.* Ka baibala o ka poe Mahometa.

L

La'bel, n. Mea hoailona ukana; hoailona omole, etc.
La'bi-al, n. Hua puanaia me na lehelehe, like me b, p.
La'bor, n. 1. Hana. SYN. work.
2. Luhi. SYN. toil.
Lab'o-ra-to-ry, n. Keena hana laau lapaau, a me na mea e ae oia ano.
La'bor-er, n. Kanaka hana; paahana; paaua. SYN. workman.
La-bö'ri-oŭs, adj. 1. Hooikaika mau.
2. Luhi. SYN. toilsome.
La-bö'ri-oŭs-ly, adv. Me ka luhi.
Lab'y-rinth, n. Wahi i pakaawili o na ala hele.
Lace, n. Lihilihi.
Lác'er-āte, v. E haehae. SYN. rend; wound.
Lác-er-ā'tion, n. Ka haehae ana.
Lach'ry-mal, adj. Pili i ka wai maka. Lachrymal duct, luaohane.
Laek, n. He nele; he hemahema. SYN. destitution.
La-cŏn'ie, adj. Pokole ma ka olelo.
Lad, n. Keiki kane. SYN. boy.
Lad'der, n. Alapii; alahaka.
Lad'ing, n. Ukana moku, etc. SYN. cargo; load.
La'dle, n. Kiaha au loihi; puna au loihi.
La'dy, n. Wahine hoopono; he lede.
Lag, v. Lohi; hoohakalia. SYN. loiter.
Lag'ging, adj. Nahili; lolohi.
La-goon', n. 1. Lokowai papa'u.
2. Kai papa'u i hoopuniia i ka aina.
Lair, n. Lua o na holoholona hihiu hae.
La'i-ty, n. Na kanaka, koe na kahunapule.
Lake, n. Lokowai nui.
Lamb, n. Hipa keiki.
Lamb'kin, n. Hipa keiki nuku.
Lamb'like, adj. Akahai, me he keiki hipa la.
Lame, adj. Oopa; opa'.
Lame'ness, n. He oopa; he opa'.
La-ment', v. E kanikau; e kumakena.
La-ment'a-ble, adj. Aloha'ino; kumakena.
Lám'en-tā'tion, n. He kanikau; he uwe.
Lamp, n. Kukui; ipu kukui.
Lamp'black, n. Lepo uahi kukui.
Lam-poon', n. Olelo hoohenehene i kakauia.
Lánçe, n. Ihe au loihi.
Lánçe, v. E o.
Lan'çet, n. Ke o a ke kauka.
Land, n. Aina.

Land, v. E hoopae iuka; e lele iuka; e pae.
Land'breeze, n. Kehau.
Land'ed, adj. Ma ka aina. Landed interest, na pono ma ka aina.
Land'höld-er, n. Konohiki.
Land'ing, n. Wahi pae waapa.
Land'lā-dy, n. Haku aina wahine.
Land'less, adj. Kaaowe.
Land'lŏek-ed, adj. Hoopuniia i ka aina.
Land'lord, n. 1. Haku aina.
2. Haku hale hookipa.
Land'mark, n. 1. He kihi aina; mokuna aina.
2. He mea i ike maopopoia ma ka aina.
Land'of'fiçe, n. Keena oihana kuai aina.
Land'-öwn'er, n. Haku aina.
Land'seāpe, n. Hiohiona aina; nanaina.
Land'slide, }
Land'slip, } n. Kaa ana o ka aina pali.
Lands'man, n. Kanaka noho ma ka aina.
Lāne, n. He alanui ololi iwaena o na pa elua.
Lán'guage, n. Olelo.
Lán'guid, adj. 1, Nipo; nipoa. SYN. listless.
2. Onawaliwali.
Lán'guish, v. E mae; e loha; luhe. SYN. droop; wilt.
Lán'guor, n. Nipoa. SYN. dullness.
Lánk, adj. Wiwi; olala. SYN. lean.
Lán'tern, n. 1. Kukui hele po.
2. Keena kukui o ka hale lama.
Láp, n. 1. Kahi o ka aahu e uhi ana i na kuli.
2. Uha'.
Láp, v. 1. E hookau kekahi maluna iki o kekahi.
2. E palu.
Láp'i-dā'ry, n. Kanaka kalai pohaku momi.
Lápse (läps), n. Ka nee ana. Lapse of time, ka nee ana o ka manawa.
Láp'stone, n. Pohaku kui o ka humuhumu kamaa.
Lär'board, n. Ka aoao hema o ka moku ke nana imua.
Lär'çe-ny, n. Aihue. SYN. theft.
Lärd, n. Aila puaa.
Lärd'er, n. Keena waiho ai.
Lärge, adj. 1. Akea. SYN. extensive.
2. Nui; nunui.

3. Lokomaikai. *A large hearted man,* he kanɛ ka lokomaikai.

Lärġe'ly, *adv.* Ma ka nui.

Lär'ġess, *n.* Makana; manawalea. present; bounty.

Lär'i-at, *n.* Kaula hoohei. SYN. lasso.

Lärk, *n.* 1. He manu mele.

2. Paani; lealea.

Lär'ynx, *n.* Ko luna o ke kania-i.

Las-çiv'i-oŭs, *adj.* Makaleho; kuko ino.

Lash, *v.* Kaula hili.

Läss, *n.* Kaikamahine. SYN. girl.

Läs'si-tüde, *n.* SYN. languor.

Läs'so, *n.* Kaula hoohei.

Läst, *n.* 1. Ka hope loa.

2. Laau kamaa.

Läst, *v.* E mau; e paa. SYN. endure.

Läst'ing, *adj.* Mau; paa.

Läst'ly, *adv.* Hope loa.

Lätch, *n.* Hao pani puka.

Läte, *adj.* Iho nei. *Late legislature,* ka ahaolelo iho nei.

Läte, *adv.* 1. Hope; lohi; lolohi.

2. Komo loa. *Late into the night,* komo loa i ka po.

Läte'ly, *adv.* Iho nei. SYN. recently. *The ship lately arrived,* ka moku i ku iho nei.

Lä'tent, *adj.* Waiho huna ana. *Latent heat,* ka wela e waiho huna ana.

Lät'er-al, *adj.* Aoao. *Lateral motion,* nee aoao aku.

Lät'er-al-ly, *adv.* Ma ka aoao.

Läth, *n.* Pili hamo puna.

Läthe, *n.* Mikini wili mea poepoe.

Läth'er, *n.* Huwa; hua'o ke sopa me ka wai.

Lät-in, *adj.* Latina. *Latin language,* Olelo Latina.

Lät'i-tüde, *n.* 1. Latitu.

2. *Latitude of speech,* ke kuokoa o ke kamailio. SYN. freedom.

Lät'ter, *adj.* and *n.* Ka hope o na mea elua.

Lät'ter-ly, *adv.* Manawa iho nei.

Lät'tiçe, *n.* Olepelepe.

Laud, *v.* E hoolea; e hoonani. SYN. praise.

Laud'a-ble, *adj.* Ku i ka mahaloia. SYN. praiseworthy.

Läugh (läf), *v.* E akaaka.

Läugh'ing-stöck, *n.* Kumu hoohenehene.

Läugh'ter, *n.* Akaaka.

Läunch, *v.* 1. E hoolana moku; a waapa paha.

2. Hoolei. SYN. throw. *Launch a spear,* e hoolei i ka ihe.

3. E komo loa. SYN. enter deeply. *Launch out into a subject,* e komo loa iloko o ke kumu manao.

Läunch, *n.* Ka waapa nui loa o ka moku.

Läun'dress, *n.* Wahine holoi lole.

Läun'dry, *n.* Hale holoi lole.

Lä'va, *n.* Pohaku pele; a-a'

Läv'a-to-ry, *n.* Wahi holoi kino. SYN. bath.

Läve, *v.* E auau; e holoi. SYN. bathe.

Läv'er, *n.* Pa holoi.

Läv'ish, *adj.* Pakela; mauna; maunauna. SYN. prodigal; wasteful.

Läv'ish-ly, *adv.* Maunauna wale.

Law, *n.* Kanawai.

Law'breäk'er, *n.* Mea hoohaki kanawai.

Läw'ful, *adj.* Ku i ke kanawai. SYN. legal.

Law'ful-ly, *adv.* Ma o ke kanawai la; mamuli o ke kanawai. SYN. legally.

Law-giv'er, *n.* Mea haawi kanawai. SYN. legislator.

Law'less, *adj.* Manao ole i ke kanawai; kanawai ole.

Law'less-ly, *adv.* Me ke kanawai ole.

Lawn, *n.* Pahale i uhiia i ke mauu.

Law'sŭit, *n.* He hoopii kanawai.

Law'yer, *n.* He loio; he kokua ma ke kanawai.

Läx, *adj.* Palaleha.

Läx'a-tive, *n.* Laau hoonaha'.

Läx'i-ty, *n.* Ano palaka; hookuu wale. *Laxity of principle,* palaka ma ka noho ana.

Läy, *v.* 1. E waiho. SYN. place. *Lay on the table,* e waiho ma ka papa.

2. E hoomoe. *Lay brick,* e hoomoe pohaku ula.

3. E hanau hua.

4. *Lay off and on,* e kalewa. *Lay to,* e poholua. *Lay in wait,* e halua; e haluapo; e hoomahua. *Lay out land for a house,* e kuene; hookuene.

Läy, *n.* 1. He mele.

2. Mahele uku ma ka moku o kohola'.

Läy'er, *n.* He kulana. *Layer of boards,* kulana papa laau.

Läy'man, *n.* He kanaka aole kahuna pule.

La'zi-ly, *adv.* Me ka molowa; loma loma; nanea wale.

La'zi-ness, *n.* Palaualelo; molowa mau.

Lä'zy, *adj.* Molowa; palaualelo.

Lĭm'bo, *n.* Wahi hoopaa; hale paahao.

Lĕad, *n.* Kepau.

Lĕad, *v.* E kai; e alakai.

Lĕad'en, *adj.* 1. Kepau.

2. *A leaden sky,* he aouli koho u'-a la.

Lĕad'er, *n.* He alakai.

Lĕnf, *n.* He lau.

Lĕaf'less, *adj.* Lau ole.

Lĕaf'let, *n.* Lau hou.

Lĕaf'y, *adj.* Uliuli i na lau; paapu i na lau.

Lĕague (leeg), *n.* 1. Setadia; e kolu mile.

2. He kuikahi. SYN. confederacy.

Lĕak, *n.* 1. He wahi kulu.

2. Wahi e komo ai ka liu.

Lĕak'aġe, *n.* Mea kulu; he liu.

Lĕak'y, *adj.* Kulu; liu. *A leaky house,* he hale kulu. *A leaky ship,* he moku liu.

Lĕan, *n.* or *adj.* Wiwi; olala; kaha ole.

Lĕan, *v.* E hi-o'; e hilinai; e kalele.

Lĕap, *v.* E lele.

Lĕap′year, n. Makahiki lele.
Lĕarn, v. E ao; e imi naauao.
Lĕarn′ed, adj. Naauao; iwaiwa·
Lĕarn′er, n. Mea imi naauao.
Lĕarn′ing, n. Ka naauao i loaa mamuli o ka imi.
Lĕase, n. Palapala hoolimalima aina etc.
Lĕase, v. E hoolimalima aina.
Lĕase′hold, n. Ka waiwai i paa ma ka hoolimalima.
Lĕash, n. Kaula hoopaa ilio.
Lĕast, adj. Uuku loa.
Lĕath′er, n. Ili hooluia.
Lĕath′ern, adj. Ili. Leathern girdle, kaei ili.
Lĕave, n. Ka ae. SYN. permission.
  2. Ka hele aku. He took his leave, ua hele aku oia. SYN. departure.
Lĕave, v. 1. E haalele. SYN. depart.
  2. E hooilina. SYN. to will property.
Lĕav′en, n. Hu berena.
Lĕave′tăk′ing, n. Ka haawi ana i ke aloha hookaawale.
Lĕav′ings, n. pl. Na koena i koe; na koena i haalele ia.
Lĕch′er, n. Kanaka makaleho.
Lĕch′er-ŏus, adj. Makaleho.
Lĕc′ture, n. He haiao.
Lĕc′tur-er, n. Mea haawi i haiao.
Lĕdge, n. Pali pohaku; anuu.
Lĕd′ger, n. Buke nui o na helu kalepa.
Lĕd′ger-line′, n. Oa pokole.
Lee, n. Aoao malalo o ka makani.
Leer, v. E mio. SYN. lay back the ears.
Lees, n. Oka waina.
Lee′shore, n. Kahakai malalo o ka makani.
Lee′ward, n. Malalo.
Lee′wăy, n. Holo hope.
Lĕft, adj. Hema.
Lĕft′hănd′ed, adj. Maa i ka lima hema, lima.
Lĕg, n. Wawae.
Lĕg′a-çy, n. Waiwai i hooilina ia.
Lĕg′al, adj. Ku i ke kanawai.
Lē′gal-īze, v. 1. E haawi ka mana o ke kanawai.
  2. E apono mamuli o ke kanawai.
Lē′gal-ly, adv. Mamuli o ke kanawai. SYN. lawfully.
Leg-a-tee′, n. Nana ka waiwai i hooilinaia.
Le-gā′tion, n. 1. Elele aupuni me kona poe ukali.
  2. Keena oihana o ka elele aupuni.
Lĕg′bāil, n. Ka mahuka ana. To give leg bail, e mahuka. SYN. flight.
Le′gend, n. 1. He olelo o ka wa kahiko.
  2. He olelo pokole i kakau ia.
Lĕ-ġĕn′da-ry, adj. 1. Maopopo ole no ka wa kahiko.
  2. Akaka ole o ka oiaio.
Lĕġ′i-ble, adj. Maopopo i ka heluhelu.
Lĕġ′i-bly, adv. Me ka moakaka i ka heluhelu.
Lĕġ′is-lāte, v. E kau i kanawai; e hooholo kanawai.

Lĕġ′is-lā′tion, v. Ke kau ana i kanawai.
Lĕġ′is-lā′tive, adj. Kau kanawai. Legislative assembly, aha kau kanawai.
Lĕġ′is-lā′tor, n. Kanaka hana kanawai; lala o ka ahaolelo kau kanawai.
Lĕġ′is-lā′ture, n· Aha Olelo Kau Kanawai.
Le-ġit′i-mate, adj. Ku i ke kanawai.
Leis′ure, n. Wa kaawale.
Leis′ure-ly, adv. Malie.
Lĕm′on, n. Hua lemona.
Lĕm′on-āde′, n. Wai lemona.
Lĕnd, v. 1. E haawi lilo ole.
  2. E kokua. To lend a hand, e kokua.
Lĕnd′er, n. 1. Mea haawi.
  2. Money lender, mea hoolimalima dala.
Lĕngth, n. Loihi; loa.
Lĕngth′en, v. E hooloihi.
Lĕngth′wise, adv. Ma ka loa.
Lĕngth′y, adj. Loihi. SYN. long.
Lēn′i-en-çy, n. Ke ahonui. SYN. forbearance.
Lēn′i-ent, adj. Ahonui. SYN. forbearing.
Lēn-i-ty, n. Ahonui. SYN. mercy.
Lĕns, n. Aniani hooakoakoa kukuna malamalama. Magnifying lens.
Lē′o-nine, adj. Mehe liona la.
Lĕp′er, n. He lepera.
Lĕp′ro-sy, n. Mai lepera; mai pake; mai alii.
Lĕp′roŭs, adj. Pili ka mai pake.
Lĕss, adj. Emi iho.
Les-see′, n. Mea hoolimalima aina, a hale paha.
Lĕss′en, v. E hooemi iho.
Lĕs′son, n. 1. He haawina.
  2. Olelo ao.
Lĕst, conj. O.
Lĕt, v. 1. 1. Let there be light, i malamalama.
  2. O. Let us play, O, kakou i ka paani.
  3. E ae. SYN. permit.
  4. Ina. Let us go, ina kakou e hele.
  5. E. Let us pray, e pule kakou.
Lĕth′ar-ġy, n. Ano hiamoe. SYN. dullness.
Lĕt′ter, n. 1. Hua palapala.
Le-vănt′, n. Na aina o ka hikina e pili ana ma ke Kaiwaenahonua.
Lĕv′ee, n. 1. Anaina hoolauna o ka poe hanohano.
  2. Pale wai.
Lĕv′el, avj. Iliwai; _aumania; palahalaha.
Lĕv′er, n. He koo; he une.
  2. Lever for heavy articles, lohai.
Le′vite, v. He Levi.
Lĕv′i-ty, n. Lealea pono ole.
Lĕv′y, v. E hookupu.
Lewd, adj. Haukae; paumaele.
Lĕx′i-cŏġ′ra-pher, n. Kanaka hana buke unuhiolelo.
Lĕx′i-con, n. Buke hai i ke ano o na huaolelo.
Li′a-bil′i-ty, n. Ku. Liability to sickness, ku i ka mai.

Li'a-bĭl'i-ties, *n.* Na ai-e'.
Li'a-ble, *adj.* Ku.
Li'ar, *n.* Mea wahahee.
Li'bel, *n.* Libela; olelo hooino i kakauia.
Li'bel-lant, *n.* Ka mea e hoopii ana no ka libela.
Li'bel-ler, *n.* Mea kakau olelo hooino.
Li'bel-loŭs, *adj.* Olelo kakau hooino.
Lĭb'er-al, *adj.* Manawalea; lokomaikai. SYN. generous; bountiful.
Lĭb'er-al'i-ty, *n.* Ka manawalea. SYN. generosity.
Lĭb'er-al-ly, *adj.* Me ka aua ole.
Lĭb'er-āte, *v.* E hookuu; hoohemo. SYN. free.
Lĭb'er-ā'tor, *n.* Mea nana e hookuu.
Lĭb'er-tine, *v.* He hooipoipo. Mea hooko i na kuko ino.
Lĭb'er-ty, *n.* 1. Ke kuokoa. SYN. freedom.
2. Ka kookuu ana. *Liberty to go,* ka hookuu ana e hele.
Li-bĭd'i-noŭs, *adj.* Kuko ino; hookamakama.
Li-brā'ri-an, *n.* Mea malama waihona buke.
Li'bra-ry, *n.* He waihona buke.
Lice, *n. pl.* Uku poo.
Li'cense, *n.* 1. Laikini; palapala ae.
2. Ke ko ana mamuli o na kuko ino.
Li'cense, *v.* E haawi i laikini; e haawi i palapala ae.
Li-cĕn'ti-ate, *n.* Ka mea nana ka palapala ae e lawelawe mamuli o kekahi o na oihana naauao.
Li-cĕn'tioŭs, *adj.* Kuko ino; hookamakama.
Li-cĕn'tioŭs-ness, *n.* Ka hooko ana i na kuko ino.
Lĭck, *v.* E palu.
Lĭd, *n.* Ke poi; ke pani. SYN. cover.
Lie, *n.* He wahahee; he olelo hoopunipuni. SYN. untruth.
Lie, *v.* E wahahee; e hoopunipuni.
Lie, *v.* E moe.
Li'en, *n.* He kuleana ma ka waiwai o hai, no ka aie'; he kuleana ma ka moraki.
Lieu-tĕn'ant, *n.* Lutanela; luna koa.
Life, *n.* Ola.
Life'blŏod, *n.* Ke koko o ke ola.
Life'boat, *n.* Waapa hoopakele ola.
Life'guärd, *n.* Koa kiai ola.
Life'less, *adj.* Ola ole; make.
Life'lŏng, *adj.* A hala ke ola.
Life'pre-sĕrv'er, *n.* Mea hoopakele ola.
Life'time, *n.* Wa o keia ola; wa ola.
Lift, *v.* E hoala; e hapai ae.
Lift, *n.* 1. He kokua. *To give a lift,* e kokua.
2. Ka hapai ana. *A heavy lift,* he hapai kaumaha.
Lig'a-türe, *n.* He mea nakii; mea nakinaki pu a paa
Light, *n.* He ao; he malamalama.

Light, *adj.* 1. Mama.
2. Iki. *A light rain,* he u'-a iki. SYN slight.
3. *Light minded,* puni lealea.
4. Palupalu. *Light soil,* lepo palupalu
5. *Light weight,* paona mama.
Light, *v.* 1. E hoo-a'; e kuni.
2. E hoomalamalama.
3. E loaa wale. *To light upon* or t· *happen to find,* e loaa wale.
4. E hookau aku; e kau aku. SYN alight.
Light'en, *v.* 1. E hoomalamalama.
2. E hoo-mama.
3. E hoolalelale; hoo-eueu.
Light'er, *n.* Waapa nui, halihali uka na.
Light-hĕad'ed, *adj.* 1. Poniuniu hiki ole ke noonoo.
2. Ulala; ano pupule.
Light-heärt'ed, *adj.* Lea ka naau.
Light'house, *n.* Hale lama.
Light-in'fan-try, *n.* Na koa hele wa wae i makaukau no ka hele mama.
Light'ly, *adv.* 1. Malie. *Tread lightly* e hehi malie. SYN. softly.
2. *To talk lightly,* e kamailio ano ole.
3. *To think lightly of,* e manao ole aku
Light'mind'ed, *adj.* Puni lealea.
Light'ning, *n.* Uila.
Like, *adj.* Like, pe; penei.
Like, *n.* Ka iike.
Like, *v.* 1. Ono. SYN. fond of.
2. Makemake. SYN. wish.
Like'li-hŏod, *n.* He paha. *No likeli·hood of rain,* aole paha he u'a. SYN probability.
Like'ly, *adj.* 1. Paha. *Not likely,* aol· paha.
2. Hoopono; kuonoono. *A likely boy* he keiki kuonoono.
Like'mind'ed, *adj.* Lokahi ka manao
Lik'en, *v.* E hoohalike.
Like'ness, *n.* Kohu like; kii koh· like. SYN. resemblance.
Like'wise, *adv.* No hoi; pela. SYN also.
Lik-ing, *n.* Makemake.
Li-li-pu'tian, *adj.* Aa; iii. SYN small in size.
Lil-y, *n.* Pua lilia.
Limb (lim), *n.* La'la'.
Lim'ber, *adj.* Pelu wale; napenape SYN. flexible.
Lim'bo, *n.* Wahi hoopaa; hale paahao
Lime, *n.* 1. He puna.
2. Hua lemi.
Lime'kiln, *n.* Imu hoomoa puna.
Lime'stone, *n.* Pohaku puna.
Lim'it, *n.* Palena; mokuna.
Lim'it, *v.* E kau palena, e hoohaiki.
Lim'i-tā'tion, *n.* Ke kau palena ana ka palena.
Lim'it-less, *adj.* Palena ole.
Limp, *v.* E hookuoi; e opa' ma ka hele
Limp, *adj.* Napenape; palupalu; alualu·
Lim'pĭd, *adj.* Aiai. SYN. clear.

Linch'pin, *n.* Hao hoopaa huila i ka paipaikomo o ke kaa.

Line, *n.* 1. He kaha (Geom.)
2. Kaula. SYN. rope.
3. Aho. SYN. fishing line.
4. Lalani; rank. *Line of soldiers,* lalani koa.
5. *Line of poetry,* lalani mele.
6. Ano. *Line of goods,* he ano waiwai kuai.
7. He hapa-12 o ka iniha.
8. Palapala pokole. *Write a line,* kakau i palapala pokole, *or* kakau i wahi leta iki.
9. Ka Poaiwaena-honua. SYN. Equator.

Line, *v.* E uhi oloko.

Lin'e-āge, *n.* Kuauhau.

Lin'e-al, *adj.* Ma ke kuauhau pololei.

Lin'e-a-ment, *n.* Helehelena kanaka. SYN. feature.

Lin'e-ar, *adj.* Loa. *Linear measure,* ana loa.

Lin'en, *n.* Lole lilina; lilina.

Lin'ger *v.* E kakali; e lolohi; kawele.

Lin'ger-ing, *adj.* loihi; kawele. *Lingering sickness,* he mai loihi; mai kawele.

Lin'gual, *n.* 1. He hua palapala i puanaia e ke alelo.
2. *adj.* No ke alelo.

Lin'guist, *n.* Mea akamai ma na olelo.

Lin'i-ment, *n.* Laau hamo.

Lit'i-gā'tion, *n.* Hoopii kanawai.

Link, *n.* He pauku kaulahao; pauku.

Link, *v.* E hoohui; e hookui pu. SYN. join.

Lint, *n.* Pulupulu lilina, mea lapaau eha.

Li'on, *n.* He liona.

Li'on-ess, *n.* Liona wahine.

Li'on-ize, *v.* E hoo-hanohano.

Lip, *n.* 1. Lehelehe.
2. He kae. SYN. edge.

Liq'ui-fy, *v.* E hooheehee.

Liq'uid, *n.* Mea hee; heehee.

Liq'ui-dāte, *v.* 1. E hoo-hee.
2. E hookaa. SYN. settle, pay.

Liq'ui-dā'tion, *n.* Ka hookaa ana. SYN. payment.

Liq'uor (lik-er), *n.* 1. Na wai ona.
2. Kela me keia ano wai.

Lisp, *v.* E puana hemahema i na hua olelo.

List, *n.* 1. He papahelu. *List of names,* papa helu o na inoa. SYN. roll; catalogue; register.
2. He wahi i hookaawale ia no ke kukini, a paio, a hakaka paha. *To enter the lists,* e komo i ke kukini.

List'en (lis'n), *v.* E hoolohe; e haka pono.

List'en-er, *n.* 1. He mea e lohe ana.
2. He hakilo; kiu. SYN. eaves-dropper.

List'less, *adj.* Kualana; nanea.

List'less-ly, *adv.* Manaka'; manao ole.

Lit'er-al, *adj.* Pili loa i ka olelo. *A literal translation,* he unuhi olelo i pili loa i ka olelo i kakauia.

Lit'er-al-ly, *adv.* Pili loa i ka hua olelo.
2. Oiaio.

Lit'er-a-ry, *adj.* Naauao ma na buke; imi buke.

Lit'er-ā'ti, *n. pl.* He poe lilo loa i ka imi buke.

Lit'er-a-tūre', *n.* Na palapala a pau o kela me keia ano.

Lithe, *adj.* Mama. SYN. nimble; supple.

Lith'o-graph, *n.* Kii i kahaia ma ka pohaku.

Li-thŏg'ra-phy, *n.* Ke kaha ana ma ka pohaku.

Lit'i-gant, *u.* Mea hoopii kanawai.

Lit'i-gā'tion, *n.* Hoopii kanawai.

Li-ti'gious, *adj.* Maa i ka hoopii kanawai.

Lit'ter, *v.* E kiola wale. *To litter up a room,* e kiola wale i kela me keia mea ma ke keena.

Lit'ter, *n.* 1. He manele.
2. Ohana holoholona keiki.

Lit'tle, *adj.* Uuku; liilii.

Lit'to-ral, *adj.* E pili ana i kahakai; no ke kai.

Live, *v.* 1. E ola.
2. E noho; e noho paa.

Live'li-hoŏd, *n.* Oihana e pono ai ka noho ana.

Live'lŏng, *adj.* Loihi launa ole. *The livelong day,* la loihi launa ole.

Live'ly, *adj.* Hoihoi; makaala.

Liv'er, *n.* 1. Mea e noho ana. SYN. dweller.
2. Mea e hoolako ana i ka ai.
3. Ake paa.

Liv'er-y-stā'ble, *n.* Hale hoolimalima lio.

Live'stŏck, *n.* Na holoholona laka.

Liv'id, *adj.* Hauliuli, me he palapu la.

Liv'ing, *n.* Na loaa i lawa no ka noho ana. SYN. support. E lawa ka loaa no ka noho'na.

Liz'zard, *n.* He moo.

**Lō! *interj.* Aia hoi! SYN. behold.

Lōad, *n.* Haawe. SYN. burden.
2. *Ship load,* piha moku; *cart load* piha kaa.

Lōad, *v.* 1. E hooili ukana.
2. E hoopiha. *Load a gun,* e hoopiha i ka pu.

Lōad'stŏne, *n.* Pohaku mageneta.

Lōaf, *n.* He popo mea ai.

Lōaf, *v.* E a'ea wale.

Lōaf'er, *n.* He a'ea haukae.

Lōam, *n.* Lepo momona.

Lōam'y, *adj.* Momona. like me ka lepo.

Lōan, *n.* 1. Mea i haawiia no ka manawa.
2. Dala hoo-aie'.

Lōathe (lōthe), *v.* E hoopailua. SYN. abhor.

Lōath'sŏme, *adj.* Hoopailua.

Lŏb'by, *n.* 1. Ke keena mawaho ae o ke keena ahaolelo.

Lŏb'by, *v.* E paipai bila kanawai.

Lōbe, *n.* Ko lalo o ka pepeiao.

Lŏb′ster, *n.* He ula.
Lō′eal, *adj.* No kauwahi.
Lo-eā′l′i-ty, *n.* Kauwahi.
Lō′eate, *v.* E hoonoho.
Lo-eā′tion, *n.* 1. Wahi. SYN. place.
2. Ka hoonoho ana.
Loeh, *n.* 1. He loko. SYN. lake.
2. He kaikuono. SYN. bay.
Lŏek, *n.* 1. Laka. Door lock, laka puka.
2. Owili lauoho. SYN. lock of hair.
3. Loko hoopaa wai ma ka auwai nui.
Lŏek, *v.* 1. E ki a paa.
2. Lock arms, e hookui pu i na lima.
Lŏek′er, *n.* Holowaa i ki ia.
Lŏek′et, *n.* Mea milimili, waiho kii.
Lŏek′-smith, *n.* Kanaka hana laka.
Lŏek′-up, *n.* Halewai.
Lŏ′eo-mō′tion, *n.* Ka hele ana ma na kauwahi.
Lŏ′eo-mō′tive, *n.* Enikini kaa mahu.
Lŏdge, *n.* 1. Hale noho iki.
2. Hale halawai o na aha malu′.
Lŏdge, *n.* 1. E noho iki; noho no ka wa pokole.
2. E ku. SYN. strike; hit.
3. Lodge a complaint, e waiho mai i kumu hoopii.
Lŏdg′er, *n.* Ohua hale; mea e noho ana.
Lŏdg′ings, *n. pl.* Wahi noho.
Lŏft, *n.* Keena oluna. Sail loft, keena humuhumu pea.
Lŏf′ty, *adj.* 1. Kiekie. SYN. elevated.
2. Hookano; haakei. SYN. proud.
Lŏg, *n.* Pauku laau.
Lŏg′a-rithm, *n.* Huhui helu.
Lŏg′-book, *n.* Buke mooleio no ka hoohoio moku.
Lŏg′-house, *n.* Hale i kukuluia me na pauku laau.
Lŏg′ie, *n.* Ka ike o ke kukulu manao.
Lŏg′ie-āl, *adj.* Kukulu manao.
Lo-gi′çian, *n.* Mea akamai i ke kukulu manao.
Loin, *n.* Puhaka.
Loi′ter, *v.* E hoololohi; nahili; manuka′.
Loi′ter-er, *n.* He nahili; mea hoohakalia wale.
Lŏll, *v.* E hoonanea; e luana wale.
Lōne′li-ness, *n.* Mehameha o ka noho ana.
Lōne′ly, ⎫ *adj.* Mehameha.
Lōne′some, ⎭
Lŏng, *adj.* Loa; loloa; loihi.
Lŏng, *v.* E iini.
Lon-gēv′i-ty, *n.* Ka loihi o ke ola.
Lŏng-hēad′ed, *adj.* Akamai i ka noonoo e mamua; poonoo. SYN. shrewd; discerning.
Lŏng′ing, *n.* Ka iini o ka naau.
Lŏn′gi-tūde, *n.* Lonitu.
Lŏn′gi-tū′di-nal, *adj.* Loa.
Lŏng′lived, *adj.* Ola loihi.
Lŏng-sŭf′fer-ing, *adj.* Ahonui; hoomanawanui. SYN. patient.
Lŏng-wind′ed, *adj.* 1. Mau ke aho.
2. Loihi a hooluhi. A long winded speech, he haiolelo loihi a hooluhi.

Lŏŏk, *v.* 1. E nana. SYN. see.
2. Look for, e imi; e huli.
Loŏk, *n.* Ka nana ana o ka maka.
Loŏk′ing-glàss, *n.* He aniani nana.
Loŏk′out, *n.* 1. He wahi naha; wahi kiai; he aleo.
2. To be on the lookout, e hakilo; e kiai; e makaala.
Loŏm, *v.* E hoea mai ma kahi mamao.
Loŏm, *n.* Mikini hana lole.
Loŏse, *v.* 1. E wehe ae; e hoohemo.
2. E kala; e hookuu.
Loŏse, *adj.* 1. Oluolu; alualu. SYN. not tight.
2. Hemo. SYN. not fast.
3. Ino; pono ole. Loose habits, na hana maa ino. A loose life, he noho′na pono ole.
Loŏse′ly, *adv.* Kapulu. To do work loosely, e hana kapulu i ka hana.
Loŏs′en, *v.* 1. E hooluolu; hooalualu. Loosen the jib sheet, e hoo alualu i ke kaula pea ihu.
2. E hoopalupalu. Loosen the soil, e hoopalupalu i ka lepo.
3. E hemo; e wehe ae.
Lo-quā′çioŭs, *adj.* Walaau mau.
Lo-quāç′i-ty, *n.* Ka walaau mau.
Lôrd, *n.* 1. Haku.
2. Inoa hanohano.
Lôrd, *v.* E hookiekie.
Lôrd′ly, *adj.* Haaheo; hookano; hookiekie.
Lôrd′ship, *n.* Inoa hanohano.
Lōre, *n.* Naauao; ike. SYN. learning.
Lŏse. *v.* 1. E nalowale; e lilo.
2. E poho′.
3. E haule.
Lŏs′er, *n.* 1. Ka mea nana ka poho′.
2. Ka mea nana ka mea i haule.
Lŏss, *n.* 1. Ka nalowale ana; ka haule ana.
2. Ka poho′; ka poino.
Lŏt, *n.* 1. He pa.
2. He mahele; haawina.
3. He hoailona.
Lŏth, *adj.* Hoowaha′waha′; makemake ole.
Lŏ′tion, *n.* Laau wai hamo.
Lŏt′ter-y, *n.* Kekahi ano pili waiwai.
Loud, *adj.* Nui ka leo; kani nui.
Loud′ly, *adv.* Aaina; me ke kani nui.
Lounge, *n.* He punee.
Lounge, *v.* 1. E hiolani; e luana wale.
2. E aea wale. SYN. loaf.
Loung′er, *n.* 1. Mea hoonanea wale.
2. Mea noho wale; he aea haukae. SYN. loafer.
Louse, *n.* He uku poo.
Lous′y, *adj.* Paapu i na uku.
Lout, *n.* Kanaka hemahema; he kuaaina.
Lŏv′a-ble, *adj.* Ku i ke aloha ia.
Lŏve, *n.* Aloha. SYN. affection.
Lŏve′lĕt′ter, *n.* Palapala hooipoipo; palapala aloha.
Lŏve′li-ness, *n.* Ano ku i ke aloha.
Lŏve′ly, *adj.* Onaona; ku i ke aloha.

Lòv'er, *n.* Mea aloha; he ipo.
Lòvc'-sŏng, *n.* Mele o ka puuwai.
Lŏv'ing, *adj.* Aloha.
Lŏv'ing-kind'ness, *n.* Lokomaikai.
Lŏw, *adj.* 1. Haahaa.
  2. Haumia; pelapela. SYN. vile.
Lŏw'born, *adj.* Hanauia ma ke kulana haahaa. SYN. baseborn.
Lŏw'bred, *adj.* Kuaaina; naaupo.
Lŏw'er, *v.* E hoohaahaa; e hookuu iho.
Lŏw'er, *v.* 1. E pouli mai.
  2. E hakumakuma. SYN. frown.
Lŏw'er-y, *adj.* Pouliuli; hakumakuma.
Lŏw'land, *n.* Aina haahaa.
Lŏw'li-ness, *n.* Akahai; haahaa o ka naau.
Lŏw'ly, *adj.* Akahai; haahaa. SYN. meek.
Lŏw'spïr'it-ed, *adj.* 1. Luuluu; kaumaha ka naau. SYN. depressed.
  2. Apiki. SYN. mean.
Lŏy'al, *adj.* Kupaa.
Lŏy'al-ty, *n.* Ka manao kupaa.
Lŏz'enge, *n.* 1. Mea ono kopaa.
  2. Huina-ha-like, like ole nae na aoao. SYN. rhomb.
Lŭb'ber, *n.* Kanaka puipui a molowa; kanaka hawawa.
Lŭb'ber-ly, *adj.* Kapulu; hemahema; lomaloma. SYN. awkward.
Lŭ'bri-cāte, *v.* E hamo i pahee.
Lŭ'çid, *adj.* 1. Molaelae; moakaka; aiai. SYN. clear; bright.
  2. *Lucid interval,* wa noonoo pono o ka mea pupule. SYN. sane.
Lŭck, *n.* Mea ulia wale; laki. *Good luck,* he pomaikai i ka ulia wale. *Bad luck,* he poino i ulia wale; laki ole.
Lŭck'y, *adj.* Pomaikai; laki.
Lŭck'i-ly, *adv.* Pomaikai maoli.
Lŭ'era-tive, *adj.* Puka; nui mai o ke dala.
Lŭ'ere, *n.* Dala puka; waiwai puka.
Lŭ'di-croŭs, *adj.* Lea; ku i ka akaaka. SYN. laughable.
Lŭff, *v.* E hoopii i ka makani.
Lŭg, *v.* E halihali me ke kaumaha.
Lŭg'gage, *n.* Ukana pili kino. SYN. baggage.
Lu-gŭ'bri-oŭs, *adj.* Haloiloi; kumakena. SYN. mournful.
Lŭke'warm, *adj.* Malili; pumahana.
Lŭll, *v.* E hoo-na'. SYN. quiet.
  2. E malie mai. *The wind has lulled,* ua malie mai ka makani.
  3. E hoomalielie. SYN. calm.

Lŭl'a-bȳ, *n.* Mele hoo-na keiki liilii.
Lum-bā'go, *n.* He hui ma ka puhaka.
Lŭm'ber, *n.* Kela me keia ano papa laau.
Lŭm'ber-rōom, *n.* Keena waiho ukana.
Lŭ'mi-nā'ry, *n.* Mea hoomalamalama; he lama.
Lŭ'mi-noŭs, *adj.* Malamalama; aiai. SYN. bright.
Lŭmp, *n.* He puu.
Lŭmp'y, *adj.* Puupuu; hakuhaku.
Lŭ'na-çy, *n.* Pupule. SYN. insanity.
Lŭn'ar, *adj.* Pili no ka mahina.
Lŭ'na-tic, *n.* He pupule.
Lŭnch, *n.* He wahi paina iki.
Lŭnch'eon, *n.* Ka ai o ka paina iki.
Lŭng, *n.* Ake mama.
Lŭrch, *n.* 1. Ka huli kuhewa o ka moku ma kona aoao.
  2. Ka haalele wale ana iloko o ka pilikia. *To leave in the lurch,* e haalele iloko o ka pilikia.
Lŭre, *v.* E onou; e hoohalua; e hoowalewale. SYN. entice.
Lŭ'rid, *adj.* Pouliuli; panopano.
Lŭrk, *v.* E hoomakakiu; e pee.
Lŭrk'ing-plāçe, *n.* Wahi e pee ai; wahi e hoomakakiu.
Lŭs'çioŭs, *adj.* Ono loa; mikomiko.
Lŭst, *n.* Kuko hewa; makaleho.
Lŭst'ful, *adj.* Piha i na kuko hewa; makaleho.
Lŭst'i-ly, *adv.* 1. Ikaika. *To work lustily,* e hana ikaika.
  2. Nui. *To shout lustily,* e hooho nui.
Lŭs'trous, *adj.* Alohilohi; hinuhinu; anapanapa.
Lŭst'rum, *n.* He wa; elima makahiki.
Lŭst'y, *adj.* Ikaika; puipui. SYN. strong.
Lux-ū'ri-ançe, *n.* Nui o ka ulu.
Lux-ū'ri-ant, *adj.* 1. Kawowo. *Luxurant growth,* kawowo ka ulu ana.
  2. Ikaika ma ka ulu ana; ulu a nui.
Lux-ū'ri-āte, *v.* 1. E hoo-oluolu; e hoonanea.
  2. E hauoli nui.
Lux-ū'ri-oŭs, *adj.* 1. Pakela ai. SYN. luxurious living.
  2. Hoohiehie.
Lŭx'u-ry, *n.* Mea e hoohiehie ai ka noho ana.
Ly-çē'um, *n.* 1. Ahahui Iini Naauao
  2. Hale o ka ahahui Imi Naauao.
Lȳe (lì), *n.* Wai lehu ahi.
Lȳre, *n.* Lira hookani. SYN. harp.

M

Mac-ăd'am-īze, *n.* E kapili alanui i na pohaku iliili.

Mach'i-nā'tion (măk-i-na'tion), *n.* Hana malu' kupono ole. SYN. intrigue; stratagem.

Ma-chine', (ma-sheen'), *n.* Mikini; mea kokua i ka hana a ka lima.

Ma-chin'er-y, *n.* Na mikini o kela me keia ano.

Ma-chin'ist, *n.* Kanaka hana mikini.

Măd, *adj.* 1. Huhu loa.
2. Pupule.

Măd'ăm, *n.* Inoa kahea no ka wahine.

Măd'house, *n.* Hale pupule. SYN. insane asylum.

Măd'ly, *adv.* Me ka ino loa. SYN. insanely. Pupule.

Măd'ness, *n.* Ano pupule; ano hehena; ulala. SYN. insanity.

Măg'a-zine', *n.* 1. Hale hoo-ahu. SYN. storehouse.
2. Buke i paila i kela me keia manawa, buke hooiliili kumu manao.

Măg'got, *n.* Ke ilo.

Măg'got-y, *adj.* Paapu i na ilo.

Mā'gi, *n.* Ka poe Magoi o ka Hikina.

Măg'ie, *n.* Hana kilokilo.

Ma-gi'cian, *n.* Kanaka kilokilo.

Măg'is-tē'ri-al, *adj.* 1. Pili i ka oihana lunakanawai.
2. Haaheo; hookiekie. SYN. arrogant.

Măg'is-tra-cy, *n.* 1. Oihana lunakanawai.
2. Ka papa lunakanawai.

Măg'is-trate, *n.* Luna hooko kanawai.

Măg'na-Ĉhär'tà, *n.* He kumu kanawai aupuni.

Măg'na-nim'i-ty, *n.* Ano lokomaikai. SYN. generosity.

Mag-năn'i-moŭs, *adj.* Lokomaikai. SYN. generous.

Mag-năn'i-mous-ly, *adv.* Me ka lokomaikai. SYN. generously.

Măg'nate, *n.* Kanaka hanohano; kanaka koikoi.

Măg'net, *n.* Pohaku ume hao.

Măg-nět'ic, *adj.* Mana ume.

Măg'net-ism, *n.* Ka mana ume.

Măg'net-īze, *v.* E hookomo i ka mana ume; e ume.

Măg-nif'i-çençe, *n.* Ke kamahao.

Măg-nif'i-çent, *adj.* Kamahao.

Mag'ni-fi-er, *n.* Aniani hoomahuahua ike.

Măg'ni-fy, *v.* 1. E hoomahuahua i ka ike o ka maka.
2. E hoolea; hoonani. SYN. praise; exalt.

Măg'ni-tūde, *n.* Ka nui. SYN. bulk; greatness. *Magnitude of the undertaking*, ka nui o ka hana.

Ma-hŏg'a-ny, *n.* He kumu laau ano like me ke kou.

Ma-hŏm'et-an, *n.* He Mahometa.

Māid,⎫ *n.* Wahine opio mare ole.
Māid'en,⎰

Māid'en-hair, *n.* He iwaiwa.

Māil, *n,* 1. Pale umauma metala.
2. Eke leta.

Māil, *v.* E hookomo ma ke eke leta. SYN. post.

Māil'a-ble, *adj.* Kupono ke halihali ia ma ke eke leta.

Māim, *v.* E moku na lala; e hana ino i ke kino. SYN. mutilate.

Māin, *adj.* 1. Nui. SYN. mighty.
2. Ano nui; hapa nui. SYN. chiefly; principally. *Mainly devoted to agriculture*, lilo nui i ka mahiai.

Māin'mast, *n.* Ke kia nui o ka moku.

Māin'sāil, *n.* Ka pea hope; ka pea nui.

Māin-tāin', *v.* 1. E malama mau. SYN. sustain.
2. E hoolako. SYN. support. *Maintain a family*, e hoolako i ka ohana.

Māin'te-nançe, *n.* 1. Ka hoolako ana i na mea e pono ai ke ola.

Māize, *n.* Kurina. SYN. Indian corn.

Ma-jĕs'tie, *adj.* Ihiihi; kamahao.

Măj'es-ty, *n.* Hanohano nui; he kamahao. *His Majesty, the King*, ka mea kamahao, ka Moi.

Mā'jor, *n.* Mekia; luna koa.

Ma-jŏr'i-ty, *n.* 1. Ka hapa nui.
2. Ka wa oo ma ke kanawai.

Māke, *v.* 1. E hana; e kukulu. SYN. construct.
2. E kaohi. SYN. compel.
3. E loaa. SYN. earn; gain. *Make money*, e loaa i dala.
4. *To make a complaint*, e waiho mai i kumu hoopii.
5. *To make a calculation*, e helu; e noonoo helu.
6. *To make known*, e hooakaka; e hoolaha.
7. Lilo. SYN. become. *A good boy will make a good man*, e lilo ana ke keiki maikai i kanaka maikai.
8. *Make choice of*, e koho. SYN. choose.
9. *Make free with*, e lawewale.
10. *Make good*, (a) E hooko. *Make good a promise*, e hooko i ka olelo. (b.) *Make good a loss*, e hoihoi i ka poho.
11. *Make light of*, e manao ole aku. SYN. to be indifferent to.

12. *Make much of,* e manao nui aku.
SYN. to esteem highly.
13. *Make out,* e hoomaopopo; akaka.
SYN. understand. *To make out the meaning,* e hoomaopopo i ke ano.
14. *Make out a case,* e hooia i ka aoao hoopii.
15. *Make over property,* e hoolilo waiwai. SYN. to deed property; to convey.
16. *Make sail,* e huki i na pea.
17. *Make up,* (a) e hoolaulea. SYN. reconcile. (b) E hoo-puolo. SYN. make up a bundle. (c) *Make up a deficit,* e hooponopono mai i ka mea i koe. (d) *Make up accounts,* e hooponopono i na helu.
18. *Make water,* (a) e liu. SYN. leak; (b) mimi. SYN. urinate.
Mak'er, n. Mea nana e hana.
Make'shift, n. He mea ku i ka wa.
Mal'ad-min'is-tra'tion, n. Ke ko pono ole ana i na hana o ka oihana.
Mal'a-dy, n. He mai. SYN. sickness
Ma-la'ri-a, n. Ea ino nana mai ka mai.
Mal'con-tent', n. Mea ohumu mau.
Mãle, n. He kane.
Mãl'e-dic'tion, n. Olelo hailiili; olelo hooino.
Mãl'e-fac'tor, n. Kanaka hoohaki kanawai.
Ma-lev'o-lent, adj. Manao ino; naau keemoa; opu ino.
Mal-fea'sance, n. Ka hana pono ole. *Malfeasance in office,* ka hana pono ole ma ka oihana.
Mal'ice, n. Ka manao ino; opu ino.
Ma-li'cioŭs, adj. SYN. malevolent.
Ma-li'cious-ly, adv. Me ka manao ino.
Ma-lign' (ma-line), v. E akiaki; e niania. SYN. traduce; slander.
Ma-lig'nant, adj. 1. Akiaki; niania. 2. Hoopilikia ola; ino loa. *A malignant disease,* he mai ino loa. SYN. virulent.
Ma-lig'ni-ty, n. 1. Niania; opu ino. SYN. malice.
Ke ano make. SYN. virulence.
Mãl'le-a-ble, adj. Hiki ke kuiia a lahilahi.
Mãl'let, n. Hamale laau.
Mal-prac'tice, n. 1. Lapaau hewa.
2. Hana, pono ole.
Mal-treat', v. E hana ino aku; e hoomaau.
Mal-treat'ment, n. 1. Ka hana ino ana.
2. Ka lapaau hewa ana.
Mãm'mon, n. Mamona; ka waiwai o keia ao.
Mãn, n. Kane; kana'ka.
Mãn, v. E hoolako i na ka'naka.
Mãn'a-cles, n. Kupee lima hoopaahao.
Mãn'age, v. 1. E hooponopono; e malama pono. *Manage affairs,* e hooponopono i ka oihana.
2. *Manage to do without,* e hoomanawanui i ka nele.

Mãn'age-a-ble, adj. 1. Hiki ke hooponopono ia.
2. Hiki ke hoolakalakaia.
Mãn'age-ment, n. 1. Ka hooponopono ana. *Poor management,* hooponopono hemahema.
2. Papa luna hooponopono.
Mãn'a-ger, n. Luna hooponopono.
Man-dā'mus, n. Palapala kauoha o ka aha hookolokolo.
Mãn'da-rin, n. Luna aupuni o Kina.
Mãn'dāte, n. He kauoha. SYN. command.
Mãn'da-to-ry, adj. Me ke kauoha.
Mãne, n. Hulu a-i' o na holoholona.
Ma-neū'ver, n. 1. He hana maalea. SYN. stratagem.
2. *Military maneuver,* ka hana o ka oihana koa.
Mãn'ful, adj. Hookanaka. SYN. manly.
Mãn'ful-ly, adv. Me ka hookanaka. SYN. nobly.
Mãn'ger, n. Pahu hanai holoholona.
Mãn'gle, v. Haihai a weluwelu
Mãn'hood, n. Ke kulana kanaka makua.
Ma'ni-ac, n. Kanaka pupule loa. SYN. madman.
Mãn'i-fest, adj. Moakaka; akakalea. SYN. obvious; evident.
Mãn'i-fest, n. He pepa hoike ukana moku.
Mãn'i-fest, v. E hoike. SYN. exhibit; show.
Mãn'i-fes-tā'tion, n. Ka hoike ana.
Mãn'i-fest-ly, adv. Maopopolea. SYN. evidently.
Mãn'i-fold, adj. Lehulehu.
Ma-nip'u-lāte, v. E mili; e lawelawe me ka lima. SYN. handle.
Man-kind', n. Ka'naka.
Mãn'li-ness, n. Ke ano hookana'ka.
Mãn'ly, adj. Hookanaka. SYN. noble.
Mãn'ner, n. 1. Ano. SYN. sort.
2. *Manners,* ano launa. *Good manners,* ano launa maikai, pihalula.
Mãn'of-war', n. Moku manuwa'.
Mãnse, n. 1. Hale noho no ke kahuna pule.
2. Aina mahi. SYN. farm.
Mãn'sion, n. Hale noho akea.
Mãn'slaugh-ter, n. Lawe ola; pepehi kana'ka.
Mãn'tel, n. Holowaa ma ka paia o ka hale.
Mãn'tle, n. He lole koloka; he kihei aahu.
Man-til'la, n. He koloka no ka wahine.
Mãn'u-al, adj. Lima. *Manual labor,* hana lima.
Mãn'u-al, n. Buke liilii, paa lima.
Mãn'u-fac'to-ry, n. Hale oihana hana lima.
Mãn'u-fac'ture, v. E hana, ina me ka lima, a mikini paha.
Mãn'u-fac'ture, n. Ka mea i hanaia e ka lima, a mikini paha.

Măn'u-făc'tur-er, n. Kanaka hana i kela me keia mea.

Măn'u-mit', v. E hookuu mai ka noho ana kuapaa. Syn. free.

Ma-nūre', n. Mea hoomomona lepo; kukae.

Măn'u-script, n. Pepa i kakau lima ia.

Ma'ny (mě-ny), adj. Lehulehu; makena; nuiwale.

Măp, n. Palapala aina.

Măr, v. E hooki-na'; e hana ino i kekahi mea.

Ma-rąud'er, n. He powa'; kanaka pakaha. Syn. robber.

Măr'ble, n. Pohaku mabela.

Mărch, n. 1. Maraki.
2. Huakai o na koa.

Măre, n. Lio wahine.

Măr'gin, n. He kae; he lihi. Syn. border.

Ma-rīne', adj. 1. O ke kai. A marine view, ke nanaina o ke kai.
2. Marine hospital, hale mai no na luina.

Ma-rīne', n. Na moku. Merchant marine, na moku kalepa.
2. He koa o ka moku manuwa.

Măr'i-ner, n. Kanaka holo moana; sela; luina. Syn. seaman; sailor.

Măr'i-tal, adj. No ke kane mare.

Măr'i-time, adj. Pili i ka moana; pili i ke kai. Syn. nautical. Maritime nations, na lahui booholo moana.

Mărk, n. 1. He hoailona; he kaha.
2. He mea kaulana. Syn. distinction. A man of mark, he kanaka kaulana.

Mărk, v. 1. E kaha; e hoailona.
2. E haka pono; e noonoo pono. Syn. heed; observe.

Măr'ket, n. 1. Hale makeke.
2. Makeke; he kuai akea; oihana kalepa.

Măr'ket-man, n. Kanaka o ka makeke.

Măr'ket-ing, n. Ke kuai ana ma ka makeke.

Mărks'man, n. Kanaka ki pu.

Măr'ma-lāde, n. Mea ono i hanaia me na hua ai.

Măr'riage, n. Ka mare. Syn. matrimony; wedlock.

Măr'riage-a-ble, adj. Kupono ke mare.

Măr'row, n. Ka lolo o ka iwi.

Măr'ry, v. E mare.

Mărsh, n. Aina po'ho-poho'.

Măr'shal, n. 1. Ilamuku.
2. He alakai nui o ka huakai.
3. Alihi kaua nui, ma Europa.

Măr'shal, v. E hoonohonoho pono. Marshal troops, e hoonohonoho pono i na puali kaua.

Mărsh'y, adj. Po'ho-poho'.

Mărt, n. Syn. market.

Măr'tial, adj. Koa.

Măr'tyr, n. Mea hoike no ka oiaio, a i ka make.

Măr'tyr-dom, n. Ka hoomake ana no ka oiaio.

Măr'vel, v. E haohao.

Măr'vel-ous, adj. Kupaianaha.

Măs'cu-līne, adj. Kane. Syn. male.

Măsh, v. 1. E hoo-pe; e kui a ŏeŏe.

Măsk, n. He uhi no ka maka; he uhi.

Mă'son, n. Kanaka hamo puna.

Mă'son-ry, n. 1. Ka mea i kukuluia me ka puna.
2. Oihana hamo puna.

Măss, n. 1. He ahu; he ahua. The masses, ka lehulehu.
2. He pule o ka hoomana Roma.

Măs'sa-cre, a' E luku wale.

Măss'ive, adj. 1. Paa; ikaika.
2. Nunui. Syn. bulky.

Măst, n. Kia moku.

Măs'ter, n. Kumu; haku.

Măs'ter, v. E lanakila; e hoopio. Syn. conquer. Master a difficulty, e lanakila maluna o ka pilikia.

Măs'ter-ly, adj. Mikioi; akamai. In a masterly manner, ma ke ano akamai.

Măs'ter-pięçe, n. Hana i oi; hana pookela.

Măs'ter-y, n. 1. Ka lanakila.
2. He akamai a wali. Syn. chew.

Măs'tiff, n. He ilio nui.

Măt, n. Moena.

Mătch, n. 1. He kukaepele hoo-a ahi.
2. He lua like.
3. He mare.
4. He paio. Syn. contest.

Mătch, v. 4. E imi i ka like.
2. E aumeume ma ka paio.

Mătch'less, adj. Lua ole. Syn. peerless; unequaled.

Mătch'măk'er, n. 1. Mea hana kukaepele.
2. Mea hookonokono mare.

Mătch'plāne, n. Koi hole papa.

Māte, n. 1. He hoa; kokoolua. Syn. companion.
2. Hulipahu.

Ma-tē'ri-al, n. Mea; materia.

Ma-tēr'nal, adj. Makuahine. Maternal love, aloha makuahine.

Ma-tēr'ni-ty, n. Kulana makuahine.

Măth'e-măt'ic-al, adj. Pili i na helu.

Măth'e-măt'ic-al-ly, adv. Mamuli o na helu.

Măth'e-mă-tī'çian, n. Mea akamai ma na helu.

Măth'e-măt'ies, n. Na helu.

Mā'tins, n. pl. Pule kakahiaka.

Măt'ri-çide, n. Mea hoomake makuahine.

Ma-triç'u-lāte, v. E kakau inoa ma ka papa inoa o ke kula nui, a ahahui paha.

Măt'ri-mō'ni-al, adj. Mare. Syn. connubial.

Măt'ri-mo-ny, n. Ka mare. Syn. marriage.

Mā'tron, n. 1. Wahine mare.
2. Luna wahine hooponopono.

Măt'ter, n. 1. Mea kino. Syn. material.
2. Pilau o kahi eha. Syn. pus.
3. Pilikia. Syn. difficulty.
4. No matter, mea ole.

Măt'ting, n. Moena; na lako hana moena.
Măt'tock, n. He kipikua.
Măt'tress, n. Pela moe.
Ma-tūre', adj. 1. Oo. SYN. ripe.
2. Mature reflection, noonoo pono.
Ma-tū'ri-ty, n. 1. Wa oo.
2. Ka piha o ka manawa.
3. The maturity of a note, ka wa hookaa o ka bila aie.
Mau'so-lē'um, n. Hale kupapau nani.
Măw, n. Opu holoholona.
Măx'im, n. Olelo naauao. SYN. proverb.
Măx'i-mum, adj. Ka nui loa.
Măy, n. Mahina o Mei.
May, v. 1. Aeia. SYN. to be permitted.
2. Malia; paha. He may have gone, malia ua hala oia.
May'or (mär), n. Ke poo o ke kulanakauhale.
Māze, n. He wahi pakaawili; mea eehia.
Mā'zy, adj. Pakaawili.
Mĕ, pron. Ia'u.
Mĕad'ow, n. Aina kula i paa i ka mauu.
Mĕa'ger, adj. 1. Wiwi; olala.
2. lawa ole; kupono ole.
Mĕa'ger-ly, adv. Kupono ole.
Mĕal, n. 1. Palaoa o kela me keia ano.
2. He pa-i'na.
Mĕal'y, adj. Maha'ha'.
Mĕan, adj. 1. Haahaa; pi; uahoa.
2. Iwaenakonu. Mean point, kiko waena konu.
Mĕan, v. E manao.
Mĕans, n. pl. Kumu. Means of instruction, kumu o ka hoonaauao.
Me-ăn'der, v. E kahe i-o ia nei.
Mĕan'ing, n. Ke ano.
Mĕan'ness, n. Apiki; ano uahoa; ino.
Mĕan'time, } adv. Ia wa no; ia manawa.
Mĕan'while, }
Mĕa'sles n. pl. Mai ula.
Mĕas'ur-a-ble, adj. Hiki ke anaia.
Mĕas'ure, n. Ana. To take measures, e hoomakaukau.
Mĕas'ure-less, adj. Palena ole. SYN. boundless.
Mĕas'ure-ment, n. Ke ana ana.
Mĕat, adj. I'o.
2. He ai o kela me keia ano. Meat and drink, na mea ai me na mea inu.
Me-chăn'ic, n. He kanaka lawelawe ma kekahi o na oihana hana lima.
Me-chăn'ic-al, adi. Hana lima. Mechanical skill, akamai ma ka hana lima.
Me-chăn'ic-al-ly, adv. Mehe mikini la; me ke komo pu ole o ka noonoo.
Me-chăn'ics, n. pl. Ka ike no ka mana motio.
Mĕch'an-ĭsm, n. 1. Na hakina mikini.
2. Ke kukulu ana o ka mikini.
Mĕd'al, n. He medala; he metala hoomanao, hooapono.
Mĕd'dle, v. E lalama; e lalau wale i ko hai.

Mĕd'dler, n. Mea apa; mea lalauwale. SYN. busybody.
Mĕd'dle-sŏme, adj. Lalama; apa; lalau wale.
Mĕ'di-ā'tion, n. Ka uwao ana.
Mĕ'di-ā'tor, n. Mea uwao.
Mĕ'di-a-tō'ri-al, adj. Uwao. Mediatorial office, oihana uwao.
Mĕd'i-cal, adj. Lapaau. Medical profession, oihana lapaau.
Me-dic'i-nal, adj. Ano laau lapaau.
Mĕd'i-cine, n. Laau lapaau; kela me keia mea e ola ai ke kino.
Mĕ'di-ŏc'ri-ty, n. Kulana iwaena.
Mĕd'i-tāte, v. E noonoo; e mumule. SYN. contemplate.
Mĕd'i-tā'tion. n. Ka noonoo nui ana.
Mĕ'di-um, n. 1. He kumu. SYN. means.
2. Ka mea mawaena. SYN. middle.
Meed, n. Uku. SYN. reward. Meed of praise, uku mahalo.
Meek, adj. Akahai; haahaa ma ka naau.
Meek'ly, adv. Me ke akahai.
Meek'ness, n. Ka haahaa o ka naau; ke akahai.
Meet, v. E halawai pu.
Meet, adj. Kupono; kohu; SYN. fit; suitable.
Meet'ing, n. He halawai.
Meet'ing-house, n. Hale halawai.
Mĕl'an-chŏl'y, adj. Luuluu.
Mel-lif'lu-oŭs, adj. Nahenahe; kolonahe.
Mel'low, adj. 1. Pala. SYN. ripe.
2. Oneae. SYN. light. Light soil, lepo oneae.
3. Nahenahe; unahe. SYN. mellifluous.
4. Konane; konale. SYN. soft; soft moonlight.
Me-lŏ'dioŭs. SYN. mellifluous.
Mĕl'o-dy, n. He leo mele; mele olioli.
Mĕl'on, n. Ipu ai maka.
Mĕlt, v. E hoo-heehee.
Mĕm'ber, n. Hoa; la'la'.
Mĕm'ber-ship, n. Ka noho'na hoa, a la'la' paha.
Mĕm'brane, n. Ili lahilahi.
Me-mĕn'to, n. Mea hoomanao.
Mĕ'moir, n. Moolelo hoomanao.
Mĕm'o-ra-ble, adj. Ku pono ke hoomanaoia; kaulana.
Mĕm'o-răn'dum, n. Kakau lima hoomanao.
Me-mō'ri-al, n. 1. He mea hoala manao; he paipai manao.
2. Palapala hoopii no ka pomaikai.
Me-mō'ri-al-ize, v. E kakau i palapala hoopii. SYN. petition.
Mĕm'o-rize, v. E hoopaa naau. SYN. commit to memory.
Mĕm'o-ry, n. Ka mana hoomanao.
Mĕn'ace, v. E hooweliweli. SYN. threaten.
Men-ăg'e-rie (men-azh'e-ry). n. 1. He hoikeike o na holoholona hihiu. Hale no na holoholona hihiu.

Mĕnd, *v.* 1. E hana hou; kapili hou.
2. E ola hou.

Men-dā′çioŭs, *adj.* Wahahee; hoopunipuni. SYN. lying; false.

Men-dāç′i-ty, *n.* Ano wahahee; maa i
ka hoopunipuni.

Mĕn′di-cant, *n.* Kanaka noi wale; he
makilo. SYN. beggar.

Me′ni-al, *adj.* Haahaa; kohu ole. *Me-
nial employment,* hana kohu ole.

Me′ni-al, *n.* Kauwa. SYN. servant.

Mĕn′su-rā′tion, *n.* Ke ana ana.

Mĕn′tal, *adj.* O ka noonoo. *Mental pur-
suits,* na hana o ka naau.

Mĕn′tal-ly, *adv.* Ma ka naau.

Mĕn′tion, *v.* E hai.

Mĕn′tor, *n.* Mea ao aku; he kakaolelo.

Me-phit′ie, *adj.* Ino; kue i ke ola kino.
Mephitic air, ea ino; ea hoomake. SYN.
foul.

Mĕr′can-tĭle, *adj.* Kalepa. *Mercantile
community,* ka poe kalepa. SYN. commercial.

Mĕr′çe-na-ry, *adj.* Alunu; puniwaiwai. SYN. avaricious.

Mĕr′chan-dise, *n.* Waiwai kalepa.

Mĕr′chant, *n.* He kalepa; kanaka kalepa.

Mĕr′chant-a-ble, *adj.* Kupono i ke kalepa; hiki ke kuai.

Mĕr′chant-man, *n.* Moku kalepa.

Mĕr′çi-ful, *adj.* Ahonui; lokomaikai.

Mĕr′çi-ful-ly, *adv.* Me ke ahonui.

Mĕr′çi-less, *adj.* Lokoino.

Mĕr′eu-ry, *n.* 1. Wai dala. SYN quick-
silver.
2. Inoa o kekahi o na hoku hele.

Mĕr′çy, *n.* Ahonui; lokomaikai.

Mĕr′çy-seat, *n.* Noho aloha.

Mĕre, *adj.* Wale no. *Mere pretense,* he
hookamani wale no.

Mĕre′ly, *adj.* Wale no. *Merely want to
know,* makemake wale no o ike.

Me-rid′i-an, *n.* Awakea; kaha awakea.

Mĕr′it, *n.* Kumu mahalo.

Mĕr′it, *v.* E pono ke loaa.

Mĕr′i-tō′ri-ous, *adj.* Mahaloia.

Mĕr′ri-ly, *adv.* Me ka olioli. SYN.
gaily.

Mĕr′ri-ment, *n.* Lealea kupono; olioli.
SYN. gaiety.

Mĕr′ry, *adj.* Olioli; lealea. SYN. gay.

Mĕsh, *n.* He maka upena.

Mĕss, *n.* 1. Mahele ai.
2. Poe o ka papaaina hookahi.

Mĕs′sage, *n.* Olelo hoou′na.

Mĕs′sen-ger, *n.* Mea i hoounaia; he
elele.

Mĕs-si′ah, *n.* Ka Mesia; Kristo.

Mĕss′māte, *n.* Hoa papa aina.

Mĕt′al, *n.* Metala.

Me-tăl′lie, *adj.* Metala. *Metallic lustre,*
hinuhinu o ka metala.

Mĕt′al-lif′er-ous, *adj.* Paapu i ka
metala.

Me-tăl′lur-gy, *n.* Oihana hookaawale
metala.

Mĕt′a-môr′phōse, *v.* E hoo-aano
SYN. transformation.

Mĕt′a-phor, *n.* Olelo hoohalike.

Mĕt′a-phŏr′ie-al, *adj.* Ma ke ano hoohalike.

Mĕt′a-phy̆-şi′çian, *n.* Poe imi no ka
naau a me kona ano.

Mĕt′a-phy̆ş′ics, *n.* Huli naau; ka ike
e pili ana i ka naau.

Mēte, *v.* E mahele aku; e ana aku.

Mēte, *n.* 1. He mahele.
2. Mokuna aina; palena.

Me′te-or, *n.* Hoku lele.

Me′te-or-ŏl′o-gy, *n.* Kaike e pili ana
i ka lewa; ke ea; me ko laila mau hiohiona.

Me′ter, *n.* He ana. SYN. measure.

Mē-thinks′, *v. impers.* Manao au.

Mĕth′od, *n.* Ka hoonohonoho mikioi.

Me-thŏd′iç-al, *adj.* Ano mikioi; mamuli o na rula.

Me-thŏd′ie-al-ly, *adv.* Me ka mikioi;
like me ka rula.

Me-trŏp′o-lis, *n.* Kulanakauhale nui.

Mĕt′ro-pŏl′i-tan, *adj.* No ke kulanakauhale nui.

Mĕt′tle, *n.* Aa nui; pihoihoi. SYN.
spirit.

Mĕt′tle-some, *adj.* Aa nui; hookano.
SYN. spirited. *A mettlesome horse,* he lio
hookano.

Mew, *v.* E owao, me he popoki la.

Mī-āş′mä, *pl.* **Mi-āş′ma-ta,** *n.* Na huna ino e lana ana iloko o ke ea; mea
hoomake.

Mi′ero-scōpe, *n.* Ohe nana mea makalii.

Mi′ero-scŏp′ie, *adj.* Makalii loa; na
ka ohe e hoike mai.

Mid′day, *n.* Awakea. SYN. noon.

Mid′dle, *n.* Ko waenakonu.

Mid′dle-āged, *adj.* Iwaena o ka wa ui
me ka wa elemakule.

Mid′dling, *adj.* Mawaena o ka maikai
me ka ino, etc.

Mid′night, *n.* Ke aumoe.

Mid′ship-man, *n.* Luina opio o ka ma-
nuwa′.

Mid′ships, *n.* Iwaena o ka moku.

Midst, *n.* Ko waenakonu.

Mid′sŭm′mer, *n.* Iwaenakonu o ke
kau.

Mid′way, *n.* Mawaenakonu.

Mid′wife, *n.* He pale keiki.

Mid′win′ter, *n.* Iwaena o ka hooilo.

Mien, *n.* Helehelena. SYN. countenance.
Lofty mien, helehelena haaheo.

Miff, *n.* He ukiuki pau koke.

Might, *n.* Mana; ikaika. SYN. power.

Might′i-ly, *adv.* Me ka mana nui.

Might′y, *ad .* Mana; ikaika; nui. SYN.
powerful.

Mi′grāte, *v.* E hele mai kahi aina a i
kahi aina e noho ai.

Mi′gra-tō′ry, *adj.* Kuewa wale.

Milch, *adj.* Waiu. *Milch cow,* bipi haawi
waiu.

Mild, *adj.* Oluolu; nahenahe; palupalu; ahe. SYN. gentle; placid.

Mil'dew, *n.* Ponalo.

Mild'ly, *adv.* Oluolu; nahenahe.

Mild'ness, *n.* 1. Ka oluolu. SYN. clemency.
2. Akahai. SYN. gentleness.

Mile, *n.* He mile.

Mile'age, *n.* 1. Ka helu o na mile.
2. Uku mile.

Mile'post, *n.* Kia kuhikuhi mile.

Mile'stone, *n.* Pohaku kuhikuhi mile.

Mil'i-ta-ry, *adj.* Koa.

Mil'i-ta-ry, *n.* Na papa koa o kela me k eiaano.

Mil'i-tate, *v.* E ku-e'. SYN. conflict.

Mi-li'tia, *n.* Na koa ku i ka wa.

Milk, *n.* Waiu.

Milk, *v.* E uwi waiu.

Milk'maid, *n.* Wahine uwi bipi.

Milk'-man, *n.* 1. Kanaka uwi bipi.
2. Kanaka kuai waiu.

Milk'-pail, *n.* Bakeke uwi waiu.

Milk'sop, *n.* Kanaka lauwili wale.

Milk'y, *adj.* Me he waiu la.

Milk'y-way, *n.* Ka leileiona; leileiaka.

Mill, *n.* 1. Mikini wili.
2. he hapa-umi keneta.

Mill'dam, *n.* Paku wai no ka wili.

Mil-lěn'i-al, *adj.* Pili i ka milenio.

Mil-lěn'i-um, *n.* Ka milenio.

Mil'ler, *n.* Kanaka wili palaoa.

Mil'li-ner, *n.* Wahine hana a kuai papale.

Mil'li-ner-y, *n.* Na kahiko no ke poo.

Mil'lion, *n.* Miliona.

Mil'lion-aire', *n.* He ona miliona.

Mill'race, *n.* Ha wai no ka wili.

Mill'stone, *n.* Pohaku wili palaoa.

Mim'ic, *v.* E hana wale; e hoohenehene.

Mince, *v.* 1. E kui me ka pahi kui.
2. E hooahaaha.

Mind, *n.* 1. Ka naau; ka noonoo.
2. Manao. SYN. will; thought.

Mind, *v.* 1. E hoolohe; e haliu.
2. Malama. SYN. to be careful.

Mind'ful, *adj.* 1. Ano hoolohe. SYN. heedful.
2. Ano makaala; kuoo. SYN. attentive.

Mine, *pron.* No'u; na'u; ko'u; ka'u.

Mine, *n.* Lua eli waiwai. *Gold mine*, lua eli gula.

Min'er, *n.* Kanaka eli waiwai.

Min'er-al, *n.* Minerala; pohaku metala.

Min'er-ăl'o-ģist, *n.* Kanaka ike ma na minerala.

Min'er-ăl'o-ġy, *n.* Ka ike no na minerala.

Min-ġle, *v.* E kaawili pu; e hui pu.

Min'i-a-ture, *n.* 1. Kii makalii i penaia.
2. Mea makalii, ano like.

Min'i-mum, *n.* Haawina emi loa; hapa uuku loa.

Min'is-ter, *n.* 1. Kauwa. SYN. servant.
2. Kahunapule. SYN. clergyman.
3. Kuhina Aupuni.
4. Kuhina elele.

Min'is-ter, *v.* E lawelawe; e hoolako.

Min'is-te̅'ri-al, *adj.* 1. Oihana kahunapule.
2. Oihana kuhina.

Min'is-tra'tion, *v.* Ka lawelawe ana.

Min'is-try, *n.* 1. Oihana kahunapule.
2. Papa o na kuhina.

Mi'nor, *n.* He keiki ma ke kanawai.

Mi'nor, *adj.* Emi iho; uuku iho.

Mi-nŏr'ĭ-ty, *n.* 1. Wa keiki ma ke kanawai.
2. Ka hapa uuku.

Min'strel, *n.* Mea hookani pila.

Min'strel-sy, *n.* Hookani pila; mele; poe mele.

Mint, *n* 1. Hale hana dala o ke aupuni.
2. He laau ala.

Min'u-end, *n.* Helu hoolawe.

Mi'nus, *adj.* Emi. *Minus sign*, kaha emi.

Min'ute (min-ĭt), *n.* 1. He minute.
2. Moolelo halawai.

Mi-nūte', *adj.* Uuku loa; makalii.

Min'ute-gun, *n.* Pu kanikau.

Mi-nūte'ly, *adv.* No na mea liilii.

Mi-nū'ti-ae, *n. pl.* Na mea liilii.

Minx, *n.* Kaikamahine mahaoi.

Mir'a-cle, *n.* Hana mana.

Mi-răc'u-loŭs, *adj.* Mana kupaianaha.

Mire, *n.* Lepo kelekele; nenelu.

Mir'ror, *n.* Aniani nana; he kilo. SYN. looking glass.

Mirth, *n.* Lealea; olioli. SYN. merriment; hilarity.

Mirth'ful, *adj.* Lea; lealea. SYN. merry; gay.

Mir-y, *adj.* Po'hopoho'; kelekele.

Mis'an-thrōpe, *n.* Kanaka nanau.

Mis'an-thrŏp'ic, *adj.* Nanau.

Mis-ăn'thro-py, *n.* Naau nanau; aloha ole i kanaka.

Mis-ăp'pli-eā'tion, *n.* Ka pili pono ole; pili hewa.

Mis'ap-plȳ' *v.* E hoopili hewa; e hoolilo hewa.

Mis-ăp'pre-hěnd', *v.* E kuhihewa. SYN. misunderstand.

Mis-ăp'pre-hěn'sion, *n.* Ke kuhikewa. SYN. misunderstanding.

Mis'be-cōme', *v.* Ku pono ole; kohu ole.

Mis'be-hāve', *v.* E hana pono ole.

Mis'be-hāv'ior, *v.* Hana kupono ole. SYN. misconduct.

Mis-eăl'eu-lāte, *v.* E noonoo hewa.

Mis-call', *v.* E kapa hewa.

Mis-car'ry, *v.* 1. E ko pono ole.
2. E hala hi.

Mis'cel-lā'ne-oŭs, *adj.* Kela me keia.

Mis'cel-la-ny, *n.* Kela me keia manao i pai ia.

Mis-chance', *n.* Kuhihewa; poino. SYN. misfortune.

Mis'chief (chif), *n.* 1. Hana apa; mahaoi.
2. Hana kolohe.
3. Poho'; poino. SYN. damage.

Mis′chiev-oŭs, *adj.* Mahaoi; kolohe; apa.

Mis′con-cēive′, *v.* E kuhihewa. SYN. misapprehend.

Mis′con-cĕp′tion, *n.* Ke kuhihewa.

Mis-cŏn′duct, *n.* Ka hewa o ka hana. SYN. misbehavior.

Mis′con-strŭc′tion, *n.* Wehewehe hewa.

Mis′con-strŭe′, *v.* E wehewehe hewa.

Mis′cre-ant, *n.* Kanaka kolohe loa.

Mis-deed′, *n.* Hana kolohe.

Mis′de-mēan′or, *v.* 1. Hana hewa.
2. Ofeni ma ke kanawai. SYN. offense.

Mis′di-rĕct′, *v.* 1. E kuhikuhi hewa.
2. E kakau hewa.

Mis′em-ploy′, *v.* E lawelawe hewa.

Mi′ser, *n.* Kanaka pi; kanaka puniwaiwai; alunu.

Mis′er-a-ble, *adj.* Oki loa.

Mis′er-a-bly, *adv.* Oki loa.

Mi′ser-ly, *adv.* Pi; alunu; puniwaiwai.

Mis′er-y, *n.* Luuluu; oki loa; ehaeha. distress; wretchedness.

Mis-for′tūne, *n.* Poino; popilikia. SYN. calamity.

Mis-give′, *v.* E haohao; kanalua. SYN. doubt.

Mis-giv′ing, *n.* He kanalua. SYN. distrust.

Mis-gŏv′ern, *v.* E hoomalu pono ole.

Mis-guide′, *v.* E alakai hewa. SYN. mislead.

Mis′hap, *n.* Pilikia ulia wale. SYN. accident.

Mis′im-prove′, *v.* E lawelawe hewa. SYN. misuse.

Mis′in-fŏrm′, *v.* E hai hewa; e hoakaka hewa.

Mis′in-tēr′pret, *v.* E unuhi hewa; wehewehe hewa.

Mis-jŭdge′, *v.* E hooholo hewa i ka manao.

Mis-lāy′, *v.* E waiho wale aku. SYN. misplace.

Mis-lēad′, *v.* E alakai hewa. SYN. misguide.

Mis-mān′age, *v.* E hooko pono ole.

Mis-mān′age-ment, *n.* Ka hooko pono ole ana.

Mis-nāme′, *v.* E kapa hewa.

Mis-nŏ′mer, *n.* He inoa kupuno ole.

Mis-plāce′, *v.* E waiho ma kahi kupono ole. *Misplaced confidence,* paulele ma ka mea kupono ole.

Mis-print′, *n.* Pai hewa.

Mis′pro-nounce′, *v.* E puana hewa.

Mis′pro-nŭn′çi-ā′tion, *n.* Ka puana hewa ana.

Mis-quōte′, *v.* E hai like ole me ka olelo.

Mis-rĕp′re-sĕnt′, *v.* E hoike hewa.

Mis-rūle′, *n.* Haunaele; malu ole.

Miss, *n.* 1. Wahine mare ole.
2. He haule. *A miss in spelling,* he haule ma ke pela ana.
3. Halahi. *A miss in firing,* halahi ma ke ki pu ana.

Miss, *v.* E haule. *Miss an opportunity,* e haule ka wa k upno.

Mis′sile, *n.* He mea hoolei; mea ki.

Mis′sing, *adj.* Nalo; haule.

Mis′sion, *n.* 1. He hana i hoounaia o hana.
2. He poe i hoouna ia no kekahi hana.

Mis′sion-ā′ry, *n.* Misionari; elele o ka euanelio.

Mis′sive, *n.* He palapala hoouna.

Mis-spĕll′, *v.* E pela hewa; e hookuikui hewa.

Mis-spĕnd′, *v.* E hoomaunauna; e uhauha. SYN. waste.

Mis-stāte′, *v.* E hai hewa; hoakaka hewa.

Mis-stāte′ment, *n.* He hooakaka hewa.

Mist, *n.* He noe; u′-a liilii.

Mis-tāke′, *n.* Kuhihewa; lalau.

Mis-tāk′en, *adj.* Kuhihewa. *If I am not mistaken,* i ole au e kuhihewa; or, ke ole au e kuhihewa.

Mis′trans-lā′tion, *n.* Olelo i unuhi hewa ia.

Mis′tress, *n.* 1. Wahine mare.
2. Wahine poo oihana.
3. *School mistress,* kumukula wahine.

Mis-trŭst′, *v.* E kanalua; e haohao. SYN. doubt; suspect.

Mis-trŭst′ful, *adj.* Kanalua. SYN. suspicious.

Mist′y, *adj.* Paa i ka noe.

Mis-ŭn′der-stănd′, *v.* E maopopo ole.

Mis-ŭn′der-stănd′ing, *n.* He kumu o ke kuhihewa.

Mis-ūs′age, *n.* Ka lawelawe hewa.

Mis-ūse′, *v.* E lawelawe hewa; e hana pono ole.

Mite, *n.* 1. He huna.
2. Mea kolo makalii loa.

Mi′tre, *n.* 1. Papale bihopa.
2. He hookui lepe i na apana laau elua.

Mi′ter, } *v.* E hookui lepe.
Mi′tre, }

Mi′ter-box, *n.* Pahu oki lepe.

Mit′i-gāte, *v.* E hoemi eha. SYN. alleviate.

Mit′i-gā′tion, *n.* Ka hooemi ana.

Mit′ten, *n.* Mikini lima.

Mit′ti-mus, *n.* Palapala hoopaa lawehala.

Mix, *v.* 1. E kawili pu; e hoohui. SYN. mingle.
2. E hoohuikau.

Mix′tūre, *n.* Ka mea i kawili pu ia.

Miz′zen-māst, *n.* Kia hope.

Moan, *v.* E uhu′; e uwe.

Mōat, *n.* He auwaha hohonu e hoopuni ana i ka pa-kaua.

Mŏb, *n.* He uluaoa; poe hoohaunaele.

Mŏ′bile, *adj.* Onioni; luliluli.

Mŏe′ça-sin, *n.* Kamaa inikini.

Mŏck, *v.* E hoomaewaewa. SYN. ridicule.

Mode, *n.* Ano. *The prevailing mode,* ke ano i ike mau ia nei. SYN. manner.

Mŏd′el, *n.* He ana hoohalike

Mŏd'el, *v.* E hana i like.
Mŏd'er-āte, *v.* E hooemi. *Moderate your desires,* e hooemi i kou mau kuko.
Mŏd'er-ate, *adj.* Kupono. *A moderate wind,* he makani kupono.
Mŏd'er-ā'tion, *n.* Akahai.
Mŏd'er-ā'tor, *n.* Luna hoomalu.
Mŏd'ern, *adj.* No keia au; no keia wa.
Mŏd'est, *adj.* Akahai.
Mŏd'est-ly, *adv.* Me ke akahai.
Mŏd'es-ty, *n.* Ke ano akahai.
Mŏd-i-cum, *n.* Wahi lihi iki; wahi hapa uuku.
Mŏd'i-fi-cā'tion, *n.* Ka hoo-ano e ana; hoololi ana.
Mŏd'i-fy, *v.* 1. E hoo-ano e. SYN. vary.
2. E hooemi. SYN. moderate.
Mŏd'u-lāte, *v.* E hoololi i ka leo.
Mŏd'u-lā'tion, *n.* Ka hoololi ana i ka leo.
Mo-hăm'me-dan, *n.* He Mahometa.
Moi'e-ty, *n.* He hapa-lua; kekahi o na hapa like elua.
Mŏist, *adj.* 1. Ma-u'; kokoou; kawa'u.
2. *Moist outside as dried meat, etc.,* pikalikali; pilalilali.
Mŏist'en, *v.* E hoo-ma-u'.
Mŏist'ure, *n.* Kawa'u.
Mō'lar, *n.* Niho nui.
Mo-lás'ses, *n.* Molakeke.
Mōld, } *n.* 1. Lepo momona.
Mŏuld, } 2. Punahelu.
3. He ana, no ka hooheehee metala.
Mōld, } *v.* 1. E hana. SYN. make.
Mŏuld, } 2. E hana metala ma ka hooheehee ana.
3. E popo. SYN. decay.
Mōld-y, *adj.* Punahelu.
Mo-lēst', *v.* E hoo-mea; hoopilikia.
Mŏl'es-tā'tion, *n.* Ke keakea ana; hoopilikia ana.
Mŏl'i-fy, *v.* E hooluolu; hoo-maalili. SYN. appease.
Mō'ment, *n.* 1. Wa pokole loa
2. Ano nui. SYN. importance.
Mō'ment-ā'ri-ly, *adv.* I keia wa koke no.
Mō'ment-ā'ry, *adj.* Kuhewa; no ka wa pokole.
Mo-ment'oŭs, *adj.* Ano nui; koikoi. SYN. important.
Mo-ment'um, *n.* Ka nee ana.
Mŏn'ärch, *n.* He Moi. SYN. sovereign.
Mo-närch'ie-al, *adj.* Moi. *Monarchical government,* aupuni moi.
Mŏn'arch-y, *n.* 1. Ohana moi.
2. Aupuni moi.
Mŏn'as-tēr'y, *n.* Hale o ka poe moneka.
Mŏn'day, *n.* Monede; poakahi.
Mŏn'e-tā'ry, *adj.* Pili i ke dala.
Mŏn'ey, *n.* Dala.
Mŏn'eyed (mŭn'ĭd), *adj.* 1. Lako i na dala.
2. Lala. *Moneyed interests,* na pomaikai dala.

Mŏn'ey-less, *adj.* Dala ole. SYN. penniless.
Mŏn'ey-măt'ter, *n.* Mea pili i ke dala.
Mŏn'ey-or'der, *n.* Palapala kikoo dala.
Mŏn'i-tor, *n.* Kumu-ao.
Mŏnk, *n.* Kanaka haipule, noho mehameha; moneka.
Mŏn'key, *n.* He keko.
Mŏn'o-ehro-măt'ie, *adj.* Waihooluu hookahi.
Mō-nŏg'a-my, *n.* Ka hiki ana ke mare i hookahi wale no wahine.
Mŏn'ō-gram, *n.* Na hua mua o ka inoa i kuawili pu ia.
Mŏn'o-mā'ni-a, *n.* Ke ano noonoo pupule ma ke kumu hookahi wale no, pololei ka noonoo ma na mea e.
Mŏn'o-mā'ni-ăe, *n.* Mea i pupule ma kekahi mea.
Mo-nŏp'o-lize, *v.* E lawe pau loa.
Mo-nŏp'o-ly, *n.* Ka pono a pau o kekahi mea, a waiwai paha.
Mŏn'o-sȳl'la-ble, *n.* Hua olelo mamala hookahi.
Mŏn'ō-thē'ism, *n.* Ka manaoio i ke akua hookahi.
Mŏn'o-tōne, *n.* Leo kahi; leo kauo.
Mo-nŏt'o-noŭs, *adj.* Luhi, no ka hana mau.
Mon-soōn', *n.* He makani ma ka moana Inia.
Mŏn'ster, *n.* Mea weliweli. *A monster of iniquity,* he mea weliweli ma ka hana hewa.
Mŏn'stroŭs, *adj.* Weliweli.
Mŏnth, *n.* He mahina; malama.
Mŏnth'ly, *adv.* Kela me keia mahina.
Mŏn'u-ment, *n.* Kia hoomanao.
Mood, *n.* Ano. *Pleasant mood,* ano oluolu.
Mood'y, *adj.* Nunuha. SYN. sullen.
Moon, *n.* Mahina.
Moon'light, } *n.* Malamalama o ka
Moon-shine, } mahina.
Moor, *v.* E hoopaa moku i ka uwapo.
Moor'ings, *n.* Na lako hoopaa moku.
Moot, *v.* E paio. SYN. debate.
Mŏp, *n.* Welu holoi papa.
Mŏp'board, *n.* Papa pale o ke keena.
Mope, *v.* E noho wale; e loma. SYN. to idle.
Mŏr'al, *n.* Olelo ao.
Mŏr'al, *adj.* Hoopono; noho pono.
Mo-răl'i-ty, *n.* Ka noho pono; ka hoopono.
Mŏr'al-ize, *v.* E hoopuka i olelo ao.
Mŏth'er-wit, *n.* Noili; maiele.
Mŏr'als, *n. pl.* Na alo hoopono o keia noho'na.
Mo-ráss', *n.* Aina po'hopoho'. SYN. marsh.
Mŏr'bid, *adj.* Mai. *Morbid state of mind,* mai ma ka naau.
More-ō'ver, *adv.* Eia hoi; eia hou. SYN. furthermore.
Mŏrn, } *n.* Kakahiaka.
Mŏrn'ing, } *n.* Kakahiaka.

Mo-rōse′, *adj.* Nainai; nunuha. SYN. sullen; crabbed.
Mo-rōse′ness, *n.* Ano nunuha; ano nainai.
Mŏr′row, *n.* Apopo.
Mŏr′sel, *n.* Hu′na; wahi hakina iki.
Mŏr′tal, *adj.* E make ana; e make ai. *A mortal wound,* he eha e make ai.
Mŏr′tal, *n.* He kanaka.
Mor-tăl′i-ty, *n.* Ka make ana.
Mŏr′tal-ly, *adv.* E make ai. SYN. fatally.
Mŏr′tar, *n.* 1. Puna hamo.
2. Ipu kui laau lapaau.
3. Pu ki poka′ pahu′.
Mŏrt′gage (mor′gage), *n.* Moraki; palapala hoopaa waiwai.
Mŏrt′ga-gee′, *n.* Ka mea nana ka moraki.
Mŏrt′ga-ger, *n.* Mea moraki waiwai.
Mŏr′ti-fi-cā′tion, *n.* Palaho.
2. Hilahila. SYN. shame.
Mŏr′ti-fȳ, *v.* 1. E palaho.
2. E hoohilahila. SYN. put to shame.
Mŏr′tise, *n.* He puka ho′le.
Mos-quī′to (mus-kē′to), *n.* Makika.
Mŏss, *n.* Limu.
Mŏss′y, *adj.* Paa i ka limu.
Mōte, *n.* He pula.
Mŏth, *n.* He mu.
Mŏth′er, *n.* Makuahine.
2. Linalina vinika.
Mŏth′er-less, *adj.* Makuahine ole.
Mŏth′er-ly, *adj.* Makuahine. *Motherly love,* aloha makuahine.
Mŏth′er-wit, *n.* Noili; maiele.
Mo′tion, *n.* 1. Motio; ka nee ana.
2. *Motion of wings,* kapalili ana o na eheu.
3. *Motion of the blood,* ka pana ana o ke koko.
4. He manao. *To make a motion,* e waiho mai i manao. *To second a motion,* e kokua i ka manao.
5. *Motion of the hands,* ka paipai ana o na lima.
Mo′tion-less, *adj.* Oni ole; malie.
Mo′tive, *n.* Ke kumu e hana ai.
Mo′tive-pow′er, *n.* Ka mana hoo-nee.
Mo′tor, *n.* Ka mana e nee ai.
Mŏt′to, *n.* Olelo hoopili.
Mound, *n.* He puu; he ahua.
Mount, *v.* 1. E pii.
2. E ee. *Mount a horse,* ee maluna o ka lio.
3. *Mount a picture,* e hookomo ke kii ma kona pahu.
4. *Mount guard,* e hoonoho i kiai.
Mount′ain, *n.* Mauna; kuahiwi.
Mount′ain-eer′, *n.* Kanaka o kuahiwi.
Mount′ain-eer′ing, *n.* Ka maa i ka pii kuahiwi.
Mŏunt′ain-ous, *adj.* Mauna.
Mount′ain-tŏp, *n.* Wekiu o ka mauna; piko o ka mauna; kualono.
Mount′e-bănk, *n.* Poe akena wale. SYN. quack.
Mŏurn, *v.* E kanikau; e kaniuhu; uwe.

Mŏurn′er, *n.* Mea kanikau.
Mŏurn′ful, *adj.* Luuluu; kaumaha.
Mŏurn′ing, *n.* 1. Uwe; kanikau; kumakena.
2. Lole kanikau.
Mouse, *n.* Iole liilii.
Mous′er, *n.* Mea hopu iole; Popoki.
Moŭs-tache′ (mŭs-tash′), *n.* Umiumi o ka lehelehe.
Mouth, *n.* 1. Waha.
2. Nuku. *Mouth of a river,* ka nuku o ka mŭliwai.
Mouth′ful, *n.* He piha waha; he olopu.
Mouth′piēçe, *n.* 1. He wahaolelo. SYN. spokesman.
2. Mea paa i ka waha.
Mŏv′a-ble, *adj.* Hiki ke hoonee ia.
Mŏve, *v.* 1. E nee; hoo-nee.
2. E manao. *Move an adjournment,* e manao e hoopanee.
3. E hoolalelale. SYN. stir up.
Mŏve′ment, *n.* 1. Ka nee ana.
2. Ka hana ana.
3. Ka naha ana o ka laau.
Mŏv′er, *n.* 1. Ka mea e nee ana.
2. Mea hapai manao, a olelo hooholo paha. *The mover of a resolution,* ka mea e hapai ana i ka olelo hooholo.
Mŏv′ing, *adj.* 1. E nee ana. *A moving body,* he kino nee.
2. Hooala manao. *A moving speech,* he haiolelo hooala manao.
Mŏw, *v.* E oki me ka pahi mauu; e oki me ka mikini.
Mŏw′er, *n.* Mea oki mauu; mikini oki mauu.
Mŭch, *adv.* or *adj.* Nui; makena.
Mŭ′çi-lage, *n.* Wai hoopipili.
Mŭck, *n.* Opala pilau.
Mŭ′cus, *n.* Wale; hupe′.
Mŭd, *n.* Kelekele.
Mŭd′dle, *n.* Kuawili o ka noonoo.
Mŭd′dy, *adj.* 1. Paele i ka lepo. *Muddy shoes,* kamaa paele i ka lepo.
2. Kelekele. *Muddy roads,* alanui kelekele.
Mŭff, *n.* Huluhulu hoopumehana i na lima.
Mŭf′fler, *n.* Kaei hoomahana i ke poo me ka a-i.
Mŭg, *n.* Kiaha pohaku.
Mu-lăt′to, *n.* He hapa nika.
Mŭl′ber-ry, *n.* Laau lau lole; laau silika.
Mŭlet, *v.* E kau i ka uku hoopai. SYN. fine.
Mūle, *n.* Hoki.
Mū′let-eer′, *n.* Kahu hoki.
Mŭl′ish, *adj.* Oolea; nunuha. SYN. stubborn.
Mŭl′let, *n.* He i′-a; ke anae; amaama.
Mŭl′ti-fā′ri-oŭs, *adj.* Lehulehu o na ano.
Mŭl′ti-ple, *n.* Helu komo ia.
Mŭl′ti-pli-cănd′, *n.* Helu hoonui ia.
Mŭl′ti-pli-cā′tion, *n.* Ka hoonui.
Mŭl′ti-pliç′i-ty, *n.* Ka lehulehu o na ano.

Mŭl′ti-pli′er, *n*, Helu hoonui.
Mŭl′ti-plȳ, *v.* E hoonui; e hoomahuahua.
Mŭl′ti-tūde, *n.* Heluna nui; ka lehulehu.
Mŭm, *adj.* Mumule.
Mŭm′ble, *v.* E nokenoke.
Mŭmps, *n.* Mai pehu ma ka papalina.
Mŭnch, *v.* E naunau.
Mŭn′dane, *adj.* No ka honua.
Mu-nic′i-pal, *adj.* Pili i ke kulanakauhale. *Municipal government,* ka hoomalu ana o ke kulanakauhale.
Mu-nic′i-pāl′i-ty, *n.* Kau wahi o ke kulanakauhale.
Mu-nif′i-çent, *adj.* Manawalea; lokomaikai. SYN. liberal; bountiful.
Mu-ni′tion, *n.* Lako kaua.
Mŭr′der, *n.* Pepehi kanaka me ka manao ino.
Mŭr′der-er, *n.* Kanaka pepehi kanaka.
Mŭr′der-oŭs, *adj.* Make. *Murderous weapon,* mea e make ai.
Mŭrk′y, *adj.* Pouliuli.
Mŭr′mur, *v.* 1. E ohumu; e hoohalahala.
2. E oeoe.
Mŭs′çle, *n.* I′-o; i′-o huki.
Mŭs′cu-lar, *adj.* Puipui; ikaika. SYN. strong.
Muse, *v.* E nalu iho; e mumuli. SYN. meditate.
Mu-se′um, *n.* Waihona mea hoikeike; museuma.
Mu′sic, *n.* Mele; memele; leo mele.
Mu′sic-al, *adj.* 1. Mele; hookani. *Musical instruments,* mea hookani.
2. Ake mele. *A musical mind,* he naau ake mele.
Mu-si′çian, *n.* 1. Mea hookani pila.
2. Mea haku mele. SYN. composer.
Mŭs′ket, *n.* Pu ki-poohiwi.
Mŭs′ket-eer′, *n.* Koa halihali pu ki-poohiwi.
Mŭs′ket-ry, *n.* Na pu ki-poohiwi o kela me keia ano.

Mŭsk′mĕl′on, *n.* Ipu ala.
Mŭs′lin, *n.* Lole makalena.
Mŭs′sul-man, *n.* He Mahometa. SYN. Mahommedan.
Mŭst, *aux. v.* He mea pono.
Mŭs′tard, *n.* Hua makeke.
Mŭs′ter, *v.* E hoakoakoa. SYN. collect.
Mŭs′ter-rŏll, *n.* Papa inoa o ka puali koa.
Mŭst′y, *adj.* Paa i ka punahelu; pou′-kiu′ki.
Mū′ta-bĭl′i-ty, *n.* Ano hee; ano pau wale; loli wale.
Mū′ta-ble, *adj.* Loli wale; muhee. SYN. changeable.
Mu-tā′tion, *n.* Ka loli ana. SYN. change.
Mūte, *adj.* Aa; kuli; leo ole. SYN. dumb.
Mū′ti-lāte, *v.* E oki ino; e hoomumuku.
Mū′ti-lā′tion, *n.* Ka oki ino ana.
Mū′ti-neer′, *n.* Koa kipi; luina hoole hana.
Mū′ti-noŭs, *adj.* Kipi; hoole hana.
Mū′ti-nȳ, *n.* Ke kipi o na koa, a o na luina paha.
Mŭt-ter, *v.* E ohumu; e namunamu.
Mŭt′ton, *n.* I′-o hipa.
Mū′tū-al, *adj.* Like; kaulike. *Mutual love,* aloha like. *Mutual benefit,* pomaikai kaulike.
Mū′tū-al-ly, *adv.* Like. *Mutually benefited,* pomaikai like.
Mŭz′zle, *n.* Nuku. *Muzzle of the ox.* ka nuku o ka bipi kauo
Mŭz-zle, *v.* E hoa i ka nuku, a ihu paha.
Mȳr′i-ad, *n.* Manomano; lehulehu.
My-sĕlf′, *pron.* Owau no.
Mys-tē′ri-oŭs, *adj.* Eehia; nalo; pohihihi.
Mȳs′te-ry, *n.* Mea pohihihi; mea eehia.
Mȳs′ti-fȳ, *v.* E hoopohihihi wale.
Mȳth, *n.* He kaao o ka wa kahiko.
Mȳ-thŏl′o-gȳ, *n.* Na kaao e pili ana i na akua o ka wa kahiko.

N

Nȧb, *v.* E hopu. SYN. sieze. *To nab a thief,* e hopu i ka aihue.
Nȧ′bob, *n.* 1. He kiaaina ma Inia.
2. Kanaka waiwai koikoi.
Nȧg, *n.* He lio.
Nȧil, *n.* 1. Kui kakia.
2. Maiuu; mikiau.
Nȧil, *v.* E kakia kui.
Nȧil′brush, *n.* Balaki hoomaemae mikiau.

Nȧ′ked, *adj.* Olohelohe; kohana.
Nȧ′ked-ness, *n.* He olohelohe; kohana.
Nȧme, *n.* He inoa. *To make a name,* e hookaulana ai i ka inoa.
Nȧme, *v* E hai i ka inoa; e kahea inoa; e haawi i inoa.
Nȧme′less, *adj.* Inoa ole.
Nȧme′ly, *adv.* Oia hoi.
Nȧme′sȧke, *n.* He poe inoa like.
Nȧp, *n.* Kuluhiamoe; hiamoe iki.

Nāpe, *n.* Ke ami o ka a-i'.
Nāp'kin, *n.* Kawele lima no ka papa-aina.
Nar-cōt'ic, *n.* Laau hoohiamoe.
Nar-rāte', *v.* E hai; e haku; e olelo. SYN. relate.
Nār'ra-tive, *n.* Kaao; moolelo. SYN. story.
Nar-rā'tor, *n.* He haku kaao; mea nana e hai.
Nār'row, *adj.* Ololi; haiki; pilikia.
Nār'row-ly, *adv.* 1. Mahunehune. *Narrowly escaped,* pakele mahunehune. SYN. barely.
2. Pono loa. SYN. closely. *Narrowly watched,* kiai pono loa ia.
Nār'rows, *n.* He kowa. SYN. strait.
Nā'sal, *adj.* No ka ihu. *Nasal tones,* leo kani no ka ihu.
Nās'cent, *adj.* Hoomaka ulu; hoomaka ola.
Nās'ty, *adj.* Pelapela; haukae.
Nā'tal, *adj.* Hanau. *Natal day,* la hanau.
Nā'tion, *n.* Lahui; aupuni.
Nā'tion-al, *adj.* No ke aupuni. *National holiday,* la kulaia o ke aupuni.
Nā'tion-āl'i-ty, *n.* Lahui. *Of what nationality?* No ka lahui hea.
Nā-tive, *adj.* Maoli. *A native man,* he kanaka maoli.
2. *Native land,* one hanau.
Na-tiv'i-ty, *n.* Ka hanau ana. *Land of his nativity,* one hanau.
Nat'u-ral, *adj.* 1. Maoli; honu'a.
2. Kupono i ke ano mau.
Nat'u-ral-ist, *n.* Kanaka imi ma ke ano o na mea ulu me na holoholona.
Nat'u-ral-ize, *v.* E hoo-ku'pa.
Nat'u-ral-ly, *adv.* Maoli. *Naturally so,* pela maolo no.
Nat'ure, *n.* 1. Ke ao nei. *Nature's God,* Ke Akua o ke ao nei.
2. Na hana o Ke Akua.
3. Ano maoli.
4. *In a state of nature,* like me ka wa i hanauia.
5. *According to nature's laws,* e like me na kanawai maoli.
Naught (nawt), He ole.
Naught'y, *adj.* Kolohe; ino.
Nau'se-ā, *n.* Poluea; liliha; polo'na.
Nau'se-āte, *v.* E poluea.
Nau'se-oŭs, *adj.* Hoopailua; liliha.
Nau'ti-cal, *adj.* Pili i ka hooholomoku.
Nau'ti-lus, *n.* Auwaalalua.
Nā'val, *adj.* Pili i na moku; *naval affairs,* na oihana moku.
Nā'vel, *n.* Ka piko o ka opu.
Nāv'i-ga-ble, *adj.* Hiki ke hooholoia na moku.
Nāv'i-gāte, *v.* E hooholo moku.
Nāv'i-gā'tion, *n.* Ka hooholo moku. *Head of navigation,* ka palena o ka hiki ke hooholo moku.
Nāv'i-gā'tor, *n.* Mea hooholo moku.
Nā'vy, *n.* Au-moku; ulumoku; na moku o ke aupuni.

Nēap'tide, *n.* Kai make.
Near, *adj.* Kokoke; kokoke loa.
Nēar'ly, *adv.* Aneane.
Near-sight'ed, *adj.* Ike powehiwehi.
Nēat, *adj.* Mikioi; aulii; palawaiki.
Nēb'u-la, *n.* Huhui hoku mehe ao la i ka ike o ka maka.
Nēc'es-sa-ries, *n. pl.* Na lako ku i ke ola kino.
Nēc'es-sa-ry, *adj.* Ku pono i ke ola kino. SYN. indispensable.
2. Kupono.
Ne-cēs'si-tāte, *v.* E kono; e kaohi. SYN. compel.
Ne-cēs'si-ty, *n.* 1. Ka nele. SYN. want.
2. Ka mea e pono ai. *Air is a necessity,* he mea e pono ai ke ea.
3. Ka mea i hookauia. *Necessity is laid upon me,* ua hookauia keia maluna o'u.
Nēck, *n.* A-i'.
Nēck'er-chief, *n.* Hainaka' a-i'.
Nēck'lace, *n.* Lei a-i'.
Ne-erōl'o-gy, *n.* Papa inoa o ka poe i make.
Nēc'ro-mān'cer, *n.* Kanaka kilokilo; kahuna hoomanamana. SYN. conjurer; sorcerer.
Need, *n.* He nele; he mea e pono ai. SYN. necessity.
Need, *v.* Pilikia no ka nele; e nele.
Need'ful, *adj.* E pono ai. *Needful supplies,* na lako e pono ai. SYN. necessary.
Nee'dle, *n.* Kuikele; kui humuhumu.
Need'less, *adj.* Makehewa; waiwai ole. *Needless expense,* lilo makehewa. SYN. useless.
Need'y, *adj.* Nele; hune; kohana. SYN. destitute.
Needs, *n.* Na nele; na mea e pono ai. SYN. necessities.
Ne-fā'ri-oŭs, *adj.* Hewa loa.
Nēg'a-tive, *adj.* Emi. *A negative quantity,* he kuanite emi. SYN. minus.
2. *Negative answer,* he pane hoole.
Nēg'a-tive, *n.* 1. He hoole. *The negative,* ka aoao hoole.
2. He aniani pai kii pepa.
Neg-lēct', *v.* 1. E waiho wale. SYN. slight.
2. E haalele wale me ke kokua ole. *Neglect the family,* e haalele wale i ka ohana me ke kokua ole.
Neg-lēct'ful, *adj.* Malama ole; haalele wale.
Nēg'li-gence, *n.* Ke ano malama ole; waiho wale.
Nēg'li-gent, *adj.* Kapulu. SYN. neglectful.
Nēg'li-gent-ly, *adv.* Me ke kapulu; malama ole.
Ne-gō'ti-a-ble, *adj.* Hiki ke hooliloia.
Ne-gō'ti-āte, *v.* 1. E hooholo. *Negotiate a treaty,* e hooholo i olelo kuikahi.
2. E hoolilo.

Ne-gö'ti-ā'tion, Ka hooholo ana. SYN, transaction.
2. Ka hana i hooholoia.
3. Ka hoolilo ana.
Ne'gress, n. He wahine nika.
Ne'gro, n. He nika; nege'ro.
Neigh (nāy), E ihihi'.
Neigh'bor, n. He hoalauna; hoa noho.
Neigh'bor-hŏŏd, n. Kauhale; kahi kokoke.
Neigh'bor-ing, adj. E kokoke ana.
Neigh'bor-ly, adj. Launa.
Nēith'er, conj. Aole kela, aole keia; aole hoi.
Nēph'ew (nĕf'u), n. Keikikane o ka hoahanau.
Nērve, n. Aalolo. A man of nerve, he kanaka wiwo ole. A nervous man, he kanaka pihoihoi.
Nērve, v. E aa; e hookomo i ka ikaika o ka manao; hooikaika i ka manao.
Nērve'less, adj. Ikaika ole.
Nērv'oŭs, adj. Pihoihoi wale; kapalili wale.
Nērv'oŭs-ness, n. Ke ano pihoihoi wale.
Nēst, n. Punana hua.
Nēst'egg, n. Ka hua i koe ma ka punana.
Nēst'le, v. E moe pili pu; e hoopipili ma ka moe ana.
Nĕt, n. 1. He upena.
2. He ko'ko'.
Nĕt, adj. Puka. Net gain, waiwai puka.
Nĕt, v. E puka. SYN, gain.
Neŭ-rāl'ġi-a, n. Hui ma na aa lolo.
Neŭ'ter, } adj. Kaaokoa; aole no kela aole no keia.
Neŭ'tral, }
Neŭ-trāl'i-ty, n. Ke kaaokoa ana.
Neŭ'tral-ize, v. E hoolilo i mea ole.
Nĕv'er, adv. Aole loa.
Nĕv'er-the-lĕss', adv. Aka nae; aka hoi. SYN, yet; however.
New, adj. Hou. SYN, novel; fresh.
New-eóm'er, a. He mea i hiki hou mai.
New-fän'gled, adj. Ano hou. Newfangled notions, na mea ano hou.
New'ly, adv. Akahi no. Newly arrived, a kahi no a hiki mai. SYN, recently.
News, n. Nu hou.
News'boy, n. Keiki kuai nupepa.
News'mŏng'er, n. Kanaka kuai nuhou; kuai nupepa.
News'pā-per, n. He nu-pepa.
News'ständ, n. Wahi kuai nupepa.
Nĕxt, adj. Kekahi ae.
Nib, n. Maka kila.
Nib'ble, v. E nalinali; e namunamu.
Niçe, adj. Aulii; mikioi; hiehie. SYN, neat.
Niçe'ly, adv. Hiehie; eleu.
Nick, n. 1. He kumumu.
2. Nick of time, wa kupono. SYN, the right time.
Nick'el, n. 1. He metala keokeo, like me ke kala.
2. He apana dala; elima keneta.

Nick'näcks, n. Kela mea keia mea liilii ano milimili.
Nick'name, n. Inoa kapakapa.
Nieçe, n. Ke kaikamahine o ka hoahanau.
Nig'gard, n. Kanaka pi; kanaka ii. SYN, miser.
Nig'gard-ly, adj. Ii. SYN, stingy.
Nigh (ni), adj. Kokoke.
Night, n. Po.
Night'cap, n. Uhi poo no ka po.
Night'fall, n. Ka uhi mai ana o ka po; ahiahi.
Night'gown, n. Lole moe.
Night'ly, adv. I kela po i keia po.
Night'māre, n. Moe hewa; moe ino.
Night'watch, v. 1. Kiai po.
2. Hora kiai o ka po.
Nim'ble, adj. Kaukaulele; mama.
Nim'bly, adv. Mama; kaukaulele.
Nim'bus, n. Luakalai. SYN, halo.
Nine, adj. Eiwa.
Nine'fold, adj. Pa-iwa.
Nine'teen, adj. Umikumamaiwa.
Nine'ty, adj. Kanaiwa.
Nin'ny, n. Kanaka ike ole.
Ninth, adj. Hapa-iwa; ka iwa.
Nip, v. E iniki; e umiki. SYN, pinch.
Nip'pers, n. Upa umiki.
Nip'ple, n. 1. Maka wai-u.
2. Gun nipple, maka o ka pu.
Nō, adv. Aole.
No-bil'i-ty, n. 1. Na 'lii.
2. Ano koikoi. Nobility of intellect, ke ano koikoi o ka manao.
Nō'ble, n. He alii
Nō'ble, adj. Hanohano; mahaloia; hoopono. SYN, illustrious; honorable.
Nō'ble-man, n. SYN, noble.
Nō'ble-ness, n. Ke ano hanohano; ano hoopono.
Nō'bly, adv. Maikai maoli; me ka lokomaikai nui.
Nō'bod-y, n. Mea ole; aohe mea.
Noe-tūr'nal, adj. Ma ka po.
Nŏd, v. E kunou; e kimo ke poo.
Noise, n. Walaau; kamumu.
Noise'less, adj. Malie; palanehe.
Nois'i-ly, adv. Halulu; kamumu; walaau.
Noi'sŏme, adj. Pilau; hauna. SYN, offensive.
Nois'y, adj. Walaau.
Nō'mad, n. Kanaka kuewa wale.
No-mād'ie, adj. Noho paa ole; kuewa.
Nō'men-elāt'ŭre, n. Ke kulana o ke hoo-kau inoa.
Nŏm'i-nal, adj. Ma ka inoa wale no.
Nŏm'i-nal-ly, adv. Ma ka inoa wale no. He is nominally the owner, he ona no oia ma ka inoa wale no.
Nŏm'i-nāte, v. E koho inoa; e hookoho.
Nŏm'i-nā'tion, n. Ke kohoia'na.
Nŏm'i-nee', n. Ka inoa i kohoia.
Nŏn'āge, n. Oo ole na ka kanawai.
Nŏn'at-tĕnd'ance, n. Ka hele ole mai.

Non-chal-ance (nōng′shäl′lŏngs), *n.* Ano mahaoi.
Nŏn′con-dúct′or, *n.* Mea kai ole. *Non-conductor of heat*, mea kai ole i ka wela.
Nŏn′con-fôrm′i-ty, *n.* Ke kulike ole; ka hana like ole.
Nŏn′de-script, *n.* Mea i akaka ole ia kona ano.
None (nun), *pron.* Aole hookahi; aohe.
Non-en′ti-ty, *n.* Mea ole loa. SYN. a nobody.
Nŏn′es-sĕn′tial, *n.* He mea ano ole; aole ano nui.
Nŏne′sŭch, *n.* Mea aohe kona lua.
Nŏn′ex-ist′ençe, *n.* Ka ole loa no.
Nŏn fûl-fĭll′ment, *n.* Ke ko ole ana.
Nŏn′ob-sĕrv′ançe, *n;* Ke ko ole ana; ka malama ole.
Non-pây′ment, *n.* Ka uku ole; hookaa ole.
Nŏn′plus, *v.* E hoo-hoka.
Non-rĕs′i-dent, *n.* Mea noho paa ole ma kona wahi.
Nŏn′re-sĭst′ançe, *n.* Ke ku-e′ ole.
Nŏn′sense, *n.* Olelo ano ole; olelo lapuwale.
Non-sĕn′sie-al, *adj.* Lapuwale; ano ole.
Nŏn′sŭit, *n.* Hoopau ana o ka hoopii.
Noöd′le, *n.* Kanaka kaialile; naaupo.
Nook, *n.* 1. He kuono.
2. Kahi nalo.
Noŏn, *n.* Awakea.
Noŏn′day ⎫ *n.* Awakea.
Noŏn′tide ⎭
Noŏn′ing, *n.* Ka hora hoomaha ma ke awakea.
Noöse, *n.* He pahele; hele; nipuu.
Nŏr, *conj.* Aole hoi.
Nŏr′mal, *adj.* 1. Kulike me na rula; na loina.
2. Ao kumu. *Normal school*, kula ao kumu.
North, *n.* Akau.
Nŏrth-êast′, *n.* Hikina Akau
Nŏrth′er′ly, *adj.* Ma ka akau aku.
Nŏrth′ern, *adj.* Akau.
Nŏrth′ward, *adv.* I ka Akau aku. *He went northward*, hele Akau aku nei oia.
Nŏrth-wĕst, *n.* 1. Ke Komohana Akau.
2. *North-west lumber*, papa noweki.
Nŏse, *n.* Ihu.
Nŏse′gay, *n.* He pu-a′ pua.
Nŏs′trïl, *n.* Puka ihu.
Nŏt, *adv.* Aole.
Nŏ′ta-ble, *adj.* Kaulana.
Nŏ′ta-ry, *n.* Luna hooia palapala.
No-tā′tion, *n.* Ke kakau helu.
Nŏtch, *n.* 1. He kumumu; nihomole; SYN. nick.
2. He mawae hohonu mawaena na kuahiwi. SYN. gap.
Nŏte, *n.* 1. He leta pokole.
2. Olelo wehewehe; olelo hoomanao.
Nŏte, *v.* 1. E kakau hoomanao.
2. E noonoo pono. SYN. mark.
Nŏte′-boŏk, *n.* Buke kakau hoomanao.
Nŏt′ed, *adj.* Kaulana.

Nŏth′ing, *adv.* Aohe no; mea ole.
Nŏ′tiçe, *n.* 1. He olelo hoakaka; olelo hoolaha.
2. E ike. *To take no notice*, aole no e ike.
Nŏ′tiçe, *v.* E nana. SYN. look at.
Nŏ′tiçe-a-ble, *adj.* Maopopo i ka ike.
Nŏ′ti-fi-eā′tion, *n.* Ka hoolaha ana; ke kukala ana.
Nŏ′ti′fy, *v.* E kukala.
Nŏ′tion, *n.* Manao ulu wale. SYN. fancy.
Nŏ′tion-al, *adj.* Piha i na manao ulu wale.
Nŏ′to-ri′e-ty, *n.* Ke kaulana ino.
No-tō′ri-oŭs, *adj.* Kaulana ino; wawa ino.
No-tō′ri-oŭs-ly, *adv.* Wawaia.
Nŏt′with-ständ′ing, *conj.* Aka nae. SYN. still.
Noun, *n.* He hai-inoa.
Noŭr′ish, *v.* E hanai; e hoo-ulu.
Noŭr′ish-ment, *n.* Ai mea e ulu ai.
Nŏv′el, *adj.* Hou. SYN. new.
Nŏv′el, *n.* Kaao.
Nŏv′el-ist, *n.* Mea haku kaao.
Nŏv′el-ty, *n.* Ke ano hou; kekahi mea hou.
No-vĕm′ber, *n.* Novemaba.
Nŏv′içe, *n.* Mea maa ole.
Now, *adv.* A no la; i keia wa.
Now′a-days, *adv.* I keia mau la.
Nŏ′where, *adv.* Wahi ole.
Nŏ′wise, *adv.* Aole loa. *"There shall in nowise enter therein,"* aole loa e komo malaila. SYN. by no means.
Nŏx′ioŭs (nŏk′shus), *adj.* Poino ai ke ola.
Nŏz′zle, *n.* Nuku o ka ohewai.
Nŭ′cle-ŭs, *n.* Ke kikowaena kahi e uluulu ai na mea e.
Nŭde, *adj.* Olohelohe; kapa ole. SYN. naked.
Nŭ′di-ty, *n.* Ka hune; olohelohe. SYN. nakedness.
Nu′ga-to-ry, *adj.* Mana ole.
Nŭg′get, *n.* Pohaku metala.
Nŭi′sançe, *n.* He ino haukae; mea hoopilikia wale.
Nŭll and void, *n.* Noa.
Nŭl′li-fŷ, *v.* E hoo-noa; e lilo i mea ole.
Nŭmb, *adj.* Maeele; lolo.
Nŭm′ber, *n.* He helu.
Nŭm′ber-less, *adj.* Lehulehu wale; nui wale.
Nŭmb′ness, *n.* Ka maeele o ke kino.
Nu′me-ral, *n.* Hua helu.
Nŭ′mer-ā′tion, *n.* Ka helu ana; ka numera.
Nŭ′mer-ā′tor, *n.* Hoohelu.
Nu-mĕr′ie-al, *adj.* Pili i na helu.
Nŭ′mer-oŭs, *adj.* Lehulehu; nui.
Nŭ′mis-măt′ies, *n.* Ka ike no na ano dala maoli i hoopukaia.
Nŭm′skull, *n.* Mea naaupo; ike ole.
Nŭn, *n.* He virikini ma ka hoomana Roma.
Nŭn′ner-y, *n.* Hale noho no na virikini.

Nŭp'tial, *n.* Mare. *Nuptial day,* la mare.
Nŭp'tials, *n. pl.* Ka mare ana. SYN. wedding.
Nûrse, *n.* 1. Kahu hanai.
  2. Mea lawelawe no ka poe mai.
Nûrse, *v.* 1. E hanai.
  2. E malama i ka poe mai.
  3. *Nurse wrath,* e hoomauhala.
Nûrs'er-y, *n.* 1. Keena no kamalii.
  2. Kihapai hoo-ulu mea kanu.

Nûrt'ûre, *v.* E malama; e hanai; e hoonaauao.
Nŭt, *n.* Hua paakiki.
Nŭt'-crăck'er, *n.* Upa wawahi hua paa-kiki.
Nŭt'meg, *n.* Hua ala.
Nŭ'tri-ment, *n.* Ai e pono ai ke ola kino. SYN. nourishment.
Nu-tri'tioŭs, *adj.* Hooikaika. *Nutritious food,* ai hooikaika kino.

O

Ọar, *n.* Hoe waapa. *Steering oar* hoe hookele.
Ō'a-sis, *n.* Wahi uliuli ma ka wao-one.
Ọat, *n.* Hua oka.
Ọath, *n.* Olelo hoohiki.
Ọat'meal, *n.* Palaoa o ka hua oka.
Ŏb'du-ra-cy, *n.* Ano paakiki o ka naau.
Ŏb'du-rate, *adj.* Paakiki. SYN. hard; callous.
O-bë'di-ençe, *n.* Ka hoolohe; malama kauoha.
O-bë'di-ent, *adj.* Hoolohe; malama.
O-bei'sançe, *n.* Ke kulou ana. SYN. bow.
O-bëse', *adj.* Puipui loa. SYN. corpulent.
O-bës'i-ty, *n.* Ka puipui loa o ke kino.
O-bey', *v.* E hoolohe; e malama.
O-bit'u-a-ry, *n.* Olelo hoike make.
Ŏb'ject, *n.* 1. Mea ike maka ia
  2. Mea i kau ia ai ka manao; ke kumu.
Ob-jëct', *v.* E ku-e'; e hoohalahala; kuipehi.
Ob-jëc'tion, *n.* Kumu ku-e; kumu hoohalahala.
Ob-jëc'tion-a-ble, *adj.* Kupono ole; hoohalahalaia.
Ob-lā'tion, *n.* He mohai.
Ŏb'li-gā'tion, *n.* 1. Aie'. SYN. debt.
  2. Pono. *Parental obligation,* ka pono a ka makua i ke keiki.
Ob-lig'a-to-ry, *adj.* Ili ka pono: he pono. *The payment of debts is obligatory,* he pono ke hookaa i na aie.
O-blige', *v.* 1. E kaohi; e kono. SYN. compel.
  2. E oluolu. SYN. please.
  3. E kokua. SYN. assist. *Oblige me with a loan,* e kokua mai i wahi dala.
O-blig'ing, *adj.* Oluolu; kokua.
Ob-lique' (ob-lïke), *adj.* Hio'. *Oblique line,* kaha hi-o'.
Ob-liq'ui-ty, *n.* Ka aui ana mai ka pololei.

Ob-lit'er-āte, *v.* E holoi aku; e anai aku. SYN. efface; erase.
Ob-liv'i-oŭs, *adj.* Ike ole mai; poina wale. SYN. forgetful.
Ŏb'long, *adj.* Huina-ha-loa.
Ŏb'lo-quy, *n.* Olelo hoomaewa; olelo akiaki. SYN. reproach; calumny.
Ob-nŏx'ious, *adj.* Ku ole i ka makemake; hoowahawahaia.
Ob-sçëne', *adj.* Pelapela; haumia.
Ob-sçën'i-ty, *n.* Olelo haumia; olelo pelapela.
Ob-seûre', *adj.* 1. Powehiwehi; maopopo ole.
  2. Haahaa; kaulana ole; ike ole ia.
Ob-seûre'ly, *adv.* Me ka powehiwehi.
Ob-seûr'i-ty, *n.* 1. He powehiwehi; molehulehu.
  2. Ka haahaa o ka noho ana; ka ike ole ia'ku.
Ŏb'sē-quies, *n.* Na hana o ka hoolewa kino kupapau. SYN. funeral rites.
Ob-sé'qui-oŭs, *adj.* Hoopilimeaai; kuapelu wale.
Ob-sẽrv'a-ble, *adj.* Noonooia; ikeia.
Ob-sẽrv'ançe, *n.* Ka malama ana. SYN. the keeping of.
Ŏb'ser-vā'tion, *n.* 1. Noonoo pono; haka pono. *A man of observation,* he kanaka haka pono.
  2. He olelo. SYN. remark.
Ob-sẽrv'a-to-ry, *n.* Hale nana hoku; ao-hoku, etc.
Ob-sẽrve', *v.* 1. E hakapono; e hakilo. SYN. watch narrowly.
  2. E olelo. SYN. remark.
Ob-sẽrv'er, *n.* Mea haka pono; mea hakilo.
Ŏb'so-lēte', *adj.* No ka wa i hala.
Ŏb'sta-cle, *n.* Kumu keakea; kumu alalai.
Ŏb'sti-nate, *adj.* Hoaano; paakiki; a-i oolea.
Ob-strĕp-er-oŭs, *adj.* Wahakole; wahapaa; waha ukele.

Ob-strŭct′, v. E keakea; e alalai. SYN. hinder.

Ob-strŭc′tion, n. Kumu keakea; kumu alalai. SYN. hindrance.

Ob-tāin′, v. E loaa. SYN. get.

Ob-tāin′a-ble, adj. Hiki ke loaa.

Ob-tūse′, adj. 1. Paakiki ma ka noonoo. SYN. dull.
2. Obtuse angle, huina peleleu.

Ob-tūse′ness, n. 1. Ka paakiki o ka noonoo.
2. Ka oi ole.

Ob′vi-āte, v. E hookaaokoa aku; e hookaawale ae.

Ob′vi-oŭs, adj. Maopopo lea; moakaka. SYN. evident.

Ob′vi-ous-ly, adv. He oiaio; he moakaka. SYN. clearly; evidently.

Oc-eā′sion, n. 1. Wa. A suitable occasion, he wa kupono. SYN. opportunity.
2. Kumu. Give occasion, haawi i kumu.

Oc-eā′sion-al, adj. I kekahi wa; kawalawala.

Oc-eā′sion-al-ly, adv. I kekahi wa. SYN. sometimes.

Oc′ci-dent, n. Ke komohana. SYN. west.

Oc′ci-put, n. Panepoo.

Oc-cült′, adj. Pohihihi; hunaia.

Oc′eul-tā′tion, n. Ka nalo ana o kekahi ao o ka lani i kekahi ao.

Oc′eu-pän′çy, Ka noho paa ana

Oc′eu-pant, n. Mea e noho ana.

Oc′eu-pā′tion, n. Hana; oihana. SYN. employment.

Oc′eu-py, 1. E noho; e komo. Occupy a house, e komo i ka hale.
2. E ko pono; hoopaa pono. Occupy the time, ke ko pono i ka manawa.
3. E paa i ka hana. I am occupied, paa wau i ka hana.

Oc-eür′, v. 1. Ikeia; SYN. happen.
2. Ala mai. The;thought occured to me, ala mai la ka manao iloko o′u.

Oc-eür′rençe He ulia. SYN. incident.

O′çean (ō′shun), n. Ka moana.

O-çe-än′ie, aaj. Moana.

Oc′ta-gon, n. Huina lehulehu, aoao ewalu.

Oc-täg′o-nal, adj. Huina ewaln.

Oc′tave, n. Na leo ewalu o ke mele.

Oc-tä′vo, n. He buke nona na opi ekolu i ke kalana hookahi.

Oc-tō′ber, n. Okatoba.

Oc′to-ge-nā′ri-an, n. Kane a wahine paha i kanawalu ai na makahiki.

Oc′u-lar, adj. Maka. Ocular demonstration, ike maka.

Oc′u-list, n. Kanaka lapaau maka.

Ŏdd, adj. 1. Like ole; kaupaewa.
2. Ano e; ku i ka aka.

Ŏdd′i-ty, n. Mea ano e; ano e.

Ŏdd′ly, adv. Ano e. SYN. singularly. Oddly enough, eia ka mea ano e.

Ŏdds, n. pl. Ka oi o i ka pomaikai.

O′di-oŭs, adj. Inainaia; pelapela; hoopailua.

O′di-um, n. Inaina; huahua. SYN. hatred; reproach.

O′dor, n. 1. He ala. SYN. fragrance.
2. Hauna; pilau. SYN. offensive odor.

O′dor-if′er-oŭs, adj. 1. Ala. SYN.
O′dor-oŭs, adj. fragrant.
2. Pilau. hauna

Ŏf, prep. O; a.

Ŏff, adv. Aku.

Of-fençe′, n. Ofeni; hana kolohe.
Of-fênse′,

Of-fĕnd′, v. 1. E ku-e. Offend against the laws, e kue i na kanawai.
2. E hoohulu; hoonaukiuki.

Of-fĕnd′er, n. Lawehala.

Of-fĕn′sive, adj. 1. Ku-e.
3. n. Ka aoao hoouka.

Ŏf′fer, v. E makaukau e haawi.

Ŏf′fer, n. Haawina.

Ŏf′fer-ing, n. Haawina; mohai.

Ŏff′hănd, adv. Me ka makaukau ole e mamua.

Ŏf′fiçe, n. Oihana; keena oihana.

Ŏf′fi-çer, n. He luna; luna oihana.

Of-fi′çial, adj. Me ka mana o ka oihana

Of-fi′çial, n. Luna.

Of-fi′çi-āte, v. E hooko mamuli o ka oihana.

Of-fi′çioŭs, adj. Mahaoi; komo wale ma ko hai pono. SYN. meddlesome.

Ŏff′ing, n. Mawaho ae o ka moana.

Ŏff′scŏur-ing, n. Opala; mea hoowa hawahaia.

Ŏff′sĕt, v. E pale. Offset a bill, e pale i ka bila ale.
2. E hoo-kaulike.

Ŏff′spring, n. Na keiki; na mamo

Ŏft′en, adv. Pinepine.
Ŏft′en-times,

Og′le, v. E awihi. SYN. look askance

Oh! interj. Auwe!

Oil, n. Aila.

Oil, v. E kahinu; e hamo me ka aila.

Oil′cloth, n. Lole hooma-uia i ka aila

Oil′cŏl-or, n. Hooluu i kaawiliia me ka aila.

Oil′y, adj. Me he aila la; paapu i ka aila

Oint′ment, n. Laau hamo; aila poni

Ŏld, adj. 1. Kahiko.
2. Apulu. SYN. worn out, (spoken o things only).
3. Old man, kanaka elemakule.
4. Old woman, luwahine.

Ŏld-fäsh′ioned, adj. No ka wa kahi ko.

O′le-äg′in-ous, adj. SYN. oily.

Ol-fäc′to-ry, adj. No ka hŏni.

Ŏl′ive, n. He oliva.

Ō-mē′ga, *n.* Hua palapala hope o ka olelo Helene.

Ŏm′e-let, *n.* Hua moa kaawiliia a hoomoaia.

Ō′men, *n.* He ouli; he hoailona.

Ŏm′i-noŭs, *adj.* 1. E hoailona ana i ka pomaikai.

2. E hoailona ana i ka poino.

O-mit′, *v.* E kapai, e waiho. SYN. leave out.

Ŏm′ni-bus, *n.* Kaa nui halihali ohua.

Om-nip′o-tence, *n.* Mea mana loa.

Om-nip′o-tent, *adj.* Mana loa.

Ŏm′ni-prĕş′ent, *adj.* Ma na wahi a pau.

Om-nis′cient, *adj.* Ike i na mea a pau.

Om-niv′o-roŭs, *adj.* Ai i na mea a pau.

Ŏn, *prep.* 1. Maluna. *On the horse,* maluna o ka lio.

2. Ma. *On the road* ,ma ke alanui.

3. No. *On this account,* no keia mea.

4. I. *On hearing this,* i ka lohe ana i keia.

Ŏn, *adv.* Imua. *Move on,* e nee imua. SYN. forward.

Once (wuns), *adv.* 1. I kekahi wa.

2. Koke; a no. *Go at once,* e hele koke.

One (wun), *adj.* Hookahi; kekahi.

One′ness, *n.* Ka lokahi.

Ŏn′er-oŭs, *adj.* Luhi; kaumaha. SYN. heavy; burdensome.

One-sid′ed, *adj.* Kapakahi; ewaewa.

Ŏn′ion (un′yun), *n.* Akaakai.

Ŏn′ly, *adv.* Wale no.

Ŏn′set, *n.* Ka hoouka. SYN. assault.

Ō′nus, *n.* Kaumaha. SYN. burden.

Ŏn′ward, *adv.* Imua.

Ooze (ūze), *n.* Lepo kelekele lahilahi.

Ooze, *v.* E kulu malie; e kahe liilii.

O-pāque′ (ō-pāk), *adj.* Paa; hiki ole i ka malamalama ke komo.

Ō′pen, *v.* 1. E hamama; e wehe.

2. E mohala. SYN. unfold.

3. E makili. *To open the mind,* e hoomakili i ka naau.

Ō′pen-ing, *n.* 1. Puka; wahi hamama.

2. Wahi e komo ai.

3. *Opening in the woods,* kipuka.

Ō′pen-ly, *adv.* Akea.

Ŏp′er-āte, *v.* 1. E hana. SYN. work.

2. E naha, *medical.*

Ŏp′er-ā′tion, *n.* 1. Ka hana ana.

2. Ka naha′o ka laau.

Ŏp′er-a-tor, *n.* Mea lawelawe; mea hana.

Oph-thál′mi-â, } *n.* He mai o ka maka.
Oph-thál′my, }

Ō′pi-āte, *n.* Laau hoo-hiamoe.

O-pine′, *v.* Manao. SYN. think.

O-pin′ion, *n.* He manao. SYN. thought.

O-pin′ion-ā′ted, *adj.* Paakiki ma kona manao iho.

Ō′pi-um, *n.* Opiuma.

Op-pō′nent, *n.* Mea alai; mea ku-e.

Ŏp′por-tūne′, *adj.* Ku; kupono. SYN. timely.

Ŏp′por-tūne′ly, *adv.* I ka wa kupono.

Ŏp′por-tū′ni-ty, *n.* Wa kupono.

Op-pōse′, *v.* E ku-e′; e keakea; e alai.

Op-pōş′er, *n.* Mea ku-e′; mea keakea.

Ŏp′po-site, *adj.* Kupono i ke alo; ku-e. *Opposite side,* aoae kue; kela aoao.

Ŏp′po-şi′tion, *n.* 1. Ke ku-e; ke keakea.

2. The opposition, ka aoao ku-e′.

Op-prĕss′, *v.* E hookaumaha; e hooluhi.

Op-prĕs′sion, *n.* 1. Hookaumaha; hooluhi hewa.

2. Luuluu; hoii.

Op-prĕs′sive, *adj.* 1. Kaumaha; luhi; luuluu. SYN. burdensome.

2. *Oppressive weather,* wa wela.

Op-prĕs′sor, *n.* Mea nana e hooluhi.

Op-prō′bri-oŭs, *adj.* Ino. *Opprobrious language,* olelo ino.

Op-prō′bri-um, *n.* Hoowahawaha. SYN. disgrace.

Ŏp′tie, } *adj.* No ka maka. *Optical delusion,* he hihio o ka maka.
Ŏp′tie-al, }

Op-ti′cian, *n.* Kanaka hana i na mea no ka maka.

Ŏp′ties, *n.* Ka ike e pili ana i na maka.

Ŏp′tion, *n.* Mana koho. SYN. choice.

Ŏp′tion-al, *adj.* Mamuli o ka manao.

Ŏp′ū-lence, *n.* Waiwai nui. SYN. wealth.

Ŏp′ū-lent, *adj.* Waiwai loa. SYN. wealthy.

Ŏr, *conj.* Paha; i ole.

Or′a-ele, *n.* 1. Olelo kuhihewa ole; olelo paa.

2. Kanaka kuhihewa ole; pololei mau.

3. *The oracles of God,* na olelo oiaio o Ke Akua.

Ō′ral, *adj.* Waha. *Oral instruction,* ao waha.

Ŏr′ange, *n.* Alani.

O-rā′tion, *n.* Hai-olelo.

Ŏr a-tŏr′ie-al, *adj.* Hai-olelo.

Ŏr′a-to-ry, *n.* Ka hai-olelo.

Ŏrb, *n.* Kino poepoe. SYN. globe.

Ŏr′bit, *n.* 1. Ke ala hele o na hoku.

2. Ka lua no na maka.

Ŏr′chard, *n.* Kihapai laau hua.

Ŏr′chĕs-tra, *n.* Papa puhi ohe.

Or-dāin′, *v.* 1. E kauoha. SYN. decree.

2. E hookahuna.

Or-dē′al, *u.* He hoao. SYN. trial.

Ŏr′der, *n.* 1. He kauoha. SYN. command.

2. Ka hoonohonoho pono.

3. Kulana; papa.

4. Bila kikoo dala. SYN. check; draft;

Ôr'der, v. E kono; e kena; e kauoha.

Ôr'der-ly, n. He koa lawelawe no ka luna koa.

Ôr'der'ly, adv. Ano pono; ano maikai.

Ôr'di-nançe, n. Rula; kauoha; kanawai.

Ôr'di-na-ri-ly, adv. Ma ke ano mau, SYN. usual; common.

Ôr'di-na-ry, adj. Ano mau; maa.

Ôr'di-nã'tion, n. Ka hookahuna ana.

Ôrd'nançe, n. Na pu-kaua nui.

Ôre, n. Pohaku metala.

Ôr'gan, n. 1. Pila hookani; ogana.
2. Nupepa waha. Government organ, nupepa waha o ke aupuni.
3. He lala. An organ of the body, he lala o ke kino.

Or-gän'ic, adj. Pili i ka lala.

Ôr'gän-ist, n. Mea nana e hookani ogana.

Ôr'gan-i-zã'tion, n. He hui; ka hoohui ana.

Ôr'gan-ize, v. E hui; e kukulu i hui.

Ôr'gies, n. pl. Na hana u'hau'ha.

Ô'ri-ent, n. Ka Hikina. SYN. east.

Ô'ri-ênt'al, adj. No ka Hikina. SYN. eastern.

Ô'ri-ên'tal-ist, n. Kanaka i akamai ma na olelo o ka Hikina.

Ôr'i-fiçe, n. Puka hookahe.

Ôr-i-gin, n. Ke kumu.

O-rïg'in-al, adj. 1. Mua; kino hou.
2. Nona iho. Original thought, noonoo nona iho.

O-rïg'i-näl'i-ty, n. Ano hou; ano makamua.

O-rïg'i-nãte, v. E hookumu.

O-rïg'i-na-tor, n. Mea nana i hookumu.

Ôr'na-ment, n. Mea e kahiko ai.

Ôr'na-ment, v. E kahiko.

Ôr'na-mênt'al, adj. Kahiko a nani.

Or-nãte', adj. Nani; aulii.

Ôr'ni-thôl'o-gist, n. Kanaka ike no na manu.

Ôr'ni-thôl'o-gy, n. Ka ike no na manu.

Ôr'phan, n. Keiki makua ole.

Ôr'tho-dox, adj. Pono ma ka manaoio.

Ôr'tho-dox-y, n. Ka pono o ka manaoio.

Ôr'tho-e-py, n. Ka puana pololei i na hua olelo.

Or-thôg'ra-py, n. Ke pela ana i na huaolelo.

Ôs'çil-lãte, v. E lewalewa; e kapalili. SYN. vibrate.

Ôs'çil-a-to-ry, adj. Lewa; luli; lulilului. SYN. vibratory.

Ôs'eu-late, v. E honi. SYN. kiss.

Ôs'se-ous, adj. Me he iwi la. SYN. bony.

Ôs'si-fi-cã'tion, n. Ka lilo ana i iwi.

Ôs'si-fÿ, v. E lilo i iwi.

Os-tën'si-ble, adj. Hoakakaia; hoikeia. The ostensible reason, ke kumu i hoakakaia.

Ôs'ten-tã'tious, adj. Hookahakaha wale.

Ôs'tra-çise, v. E kipaku. SYN. bænish.

Ôth'er, adj. 1. E; e ae.
2. Ka lua. The one—the other, ka mua, ka lua.

Ôth'er-wïse, adv. 1. I ole ia. SYN. or else.
2. Ma kekahi ano e ae. SYN. some other way.

Ought (awt), v. imp. E pono; kupono.

Our, } pron. Ko kakou; ko makou.
Ours, }

Our-selves', pron. Kakou iho.

Oust, v. E hookuke; e kipaku. SYN. eject.

Out, adv. 1. Iwaho. Out of the house, iwaho o ka hale.

Out-bid', v. E koho kiekie ae.

Out'break, v. 1. Ka pahu' ana. SYN. eruption.
2. Puupuu ana. SYN. eruption on the body.
3. Ke kipi. SYN. insurrection.

Out'burst, n. Ka poha' ana.

Out'east, n. He kuewa; aea haukae.

Out'ery, n. Uwa; wawa nui.

Out-do', v. E kela. SYN. excel.

Out'er-môst, adj. Ko waho loa; mawaho loa.

Out'fit, n. Na lako e pono ai; na mea makaukau.

Out'go, n. Ka lilo.

Out'go-ing, Puka ana iwaho.

Out-grôw', v. E ulu ae, a haalele. Outgrow childish habits, e ulu ae, a haalele i na hana kamalii.

Out-Hër'od, v. E kela loa ma ka lokoino. Out-Herod Herod himself, e kela imua o Herode ma ka lokoino.

Out'house, n. Hale lilili.

Out-länd'ish, adj. Lalau; hawawa.

Out-lâst', v. E oi ka paa; e mau aku.

Out'law, n. Kanaka mawaho o ka malu o ke kanawai.

Out'lãy, n. Ka lilo.

Out'let, n. Wahi hookahe aku.

Out'line, n. Ke kaha owaho.

Out-live', v. E oi ke ola.

Out-nûm'ber, v. E oi ka nui; oi ka heluna.

Out'pôst, n. Kahua kiai.

Out'pôur, v. E ninini; e hookahe.

Out'rage, v. E powa; e lima ikaika; e hana mainoino.

Out'rage, n. He hana mainoino.

Out-rä'geoûs, adj. Mainoino loa; hewa loa.

Out-ride', v. E mama ae ma ka holo ana.

Out'rïd-er, n. Poe ukali.

Out'right, *adv.* A no; koke. *Killed outright,* pepehi koke ia. SYN. immediately.

Out-run', *v.* E mama oi.

Out-sail', *v.* E oi ma ka holo.

Out'set, *n* Kinohou; ka hoomaka ana.

Out-shine', *v.* 1. E alohilohi a oi.
2. E oi i ke akamai. SYN. excel, surpass.

Out'side, *adv.* Mawaho; iwaho. *The outside,* ko waho.

Out-stand'ing, *adj.* Kaa ole. SYN. unpaid.

Out-stretch', *v.* 1. E kikoo aku.
2. E uhola; e hoohola.

Out-strip', *v.* E haalele ihope. SYN. out-run.

Out-talk', *v.* Kela i ke kamailio.

Out-vote', *v.* E puka ma ka balota.

Out-walk', *v.* E haalele ihope ma ka hele wawae.

Out'ward, *adv.* 1. Mawaho; iwaho.
2. Aku. *Outward bound vessels,* na moku e hele aku ana.

Out'ward-ly, *adv.* Ma ko waho.

Out-wear', *v.* Oi i ka lawelawe ana.

Out-weigh', *v.* E kaumaha ae.

Out-wit', *v.* E hoopuni me ka maalea.

O'val, *adj.* Hualala.

Ov'en, *n.* Imu; oma; umu.

O'ver, *prep.* 1. Maluna'e. SYN. above.
2. Ma o ae; ma kela aoao. SYN. across. *Over and over,* kaaihe.

O'ver-alls, *n.* Na lole wawae hana.

O'ver-anx'ious, *adj.* Pihoihoi pono ole.

O'ver-awe', *v.* E hooweliweli; e hoomaka'uka'u.

O'ver-bal'ance, *v.* E kaumaha pono ole.

O'ver-bear'ing, *adj.* Hookiekie; hookaumaha.

O'ver-board', *adv.* Iloko o ke kai. *To fall overboard,* e haule iloko o ke kai.

O'ver-bur'den, *v.* E hookaumaha pono ole.

O'ver-cast', *v.* 1. E pouli i na ao.
2. E humuhumu.

O'ver-charge', *v.* E hoo-uku pono ole.

O'ver-coat, *n.* Kuka nui.

O'ver-come', *v.* 1. E lanakila; e hoopio. SYN. conquer.
2. E pio. SYN. conquered.

O'ver-do', *v.* E hana a oi i ka mea kupono.

O'ver-alls, *n.* Na lolewawae hana.

O'ver-done', *adj.* Ahulu. *Food overdone,* ai ahulu.

O'ver-draw', *v.* 1. E kikoo a oi aku i ke dala i hoomoeia.
2. E hai a oi i ka mea oiaio.

O'ver-flow', *v.* E manini; e hu; huliamahi.

O'ver-grow', *v.* 2. E hihi wale ma ka ulu ana.
2. *An overgrown boy,* he keiki hiki wawe ma ka ulu ana.

O'ver-hang', *v.* E kau pono maluna'e o ke poo.

O'ver-haul', *v.* 1. E huli; e imi no na kina. SYN. examine.
2. E hahai a loaa. SYN. overtake.

O'ver-head', *adj.* Maluna'e o ke poo.

O'ver-hear', *v.* E lohe wale.

O'ver-joyed', *p. p.* Piha i ka hauoli.

O'ver-land, *adj.* Ma ka aina.

O'ver-lay', *v.* E hamo; e hoohola.

O'ver-leap', *v.* 1. E lele maluna ae.
2. E lanakila ae. *Overleap all obstacles,* e lanakila maluna'e o na pilikia a pau.

O'ver-load', *v.* E hoopiha pono ole; e hoopiha loa.

O'ver-look', *v.* 1. E kiai; e hoopono-pono. SYN. oversee.
2. E waiho me ka hoopai ole.

O'ver-match', *v.* E ikaika ae maluna.

O'ver-night', *adv.* A hala ka po.

O'ver-per-suade', *v.* E kauo i ka makemake.

O'ver-plus', *n.* Ke koena i koe. SYN. surplus.

O'ver-pow'er, *v.* E hoopio; e pio. SYN. overcome.

O'ver-rate', *v.* E manao nui kupono ole; e koho nui kupono ole. *He overrates his strength,* koho nui kupono ole oia i kona ikaika. *He overrates his abilities,* manao nui kupono ole oia i kona akamai.

O'ver-reach', *v.* E hoopuni wale.

O'ver-rule', *v.* 1. E hooholo ku-e'.
2. E hoomalu.

O'ver-run', *v.* E uhi paapu; e hooholo nui.

O'ver-see', *v.* E hooponopono.

O'ver-seer', *n.* Luna; luna hooponopono.

O'ver-set', *v.* E kahuli; e hanini.

O'ver-shad'ow, *v.* E kau mai ka malumalu.

O'ver-shoot', *v.* 1. E hala ka maka ma ke ki ana; halahi.
2. E kela imua o ka mea kupono

O'ver-sight, *n.* 1. Palaka.
2. Ka hooponopono ana.

O'ver-sleep', *v.* E hiamoe loa.

O'ver-spread', *v.* E uhi; e uhola; hohola.

O'ver-step', *v.* E hoohala i ka mea kupono.

O'ver-stock', *v.* E hoopiha loa a pono ole.

O'ver-strain', *v.* E hooikaika ino. SYN. overtask.

O-vert', *adj.* Akea. SYN. open to view.

O'ver-take', *v.* E hahai a loaa.

O'ver-task', *v* E hooluhi pono ole.

O'vert-ure, *n.* 1. E waiho mai i manao. SYN. proposal; offer.
2. He mele hoomaka.

Ō'ver-tûrn', v. E hooauhuli; hooka-huli.

Ō'ver-ween'ing, adj. 1. Nui pono ole. *Overweening ambition,* ake nui pono ole o ka naau.
2. Hookano. SYN. arrogant.

Ō'ver-whĕlm', v. E popoi. *Troubles overwhelm,* popoi mai na popilikia.
2. Pauhia. *Overwhelmed with work,* pauhia i ka hana.
3. E piho; palemo. *Overwhelmed in the sea,* palemo ma ka moana

Ō'ver-wŏrk', n. Hana luhi loa.

O'ver-wrought' (rąwt), p p. Oi kupono ole ma ka hana, a ma ka noonoo paha. *Overwrought imagination,* he hihio pono ole o ka noonoo.

Ōwe (ō), v. E aie.

Ōw'ing to, p. a. No. *On account of; owing to various reasons,* no na kumu he nui.

Owl, n. Puueo.

Owl'ish, adj. Me he puueo la.

Ōwn, adj. Ponoi'.

Ōwn, v. 1. E loaa. *To own a horse,* e loaa i lio.
2. E ae. SYN. confess.

Ōwn'er, n. Ka mea nona. *The owner of the horse,* ka mea nona ka lio.

Ŏx, n. Bipi kauo.

Ŏx'en, n. pl. Na bipi kauo.

Ŏx'y-ġen, n Ea mama, mea e pono ai ke ola kino.

Oys'ter, n. Olepe.

P

Pāçe, n. Kikoo wawae; he ana, ekolu kapuai.

Pā'çer, n. Lio holo peke.

Pa-çĭf'ic, adj. Oluolu; lai; malie. SYN. mild; peaceful.

Pāç'i-fy, v. E hoo-na'; hooluolu; hoolaulea.

Pāck, n. 1. He haawe.
2. He pu-a'.

Pāck, v. 1. E hoo-o; e hao. *Pack a trunk,* e hao i ka pahu
2. E hookikina.

Pāck'aġe, n. 1. He puolo; he ope.
2. Pahu.

Pāck'et, n. 1. Puolo liilii.
2. Moku kalepa.

Pāck'hôrse, n. Lio hoo-unauna.

Pāck'săd'dle, n. Noho lio hoo-unauna.

Pāck'thrĕad, n. Lopi nakii puolo.

Pād, n. Uluna liilii.

Pād'dle, n. Hoe waa.

Pād'dle, v. E hoe.

Pād'dock, n. Pa holoholona.

Pād'lock, n. Laka lou.

Pae'an, n. Mele hoonani.

Pā'ġan, n. Pegana; kanaka hoomana-kii.

Pā'ġan-ism, n. Hoomanakii.

Pāġe, n. 1. Aoao.
2. Keiki lawelawe no ka poe hanohano.

Pā'ġeant, n. Hoike hookahakaha.
Pā'ġeant-ry, } n. Hoike hookahakaha.

Pa-ġō'da, n. Heiau hoomanakii ma ka Hikina.

Pāil, n. Bakeke.

Pāil'ful, n. Piha bakeke.

Pāin, n. Eha; hui; ehaeha.

Pāin'ful, adj. 1. Hui; eha.
2. Kaumaha; luuluu. SYN. sorrowful.

Pāin'ful-ly, adv. Ehaeha; luuluu; luhi.

Pāin'less, adj. Eha ole.

Pāins, n. pl. Ke akahele; ano mikioi. *To take pains,* e akahele loa.

Pāint, n. He pena.

Pāint, v. 1. E hamo pena.
2. E pena kii.
3. *Paint one's cheeks for beauty,* nounounea.

Pāint'er, n. 1. Mea hamo pena.
2. Mea pena kii.
3. Kaula hoopaa waapa.

Pāint'ing, n. Kii i penaia.

Pāir, n. He pa. *A pair of shoes,* he pa kamaa.

Pāir, v. E kaulua.

Pāl'açe, n. Hale nui a nani.

Pa-lăn-keen' } n. He manele.
Pa-lăn-quĭn' }

Pāl'at-a-ble, adj. Ono, ke ai.

Pāl'ate, n. Kileo.

Pa-lā'tial, adj. Kamahao. *A palatial residence,* he hale noho kamahao.

Pa-lā'ver, n. Walaau; he kuka' pu.

Pāle. adj. Haikea; hakeakea.

Pāle, n. 1. He laau pa.
2. Wahi hoopuniia.

Pāle'ness, n. (*From sickness.*) Lanakea.

Pāl'ette, n. Papa kaawili pena no ka pena kii.

Pāl'ing, n. Laau pa.

Pąll, n. Kapa uhi kupapau.

Pąll, v. Ono ole; liliha.

Pal-lā′di-um, *n.* He pa-kaua; he puuhonua. *The purity of the ballot the palladium of our political rights,* ka makamae o ke koho balota ka puuhonua ia o ko kakou pono aupuni.

Pāl′let, *n.* Bela moe inoino.

Pāl′li-āte, *v.* E hooemi i ka hewa. SYN. extenuate.

Pāl′li-ā′tion, *n.* Ke kumu e emi ai ka hewa.

Pāl′lid, *adj.* SYN. pale; wan.

Pālm, *n.* 1. He kumu loulu.
2. Ka po′ho lima.

Pālm′y, *adj.* Kuonoono; kuapapa. SYN. prosperous.

Pāl′pa-ble, *adj.* 1. Moakaka. SYN. evident.
2. Hiki ke ha′ha′ia.

Pāl′pi-tāte, *v.* E konikoni; e kapalili.

Pāl′pi-tā′tion, *n.* Ke kapalili. *Palpitation of the heart,* ke kapalili o ka houpo.

Pāl′sied, *adj.* Loohia i ka mai lo′lo′.

Pāl′sy, *n.* Mai lolo.

Pāl′try, *adj.* Mea ole; pupuka.

Pām′pas, *n. pl.* Na aina papu akea ma Amerika Hema.

Pām′per, *v.* 1. E pakela ai.
2. E hoomilimili; hoomalimali.

Pām′phlet, *n.* He palapala i humuhumuia.

Pān, *n.* Pa tini.

Pān′a-çē′a, *n.* Kumu hoola nui. SYN. sovereign remedy.

Pān′eāke, *n.* Palaoa parai. SYN. griddle cake.

Pān′de-mō′ni-um, *n.* 1. Keena kuka′ o na diabolo.
2. He uluaoa; haunaele nui.

Pān′der. *n.* He weawea; mea alakai hewa.

Pāne, *n.* Apana aniani.

Pān′e-ġȳr′ic, *n.* Haiolelo hoolea. SYN. eulogy.

Pān′el, *n.* 1. Papa lahilahi o ka puka komo.
2. Papa inoa o ka poe jure.

Pāng, *n.* He umii; he hui.

Pān′ic, *n.* Maka′u kuhewa mai.

Pān′o-ply, *n.* Na kahiko kaua.

Pān′o-rā′ma, *n.* He nanaina akea.

Pānt, *v.* 1. E naenae; paupauaho.
2. E ahaha′. *The dog pants,* ahaha ka ilio.

Pān′ta-lēts′, *n.* Lole wawae kaikamahine.

Pān′ta-lōons′, *n.* Lole wawae.

Pān′the-ism, *n.* Ka manaolo o ke akua na mea a pau.

Pān′try, *n.* Keena waiho pa.

Pāp, *n.* Ai wali.

Pā′pa-çy, *n.* Ka hoomana o Roma.

Pā′pal, *adj.* Po′pe.

Pā′paw, } Pa-pai′a, } *n.* Hei; milikana.

Pā′per, *n.* 1. Pepa; kalana.
2. Nupepa.
3. Manao i hakuia; kumu manao.

Pap-poose′, *n.* Keiki liilii inikini.

Pa-pȳr′us, *n.* Naku o Aigupita.

Pār, *n.* Like. SYN. equality. Kulana like.

Pār′a-ble, *n.* Olelo nane.

Pa-rāde′, *n.* Hookahakaha; haanou.
2. *Military parade,* paikau.

Pa-rāde, *n.* E haanou; E hookehakeha.

Pār′a-dīse, *n.* Paredaiso.

Pār′a-dox, *n.* Mea e haohao ai, he oiaio nae.

Pār′a-gon, *n.* Mea pookela.

Pār′a-graph, *n.* He pauku olelo.

Pār′al-lax, *n.* Ka nee ana o na ao o ka lani ke ikeia mai kauwahi, a mai kauwahi aku.

Pār′al-lel, *n.* Kaha moe like.

Pār′al-lel, *adj.* Moe like.

Pār′al-lēl′o-gram, *n.* Huina-ha; aoao like lua.

Pār′al-lēl′o-pī′ped, *n.* Pa-ili-ono, aoao like lua.

Par-āl′y-sis, *n.* Mai lolo.

Pār′a-lȳt′ic, *adj.* Loohia i ka mai lolo.

Pār′a-lȳse, *v.* 1. E loohia i ka mai lolo.
2. E hoomake manao.

Pār′a-mount, *adj.* Ano nui; koikoi.

Pār′a-mour, *n.* He ipo.

Pār′a-pet, *n.* He papu; he ahua kaua.

Pār′a-sīte, *n.* 1. He hoopilimeaai. SYN. sycophant.
2. Uku hoopili i ke kino.
3. He laau hihi e ulu ana ma na kumulaau.

Pār′a-sol, *n.* Mamalu liilii pale la.

Pār′boil, *v.* E hoo-baila iki.

Pār′çel, *n.* 1. Puolo liilii. SYN. package.
2. *To parcel out,* e mahele aku.

Pārch, *v.* 1. E papaa. SYN. scorch.
2. *Parched with thirst,* make wai loa.

Pārch′ment, *n.* Ili lahilahi; mea kakau.

Pār′don, *n.* Ka huikala.

Pār′don, *v.* E kala i ka hewa.

Pār′don-a-ble, *adj.* Hiki ke kalaia.

Pāre, *v.* E koli; e kolikoli.

Pā′rent, *n.* Makua. *Parent-in-law,* hunowai.

Pa-rēnt′al, *adj.* Makua. *Parental authority,* ka mana makua.

Pa-rēn′the-sis, *n.* Kaha apo.

Pār′en-thēt′ic-al, *adj.* Apoia i na kaha apo.

Pār′ing, *n.* Mea i koliia.

Pār′ish, *n.* Apana ekalesia.

Pa-rish′on-er, *n.* Lala o ka apana ekalesia.

Pār′ity, *n.* Ke ano like.

Pārk, *n.* 1. Kihapai hooluolu.
2. Kahi i hooiliiliia′i o na lako kaua o kela me keia ano.

Pār′lançe, *n.* Ke kamailio ana. *Common parlance,* ke ano i kamailio mau ia.

Pār′ley, *v.* E kuka′ pu.

Pār′lia-ment, *n.* Ahaolelo o Beritania.

Pär′lia-mĕnt′a-ry, *adj.* Ku like me na hana o ka ahaolelo.

Pär′lor, *n.* Keena hookipa.

Pa-rō′chi-al, *adj.* Pili i ka apana ekalesia.

Pa-rōle′, *n.* He ae waha.

Pär′ox-ysm, *n.*1. He umii; hui kuhewa mai.

2. Kupaka.

Pär′ri-cide, *n.* Mea pepehi makua.

Par′rot, *n.* Manu aloha; parota.

Par′ry, *v.* E pale; e hookapae. SYN.

Pär′si-mō′ni-oùs, *adj.* Pi; aua; ii; SYN. stingy; penurious.

Pär′si-mo-ny, *n.* Pi; aua; alunu.

Pär′son, *n.* Kahu ekalesia.

Pär′son-āge, *n.* Kahi e noho ai o ke kahu ekalesia.

Pärt, *n.* He hapa; he haawina; mahele.

Pärt, *v.* 1. E mahele. SYN. divide.

2. E hoolilo aku. *Part with property,* e hoolilo aku i ka waiwai.

3. E hookaawale aku. *Part with friends,* e hookaawale aku mai na hoa.

Par-tāke′, *v.* E komo pu. *Partake of benefits,* e komo pu ma na pomaikai.

2. E ai pu. *Partake of the feast,* e ai pu i ka ahaaina.

Par-tāk′er, *n.* Mea komo pu.

Pär′tial, *adj.* 1. Hapa. *A partial report,* he hoike hapa.

2. Ewaewa; kapakahi; kaulike ole.

Pär-tial′i-ty, *n.* Ka paewaewa; kaulike ole.

Pär′tial-ly, *adv.* Hapa; me ka ewaewa.

Par-tic′i-pant, *n.* SYN. partaker.

Par-tic′i-pāte, *v.* SYN. partake.

Par-tic′i-pā′tion, *n.* Ke komo pu ana. SYN. partaking.

Par-tic′i-pā′tor, *n.* SYN. partaker.

Pär′ti-cle, *n.* He huna; he mole.

Par-tic′u-lar, *adj.* 1. Kekahi mea hookahi.

2. Mikioi; akahele.

Par-tic′u-lars, *n. pl.* Na huna liilii. SYN. details.

Par-tic′u-lar-īze′, *v.* E hai i na kumu liilii. SYN. detail.

Pär′ti-san, *n.* Mea ukali; haumana.

Par-ti′tion, *n.* 1. Ka mahele ana.

2. He paku. *Partition of the room,* ka paku o ke keena.

Pärt′ly, *adv.* Iki. SYN. in a measure. *Partly learned,* paa naau iki.

Pärt′ner, *n.* Hoa; hoa-hana.

Pärt′ner-ship, *n.* Hui oihana.

Pär′ty, *n.* 1. He poe. *A party of boys,* he poe keiki.

2. Poe ahaaina; poe hoolauna.

3. He aoao.

Pär′ty-col′ored, *n.* Onionio. SYN. variegated.

Päss, *v.* E maalo ae.

Päss, *n.* 1. Wahi haahaa mawaena o na kuahiwi i hiki ke hele ia.

2. Palapala ae e hele. SYN. passport.

3. He ano; kulana. SYN. state; condition.

Pàss′a-ble, *adj.* 1. Hiki ke hele ia.

2. Hiki no; e aho ia.

Päs′sage, *n.* 1. Ka hele ana; ka holo ana; ka lele ana.

2. Ka hooholo loa′na. *Passage of a bill,* ka hooholo loa′na o ka bila.

3. He olelo. *Passage in the book,* he olelo iloko o ka buke.

Päs′sage-wāy′ *n.* Kahi e hele ai.

Pàss′book, *n.* Buke baneko helu dala.

Päs′sĕn-ger, *n.* Ohua; ee moku.

Päs′sion, *n.* Huhu wela.

Päs′sion-āte, *adj.* 1. Huhu wale; hikiwawe i ka huhu.

2. Ikaika loa, nui loa. *Passionately grieved,* kaumaha nui loa.

Päs′sive, *adj.* Noho wale; ku-e′ ole. *Passive obedience,* hoolohe hoomanaka′.

Pàss′ō-ver, *n.* Moliaola.

Pàss′port, *n.* Palapala hoapono; palapala kuhikuhi kino.

Pàss′word, *n.* Hua olelo huna′. SYN. countersign.

Pàst, *n.* Wa i hala.

Pàst, *adj.* Hala.

Pàste, *n.* Mea hoopipili.

Pàste′bōard, *n.* Pepa manoanoa.

Pàs′time, *n.* Mea hoonanea; paani. SYN. sport; amusement.

Pàs′tor, *n.* Kahu ekalesia.

Pàs′tor-āte, *n.* Oihana kahu ekalesia.

Päs′try, *n.* Kela me keia ano palaoa ono.

Pàst-ur-āge, *n.* 1. Oihana hanai holoholona.

2. Aina holoholona.

3. Ai na na holoholona.

Pàst-ūre, *n.* Kula holoholona.

Pàst′ūre, *v.* E hanai holoholona.

Pàt, *v.* E paipai oluolu me ka lima.

Pàt, *adv.* Kupono. SYN. fit; seasonable.

Pàtch, *n.* 1. Poho lole; apana lole.

2. Apana. *A patch of grass,* he apana aina.

Pàtch, *v.* E poho; e kapili hou.

Pàtch′work, *n.* 1. Lole apana.

2. Hana kapulu.

Pàte, *n.* Poo. SYN. head.

Pàt′ent, *n.* Palapala hookuleana.

Pàt′ent, *adj.* Moakaka. SYN. evident.

Pàt′ĕnt-ee′, *n.* Mea nana ka palapala hookuleana.

Pàt′ent-of′fice, *n.* Keena oihana hoopuka palapala hookuleana.

Pàt′ent-rights′, *n.* Na pono o ka palapala hookuleana.

Pa-tēr′nal, *adj.* Pili i ka makuakane.

Pa-tēr′ni-ty, *n.* Ke kulana makuakane.

Pàth, *n.* Ala; alanui.

Pa-thĕt′ic, *adj.* Manaonao; menemene.

Pa-thōl′ò-gy, *n.* Ka ike no na mai.

Pä′thos, *n.* Mea ho-ala i ka manaonao.

Päth′wāy, *n.* Alanui; kuamoo.

Pä′tience (shens), *n.* Ahonui; hoomanawanui.

Pā'tient, n. Mea i lapauia.
Pā'tient, adj. Ahonui; hoomanawa-nui.
Pā'tient-ly, adv. Me ke ahonui.
Pā'tri-ärch, n. He poo ohana o ka wa kahiko.
Pa-tri'çian, n. He alii. SYN. noble.
Pät'ri-mō'ny, n. Waiwai o ka makua i hoolinaia i ke keiki.
Pät'ri-ot, n. Kanaka makee aupuni.
Pät'ri-ŏt'ie, adj. Aloha aina; makee aupuni.
Pät'ri-ot-ism, n. Ke aloha aina.
Pa-trōl', n. He kiai kaahele.
Pät'ron, n. Mea kokua; mea hoopomaikai.
Pät'rŏn-age, n. Ke kokua ana; ka hoopomaikai ana.
Pät'ron-ize, v. E kokua; e hoopomaikai.
Pät'ter, v. 1. E nakulukulu. SYN. patter as rain.
2. Kamumu; nakeke. SYN. patter of feet.
Pät'tern, n. Ana hoohalike;kumu hoohalike.
Pau'çi-ty, n. He kakaikahi; he uuku.
Pau'per, n. Mea ilihune.
Pau'per-ism, n. Ka nele; ka hune. SYN. indigence.
Pause, n. 1. Kiko hoomaha leo.
2. He maha iki; wahi ku.
Pause, v. 1. E uoki; e ku a nana iki.
2. E maha iki.
Pāve, v. E kipapa.
Pāve'ment, n. He kipapa pohaku.
Pa-vil'ion, n. Hale lewa; hale lole.
Paw, n. Wawae o ka ilio; popoke; a me na holoholona o ia ano.
Pawn, n. E panai kekahi waiwai liilii no ke dala.
Pawn'brō'ker, n. Kanaka panai waiwai.
Pāy, v. 1. E uku.
2. Puka. The business pays, puka ka oihana.
Pāy'day, n. La kikoo; la hookupu.
Pāy'mäs-ter, n. Luna uku dala.
Pāy'ment, n. Ka uku ana; ka hookaa ana.
Péa (pē), n. He pi; hua ai.
Peaçe, n. Maluhia; kuikahi.
Peaçe'a-ble, adj. Oluolu; kuikahi.
Peaçe'a-blÿ, adv. Me ka oluolu.
Peaçe'ful, adj. 1. Oluolu; maliu; malie.
2. Kuapapa.
Peaçe'mäk'er, n. Mea uwao.
Peaçe'of'fi-çer, n. He makai.
Peach, n. Hua piki.
Péa'jäek-et, n. Pili lakeke.
Peak, n. 1. Wekiu mauna; piko mauna.
2. Laau oluna o ka pea hope.
Peal, n. Leo haalulu.
Peal, v. E haalulu.
Pēa'nut, n. Pinaki.
Pēarl, n. He momi.

Pēarl'y, n. Me he momi la.
Pēas'ant, n. He makaainana.
Pēas'ant-ry, n. Na makaainana.
Peb'ble, n. Iliili; paiwi.
Pēc'ca-dil'lo, n. Hewa liilii; kina'. SYN. fault.
Pēck, n. Peka; hapa-ha o ka busela.
Pēck, v. E kiko.
Pēc'u-lāte, v. E aihue; e apuka. SYN. embezzle.
Pe-eūl'iar, adj. 1. Ano e. SYN. singular.
2. Kupono. SYN. appropriate.
3. Pili i ka mea hookahi; papa paha; ano paha. Peculiar to the class, pili i kela papa wale no.
Pe-eūl'iar'i-ty, n. He mea ano e.
Pe-eūn'ia-ry, adj. Dala. Pecuniary assistance, kokua dala. Pecuniary matters, na mea pili i ke dala.
Pēd'a-gōgue, n. Kumu kula. SYN. teacher.
Pēd'ant, n. Mea e akena ana i kona ike.
Pe-dänt'ie, adj. Hookelakela i ka ike.
Pēd'dle, v. E piele; e maau'auwa'.
Pēd'dler, n. He piele; mea maauauwa.
Pēd'es-tal, n. Kahua no ke kia hoomanao; kii kalaiia, etc.
Pe-dēs'tri-an, n. Kanaka hele wawae.
Pe-dēs'tri-an-ism', n. Ka hele wawae ana.
Pēd'i-gree, n. He kuauhau.
Peel, n. Ka ili o ke kahi mau hua ai.
Peel, v. E ihi; e maihi.
Peep, v. 1. E kiei; e halo'; e naei.
2. E piopio; ioio. SYN. peep as chickens.
3. Peep of day, ke alaula.
Peer, n. He hoa.
2. Peer of the realm, he 'lii o ke aupuni.
Peer'age, n. Kulana alii; papa alii.
Peer'less, adj; Lua ole; pookela. SYN. matchless; unequaled.
Peev'ish, adj. Nainai; na ole; huhu wale. SYN. irritable; cross.
Pēg, n. Pine laau.
Pēll-mēll', n. and adv. Huikau.
Pel-lū'çid, adj. Moakaka; aiai. SYN. transparent.
Pēlt, n. Ili holoholona.
Pēlt, v. E kipehi.
Pēn, v. 1. E kakau.
2. E hoopaa iloko o ka pa.
Pēn, n. 1. Peni kakau. Steel pen, maka kila. Quill pen, peni hulu.
2. Pa. Pig pen, pa puaa.
Pē'nal, adj. Hoopai. Penal servitude, hana hoopai.
Pēn'al-ty, n. Hoopai.
Pēn'ançe, n. Hoopai huikala.
Pēnçe } n. Na peni dala.
Pēn'nies }
Pēn'çil, n. Peni. Slate pencil, peni pohaku. Lead pencil, peni kepau; penikila.
2. Huhui kukuna malamalama.
Pēn'dant, n. Mea e lewa ana.

Pĕnd′ing, *adj.* and *prep.* E waiho nei.
A *pending suit*, ka hihia e waiho nei.
Pending the decision, e kali ana i ka olelo hooholo.

Pĕnd′u-loŭs, *adj.* Lewa wale; lewalewa

Pĕnd′u-lum, *n.* Hao lewa o ka wati.

Pĕn′e-trāte, *v.* E komohia iloko.

Pĕn′e-trā′tion, *n.* 1. Ke komo loa′na. 2. Noeau. SYN. sagacity.

Pĕn′hold-er, *n.* Au o ka peni.

Pen-in′su-lä, *n.* Ane-moku.

Pĕn′i-tençe, *n.* Mihi; walania.

Pĕn′i-tent, Mea mihi.

Pĕn′i-tĕn′ti-a-ry, *n.* Hale paahao.

Pĕn′i-tent-ly, *adv.* Me ka mihi oiaio.

Pĕn′knife, *n.* Pahi koli peni.

Pĕn-man, *n.* Mea kakau lima.

Pĕn-man-ship, *n.* Kakau lima.

Pĕn′nant, } *n.* Hae ololi, loloa.
Pĕn′non, }

Pĕn′ni-less, *adj.* Dala ole.

Pĕn′ny, *n.* He peni; dala Britania.

Pĕn′ny-a-lïn′er, *n.* 1. Mea haku no ka nupepa. 2. Mea haku manao lapuwale.

Pĕn′sion, *n.* 1. Kokua makahiki mai ke aupuni. 2. Kula hanai ma Farani.

Pĕn′sion-er, *n.* Mea i kokua mau ia.

Pĕn′sïve *adj.* Poonoo; mumule; nalu.

Pĕn′ta-gon, *n.* Huina aoao elima.

Pĕn′ta-teŭçh (pen′ta-tuke), *n.* Na buke mua elima o ka Baibala.

Pĕ′nŭlt, *n.* Ka mamala e pili ana i ka mamala hua-olelo hope loa.

Pe-nū′ri-oŭs, *adj.* Aua; pi. SYN. parsimonious.

Pĕn′u-ry, *n.* Ka nele; hune. SYN. poverty; want.

Pēo′ple, *n.* 1. Lahui. *The people*, ka lahui. 2. Poe. *Some people*, kekahi poe.

Pēo′ple, *v.* E hooulu lahui.

Pĕp′per, *n.* He laau nioi; he pepa mea hoomiko.

Pĕp′per-corn, *n.* Ka hua o kekahi ano pepa.

Pĕp′per-y, *adj.* 1. Miko loa i ka pepa. 2. Hikiwawe i ka huhu. SYN. irritable.

Pĕr′ad-vĕnt′ūre, *adv.* Malia paha; ina paha. SYN. perhaps.

Per-am′bu-lāte, *v.* E kaahele wawae.

Per-am′bu-lā′tor, *n.* Mikini ana loa.

Pĕr-çeive′, *v.* 1. E hoomaopopo. SYN. discern. 2. E makili. *Perceive internally.*

Per-çĕnt′age, *n.* Pa-keneka; hapa haneri.

Per-çĕp′ti-ble, *adj.* Hiki ke hoomaopoia.

Per-çĕp′tion, *n.* 1. Ka noonoo. 2. Ka hoomaopopo ana.

Per-çĕp′tive, *adj.* Hoomaopopo; noonoo. *Perceptive qualities*, mana hoomaopopo.

Pĕrch, *a.* Wahi e kau ai ka manu.

Pĕrch, *v.* E kau me he manu la.

Per-chânçe′, *adv.* Malia; malia paha. SYN. perhaps.

Pĕr′co-lāte, *v.* E kulu. SYN. filter.

Per-di′tion, *u.* Ka poino mau loa.

Per-e′gri-nā′tion, *n.* Ka hele auwana io ia-nei.

Pĕr-ĕmp′to-ry, *adj.* Loa; paa. *A peremptory command*, he kauoha paa.

Pĕr-ĕn′ni′al, *adj.* Mau. SYN. perpetual.

Pĕr′feet, *adj.* Hemolele; kina′ ole.

Per-fĕet′, *v.* E hooko pono.

Per-fĕc′tion, *n.* Ke ano hemolele; kina′ ole.

Pĕr′feet-ly, *adv.* Me ka pololei loa; pono loa.

Per-fĭd′i-oŭs, *adj.* Maalea; hoopunihei. SYN. treacherous.

Per-fĭd′i-ous-ly, *n.* Me ka maalea; ano hoohalua. SYN. treacherously.

Pĕr′fi-dy, *n.* Maalea; ano punihei. SYN. treachery.

Pĕr′fo-rāte, *v.* E hou i puka; e wili i puka.

Pĕr′fo-rā′tion, *n.* 1. Ka puka i hou ia, etc. 2. Ka hou ana; ka wili ana.

Per-fôrm, *v.* E hooko. SYN. achieve.

Per-fôrm′ançe, *n.* 1. Ka hooko ana. 2. Hana.

Per-fôrm′er, *n.* 1. Mea e hooko ana. 2. Mea keaka; hookani pila, etc.

Pĕr′fūme, *n.* Mea ala; he ala.

Per-fūme′, *v.* E hoo-pe′.

Per-fūm′er-y, *n.* Kela me keia mea ala.

Per-hăps′, *adv.* Paha; malia paha; anoai.

Pĕr′i-eär′di-um, *n.* Ka ili lahilahi e hoopuni ana i ka puuwai.

Pĕr′i-gee, *n.* Ka hookoke loa′na o ka mahina i ka honua ma kona ala hele.

Pĕr′i-hē′li-on, *n.* Ke kokoke loa′na o ka hoku hele i ka la, ma kona ala hele.

Pĕr′il, *n.* Popilikia.

Pĕr′il-oŭs, *adj.* Pilikia; paapu i na popilikia.

Pe-rĭm′e-ter, *n.* Ke ana puni o kekahi mea.

Pĕ′ri-od, *n.* 1. Kiko-kahi. 2. He wa.

Pĕ′ri-ŏd′ie-al, *n.* He palapala i pai manawa ia.

Pĕ′ri-ŏd′ie-al, *adj.* Kela me keia manawa.

Pĕ′ri-ŏd′ie-al-ly, *adv.* I kela me keia wa.

Pe-riph′er-y, *n.* Ke ana-puni o ka poai.

Pĕr′ish, *v.* E make.

Pĕr′ish-a-ble, *adj.* Mae wale; popo wale.

Pĕr′jure, *v.* E hoohiki wahahee.

Pĕr′jur-er, *n.* Mea hoohiki wahahee.

Pĕr′ju-ry, *n.* Ka hoohiki wahahee.

Pĕr′ma-nençe, } *n.* Ka paa; ke ano
Pĕr′ma-nen-çŷ, } mau.

Pĕr'ma-nent, *adj.* Paa; mau. SYN. lasting.

Pĕr'ma-nĕnt-ly, *adv.* Paa; mau. *Stay permanently,* e noho paa.

Pĕr'me-a-ble, *adl.* Hiki ke komoia; hiki ke hoo-u'ia.

Pĕr'me-āte, *v.* E hoo-u; e komo.

Per-mis'si-ble, *adj.* Ae ia.

Per-mis'sion, *n.* Ka ae. SYN. consent.

Per-mit', *v.* E ae. SYN. allow.

Pĕr'mit, *n.* He palapala ae. SYN. license.

Per-ni'çioŭs, *adj.* Ino; hooeha; poino. SYN. hurtful.

Pĕr-o-rā'tion, *n.* Na olelo hope o ka hai olelo.

Pĕr'pen-dīc'u-lar, *adj.* Kupono; kupololei.

Pĕr'pen-dīc'u-lár'i-ty, *n.* Ke kupono; ku pololei.

Pĕr'pe-trāte, *v.* E hoo-ko ma kekahi mea ino. *Perpetrate a crime,* e hana i karaima.

Pĕr'pe-trā'tor, *n.* Ka mea nana e hana. *The perpetrator of the theft,* ka mea nana e aihue.

Per-pĕt'u-al, *adj.* Mau loa. SYN. everlasting.

Pĕr-pĕt'u-āte, *v.* E hoomau.

Pĕr'pe-tū'i-ty, *n.* Ka mau ana.

Per-plĕx', *v.* E hoopilihua; hookuawili.

Per-plĕx'ing, *adj.* Hookuawili; anoninoni; pioo.

Per-plĕx'i-ty, *a.* Mea hoolauwili ai.

Pĕr'qui-ṣite, *n.* Koina.

Pĕr'se-cūte, *v.* E hooino; hoomaau'.

Pĕr'se-cū'tion, *n.* Ka hoomaau'; hooino.

Pĕr'se-cu-tor, *n.* Mea hoomaau'; mea hooino.

Pĕr'se-vēr'ance, *n.* Hoomanawanui.

Pĕr'se-vēre', *v.* E hoomanawanui.

Pĕr'se-vēr'ing-ly, *adv.* Me ka hoomanawanui.

Per-sist', *v.* E hoomau. SYN. continue.

Per-sist'ençe, *n.* Ka hoomau ana. SYN. perseverance.

Per-sist'ent, *adj.* Kupaa,

Pĕr'son, *n.* 1. Ke kino.
2. Mea. *Some person,* kekahi mea. *First person,* ka mea e kamailio ana. *Second person,* ka mea i kamailio ia. *Third person,* ke kumu o ke kamailio.

Pĕr'son-age, *n.* 1. Mea hanohano.
2. Poe.

Pĕr'son-al, *adj.* Pili kino.

Pĕr'son-ăl'i-ty, *n.* 1. He ano ku okoa.
2. He olelo pili kino.

Pĕr'son-ăl-ly, *adv.* Iho. *Personally responsible,* maluna iho o'u ka haawe.

Pĕr'son-āte, *v.* E ku no kekahi mea e. SYN. represent. *The lawyer personates his client,* ke ku nei ka loio no kona mua.

Per-spĕc'tive, *n.* Ka nanaina.

Pĕr'spi-cū'i-ty, *n.* Moakaka.

Per-spic'u-oŭs, *adj.* Moakaka. SYN. plain.

Pĕr'spi-rā'tion, *n.* Hou. SYN. sweat.

Per-spire', *n.* E kahe ka hou.

Per-suāde', *v.* E koi; e kono.

Per-suā'sion, *n.* Ke koi ana.

Per-suā'sive, *adj.* Mana i ka hoohuli manao.

Pĕrt, *adj.* Pakike'.

Per-tāin', *v.* E pili. SYN. belong.

Pĕr'ti-nā'çioŭs, *adj.* Mahaoi; paakiki. SYN. stubborn.

Pĕr'ti-nāç'i-ty, *n.* Ke ano mahaoi; kupaa ma kekahi mea.

Pĕr'ti-nent, *adj.* Pili pono. SYN. appropriate.

Pĕrt'ly, *adv.* Me ka pakike'.

Per-tŭrb', *v.* 1. E hoopihoihoi; e hopohopo.
2. E hoolauwili.

Pĕr'tur-bā'tion, *n.* 1. Hopohopo; pilihua.
2. Ka lauwili ana.

Pe-rū'ṣal, *n.* Ka heluhelu noonoo.

Pe-rūṣe', *v.* E heluhelu noonoo.

Per-vāde', *v.* E puni.

Per-vērse', *adj.* Kekee; oolea.

Per-vēr'sion, *n.* Ka hoo-kekee ana.

Per-vēr'si-ty, *n.* Ke ano kekee; ano oolea.

Per-vērt', *v.* E hoohuli mai ka pono; mai ka pololei.

Pes'si-mist, *n.* Mea manao ino wale.

Pĕst, *n.* He ahulau.

Pĕs'ter, *v.* E hoonaukiuki; e hanawale; e hoo-mea.

Pĕst'-house, *n.* Hale mai no na mai laha.

Pĕs'ti-lençe, *n.* Mai ahulau.

Pĕs'ti-lent
Pĕs'ti-lĕn'tial } *adj.* Ino; haukae.

Pĕs'tle, *n.* Pohaku kui.

Pĕt, *n.* 1. He milimili; punahele; pokii.
2. Nunuha. SYN. pout.

Pe-ti'tion, *n.* He noi; palapala noi.
2. Palapala hoopii.

Pe-ti'tion-er, *n.* Mea noi; mea hoopii no ka pomaikai.

Pĕt'ri-făc'tion, *n.* Mea i lilo i pohaku.

Pĕt'ri-fÿ, *v.* E lilo i pohaku.

Pe-trō'le-um, *n.* Aila honua.

Pĕt'ti-eōat, *n.* He pa-u'.

Pĕt'ti-fŏg'ger, *n.* Loio hawawa.

Pĕt'tish, *adj.* Nunuha; nainai.

Pĕt'ty, *adj.* Liilii; mea ole.

Pĕt'u-lançe, *n.* Nainai; nunuha.

Pĕt'u-lant, *adj.* Nainai; na ole; ohumu wale. SYN. peevish; cross.

Pew, *n.* He noho ma ka luakini.

Pew'ter, *n.* Piula; piuta.

Phăn'taṣm, *n.* He ouli; he hihio.

Phăn'tom, *n.* He lapu; he akua.

Phăr'i-see, *n.* He Paresaio.

Phăr'ma-eō'pœ-ia, *n.* Buke hoike no ka hana ana i na laau lapaau.

Phăr'ma-çy, *n.* Oihana hoomakaukau laau lapaau.

Phāṣe, n. Nanaina; ano. SYN. appearance.
Phe-nŏm-i-non, n. He ouli; mea ano e.
Phial, n. Omole liilii. SYN. vial.
Phil'an-thrŏp'ie, adj. Aloha i kanaka; manawalea; ano kokua. SYN. benevolent.
Phi-lăn'thro-pist, n. He mea i aloha i kanaka; mea i kokua aloha aku.
Phi-lăn'thro-py, n. Ke aloha i kanaka.
Phi-lŏl'o-ġist, n. Mea akamai i ka huli olelo.
Phi-lŏl'o-ġy, n. Huli olelo.
Phi-lŏs'o-pher, n. Kanaka ake-akamai.
Phil'o-sŏph'ie, adj. Akeakamai.
Phi-lŏs'o-phize, v. E noonoo no ke kumu o kela me keia mea.
Phi-lŏs'o-phy, n. Akeakamai.
Phiz, n. Helehelena.
Phlĕgm (flem), n. Wale.
Pho-nĕt'ie, adj. Pili i na leo hua palapala.
Pho-nĕt'ies, n. Ka ike e pili ana i ka leo kanaka.
Pho-nŏg'ra-phy, n. Kakau hoailona leo.
Phŏs'pho-rŭs, n. Laau hoomalamalama.
Pho'to-graph, n. Kii i paila.
Pho-tŏg'ra-phy, n. Oihana pai kii.
Pho-tŏm'e-ter, n. Mea ana malamalama.
Phrāṣe, n. Mamala olelo.
Phrā'ṣe-ŏl'o-ġy, n. Ke ano o ka olelo.
Phre-nŏl'o-ġy, n. Ka ike e pili ana i ka lo'lo.
Phrĕn'ṣy, n. Pupule. SYN. madness.
Phthiṣ'ie (tiz'ik), n. Naenae.
Phyṣ'ie, n. Laau lapaau.
Phyṣ'ie-al, adj. 1. Kino. Physical pain, eha kino.
2. No na helehelena. Physical geography, he hoike no na helehelena o ka honua.
Phy-ṣi'çian, n. Kauka lapaau. SYN. doctor.
Phyṣ'ies, n. pl. Ka ike e pili ana no na mea kino a pau.
Phyṣ'i-ŏg'no-my, n. 1. Ka helehelena.
2. Ka hoakaka ana i ke ano o ke kanaka mai kona mau helehelena.
Phyṣ'i o-lŏġ'ie-al, adj. Pili i ke ola kino.
Phyṣ'i-ŏl'o-ġist, n. Mea imi i na loina no ke ola kino.
Phyṣ'i-ŏl'o-ġy, n. Ka ike no ke ola kino.
Pĭ-ăn'ist, n. Mea hookani piana.
Pĭ-ă'no,
Pĭ-ă'no-fŏrte', } n. He piana.
Pĭ-ăz'zà, n. Lanai hale. SYN. verandah.
Piek, v. 1. E ohi. Pick fruit, e ohi i na hua.
2. E wae. SYN. choose.

3. E wehe. Pick a lock, e wehe i ka laka.
Pick, n. Mea i wae ia; ka mea oi o ka maikai.
Pick'ax, n. Kipikua.
Pick'et, n. 1. Koa kiai ma ke kaua.
2. Laau pa.
Pick'le, n. 1. He kai.
2. Hua ai i hoomikoia i ka vinika.
Pick'pŏck'et, n. Kaili pakeke; aihue pakeke.
Piç'nie, n. Ahaaina hoonanea.
Pĭc-tō'ri-al, n. Buke kii; nupepa kii.
Piet'ûre, n. He kii.
Piet'ûre, v. E noonoo mehe kii la.
Pĭc-tûr-ĕsque', adj. Me he kii la.
Pie, n. He pai; mea ono.
Pieçe, n. 1. He apana.
2. Haiolelo. kumumanao.
3. He apa'. Piece of cloth, apa' lole.
Pieçe'meal, adj. Pauku.
Pieçe'work, n. Ukupau.
Piĕr, n. Kahua uapo; he uapo moku.
Pierçe, v. E hou.
Pi'e-ty, n. 1. Aloha. Filial piety, aloha o ke keiki i ka makua.
2. Haipule.
Pig, n. 1. Puaa keiki.
2. Auka metala.
Pig'eon, n. Manu nunu.
Pig'eon-hole, n. Holowaa waiho pepa.
Pike, n. 1. He ihe.
2. Inoa o kekahi i-a.
Pile, n. 1. He ahua.
2. He pou loihi.
Pile, v. E hooahu; e hooiliili; e paila.
Pileṣ, n. He mai.
Pil'fer, v. E aa'ma; aihue i na mea liilii.
Pil'fer-er, n. Mea aama. SYN. petty thief.
Pil-gär'lie, n. He kuewa. SYN. vagabond.
Pil'grim, n. Mea hele malihini.
Pil'grim-aġe, n. Ka hele malihini ana.
Pill, n. Hua ale.
Pil'laġe, v. E hao wale. SYN. plunder.
Pil'lar, n. He kia; he pou.
Pil'lŏw, n. Uluna.
Pil'lŏw-eâse, n. Eke uluna.
Pi'lot, n. Pailoka; alakai.
Pi'lot-aġe, n. 1. Uku pailoka.
2. Ke alakai ana.
Pimp, n. Weawea.
Pim'ple, n. Puupuu liilii ma ka ili.
Pin, n. Kui pine.
Pin, v. E hoopaa me ke kui pine.
Pin'çerṣ,
Pinch'erṣ, } n. Upa' umii.
Pinch, v. 1. E iniki; e umiki.
2. E mio.
Pin'eush'ion, n. Uluna kui pine.
Pine, n. Laau paina.
Pine, v. E hookii.
Pine'-äp'ple, n. Hala kahiki.
Pin'ion, n. 1. Eheu. SYN. wing.
2. Niho pokakaa.
Pin'-mŏn'ey, n. Dala no ka wahine.

Pin'na-cle, *n.* Wahi oioi. *Pinnacle of the temple,* wahi oioi o ka luakini.
Pint, *n.* Paina; hapaha kuata.
Pi'o-neer', *n.* Kanaka komo mua ma ka aina, a hana paha.
Pi'oŭs, *adj.* Haipule.
Pipe, *n.* Ohe; ohe puhi. *Water pipe,* ohe wai.
2. *Tobacco pipe,* ipu baka.
3. Pu makani.
Piq'uant (pi'kant), *adj.* Awahia; mulea.
Pique (pēek), *n.* Hoomauhala, opu ino. SYN. grudge.
Pi'ra-cy, *n.* Powa moku.
Pi'rate, *n.* He powa moku.
Pi-răt'ic-al, *adj.* Powa. *A piratical craft,* he moku powa.
Pis'tol, *n.* Pu panapana.
Pit, *n.* He lua.
Pit'a-păt, *adv.* Kapalili. *My heart goes pitapat,* kapalili kuu puuwai, *or* kapalili kuu houpo.
Pitch, *n.* 1. Kepau hamo.
2. Ka loli ana o ka leo. *A high pitch of voice,* he leo kiekie.
Pitch, *v.* 1. E hoolei; e kiola. SYN. toss.
2. E kukulu.
3. E hoopi'nana. SYN. pitch, as a vessel in a storm.
4. *Pitch a tune,* e hoomaka i ka leo mele.
Pitch'er, *n.* 1. He pika.
2. Mea hoolei kinipopo.
Pitch'fork, *n.* O kiola mauu.
Pit-e'oŭs, *adj.* Kaumaha; kumakena.
Pit'fall, *n.* Lua pahele.
Pith, *n.* 1. Iho.
2. I'o. *The pith of the remark,* ka i-o o ka olelo.
Pith-y, *adj.* Noeau; i-o.
Pit'i-a-ble, *adj.* Ku i ka hoomae-ele.
Pit'i-a-ble, *adj.* 1. Ano hoo-mae-ele.
2. Haahaa. SYN. low; mean.
Pit'i-less, *adj.* Aloha ole; menemene ole.
Pit'saw, *n.* Pahiolo lua.
Pit'tance, *n.* Loaa uuku; loaa lawa ole.
Pit-y, *n.* Aloha hoomae-ele; aloha menemene. SYN. compassion; sympathy.
Piv'ot, *n.* He pine mea e kaa ai.
Plă'ea-ble, *adj.* Hiki ke hoolauleaia.
Pla-eärd', *n.* Palapala hoolaha.
Plă'eate, *v.* E hoomalielie; hoolaulea. SYN. appease.
Plăçe, *n.* Wahi.
Plăçe, *v.* E hoonoho; e waiho.
Plăç'id, *adj.* Malie; oluolu; na. SYN. calm.
Plăç'id-ly, *adv.* Me ka malie. SYN. calmly.
Plă'gia-rism, *n.* Ka lawe wale ana i ka olelo a hai i kakau ai.
Plă'gia-rist, *n.* Mea lawe wale i ka olelo a hai i kakau.
Plăgue, *n.* 1. Mai ahulau.
2. Mea hoopilikia wale.

Plăin, *n.* Aina papu; aina malaelae.
Plăin, *adj.* Akaka. SYN. evident.
Plăin'ly, *adv.* Moakaka.
Plăin'tiff, *n.* Aoao nana ka hoopii kanawai.
Plăint'ive, *adj.* Uhu; kaniuhu. SYN. mournful.
Plăit, *v.* E ulana. SYN. braid.
Plăn, *n.* Kii hoike ano.
2. He manao hoo-ko.
Plăne, *n.* 1. Ili laumania.
2. Koi kahi.
Plăn'et, *n.* Hoku hele.
Plăn'et-a-ry, *adj.* Pili i na hoku hele.
Plănk, *n.* Papa manoanoa.
Plănt, *n.* Mea kanu; mea ulu.
Plănt, *v.* E kanu.
Plănt'ain, *n.* Maia popolu.
Plan-tā'tion, *n.* Mahina ai. *Sugar plantation,* mahi ko.
Plănt'er, *n.* Kanaka mahiai.
Plăs'ter, *n.* Puna hamo; laau hamo.
Plăs'ter-er, *n.* Kanaka hamo puna.
Plăte, *n.* 1. Pa.
2. *Timber plate,* lohelau.
Pla-teau' (pla-tō'), *n.* Aina papa kiekie.
Plăte'ful, *n.* Piha pa.
Plăt'form, *n.* 1. He awai.
2. Palapala hoike manao hooholo.
Plăt'ter, *n.* Pa palahalaha.
Plaud'it, *n.* Mahalo; leo hoano.
Plau'si-ble, *adj.* Pono i ka mana'ku.
Plăy, *n.* 1. Paani; lealea; hoonanea. SYN. sport.
2. Hana keaka.
3. He akea. SYN. scope. *Give full play,* e hoakea.
Plăy'-aet'or, *n.* Kanaka keaka.
Plăy'-bill, *n.* Palapala hoolaha keaka.
Plăy'-fĕl'low, *n.* Hoa paani. SYN. playmate.
Plăy'ful, *adj.* Piha i ka paani. SYN. sportive.
Plăy'mate, *n.* Hoa paani.
Plăy'thing, *n.* Mea paani.
Plăy'wright, *n.* Mea haku kike'keaka.
Plĕa, *n.* Olelo pale.
Plĕad, *v.* 1. E noi haahaa; e koi.
2. E palo olelo.
Plĕad'er, *n.* 1. He loio. SYN. advocate.
2. Mea koi ikaika.
Plĕas'ant, *adj.* Oluolu; malie; kalaelae.
Plĕas'ant-ly, *adv.* Me ka oluolu.
Plĕas'ant-ry, *n.* Hana hoolealea; olelo hoo-oluolu.
Plĕase, *v.* E oluolu; e hoo-oluolu.
Plĕas'ing, *adj.* Oluolu; lea.
Plĕas'ure, *n.* Lealea; olioli.
Ple-bē'ian, *adj.* Kuaaina. SYN. vulgar.
Plĕdge, *n.* Mea panai.
Plĕdge, *v.* 1. E waiho ma ke ano panai.
2. E hoohiki.

Plĕn-i-po-tĕn'ti-a-ry, *n.* He eleleme ka mana akea.
Plĕn'i-tūde, *n.* Ka piha; ka nui. SYN. fullness.
Plĕn'te-oŭs,⎰ *adj.* Lawa; mahuahua;
Plĕn'ti-ful, ⎱ lako.
Plĕn'ty, *n.* Ka lawa pono; ka lako pono.
Pleŭ'ri-sy, *n.* Mai umii.
Pli'a-ble, *adj.* 1. Nolunolu. SYN. flexible.
2. Lauwili.
Pli'ant, *adj.* Hoolohe.
Plight, *v.* E haawi i ka olelo ae.
Plight, *n.* Ka noho'na. SYN. condition. *A sorry plight,* inoino ka noho'na.
Plŏd, *v.* 1. E maalo ae me ka luhi.
2. E hoomau me ka hoomanawanui.
Plŏt, *n.* 1. Hana kipi; hana hoohalua.
2. Apana. *Plot of ground,* apana aina.
Plŏt, *v.* 1. E kipi malu'.
2. E kahakaha i kii o ka aina.
Plŏt'ter, *n.* Kanaka kipi; kanaka hoohalua.
Plŏ'ver, *n.* Manu kolea.
Plow ⎰
Plough ⎱ *n.* Oo-palau.
Plow'man ⎰
Plough'man ⎱ *n.* Kanaka palau aina.
Plow'share ⎰ *n.* Ka hao o ka oo-pa-
Plough'share⎱ lau.
Plŭck, *v.* 1. E ohi. SYN. pick.
2. E uhuki. SYN. pull.
Plŭck, *n.* Aa; koa. SYN. courage.
2. Ake paa.
Plŭg, *n.* 1. He umoki.
2. Pepee. *Plug of tobacco,* pepee baka.
Plŭg, *v.* E hoopaa me ka umoki.
Plŭ'mage, *n.* Na hulu manu.
Plŭmb, *v.* E hookupono; e hoo-ku pololei.
Plŭmb'er, *n.* Kanaka hana ma na mea kepau, etc.
Plŭmb'line, *n.* He kaula me ka poka' mea hoo-kupono.
Plūme, *n.* Hulu no ka papale; hulu manu.
Plŭm'met, *n.* SYN. plumb line.
Plŭmp, *adj.* 1. Momona; puipui; nemunemu.
2. Huake; kaekae.
Plŭn'der, *n.* Waiwai i hao ia.
Plŭn'der, *v.* E hao; e pakaha.
Plŭn'der-er, *n.* He pakaha; powa.
Plŭnge, *v.* 1. E lu; e kimo.
2. E hoo-u'.
Plū'ral, *adj.* Oi i ka hookahi; lehulehu.
Plu-rǎl'i-ty, *n.* Ka lehulehu; ka oi.
Plŭs. Hui; hoailona o ka hoouluulu.
Pneū-mǎt'ics (nū), *n.* Ka ike no ke ea me kona ano.
Pneū-mō'ni-à, *n.* He wela ma ke ake mama.
Pōach, *v.* 1. E hoomoa hua moa ma ka hoo-naha' ana iloko o ka wai baila.
2. E aihue i na holoholona liilii ma ka aina o hai.

Pŏck'et, *n.* Eke ma ka lole komo; he pakeke.
Pŏck'et-bŏŏk, *n.* Buke lawe pakeke.
Pŏck'et-knife, *n.* Pahi pelu. SYN. jack knife.
Pŏd, *n.* Aa; wahi' o kekahi mau hua.
Pō'em, *n.* He mele.
Pō'et, *n.* He haku-mele.
Pō'et-ess, *n.* Wahine haku mele.
Po-ĕt'ic, ⎰ *adj.* Memele.
Po-ĕt'ic-al,⎱
Pō'et-ry, *n.* Mele. SYN. verse.
Poign'ant (poin) *adj.* Nui loa. *Poignant grief,* ehaeha nui loa o ka naau.
Point, *n.* 1. He piko; welau.
2. Kumu-manao. SYN. subject matter.
3. He lae.
Point, *v.* E kuhikuhi.
Point'blank', *adj.* Kokoke loa; kupono i ke alo.
Point'ed, *adj.* 1. Oi; winiwini. SYN. sharp.
2. Pili pono. *A pointed remark,* he olelo pili pono.
Point'er, *n.* 1. Laau kuhikuhi.
2. Ilio hahai holoholona.
Point'ing, *n.* Ke kau pono ana i na kiko.
Poi̇̄s'on, *n.* Laau make; akua hanai.
Poi̇̄s'on-er, *n.* Mea hanai laau make.
Poi̇̄s'on-oŭs, *adj.* Make.
Pōke, *v.* E hou.
Pō'ker, *n.* Hao hoala ahi.
Pō'lar, *adj.* Pili i na welau o ka honua. *Polar regions,* na wahi ma na welau.
Pōle, *n.* 1. He oa; aho.
2. He pahu. *Flag pole,* pahu hae.
3. He ana.
4. He Welau. *North Pole,* Welau Akau. North Star.
Pōle'star, *n.* Ka Hoku-paa. SYN. North Star.
Po-lice' (po-lees'), *n.* Na makai.
Po-lice'man, *n.* He makai.
Pŏl'i-cy, *n.* 1. He manao hooko.
2. Palapala panai ola.
Pŏl'ish, *n.* 1. Lepo anai.
2. He hinuhinu.
3. Ano hoohiehie; ano keonimana.
Po-lite', *adj.* Ano oluolu; ano keonimana; pihalula.
Po-lite'ness, *n.* Ke ano oluolu o ka manao.
Po-lite'ly, *adv.* Pihalula.
Pŏl'i-tie, *adj.* Kupono; noeau. SYN. prudent.
Po-lit'ie-al, *adj.* Pili i ka oihana aupuni; kalai aina. *Political economy,* ka-lai aina.
Pŏl'i-ti'çian, *n.* Kanaka makee oihana aupuni.
Pŏl'i-ties, *n.* Ka ike e pili ana i ka oihana aupuni.
Pŏll, *n.* Ke poo. *Poll tax,* auhau kino.
Pŏlls, *n. pl.* Papa inoa o ka poe koho balota. *At the polls,* ma ke kahua koho.
Pol-lūte', *n.* E hoohaumia. SYN. defile; corrupt.

Pol-lū'tion, *n.* Haumia; paumaele. SYN. corruption.

Pol-troon', *n.* He maka'uwale haukae.

Po-lyg'ä-mist, *n.* Mea mare lehulehu.

Po-lyg'ä-my, *n.* Mare lehulehu.

Pŏl'y-gon, *n.* Huina lehulehu.

Pŏl'y-nō'mi-al, *n.* Kuanite mahele lehulehu.

Pol'y-syl'la-ble, *n.* Hua-olelo mamala lehulehu.

Pŏl'y-thē'ism, *n.* Manaoio i na akua he lehulehu.

Po-māde', } *n.* Aila hamo lauoho.
Po-mā'tum, }

Pŏm'mel, *n.* Omuku noho lio.

Pŏm-mel, *v.* E kui. SYN. pound.

Po-mŏl'o-gy, *n.* Ka ike e pili ana i na hua o ka aina me ka hooulu ana.

Pŏmp, *n.* Hoohiehie; hookahakaha.

Pŏmp'ous, *adj.* Hookeha.

Pŏnd, *n.* He kiowai; loko wai uuku.

Pŏn'der, *v.* E nalu; e poonoo. SYN. consider.

Pŏn'der-ous, *adj.* Kaumaha loa. SYN. heavy.

Pŏn'tiff, *n.* Kahuna Nui.

Po'ny, *n.* Lio punahele.

Poo'dle, *n.* Ilio liilii.

Pool, *n.* He kiowai; loko.

Poor, *adj.* 1. Ilihune; nele. SYN. destitute.
2. Olala; wiwi. SYN. lean.
3. Inoino. SYN. inferior.
4. Kupono ole. SYN. worthless.
5. Onawaliwali. SYN. ill.

Poor'ly, *adv.* 1. Onawaliwali.
2. Hemahema. *Poorly done*, hemahema ka hana.
3. *Think poorly of*, manao ole ia'ku.

Pŏp, *v.* E poha'; e leleponi.

Pōpe, *n.* Ke poo o ka hoomana katolika.

Pōp'er-y, *n.* Hoomana katolika.

Pŏp'u-lace, *n.* Na makaainana.

Pŏp'u-lar, *adj.* Oluolu i ka lahui; ku i ka makemake o ka lehulehu.

Pŏp'u-lär'i-ty, *n.* Ka hilinai o ka lehulehu.

Pŏp'u-lāte, *v.* E hoopiha ka aina i kanaka.

Pŏp'u-lā'tion, *n.* Na kanaka o ka aina.

Pŏp'u-lous, *adj.* Paapu i kanaka.

Pŏrch, *n.* Lanai hale.

Pōre, *n.* Pukapuka ili.

Pōre, *v.* E haka pono; e noonoo.

Pŏrk, *n.* I'o puaa.

Pŏrk'er, *n.* He puaa.

Pōr'ous, *adj.* Pukapuka.

Pōr'poise (pus), *n.* Naia.

Pōrt, *n.* 1. Awa ku moku. SYN. harbor.
2. Aoao hema o ka moku.

Pŏrt'a-bil'i-ty, *n.* Hiki ke halihali ia.

Pōr'ta-ble, *adj.* Hiki ke laweia.

Pŏrt'al, *n.* Ipuka; kahi e komo ai.

Por-tĕnd', *v.* E hoike e mamua. SYN. presage.

Pŏr'tĕnt, *n.* He ouli o ka poino.

Por-tĕnt'ous, *adj.* Paapu i na ouli o ka ino.

Pŏr'ter, *n.* 1. Kiai puka.
2. Kanaka hali ukana.
3. He ano bia.

Pŏrt'fō'li-o, *n.* He ope waiho pepa.

Pŏrt'hōle, *n.* Puka ki-pu o ka moku manuwa.

Pŏr'ti-co, *n.* He lanai no ka puka komo.

Pŏr'tion, *n.* Haawina; mahele; hapa.

Pŏr'tion-less, *adj.* Mahele ole.

Pŏrt'ly, *adj.* Puipui.

Pŏrt-măn'teau, *n.* Eke lawe lole.

Pŏr'trait, *n.* Kii helehelena.

Pŏr-trāy', *v.* E pena i ke kii.
2. E hoike lea.

Pōse, *n.* Ke ano o ke ku ana.

Pŏṣ'er, *n.* Ninau pohihihi.

Po-ṣi'tion, *n.* 1. Wahi. SYN. place.
2. Kulana. *Position in society*, kulana iwaena o kanaka.

Pŏṣ'i-tive, *adj.* Akaka; maopopo
2. *Positive quantity*, kuanite hui.

Pŏṣ'i-tive-ly, *adv.* Me ka maopopo lea; oiaio maoli.

Pŏṣ'se Cŏm-i-tā'tus, *n.* He puali makaainana e kokua ana i na lima o ke kanawai.

Pos-sĕṣṣ', *v.* E loaa; e loaa ponoi.

Pos-sĕṣ'sion, *n.* Ka loaa ana. *In his possession*, aia ma kona lima; aia i iaia.

Pos-sĕṣ'sions, *n. pl.* Na waiwai ponoi.

Pos-sĕṣ'sor, *n.* Ka ona; ka haku.

Pŏs'si-bil'i-ty, *n.* Ka hiki ana paha.

Pŏs'si-ble, *adj.* Paha. SYN. perhaps.

Pŏst, *n.* He pou.
2. He elele.

Pŏst, *v.* 1. E hoonoho. *Post guards*, e hoonoho i poe kiai.
2. E hookomo i ka eke leta. SYN. mail.
3. E hookomo ma ka Ledger.
4. E imi; e hoonauao.

Pŏst'age, *n.* Uku leta; poo leta.

Pŏst'al, *adj.* Pili i ka oihana lawe leta.

Pŏst'dāte, *v.* E kakau mahope o ka manawa.

Pŏst'di-lū'vi-an, *adj.* Mahope mai o kaiakahinalii.

Pŏst'er, *n.* Palapala hoolaha.

Pos-tē'ri-or, *adj.* Mahope mai.

Pos-tē'ri-ors, *n. pl.* Kikala.

Pos-ter'i-ty, *n.* Na mamo. SYN. descendants.

Pŏst'hāste, *adv.* Me ka awiwi loa.

Pŏst'hu-mous, *adj.* Mahope mai o ka make ana. *A posthumous child*, he keiki i hanauia mahope mai o ka make ana o ka makuakane.
2. *Posthumous works*, na buke i paiia mahope mai o ka make ana o ka mea nana i kakau.

Pŏst'märk, *n.* Hoailona pai o ka hale leta.

Pŏst'mȧst'er, *n.* Luna leta.

Pŏst'mis'tress, *n.* Luna leta wahine.

Pŏst-môr′tem, *adj.* Mahope o ka ma-ke. *Postmortem examination*, ka imi ana i ke kumu o ka make ana.

Pŏst′ŏffice, *n.* Hale leta.

Pŏst′pāid, *adj.* Ukuia ka uku leta.

Pŏst′pōne, *v.* E hoopanee.

Pŏst-pōne′ment, *n.* Ka hoopanee ana.

Pŏst′script, *a.* Olelo pakui no ka pa-lapala.

Pŏst′ūre, *n.* Ke ano o ke ku ana; ka moe ana. SYN. attitude.

Pŏt, *d.* Ipu no kela me keia hana. *Iron pot*, ipu-hao.

Pŏt, *v.* E hookomo ma ka ipu.

Pŏ′ta-ble, *adj.* Kupono ke inuia. SYN. drinkable.

Po-tā′to, *n.* Uala. *Sweet potato*, uala maoli. *Irish or white potato*, uala ka-hiki.

Pŏ′tent, *adj.* Mana. SYN. powerful.

Pŏ′tent-āte, *n.* He moi. SYN. sover-eign.

Pŏ′tion, *n.* Laau inu.

Pŏt′luek, *n.* He paina o na mea ai i loaa ma ka lima.

Pŏt′taḡe, *n.* He supa.

Pŏt′ter, *n.* Kanaka hana ipu lepo.

Pŏt′ter-y, *n.* Kela me keia ano ipu lepo.

Pŏt-văl′iant, *ad.* Aa , no ka ona.

Pouch. *n.* Aa moni; eke.

Poul′tiçe, *n.* Laau hamo; mea hooe-mi pehu.

Poul′try, *n.* Na manu o ka pa manu.

Pounçe, *v.* E poi; e popoi.

Pound, *n.* 1. He paona.

2. He dala gula o Beretania. SYN. sovereign.

3. Pa aupuni.

Pound, *v.* E kui.

Pound′keep′er, *n.* Luna pa-aupuni.

Pōur, *v.* E ninini; e hookahe.

Pout, *v.* E o iwaho ka lehelehe; e nu-nuha.

Pŏv′er-ty, *n.* He nele; he hune. penury; want; indigence.

Pow′der, *n.* 1. Pauda ki-pu.

2. Lepo wali; lepo aeae.

3. Laau a ke kauka.

Pow′er, *n.* Mana.

Pow′er-ful, *adj.* Mana nui.

Pow′er-less, *adj.* Mana ole.

Prăc′ti-ea-bĭl′i-ty, *n.* Ka hiki. SYN. possibility.

Prăc′ti-ea-ble, *adj.* Hiki. SYN. pos-sible.

Prăc′ti-eal, *adj.* 1. Lawelawe mau.

2. Makaukau ma ka lawelawe ana. *A practical man*, he kanaka makaukau ma ka lawelawe ana.

Prăc′tise, *n.* 1. Hana mau. SYN. habit.

2. Ka lawelawe mau ana.

Prăc′tise, *v.* E hana mau; e lawelawe nui; e hoomaamaa.

Prac-ti′tion-er, *n.* Mea lawelawe ma kekahi o na oihana naauao.

Prāi′rĭe, *n.* Aina papu akea.

Prāiṣe, *n.* Mahalo; hoolea; hoonani.

Prāiṣe′wŏr-thy, *adj.* Ku i ka maha-loia.

Prănçe, *v.* E lelelele.

Prănç′er, *n.* Lio lelelele.

Prănk, *n.* Hana paani; hana lealea. SYN. frolic.

Prāte, *v.* E walaau wale.

Prāt-tle, *v.* Ka walaau o kamalii liilii.

Prăt′tler, *n.* Keiki liilii hoomaka wa-laau.

Prāy, *v.* E pule; e noi. SYN. supplicate.

Prāy′er, *n.* He pule; he noi. SYN. supplication.

Prāy′er-ful, *adj.* Haipule.

Prāy′er-less, *adj.* Pule ole; hooma-loka.

Prēach, *v.* E hai-olelo.

Prēach′er, *n.* He hai-olelo; kahuna pule.

Prē-ăd′am-īte, *adj.* Mamua′e o Adamu

Prē′am-ble, *n.* Olelo mua.

Pre-eā′ri-oŭs, *adj.* 1. Maopopo ole; loli wale. SYN. uncertain.

2. Paa ole.

3. Mahunehune. *In a precarious con-dition*, ola mahunehune.

Pre-eaū′tion, *n.* Ka hoomakaukau e. *To take the precaution*, e hoomakaukau e.

Pre-çēde′, *v.* E hele mamua.

Pre-çēd′ençe, | . Ke kulana oi.

Pre-çēd′en-çy, |

Prēç′e-dent, *n.* He ana hoohalike.

Pre-çēd′ing, *adj.* Mamua′e.

Prē′çept, *n.* Kauoha; olelo ao. SYN. maxim.

Pre-çēpt′or, *n.* Kumu-ao. SYN. teacher.

Prē′çinet, *n.* 1. Palena; mokuna. SYN. boundary.

2. He kauwahi.

Prē′çioŭs, *n.* Makamae; hiwahiwa.

Prēç′i-piçe, *n.* Pali.

Pre-çĭp′i-tan-çy, *n.* Pupuahulu; kiki.

Pre-çĭp′i-tāte, *v.* 1. E kiola iho. SYN. cast down.

2. E pupuahulu.

3. E hoohikilele.

Pre-çĭp′i-tā′tion, *n.* Ka hoohikilele ana.

Pre-çĭp′i-toŭs, *adj.* Palipali.

Pre-çiṣe′, *adj.* Kupono loa; pololei loa.

Pre-çiṣe′ly, *adv.* Like loa; ku like maoli. *Precisely so*, pela maoli no.

Pre-çiṣ′ion, *n.* Ke kupono loa; pololei loa.

Pre-çlūde′, *v.* E hoo-ke′; hookaaokoa.

Pre-eō′çioŭs, *adj.* Ulu wawe o ka noonoo.

Pre-eōç′i-ty, *n.* Ka ulu wawe o ka noo-noo.

Prē′eon-çēive′, *v.* E hooholo e ma ka manao.

Prē′çon-çērt′, *v.* E noonoo, a hooholo e mamua.

Pre-eūr′sor, *n.* 1. He elele. SYN. forerunner.

2. He ouli. SYN. harbinger.

Prĕd′a-to-ry, *adj.* Powa; pakaha.
SYN. plundering.

Prĕd′e-cĕs′sor, *n.* Mea noho mua. *Predecessor in office,* mea noho mua ma ka oihana.

Pre-dĕs′ti-nāte, } *v.* E wae e mamua.
Pre-dĕs′tine, } SYN. foreordain.

Prĕ′de-tĕr′mīne, *v.* E hooholo e mamua.

Pre-die′a-ment, *n.* Pilikia.

Pre-dict′, *v.* E wanana; hai e mamua.* SYN. foretell.

Pre-dic′tion, *n.* He wanana. SYN. prophesy.

Prĕ′di-lēc′tion, *n.* Ka huli e o ka manao. SYN. partiality.

Prĕ′dis-pōse′, *v.* E hilinai e ka manao.

Prĕ′dis-po-si′tion, *n.* He hilinai e.

Pre-dŏm′i-nant, *adj.* Pookela; oi i-mua o na mea e.

Pre-dŏm′i-nāte, *v.* E kela; e oi.

Prē-ĕm′i-nençe, *n.* Ka noho pookela ana.

Prē-ĕm′i-nent, *adj.* Pookela.

Prē-ĕmpt′, *v.* E loaa i ka pono o ke kuai mua.

Prē-ĕmp′tion, *n.* Ka pono o ke kuai mua.

Prē′en-gāġe′, *v.* E hoopaa e; e lilo e.

Prē′en-gāġe′ment, *n.* Ka hoopaa e ana; lilo e ana.

Prē′ex-ist′, *v.* E ola e; e waiho e.

Prē′ex-ist′ent, *adj.* Ola ana mamua; e waiho ana mamua.

Prĕf′açe, *n.* Olelo hoakaka mua.

Pre-fĕr′, *v.* E aho.

Prĕf′er-a-ble. *adj.* Aho ia.

Prĕf′er-ançe, *n.* Ke koho ana; ka oi ma ke koho.

Pre-fĕr′ment, *n.* Ka hookiekie an′ae ma ka oihana.

Pre-fiġ′ūre, *v.* E hoike e ma na hoailona.

Pre-fix′, *v.* E kakau mamua iho.

Prĕġ′nan-çy, *n.* Hapai keiki.

Prĕġ′nant, *adj.* 1. Hapai.
2. Paapu; piha. SYN. full.

Pre-jūdġe′, *v.* E hooholo e mamua o ka lohe ana.

Prĕj′u-diçe, *n.* Manao ino; manao kue.

Prĕj′u-di′çial, *adj.* Kue i ka pono.

Prĕl′ate, *n.* Kahuna kiekie o ka ekalesia Roma.

Pre-lim′i-na-ry, *adj.* Mua; hoomakaukau. SYN. preparatory.

Prĕ′lūde, *n.* 1. He mele hoomaka aha mele.
2. Hana hoomakaukau; olelo mua.

Prĕ′ma-tūre′, *adj.* Mamua o ka wa kupono.

Prĕ′ma-tūre′ly, *adv.* Mamua′e o ka manawa.

Pre-mĕd′i-tāte, *v.* E noonoo e mamua.

Pre-mĕd′i-tāt′ed, *adj.* Noonoo e ia.

Prē′mier, *n.* Kuhina nui; ka mua.

Prĕm′is-es, *n.* Ka hale me kona pa.

Prē′mi-um, *n.* 1. Makana apono. SYN. reward; prize.
2. Uku makahiki no ka panai ola.

Prē′mo-ni′tion, *n.* He halia; he hihio no na mea e hiki mai ana.

Prē-ŏe′cu-pȳ, *v.* 1. E lilo e; e hoopaa e.
2. E komo e.

Prĕp′a-rā′tion, *n.* Ka hoomakaukau ana.

Pre-pâr′a-to-ry, *adj.* Hoomakaukau

Pre-pāre′, *v.* E hoomakaukau; e lolii; e liuliu.

Prē-pāȳ′, *v.* E uku e.

Pre-pŏn′der-āte, *v.* E kaumaha oi; e koikoi oi aku. SYN. outweigh.

Prĕp′o-si′tion, *n.* Inaleo.

Prē′pŏs-sĕss′ing, *adj.* Onaona; nakui.

Pre-pŏs′ter-oŭs, *adj.* Lapuwale. SYN. absurd.

Prē-rĕq′ui-sīte, *n.* He mea e pono ai.

Pre-rŏġ′a-tive, *n.* Pono pili paa. *Royal prerogative,* pono pili paa i ka Moi.

Prē-sāġe′, *v.* E hoike e mai; e wanana.

Prĕs′by-tĕr-y, *n.* Aha luna kahiko.

Prē′sçi-ençe, *n.* Ka ike no na mea e hiki mai ana. SYN. foresight.

Pre-scribe′, *v.* 1. E hoonoho i kanawai; a rula paha.
2. E haawi i laau lapaau.

Pre-scrip′tion, *n.* Olelo kuhikuhi laau lapaau.

Pre-scrip′tive, *adj.* Mai kahiko mai. *Prescriptive right,* pono mai kahiko mai.

Prĕs′ençe, *n.* 1. Ke alo. *Royal presence,* alo Moi.
2. *Presence of mind,* makaukau o ka noonoo; pilihua ole.

Prĕs′ent, *n.* 1. He makana.
2. *The present,* ke au e hele nei.

Prĕs′ent, *adv.* Eia; maanei; ke noho nei.

Pre-sent′, *v.* 1. E haawi. SYN. give.
2. E hoike. SYN. show.

Pre-sĕnt′a-ble, *adj.* Kohu pono; kupono ke ku imua.

Prĕ′sen-tā′tion, *n.* Ka haawi ana; ka lohe ana.

Pre-sĕn′ti-ment, *n.* He halia. SYN. premonition.

Prĕs′ent-ly, *adv.* Kokoke. SYN. soon; shortly.

Prĕs′er-vā′tion, *n.* Ka hoomalu ana; ka malama ana.

Pre-sĕrve′, *v.* 1. E malama.
2. E hoomoa i mea ono mai na hua ai.

Pre-sĕrve′, *n.* Mea ono i hoomoaia mai na hua ai.

Pre-sĕrv′er, *n.* Kahu malama; mea nana e hoopakele.

Pre-side′, *v.* E noho i poo.

Prĕs′i-den-çy, *n.* 1. Hoomalu peresidena.
2. Ka oihana peresidena. *Under the presidency of,* malalo o ka hoomalu peresidena ana o.

Prĕs′i-dent, *n.* Peresidena.

Prĕṣ'i-dĕn'tial, *adj.* Pili i ka oihana peresidena.

Prĕss, *v.* 1. E kaomi; e uwi. SYN. squeeze.

2. E hoo-ke'. SYN. crowd.

3. E kono ikaika. SYN. urge.

4. E hii; hiipoi. SYN. embrace.

Prĕss, *n.* 1. Mikini kaomi.

2. He pai palapala.

3. Na palapala i paiia o na ano a pau.

4. Puuluulu o kanaka. SYN. crowd.

Prĕss'ing, *adj.* E kono ana; e kaohi ana.

Prĕss'ure, *n,* Ke kaomi ana; ke kaohi ana.

Prĕs-tíge', *n.* Ke kaulana.

Prĕs'to, *adv.* Emoole.

Pre-ṣūme', *v.* 1. E manao wale. SYN. suppose.

2. E mahaoi; e lalau; ho-aa'no.

Pre-ṣŭmp'tion, *n.* 1. Ka manao wale. SYN. supposition.

Pre-ṣŭmp'tu-oŭs, *adj.* Ho-aa'no.

Pre-tĕnd', *v.* E hookamani. SYN. feign.

Pre-tĕnse', *n.* Hoopohala.

Pre-tĕn'sion, *n.* Manao wale; manao hookamani.

Prē'ter-nät'u-ral, *adj.* Eehia; kupai-anaha. SYN. supernatural.

Prē'text, *n.* Kumu hoopohala. SYN. pretense.

Prĕt'ty, *adj.* 1. Maikai; hoonu'anu'a.

2. *Pretty good,* maikai iki. *Pretty bad,* ino no.

Pre-vāil', *v.* E laha; e lanakila.

Pre-vāil'ing, *adj.* 1. Lanakila; laha.

2. Mau. *Prevailing wind,* makani mau.

Prĕv'a-lençe, *n.* Ka laha ana.

Prĕv'a-lent, *adj.* Laha. *Prevalent sickness,* mai laha.

Pre-vär'i-eāte, *v.* E hauhili ma ka olelo.

Pre-vär'i-eā'tion, *n.* Olelo hauhili.

Pre-vĕnt', *v.* E keakea; e pale.

Pre-vĕn'tion, *n.* Ke keakea ana; ka pale ana.

Pre-vĕnt'ive, *n.* Kumu keakea; kumu pale.

Prĕ'vi-oŭs, *adj.* Mua. *Move the previous question,* e ninau a no.

Prĕ'vi-ous-ly, *adv.* Mamua iho.

Prey, *n.* Waiwai pio; mea pio.

Prey, *v.* E hao; e pakaha. *Beast of prey,* holoholona ai holoholona.

Priçe, *n.* Kumukuai.

Priçe, *v.* E ninau i ke kumukuai.

Priçe-eŭr'rent, *n.* Kumukuai o ka mākeke.

Priçe'less, *adj.* Makamae. SYN. precious.

Prick, *v.* E hou me ka mea oioi.

Prick'er, *n.* Mea oioi. SYN. brier.

Prick'ly-peâr', *n.* Panini; pa-bipi.

Pride, *n.* Haaheo; hookiekie.

Priĕst, *n.* Kahuna pule.

Priĕst'eraft, *n.* Hoomana hookamani.

Priĕst'hŏŏd, *n.* Oihana kahunapule.

Priĕst-rĭd'den, *adj.* Malalo loa o ka mana o ke kahuna pule.

Prig, *n.* Mea akena wale.

Prig'gish, *adj.* Akena wale.

Pri'ma-ry, *adj.* Mua; kumu mua.

Prime, *adj.* 1. Mua; nui. *Prime cause,* kumu nui; kumu mua. SYN. chief.

2. Oi o ka maikai.

3. *Prime of life,* wa oo; wa ikaika.

Prim'er, *n.* Buke A; kumumua.

Pri-mē'val, *adj.* No kinohi.

Prim'ing, *n.* 1. Pauda ki pu.

2. Ka hamo mua ana o ka pena.

Prim'i-tive, *adj.* Kinohou.

Prim'ness, *n.* Ano hookiekie.

Pri'mo-gĕn'i-tor, *n.* Kupuna mua.

Pri'mo-gĕn'i-türe, *n.* Ka pono o ka hanau mua. SYN. birthright.

Prinçe, *n.* Keiki moi; he alii.

Prinçe'ly, *adj.* 1. Me he moi la.

2. Kamahao; nani. *A princely gift,* he makana nani.

Prin'çess, *n.* He alii wahine.

Prin'çi-pal, *adj.* Nui. Mua. SYN. chief.

Prin'çi-pal, *n.* 1. Ke poo o ke kula nui.

2. Kumupaa.

Prin'çi-ple, *n.* Loina; oiaio; mole. *A man of principle,* he kanaka kupaa ma ka oiaio.

Prink, *v.* E kahiko i ke kino a nani.

Print, *v.* E pai.

Print, *v.* 1. He meheu.

2. Lole kalakoa.

3. He kii.

Print'er, *n.* Kanaka pai palapala.

Print'ing, *n.* Ke pai ana.

Print'ing-ŏf'fiçe, *n.* Hale pai palapala.

Print'ing-pā'per, *n.* Pepa pai palapala.

Print'ing-prĕss', *n.* Mikini pai palapala.

Pri'or, *adv.* Mamua ae. SYN. previous.

Pri-ŏr'i-ty, *n.* Ka mua. *Priority of birth,* ka mua ma ka hanau ana.

Priṣm, *n.* Kinopaa aoao like lua, ili laumania.

Priṣ'on, *n.* Hale paahao.

Priṣ'on-er, *n.* He paahao.

Pris'tine, *adj.* No kinohi. SYN. primeval.

Pri'va-çy, *n.* Kahi mehameha; kahi malu'.

Pri'vate, *adj.* Mehameha; malu'; huna ia.

Pri'vate, *n.* He koa maoli.

Pri-vā'tion, *n.* He nele.

Priv'i-lege, *n.* He pono; he pomaikai.

Priv'i-ly, *adj.* Malu'. SYN. secretly.

Priv'y, *n.* Hale liilii.

Priv'y, *adj.* 1. Malu'. *Privy council,* Aha kuka' malu'.

2. Ike malu'; ae malu'.

Prize, *n.* Uku makana no ka oi.

Prize, *v.* E manao nui aku; e kau nui ka manao.

Prize'-fight'er, *n.* Mea hakaka, aume-ume paha, no ka makana.
Pro and con. Kokua a kue.
Prŏb'a-bil'i-ty, *n.* Ka oiaio paha.
Prŏb'a-ble, *adj.* Oiaio paha; oiaio i ka nana'ku.
Prŏb'a-bly, *adv.* Pela paha; oiaio paha.
Pro'bate, *n.* Ka hooia ana i na palapala hooilina. *Probate court,* aha hooia palapala hooilina.
Pro-bā'tion, *n.* 1. He wa hoao.
2. He hoao; hooia.
Pro-bā'tion-a-ry, *adj.* Hoao; hooia.
Probe, *n.* He kui-hou a ke kauka.
Probe, *v.* E hookomo i ke kui hou.
Prŏb'i-ty, *n.* Oiaio; hoopono. SYN. honesty.
Prŏb'lem, *n.* Manaohai; nanehai.
Prŏb'lem-ăt'ic, *adj* Maopopo ole.
Pro-bŏs'çis, *n.* He nuku loloa.
Pro-çēd'ūre, *n.* Ka holo ana o ka hana.
Pro-çēed', *v.* 1. E hele imua; maalo ae.
2. *Proceed from,* e puka mai no loko ae.
Pro-çeed'ing, *n.* Ka hana.
Prō'çeeds, *n.* Na loaa. SYN. avails.
Prŏç'ess, *n.* 1. He hana. *A legal process,* he hana o ke kanawai.
2. *Process of time,* ka nee ana o ka manawa.
3. *Process of thought,* ka holo ana o ka noonoo.
Pro-çĕs'sion, *n.* He huakai hele.
Pro-claim', *v.* E hoolaha. SYN. publish.
Prŏc'la-mā'tion, *n.* He olelo hoolaha; olelo kukala.
Pro-cliv'i-ty, *n.* Ka hilinai ana. SYN. propensity.
Pro-crăs'ti-nāte, *v.* E hookaulua. SYN. put off; delay.
Pro-crăs'ti-nā'tion, *n.* Ka hookaulua ana.
Pro-cūr'a-ble, *adj.* Hiki ke loaa; loaa no.
Pro-cūre', *v.* E loaa. SYN. obtain.
Prŏd'i-gal, *adj.* Uhauha; maunauna.
Prŏd'i-găl'i-ty, *n.* Ka uhauha; ka pakela. SYN. profusion; extravagance.
Pro-di'gious, *adj.* Nui launa ole.
Prŏd'i-gy, *n.* Mea kupaianaha.
Pro-dūce', *v.* 1. E hoohua mai.
2. E waiho mai. SYN. bring forward.
Prŏd'uçe, *n.* 1. Na hua. SYN. fruit.
Pro-dūç'er, *n.* Mea nana e hoohua.
Prŏd'uct, *n.* 1. Hua. SYN. fruit.
2. Hualoaa.
Pro-dŭç'tion, *n.* 1. Hua; ka hoohua ana.
2. Ka waiho ana mai.
Pro-dŭct'ive, *adj.* Hua nui.
Prŏf'a-nā'tion, *n.* Ka hana ino ana i na mea laa.
Pro-fāne', *v.* 1. E hana ino.
2. E hana ino i na mea laa.
3. E hoohaumia.

Pro-fāne', *adj.* 1. Laa ole. SYN. secular.
2. Kuamuamu.
Pro-fān'i-ty, *n.* 1. Ka lawe ino ana i ka inoa o Ke Akua.
2. Ka hoohaumia ana i na mea laa.
Pro-fĕss', *v.* E hooia me ka waha.
Pro-fĕs'sion, *n.* 1. Ka hooia ana me ka waha.
2. He oihana naauao.
Pro-fĕs'sion-al, *adj.* Pili oihana. *Professional services,* Kokua pili oihana.
Pro-fĕs'sor, *n.* 1. Mea e hooia ana.
2. Kumu-ao no na lala kiekie o ka ike.
Pro-fĕs'sor-ship, *n.* Oihana kumu-ao ma ke kula nui.
Prŏf'fer, *v.* E haawi.
Pro-fi'çien-çy, *n.* Ka makaukau. *A great degree of proficiency,* makaukau maoli.
Pro-fi'çient, *adj.* Makaukau; akamai.
Prō'fīle, *n.* He kaha helehelena.
Prŏf'it, *v.* E ao; e puka.
Prŏf'it, *n.* Puka; waiwai; pomaikai.
Prŏf'it-a-ble, *adj.* Waiwai; makepono; pomaikai.
Prŏf'it-a-bly, *adv.* Me ka makepono.
Prŏf'li-ga-çy, *n.* Ano uhauha.
Prŏf'li-gate, *adj.* Uhauha.
Pro-found', *adj.* Hohonu.
Pro-found'ly, *adv.* 1. Loa. *Profoundly sorrowful,* kaumaha loa.
2. Hohonu. *Profoundly wise,* hohonu ka ike. *Profoundly skilled,* hohonu ke akamai.
Pro-fŭn'di-ty, *n.* Ka hohonu. SYN. depth.
Pro-fūse', *adj.* Pakela loa; makena wale. SYN. lavish.
Pro-fū'sion, *n.* Paapu wale; makena loa.
Pro-gĕn-i-tor, *n.* He kupuna.
Prŏg'e-ny, *n.* Na keiki. SYN. offspring.
Prog-nŏs'ti-cāte, *v.* E hoike e mamua. SYN. foretell.
Prog-nŏs'ti-cā'tion, *n.* Ka wanana ana.
Prō'gram, } *n.* Papa hoike no na
Prō'grămme, } hana.
Prŏg'ress, *n.* 1. Ka holomua.
2. Ka nee ana imua.
Pro-grĕss', *v.* E nee imua.
Pro-grĕs'sion, *n.* Ka nee ana imua.
Pro-grĕs'sive, *adj.* Holo mua.
Pro-hib'it, *v.* E pa'pa'; e hookapu.
Prō'hi-bi'tion, *n.* Ka papa ana; ka hookapu ana.
Pro-hib'i-to-ry, *adj.* Hookapu.
Pro-jĕct', *v.* 1. E kikoo iwaho; e kiola.
2. E hoomakaukau hana. SYN. to plan.
Prŏj'ect, *n.* Hana i noonoo ia. SYN. plan.
Pro-jĕc'tile, *n.* Mea lele.
Pro-jĕct'ing, *adj.* E o ana iwaho.
Pro-jĕc'tion, *n.* 1. Mea e o ana iwaho.
2. Ka hoolele ana. SYN. throwing forward.
Pro-lif'ic, *adj.* Hua nui; hana nui.

Prŏ′lix, *adj.* Loihi a luhi.
Pro-lŏng′, *v.* E hooloihi; hookaulua·
Prŏ′lon-gā′tion, *n.* Ka hooloihi ana.
Prŏm′e-nāde′, *v.* E holoholo.
Prŏm′i-nence, *n.* Ka hookiekie ana'e.
Prŏm′i-nent, *adj.* Kiekie; ohuku. *A prominent man*, he kanaka kiekie; kanaka koikoi.
Prŏm′i-nent-ly, *adv.* Me ka maopopo lea. *To bring prominently forward*, e hoike maopopo lea mai.
Pro-mis′cu-oŭs, *adj.* Huikau.
Prŏm′ise, *n.* He olelo paa.
Prŏm′is-so-ry Note, *n.* Bila hooaie′.
Prŏm′on-to-ry, *n.* Lae kiekie.
Pro-mōte′, *v.* 1. E kokua; e hooikaika.
2. E hookiekie ae ma ka oihana.
Pro-mŏt′er, *n.* Mea e kokua ana.
Pro-mō′tion, *n.* Ka hookiekie ana'e.
Prŏmpt, *adj.* Makaukau; kuoo. SYN. ready.
Prŏmpt, *v.* E paipai.
Prŏmpt′i-tŭde, *n.* Ke ano kuoo; makaukau.
Prŏmpt′ly, *adv.* Me ka hakalia ole.
Pro-mŭl′gāte, *v.* E hoolaha. SYN. proclaim.
Prŏ′mul-gā′tion, *n.* Ka hoolaha ana.
Prōne, *adj.* 1. Moe alo ilalo.
2. Maa; walea.
Prŏng, n. Manamana.
Prō′noun, *n.* Pani inoa.
Pro-noŭnce′, *v.* E puana leo.
Prō-noŭnced′, *adj.* Ike lea ia. *A pronounced liar*, he kanaka wahahee i ike lea ia.
Pro-nŭn′çi-ā′tion, *n.* Ka puana leo.
Prŏŏf, *n.* 1. Olelo hooia; ka hooia ana.
2. He pai mua, i mea hooponoponoia.
Prŏŏf, *adj.* Paa. *Water proof*, paa i komo ole ai ka wai.
Prŏŏf′sheet, *n.* He pepa i pai mua ia no ka hooponopono ana.
Prŏp, *n.* He koo; he uuu; makia. SYN. support.
Prŏp′a-gāte, *v.* E hoolaha. SYN. disseminate.
Prŏp′a-gā′tion, *n.* Ka hoolaha ana.
Pro-pĕl′, *v.* E hoonee imua.
Pro-pĕl′ler, *n.* 1. Mea e hoonee imua.
2. Mokumahu me ka huila kaa mahope.
Pro-pĕn′si-ty, *n.* Ka hilinai ana. *Propensity to evil*, ka hilinai ana i ka hewa.
Prŏp′er, *adj.* Kupono. SYN. suitable; fit.
2. *Proper noun*, inoa pili kino; inoa maoli.
Prŏp′er-ly, *adv.* Kupono.
Prŏp′er-ty, *n.* 1. Waiwai. *Personal property*, waiwai pili kino.
2. Ano. SYN. quality.
Prŏph′e-cў, *n.* Olelo wanana. SYN. prediction.
Prŏph′e-sў, *v.* E wanana. SYN. predict.
Prŏph′et, *n.* He kaula.
Pro-phĕt′ic, *adj.* Wanana ia.

Pro-pĭn′qui-ty, *n.* Ke kokoke. SYN. neighborhood.
Pro-pi′ti-āte, *v.* E hoolaulea.
Pro-pi′ti-ā′tion, *n.* He kalahala.
Pro-pi′tioŭs, *adj.* Laulea; oluolu.
Pro-pŏr′tion, *n.* 1. Kaukolu.
2. Ka hookaulike.
Pro-pŏr′tion-al, *adj.* Hookaulike.
Pro-pŏr′tion-āte, *adj.* Kaulike. *A proportionate quantity*, he kuanite kau like.
Pro-pōs′al, *n.* He manao e hai aku; he noi e mare.
Pro-pōse′, *v.* E hai manao; e noi. *Propose marriage*, e noi e mare.
Prŏp′o-si′tion, *n.* Manaohai.
Pro-pound′, *v.* E waiho mai.
Pro-pri′e-tor, *n.* He haku; he ona.
Pro-pri′e-tor-ship, *n.* Ka noho haku ana.
Pro-pri′e-ty, *n.* Ka pono; ka mea ku pono.
Prŏ′ro-gā′tion, *n.* Ka hoopau ana. *Prorogation of Legislature*, ka hoopau ana o ka Ahaolelo.
Pro-rōgue′, *v.* E hoopau. *Prorogue Legislature*, e hoopau i ka Ahaolelo.
Pro-scribe′, *v.* E hoahewa e make; e kipaku mawaho ae o ka mana o ke kanawai.
Prōse, n. Kela me keia ano olelo, koe ke mele.
Prōs′e-cūte, *v.* 1. E hoopii kanawai.
2. E hoomau ma ka hooikaika.
Prŏs′e-cū′tion, *n.* 1. Ka hoopii ana.
2. Ka aoao hoopii.
3. Ka hooikaika ana.
Prŏs′e-lўte, *v.* E kaana.
Prŏs′peet, *n.* Nanaina.
Pro-spĕet′ive, *adj.* Pili i ka wa e hiki mai ana.
Pro-spĕet′us, *n.* He olelo hoakaka mua no kekahi hana.
Prŏs′per, *v.* E holomua; e kuonoono.
Pros-pĕr′i-ty, *n.* Pomaikai; kuonoono.
Prŏs′per-oŭs, *adj.* Kuonoono; pomaikai.
Prŏs′ti-tūte, *n.* Wahine hookamakama.
Prŏs′ti-tūte, *v.* 1. E hookamakama.
2. E hoohaahaa; hoohaumia.
Prŏs′trāte, *adj.* 1. Hina ilalo; kulai ia.
2. Luuluu.
Prŏs′trāte, *v.* E kulou; e kulai iho.
Pros-trā′tion, *n.* 1. Luuluu.
2. Ke kulai ana; moe ana ma ke alo.
Prōs′ў, *adj.* Luhi ma ka olelo; ma ke kakau paha.
Pro-tĕet′, *v.* E hoomalu; e malama.
Pro-tĕe′tion, *n.* Mea e malu ai; kumu hoomalu; ka hoomalu ana.
Pro-tĕet′or, *n.* Kahu malama.
Pro-tĕet′or-ate, *n.* Ka hoomalu ana.
Prŏ′te-ge′ (prŏ′tăy-zhăy), *n.* Keiki hanai; punahele.
Pro-test′, *n.* He olelo hoohalahala; he olelo hoole.

Pro-tĕst′, *v.* E hoohalahala; e hoole.
Prŏt′est-ant, *n.* Mea ku-e′ i ka ekalesia o Roma; he hoole pope.
Prŏt′est-ant-ism, *n.* Hoole pope.
Prŏt′es-tā′tion, *n.* Ka hoole hoohiki.
Prō′to-col, *n.* Ke kakau mua o ke kuikahi.
Pro-trăet′, *v.* E hoomau aku a loihi.
Pro-trŭde′, *v.* 1. E hoo-o′ iwaho; e ohuku.
2. E lewalewa. SYN. hang out.
Pro-tu′ber-ançe, *n.* He puu; mea oi iwaho
Prŏud, *adj.* Hookano; haanui.
Prŏud′ly, *adv.* Me ka hookano; ka hookiekie.
Prove, *v.* E hooia; e hoao.
Prŏv′en-der, *n.* Ai na na holoholona.
Prŏv′erb, *n.* Olelo ao.
Pro-vēr′bi-al, *adj.* Olelo nui ia; wawa ia.
Pro-vide′, *v.* E hoomakaukau; hoolako; e lolii. SYN. prepare.
Pro-vid′ed, *conj.* Ina nae. SYN. on condition; with the understanding.
Prŏv′i-dençe, *n.* Ka lima o Ke Akua.
Prŏv′i-dent, *adj.* Hoomakaukau e mamua.
Prŏv′i-dĕn′tial, *adj.* Na ka lima o Ke Akua.
Pro-vid′er, *n.* Mea hoomakaukau; hoolako.
Prŏv′inçe, *n.* 1. He mahele o ke aupuni i mamao aku mai ke poo oihana.
2. He mahele o ka oihana.
3. He panalaau.
Pro-vin′çial-ism, *n.* Olelo kuaaina.
Pro-vis′ion, *n.* 1. He ai i hoomakaukauia.
2. Ka hoomakaukau ana.
Pro-vis′ion-al, *adj.* Ku i ka wa.
Pro-vi′so, *n.* He olelo ku i ka wa.
Prŏv′o-cā′tion, *n.* Kumu hoonaukiuki.
Pro-vōke′, *v.* 1. E hoonaukiuki; e hoohuhu.
2. E hooeueu; hoolalelale. SYN. incite.
Pro-vōk′ing, *p. a.* Ukiuki.
Prŏv′ost-mär′shal, *n.* Luna hopu koa mahuka.
Prow, *n.* Ka ihu o ka moku. SYN. bow.
Prow′ess, *n.* Koa. SYN. valor.
Prowl, *v.* E kokolo me he holoholona hihiu la.
Prŏx′i-māte, *adj.* Kokoke; ane.
Prox-im′i-ty, *n.* Kahi kokoke. SYN. vicinity.
Prŏx′i-mo, *n.* He hope; he agena.
Prŏx′y, *n.* He panai o kekahi mahina′e.
Pru′dençe, *n.* Noonoo akahele. SYN. discretion.
Pru′dent, *adj.* Akahele ma ka noonoo; noeau.
Pru′dent-ly, *adv.* Me ke akahele; me ka noonoo. SYN. discreetly.
Prūne, *v.* E oki i na lala. SYN. trim.

Prȳ, *v.* 1. E hoomakakiu.
2. E ohiki; e mahiki; e unu.
Psălm (säm), *n.* Halelu.
Psălm′ist, *n.* Mea haku halelu.
Psạl′ter (sawl′ter), *n.* Ka buke o na Halelu.
Pshạw, *interj.* Ka! Kahaha!
Psȳ-chŏl′o-gy, *n.* Ka ike e pili ana i ka uhane o kanaka.
Pū′ber-ty, *n.* Wa oo.
Pŭb′lie, *n.* Ka lahui; ke akea. *Public interest,* na pono o ka lahui. *In public,* ma ke akea.
Pŭb′li-can, *n.* 1. Kanaka kuai waiona.
2. He luna auhau, ma ka baibala.
Pŭb′li-cā′tion, *n.* 1. Kela me keia palapala.
2. Ka hoolaha ana.
3. Mea i hoolahaia.
Pub-lie′i-ty, *n.* Ka hoo-akea ana; ka laulaha.
Pŭb′lie-ly, *adv.* Ma ke akea; imua o ka lehulehu.
Pŭb′lie-spir′it-ed, *adj.* Makee i ka pono o ka lehulehu.
Pŭb′lish, *v.* 1. E hoolaha; e kukala. SYN. proclaim.
2. E hoopuka.
Pŭb′lish-er, *n.* Mea hoopuka palapala.
Pŭek′er, *v.* E mio; minoi; muki.
Pŭd′ding, *n.* He pudina; mea ai.
Pŭd′dle, *n.* Kiowai.
Pu′er-ile, *adj.* Kohu kamalii. SYN. childish.
Pŭff, *v.* E puhi; e punoho.
2. E haanou. SYN. brag.
Pŭff, *n.* 1. He olelo hoomalimali.
2. Puahiohio.
Pŭg, *n.* Keko; ilio liilii me ka ihu pe′ pe.
Pŭ′gil-ism, *n.* Mokomoko.
Pŭ′gil-ist, *n.* Mea akamai i ka moko moko.
Pŭg-nā′çioŭs, *adj.* Hikiwawe i ka hakaka wale.
Pu-is′sant, *adj.* Ikaika; mana. SYN. mighty; powerful.
Pūke, *v.* E luai; hoolualuai. SYN. vomit.
Pŭll, *v.* 1. E huki; e uhuki.
2. E hoe. SYN. row.
3. *Pull fruit from a tree,* e lou′lu.
Pŭl′let, *n.* Moa wahine opio.
Pŭl′ley, *n.* He pokakaa; he balaka. SYN. block.
Pŭl′mo-na-ry, *adj.* Pili i ke ake mama.
Pŭlp, *n.* Ka i-o o na hua ai.
2. Kela me keia mea palupalu.
Pŭl′pit, *n.* He awai luakini.
Pŭl′säte, *v.* 1. E pana. SYN. beat.
2. Koni. SYN. throb.
Pul-sā′tion, *n.* He pana; he koni.
Pŭlse, *n.* Ka pana.
Pŭl′ver-i-zā′tion, *n.* Ka hooaeae ana o na mea kino paa.

Pŭl-ver-īze, v. E aokaoka.

Pŭm'ĭçe, n. Pohaku pele lana ma ka wai.

Pŭmp, n. He pauma.

Pŭmp, v. 1. E pauma.

2. E nieniele maalea.

Pŭmp'kin, n. Ipu pu.

Pŭn, n. Olelo ano lua.

Pŭnch, n. 1. He hao hou puka.

2. He kui.

Pŭnch, v. E hou. SYN. poke.

Pŭnet'u-al, adj. Kuoo; inakaala; ku i ka manawa.

Pŭnet'u-ăl'i-ty, n. Ka makaala i ka wa kupono.

Pŭnet'u-āte, v. E hookomo i na kiko.

Pŭnet'u-ā'tion, n. Ke kiko ana.

Pŭnet'ūre, n. He pukapuka.

Pŭn'ġent, adj. Awahia.

Pŭn'ish, v. E hoopai; e hili; e hahau. SYN. chastise; correct.

Pŭn'ish-a-ble, adj. Ku i ka hoopai.

Pŭn'ish-ment, n. Ka hoopai.

Pū'ny, adj. Aa; wiwi; nawaliwali.

Pŭp } n. Ilio keiki.
Pŭp'py }

Pū'pĭl, n. 1. Haumana.

2. Onohi maka.

Pŭrr, v. E nunulu.

Pur'chase, v. E kuai; e loaa ma ke kuai ana. SYN. buy.

Pur'chase, n. Ke kuai ana.

Pur'chas-er, n. Mea nana e kuai. SYN. buyer.

Pūre, adj. Maemae; makamae.

Pūre'ly, adv. 1. Me ka maemae.

2. Wale no. SYN. merely.

Pur'ga-tive, n. Laau hoo-naha'.

Pūrġe, v. 1. E hoomaemae; e kala.

2. E naha'; hoo naha'.

Pū'ri-fi-cā'tion, n. Ka hoomaemae ana.

Pū'ri-fi'er, n. Mea hoomaemae.

Pū'ri-fȳ, v. E hoomaemae; e hiuwai.

Pū'ri-ty, n. Ka maemae.

Pur-loin', v. E kaili; e aihue. SYN. pilfer.

Pur-loin'er, n. Mea kaili wale.

Pûr'ple, n. Lole makue; poni; uliuli.

Pûr'ple, adj. Poni.

Pûr'port, n. Ano. SYN. meaning.

Pûr'pose (pus), n. Manao paa. SYN. intention.

Pûr'pose, v. E manao paa. SYN. intend.

Pûr'pose-ly, adv. Me ka manao e ma-mua. SYN. intentionally.

Pûrṣe, n. Aa moni; eke dala.

Pûrse'proud, adj. Hookiekie mamu-li o ka waiwai.

Pûrs'er, n. Luna uku dala moku.

Pur-sū'ant, adj. Mamuli o. SYN. con-formably.

Pur-sū'er, n. Mea hahai; mea alualu.

Pur-sūe', v. 1. E hahai; e alualu.

2. To pursue study, e hahai mamuli o ka ike.

Pur-sūit', n. 1. Ka hahai ana; ka alu-alu ana.

2. He oihana. SYN. calling; occupa-tion.

Pur-vey', v. E hoolako i ai.

Pur-vey'or, n. Kuene; mea hoolako i kela me keia mea e pono ai. SYN. steward.

Pŭs, n. Palahehe.

Pŭsh, v. E koo; e pahu.

Pŭsh'ing, adj. Makaala; mikiala. SYN. energetic.

Pū'sil-la-nĭm'i-ty, n. Maka'u wale. SYN. cowardice.

Pū'sil-lăn'i-moŭs, adj. Maka'u wale. SYN. cowardly.

Pŭss, n. Popoki; owao. SYN. cat.

Pŭs'tūle, n. Puupuu liilii. SYN. pimple.

Pŭt, v. E waiho.

Pū'tre-fāe'tion, n. He palaho'.

Pū'tre-fȳ, v. E palaho'.

Pū'trid, adj. Palaho'.

Pŭt'ty, n. He pati; mea hoopaa aniani.

Pŭz'zle, v. E hoohuahualau; e hoopo-hihihi.

Pŭz'zling, adj. Pohihihi; hoohuahua-lau.

Pȳg-my, n. He keko; mea iii.

Pȳr'a-mid, n. Puuoa; piramida.

Pȳ-rŏm'e-ter, n. Mea ana wela nui.

Pȳr'o-tĕch'ny, n. Oihana hana ahika-olele.

Pȳr'o-tĕch'nist, n. Kanaka hana i na ahikaolele.

Q

Quăck, *n.* 1. Leo o ka manu ka'ka'.
2. Kauka hemahema.

Quăck'er-y, *n.* Ka akena wale ma ka ke lapaau.

Quad'ran-gle, *n.* He huina-ha.

Quad'rant, *n.* 1. Ka hapaha' o ka poai.
2. Mea ana kiekie.

Quad-răt'ic, *adj.* Pili i ka huinaha' like.

Quad-răt'ic e-qua'tion, *n.* Hoohalike mana elua.

Quad'ri-lăt'er-al, *n.* Ili aoao eha'.

Qua-drille', *n.* He hula pa-ha'.

Quad-rill'ion, *n.* Kuaderiliona.

Quad-roōn', *n.* He hapa nika.

Quad-rū'ma-noŭs, *n.* Lima eha'.

Quad'ru-ped, *n.* Holoholona wawae eha'.

Quad-rū'ple, *adj.* Pa-ha'.

Quăff, *v.* E inu a nui.

Quăg'mīre, *n.* Nenelu poho'. SYN. bog.

Quăint, *adj.* 1. Ano e; ano hoakaaka. *A quaint expression,* he olelo ano e. SYN. odd; whimsical.
2. Kahiko; no ka wa kahiko. SYN. antique.

Quāke, *v.* E haalulu; e naueue. SYN. tremble.

Quāk'er, *n.* He ano hoomana. SYN. Friend.

Qual'i-fi-câ'tion, *n.* 1. Ka makaukau.
2. Ka hoo-koe; hoohaike.

Qual'i-fi-er, *n.* 1. Hua olelo hookupono.
2. Mea e hoomakaukau ana.

Qual'i-fy, *v.* 1. E hoomakaukau mamuli o ka imi.
2. E hoohaiki; e hookupono.

Qual'i-ty, *n.* 1. Ano. *A good quality,* he ano maikai.
2. Kulana kiekie.

Quălm, *n.* 1. Poluea. SYN. nausea.
2. *Qualms of conscience,* ka hoopai o ka lunaikehala.

Quălm'ish, *adj.* Poluea. SYN. sick at the stomach.

Quan'da-ry, *n.* He pilikia no ka maopopo ole.

Quan'ti-ty, *n.* 1. Ka nui.
2. He kuanite.

Quar'an-tīne, *n.* Ka hoomalu ana, no ka mai ahulau.

Quar'rel, *v.* He hakaka; kumu ku-e'.

Quar'rel-sóme, *adj.* Hakaka; huhu wale.

Quar'ry, *n.* 1. Lua kalai pohaku.
2. Ka loaa ma ke ki holoholona.

Quart, *n.* Hapaha galani; kuata.

Quar'ter, *n.* 1. Hapaha.
2. Kau-wahi.
3. He ahonui i ka enemi ma ke kaua.

Qua-tēr'ni-on, *n.* Eha'; he kauna. *Quaternion of soldiers,* eha' poe koa.

Quar'ters, *n.* Wahi noho.

Quar'ter-day, *n.* La hookaa aie.

Quar'ter-dĕck', *n.* Oneki o hope o ka moku, no na 'lii moku.

Quar'ter-ly, *adj.* Kela me keia hapaha.

Quar'ter-ly, *n.* Buke i paiia ma kela me keia hapa-ha.

Quar'ter-măs'ter, *n.* Luna hoomakaukau, hoolako, no ka puali koa.

Quar-tĕtte' }
Quar-tĕt' } *n.* Leo mele me na leo eha'.

Quar'to, *n.* He buke me na lau eha i ke kalana.

Quăsh, *v.* E hoopau. *Quash an indictment,* e hoopau i ka hoopii.

Quā'ver, *n.* 1. He haalulu o ka leo.
2. He leo mele.

Quay (kē), *n.* Uapo ku moku. SYN. wharf.

Queen, *n.* Moi wahine.

Queen dŏw'a-ger, *n.* Alii wahine, kane make.

Queer, *adj.* Ano e. SYN. odd; singular.

Quĕll, *v.* E hoopio. *Quell an insurrection,* e hoopio i ke kipi.

Quĕnch, *v.* 1. E kena. SYN. satisfy.
2. E kinai. *Quench fire,* e kinai i ke ahi me ka wai.

Quĕnch'a-ble, *adj.* Hiki ke kinaiia.

Quĕr'ist, *n.* Mea nieniele.

Quĕr'u-loŭs, *adj.* Nainai; na ole. SYN. complaining.

Quē'ry, *n.* He niele; he ninau.

Quĕst, *n.* Ka imi ana. SYN. search.

Quĕs'tion, *n.* 1. He ninau.
2. Kumu kanalua; kumu paio.

Quĕs'tion-a-ble, *adj.* Kanalua ia.

Quĕs'tion-er, *n.* Mea ninaninau.

Quib'ble, *n.* He olelo hauhili.

Quib'bler, *n.* Mea hauhili ma kana olelo.

Quick, *adj.* 1. Wikiwiki; mama.
2. Aapo. SYN. ready. *Quick to answer,* makaukau ma ka haina.

Quick'en, *v.* E hoo-eueu; hoolalelale.

Quick'lime, *n.* Puna i hoo-hu ole ia.

Quick'ly, *adv.* 1. Awiwi; mama.
2. Hopuhopualulu. SYN. hastily.

Quick'ness, *n.* Ka mama; ka hikiwawe.

Quick'sand, *n.* One poho'.

Quick'sïl'ver, n. Wai-dala.
Quick'-wit'ted, adj. Noili; maiele.
Quid, n. He pepee baka nau.
Quid'nunc, n. He holoholo olelo. SYN. gossip.
Qui-ēs'çent, adj. Malie; maha.
Qui'et, adj. 1. Malie; malielie; na. SYN. calm; tranquil.
2. Pohala.
Qui'et-ly, adv. Nihi; malie.
Qui'e-tūde, n. Ka malie; ka maha.
Qui-ē'tus, n. 1. Ka pio ana.
2. Make.
Quill, n. Hulu nui o ka manu.
Quill'pen, n. Peni hulu.
Quilt, n. Kapa apana. SYN. bed-quilt.
Qui'nïne, n. Laau lapaau fiva.
Quin-tëtte', } n. Leo mele me na leo elima.
Quin-tet, }
Quin-tü'ple, adj. Pa-lima.
Quire, n. He ope pepa, 24 kalana.
Quit, v. E ho-o'ki; e haalele. Quit the house, e haalele i ka hale.
Quit'claim, n. Palapala haalele kule-ana.

Quïte, adv. 1. Loa. Quite late, lohi loa; komo loa i ka po.
2. Quite lately, aohe liuliu.
3. Quite the thing, oia maoli no.
Quiv'er, n. He aa pua.
Quiv'er, v. 1. E hulili; e anapa.
2. E kapalili. Wings quiver, kapalili na eheu.
3. Haukeke. Lips quiver, haukeke na lehelehe.
4. E haalulu. SYN. quaver.
Quiz, v. E hoohuahualau; e loiloi.
Quön'dam, adj. No ka wa i hala. Quondam friend, he hoa o ka wa i hala.
Quö'rum, n. Ka hapa e lawa pono ai ka hana.
Quöta, n. Mahele kau-like.
Quo-tā'tion, n. 1. He olelo i unuhiia no loko mai o kekahi olelo e.
2. Market quotations, he papa hoike kumu kuai.
Quöte, v. E unuhi; e lawe i ko hai olelo.
Quöth, v. I akula; wahi. Quoth he, wahi ana.
Quö'tiënt, n. Helu puka.

R

Răb'bet, v. E hole i ka papa.
Rab'bit, n. Lapika; iole kahiki.
Rab'ble, n. He puulu kanaka; uluaoa.
Rab'bid, adj. Hehena; haehae.
Răçe, n. 1. He kukini; heihei.
2. He mamo. The five races of mankind, na mamo elima o kanaka.
Răçe'eöurse, n. Kahua heihei.
Răçe'horse, } n. Lio heihei.
Răç'er, }
Rack, v. E kupaka. Racked with pain, kupaka i ka eha.
Rack'et, n. Kamumu nui; walaau nui.
Ră'di-ançe, n. Malamalama alohilohi.
Ră'di-ant, adj. 1. Huali; olinolino; alohilohi.
2. Radiant with delight, alohilohi ka maka i ka hauoli.
Ră'di-āte, v. E kaa; e hohola.
Ră'di-ā'tion, n. Ke kaa ana; ka hohola ana.
Ră'di-ā'tor, n. Mea hohola i ka mala-malama, a wela paha.
Răd'i-cal, adj. Mai ke kumu mai. Radical change, he hoololi mai ke kumu mai.
Răd'i-cal, n. He kumu. SYN. root.

Răd'i-cal-ly, adv. Mai ke kumu mai. Radically wrong, hewa mai ke kumu mai.
Ră'di-ŭs, n. Kaha hanai.
Răf'fle, n. He ano piliwaiwai.
Răft, n. He huina laau hoolana ma ka wai; he lana laau.
Răft'er, n. He oa hale.
Răg, n. Welu.
Răg'a-mŭf'fin, n. Mea pupuka ino.
Răge, n. 1. Huhu nui; keeo.
2. Kupikipiki-o'. The ocean's rage, ke kupikipikio o ke kai.
Răg-ged, adj. Weluwelu; haehaeia.
Răg'man, n. Kanaka kuai welu.
Răid, v. E pakaha; e komo ma ke ano enemi.
Răil, n. He kaola. Iron rail, kaola hao.
Răil'ler-y, n. Olelo loiloi; olelo paani. SYN. banter.
Răil'ing, n. 1. Paku' laau; he pa.
2. Olelo kuamuamu.
Răil'road, } n. Alanui hao. SYN. tramway.
Răil'way, }
Răi'ment, n. Lole komo. SYN. clothing; garments.
Răin, n. U'-a.
Răin'bow, n. Anuenue.

Rāin'-gāuge, *n.* He apu ana i ka nui o ka u-a.

Rāin'y, *adj.* U'-a,

Rāin'y-sēa'son, *n.* Kuaua.

Rāise, *v.* 1. E hoala; e hapai ae. SYN. lift.

2. E ulu; hoo-ulu.

3. E leha'e. *Raise the eyes,* e leha'e i na maka.

Rāis'in, *n.* Hua waina maloo.

Rāke, *n.* 1. Hapuku; kahi opala.

2. Kanaka uhauha.

Rāl'ly, *v.* E alu mai; e eu; e hoo-eueu.

2. Hoohenehene; loiloi.

Rām, *n.* 1. Hipa kane. He nuku hao no ka moku kaua.

3. Kekahi ano pauma.

Ram, *v.* E hou; e pahu.

Rām'ble, *n.* E holoholo; e makaikai. SYN. stroll.

Rām'bler, *n.* Mea holoholo; mea makaikai.

Rām'bling, *n.* 1. Ka holoholo ana.

2. *A rambling thought,* he manao auwana wale, pili ole.

Rām'part, *n.* Ka pa o ka pa-kaua.

Rām'rod, *n.* Hao hoopiha pu.

Ranch, *n.* Wahi hanai holoholona.

Răn'cid, *adj.* Polopolona.

Răn'cor, *u.* Inaina nui; opu ino. SYN. enmity.

Răn'cor-oŭs, *adj.* Opu ino; naaukeemoa.

Răn'dom, *adj.* Wale. *Random talk,* kamailio wale.

Rānge, *n.* 1. Lalani. SYN. row.

2. *Within range of the gun,* ma kahi i hiki ai ka pu.

3. *Within range of vision,* ma kahi i hiki ai ka maka.

4. Kahi e holoholo ai; he aina kula. *A cattle range,* he aina kula no na holoholona.

Rānge, *v.* E holoholo. *The cattle range over the pastures,* holoholo na bipi ma ke kula.

Rank, *adj.* 1. Hauna. SYN. strong.

2. Ulu nui; hihi.

Rănk, *n.* He kulana; he papa.

Rănk, *v.* E ku ma ke kulana.

Rănk'le, *v.* 1. E hoo-uluhua.

2. E hoopehu. SYN. fester.

Răn'sack, *v.* E imi ma na wahi a pau.

Răn'som, *n.* Uku panai.

Răn'som, *v.* E hoola panai.

Rant, *n.* Olelo haanui; walaau; wahapaa.

Rant'er, *n.* He wahapaa; waha kole.

Răp, *v.* E kui; e kikeke. SYN. knock.

Ra-pā'cioŭs, *adj.* Hao wale; alunu.

Ra-pāç'i-ty, *n.* Alunu; puniwaiwai.

Rāpe, *n.* Pue wahine.

Răp'id, *adj.* Mama; hikiwawe; kiki.

Răp'ids, *n.* Kahi e kahe awiwi ai ka muliwai.

Ra-pīd'i-ty, *n.* Ka mama; ka hikiwawe.

Răp'id-ly, *adv.* Mama; wawe; hikiwawe.

Răp'ine, *n.* Ka hao wale ana; ka powa ana.

Răpt'ūre, *n.* Hauoli nui.

Răpt'ur-oŭs, *adj.* Piha i ka kauoli.

Rāre, *adj.* 1. Ike pinepine ole ia; milimili. SYN. choice.

2. Moa iki. SYN. underdone.

Rār'e-fāc'tion, *n.* Ka hoo-mama ana o ke ea.

Rār'e-fȳ, *v.* E hoolilo a mama.

Rāre'ly, *adv.* Kakaikahi loa.

Rār'i-ty, *n.* 1. He mea ike pinepine ole ia; mea milimili.

2. Ke ano mama; ano lahilahi.

Rās'cal, *n.* Kanaka kolohe; kanaka apiki.

Rās-cal'i-ty, *n.* Hana kolohe; hana apiki.

Rāsh, *adj.* Hoaano. SYN. foolhardy.

Rāsh'ly, *adv.* Me ka noonoo ole.

Rāsp, *n.* He apuapu nui.

Rāsp'ber-ry, *n.* He akala.

Rāsp'ing, *adj.* Okalakala.

Răt, *n.* Iole nui.

Rāte, *n.* 1. Kumukuai. SYN. price.

2. Ka holo ana; ka nee ana. SYN. movement.

3. Ratio; kulana.

Rāth'er, *adv.* 1. E aho.

2. Iki. *Rather small,* uuku iki.

Răt'i-fi-cā'tion, *n.* Ka apono ana.

Răt'i-fȳ, *v.* E apono ma ke kakau lima.

Rā'tio (shō), *n.* Ke kaulike; rati'o.

Rā'tion, *n.* He mahele ai.

Rā'tion-al, *adj.* Noonoo; ku i ka noonoo.

Rā'tion-al-ly, *adv.* Me ka noonoo.

Răt'line, *n.* Kaula liilii o ka likini moku.

Răt-tōōn', *n.* Oha'ko.

Răt'tle, *n.* Mea paani hoonakeke.

Răv'age, *v.* E luku; e hooneoneo. SYN. devastate.

Răv'ā-ger, *n.* Mea luku. SYN. plunderer.

Rāve, *v.* E pupule loa; e kamailio pupule.

Rā'ven, *n.* Manu koraka.

Răv'en-oŭs, *adj.* 1. Hae. SYN. voracious.

2. *Ravenously hungry,* pololi loa.

Ra-vīne', *n.* Kahawai.

Răv'ing, *adj.* Hehena.

Răv'ish, *v.* 1. E pue; e lima ikaika.

2. *Ravished with delight,* piha i ka hauoli.

Rạw, *adj.* 1. Maka; kole.

2. *Raw material,* na lako maoli.

3. Anuanu; opili. SYN. blustering.

Rạw'bōned, *adj.* Olala.

Rạw'hide, *n.* Ili maka; laau hili.

Rāy, *n.* Kukuna.

Rāy'less, *adj.* Pouli; poeleele.

Rāze, *v.* E hooauhuli; hoohiolo. SYN. demolish.

Rā'zor, *n.* Pahi umiumi.

Rā'zor-strŏp, *n.* Ili hoo-kala pahi-umiumi.

Reach, *v.* 1. E kikoo; e o aku.
2. E homai.
3. E hohola. *Reach far and wide,* e hoholo ma o a maanei.

Reach, *n.* 1. Ma kahi e hiki ai. *Within reach of the arm,* ma kahi e hiki ai ka lima.
2. Ma kahi kokoke.

Rē-āet', *v.* E ili hou; e hoi hou.

Rē-āe'tion, *n.* Ka hoi hou ihope.

Read, *v.* E heluhelu.

Read'a-ble, *adj.* Kupono ke helu he-luia.

Read'er, *n.* 1. Mea heluhelu.
2. Buke heluhelu.

Read'i-ly, *adv.* Me ka hikiwawe; me ka makaukau.

Read'i-ness, *n.* Ka makaukau; ka hi-kiwawe.

Read'ing, *n.* He mea heluhelu; ka he-luhelu ana.

Rē'ad-jŭst', *d.* E hooponopono hou.

Rē'ad-jŭst'ment, *n.* Ka hooponopono hou ana.

Rē'ad-mis'sion, *n.* Ka hookomo hou ana.

Rē'ad-mīt', *v.* E hookomo hou.

Read'y, *adv.* Makaukau; lolii; mio.

Rē'af-fīrm', *v.* E hai hou; e i hou.

Rē-al, *adj.* Oiaio; maoli. SYN. genuine.

Rē-āl'i-ty, *n.* Ka oiaio. SYN. truth; fact.

Rē'al-i-zā'tion, *n.* Ke ko ana.

Rē'al-ize, *v.* 1. E ko. SYN. accomplish.
2. E loaa. SYN. find.
3. E hoomaopopo. SYN. appreciate.
4. E puka. SYN. gain.

Rē'al-ly, *adv.* He oiaio. SYN. verily; truly.

Realm, *n.* Aupuni moi.

Rēam, *n.* He puolo pepa, *20 quires.*

Rēam'er, *n.* He wili e hana a nui ka puka.

Rē-ăn'i-māte, *v.* 1. E hoihoi mai i ke ola.
2. E hoohoihoi.

Rēap, *v.* E ohi.

Rēap'er, *n.* Mea ohi; mikini oki pa-laoa.

Rē'ap-pēar', *v.* E hoea hou mai.

Rē'ap-pēar'ançe, *n.* Ka hoea hou ana mai.

Rē'ap-point', *v.* E koho hou no ka oihana.

Rēar, *n.* 1. Ko hope. *Rear of the house,* ko hope o ka hale.
2. *Rear of an army,* hunapaa.
3. Ke kua.

Rēar, *v.* 1. E hanai. SYN. raise.
2. E ao. SYN. teach.
3. E hoala; e kukulu. SYN. raise; elevate.
4. E ku ma na wawae hope.

Rē'as-çend', *v.* E pii hou ae.

Rēa'son, *n.* 1. Ka noonoo kanaka.
2. He kumu. SYN. motive.

Rēa'son, *v.* E noonoo pu; e no aku.

Rēa'son-a-ble, *adj.* Kupono; ku i ka noonoo.

Rēa'son-a-ble-ness, *n.* Ke kupono; ku i ka noonoo.

Rēa'son-a-bly, *adv.* Ma ka mea ku-pono.

Rēa'son-er, *n.* Mea alakai i ka noo-noo.

Rēa'son-ing, *n.* Ke alakai ana i ka noonoo.

Rē'as-sēm'ble, *v.* E akoakoa hou.

Rē'as-sērt', *v.* E hai hou. SYN. reaf-firm.

Rē'as-sūme', *v.* E hapai hou; e lawe hou. SYN. resume.

Rē'as-sūre', *v.* E hoopau i ke kanalua; e hoopau i ka pihoihoi.

Rē'at-tēmpt', *v.* E hoao hou.

Re-bāte', *n.* Ka hooemi ana. *Rebate on duties,* ka hooemi ana mai ka auhau dute.

Re-bĕl', *v.* E kipi.

Rĕb'el, *n.* He kipi.

Re-bĕl'lion, *n.* Ke kipi i ka aupuni.

Re-bĕl'lious, *adj.* Kipi; hookuli.

Re-bound', *v.* 1. E lele hou mai.
2. E kupinai.

Re-bŭff', *n.* Kumu keakea.

Re-build', *v.* E kukulu hou.

Re-būke', *v.* E ao; e papa'ku.

Re-bŭt,, *v.* E pale i ka olelo hoike.

Re-call', *v.* 1. E kahea hou mai.
2. E hoihoi mai.
3. E hoomanao. SYN. recall to mind.

Re-cānt', *v.* 1. E hoihoi mai i ka ma-nao. SYN. retract.
2. E haalele i ka manaoio.

Rē'can-tā'tion, *n.* Ka haalele ana i ka manao.

Rē'ca-pit'u-lāte, *v.* E helu hou mai ka mua mai.

Rē'ca-pit'u-lā'tion, *n.* Ka heluna nui.

Re-căp'ture, *v.* E hopu hou.

Re-cēde', *v.* E ku emi ihope; e hoi ihope.

Re-cēipt', *n.* 1. Palapala hookaa.
2. Ka loaa ana. SYN. reception.
3. He rula no kekahi mau hana.
4. Kahi e hoo-kaa ai.

Re-cēiv'a-ble, *adj.* Loaa mai. *Bills receivable,* na bila loaa mai.

Re-cēive', *v.* E loaa.

Re-cēiv'er, *n.* Mea e loaa ana; mea malama.

Rē'çent, *adj.* Iho nei. *Recent arrival,* ke ku ana iho nei.

Rē'çent-ly, *adv.* A no iho nei.

Re-çĕp'ta-cle, *n.* Wahi hoahu.

Re-çĕp'tion, *n.* 1. Ka loaa ana.
2. Ke kipa ana.

Re-cĕss', *n.* 1. Wa hoomaha pokole.
2. He kuono iloko o ke keena.

Rĕç'i-pe, *n.* Rula wehewehe no kekahi mau hana. *Recipe for cooking,* rula no ke kuke ana.

Re-çĭp′i-ent, *n.* Mea nana e loaa.

Re-çĭp′ro-cāte, *v.* E haawi aku ha-awi mai; e panai like.

Re-çit′al, *n.* Ka hai waha ana.

Rĕç-i-tā′tion, *n.* Ka hai ana.

Re-çite′, *v.* E hai waha; e hai paa naau. SYN. repeat.

Rĕck′less, *adj.* Noonoo ole. SYN. rash.

Rĕck′less-ly, *adv.* Me ka noonoo ole. SYN. rashly.

Rĕck′on, *v.* E noonoo; e helu.

Rĕck′on-ing, *n.* 1. Ka hooponopono ana i ka helu.
2. Ka helu ana; helu.

Re-claim′, *v.* 1. E hoohuli mai.
2. E loaa hou. SYN. recover.
3. *Reclaim poor land*, e hoomomona i ka aina panoa.

Re-claim′a-ble, *adj.* Hiki ke hoohu-liia.

Re-cline′, *v.* E hilinai aku; e moe iho.

Re-clin′ing, *n.* Ka hilinai ana; ka moe iho ana.

Re-cluse′, *n.* Kanaka noho mehameha.

Rĕc′og-ni′tion, *n.* Ka hoomaopopo ana; ka ike ana.

Re-cŏg′ni-zance, *n.* Ano bona i ka-kauia.

Rĕc′og-nize, *v.* E hoomaopopo; e ike aku.

Re-coil′, *v.* E kuemi ihope.

Rĕc′ol-lĕct′, *v.* E hoomanao. SYN. remember.

Rĕc′ol-lĕc′tion, *n.* Ka hoomanao ana.

Rĕ′com-mĕnçe′, *v.* E hoomaka hou.

Rĕc′om-mĕnd′, *v.* E apono.

Rĕç′om-men-dā′tion, *n.* Ka apono ana. *Letter of recommendation*, palapa-la apono.

Rĕ′com-mit′, *v.* 1. E hoihoi hou. *Re-commit a bill*, e hoihoi hou i ka bila.
2. E hana hou.

Rĕc′om-pense, *n.* He uku hana. SYN. reward.

Rĕc′on-çile, *v.* E hookuikahi; hoo-laulea.

Rĕc′on-çil′i-ā′tion, *n.* Ka hookuikahi ana.

Rĕc′on-dite, *adj.* 1. Pohihihi; mao-popo ole.
2. Huna′ia mai ka noonoo. SYN. abstruse.

Re′con-dŭct′, *v.* E kai hou; e alakai hou.

Re-cŏn′noĭs-sänçe, *n.* Ke kiu ana i ka aina.

Rĕ′con-noi′tre, *v.* 1. E kiu; hooma-kakiu.
2. E hakilo.

Re-cŏn′quer (kon′ker), *v.* E hoopio hou.

Rĕ′con-sĭd′er, *v.* E noonoo hou.

Rĕ′con-sĭd′er-ā′tion, *n.* Ka noonoo hou ana.

Re-côrd′, *v.* E kakau ma ke ano moo-lelo.

Rĕc′ôrd, *n.* He moolelo kakau. *Court of record*, aha kakau. *Record of evi-dence*, moohihia.

Re-côrd′er, *n.* Luna kakau palapala.

Re-count′, *v.* E hai liilii mai.

Re-course′, *n.* Wahi launa. SYN. resort. *Recourse to books*, e launa me na buke.

Re-cov′er, *v.* 1. E loaa hou ka mea i lilo.
2. E ola hou; konakonea. SYN. get well.

Re-cóv′er-y, *n.* 1. Ka loaa hou ana o ka mea i lilo.
2. Ke ola hou ana.

Rĕc′re-ant, *adj.* Huli hoi ihope; ku-makaia. *Recreant to a trust*, kumakaia i kekahi pono.

Rĕc′re-āte, *v.* E hoo-oluolu; e hoona-nea. E paani.

Rĕc′re-ā′tion, *n.* Ka hoo-oluolu ana; ka paani ana.

Re-crim′i-nāte, *v.* E nuku aku nuku mai.

Re-crim′i-nā′tion, *n.* Ka nuku aku nuku mai.

Re-erŏss′, *v.* E hele hou i kela aoao.

Re-cruit′, *v.* 1. E hooikaika hou i ke kino.
2. E kepa.

Re-cruit′, *n.* He koa hou; mea kepa hou.

Re-cruits′, *n. pl.* Kela lako keia lako.

Rĕct′an-gle, *n.* Huina kupono.

Rĕct-an′gu-lar, *adj.* Huina kupono.

Rĕc′ti-fi-cā′tion, *n.* Ka hooponopono ana; ka hoopololei ana.

Rĕc′ti-fy, *v.* 1. E hooponopono. SYN. correct.
2. E hoopololei. SYN. straighten.
3. E hoomaemae; hoo-aiai. SYN. clarify.

Rĕc′ti-lĭn′e-ar, *adj.* Kaha pololei.

Rĕc′ti-tūde, *n.* Ka hoopono. SYN. uprightness.

Rĕc′tor, *n.* 1. He kahu ekalesia.
2. Puuku nui o ke kula nui.

Re-cŭm′bent, *adj.* Moe hilinai. SYN. reclining.

Re-cŭ′per-āte, *v.* E hooikaika hou.

Re-cŭr′, *v.* 1. E hoihou. *Recur to a subject*, e hoi hou i ke kumumanao.
2. E ike hou ia.

Re-cŭr′rence, *n.* Ka ike hou; hoi hou.

Rĕd, *adj.* Ulaula.

Rĕd′den, *v.* E ha′ulaula.

Rĕd′dish, *adj.* Haulaula.

Re-deem′, *v.* 1. E hoola panai.
2. E uku panai.
3. *Redeem a pledge*, e hooko i ka olelo hoohiki.

Re-deem′er, *n.* Ka Hoola.

Re-dĕmp′tion, *n.* 1. Ke Ola.
2. Ka uku panai ana.
3. Ka hooko ana.

Rĕd′hŏt, *adj.* Enaena.

Rĕd′ness, *n.* Ka ulaula.

Rĕd′o-lent, *adj.* Moaniani.

Re-doŭb′le, *v.* E papalua.

Re-doubt′ (dowt), n. He papu iloko o kekahi pakaua.

Re-dound′, v. E kokua mamuli o kekahi mea. *Redound to his glory,* e kokua mamuli o kona nani.

Re-dress′, v. E hooponopono i na pilikia.

Re-dress′, n. Ka hoihoi ana o ka poino.

Re-duce′, v. 1. E hoo-emi. 2. E hoopio. SYN. conquer.

Re-duc′tion, n. 1. Ka hoo-emi. 2. Ka lawe pio ana.

Re-dun′dant, adj. Pakela; keu.

Reed, n. 1. He ohe; ohe kani. 2. He naku; akaakai. SYN. rush.

Reef, v. E li. *Reef the sail,* e li ka pea.

Reef, n. Ae-kai; kuanalu.

Reek, v. E punohu.

Reel, v. 1. E hele hikaka; e kunewanewa. 2. *Reel from weakness,* e kaalele. 3. E wili. SYN. wind.

Reel, n. He pokakaa wili.

Re′e-lèet′, v. E koho hou.

Re′em-bärk′, v. E ee hou maluna o ka moku.

Re′en-äct′, v. E hana hou; hooholo hou.

Re′en-förce′, v. 1. E hooikaika hou. 2. E hoopiha hou mai.

Re′en-gäge′, v. 1. E hoopaa hou. 2. E hoolimalima hou.

Re′en-list′, v. E kakau inoa hou no ke komo ana ma ka puali koa.

Re-ën′ter, v. E komo hou aku.

Re′es-tab′lish, v. E hookahua hou.

Reeve, v. E hookomo i ka piko o ke kaula. *Reeve the end of the rope through the block,* e hookomo i ka piko o ke kaula ma ka balaka.

Re′ex-äm′i-nä′tion, n. 1. Ka ninau hou ana. 2. Ka huli hou ana.

Re′ex-äm′ine, v. E ninau hou; e hoike hou. *Re-examine accounts,* e huli hou i na helu.

Re-fec′to-ry, n. Keena paina.

Re-fer′, v. 1. E kuhikuhi. 2. E waiho. *Refer to a committee,* e waiho i ke komite.

Ref′er-ee′, n. Mea uwao; mea hooholo i ka pono iwaena o na aoao elua.

Ref′er-ence, n. 1. He kuhikuhi. 2. Ka waiho ana. 3. Ka pili ana. *No reference to the subject,* aole pili i ke kumu manao.

Ref′er-en-ces, n. 1. Palapala hoike. 2. Olelo kuhikuhi.

Re-fine′, v. E hoomaemae.

Re-fined′, adj. 1. Maemae; mikioi. 2. Hoomaemaeia.

Re-fine′ment, n. Ka maemae; ka mikioi.

Re-fin′er, n. Mea hoomaemae.

Re-fin′er-y, n. Wahi hoomaemae.

Re-fit′, v. 1. E hoolako hou; hooponopono hou. 2. E kakia hou. SYN. repair.

Re-flĕct′, v. 1. E noonoo; poonoo. SYN. consider. 2. Anaha. 3. E kau apono, e kau ahewa paha.

Re-flĕc′tion, n. 1. Poonoo. 2. Anaha; anahanaha. 3. He kina′.

Re-flĕct′or, n. He mea e anaha ai i na kukuna malamalama.

Re-förm′, v. E huli hou; hoohuli hou.

Re-förm′, n. He hana hou, ku i ka pono.

Rĕf′or-mä′tion, n. 1. Ka hoohuli hou ana. 2. Ka imi hou ana i ka pono.

Re-för′ma-to-ry, n. Wahi hoopololei. *Reformatory school,* kula hoopololei.

Re-fräct′, v. E aui. *Water refracts light,* e aui ae ke kukuna malamalama i ka wai.

Re-fräc′tion, n. Ka aui ana.

Re-fräct′o-ry, adj. Nuha; paakiki.

Re-fräin′, v. E kaaokoa aku; e ho-o′ki.

Re-fräin′, n. Ke ano o ke mele.

Re-frĕsh′, v. E hoo-oluolu.

Re-frĕsh′ing, adj. Oluolu.

Re-frĕsh′ment, n. Mea e oluolu ai.

Re-frĕsh′ments, n. pl. Na mea ai, me na mea inu.

Re-frig′er-ä′tor, n. He pahu hooanuanu.

Rĕf′uge, n. He puuhonua; wahi lu′lu.

Rĕf′u-gee′, n. He kuea; kuewa.

Re-ful′gent, adj. Alohilohi; huali. SYN. radiant.

Re-fund′, v. E pani hou. SYN. repay; restore.

Re-füs′al, n. He hoole. He ae ole.

Re-füse′, v. E hoole; e ae ole.

Ref′use, n. Koena opala.

Rĕf′u-tä′tion, n. Ka pale ana i ka olelo.

Re-fute′, v. E pale olelo.

Re-gäin′, v. E loaa hou. SYN. recover.

Rĕ′gal, adj. Hanohano moi.

Re-gäle′, v. E hooluolu. SYN. refresh.

Re-gä′li-a, n. pl. 1. Na kahiko alii. 2. Na kahiko o ke kulana. SYN. insignia.

Re-gärd′, v. E maliu; e hoolohe.

Re-gärd′, n. Manao mahalo; manao aloha.

Re-gärd′ful, adv. 1. Imi i ka pomaikai. SYN. considerate. 2. Manao nui. SYN. mindful.

Re-gärd′less, adj. Manao ole aku. *Regardless of expense,* manao ole aku i ka lilo; helu ole i ka lilo.

Re-gät′ta, n. Heihei moku; heihei waapa.

Rĕ′gen-cy, n. Ka noho ′na o ka hope moi.

Re-gĕn′er-ate, adj. Hoo-hanau hou ia.

Re-gĕn′er-ate, v. E hoo-hanau hou.

Re-gĕn′er-ä′tion, n. Ka hanau hou.

Rĕ′gent, n. Hope moi.

Rĕg′i-çide, n. Pepehi alii; mea pepehi moi.

Re-gime′, (rā-zheem′) *n.* Ke ano o ka hoomalu ana.

Rĕg′i-men, *n.* Ka noho'na i loaa ka ikaika kupono o ke kino.

Rĕg′i-mĕnt, *n.* He regimana koa.

Rĕg′i-mĕnt′als, *n.* Na aahu koa.

Re′gion, *n.* Wahi. *Region of country,* wahi o ka aina.

Rĕg′is-ter, *n.* 1. He papa kuhikuhi. SYN. catalogue.
2. Kapuahi hoomahana hale.
3. He pani ea no ke kapuahi hao.
4. He buke kakau. *Marriage register,* buke kakau mare.
5. Ka hiki ana o ka leo mai ka haahaa loa a i ke kiekie loa.

Rĕg′is-ter, *v.* E kakau. SYN. record.

Rĕg′is-trär, *n.* Luna kakau; puuku. *Registrar of public accounts,* puuku nui o ka waihona aupuni.

Rĕg′is-trā′tion, *n.* Ke kakau ana. SYN. recording.

Rĕg′is-try, *n.* He buke no ke kakau ana i kela me keia mea.

Rĕg′nant, *adj.* E noho alii ana.

Re-grĕt′, *n.* Mamina; minamina; menemene.

Re-grĕt′ful-ly, *adv.* Me ka minamina.

Rĕg′u-lar, *adj.* Mau; walea. *Regular proceedings,* na hana ku mau.

Rĕg′u-lär′i-ty, *n.* Ke ano mau; ma ke ano i maa.

Rĕg′u-lär-ly, *adv.* Ma ke ano mau; ma ke ano i maa.

Rĕg′u-lāte, *v.* E hooponopono. SYN. adjust.

Rĕg′u-lā′tion, *n.* 1. Ka hooponopono ana. SYN. adjustment.
2. He rula. SYN. rule.

Rĕg′u-lā′tor, *n.* Mea hooponopono.

Rĕ′ha-bil′i-tāte, *v.* E hoihoi hou i na pono i lawe ia'ku.

Re-hērs′al, *n.* 1. He hai hoomakaukau.
2. E hai. SYN. recite.

Reign, *n.* Ka noho alii ana.

Re′im-bûrse′, *v.* E hoihoi i ka poho. SYN. repay.

Re′im-bûrse′ment, *n.* Ka hoihoi ana i ka poho.

Rein, *n.* He kaula waha. *To give reins to,* e hooko mamuli o ke kuko. *To take the reins,* e alakai.

Rē′in-fôrce′, *v.* See re-enforce.

Reins, *n.* Ka puhaka.

Rē′in-sẽrt′, *v.* E hookomo hou.

Rē′in-stāte′, E hoihoi hou ma ka oihana.

Rē′in-vĕst′, *v.* Hoomoe hou i ka waiwai. *Reinvest money,* e hoomoe hou i ke dala.

Re-ĭt′er-āte, *v.* E hai pinepine; e kukaiolelo.

Re-ĭt′er-ā′tion, *n.* He pinepine ka hai ana.

Re-jĕct′, *v.* E hoole; e hoowaha'waha′.

Re-jĕc′tion, *n.* Ka hoole ana; ka hoowahawaha.

Re-jŏice, *v.* E hauoli.

Re-jŏic′ing, *n.* Ka hauoli.

Re-jŏin′, *v.* 1. E hui hou.

Re-jŏin′der, *n.* Haina; olelo pane. SYN. reply.

Re-jü′ve-nāte, *v.* E hoi hou i ka wa ui.

Re-kĭn′dle, *v.* 1. E hoo-a hou.
2. E hoala hou.

Re-lāpse′, *v.* 1. E haule hou ihope.
2. *Relapse into sickness,* e hopilo.

Re-lāte′, *v.* E hai. SYN. tell.

Re-lāte′ to ⎱ E pili; e pili ana. SYN.
Re-lāt′ing to ⎰ pertaining to.

Re-lā′tion, *n.* 1. Ka hai ana. SYN. narration.
2. He pili. *No relation to the subject,* aohe pili i ke kumu manao.
3. He pili koko.

Re-lā′tion-ship, *n.* Ka pili koko; ka pili.

Rĕl′a-tive, *n.* He pili koko; makamaka.

Rĕl′a-tive, *adj.* E pili ana.

Re-lăx′, *v.* 1. E alu; e hooalu. SYN. loosen.
2. E hooemi. *Relax exertion,* e hooemi i ka hooikaika.
3. E hookuu; e hooluolu. *Relax the mind,* e hooluolu i ka noonoo.

Rĕl′ax-ā′tion, *n.* Ka hoo-alu ana; hooluolu ana, hoonanea.

Re-lāy′, *n.* He poe hou mai. *Relay of horses,* he mau lio hou mai.

Re-lēase′, *v.* 1. E hookuu; e wehe.

Re-lĕnt′, *v.* E mihi.

Re-lĕnt′less, *adj.* Mihi ole; paakiki.

Rĕl′e-vant, *adj.* Pili pono; ku. SYN. applicable.

Re-lī′a-ble, *adj.* Pauleleia; oiaio. SYN. trustworthy.

Re-lī′ance, *n.* Paulele. SYN. trust; confidence.

Rĕl′ic, *n.* 1. Mea hoomanao. SYN. memento.
2. Kino kupapau.

Rĕl′ict, *n.* Wahine kane make. SYN. widow.

Re-lĭef, *n.* 1. Kokua. SYN. assistance.
2. Maha. *Relief from pain,* maha mai ka eha.

Re-lĭeve′, *v.* 1. E kokua. SYN. assist.
2. E hoopakele.
3. E haawi i ka maha.

Re-lĭg′ion, *n.* Ka hoomana. SYN. piety.

Re-lĭ′giŏŭs, *adj.* Haipule; manaoio.

Re-lĭn′quish, *v.* E haalele iho; e waiho ae. SYN. resign.

Re-lĭn′quish-ment, *n.* Ka haalele ana.

Rĕl′ish, *v.* E ono. *Relish food,* e ono ai.

Rĕl′ish-a-ble, *adj.* Mikomiko.

Re-lōad′, *v.* 1. E hoouka hou i ka ukana.
2. E hoopiha hou.

Re-lŭc′tance, *n.* Ka aua o ka manao.

Re-lŭc′tant, *adj.* Aua; makemake ole.

Re-lŭc′tant-ly, *adv.* Me ka aua.

Re-lȳ′, *v.* E paulele; e hilinai.

Re-máin′, v. 1. E koe.
2. E noho.
Re-máin′der, n. Ke koena.
Re-máins′, n. pl. 1. Na huna i koe.
2. Kino kupapau. SYN. corpse.
Re-mánd′, v. E hoihoi. Remand to jail,
e hoihoi i ka hale paahao.
Re-márk′, n. He wahi olelo.
Re-márk′a-ble, adj. Kupaianaha.
Re-márk′a-bly, adv. Loa. Remarkably
good, maikai loa.
Rĕm′e-dy, n. 1. He mea e pono ai.
2. Mea e pakele ai.
3. Lauu lapaau.
Rĕm′e-dy, v. E hooponopono. Remedy
a mistake, e hooponopono i ke kuhihe-
wa.
Re-mĕm′ber, v. E hoomanao. SYN.
recollect.
Re-mĕm′brance, n. Ka hoomanao.
SYN. recollection.
Re-mínd′, v. E paipai: e hoala manao.
Rĕm′i-nis′çençe, n. Mea hoala manao.
Re-míss′, adj. Palaka.
Re-mís′sion, n. 1. Ke kala ana.
2. Ka hookuu ana; ka hoihoi ana.
Re-mít′, v. 1. E hooili.
2. E hookuu. Remit taxes, e hookuu
auhau.
Re-mít′tançe, n. 1. Ka hooili ana; ka
hookuu ana.
2. Dala i hooiliia.
Rĕm′nant, n. Koe′na.
Re-môd′el, v. E kalai hou; e kaha-
kaha hou.
Re-môn′strançe, n. Olelo pa′pa′; olelo
ao.
Re-môn′strāte, v. E pa′pa′. SYN. ex-
postulate.
Re-môrse′, n. Manao walania.
Re-môrse′ful, adj. Walania; kaumaha.
Re-môrse′less, adj. Lokoino; aloha
ole. SYN. cruel; pitiless.
Re-môte′, adj. Kaawale loa; mamao.
Re-môte′ness, n. Ke kaawale loa.
Re-mount′, v. E ee hou; e pii hou ae.
Re-mov′al, n. 1. Ka lawe ana′ku.
2. Ka haalele ana i kauwahi. SYN.
departure.
3. Ke kapai ana. Removal from office,
ke kapai ana mai ka oihana.
Re-move′, v. 1. E lawe aku.
2. E haalele; e hele aku.
3. E hoohemo; e kapai.
Re-mü′ner-āte, v. E uku; e hoihoi i
ka poho′. SYN. recompense.
Re-mü′ner-ā′tion, n. He uku. SYN.
pay.
Re-mü′ner-ā′tive, adj. Puka; waiwai.
Ren-cŏn′tre, } n. He halawai ku-e′;
Ren-coun′ter, } he hakaka.
Rĕnd, v. E haehae; e uhae. SYN. tear.
Rĕn′der, v. 1. E haawi. SYN. give.
2. E unuhi. SYN. translate.
3. E wehewehe. SYN. explain.
4. E hoomaemae; hooaiai. SYN. clarify.

Rĕn′der-ing, n. Ke ano o ka unuhi
ana.
Rĕn′dez-vous (ren-dĕ-vū), n. He
wahi e akoakoa ai.
Rĕn′e-gāde, n. 1. He aea haukae.
2. Mea haalele wale i kona manaoio.
3. Koa mahuka. SYN. deserter.
Re-new′, v. 1. E hana hou. SYN. ren-
ovate.
2. E hoomaka hou. SYN. begin again.
3. E haawi hou i bila aie.
Re-new′al, n. Ka hana hou ana; haawi
hou ana etc.
Re-nounçe′, v. E haalele loa; e hoole
loa.
Rĕn′o-vāte, v. E hana hou; hoomae-
mae.
Rĕn′o-vā′tion, n. Ka hoomaemae ana.
Re-nown′, n. Kaulana. SYN. fame.
Re-nowned′, adj. Kaulana. SYN.
celebrated; famous.
Rĕnt. n. 1. He nahaehae; he mawae.
2. Uku aina; uku hale.
Rĕnt, v. E hoolimalima aina, a hale
paha.
Rĕnt′al, n. Ka hoolimalima ana i ka
aina, etc.
Rĕnt′rŏll, n. Papa inoa o na hoa-aina.
Re-nŭn′çi-ā′tion, n. Ka haalele loa na.
Re-ŏç′eu-pỹ, v. E komo hou aku.
Re-ō′pen, v. E wehe hou ae.
Re-ôr-gan-ize, v. 1. E kukulu hou.
Reorganize the company, e kukulu hou
i ka hui.
2. E hooponopono hou.
Re-ôr′gan-i-zā′tion, n. Ke kukulu-
hou ana; ka hooponopono hou ana.
Re-pāid, v. Feel repaid for trouble,
hoihoi ia mai ka poho′o ka luhi.
Re-pāint′, v. E pena hou.
Re-pāir′, v. 1. E hana hou.
2. E kakia hou; kapili hou.
3. E hele. SYN. resort to; go.
Rĕp′a-rā′tion, n. He pani no ka poho′.
Rĕp′ar-tee′, n. He pane akamai.
Re-pâss′, v. E naue hou ae; e maalo
hou ae.
Re-pâst′, n. He pai hou.
Re-pāy′, v. E uku hou; e pani hou.
Re-pāy′ment, n. Ka uku hou ana.
Re-pēal′, v. E hoopau; hoonoa. SYN.
abrogate.
Re-pēat′, v. 1. E hai pinepine; e hai
hou.
2. E hana hou.
3. Repeat over and over, kukai olelo.
Re-pēat′ed-ly, adv. Pinepine. SYN.
frequently.
Re-pēat′er, n. 1. He wati liilii hoo-
kani hora.
2. Pupanapana kani lehulehu; he
revolver.
Re-pĕl′, v. E pale; e hoo-kue.
Re-pĕl′lent, adj. Ku-e.
Re-pĕnt′, v. E mihi.
Re-pĕnt′ançe, n. Ka mihi no ka hewa.
Re-pĕnt′ant, adj. Mihi; kaumaha no
ka hewa. SYN. penitent.

Re-peo'ple, v. E hooulu lahui.
Rep'e-ti'tion, n. 1. Ke kuawili o ka olelo.
2. Ka hana hou ana.
Re-pine', v. E ohumu hewa.
Re-pin'ing-ly, adv. Me ka ohumu ahewa.
Re-plače', v. E hoihoi hou; e pani hou.
Re-plant, v. E kanu hou.
Re-plen'ish, v. 1. E hoopiha hou mai. SYN. refill.
2. E hoolako hou. SYN. supply again.
Re-plete', adj. Paapu loa; piha loa.
Re-ple'tion, n. Ka piha ana a piha loa.
Re-ply', v. E pane; e kike'. Reply quickly. apaapani.
Re-port', n. 1. Olelo hoike.
2. He lono. SYN. common report.
3. He kani; he poha'.
Re-port'er, n. Mea kakau hunahuna mea hou no ka nupepa.
Re-pose', n. Hiamoe; maha.
Re-pos'i-to-ry, n. He waihona.
Re'pos-sess', v. E loaa hou; e komo hou.
Rep're-hend', v. E pa'pa'; e ao.
Rep're-hen'si-ble, adj. Hooahewaia.
Rep're-sent', v. E hoike; e hoailona; e kuhikuhi.
Rep're-sen-ta'tion, n. 1. Ke ku ana no hai.
2. He aka; he hoailona.
Rep're-sent'a-tive, n. 1. Luna ma-kaainana.
2. He hope.
3. He hoailona.
Re-press', v. E uumi; e kinai.
Re-press'ive, adj. Kaohi. Repressive measures, na kanawai kaohi.
Re-prieve', v. E hoopanee i ka hoopai.
Rep'ri-mand, v. E ao ikaika aku no ka hewa.
Re-print', v. E pai hou.
Re'print, n. He palapala i pai hou ia.
Re-pris'al, n. He pani no ka poho'.
Re-proach', n. He kumu e hoahewa ai.
Re-proach'ful, adj. Hoahewa.
Rep'ro-bate, n. Mea lilo loa i ka hewa.
Re'pro-duçe', v. 1. E hoohua hou mai.
2. E hoike hou.
Re'pro-duc'tion,n. Ka hoohua hou mai; ulu hou mai.
Re-proof', n. Olelo ao; olelo pa'pa'. SYN. rebuke.
Re-prove', v. E pa'pa'; e ao no ka he-wa.
Rep'tile, n. He moo: nahesa; mea kolo.
Re-pub'lic, n. He aupuni makaainana.
Re-pub'li-can-ism, n. Na loina o ke aupuni makaainana.
Re-pub'li-cä'tion, n. Ke pai hou ana.
Re-pub'lish, v. E pai hou; e hoolaha hou.
Re-pu'di-äte, v. E hoole hoowaha'-waha'.

Re-pug'nançe, n. Ka hoopailua i ka manao.
Re-pug'nant, adj. Hoopailua i ka na-au.
Re-pulse', v. E pale ku-e'; e kipaku. SYN. repel.
Re-pul'sive, adj. Inoino; pupuka.
Re-pur'chase, v. E kuai hou mai.
Rep'u-ta-ble, adj. Inoa maikai. A reputable man, he kanaka inoa maikai. SYN. respectable.
2. Kupono; kuonoono. A reputable business, he oihana kuonoono.
Rep'u-ta'tion, n. Inoa imua o ha lehu lehu. A bad reputation, he inoa ino imua o ka lehulehu.
Re-pute' n. Inoa ma ke akea.
Re-put'ed, adj. Oleloia. A reputed thief, oleloia he aihue.
Re-quest', n. He noi.
Re'qui-em, n. Leo mele kanikau.
Re-quire', v. E koi; e kaohi; e kono.
Re-quire'ment, n. Ke koi ana; ka mea i konoia.
Req'ui-site, v. Mea e pono ai. SYN. necessity.
Req'ui-si'tion, n. He kaohi; he ololo e kono ana.
Re-quite', v. E hoopai; e uku.
Re-scind', v. E hoololi; hoonoa. SYN. revoke.
Res'eue, v. E hoopakele.
Re'search, n. He hooikaika ma ka imi.
Re-sell', v. E kuai hou aku.
Re-sem'blançe, n. Ka hoohalikelike; ano like. SYN. likeness.
Re-sem'ble, v. E hoohalike; kulike.
Re-sent', v. E ku-e me ka ukiuki.
Re-sent'ful, adj. Ukiuki.
Re-sent'ment, n. Manao ukiuki; hu-hu. SYN. displeasure.
Re-serve', v. E hookoe; hookaawale.
Re-serve', n. 1. He ano ihiihi; hoo-kiekie.
2. Ka mea i koe.
Re-served', adj. Ihiihi; launa ole.
Res'er-vä'tion, n. 1. Mea i hookoe ia.
2. Indian reservation, aina i hookoe ia no na Inikini.
Res'er-voir, n. Waihona wai.
Re-ship', v. 1. E hooili hou ma ka mo-ku.
2. E kepa hou.
Re-side', v. E noho paa. SYN. dwell; live
Res'i-dençe, n. Wahi noho paa.
Res'i-dent, n. Kamaaina.
Re-sid'u-a-ry, adj. Pili i ke koena. Residuary legatee, hoooilina no ke koe-na waiwai.
Res'i-düe, n. Ke koena. SYN. remain-der.
Re-sign', v. E haalele. Resign office, e haalele i ka oihana.
Res'ig-nä'tion, n. 1. Ka haalele ana.
2. Ka waiho aku ana.
3. Ka ae hoomanawanui o ka naau.

Re-signed', adj. Naau pepe.
Re-sist', v. E pale; e hoo-ku-e'.
Re-sist'ance, n. Ka hooku-e' ana; ka pale ana.
Re-sist'less, adj. Hiki ole ke hooku-e' ia. SYN. irresistible.
Rĕs'o-lute, adj. Kupaa; oni-paa; wiwo ole. SYN. firm; determined.
Rĕs'o-lute-ly, adv. Wiwo ole. Resolutely resist temptation, e kue' wiwo ole i ka hoowalewale ia mai.
Res'o-lū'tion, n. 1. Olelo hooholo.
2. Onipaa, wiwo ole o ka naau.
Re-sólve', v. E hooholo i ka manao; e paa i ka manao.
Rĕs'ó-nant, adj. Kani.
Re-sôrt', n. Kahi e akoakoa ai; kahi e hele pinepine ai.
Re-sôrt', v. 1. E akoakoa; e hele pinepine.
2. E hana. Resort to stern measures, e hana me ka lima oolea.
Re-sound', v. E kani.
Re-sound'ing, adj. Kani.
Re-source', n. Kahi e loaa ai.
Re-spĕct', v. E haawi i ka mahalo.
Re-spĕct', n. 1. Manao mahalo.
2. Pili ana. SYN. reference.
Re-spĕct'a-bīl'i-ty, n. Ke ano ku i ka mahalo.
Re-spĕct'a-ble, adj. Ku i ka mahalo; kuonoono.
Re-spĕct'a-bly, adv. Mahalo. Respectably connected, pili mahalo aku.
Re-spĕct'ed, adj. Mahaloia; manao nui ia.
Re-spĕct'ful, adj. Ano mahalo; ano haahaa.
Re-spĕct'ful-ly, adv. 1. Haahaa. Respectfully request, e noi haahaa.
2. Me ke mahalo.
Re-spĕct'ive, adj. Pakahi. Their respective friends, ko lakou mau hoa pakahi.
Re-spĕct'ive-ly, adv. Pakahi. SYN. individually.
Rĕs'pi-rā'tion, n. Ka hanu ana.
Re-spire', v. E hanu. SYN. breathe.
Rĕs'pite, n. Hoohakalau. SYN. delay.
Re-splĕn'dent, adj. Alohilohi.
Re-spŏnd', v. 1. E pane hou. SYN. reply.
2. E kulike. SYN. suit.
Re-spônse', n. He pane no ka olelo.
Re-spŏn'si-bīl'i-ty, n. Ku i ka hookololokolo; ili ke kaumaha o kekahi mea. SYN. accountability.
Re-spŏn'si-ble, adj. Ku i ka hookololokolo. He is responsible for his actions, ku oia i ka hookololokolo no kana mau hana.
Rĕst, n. 1. E maha; e palekana.
2. He koo. SYN. support.
3. Koena. SYN. remainder.
4. Kaha hoomaha ma ke mele.
Rĕst, v. E hoomaha.
Rĕst'au-rant, n. Hale paina.
Rĕst'ful, adj. Oluolu; maha.

Rĕs'ti-tū'tion, n. Ka hoihoi hou ana.
Rĕs'tive, adj. Pihoihoi; puiwa. A restive horse, he lio pihoihoi.
Rĕst'less, adj. Uluku'; haulani; hina.
Rĕs'to-rā'tion, n. Ka hoihoi hou ana.
Re-stôr'a-tive, n. Laau hooikaika kino.
Re-stôre', v. 1. E hoihoi. SYN. return.
2. Restore to health, e haawi hou i ka ikaika kino.
Re-stôr'er, n. Mea nana e hoihoi.
Re-strāin', v. E kaohi; e hoopaa; e keakea.
Re-strāint', n. Ke kaohi ana; ke hoopaa ana.
Re-strict, v. E hoohaiki. SYN. limit.
Re-stric'tion, n. Ka hoohaiki ana. SYN. limitation.
Re-sŭlt', n. Hopena.
Re-sūme', v. E hapai hou. Resume work, e hapai hou i ka hana.
Re-sŭmp'tion, n. Ka hapai hou ana.
Rĕs'ur-rĕc'tion, n. 1. Ke ala hou ana mai ka make mai.
2. Ka hoala hou ana.
Re-sŭs'çi-tāte, v. E hoola hou.
Re-sŭs'çi-tā'tion, n. Ka hoola hou ana.
Re-tāil', v. 1. E kuai liilii aku.
2. Retail gossip, e holoholo olelo.
Re'tail, n. Ke kuai liilii.
Re-tāil'er, n. 1. Kalepa kuai liilii.
2. Retailer of gossip, he holoholo olelo.
Re-tāin', v. E hookoe; e hoopaa.
Re-tāin'er, n. 1. He ohua; he poe ukali.
2. Uku hoopaa loio.
Rĕ-tāke', v. E hopu hou; e lawe hou.
Re-tăl'i-āte, v. E hana aku hana mai.
Re-tăl'i-ā'tion, n. Ka hana aku hana mai.
Re-tärd', v. E hoohakalia; e hoololohi.
Re-tĕn'tion, n. Ka hookoe ana; ka hoopaa ana.
Re-tĕn'tive, adj. Hoopaa; apo. A retentive mind, he naau apo; naau hoopaa.
Rĕt'i-çençe, n. Ke ano mumule; kamailio ole.
Rĕt'i-çent, adj. Noho malie; kamailio ole.
Rĕt'i-cule, n. Eke lawe mea humuhumu.
Rĕt'i-nà, n. He mea ano upena ma ka maka.
Rĕt'i-nūe, n. He poe ukali mahope o ke'lii.
Re-tire', v. 1. E hele aku. SYN. depart.
2. Hele i ka hiamoe.
3. E haalele. Retire from business, e haalele i ka oihana.
Re-tire'ment, n. 1. Kahi mehameha.
2. Ka haalele ana.
Re-tir'ing, adj. Akahai; noho malie; mahaoi ole.
Re-tôrt', n. 1. Pane huhu.
2. Ipu hooheehee metala.

Re-trāçe′, v. E hoi hou ihope.
Re-trāct′, v. E hoihoi mai i ka olelo.
Re-trāc′tion, n. Ka lawe hou ana i ka olelo.
Re-trēat′, v. E hee; e auhee.
Re-trēat′, n. Wahi malu; wahi lulu; he puuhonua. Syn. asylum.
Re-trēnch′, v. E hooemi i na lilo.
Re-trēnch′ment, n. Ka hooemi ana i na lilo.
Rĕt′ri-bū′tion, n. Ka hoopai; ka uku.
Re-trĭb′u-tive, adj. Uku e like me ka hana. Retributive justice, ke kaulike e uku ana e like me ka hana.
Re-trĭēve′, v. E loaa hou. Retrieve a reputation, e loaa hou i ka inoa maikai.
Re-trĭēv′er, n. He ilio i aoia e ki a hoihoi mai i na manu i ki ia.
Rĕt′rō-grāde, v. E ku-emi ihope; e hoi ihope.
Rĕt′rō-grĕs′sion, n. Ke kuemi ana; ka hoi ana ihope.
Rĕt′ro-spĕet, n. Ka nanaina o ka wa i hala.
Rĕt′ro-spĕct′ive, adj. No ka wa i hala.
Re-tūrn′, v. 1. E huli; e hoi hou. Syn. come back.
    2. E hoihoi. Syn. bring back; fetch back.
Re-tūrns, n. pl. He papa hoike. Election returns, ka papa hoike no ke koho balota.
Rē′u-nīte′, v. E hui hou; e hoohui hou.
Re-vēal′, v. E hoike i na mea huna′. Syn. divulge.
Rĕv′el, n. He anaina uhauha. Syn. carouse.
Rĕv′e-lā′tion, n. He hoike ana.
Rĕv′el-ry, n. Uhauha.
Re-vĕnġe′, n. He hoopai ino.
Re-vĕnġe′ful, adj. Manao inaina; manao hoopai ino.
Rĕv′e-nūe, n. Na loaa o ke aupuni.
Re-vēr′ber-āte, v. E kupinai. Syn. echo.
Re-vēr′ber-ā′tion, n. Ke kupinai ana; ke kani ana.
Re-vēre′, v. E hoomaikai.
Rĕv′er-ençe, n. He manao hoomaikai.
Rĕv′er-end, adj. 1. Hoomaikaiia.
    2. Inoa oihana no na kahunapule.
Rĕv′er-ent, n. Manao hoomaikai.
Rĕv′er-ent-ly, adv. Me ka manao hoomaikai.
Rĕv′er-ie, n. Poonoonoo; ka nalu iho ana.
Re-vēr′sal, n. Ka hoololi ana. The reversal of the decision, ka hoololi ana o ka olelo hoohola.
Re-vērse′, v. 1. E hoololi ae. Reverse the decision, e hoololi ae i ka olelo hooholo.
    2. E hookahuli. Syn. overturn; invert.
Re-vērse′, n. 1. Aoao kue. Syn. opposite.

    2. Poino. Meet with reverses, e halawai me na poino.
Re-vērs′i-ble, adj. Hiki ke hoololiia.
Re-vēr′sion, n. Ka hoihoi hou ana o na pono i ka mea nana i hoolilo aku, a i kona mau hope paha.
Re-vērt′, v. E hoi hou a i ka mea mamua.
Re-view′, v. 1. E hoi ihope. Review a lesson, e hoi ihope i ka haawina i hala.
    2. E makaikai. Review troops, e makaikai i na puali koa.
    3. E huli. Review a book, e huli i ka buke.
Re-view′, n. Ka nanaina ihope.
Re-view′er, n. Kanaka huli buke.
Re-vile′, v. E olelo ino; e hoohenehene; kuamuamu.
Re-vil′er, n. Mea kuamuamu; he wahapaa.
Re-vīse′, v. E hooponopono hou.
Re-vīs′er, n. Mea hooponopono hou.
Re-vīs′ion, n. 1. Ka hooponopono hou ana.
    2. He palapala i hooponopono hou ia.
Re-vīs′it, v. E hele hou; e makaikai hou.
Re-vīv′al, n. He ala hou ana.
Re-vīve′, v. E hoala hou.
Re-vīv′i-fў, v. E hoo-eueu; e hoolalelale.
Re-vōke′, v. E kahea hou mai. E hoopau. Syn. rescind.
Re-vōlt′, v. 1. E kipi.
    2. E hoopailua ma ka naau.
Re-vōlt′ing, adj. Hoopailua i ka naau.
Rĕv′o-lū′tion, n. 1. Ka hooauhuli ana i ke aupuni.
    2. Ke kaa ana.
    3. He nome.
Rĕv′o-lū′tion-a-ry, adj. Auhulihia.
Re-vŏlve′, v. E kaa; hookakaa.
Re-vŏlv′er, n. Pupanapana kani lehulehu.
Re-ward′, n. He uku; uku makana. Syn. recompense.
Re-ward′, n. Mea nana e uku.
Re-write′, v. E kakau kope hou.
Rhĕt′o-ric, n. Ke kakau ana, me ke kamailio ana ma na rula.
Rhe-tŏr′ic-al, adj. Pili i ke akamai o ka olelo; palolo.
Rheū′ma-tişm, n. He hui ma na ami.
Rhŏm′boid, n. Huina-ha-loa like ole na huina.
Rhŏm′bus (rom), n. Huina-ha-aoaolike; like ole nae na huina.
Rhyme (rime), n. Ke kani like o na leo o na hua olelo hope o kekahi mau lalani mele.
Rib, n. Iwi aoao. Ribs of a boat or ship, wae.
Rib′bon, n. Lipine.
Rice, n. Hua laiki.
Rich, adj. Waiwai; lako. Syn. wealthy.
Rich′es, n. Ka waiwai; na lako. Syn. wealth.

Rich'ness, n. 1. Ano waiwai; ano nani.
2. Momona. *Richness of soil*, momona o ka lepo.
Rick'et-y, adj. Paa ole; palupalu. *A rickety chair*, noho palupalu.
Rid, v. E hookaawale ae; e hoomaemae.
Rid'dance, n. Ka hookaawale ana; hoomaemae ana. *A good riddance*, he hoomaemae makepono.
Rid'dle, n. He nane.
Ride, v. E hooholo.
Rid'er, n. Mea hooholo.
Ridge, n. Kualapa.
Rid'i-cule, v. E hoohenehene; e loiloi.
Ri-dic'u-lous, adj. Ku i ka hoohenehene; naaupo.
Ri'fle, n. Pu raifela.
Ri'fle, v. 1. E powa. SYN. rob.
2. E wili. SYN. bore.
Rift, n. He owa; he mawae.
Rig, v. 1. E kukulu i ka likini o ka moku.
2. E kahiko i lole hookahakaha.
Rig'ging, n. He likini moku.
Right, adj. 1. Pono; pololei; kupono.
2. Akau. *Right side*, aoao akau.
Right, n. 1. Ka pono; ka pololei.
2. He kuleana. SYN. claim.
Right, v. E hooponopono; hoopololei.
Right'-an'gle, n. Huina kupono.
Right'eous (ri'chus), adj. Pono.
Right'eous'ness, n. Ka pono.
Right'ful, adj. 1. Maoli. *Rightful heir*, ka hooilina maoli.
2. Pono-i'.
Right'ful-ly, adv. Me ka pono maoli.
Right'-hand'ed, adj. Maa i ka lima akau.
Right'ly, adv. Pono. *Rightly judge*, koho pono.
Rig'id, adj. 1. Oolea. SYN. severe.
2. Lualua ole; oolea. SYN. stiff.
Rig'id-ly, adv. Me ka oolea; kupaa.
Rig'ma-rôle, n. Kamailio lapuwale.
Rig'or-ous, adj. 1. Oolea.
2. Anuanu. *A rigorous climate*, he kau anuanu.
Rill, n. Kahawai liilii.
Rim, n. Kae; lihilihi.
Rind, n. Ka ili owaho o ka hua ai.
Ring, n. 1. He apo; he komo.
2. He hui e aua ana i kekahi mau pomaikai no lakou iho.
Ring, v. E kani; e hookani.
Ring'lead'er, n. He alakai ma ke kolohe.
Ring'let, n. Owili lauoho.
Ring'worm (wûrm), n. He ane.
Rinse, v. E ka'ka' i ka wai.
Ri'ot, n. He haunaele. SYN. tumult.
Ri'ot-ous, adj. Hoohaunaele.
Rip, v. E wehe hou i ka humuhumu; e nahae.
Rip, n. He nahae ma ka lole.
Ripe, adj. Pala. *Fully grown*, oo. *Fully grown, but not ripe*, oo, aole nae i pala.
Rip'ple, n. He onini; kahe nahe; owe nahe.

Rise, v. 1. E ala; e eu; e ku.
2. E puka. *The sun rises*, ke puka nei ka la.
3. E pii. *Prices rise*, pii na kumukuai.
Rise, n. Ka pii ana.
Ris'i-bil'i-ty, n. Ake e akaaka.
Ris'ing, n. Ke ala ana.
2. Ke ala kue ana. SYN. insurrection.
Risk, n. He pilikia. *To take a risk*, e haawe i ka pilikia; e haawe i ka poino.
Risk'y, adj. Paapu i na pilikia.
Rite, n. He hana hoomana.
Rit'u-al, n. Buke o na hana hoomana.
Riv'al, n. Mea paio pu; hoa paio.
Riv'al, adj. Paio pu.
Ri'val-ry, n. Ka paio pu ana. SYN. competition.
Rive, v. E wawahi; e haehae. SYN. cleave; split.
Riv'er, n. Muliwai.
Riv'et, v. Kui makia.
Riv'et, v. 1. E makia me ke kui.
2. E hoopaa; e kauo. *Rivet the attention*, e kauo i ka noonoo.
Riv'u-let, n. Kahawai uuku. SYN. rill.
Road, n. Alanui; ala.
Road'stead, n. Wahi ku moku.
Road'ster, n. He lio ikaika ma ka hele.
Roam, v. E auwana hele; holoholo.
Roar, n. 1. Leo uwo; leo haalulu.
2. *Roar of the surf*, paepu o ka nalu.
Roast, v. 1. E pulehu. SYN. roast in an oven; bake.
2. Koala. SYN. roast on the coals.
Roast'er, n. Puaa liilii mea pulehu.
Rob, v. E hao wale; e powa'.
Rob'ber, n. He powa; hao wale.
Rob'ber-y, n. Hana powa; hao wale.
Robe, n. Lole hooluelue.
Ro-bust', adj. Puipui; ikaika. SYN. strong.
Rock, n. Pohaku nunui.
2. *Sunken rocks*, puko'a.
Rock, v. 1. E paipai. *Rock the cradle*, e paipai i ka moe keiki.
2. Kuoe. SYN. rock, as a ship in the calm.
Rock'er, n. Noho paipai. SYN. rocking chair.
Rock'et, n. Ahikaolele.
Rock'ing-horse, n. Lio laau paipai.
Rock'salt, n. Paakai i eliia.
Rock'y, adj. Pohaku. *Rocky land*, aina pohaku.
Rod, n. 1. Laau hahau; laau hili.
2. He roda, 16½ kapuai.
3. He laau loihi. *Fishing rod*, kamokoia.
Rogue (rōg), n. He mea apiki.
Rogu'ish, adj. Apiki; mahaoi.
Roil, v. 1. E kaawili a lepo.
2. E hoonau'kiu'ki. SYN. stir up.
Roil'y, adj. SYN. turbid.
Roll, v. 1. E olokaa. *Roll the stone*, e olokaa i ka pohaku.

2. E kakaa, *roll in the dirt*, e kakaa iloko o ka lepo.

3. E owili.

Roll′, *n.* He owili.

Roll′call, *n.* Papa kahea inoa.

Roll′ing-pin, *n.* Kui wili palaoa.

Ro′man, *adj.* No Roma.

Ro′mance, *n.* He kaao.

Ro-man′tic, *adj.* 1. Ulu wale o ka noonoo.

2. *A romantic scene*, he nanaina nani.

Romp, *n.* 1. He paani ikaika.

2. He kaikamahine mahaoi.

Rood, *n.* Hapa-ha′ o ka eka.

Roof, *n.* Hale oluna; kaupoko.

Roof, *v.* E kukulu i ke kaupoko.

Roof′less, *adj.* 1. Kaupoko ole.

2. Nele i ka hale ole.

Room, *n.* 1. He keena; lumi.

2. Wahi akea; wahi kaawale. *Make room*, e hooakea; e hookaawale.

Room′y, *adj.* Akea; kaawale. SYN. spacious.

Roost, *v.* E kau mehe moa la.

Roost′er, *n.* Moa kane. SYN. cock.

Root, *n.* He aa; he kumu.

Root, *v.* 1. E hookumu.

2. E eku.

Rope, *n.* Kaula.

Rope′mak′er, *n.* Mea hana kaula.

Rope′walk, *n.* Hale hana kaula.

Rope′yarn, *n.* Pulupulu hana kaula.

Rose, *n.* He pua rose.

Ro′se-ate, *adj.* 1. Ulaula, mehe rose.

2. Omeomeo.

Rose′bush, *n.* Kumu rose.

Ros′ter, *n.* Papa inoa o na lii koa.

Ros′trum, *n.* He awai hai-olelo.

Ros′y, *adj.* Omeomeo. SYN. roseate.

Rot, *n.* Palaho′. SYN. putrefaction.

Ro′ta-ry, } *adj.* Kaa; kakaa.
Ro′ta-to-ry, }

Ro′tate, *v.* E kaa ma ka iho.

Ro-ta′tion, *n.* 1. Ke kaa ana.

2. *Read in rotation*, e heluhelu kaahele.

Rote, *n.* 1. Ka hoopaa naau; hai paanaau. *Read by rote*, e heluhelu paanaau.

Rot′ten, *adj.* 1. Palaho; popopo; palakahuki.

2. *Rotten egg*, hua aelo.

Rot′ten-stone, *v.* Pohaku palupalu mea anai.

Ro-tund′, *adj.* Nemunemu.

Ro-tund′i-ty, *n.* Ke ano poepoe.

Rou-e′, *n.* Kanaka hoohaumia.

Rough (rŭf), *adj.* 1. Okalakala. *A rough voice*, leo okalakala.

2. Apuupuu; malualua. *A rough country*, he aina malualua.

3. Kupikipiki-o′.

4. Keemoa; niha; kamaniha. SYN. surly; crabbed.

Rough, *n.* Kanaka hakaka wale.

Rough, *v.* *To rough it* e noho e like me ka nihi; e noho hemahema.

Rough′hew (rŭf), *v.* E kalai mua.

Rough′ly, *adj.* 1. Me ka lima oolea.

2. Okalakala. *To answer roughly*, e pane okalakala.

Rough′ness, *n.* Ke ano okalakala; malualua, etc.

Rough′shod, *adj.* 1. Kamaa oolea.

2. ano oolea; paakiki. *To ride rough-shod*, e hooko me ka manao ole aku i ka ehaeha o hai.

Round, *adj.* Poepoe.

Round, *n.* 1. He puni.

2′ Laau poepoe o ke alapii.

Round, *v.* E hoo-popo; e hana a poepoe. *To round off corners*, e pohe; e pohuku.

Round′a-bout′, *adj.* Pololei ole; paewaewa.

Round′ed, *p. p.* Poheoheo.

Round′ly, *adv.* Akea; me ka wiwo ole. SYN. openly; boldly.

Rouse′, *v.* 1. E ala′e; e lalelale; e eu.

2. E hoo-ala; e hoo-eueu.

Rout, *v.* E hoo-auhee. SYN. vanquish.

Route (rūte), *n.* He ala e hele ai.

Rou-tine′, *n.* Ke ano mau o ka hana. *Daily routine*, na hana mau o ka la. SYN. round.

Rove, *v.* E hele auwana. SYN. roam.

Rov′er, *n.* Mea hele auwana; he kuheleloa.

Row, *n.* He haunaele; uluaoa. SYN. riot.

Row, *n.* Lalani.

Row, *v.* E hoe waapa.

Row′el, *n.* Ke kui o ke kepa′.

Roy′al, *adj.* Alii.

Roy′al-ly, *adv.* Me he moi la.

Roy′al-ty, *n.* 1. Ke kulana moi.

2. He mahele no ka mea nona ka pono.

Rub, *v.* E anai; hookalakala. SYN. scour.

Rub′bish, *n.* Opala.

Ru′bi-cund, *adj.* Ulaula. *A rubicund visage*, he helehelena ulaula.

Ru′by, *n.* Pohaku momi.

Rud′der, *n.* Hoeuli.

Rud′dy, *adj.* Ehu.

Rude, *adj.* 1. Mahaoi; niha.

2. Kuaaina. SYN. uncultivated.

Rude′ly, *adv.* 1. Mahaoi; niha.

2. Hemahema. *Rudely constructed*, kukulu hemahema ia.

Rude′ness, *n.* Ano kamaniha; ano mahaoi.

Ru′di-ment, *n.* He mole; kumumua. *Rudiments of knowledge*, na kumumua o ka ike.

Rue, *v.* E mihi; e mamina. SYN. regret.

Rue′ful, *adj.* Kaumaha; luuluu.

Ruf′fi-an, *n.* Kanaka lokoino; he pepehi kanaka.

Ruf′fle, *v.* 1. E hoouluhua. SYN. vex.

2. E pihapiha lole.

3. E onini mai la i ke kai.

Rug, *n.* 1. Moena wawae.

2 Pela moe.

Rug′ged, *adj.* 1. Apuupuu; malualua.

2. Puipui.

Rŭ'in, *n.* 1. Poino loa.
2. Kahua hale i helelei.
Rŭ'in-oŭs, *adj.* 1. Poino. SYN. disastrous.
2. Helelei. *In a ruinous condition,* helelei wale.
Rŭle, *n.* He loina; rula. SYN. regulation.
Rŭle, *v.* 1. E noho aupuni; noho alii.
2. E lanakila. SYN. triumph.
3. E kaha lalani.
4. E hoomalu. SYN. govern.
Rŭl'er, *n.* 1. He poo aupuni; he luna.
2. He rula laau.
Rŭm, *n.* Rama; wai ona.
Rŭm'ble, *v.* E haalulu; e nakulu.
Rŭm'bling, *adj.* Manunu'nu; nakulu.
Rŭ'mi-nāte, *v.* E hoolualuai. SYN. chew the cud.
Rŭ'mor, *n.* He lono wale.
Rŭmp, *n.* Ke kikala.
Rŭm'ple, *v.* E hoo-mimino.
Rŭn, *v.* 1. E holo; e holo mama.
2. E kahe. SYN. flow.
Rŭn, *n.* He holo.
2. He wahi kahawai uuku.
3. He kikoo nui i ke dala ma ka baneko mamuli o ka maka'u.
4. Ke kau mau ana. *A run of good luck,* ke kau mau ana o ka pomaikai.
5. Ka hahai mau ana. *Run of bad luck,* ka hahai mau ana o ka poino.

Rŭn'a-wāy, *n.* Mea mahuka.
Rŭn'ner, *n.* 1. Kanaka kukini.
2. He holua.
Ru-pee', *n.* Dala o Inia, 46 keneta.
Rŭpt'ūre, *n.* 1. He mokuahana.
2. He puu-lele. SYN. hernia.
Rŭpt'ūre, *v.* E mokuahana; e moku.
Rŭ'ral, *adj.* No kuaaina. *Rural districts,* na wahi o kuaaina.
Rŭse, *n.* Hana hoohalua; hana maalea. SYN. artifice; stratagem.
Rŭsh, *n.* 1. Naku; kaluha; akaakai.
2. He holo nui.
Rŭsh, *v.* E nei.
Rŭs'sian, *n.* Kamaaina no Rusia.
Rŭst, *n.* He popo. *Iron rust,* kukaehao.
Rŭs'tic, *n.* He kanaka no kuaaina.
Rŭs'ti-cāte, *v.* E hoonanea ma kuaaina.
Rŭs-tic'i-ty, *n.* Ke ano kuaaina.
Rŭs'tle, *v.* E nehe; nakulukulu.
Rŭst'y, *adj.* 1. Popo; popopo.
2. Poina wale; poina loa.
Rŭt, *n.* He mawae ma ke alanui. *To follow in a rut,* e hooko mau ma ke ano kahiko (mehea'la e hahai ana i ka mawae o ke alanui.)
Rŭth'less, *adj.* Menemene ole; lokoino. SYN. pitiless.

S

Săb'bath, *n.* La Sabati.
Să'ber, }
Să'bre, } *n.* He pahikaua.
Să'ble, *adj.* Eleele ;pouli.
Săc'cha-rine, *adj.* Ono, me he ko la.
Să'cer-dō'tal, *adj.* Pili i ka oihana kahuna pule.
Săck, *n.* 1. Eke. SYN. bag.
2. He ku'ka.
Săck, *v.* E luku; e powa. SYN. plunder; ravage.
Săck'ing, *n.* Lole hana eke.
Săc'ra-ment, *n.* Ahaaina a ka Haku.
Să'cred, *adj.* 1. Hoano; hemolele. SYN. holy.
2. Laa; kapu. SYN. dedicated; consecrated.
Să'cred-ness, *n.* Ke ano laa; ano kapu.
Săc'ri-fĭçe, *n.* 1. He mohai.
2. He poho'. *To sell at a sacrifice,* e kuai poho'.

Săc'ri-fĭce, *v.* E mohai; e hoopoino; hoo-poho'.
Săc'ri-lege, *n.* Ka hoohaumia ana i na mea hoano.
Săc'ri-lē'gious, *adj.* Manao hoino i na mea hoano. SYN. impious.
Săd, *adj.* Kaumaha; luuluu; ehaeha.
Săd'den, *v.* E hookaumaha i ka naau.
Săd'dle, *n.* Noho lio.
Săd'dler-y, *n.* Na lako no ka hoa ana i ka lio.
Săd'dle-tree, *n.* Laau noho lio.
Săd'ly, *adv.* Me ke kaumaha o ka naau.
Săd'ness, *n.* Kaumaha; luuluu; mokuahua; mokumokuahua.
Săfe, *adj.* 1. Malu; maluhia; lulu; palekana.
2. Pilikia ole.
Săfe, *n.* 1. Pahu waiho dala.
2. He pa waiho ai.
Săfe'-eŏn'duct, *n.* Palapala hoomalu kino ma ka hele huakai ana iloko o ka aina o ka enemi.

Safe'guard, *n.* He pale no ka poino.
Safe'ly, *adv.* Maluhia; palekana.
Safe'ty, *n.* Maluhia; malu; lulu.
Safe'ty-lamp, *n.* Kukui hoomalu ola, no ke komo ana ma na lua eli.
Safe'ty-valve', *n.* Pani hookuu mahu.
Sag, *v.* E alu; e alualu.
Sa-ga'cious, *adj.* Noeau; naauao. SYN. wise.
Sa-gac'i-ty, *n.* Noeau; naauao. SYN. wisdom.
Sage, *n.* 1. He kanaka naauao.
2. He laau ala, mea hoomiko ai.
Sage, *adj.* Naauao.
Sail, *n.* 1. He pea.
2. He hooholo ma ke kai a wai e ae paha.
Sail, *v.* E hooholo; e holo. *Sail for pleasure,* e kakele waa.
Sail'cloth, *n.* Lole hana pea.
Sail'loft, *n.* Keena hana pea.
Sail'mak'er, *n.* Mea hana pea.
Sail'or, *n.* He hooholo moku; luina.
Saint, *n.* He mea hemolele.
Saint'ly, *adv.* Hemolele.
Sake, *n.* Pono. *For the sake of the people,* no ka pono o ka lahui.
Sal'a-ble, *adj.* Lilo koke ke kuai ia.
Sal'ad, *n.* He ai mikomiko.
Sal'a-ried, *adj.* Uku paaia. *Annual salary,* uku paa o ka makahiki.
Sal'a-ry, *n.* Uku paa; uku makahiki.
Sale, *n.* He kuai lilo. *On sale,* waiho ana no ke kuai.
Sales'man, *n.* Kanaka kuai; kupakako.
Sa'line, *adj.* 1. Paakai. *Saline particles,* na hu'na paakai.
2. Miko i ka paakai.
Sa-li'va, *n.* Wale.
Sal'i-vat'ed, *n.* Hookaheia ka wale.
Sal'low, *adj.* Olenalena.
Sal'ly, *v.* 1. E puka aku mawaho.
2. E hoouka kaua.
Sal'ly-port, *n.* Puka komo o ka pakaua.
Sal'mon (sam'on), *n.* Kamano.
Sa-loon', *n.* Keena akea. *A drinking saloon,* keena inu wai-ona. *Gambling saloon,* keena pili-waiwai. *Photographic saloon;* keena pai-kii.
Salt, *n.* Paakai.
Salt, *v.* E ko-pi' i ka paakai.
Salt'cel'lar, *n.* Ipu paakai.
Sa-lu'bri-ous, *adj.* Oluolu. SYN. healthy. *A salubrious climate,* he kau oluolu.
Sa-lu'bri-ty, *n.* Ano oluolu; kupono i ke ola kino.
Sal'u-ta-ry, *adj.* Maluhia; kupono. SYN. beneficial; useful; wholesome.
Sal'-u-ta'tion, *n.* Uwe aloha; olelo aloha. SYN. greeting.
Sal-u'ta-to'ry, *n.* E haawi ana i ke aloha.
Sa-lute', *v.* E haawi ana i ka mahalo; E aloha aku; e uwe aloha.
Sal'vage, *n.* Ka uku no ka hoopakele ana i ka moku a ukana moku paha.

Sal-va'tion, *n.* Ola; Ola Mau Loa.
Salve (säv), *n.* Laau hamo eha.
Sal'ver, *n.* Pa metala.
Sal'vo, *n.* Ke kani like ana o kekahi mau pu.
Same, *adj.* Ia mea hookahi no; mea like.
Same'ness, *n.* Ka like; ka lokahi.
Sam'ple, *n.* Ana hoohalike.
San'a-to-ry, *adj.* Ku i ke ola kino. SYN. sanitary.
Sanc'ti-fi-ca'tion, *n.* Ka hoo-laa ana.
Sanc'ti-fy, *v.* E hoo-laa; e hoano.
Sanc'ti-mo'ni-ous, *n.* Hoomana hookamani.
Sanc'tion, *v.* E apono. SYN. approve.
Sanc'ti-ty, *n.* Ke ano hemolele; ano hoano.
Sanc'tu-a'ry, *n.* Wahi hoano; luakini.
Sanc'tum, *n.* Keena malu'.
Sand, *n.* O'ne.
Sand'al, *n.* Kamaa hawele.
San'dal-wood, *n.* Iliahi.
Sand'stone, *n.* Pohaku oneone; he papaakea.
Sand'wich, *n.* He mau apana berena me ka i'o mawaena.
Sand'wich, *v.* E hookomo mawaena o na mea elua.
San'dy, *adj.* 1. Oneone.
2. Ehu. *Sandy hair,* lauoho ehu.
Sane, *adj.* Lalau ole ka manao.
San'gui-na-ry, *adj.* Puni koko; hookahe koko. SYN. bloody.
San-guine, *adj.* Naau hoihoi.
San'i-ta-ry, *adj.* No ke ola kino.
San'i-ty, *n.* Ka pololei o ka noonoo.
Sap, *n.* Ka wai o na mea ulu.
Sap, *v.* E kohi malalo iho; e eli malalo iho. SYN. undermine.
Sa'pi-ent, *adj.* Naauao. SYN. wise.
Sap'ling, *n.* Kumu laau opio.
Sar'casm, *n.* Olelo loiloi. SYN. satire.
Sar-cas'tic, *adj.* Loiloi; hoohenehene. SYN. satirical; caustic.
Sar-coph'a-gus, *n.* Pahu-pohaku kupapau.
Sar'di-us, *n.* Pohaku momi; saredio.
Sar-don'ic, *adj.* Henehene hookamani. *Sardonic laugh,* akaaka hookamani.
Sash, *n.* 1. Kaei puhaka.
2. Laau aniani no ka pukamakani.
Sa'tan, *n.* Satana; Diabolo. SYN. the Devil.
Sa-tan'ic, *adj.* Ano Satana; ino loa.
Satch'el, *n.* Eke buke.
Sat'el-lite, *n.* 1. He hoku' liilii e poai ana i ka hoku' nui.
2. He hoopilimeaai.
Sa'ti-ate, *v.* E hoo-lawa; e ke'na; maona.
Sa-ti'e-ty, *n.* Ka lawa pono; ka piha pono.
Sat'in, *n.* Kilika pahoehoe.
Sat'ire, *n.* Olelo loiloi no na hana kupono ole.
Sa-tir'ic-al, *adj.* Hoohenehene ana i ka hewa.

Săt'is-făc'tion, n. 1. Ka oluolu o ka manao.
2. Ke ko ana o ka makemake.
Săt'is-făc'to-ri-ly, adv. Aponoia.
Săt'is-făc'to-ry, adj. 1. Kupono; pono. A satisfactory answer, he haina pono.
2. Ku i ka makemake.
Săt'is-fy, v. 1. E hooko i ka makemake.
2. E hooia. SYN. prove.
3. E hoo-kaa. Satisfy a claim, e hookaa i ka aie, also hoo-na'.
4. Satisfy thirst, e kena i ka makewai.
5. Satisfy hunger, e hoopau i ka pololi.
6. Satisfy the wants of a child, e hoo-na i ke keiki.
Săt'rap, n. He kiaaina ma Peresia.
Săt'u-răte, v. E hoo-ma-u'.
Săt'u-răt'ed, adj. Heo-u'ia.
Săt'ur-day, n. La hoomalolo; Poaono.
Săt'ur-nă'li-ă, n. pl. Ahaaina uhauha.
Săt'ur-nine, adj. Nanau.
Săuçe, n. Kai ono no ka mea ono.
Săuçe, v. E pakike'; e honekoa.
Săuçe'box, n. Keiki paoke'; keiki mahaoi.
Său'çer, n. Pa kiaha.
Său'çy, adj. Pakike', honekoa; mahaoi.
Săun'ter, v. E holoholo hoonanea.
Său'sage, n. I'o kaki.
Săv'age, n. He kanaka hihiu; kanaka hupo. SYN. barbarian.
Săv'age, adj. Hihiu; lokoino. SYN. barbarous; cruel.
Săv'age-ly, adv. Me ka lokoino loa.
Sa-văn'na, n. Aina papu; aina malailai. SYN. prairie; pampas.
Sa-vant' (sa-vong), n. Kanaka naauao.
Săve, v. 1. E malama. SYN. take care of.
2. E hoopakele. SYN. rescue.
3. E hoola. SYN. redeem.
Săv'ing, adj. 2. Hoomakaulii.
2. A saving clause, he olelo e pakele ai.
Săv'ing, prep. Koe. SYN. except.
Săv'ings, n. Na loaa i hoililili ia.
Săv'ior } n. 1. Ka Hoola; Iesu Kristo.
Săv'iour } 2. Mea e hoopakele ana.
Săv'or, n. 1. Liu. The savor of salt, ka liu o ka paakai.
2. He mea aia.
Săv'vo-ry, adj. Ono; mikomiko.
Săw, n. 1. He pahiolo.
2. Olelo naauao. SYN. proverb.
Săw'dust, okaoka papa.
Săw'pit, n. He lua olo papa.
Săw'yer, n. Kanaka olo papa.
Săy, v. E olelo; e i; e hai.
Săy'ing, n. He olelo.
Scăb, n. He papaa ma ka ili.
Scăb'bard, n. Wahi' pahikaua. SYN. sheath.
Scăf'fold, n. He amana. SYN. gallows; gibbet.
Scăf'fold-ing, n. Wahi e ku ai o ka poe kukulu.
Sea̤ld, v. E wela i ka wai, a mahu paha.

Sea̤ld, n. 1. He wela ma ka ili no ka wai wela, a mahu paha.
2. He mai ma ka iwi poo.
Sea̤le, n. 1. He ana. SYN. measure.
2. Na leo pă-ko-li.
3. Unahi. SYN. fish-scale.
4. He papa ana kumukuai; ana uku.
5. He anuu.
Sea̤le, v. 1. E pii iluna. SYN. mount; ascend.
2. E wehe i na unahi.
3. E ana.
Sea-lène', adj. Like ole o na aoao me na huina.
Sea̤les, n. Ana kaupaona.
Sca̤lp, n. Iwi poo.
Sca̤lp'el, n. Pahi oki a ke kauka.
Sca̤l'y, adj. Paa i na unahi.
Sea̤mp, n. Mea hana apiki. SYN. knave.
Sea̤m'per, v. E holo ki'ki'.
Sea̤mp'ish, adj. Apiki.
Sea̤n, v. E hakilo; e kiai pono.
Sea̤n'dal, n. He olelo, a he hana, hoohaumia.
Sca̤n'dal-ous, adj. Haumia; hoohihia.
Sca̤n'dal-mŏng'er, n. He wahaohi.
Sea̤nt, }
Sea̤nt'y, } adj. Lawa ole.
Sca̤nt'ling, n. Laau kua.
Sea̤pe'gŏat, n. Mea i hoopaiia no na hewa o hai.
Sea̤pe'grăçe, n. Mea apiki maoli.
Scap'u-lă, n. Ke kipoohiwi.
Sea̤r, n. Linalina; moali. Scar from burning, kalakala wela.
Sea̤rçe, adj. Kakaikahi; ike pinepine ole ia.
Sea̤rçe'ly, adv. Aneane hiki ole.
Sea̤r'çi-ty, n. Ka lawa ole; ka nele.
Sea̤re, v. E hoopuiwa. To scare away animals, e hoohemu.
Sea̤re'crow, n. He mea hoohemu manu.
Sea̤rf, n. Lole hawele a-i'.
Sca̤r'let, adj. Ulaula.
Sca̤r'let fe̤'ver, n. He fiva; fiva ula.
Sea̤th'less, adj. Poino ole. SYN. without harm.
Sea̤t'ter, v. 1. E hoohelelei. SYN. strew.
2. Hoopuehu. SYN. disperse.
Sea̤t'ter-ing, n. Helelei liilii.
Sea̤v'en-ger, n. Mea hoomaemae alanui kulanakauhale.
Sçe̤ne, n. He nanaina.
Sçe̤n'er-y, n. He nanaina ma ka aina.
Sçe̤nt, n. 1. He ala; ka honi o ka ihu.
2. He meheu. A foul scent, he pilo.
Sçe̤nt, v. 1. E moani. SYN. perfume.
2. E honi.
Sçe̤nt'less, adj. Ala ole.
Sçe̤p'ter, n. Kookoo alii.
Sche̤d'üle, n. Papa hoike; papa kuhikuhi. A schedule of prices, papa kuhikuhi kumukuai.
Sche̤me (skēme), n. He kumu hana; hana i noonooia.

SCHEME 181 SCRUPULOUS

Scheme, v. E poonoo; e noonoo hana. SYN. plan.

Schism (sizm), n. He mokuahana.

Schis-mat'ic, adj. Mokuahana.

Schol'ar, n. 1. Haumana kula. SYN. pupil.
2. Kanaka makaukau ma ka ike.

Schol'ar-ly, adj. Makaukau ma ka ike. SYN. learned.

Schol'ar-ship, n. 1. Ka makaukau o ka ike.
2. He kulana kokua ma ke kula.

Scho'li-um, n. Manao pili o ka manao hai.

School (skool), n. He kula ao.

School, v. E ao.

School'fel'low, n. He hoa kula. SYN. school-mate.

School'house, n. Hale kula.

School-ing, n. Ke ao ana ma ke kula.

School'-ma'am, n. Kumu kula wahine.

School'-mas'ter, n. Kumu kula. SYN. school teacher.

School'teach'ing, n. Oihana ao kula.

Schoon'er, 1. Kialua.
2. Kiaha nui, mea inu bia.

Sci'ence, n. 1. Ike; ike i hoonohonoho pono ia.
2. Akeakamai.

Sci'en-tif'ic, adj. Akeakamai.

Sci'en-tif'ic-al-ly, adv. Mamuli o na loina o ke akamai.

Sci'ent-ist, n. Kanaka akeakamai.

Scin-til'la, n. He huna; lihi iki.

Scin'til-late, v. E imoimo mehe hoku la; e anapanapa. SYN. twinkle.

Sci'on, n. Mamo; la'la'.

Scis'sors, n. pl. Upa' oki.

Scoff, v. E olelo haakei; e kuamuamu.

Scof'fer, n. Kanaka haakei.

Scold, a. E nuku; hookikina; wahapaa.

Scold'ing, n. He olelo huhu; olelo nuku.

Scon̄ce, n. He poo.

Scoop, n. He kioe.

Scoop, v. E kioe; e poo.

Scoop'net, n. He upena liilii paa lima.

Scope, n. 1. Ke kumu. SYN. design.
2. The scope of the eye, ka nanaina o ka maka.
3. He palena o ke kumumanao.

Scorch, v. E papaa i ka wela; e hoowela; paawela.

Score, n. 1. Iwakalua. Three-score and ten, ekolu iwakalua me ka umi.
2. He papa kakau kaha.
3. To pay up old scores, e hookaa i na aie kahiko; e hopu no na hala kahiko.

Score, v. 1. E kakau kaha. To score a game, e eo ma na kaha.
2. To score up against one, e hoomauhala.

Sco'ri-a, n A'a' pele.

Scorn, v. E hoohenehene; e hoowaha'waha'.

Scorn'er, n. He kanaka haakei.

Scorn'ful, adj. Haakei.

Scor'pi-on, n. Moo niho-awa.

Scotch, v. E paipai ka huila i kaa ole.

Scotch'man, n. Kamaaina no Sekotia.

Scot'free, adj. Hookuia me ka uku ole.

Scoun'drel, n. He mea i lilo loa i ka hewa.

Scour, v. 1. E anai; e hoohinuhinu.
2. E holo a puni me ka imi ana. Scour the country for food, e holo a puni ka aina e imi ana i ai.

Scourge (skurge), n. 1. He kaula hili.
2. He mai ahulau.
3. He hoopai.

Scout, n. He kiu no ka puali koa.

Scout, v. E loiloi; e hoohenehene. SYN. ridicule.

Scow, n. He kao; waapa nui halihali ukana.

Scowl, n. Hookuekue maka.

Scram'ble, v. E kokolo ma na kuli.
2. E hopuhopu aku.

Scrap, n. Apana liilii; hakina; huna. A scrap of news, hunahuna nuhou.

Scrap'book, n. Buke hooiliili hunahuna olelo.

Scrape, v. 1. E koli; e kolikoli.
2. E wao; wauwau. SYN. scratch.
3. E koekoe.

Scrape, n. Hihia.

Scrap'er, n. Mea koekoe; mea kolikoli.

Scratch, v. 1. E wao; e wauwau.
2. E helu. SYN. scratch as a hen.

Scratch, n. He kaha wale.

Scrawl, v. E kakau me ka pupuahulu.

Scraw'ny, adj. Iika; lii.

Scream, v. E uwa'; e uwe nui.

Screech, n. He kani okalakala.

Screen, v. 1. E pale; e huna'. SYN. shelter; hide.
2. E kanana. SYN. sift.

Screw (skru), n. 1. Kui nao; wili nao.
2. Screw of a steam ship, wili kakaa o o ka mokuahi.

Screw, v. E uma; e wili.

Screw'driv'er, n. Wili-kui-nao.

Screw'pine, n. Puhala. SYN. pandanus.

Scrib'ble, v. E kakau wale aku.

Scrib'bler, n. Mea kakau wale.

Scribe, n. Kakauolelo.

Scrimp, v. E hoohaiki ma ka hoolako ana.

Scrip, n. Palapala hoike no na mahele waiwai.

Script, n. Hua kepau ano kakau lima.

Script'ur-al, adj. Ku like me ka olelo o ka Baibala.

Script'ure, n. Baibala.

Scrof'u-la, n. Ka alaala.

Scrof'u-lous, adj. Alaala.

Scroll, n. He owili pepa.

Scroll'saw, n. Pahiolo oki kuawili.

Scrub, v. E holoi ikaika.

Scrub'by, adj. Kupu ole; ii.

Scru'ple, n. 1. Haohao o ka manao; kanalua.
2. He ana no ka laau lapaau.

Scru'pu-lous, adj. Akahele loa.

Scrŭ'ti-nize, *v.* E kiai pono; e hakilo; e kiei.

Scrŭ'ti-ny, *n.* Ke kiai pono ana; ka hakilo ana.

Seŭd, *v.* 1. E holo imua o ka makani; e kalewa.
2. E holo hee aku.

Seŭf'fle, *n.* He aumeume.

Scŭll, *n.* He hoe pokole.

Scŭll'er, *n.* Kanaka hoe pa-lua i na hoe.

Scŭl'ler-y, *n.* Wahi e waiho ai na mea o ka hale kuke.

Scŭlpt'or, *n.* Mea kalai kii.

Scŭlpt'ure, *n.* Kalai kii.

Scŭm, *n.* Hu'a; huwa'.

Scŭp'per, *n.* He puka hookahe wai no ka oneki moku.

Scŭr'ril-oŭs, *adj.* Amuamu; hailiili.

Scŭr-ril'i-ty, *n.* Olelo kuamuamu.

Scŭt'tle, *v.* 1. E hoo-piho' i ka moku.
2. E holo kiki.

Scythe (sithe), *n.* Pahi oki mauu.

Sêa, *n.* Kai.

Sêa'bôard, *n.* Kahakai. SYN. seacoast.

Sêa'breeze, *n.* Makani ahe. *Seabreeze at Lahaina*, maaa. *Seabreeze at Kona*, eka. *Seabreeze at Hilo*, malua.

Sêa'côast, } *n.* Kahakai. SYN. sea-
Sêa'side, } shore.

Sêa'fâr-ing, *adj.* Holo moana.

Sêal, *n.* 1. Ilio o ke kai.
2. He sila; hoailona pai.

Sêal, *v.* E sila.

Sêal'ing-wax, *n.* Kepau sila palapala.

Sêam, *n.* Kuina.

Sêa'man, *n.* Kanaka holo moana. He luina. SYN. sailor.

Sêa'man-ship, *n.* Ke akamai ma ka hooholo moku.

Sêam'stress, *n.* Wahine humuhumu.

Sêa'pôrt, *n.* Awa ku moku.

Sêar, *v.* E kuni i ke ahi.

Sêarch, *v.* E imi; e huli. SYN. seek; look for.

Sêarch'er, *n.* He mea imi; mea huli; haumana. SYN. inquirer.

Sêarch'wǎr'rant, *n.* Palapala imi.

Sêa'rôom, *n.* Ke akea o ka moana.

Sêa'shĕll, *n.* He pupu o kai.

Sêa'shôre, *n.* Kahakai; kaha one. SYN. seaside.

Sêa'sick, *adj.* Poluea; luai-moku.

Sêa'son, *n.* 1, Kau. *Growing season*, laaulu, *Out of season*, laawela.
2. Wa kupono.

Sêas'on, *v.* 1. E hoomiko ai.
2. E hoomaloo. *Season lumber*, e hoo-maloo papa.

Sêa'son-a-ble, *adj.* Kupono i ka wa.

Sêa'son-ing, *n.* He inai. SYN. con-diment.

Sêat, *n.* 1. He noho. SYN. chair.
2. Ke kikala.
3. Kahua. *A seat of learning*, kahua hoonaauao.

Sêa'ward, *adv.* I kai; makai.

Sêa'weed, *n.* Limu.

Sêa'wôrth-y, *adj.* Kupono ke holo moana.

Sê'cant, *n.* Kaha oki.

Se-cêde', *v.* 1. E hoo-kaaokoa aku; e oki.
2. E haalele.

Se-cês'sion, *n.* Ka hookaawale ana; ke kaaokoa ana.

Se-clûde', *v.* E hookaawale ma kahi malu'.

Se-clû'sion, *n.* 1. Kahi mehameha.
2. Ka hoo-mehameha ana.

Sêc'ond, *n.* He sekona.

Sêc'ond, *adj.* Lua. *The second day*, ka lua o na la.

Sêc'ond, *v.* E kokua. *Second the motion*, e kokua i ka manao.

Sêc'ond-â'ry, *adj.* Emi mai. *Of sec-ondary importance*, emi ka waiwai.

Sêc'ond-hând', *adj.* Aole hou loa.

Sêc'ond-râte', *adj.* Aole maikai loa; emi ka maikai.

Sê'cre-cy, *n.* Ano malu'; hai ole ia. *Sworn to secrecy*, hoohikiia no ka hai ole.

Sê'cret, *n.* Olelo huna'; mea huna'.

Sê'cret, *adj.* Malu'.

Sê'cre-tâ'ry, *n.* 1. Kakau-olelo.
2. Pahu kakau palapala.
3. Kuhina aupuni.

Se-erête', *v.* 1. E huna'. SYN. hide; conceal.
2. *Secrete one's self*, e pee. SYN. hide.

Sê'cret-ly, *adv.* Malu'.

Sêct, *n.* Aoao hoomana.

Sec-tâ'ri-an, *adj.* Pili i ka aoao hoo-mana.

Sêc'tion, *n.* 1. He mahele. SYN. di-vision.
2. He hakina; apana i okiia.

Sêct'or, *n.* Hakina poai e moe ana ma-waena o na hanai elua me ko laua pio.

Sêc'u-lar, *adj.* No ke kino. *Secular affairs*, na hana e pili i ke kino.

Se-cûre', *adj.* 1. Paa.
2. Malu; lulu.

Se-cûre'ly, *adv.* Paa.

Se-cûr'i-ty, *n.* 1. Maluhia; ka hoo-paa ana.
2. Waiwai hoopaa; palapala hoopaa.

Se-dâte', *adj.* Noho malie; pihoihoi ole.

Se-dâte'ly, *adv.* Malie.

Sêd'a-tive, *n.* Laau hooluolu eha; mea hoomalielie.

Sêd'en-tâ'ry, *adj.* Noho malie; noho i ka hale. *Sedentary occupation*, na hana e hoopaa ana i ka hale.

Sêd'i-ment, *n.* Oka; maku. SYN. dregs.

Se-di'tion, *n.* Kipi. SYN. insurrection.

Se-di'tioŭs, *adj.* Kipi; hoala kipi.

Se-dûce', *v.* 1. E hoowalewale; e alakai hewa.
2. E onou; luahele. SYN. entice.

Se-dûc'er, *n.* Mea hoowalewale; mea onou.

Se-dûc'tion, *n.* Hoowalewale; onou; ka hoohaumia ana.

Se-dŭc'tive, *adj.* Onou.

Sĕd'u-loŭs, *adj.* Hooikaika. SYN. assiduous.

See, *v.* E ike; ike maka; nana.

Seed, *n.* He anoano; hua.

Seed'ling, *n.* Mea kupu mai ke anoano.

Seeds'man, *n.* Kanaka kuai anoano.

Seed'time, *n.* Wa kanu.

Seed'y, *adj.* 1. Paapu i na anoano.
2. Apulu. SYN. shabby.

Seek, *v.* E imi; e huli. SYN. search.

Seek'er, *n.* Mea imi. SYN. searcher.

Seem, *v.* Mehe mea 'la; i ka nana'ku.

Seem'ing-ly, *adv.* I ka nana'ku.

Seem'ly, *adj.* Kupono. SYN. decorous.

Seer, *n.* He kaula. SYN. prophet.

See'saw, *n.* He mahiki; makoiele.

Seethe, *v.* E baila; e kupa; e lapalapa. *A seething caldron of lava,* he lua o ke ahi lapalapa o Pele.

Sĕg'ment, *n.* Ka hapa o ka poai i okiia i ke kaula.

Sĕg're-gāte, *v.* E hookaawale. SYN.

Sēine (seen), *n.* Upena nui.

Seis'mic, *ddj.* Pili i ka olai.

Seis'mo-graph } *n.* Mikini ana i ka
Seis-mŏm'e-ter } naueue ana o na olai.

Seize, *v.* E apo; e hopu.

Seiz'ūre, *n.* Ka apo ana; ka hopu ana.

Sĕl'dom, *adj.* Kakaikahi; pinepine ole.

Se-lĕct', *v.* E wae; e koho. SYN. choose.

Se-lĕc'tion, *n.* 1. Ka wae ana. SYN. choice.
2. He olelo i waeia; mea i waeia.

Sĕlf, *adj.* Iho. *For himself,* nona iho. *For myself,* no'u iho.

Sĕlf'-ăct'ing, *adj.* E hooko ana mamuli o ka mana iloko iho.

Sĕlf'-as-sĕrt'ing, *adj.* Mahaoi.

Sĕlf'-as-sûr'ançe, *n.* Hoaano.

Sĕlf'-con-çeit', *n.* Manao akena.

Sĕlf'-cŏn-dĕmned', *adj.* Hoahewa iaia iho.

Sĕlf'-cŏn'fi-dençe, *n.* Ka paulele iaia iho.

Sĕlf'-cŏn'sçioŭs, *adj.* Manao nui iaia iho.

Sĕlf'-con-trŏl', *n.* Ka uumi ana i na kuko.

Sĕlf'-cŭlt'ūre, *n.* Ka ao ana iaia iho.

Sĕlf'-de-çeived', *adj.* Puni iaia iho.

Sĕlf'-de-ni'al, *adj.* SYN. self-control.

Sĕlf'-de-vō'tion, *n.* Ka hoolilo ana o kehahi iaia iho no ka pono o hai.

Sĕlf'-dis-trŭst', *n.* Kanalua iaia iho.

Sĕlf'-ĕd'u-cāt'ed, *adj.* Aoia e ia iho.

Sĕlf'-es-teem', *n.* Mahalo iaia iho.

Sĕlf'-ĕv'i-dent, *adj.* Maopopo me ka wehewehe ole.

Sĕlf'-ex-ĭst'ent, *adj.* E ola ana mamuli o kona mana iho; nona iho kona ola.

Sĕlf'-im-pŏrt'ant, *adj.* Hookiekie; haano.

Sĕlf'-im-pōsed', *adj.* Hapai ia mamuli o ka makemake iho.

Sĕlf'-ĭn'ter-est, *n.* Pomaikai pili kino.

Sĕlf'ish, *adj.* Pi; alunu; aua.

Sĕlf'ish-ly, *adv.* Me ka aua.

Sĕlf'ish-ness, *n.* Alunu.

Self'-lŏve, *n.* SYN. selfishness.

Sĕlf'-māde, *adj.* Kuonoono mamuli o kona hooikaika iho.

Sĕlf'-pŏs-sĕssed', *adj.* Makaukau; pihoihoi ole.

Sĕlf'-pŏs-sĕs'sion, *n.* Ka makaukau o ka naau; ano pihoihoi ole. SYN. presence of mind.

Sĕlf'-pres-er-vā'tion, *n.* Ka malama ana o kekahi iaia iho.

Sĕlf'-re-li'ançe, *n.* Ka hilinai ana maluna ona iho.

Sĕlf'-re-prōach', *n.* Hoahewa iaia iho.

Sĕlf'-re-spĕct', *n.* Makee inoa maikai.

Sĕlf'-re-strāint', *n.* SYN. self-control.

Sĕlf'-right'eoŭs, *adj.* Pono i kona manao iho.

Sĕlf'-sāme, *adj.* Ia hookahi no. *In the self-same hour,* ia hora hookahi no.

Sĕlf'-săt'is-fied, *adj.* Hanawalea.

Sĕlf'-seek'er, *n.* Mea imi nona iho wale no.

Sĕlf'-suf-fi'çien-çy, *n.* SYN. self assurance; ano haanou; hooio.

Sĕlf'-wĭlled', *adj.* Koe-a'. SYN. stubborn; obstinate.

Sĕll, *v.* 1. E kuai aku.
2. E hoopuni wale.

Sĕl'ler, *n.* Mea nana e kuai.

Sĕm'blançe, *n.* Ka like.

Sĕm'i-ăn'nu-al, *adj.* Hapa makahiki.

Sĕm'i-an'nu-al-ly, *adv.* I kela me keia hapa makahiki.

Sĕm'i-brēve, *n.* Poo; hua mele.

Sĕm'i-çir'çle, *n.* He hapa poepoe.

Sĕm'i-çir'çeu-lar, *adj.* Hapa poepoe.

Sĕm'i-eō'lon, *n.* Kiko-koma.

Sĕm'i-di-ăm'e-ter, *n.* Hapa ana waena.

Sĕm'i-na-ry, *n.* Kula kiekie; kula nui.

Sĕn'ate, *n.* Ahaolelo kiekie.

Sĕn'a-tor, *n.* Lala o ka ahaolelo kiekie.

Sĕn'a-tō'ri-al, *adj.* Pili i ka ahaolelo kiekie.

Sĕnd, *v.* 1. E hoouna. *Send a messenger,* e hoouna i elele.
2. E hooili. *Send freight,* e hooili i ukana.
3. *Send for,* e kena.

Sĕn'ile, *adj.* Palalauhala.

Sĕn'ior, *n.* 1. Ka mua. *Senior in office,* ka mua ma ka oihana.
2. He haumana o ka papa mua ma ke kula nui.

Sĕn-iŏr'i-ty, *n.* Ka mua ma ke kulana; ma ka oihana, etc. SYN. priority.

Sen-sā'tion, *n.* 1. Ka hoomaopopo ana. *Sensation of pain,* ka hoomaopopo ana i ka eha.
2. He hana hoopihoihoi. *To create a sensation,* e hana i mea e pihoihoi ai.

Sen-sā'tion-al, *adj.* Hoopihoihoi. *A sensational report,* he lono hoopihoihoi.

Sĕnse, *n.* 1. He ike. *Sense of sight,* ka ike o ka maka.
2. Ke ano. SYN. meaning.
3. Noonoo. SYN. understanding.
4. Manao. SYN. opinion.
5. *Common sense,* noonoo maoli.
Sĕnse′less, *adj.* Noonoo ole; ike ole.
Sĕn′si-bĭl′i-ty, *n.* Ka hikiwawe ana o ka ike.
Sĕn′si-ble, *adj.* 1. Ike. *Still sensible,* ke koe nei ka ike.
2. *A sensible man,* he kanaka noonoo.
Sĕn′si-bly, *adv.* 1. Me ka noonoo. SYN. judiciously.
2. I ke ike ana. *Sensibly diminished,* ua emi mai i ke ike ana.
Sĕn′si-tĭve, *adj.* 1. Pihoihoi koke.
2. Ala koke mai o ka manao.
Sĕn′si-tĭve-ness, *n.* 1. Ke ala koke mai ana o ka manao.
2. Ano pihoihoi.
Sĕn′sū-al, *adj.* Puni lealea; puni i ko ke kino. *Sensual delights,* na lealea no ke kino.
Sĕn′sū-al-ĭst, *n.* Mea puni lealea.
Sĕn′sū-āl′i-ty, *n.* Puni lealea; lilo i ko ke kino me kona mau kuko.
Sĕn′tĕnce, *n.* 1. Hopunaolelo.
2. Olelo hoopai.
Sĕn′ti-ment, *n.* He manao. SYN. thought.
2. He manao hoala kuko; hoala iini o ka naau.
3. He manao haawi i ka mahalo. SYN. toast.
Sĕn′ti-mĕnt′al, *adj.* Manao aloha konikoni.
Sĕn′ti-men-tāl′i-ty, *n.* Manao kuko.
Sĕn′ti-nel } *n.* He koa kiai.
Sĕn′try }
Sĕp′a-rāte, *v.* E hookaawale.
Sĕp′a-rate, *adj.* Kaawale; okoa.
Sĕp′-a-rāte′ly, *adv.* Pakahi.
Sĕp′a-rā′tion, *n.* Ka hookaawale ana; ke kaaokoa ana.
Sĕp′a-rā′tor, *n.* Mea hookaawale.
Sep-tĕm′ber, *n.* Sepetemaba.
Sĕp′ul-chre (ker), *n.* Hale kupapau; ilina.
Sĕp′ul-tūre, *n.* Ka hoolewa ana. SYN. burial.
Sĕ′quel, *n.* Hopena. *The sequel will shew,* na ka hopena e hoike mai.
Sĕ′quence, *n.* 1. Mea hahai; mea pili.
2. Ka hoonohonoho ana.
Se-răgl′io (se-răl′yo), *n.* Hale o na wahine o ka Moi o Tureke.
Sĕr′aph, *n.* Anela kiekie.
Ser-e-nāde′, *n.* He mele ho'alohaloha.
Se-rēne′, *adj.* 1. Lai; malie. SYN. calm.
2. Alaneo. SYN. cloudless.
3. Maluhia. SYN. peaceful.
Se-rēne′ly, *adv.* Maluhia; malie.
Se-rēn′i-ty, *n.* 1. Ano lai; lailai.
2. *Serenity of mind,* ka maluhia o ka manao.
Sĕrf, *n.* He lopa'.

Ser′geant (sär′jent), *n.* 1. He kakiana; luna koa.
2. Loio kiekie o Beritania.
Sĕ′ri-al, *n.* He kumu manao, a kaao paha, i hoopuka liilii ia i i kela me keia manawa.
Sĕ′ries, *n.* Papa. *Series of lessons,* he papa haawina.
Sĕ′ri-oŭs, *adj.* 1. Ano koikoi; ano nui.
2. Kuoo. *A serious man,* kanaka kuoo.
Sĕ′ri-oŭs-ly, *adv.* Me ke kuoo; me ka lealea ole; ma ke ano koikoi o ka manao.
Sĕr′mon, *n.* He haiao.
Sĕr′mon-īz′er, *n.* Kanaka haiao.
Sĕr′pent, *n.* He nahesa; he moo.
Sĕr′pent-ine, *adj.* Kuawili; pakaawili. SYN. sinuous.
Sĕr′rat-ed, *adj.* Nihoniho.
Sĕrv′ant, *n.* He kauwa; mea lawelawe.
Sĕrve, *v.* 1. E lawelawe; e noho kauwa.
2. Kupono. SYN. answer. *Serve a purpose,* kupono no kekahi hana.
3. Kokua. *Serve a good turn,* e kokua lokomaikai.
Sĕrv′ice, *n.* 1. ka lawelawe ana.
2. Oihana. *Government service,* oihana aupuni.
3. He halawai. *Religious service,* halawai haipule.
4. Na lako no ka papa aina. *A silver service,* na lako kala'.
Sĕrv′ice-a-ble, *adj.* Kupono; kokua.
Sĕrv′ile, *adj.* Kuapaa; kuapelu; hoopilimeaai.
Sĕr-vil′i-ty, *n.* Ke ano hoopilimeaai.
Sĕrv′i-tŭde, *n.* Ka noho ana kauwa kuapaa. SYN. slavery.
Sĕs′sion, *n.* Ka noho ana. *School session,* ka noho ana o ke kula. *Session of Legislature,* ka noho ana o ka Ahaolelo.
Sĕss′pool, *n.* He nenelu.
Sĕt, *v.* 1. E hoonoho. *Set brick,* e hoonoho pohakuula.
2. E napoo'. *The sun sets,* ke napoo' nei ka la.
Sĕt, *adj.* 1. Paa. SYN. established. *Set principles,* na loina paa.
2. Paakiki. SYN. determined.
Sĕt, *n.* He kulana. *Set on edge,* hoomania.
Sĕt-tee′, *n.* Noho koki'. SYN. sofa.
Sĕt′tle, *v.* 1. E hooponopono. *Settle accounts,* e hooponopono i na helu. *Settled in mind,* akaku'.
2. E noho; e noho paa. *Settle in a place* e noho paa ma kauwahi. *Settle down to business,* e noho paa i ka hana.
3. E hooaiai i ka maku a i ka lepo paha.
4. E emi iho ke kahua. *The house is settling,* ke emi iho nei ke kahua o ka hale.
Sĕt′tle-ment, *n.* 1. Ka hooponopono ana.
2. Ka hoonoho ana i ka aina hou.
3. He panalaau; he kauhale.
Sĕt′tler, *n.* Mea noho paa ma ka aina hou.

Sět′tlings, *n.* He maku; he oka. SYN. dregs; sediment.

Sět′tô, *n.* He mokomoko; akoakoa.

Sěv′en, *adj.* E hiku.

Sěv′en-fôld, *adj.* Pa-hiku.

Sěv′enth, *adj.* Ka hiku; he hapahiku.

Sěv′en-teen,′ *adj.* Umikumamahiku.

Sěv′en-ty, *adj.* Kanahiku.

Sěv′er, *v.* E oki a kaawale; e moku loa; poomuku.

Sěv′er-al, *adj.* He mau; kekahi mau.

Sěv′er-al-ly, *adv.* Pakahi; okoa.

Se-vēre′, *adj.* Oolea′. *A severe man,* he kanaka oolea.
2. Ikaika; nui. *A severe cold,* he kunu ikaika.
3. Ino; anuanu loa. *Severe weather,* wa ino, wa anuanu loa.

Se-vēre′ly, *adv.* Me ka oolea; me ka paakiki.
2. Loa. *Feel the cold severely,* anuanu loa; opili loa i ke anu.

Se-věr′i-ty, *n.* 1. Ke ano oolea; ano paakiki.
2. *Severity of cold or heat,* Ikaika o ke anu; a wela paha.

Sew (sô), *n.* E humuhumu; e omau.

Sew′er (sô-er), *n* Mea humuhumu.

Sew′er (sū-er), *n.* He auwai hookahe aku i ka ino o ke kulanakauhale.

Sew′er-age
Sew′age } *n.* Ka ino i hookahela′ku.

Sew′ing (sô′ing), *n.* Kela mea keia mea humuhumu.

Sěx, *n.* Ano kane a wahine paha. *Male sex,* kane. *Female sex,* wahine.

Sex-ěn′ni-al, *adj.* Kela me keia ono makahiki.

Sěx′tant, *n.* 1. He hapa-ono o ka poai.
2. Mea ana i na huina.

Sěx′ton. *n.* Luna malama luakini.
2. Mea hookani bele o ka luakini.

Sex-tū′ple, *adj.* Pa-ono.

Sěx′u-al, *adj* Ano kane a wahine.

Shăb′bi-ly, *adv.* Kohu ole. *Shabbily dressed,* kohu ole ka aahu.
2. Apiki. *Treat shabbily* e hana apiki.

Shăb′by, *adj.* Kohu ole; weluwelu.
2. Apiki. *A shabby fellow,* he kanaka apiki.

Shăck′les, *n. pl.* Kupee no ka hoopaahao.

Shāde, *n.* 1. He malumalu.
2. Uhi maka; mea pale malamalama.

Shāde, *v.* E hoo-uhi.

Shăd′ôw. *n.* A′ka.

Shăd′y, *adj.* Malumalu.

Shăft, *n.* 1. He pua.
2. Au no ke kaa lio.
3. Iho hookakaa huila.
4. Puka e komo ai i ka lua eli waiwai.

Shăg′gy, *adj.* Huluhulu.

Shāh, *n.* Inoa moi no Peresia.

Shāke, *v.* E hoolulituli; e hoonaueue; e naue.

Shāk-y, *adj.* Naueue; naka.

Shăl′lôw, *adj.* 1. Papa′u. SYN. shoal.
2. Hapapa. *Shallow soil,* lepo hapa′pa.

Shăm, *n.* Mea hookamani; mea i-o ole.

Shăm-bleş, *n.* Wahi loli bipi; hale kuai bipi.

Shāme, *n.* Hilahila; mea hilahila.

Shāme-fāç′ed, *adj.* Maka hilahila; palaimaka.

Shāme′ful, *adj.* Hilahila.

Shāme′ful-ly, *adv.* Hilahila ole.

Shāme′less, *adj.* Hilahila ole.

Shāme′less-ly, *adv.* Me ka hilahila ole.

Sham-poō′, *v.* E lomilomi.

Shăn′ty, *n.* Hale pupupu.

Shāpe, *n.* Ke ano o ke kino; hiona.

Shāpe, *v.* E hooponopono i ke kii o kekahi mea.
2. *To shape a course,* e hoopololei i ka hele ana.
3. *Shape a course of reading,* e hooponopono i na mea e heluhelu.

Shāpe′less, *adj.* Hiona ole; ano ole o ke kii.

Shāpe′ly, *adj.* Aulii; maikai. SYN. comely.

Shāre, *n.* He mahele; haawina.

Shāre′hôld-er, *n.* Ka mea nona na mahele.

Shār′er, *n.* He hoa i komo pu ma ka mahele ana.

Shärk, *n.* Ma-no′.

Shärp, *adj.* 1. Oi. *Sharp pointed,* wana.
2. Awaawa. SYN. acid; pungent.
3. Huhu. *Speak sharp words,* e olelo huhu.
4. Akamai. SYN. keen; maalea.

Shärp′en, *v.* E hookala; e hana a oi.

Shärp′er, *n.* Kanaka maalea.

Shärp′ly, *adv.* 1. Me ka huhu.
2. Me ka ikaika. *Rebuke sharply,* e ao ikaika aku.

Shärp-sět′, *adj.* Pololoi loa. SYN. very hungry.

Shăt′ter, *v.* E nahaha liilii; e wawahi liilii.

Shāve, *v.* 1. E kahi umiumi.
2. Koli; e kolikoli.

Shāv-er, *n.* Keikikane. SYN. boy.

Shāv′ing, *n.* Pulupulu laau; mea i koliia.

Shạwl, *n.* Kihei poohiwi.

Shē, *pron.* Ia; oia (ano wahine).

Shēaf, *n.* Pu-a′ palaoa.

Shēar, *v.* E ako.

Shēar′er, *n.* Mea ako.

Shēars, *n.* 1. Upa′ nui.
2. He mau koo ekolu, mea hapai i na kino kaumaha.

Shēath, *n.* He wahi′.

Shēathe, *v.* E hookomo i ka wahi.′

Shēath-ing, *n.* Mea hoo-uhi i ko lalo o ka moku.

Shěd, *n.* 1. Hale malumalu; hale kamala.
2. He lanai.

Shěd, *v.* 1. E hookahe. *Shed rain,* e hookahe aku i ka u′-a
2. E pale.

Sheen, *n.* Wakawaka; hulali.

Sheep, n. Hipa.
Sheep'fold, n. Pa hipa. SYN. sheep-pen.
Sheep'ish, adj. Maka hilahila.
Sheep'shear'er, n. Mea ako hipa.
Sheep'skin, n. Ili hipa.
2. Palapala hookuu o ke kula nui.
Sheet, n. I. He kihei moe; kapa moe.
2. Apana pepa; kalana.
3. Kaula pea moku.
Sheet'ing, n. Lole kihei moe.
Sheet-light'ning, n. Uwila e anapa ana mai o ao.
Sheik (shāke), n. He poo mamo o Arabia.
Shelf, n. Holowaa; papa waiho mea liilii.
Shell, n. 1. He pupu. Land shell, pupu kanioe.
2. He poka' pahu'; SYN. bomb.
Shell, v. 1. E ohiki; e poalo.
2. E ki-pu i na poka' pahu'.
Shell'fish, n. Mea ola o ke kai me ka iwi mawaho; e laa ka opihi, papai, ula.
Shel'ter, n. Wahi malu; wahi lulu.
Shel'ter, v. E hoomalu.
Shel'ter-less, adj. Malu ole.
Shelve, v. 1. E waiho ma ka holowaa.
2. E moe hi-o'; waiho kapakahi.
Shep'herd, n. He kahuhipa.
Shep'herd-ess, n. He kahuhipa wahine.
Sher'iff, n. Makai nui.
Shield, n. He pale; pale kaua.
Shield, v. E hoomalu; e pale.
Shift, v. 1. E hoololi. SYN. change.
2. Shift the responsibility, e hooili ka pono maluna o hai.
Shift, n. He palule wahine; mumuku.
2. Mahele wa hana.
Shift'less, adj. Loli wale; hawawa.
Shil'ling, n. Silina.
Shil'ly-shäl'ly, adv. Ano kanalua mau; lauwili wale.
Shim'mer, v. E hulali; anapanapa.
Shin, n. Lapa wawae.
Shine, v. E malamalama.
Shin'gle, n. 1. Pili laau.
2. Iliili o kahakai.
Ship, n. Moku; moku kiakolu.
Ship, v. 1. E hooili ukana maluna o ka moku.
2. Ship a sea, e popoi ke kai maluna o ka oneki moku.
3. E kepa; hoolimalima kumakahiki.
Ship'board; adv. Maluna o ka moku.
Ship-'mäs'ter, n. Kapena moku. SYN. captain.
Ship'ment, n. 1. Hooili ukana.
2. Ukana i hooiliia.
Ship'ping, n. 1. Kela me keia ano moku.
2. Shipping news, nuhou no na moku.
Ship'shape, adj. Kohu pono. SYN. in good order.
Ship'wreck (reck), n. 1. Moku i make i ka moana.
2. Shipwreck of character, poino ka inoa maikai.

Ship'wright (rīt), n. Kanaka kapili moku.
Shirk, v. E hoopalaleha; e imi i kumu e haalele hana.
Shirt, n. Palule.
Shiv'er, v. 1. E wawahi liilii. SYN. shatter.
2. E kuu-lulu; huhulu-ii'. E opili.
Shōal, n. 1. Wahi papa'u o ke kai.
2. Shoal of fish, uulu i'a.
Shock, v. E hooilihia.
Shock, n. He naueue. Shock of earthquake, naueue o ke olai.
Shock'ing, adj. Ilihia; eehia; weliweli.
Shoe, n. Kamaa.
Shoe, v. E kapili wawae hao.
Shoe'black, n. Mea balaki kamaa.
Shoe'black'ing, n. Inika kamaa.
Shoe'mäk'er, n. Humuhumu kamaa.
Shoe'string, n. Kaula kamaa.
Shoot, v. 1. E ki. Shoot from a gun, ki pu.
2. E pana. SYN. shoot from a bow.
3. E kupu. Shoot out of the ground, e kupu ae la.
Shoot, n. He oha'; pohuli. SYN. sucker.
Shoot'ing-stär', n. Hoku lele.
Shop, n. 1. Hale oihana. Carpenter shop, hale kamena.
2. Hale kuai.
Shop'-keep'er, n. Kanaka malama hale kuai.
Shop'lift'er, n. Mea aihue i ko ka hale-kuai.
Shop'ping, n. He makaikai kuai.
Shore, n. 1. Kahakai ; kapakai. SYN. coast.
2. He koo. SYN. prop.
Shore, v. E koo. SYN. prop.
Short, adj. Pokole. Too short, ekekei'.
Short'en, v. 1. E hoopokole; e hoohaiki.
2. Shorten sail, e hookuu i ka pea.
Short'hand, n. Kakau lima hoopokole. SYN. stenography.
Short'hand'ed, adj. Lawa ole na lima hana.
Short-lived', adj. Ola pokole.
Short'ly, adv. Koke; kokoke.
Short-sight'ed, adj. 1. Ike powehiwehi.
2. Noonoo ole.
Shot, n. Poka' pukuniahi.
2. Lu.
3. Ke ki ana i ka pu; ka pana ana i ka pua.
Shote, n. Puaa liilii. SYN. pig.
Shŏt'-tōw'er, n. Hale pakui kahi e hana ai i na lu.
Shoul'der, n. Poohiwi.
Shoul'der, v. 1. E auamo; e haawe; e kaupoohiwi.
2. E hoo-ke'.
Shoul'der-blāde, n. Iwi hoehoe.
Shout, v. E hooho; e kahea leo nui.
Shove, v. E pa'hu; e koo mahope.
Shov'el, n. Kopala.
Show, n. He hoikeike. To show off, e hookelakela.

Shŏw'-bĭll, *n.* Palapala hoolaha i pai ia.

Shŏw'ease, *n.* Pahu aniani; mea hoikeike i na waiwai liilii ma ka hale kuai.

Shŏw'er, *n.* Kuau'-a; naulu.

Shŏw'er, *v.* E u'-a; e ninini wai.

Shŏw'er-y, *adj.* U'-a. *A showery day*, he la u'-a.

Shŏw'i-ly, *adv.* Hookahakaha; hoohiehie.

Shŏw'man, *n.* Kanaka hoikeike mea hou.

Shŏw'y, *adj.* Hookelakela; hiehie.

Shrĕd, *n.* Apana lole weluwelu. *Torn into shreds*, haehaeia a weluwelu.

Shrew (shrŭ), *n.* Wahine pakakeu.

Shrewd, *adj.* Akamai; ike; maalea. SYN. sagacious.

Shrewd'ly, *adv.* Me ke akamai; me ka maalea.

Shriĕk, *n.* He uwa'; uwe nui. SYN. scream.

Shrĭll, *adj.* Oioi; winiwini.

Shrĭmp, *n.* Opae.

Shrĭnk, *v.* 1. Eeke; kupau.
2. *Shrink as in washing*, pauneinei.

Shrĭv'el, *v.* E mimino.

Shrŏud, *n.* Lole kupapau.

Shrŏuds, *n.* Na kaula puueo.

Shrŭb, *n.* Laau hihi, laalaau.

Shrŭb'ber-y, *n.* Na laa laau.

Shŭd'der. *v.* E haalulu. SYN. tremble.

Shŭn, *v.* E haliu aku; e alo'.

Shŭt, *v.* E pani.

Shŭt'ter, *n.* Pani puka.

Shȳ, *adj.* Hopohopo; wiwo wale; palaimaka. SYN. timid.

Shȳ'ly, *adv.* Me ka hopohopo. SYN. timidly.

Sĭck, *adj.* 1. Mai. *Sick at the stomach*, uneunea.
2. Molowa. *Sick of such talk*, molowa no ia ano olelo.

Sĭck'en, *v.* E mai.

Sĭck'ish, *adj.* Liliha; poluea.

Sĭck'le, *n.* He pahi kakiwi.

Sĭck'ly, *adj.* Onawaliwali; omaimai.

Sĭck'ness, *n.* He mai; he nawaliwali.

Side, *n.* Aoao. *Side of head*, hua-poo.

Side, *v.* E ku ma ka aoao; e kokua.

Side'bŏard, *n.* He papa waiho pa.

Side'glănçe, *n.* Awiha.

Si-de're-al, *adj.* SYN. starry. *The siderial heavens*, na lani o na hoku'.

Side'săd'dle, *n.* Noho wahine no ka lio.

Side'wĭse, *adv.* Ma ka aoao.

Sĭ'dle, *v.* E nenee pili aoao.

Siêge, *n.* E hoopuni i ke kulanakauhale ma ke kaua.

Si-ĕs'ta, *n.* He wahi hiamoe iki.

Sieve (sĭv) *n.* He kanana.

Sift, *n.* E kanana.

Sigh (sĭ), *n.* Leo uhu'.

Sight, *n.* 1. Ka ike o ka maka. *To sight or aim*, e lena.
2. He nanaina; hiohiona.

Sight'less, *adj.* Makapo; makapaa. SYN. blind.

Sight'ly, *adj.* Nani i ka nanaina.

Sign (sin), *n.* He hoailona; ouli.

Sign, *v.* 1. E kakau inoa.
2. E kuhikuhi lima aku; e peahi.

Sig'nal, *n.* He hoailona; hae hoailona. *Pilot signal*, hae pailota.

Sig'nal, *v.* E peahi hoailona; e hoailona.

Sig'nal, *adj.* Kupanaha. SYN. remarkable.

Sig'nă-tūre, *n.* 1. Ka inoa i kakauia.
2. Ka leo ki o ka leo mele.

Sign'bŏard, *n.* Papa inoa mawaho o ka hale kuai.

Sign'er, *n.* Mea kakau inoa.

Sig'net, *n.* Hoailona pai. SYN. seal.

Sig-nĭf'i-can-çy } *n.* Ke ano nui. SYN.
Sig-nĭf'i-cançe } meaning; import.

Sig-nĭf'i-cant, *adj.* Ano nui. SYN. important.

Sig'ni-fĭ-cā'tion, *n.* Ke ano. SYN. meaning.

Sig'ni-fȳ, *v.* E hoike. *Signify a desire*, e hoike i ka makemake. SYN. show; make known.

Sign-măn'u-al, *n.* Ke kakau ana o ka lima.

Sign'post, *n.* Kia kuhikuhi.

Si'lençe, *n.* Neo; leo ole.

Si'lençe, *v.* E hamau; e hoo-neo; e hoo-malie.

Si'lent, *adj.* Neo. *Be silent*, e hamau.

Si'lent-ly, *adv.* Palanehe; palanehe ole.

Silk, *n.* He silika.

Silk'en } *adj.* 1. Palupalu me he sili-
Silk'y } ka la.
2. Silika.

Silk'wŏrm, *n.* Enuhe silika.

Sĭll, *n.* Paepae puka; laau kahua o ka hale.

Sĭl'ly, *adj.* Lapuwale; naaupo. SYN. foolish.

Sĭl'ver, *n.* Kala'.

Sĭl'ver-smĭth, *n.* Kanaka hana mea kala'.

Sĭl'ver-y, *adj.* Mehe kala' la.
2. *Silvery tones*, na leo nahenahe.

Sĭm'i-lar, *adj.* Ano like.

Sĭm'i-lăr'i-ty, *n.* Ke ano like. SYN. resemblance.

Sĭm'i-lar-ly, *adv.* Like; ano like.

Sĭm'i-le, *n.* Olelo hoohalikelike.

Si-mĭl'i-tūde, *v.* Ka like; ke ano like. SYN. likeness; resemblance.

Sĭm'mer, *v.* E lapalapa iki ma ka baila ana.

Si-mŏŏn', *n.* Makani wela o Arabia.

Sĭm'per, *v.* E akaaka ano ole; akaaka wale.

Sĭm'ple, *adj.* 1. Maopopo; akaka.
2. Akahai. *To live in a simple manner*, e noho akahai.
3. Naaupo. SYN. ignorant.

Sĭm'ple-ton, *n.* Mea ike ole; mea naaupo.

Sĭm-plĭç′i-ty, *n.* 1. Akahai o ka naau.
2. Ke ano moakaka.
3. Naaupo. SYN. ignorance.
Sĭm′pli-fy, *v.* E hoomoakaka.
Sĭm′plȳ, *adv.* Wale no. SYN. merely;
only. *The truth simply*, ka oiaio wale
no.
Sĭm′u-lāte, *v.* E kookamani; e epa.
SYN. feign.
Sĭm′u-lā′tion, *n.* Ka hookamani ana.
Sĭ′mul-tā′ne-oŭs, *adj.* 1. Like. *A si-
multaneous shout*, he hoo′ho like.
2. Wa hookahi.
Sĭ′mul-tā′ne-oŭs-ly, *adj.* I ka wa hoo-
kahi.
Sĭn, *n.* Hewa; hala.
Sĭnçe, *conj.* Oiai.
Sĭnçe, *adv.* Mahope mai.
Sĭn-çēre′, *adj.* Oiaio; hookamani ole.
Sĭn-çēre′ly, *adv.* Me ka oiaio. SYN.
truly.
Sĭn-çēr′i-ty, *n.* Oiaio. SYN. truth.
Sĭne, *n.* He kaha i kaha kupono ia mai
kehahi poo o ka pio, a i ka hanai e pili
ana i kekahi poo; he koo.
Sĭ′ne-eūre, *n.* He oihana i ukuia, aohe
nae he hana.
Sĭn′ew, *n.* Olona′.
Sĭn′ew-y, *adj.* Ikaika; puipui. SYN.
strong.
Sĭn′ful, *adj.* Hewa.
Sĭn′ful-ness, *v.* Ka hewa.
Sing, *v.* E mele; memele; e pa-ko-li.
Birds sing, memele na manu. *Sing by
note*, e pa-ko-li.
Sĭnge, *v.* E kuni ko waho i ke ahi.
Sĭng′er, *n.* Mea mele; mea memele.
Sĭng′ing, *n.* Ka pa-ko-li; ke mele ana.
Sĭng′ing-bŏŏk, *n.* Buke pa-ko-li.
Sĭng′ing-mâs′ter, *n.* Kumu ao pa-ko-li.
Sĭng′ing-school, *n.* Kula pa-ko-li.
Sĭn′gle, *adj.* 1. Hookahi.
2. Mare ole.
3. Lokahi. SYN. united.
Sĭn′gle, *v.* E wae. SYN. select.
Sĭn′gle-hând′ed, *adj.* Oia hookahi
wale no. SYN. alone.
Sĭn′gle-heärt′ed, *adj.* Oiaio; hooka-
mani ole. SYN. ingenuous.
Sĭn′gly, *adv.* Pakahi. SYN. one by one.
Sĭng′-sŏng, *adj.* Leo kauo.
Sĭn′gu-lar, *adj.* 1. Hookahi, aohe elua.
2. Ano e; kupanaha.
Sĭn′gu-lăr′i-ty, *n.* Ke ano e, aohe o ke
ano mau.
Sĭn′is-ter, *adj.* 1. Hema. *Sinister hand*,
lima hema.
2. Ewaewa. *Sinister design*, manao
hooko ewaewa.
Sĭnk, *v.* 1. E piho; e poholo ilalo.
2. *To sink a pit*, e eli i lua.
3. *Decline in strength*, emi ka ikaika o
ke kino.
4. E hoo-emi; e emi. *Prices sink*, emi
ke kumukuai.
Sĭnk, *n.* 1. He kio lepo; he nenelu po-
ho′.
2. Wahi holoi pa.

Sĭnk′ing-fŭnd, *n.* Waihona dala hoo-
emi aie.
Sĭn′less, *adj.* Hewa ole; hala ole.
Sĭn′ner, *n.* He lawehala; mea hewa.
Sĭn-of′fer-ing, *n.* Mohai hewa.
Sĭn′u-oŭs, *adj.* Kuawili. SYN. ser-
pentine.
Sĭp, *v.* E inu iki; e mukiki.
Sī′phon, *n.* He ohe pelu; mea hookahe
wai.
Sĭr, *n.* Inoa mahalo no ke keonimana.
Sire, *n.* 1. He makuakane.
2. Inoa mahalo no ka moi.
Sĭ-rŏc′co, *n.* Makani wela ma Italia
me na wahi kokoke.
Sĭr′up, *n.* Molakeke.
Sĭs′ter, *n.* 1. *Sister of a brother*, kai-
kuahine.
2. *Older sister*, kaikuaana.
3. *Younger sister*, kaikaina.
Sĭs′ter-ly, *adj.* Ano hoahanau wahine.
Sĭt, *v.* E noho.
2. *Sit a hen*, e hoomoe i ka moa.
Site, *n.* Kahua. *A house site*, he kahua
hale.
Sĭt′ting, *n.* Ka noho ana. *Sitting of
Legislature*, ka noho ana o ka Ahaolelo.
Sĭt′u-ā′ted, *adj.* 1. E waiho ana; e
moe ana.
2. *Pleasantly situated*, maikai ka no-
ho′na.
Sĭt′u-ā′tion, *n.* 1. Kauwahi; wahi. *In a
good situation*, ma kauwahi maikai.
2. He oihana. SYN. occupation.
Sĭx, *adj.* E ono.
Sĭx-fŏld′, *adj.* Pa-ono.
Sĭx′teen, *adj.* Umikumamaono.
Sĭxth, *adj.* He hapa-ono; ka ono.
Sĭx′ty, *adj.* Kana-ono.
Size, *n.* Ka nui. SYN. bulk.
Skāte, *n.* He holua no ka wawae.
Skein, *n.* Owili lopi.
Skĕl′e-ton, *n.* Na iwi a pau o ke kino;
he kino iwi.
Skĕp′tic, *n.* He ai-a′; he hoomaloka.
SYN. unbeliever.
Skĕp′ti-çism, *n.* Ka hoomaloka. SYN.
unbelief.
Skĕtch, *n.* 1. Kii i kaha iki ia.
2. He kaao; he wahi olelo iki.
Skĕtch, *v.* E kahakaha; e kakau iki.
Skew′er, *n.* He o, mea hoopaa i′-o no
ka pulehu ana.
Skĭff, *n.* He waapa liilii.
Skĭll, *n.* Akamai; noeau; ano makau-
kau.
Skĭlled, } *adj.* Akamai; makaukau.
Skĭll′ful, }
Skĭll′let, *n.* Ipu-hao uuku.
Skĭll′ful-ly, *adv.* Me ke akamai.
Skĭm, *v.* E kioi.
Skĭm′mer, *n.* Puna kioi.
Skĭn, *n.* Ili; alualu.
Skĭn, *v.* E loli i ka ili.
Skĭn′flint, *n.* Kanaka laioo; maihi ili;
kanaka pi. SYN. miser.
Skĭn′ny, *adj.* Olala.

Skip, v. 1. E lelelele.
2. E kikokikoi.
3. E haalele.

Skip'per, n. Kapena o ka moku liilii.

Skir'mish, n. He hoouka iki ma ke kaua.

Skirt, n. 1. He pa-u'.
2. Lepa o ka aahu.

Skirt, v. 1. E waiho paapu. *Rocks skirt the shore,* waiho paapu na pohaku ma kahakai.
2. Ku puuluulu. *Trees skirt the river bank,* ku puuluulu na kumulaau ma kapa muliwai.

Skit'tish, adj. Puiwa.

Skulk, v. E kolo-pee. SYN. lurk.

Skull, n. Ka pu-niu; iwi poo.

Sky, n. Ke ao-uli; na lani.

Sky'light, n. Puka hoomalamalama mai luna mai.

Sky'rock'et, n. Ahikaolele. SYN. rocket.

Slab, n. Pauku palahalaha lahilahi.

Slack, adj. 1. Alualu. SYN. loose.
2. Kaulua; palaka; palaleha. SYN. dilatory.

Slack'en, v. 1. E hooluolu; hooalualu; e ko-o'. SYN. loosen.
2. E hookaulua; palaka.

Slake, v. 1. E kena. SYN. quench.
2. E hooma-u'. *Slake lime,* e hooma-u' ka puna i ka wai.

Slam, v. 1. E papani ino.
2. E kiola ino ilalo.

Sland'er, v. E alapahi; e akiaki. SYN. calumniate; defame.

Slan'der-er, n. He paokee; kanaka aki.

Slan'der-ous, adj. Alapahi; paokee.

Slang, n. Olelo kupono ole; olelo haahaa.

Slant, v. E hi-o', e moe kapakahi.

Slant'ing, adj. Hi-o; moe kapakahi.

Slap, v. E pai me ka lima.

Slap'dash, adv. Ano kapulu; pupuahulu.

Slash, v. E okioki wale; okioki ino.

Slat, n. Aaho.

Slate, n. Papa pohaku; pili pohaku.

Slat'tern, n. Wahine kapulu.

Slaugh'ter, v. 1. E pepehi wale.
2. E luku wale.

Slaugh'ter-house, n. Hale pepehi holoholona.

Slave, n. Kauwa hooluhi.

Slave, v. E luhi wale; e luhi makehewa.

Slav'er, n. Moku powa kanaka.

Slav'er-y, n. Ka hooluhi wale ana.

Slave'trade, n. Oihana powa kanaka.

Slav'ish, adj. Luhi wale; haahaa. servile.

Slay, v. E hoo-make; e pepehi. SYN. kill.

Slay-er, n. Mea hoo-make.

Sled, n. Hee holua.

Sledge, n. Hamale nui.

Sleek, adj. Nemonemo.

Sleep, v. E moe; e hiamoe.

Sleep'er, n. 1. Mea hiamoe.
2. Laau kua no ka hale.

Sleep'i-ly, adv. Makahiamoe.

Sleep'less, adj. Uluku'; hiaa.

Sleep'y, adj. Makahiamoe.

Sleet, n. He u-a i huiia me ka hau.

Sleeve, n. Lima lole.

Sleigh (slā), n. Kaa holua holo maluna o ka hau.

Slen'der, adj. 1. Wiwi. SYN. thin.
2. Makalii; puahilo. SYN. fine.
3. *A slender hold on life,* paa mahunehune i ke ola.

Slice, n. He apana lahilahi i okiia.

Slice, v. E okioki apana.

Slide, v. 1. E hee holua; e holo pahee.
2. E kaa. *A land slide,* ke kaa ana o ka lepo.

Slight, adj. 1. Wiwi. SYN. slender.
2. Mea ole; mea iki. *Of slight importance,* mea iki wale no; mea ole.

Slight, v. 1. E kapulu. *To slight work,* e kapulu ma ka hana.
2. E manao ole aku.

Slight'ly, adv. Iki.

Slim, adj. 1. Wiwi. SYN. slender.
2. *A slim dinner,* aina lawa ole.
3. *A slim congregation,* he anaina kawalawala.

Slime, n. Nenelu.

Slim'y, adj. Walewale.

Sling, v. 1. E maa.
2. *Sling a hammock,* e hohola i ka manele.

Slink, v. E kokolo aku. SYN. sneak.

Slip, v. 1. E pakika; e poholo.
2. *Slip away,* e kolo malie aku.
3. *Slip off,* e hoopahemo.

Slip, n. 1. Lala laau mea kanu.
2. He noho ma ka luakini.
3. Apana pepa loloa.
4. He lalau; he kuhihewa. *A slip of the pen,* he lalau o ka peni.

Slip'per, n. Kamaa haahaa.

Slip'per-y, adj. Pahee; hanupanupa; lalawai.

Slip'shod, adj. 1. Komoia ke kamaa inoino.
2. Ano kapulu.

Slit, v. E oki ma ka loa; e nahae.

Sliv'er, n. He moka; he apana ololi, lahilahi.

Sloop, n. Kia-kahi.

Slop, n. 1. Wai hanini wale.
2. *Slops,* wai ekaeka.
3. *Slop over,* e hanini.

Slope, n. He lapa.

Slope, v. 1. E hi-o'.
2. E mahuka.

Slop'ing, adj. E moe hi-o' ana. SYN. slanting.

Slop'py, adj. Kelekele. SYN. muddy.

Sloth, n. He molowa; hana ole. SYN. idleness.

Sloth'ful, adj. Molowa; hiamoe wale; lomaloma. SYN. idle; lazy; sluggish.

Sloth'ful-ness, n. Hiamoe wale.

Slough (slou), n. Wahi po'hopoho'.

Slóv'en, n. Mea paumaele; mea ekaeka.
Slóv'en-ly, adj. Ekaeka; paumaele; haukae.
Slŏw, adj. 1. Lohi; lolohi.
2. Apa; nahili. SYN. dilatory.
3. Lohi o ka noonoo. SYN. dull.
Slŏw, v. E hoo-lolohi; e hooholo akahele.
Slŏw'ness, n. Ka hoohakalia; hoololohi.
Slūe, v. E hull. Slue around the log, e huli i ka laau ma kona welau.
Slŭg'gard, n. Mea hiamoe wale.
Slŭg'gish, adj. 1. Hiamoe wale; loiele.
2. Kokolo. A sluggish stream, he kahawai kokolo.
Slūice, n. Wai e kahe ana ma ka puka wai.
Slŭm'ber, n. Hiamoe. SYN. sleep.
Slŭm'ber-er, n. Mea hiamoe. SYN. sleeper.
Slŭmp, v. E poholo pu ilalo. SYN. sink through.
Slūr, n. 1. He kaha apo no na hua mele.
2. He olelo hoino. A slur upon the character, he olelo hoino no ka inoa maikai.
Slūr, v. E hoo-hapala; e hookapulu.
Slŭt, n. 1. He wahine pelapela.
2. Ilio wahine.
Slȳ, adj. Maalea. SYN. cunning.
Slȳ'ly, adv. Me ka maalea. SYN. cunningly.
Smăck, v. E muki'.
Smăck, n. Moku liilii lawai'a.
Smăll, adj. 1. Uuku; iki.
2. Iii; aa. SYN. dwarfish.
3. Haahaa. SYN. mean.
Smăll'ārms, n. Na pu kau poohiwi; na pu panapana.
Smăll'pŏx, n. Mai puupuu liilii.
Smärt, adj. Akamai; eleu; miki.
Smärt, v. E maneo; eha.
Smärt'ly, adv. Eleu; mikiala.
Smärt'ness, n. Ke akamai. SYN. skill.
Smäsh, v. E wawahi; e kipo.
Smăt'ter, v. E namunamu.
Smăt'ter-er, n. Mea hemahema ma ka ike.
Smăt'ter-ing, n. He ike uuku; ike hemahema.
Smēar', v. E hoohapala. SYN. daub.
Smĕll, n. 1. E honi. Smell the fragrance, e honi i ke ala.
2. E pilau; e hauna.
Smĕll, n. 1. The sense of smell, ka ike o ka ihu; ka honi ana.
2. A sweet smell, he ala; aala.
3. A bad smell, he pilo; pilau; hauna.
Smēlt, v. E hooheehee metala.
Smīle, n. E aka iki.
Smīl'ing, adj. 1. Oluolu. A smiling morning, he kakahiaka oluolu.
2. Hoihoi. A smiling countenance, he helehelena hoihoi.
Smīl'ing-ly, adv. Me ka hoihoi.

Smîrch, v. E hapala; e paele.
Smîrk, v. See simper.
Smîte, v. E kui; e pai; e hoopai.
Smith, n. Kanaka hana i na mea metala.
Smith'y, n. Hale hana hao, etc.
Smōke, n. He u-ahi.
Smōke, v. 1. E punohu u-ahi.
2. E puhi. Smoke tobacco, puhi baka.
3. E hoo-pi'-pi'.
Smōk'er, n. Mea puhi baka.
Smōk'y, adj. 1. Paapu i ka u-ahi.
2. Pi'pi'.
Smōl'der, v. E a pi'pi'.
Smōl'der-ing, adj. Pi'pi'.
Smōoth, adj. 1. Pahee; mania. SYN. glossy.
2. Malino; malie. SYN. calm.
Smōoth, v. 1. E hana a mania.
2. E hookaawale i na mea e keakea ana.
Smōoth'ly, adv. Pahee; keakea ole ia.
Smŏth'er, v. 1. E umi; e umi wale. SYN. strangle; stifle.
2. E paa ka hanu.
Smŭg'gle, v. E hookomo kolohe i ka waiwai iloko o ka aina, me ka uku ole i ke dute.
Smŭg'gler, n. Mea hookomo kolohe i ka waiwai.
Smŭg'gling, n. Ka hookomo kolohe i ka waiwai.
Smŭt'ty, adj. Paele i ka lepo.
Snāil, n. Pupu kanioe.
Snāil'pāced, adj. Hookaulua loa; like me ke kolo ana o ka pupu.
Snāke, n. Moo; nahesa.
Snăp, v. 1. E uhaki. Snap asunder, e uhaki mawaena.
2. E pai'na. The rope has snapped, paina ke kaula.
3. E uina. Snap the whip, e uina i ka huipa.
4. E pana. SYN. snap the fingers.
5. Kepa, as snap the teeth like a dog.
6. E kanapi, as snap the gun.
7. E keu; olelo kaki.
Snăp'pish, adj. Kaki; keu. SYN. petulant.
Snāre, n. He pahele.
Snāre, v. 1. E halua; e hoohalua.
2. Snare birds, e kawili manu.
Snärl, v. E na'na.
Snärl, n. He leo na'na.
2. He hihia. SYN. tangle.
Snătch, v. E kaili ino; e lalau ino.
Snēak, v. E kolo pee.
Snēak, n. Mea kolo pee.
Snēak'-thief, n. Mea aihue i na mea liilii.
Sneer, n. He loiloi; henehene.
Sneer'ing-ly, adv. Henehene; loiloi.
Sneeze, v. E ki'he.
Sniff, v. E hanuhanu.
Snick'er, n. He akaaka kamalii. SYN. giggle.
Snip, v. E oki; e ako.
Sniv'el, v. E hoomaka a uwe; halokoloko.

Snŏb, *n.* Kanaka akena wela.
Snŏb'bish, *adj.* Kelakela; haakei.
Snooze, *v.* E hiamoe iki. SYN. doze.
Snŏre, *v.* E no'no; e ho'ho.
Snŏr'ing, *n.* Ka no'no ana o ka ihu.
Snŏrt, *v.* E hoho; e hau.
Snout, *n.* Nuku.
Snŏw, *n.* Hau.
Snŏw, *v.* E haule mai ka kau.
Snŏw'-ball, *n.* Po'po' hau.
Snŏw'-shoe, *n.* Kamaa hele hau.
Snŏw'-stŏrm, *n.* He haule ino mai o ka hau.
Snŏw'y, *adj.* Hau; keokeo me he hau la.
Snŭb, *v.* E nuku.
Snŭb-'nŏse, *n.* Ihu kumene.
Snŭff, *v.* 1. E hau. *Snuff the wind,* e hau i ka makani.
2. E koli. *Snuff the candle,* e koli i ke kukui.
Snŭf'fers, *n.* Upa koli kukui.
Snŭg, *adj.* 1. Papaana. SYN. comfortable.
2. *Snug fit,* paikini.
Snŭg'gle, *v.* E moe pili.
Snŭg'ly, *adv.* Papaana.
Sŏ, *adv.* Pe; penei.
Sŏ, *conj.* Nolaila.
Sŏak, *v.* 1. E hoo-u'; hoo-ma-u'.
2. E omo. SYN. imbibe.
Sŏap, *n.* Sopa.
Sŏap'-sŭds, *n.* Hua o ka wai sopa.
Sŏar, *v.* E lele iluna lilo.
Sŏb, *v.* E hauhau; e uwe.
Sŏ'ber, *adj.* 1. Kuoo.
2. Ona ole.
Sŏ'ber-ly, *adv.* Me ke kuoo; me ke akaaka ole.
Sŏ'ber-mind'ed, *adj.* Kuoo.
So-bri'e-ty, *n.* 1. Ke ano kuoo.
2. Ka ona ole.
Sŏ'bri-quet (sŏ'bre-kā'), *n.* Inoa kapakapa. SYN. nickname.
Sŏ'çi-a-bĭl-i-ty, *n.* Ke ano launa pu.
Sŏ'çi-a-ble } *adj.* Launa.
Sŏ'çi-al }
Sŏ'çi-al-ly, *adv.* Ma ke ano launa.
So-çi'e-ty, *n.* 1. Ka noho pu ana o kanaka.
2. Ka launa ana.
3. He hui. *A literary society,* he hui imi naauao o na buke.
Sŏck, *n.* He kakini.
Sŏck'et, *n.* Kumu. *Socket of the eye,* makalua.
Sŏd, *n.* Papaa mauu. SYN. turf.
Sŏ'fa, *n.* He noho koki.
Sŏft, *adj.* Palupalu; pepe; wali; uouo'.
Sŏft'en, *v.* E palupalu; e hoopepe.
Sŏft'ness, *n.* Ke ano palupalu.
Soil, *n.* Lepo.
Soil, *v.* E paele i ka lepo.
Soi-ree' (swä-rā'), *n.* He anaina hoonanea ma ke ahiahi.
Sŏ'journ, *v.* E noho malihini.
Sŏ'journ-er, *n.* Mea noho malihini.

Sŏl'açe, *n.* E hooluolu; hoo-na'. SYN. cheer.
Sŏ'lar, *adj.* No ka La. *Solar heat,* wela o ka La.
Sŏl'der, *n.* Kepau kapili metala.
Sŏl'dier (sŏl-jer), *n.* He koa.
Sŏl'dier-ly, *adj.* Ano koa.
Sŏle, *n.* Poli wawae.
Sŏle, *adj.* Hookahi wale no. *Sole survivor,* ka mea hookahi wale no i pakele.
Sŏl'e-çism, *n.* He hewa ma ka olelo. SYN. barbarism.
Sŏle'ly, *adv.* Wale no. *Solely for your benefit,* no kou pono wale no.
Sŏl'emn, *adj.* Eehia; hoano.
So-lĕm'ni-ty, *n.* He hana eehia; he ano eehia.
Sŏl'em-nize, *n.* 1. E hooko i na hana ku i ka hoomana.
2. *Solemnize a marriage,* e hooko i ka oihana mare.
3. *Solemnize the mind,* e hookomo i ka eehia i ka naau.
Sŏl'emn-ly, *adv.* Me ka eehia o ka naau.
So-liç'it, *v.* 1. E kono; e hookonokono. SYN. entice.
2. E noi; e koi. SYN. request.
So-liç'i-tā'tion, *n.* 1. Ka hookonokono ana.
2. Ke koi ana.
So-liç'it-or, *n.* He loio.
So-liç'it-oŭs, *adj.* Pihoihoi; iini nui.
So-liç'i-tŭde, *n.* Iini nui o ka manao.
Sŏl'id, *n.* He kino paa; he paa.
Sŏl'id, *adj.* Paa.
So-lĭd'i-fy, *n.* E lilo i kino paa.
Sŏl'id-ly, *adv.* 1. Me ka paa loa.
2. Me ka lokahi. SYN. unanimously.
So-lil'o-quize, *v.* E nalu. *I said to myself,* nalu iho au.
So-lil'o-quy, *n.* Ka nalu ana.
Sŏl'i-ta-ry, *adj.* 1. Mehameha. SYN. lonely.
2. Neoneo. SYN. unfrequented.
Sŏl'i-tŭde, *n.* Wahi mehameha; wahi neoneo.
Sŏ'lo, *n.* Mele leo hookahi.
Sŏl'stiçe, *n.* He wahi ma ke ala hele o ka honua i mamao loa'ku ai ka la mai ka poaiwaena.
Sŏl'u-ble, *adj.* Heehee i ka wai.
So-lŭ'tion, *n.* 1. He wai a me kekahi mea e ae i kaawili pu ia.
2. He wehewehe ano.
Sŏlve, *v.* E wehewehe; e imi ninau.
Sŏlv'en-çy, *n.* 1. Ka oi o ka loaa mamua o ka lilo.
2. Ka makaukau e hookaa aie.
Sŏlv'ent, *adj.* Hiki ke hookaa i na aie.
Sŏlv'ent, *n.* He wai hoohee.
Sŏm'bre, } *adj.* 1. Pouliuli.
Sŏm'ber, }
2. Ano kaumaha.
Sŏme, *adj.* 1. Mau; kekahi. *Some persons,* kekahi poe.
2. Kauwahi. *Some portion,* kauwahi hapa.

Sóme'bŏd-y, *n.* Kekahi mea. SYN. some one.

Sóme'how, *adv.* Pehea la! *It must be done somehow,* e pono ke hanaia pehea la!

Sóm'er-saُult, } *n.* He kulou poo; ku-
Sóm'er-set, } wala.

Sóme'thing, *n.* Kekahi mea.

Sóme'time, *adv.* I kekahi wa.

Sóme'times, *adv.* I kekahi mau manawa.

Sóme'what, *adv.* Iki. *Somewhat tired,* luhi iki.

Sóme'whére, *adv.* Ma kau wahi; ma kekahi wahi.

Som-nàm'bū-lişm, *n.* Moe hewa; hele ma ka hiamoe.

Som-nàm'bu-list, *n.* Mea moe hewa.

Sŏm'no-lençe, *n.* Ke ake o ka naau e hiamoe.

Sŏm'no-lent, *adj.* Maka hiamoe. SYN. sleepy.

Sŏn, *n.* Keiki kane.

Sŏng, *n.* He mele. SYN. hymn; ballad.

Sŏng'ster, *n.* He manu memele.

Sŏng'stress, *n.* Wahine akamai i ke mele.

Sŏn'in-law, *n.* Hunona kane.

Sŏn'net, *n.* He mele pokole.

So-nō'roŭs, *adj.* Kani; kanioi.

So-nō'roŭs-ly, *adv.* Me ke kanioi.

Sŏon, *adv.* Koke; kokoke; awiwi; hiki-wawe.

Sŏot, *n.* Lepo uahi.

Soothe, *v.* E hoomalielie; hoo-na. SYN. calm.

Sŏoth'say-er, *n.* He kilo; hoopiopio.

Soŏt'y, *adj.* Paele i ka lepo uahi.

Sŏp, *n.* Hakina ai.

Sŏph'ist, *n.* Mea hoo-akamai wale ma ka olelo.

So-phist'ic-al, *adj.* Akamai wale ma ka olelo.

Sŏph'ist-ry, *n.* Ka hoo-akamai ma ka olelo.

Sŏph'o-mōre, *n.* Ka papa ekolu ma ke Kula Nui.

Sŏp'o-rif'ie, *n.* He mea hoo-hiamoe.

So-prän'o, *n.* Ka leo wahine. SYN. treble.

Sŏr'çer-er, *n.* Kahuna anaana.

Sŏr'çer-y, *n.* Anaana; hoopiopio.

Sŏr'dĭd, *adj.* 1. Alunu; puniwaiwai. SYN. covetous.

2. Paele; paumaele; haukae. SYN. filthy.

Sŏre, *adj.* Eha.

Sŏre } *adv.* Loa. *Sorely troubled,* pili-
Sŏre'ly } kia loa.

Sŏr'rŏw, *n.* Kaumaha o ka naau; ehaeha; luuluu. SYN. grief.

Sŏr'rŏw-ful, *adj.* Kaumaha; luuluu.

Sŏr'rŏw-ful-ly, *adv.* Me ka ehaeha; me ke kaumaha.

Sŏr'ry, *adj.* Minamina; mamina; mihi.

Sŏrt, *n.* He ano. SYN. kind; species.

Sôrt, *v.* E wae ma na ano; e hookaawale ma na ano.

Sŏr'tĭe, *n.* Ka puka'na mai e hoouka kaua.

Sŏt, *n.* Mea ona mau.

Sŏt'tish, *adj.* Ona mau.

Sŏt'tish-ness, *n.* He ona mau.

Soûl, *n.* Ka uhane.

Soûl'less, *adj.* Haahaa; hoo-kanaka ole.

Sound, *n.* 1. He haalulu; he leo; he kani.

2. Kaikuono papa'u.

Sound, *adj.* 1. Paa; kina' ole.

2. Oiaio maoli. *Sound advice,* olelo ao oiaio maoli.

Sound, *v.* E kani; hoo-kani; haalulu.

Sound'ings, *n.* Na wahi o ke kai i hiki ke ana ia ka hohonu.

Sound'ly, *adv.* 1. Me ka ikaika. *Whip soundly,* e hahau me ka ikaika.

2. Loa. *Sleep soundly,* e hiamoe loa.

Sound'ness, *n.* 1. Ke kina' ole; popo ole; paa.

2. Ka oiaio. SYN. truth.

Sŏup, *n.* He supa; kai.

Sŏur, *adj.* 1. Awaawa.

2. Nanau; keemoa. SYN. crabbed.

Soûrçe, *n.* Kumu.

Sŏuse, *n.* 1. He lu iloko o ka wai.

2. Na pepeiao me na wawae o ka puaa i hoomoala iloko o ka vinika.

South, *n.* Kukulu Hema.

South-ēast', *n.* Hikina Hema

Soûth'er-ly, *adj.* 1. Mai ka Hema mai *A southerly wind,* he makani mai ka Hema mai.

2. I ka Hema aku.

Soûth'ward (or sŭth'ard), *adv.* 1. I ka Hema aku.

2. *From southward,* mai ka Hema mai.

South-wēst', *adj.* Komohana Hema.

South-wēst'er, *n.* 1. Makani ino no ke Komohana Hema mai.

2. He papale nui pale ino maluna o ka moku.

Sou-ve-nir (sōōv'neer), *n.* Mea hoomanao. SYN. keep-sake.

Sŏv'er-eign (sŭv'er-in), *n.* 1. He moi.

2. Hapaha gula o Enelani.

Sŏv'er-eign, *adj.* Mana kiekie; mana loa.

Sŏv'er-eign-ty, *n.* Ka mana kiekie.

Sŏw, *n.* Puaa kumulau.

Sŏw, *v.* E lu'lu' hua; e lu.

Sŏw'er, *n.* Mea lu'lu' hua.

Spáçe, *n.* 1. Wa; kowa; wahi kaawale.

2. *Infinite space,* ke ao palena ole o Ke Akua.

Spá'çioŭs, *adj.* Akea. SYN. roomy; ample.

Spáde, *n.* Oo.

Spän, *n.* He kikoo lima.

Spän'iard, *n.* Kamaaina o Sepania.

Spän'iel, *n.* Kekahi ano ilio.

Spän'ish, *adj.* Paniolo; no Sepania.

Spänk, *v.* E pai i ke kikala.

Spänk'er, *n.* Pea hope o ka moku; ka pea nui.

Spär, *n.* He o'a moku.

Spär, *v.* E mokomoko. SYN. box.

Spär'deck, *n.* Ka oneki nui o ka moku.

Spāre, *adj* 1. Wiwi; olala. SYN. thin; lean.

2. Koe. *A spare book,* he buke i koe.

3. Kaawale. *No spare time,* aole manawa kaawale.

4. Aua. SYN. chary.

Spāre, *n.* 1. E aua. SYN. forbear.

2. E hookuu. *Spare me to go,* he hookuu ia'u e hele.

3. E kokua. *Spare a book,* e kokua mai i buke.

4. E ahonui. SYN. be merciful.

Spāre'rĭb, *n.* Kulana aoao o ka i'o puaa.

Spär'ing, *adj.* Pakiko; aua.

Spär'ing-ly, *adv.* 1. Pakiko. *Eat sparingly,* e ai pakiko.

2. Aua. *Give sparingly,* e haawi me ka aua.

Spärk, *n.* He huna ahi.

Spärk'le, *adv.* E huali; hulili; e lilelile.

Spärse, *adj.* Kawalawala.

Spärse'ly, *adv.* Kawalawala. *A sparsely settled country,* he aina i noho kawalawala ia.

Spăsm, *n.* He eha e umii ana ; hui kuhewa.

Spăs-mŏd'ie, *adj.* Kaulele; kikokikoi.

Spăt'ter, *v.* E kopipi; e mahikihiki.

Spēak, *v.* Ekemu; e kamailio; e haiolelo.

Spēak'er, *n.* 1. Mea ekemu; mea kamailio.

2. Luna-hoomalu.

Spēak'ing, *n.* Ke kamailio ana; ka haiolelo ana.

Spēak'ing-trŭm'pet, *n.* He ole.

Spēak'ing-tūbe, *n.* He ohe kamailio.

Spēar, *n.* He ihe.

Spē'çial, *adj.* Wae ia; ku i ka wa.

Spē'çial-ty, *n.* Mea i maa ai; mea i makaukau loa'i.

Spē'çie, *v.* Dala paa. *Specie payment,* uku dala paa.

Spē'çies, *n.* He ano. SYN. kind.

Spe-çif'ie, *adj.* 1. Kuhikuhi pono ia; hoopololei ia.

2. *A specific remedy,* he laau hoola maoli.

Spe-çif'ie-al-ly, *adv.* Maopopolea.

Spĕç'i-fi-eā'tion, *n.* Ke kuhikuhi pono ana.

Spĕç'i-fȳ, *v.* E kuhikuhi pono.

Spĕç'i-men, *n.* Mea hoike i ke ano.

Spē'çioŭs, *adj.* Pololei i ka nana'ku. SYN. plausible.

Spĕĕk, *n.* Kiko; kikokiko; pula.

Spĕĕk'led, *adj.* Kikokiko; kinohinohi. SYN. spotted.

Spĕĕ'ta-cle, *n.* He mea i hoikeia; nanaina.

Spĕĕ'ta-cles, *n.* Maka aniani.

Spec-tā'tor, *n.* Mea e nana ana. SYN. beholder.

Spĕĕ'tre, *n.* He uhane; uhane lapu.
Spĕĕ'ter, } SYN. ghost.

Spĕĕ'trum, *n.* Na kukuna o ka malamalama i hookaawale ia e ke aniani hookaawale.

Spĕĕ'u-lāte, *v.* 1. E hoopukapuka.

2. E poonoo; noonoo. SYN. consider; reflect.

Spĕĕ'u-lā'tion, *n.* 1. Ka hoopukapuka ana.

2; Ka noonoo wale ana. SYN. conjecture.

Spĕĕ'u-lā'tor, *n.* 1. Mea hoopukapuka.

2. Mea noonoo wale.

Speech, *n.* Olelo; haiolelo.

Speech'less, *adj.* 1. Ekemu ole; aa.

2. *Speechless from fear,* lohaloha.

Speed, *v.* E holo mama aku.

Speed, *n.* Mama ma ka holo; awiwi.

Speed'i-ly, *adv.* Me ka mama; hikiwawe.

Speed'y, *adj.* Mama; hikiwawe; awiwi.

Spĕll, *v.* 1. E hookuikui hua; e pela.

2. E hoomaha mai.

Spĕll, *n.* He manawa iki; he wa.

Spĕll'er, *n.* 1. Keiki hookuikui hua olelo.

2. Buke pe'la hua olelo.

Spĕl'ling, *n.* Ke pela hua olelo.

Spĕnd, *v.* E hoolilo aku. *Spend wastefully,* e hoomaunauna; e uhauha wale.

Spĕnd'thrift, *n.* Mea uhauha wale.

Spew, *v.* E luai. SYN. vomit.

Sphēre, *n.* 1. He poepoe. *Flattened sphere,* poepoe hawae. *A lengthened sphere,* poepoe pikoi.

2. He kulana.

Sphĕr'ie-al, *adj.* Poepoe.

Spice, *n.* Hua aia; mea hoomiko ai.

Spi'çy, *adj.* 1. Aala; mikomiko.

2. *A spicy remark,* he olelo akamai.

Spi'der, *n.* Nananana.

Spig'ot, } *n.* Umoki laau no ka pahu
Spile, }

Spike, *n.* Kui hao nunui.

Spike, *v.* 1. E kakia me ke kui hao nui.

2. *Spike a gun,* e kakia i kui hao ma ka puka ki o ka pukuniahi.

Spill, *v.* E hanini; hoo-hanini.

Spin, *v.* 1. E kaa. *Spin a top,* e kaa i ka hu.

2. E milo. *Spin rope,* e milo kaula.

Spi'nal, *adj.* Pili i ka iwi kuamoo.

Spine, *n.* Iwi kuamoo. SYN. backbone; spinal column.

Spin'ning-wheel, *n.* Pokakaa milo lopi.

Spī'ny, *adj.* Oioi; wanawana. SYN. thorny.

Spin'ster, *n.* Wahine i mare ole.

Spi'ral, *adj.* Pakaawili.

Spire, *n* Hale oioi; hale pakui.

Spir'it, *n.* 1. Uhane. SYN. soul.

2. He lapu. SYN. ghost.

3. Ano koa. SYN. courage.

4. Hoihoi o ka naau.

Spir'it-ed, adj. 1. Hoihoi. A spirited horse, he lio hoihoi.
2. Hoohoihoi; hooeueu. A spirited address, he haiolelo hooeueu.
Spir'its, n. Na wai ona.
Spir'it-u-al, adj. 1. No ka uhane. Spiritual needs, na nele o ka uhane.
2. Haipule.
Spir'it-u-al-ism, n. Ka manaoio i na lapu, na hihio, me na uhane.
Spir'it-u-al-ist, n. Kanaka i manaoio i na lapu, etc.
Spir'it-u-al-ly, adv. Haipule. Spiritually minded, naau haipule.
Spir'it-u-ous, adj. Ona. Spirituous liquors, na wai ona.
Spit, n. 1. Kuha.
2. Lae o'ne.
3. He o pulehu i'-o.
Spite, n. Hoomauhala; opu ino. SYN. malice.
Spite'ful, adj. Opu ino; keemoa. SYN. malicious.
Spit'tle, n. Kuha; wale.
Spit-toon', n. Ipu kuha.
Splash, v. E pooi ka wai; e kapeku.
Splen'did, adj. Nani; kamahao.
Splen'dor, n. He nani; he kamahao.
Splen'e-tic, adj. Nanau; keemoa. SYN. morose.
Splice, v. E hookui; e panaina.
Splint } n. 1. Laau hoopololei iwi i
Splint'er } haki.
2. He moka. SYN. fragment.
Split, v. 1. E ka'ka'. Split wood, e ka'-ka' wahie. SYN. cleave.
2. E wahi; e wawahi liilii. SYN. split to pieces.
3. E mokuahana.
Spoil, v. 1. E hao; e pakaha. SYN. rob.
2. E ino. The food is spoiled, ua ino ka ai.
Spoil, n. Waiwai pio. SYN. plunder; booty.
Spoke, n. Kukuna o ka huila.
Spoke'shave, n. Pahi koli.
Spokes'man, n. He waha-olelo.
Spo-li-a'tion, n. Ka hao wale ana.
Sponge, n. Huahuakai.
Spong'er, n. He hoopilimeaai; he lo'-ma-lo'ma-ai-halale.
Spong'y adj. Pukapuka; me he huahuakai la.
Spon-ta'ne-ous, adj. 1. Ulu wale. SYN. voluntary.
2. A spontaneous thought, he manao ulu wale.
Spon-ta'ne-ous-ly, adv. 1. Wale. To grow spontaneously, e kupu wale mai.
2. Mamuli o ka makemake. SYN. voluntarily.
Spook, n. He lapu; he mu. SYN. ghost.
Spool, n. Pokakaa wili lopi.
Spoon, n. He puna.
Spoon'ful, n. Piha puna.
Sport, n. Paani; lealea. SYN. play; fun.

Sport'ive, adj. Lea; lealea; hoihoi. SYN. merry.
Sport'ive-ly, adv. Ma ke ano paani.
Sports'man, n. 1. Kanaka ki holoholona.
2. Kanaka i puni i kela me keia hana lealea.
Spot, n. 1. Kiko; onio. A dirty spot, he paele. A bad spot, he kina'. SYN. stain; blemish.
2. Kauwahi. SYN. place; locality.
Spot, v. 1. E paele i ka lepo. SYN. soil.
2. E hakilo; kiai; kiu.
Spot'less, adj. Maemae; kina ole.
Spot'ted, adj. Onionio; kinohinohi. SYN. speckled.
Spouse, n. Mea i mare; ka wahine paha o ke kane mare; ke kane paha o ka wahine mare.
Spout, n. He nuku wai.
Spout, v. E kahe ikaika noloko mai.
Sprain, n. He hai; okupe.
Sprain, v. E anuu.
Sprawl, v. E moe moau.
Spray, v. 1. Ehu; ehukai.
2. Lala; mau lala liilii i hui ma ka lala nui.
Spread, v. 1. E uhola; e halii. Spread the bed, e halii i ka moe.
2. E hohola; e hoolaha. Spread the news, e hoolaha i ka nuhou. SYN. circulate.
3. E laha.
Spread, n. He papa aina i hoomakaukau ia me na mea ai.
Spree, n. Lealea uhauha.
Sprig, n. Laalaau.
Spright'li-ness, n. Ano hoihoi; lalelale.
Spright'ly, adj. Hoihoi; lalelale. SYN. vivacious.
Spring, v. E lele. SYN. jump.
2. E poi; popoi. SYN. pounce.
3. E puai. SYN. burst forth as water.
4. E kupu. SYN. germinate.
5. Nopu; nopunopu.
Spring, n. Punawai. Spring water, wai mapuna.
2. Ke kau makalii; kau kupulau.
3. Kila holuholu.
4. He lehe iluna.
Spring'tide, n. Kai piha.
Spring'y, adj. Holuholu; napenape. SYN. elastic.
Sprink'le, v. 1. E kapipi; e kopi.
2. E u'a iki.
Sprink'le, n. He wahi u'a iki.
Sprink'ling, n. 1. He mau paka-u'-a.
2. He wahi mea iki.
Sprit, n. He o'a pea.
Sprite, n. He uhane; lapu. SYN. ghost.
Sprout, v. E kupu; e hoo-kupu.
Sprout, n. He opuu. Sugar cane sprout, ahuahu.
Spruce, adj. Mikioi; aulii. SYN. neat.
Spry, adj. Ma'ma'. SYN. nimble.
Spunk, n. Naau koa; naau hooikaika.
Spur, n. Kepa; kui.

Spûr, *v.* 1. E hou i ke kepa.
2. E hooeueu; hoolalelale.
Spû'ri-oŭs, *adj.* Oiaio ole; hookamani.
Spûrn, *v-* 1. E kae. SYN. turn a deaf ear.
2. E kipaku me ka hoowaha'waha'
3. E keehi me ka huhu.
Spûrt, *v.* E ki'ki'.
Spût'ter, *v.* E nono-a'; nononono-a
Spȳ, *n.* He kiu.
Spȳ, *v.* 1. E hoomaka'kiu.
2. E ike ma kahi mamao. SYN. espy.
Spȳ'glass, *n.* Ohe na'na'.
Squab'ble, *n.* He hakaka; aumeume. SYN. scuffle.
Squad, *n.* Poe koa; poe koa ao paikau.
Squad'ron, *n.* 1. He mahele o ke aumoku.
2. He mahele o ka puali koa hooholo lio.
Squal'id, *adj.* Haukae; pelapela.
Squall, *n.* 1. He kikiao; makani mumuku.
2. Alala' o ke keiki.
Squal'ly, *adj.* Puahiohio.
Squa'lor, *n.* Ka haukae o ka noho'na.
Squan-der, *v.* E uhauha; e hoomaunauna.
Squâre, *adj.* 1. Huina-ha-kupono; aoao like.
2. Hoopono; pololci. SYN. just; honest.
Squâre, *n.* 1. He huina-ha-kupono, aoao like.
2. He helu i hoonui ia me ia iho; he mana.
3. Kuea kamena'.
4. Wahi akea, kaawale iloko o ke kulanakauhale.
Squâre'ly, *adv.* Pololei. *Hit squarely,* ku pololei.
Squâre'root', *n.* Kumu kuea.
Squash, *n.* Ipu pu.
Squat, *adj.* Poupou.
Squat'ter, *n.* Mea noho kuleana ole ma ka aina.
Squaw, *n.* Wahine Inikini.
Squeak, *v.* E ui; uini', e nakolo.
Squeal, *v.* E uwe, mehe puaa la.
Squeam'ish, *adj.* Poluea.
Sqeeze, *v.* 1. E uwi. *Squeeze dry,* e uwi a maloo.
2. E kaomi. *A tight squeeze,* wahi pilikia loa.
Squint'eyed, *adj.* Maka keekee.
Squirm, *v.* E onioni; kupaka; pakaawili.
Squirt, *v.* E ki wai; e kiki aku.
Stâb, *v.* E hou i ka pahi; i ka mea oioi paha.
Sta-bil'i-ty, *n.* Oni paa; kupaa; paa.
Stâ'ble, *adj.* Onipaa; paa. SYN. stanch.
Stâ'ble, *n.* Hale malama holoholona.
Stâck, *n.* He ahua; puu. *Stack of hay,* puu mauu maloo.
Stâck, *v.* E hoo-pu-a'.
Stâff, *n.* 1. Kookoo.
2. O'a. SYN. music staff.

3. Na kokua o ke generala; kiaaina, etc.
4. *Flag staff,* pahu hae.
Stâge, *n.* 1. He awai.
2. He wa; he au.
Stâge'coach, *n.* Kaa nui lawe ohua.
Stâg'ger, *v.* E hika'ka'; kunewanewa.
Stâg'ing, *n.* He wahi e ku ai o ka poe kukulu hale; amana kukulu hale.
Stâg'nant, *adj.* Lana malie a pilopilo.
Stâg'nâte, *v.* E lana malie a pilopilo. E pau ke kahe ana a inoino mai.
Stag-nâ'tion, *n.* Ka pau ana o ke kahe. Ka lana malie ana.
Stâid, *adj.* Kuoo. SYN. sedate.
Stâin, *n.* Kohu lepo; he paele; kina.
Stâin'less, *adj.* 1. Kina' ole. maemae.
2. Makamae. *A stainless reputation,* he inoa makamae.
Stâirs, *n.* Anuu.
Stâir'ease }
Stâir'way } *n.* Ala anuu,
Stâke, *n.* 1. Pahu.
2. Waiwai pili.
3. Kuleana. *A stake in the country,* he he kuleana iloko o ka aina.
4. *Reputation at stake,* e poino paha ka inoa maikai.
Stâle, *adj.* Kahiko; mananalo.
Stâlk, *n.* Kumu o ka laau liilii. *Corn stalk,* kumu kurina.
Stâlk, *v.* E hele kikoo moau.
Stâll, *n.* 1. Keena hoopaa hooloholona.
2. Wahi kuai ma ka hale makeke.
Stâl'lion, *n.* Lio kea.
Stal'wärt, *adj.* Ikaika; puipui. SYN. strong.
Stäm'mer, *v.* E uu.
Stäm'mer-er, *n.* Mea leo uu.
Stämp, *v.* 1. E hehi.
2. E pai; e kau i poo leta.
Stämp, *n.* 1. Hoailona pai.
2. Poo-leta. SYN. postage stamp.
Stäm-pêde', *n.* He auhee puiwa. SYN. panic.
Stânch, *v.* E hoopau i ke kahe ana.
Stânch, *adj.* Pili paa; kupaa. SYN. firm.
Stänch'ion, *n.* Mea koo.
Ständ, *v.* E ku. *To take a stand,* e ku.
Ständ, *n.* Kahi e ku ai.
2. He pakaukau liilii.
3. *Stand erect,* (*as hair through fear*), ku ka ehu; kakalaioa.
Ständ'ard, *n.* 1. He hae. SYN. banner.
2. He ana. SYN. measure. *A standard of value,* he ana o ka waiwai.
Ständ'ard, *adj.* Mau ka waiwai; paa ka waiwai.
Ständ'ard-beâr-er, *n.* Mea lawe hae.
Ständ'ing, *n.* He kulana. SYN. position; rank.
Ständ'ing, *p. p.* 1. E ku ana. *Standing crops,* na hua o ka aina e ku ana; aole i ohi ia.
2. Mau. *Standing committee,* komite mau.

Stän′za, n. Pauku mele; pauku himeni.

Stä′ple, n. 1. He lou.
2. Waiwai i hoohua mau ia.

Stä′ple, adj. Hoohua mau ia. *Staple productions*, waiwai i hoohua mau ia.

Stär, n. 1. Hoku.

Stär′board, n. Ka aoao akau o ka moku.

Stärch, n. Pia; mea pia lole.

Stäre, v. E haka pono ka maka.

Stär′gäz′er, n. Kilo hoku.

Stär′light, n. Malamalama hoku′.

Stärt, v. 1. E hoomaka hele.
2. E nee.
3. E puiwa.

Stärt′le, v. E hoopuiwa; hjkilele.

Stärt′ling, adj. Hoopuiwa; weliweli.

Star-vä′tion, n. Make i ka pololi; wi. loli.

Stärve, v. E hooki ai; e make i ka pololi.

Starve′ling, n. Mea wiwi; a olala paha, no ka lawa pono ole o ka ai.

Stäte, n. 1. He moku-aina.
2. *The State*, ke Aupuni.
3. Ka noho′na.
4. Hanohano.

Stäte, v. E hoakaka; e hai. *State a complaint*, e hoakaka i ka pilikia.

Stät′ed, adj. Mau. *Stated hours*, na hora mau. *Stated meetings*, na halawai ku mau.

Stät′ed-ly, adv. I kela me keia manawa.

Stäte′ly, adj. Hanohano; ihiihi; hiehie. SYN. dignified.

Stäte′ment, n. He haina; he olelo.

Stäte′room, n. Keena noho, maluna o ka moku.

Stätes′man, n. Kanaka akamai i ke kalai aina.

Stätes′man-like, adj. Noeau i ke kalaiaina.

Stä′tion, n. 1. He kahua. *Commercial station*, kahua no ka oihana kalepa.
2. *Railroad station*, kahi e ku ai na kaa alanui hao.
3. *Station house*, halewai.
4. Kulana. SYN. standing.

Stä′tion, v. E hoonoho.

Stä′tion-a-ry, adj. Paa; nee ole; hoonoho paa ia.

Stä′tion-er, n. Mea kuai i na lako no ke kakau palapala.

Stä′tion-e-ry, n. Na lako kakau palapala.

Sta-tis′tics, n. Na helu o kela me keia mea.

Stät′u-a-ry, n. Na kii i kalaiia.

Stät′ue, n. Kii kalaiia.

Stät′üre, n. Kiekie. SYN. hight.

Stät′ute, n. Kanawai. SYN. law; ordinance.

Stäve, n. Laau kapili barela.

Stäve, v. E wawahi; e kipo; e naha′ha′.

Stäy, v. 1. E noho; e kali. *Stay awhile*, e kali iki.
2. E koo; e paipai. SYN. prop.

Stäy, n. 1. He koo; he mea paipai. SYN. prop.
2. Kaula koo.

Stëad, n. Hakahaka; wahi. *In his stead*, ma kona wahi.

Stëad′fast, adj. Kupaa; wiwo ole.

Stëad′fast-ly, adv. 1. Me ka wiwo ole.
2. Me ka loli ole.

Stëad′i-ly, adv. Mau. *Steadily increase*, e mahuahua mau.
2. *Steadily gaze*, e nana me ka wiwo ole o ka maka.

Stëad-y, adj. 1. Mau. *A steady wind*, he makani mau.
2. Kupaa. *A steady man*, he kanaka kupaa.
3. Ona ole. SYN. sober.

Stëad-y, v. E hookupaa. *Steady your hand*, e hookupaa i kou lima.

Steäk, n. I-o koala.

Stëal, v. E aihue. *Steal away*, e kokolo malu aku.

Stëal′ings, n. Na mea i aihue ia.

Stëalth, n. Hana malu′.

Stëalth-y, adj. Malu′. *A stealthy act*, hana malu.
2. Kolopee; amio; amihi.

Stëam, n. Mahu.

Stëam′boat, n. Mokumahu; mokuahi.

Stëam′en′gine, n. Enikini mahu.

Stëam′er, n. 1. Mokumahu. SYN. steamboat.
2. He ipu e hoomoa ai i ka mahu.

Stëam′pack′et, n. Mokumahu holo moana.

Stëam′plow, n. He mikini mahu mea palau aina.

Stëam′tug, n. Mokumahu hookolo moku.

Steed, n. Lio mama.

Steel, n. 1. Hao kila.
2. He o hookala pahi.

Steel, v. E hoopaakiki. *Steel the heart*, e hoopaakiki i ka naau.

Steel′träp, n. Upiki hao.

Steel′yard (stil-yard), n. Ana kaupaona.

Steep, v. E hoo-u′.

Steep′le, n. He puuoa.

Steer, v. E hookele.

Steer, n. Bipi kane opio.

Steer′age, n. Wahi e noho ai na ohua o mua o ka moku.

Steers′man, n. Kanaka hookele moku; hookelewaa.

Stël′lar, adj. Pili i na hoku. SYN. siderial.

Stëm, n. 1. He kumu. *Stem of an apple*, kumu o ka ohia.
2. Ihu o ka moku; ko mua o ka moku. *From stem to stern*, mai mua a hope o ka moku.

Stëm, v. E hoo-ku-e′. *Stem the tide*, e hooikaika ku-e′ i ke au.

Stënch, n. Pilau.

Sten-ŏg′ra-phy, *n.* Kakau lima hoopokole.

Sten-tō′ri-an, *adj.* *Stentorian voice,* leo ikaika loa; leo hoo′ho.

Stĕp, *v.* 1. E hehi; e hele. *Step quietly,* e hele malie.

2. *Step a mast,* e kukulu i ke kia.

Stĕp′-fä′ther, *n.* Makuakane kolea.

Stĕp′-móth′er, *n.* Makuahine kolea.

Stĕp′ping-stŏne, *n.* Pohaku kipaepae.

Stĕ′re-ŏp′ti-cŏn, *n.* Pahu hoolele kii.

Stĕ′re-o-scōpe, *n.* Aniani nana kii.

Stĕ′re-o-tÿped, *adj.* Loli ole. *Stereotyped opinions,* na manao i loli ole.

Stĕr′ile, *adj.* Hua ole; panoa.

Stĕr′ling, *adj.* 1. Oiaio. *Sterling merit,* pono oiaio.

2. *Sterling weight,* paona kupono.

3. Pili i ke dala Beritania.

Stĕrn, *n.* Ka hope o ka moku.

Stĕrn, *adj.* Oolea. SYN. severe; rigorous.

Stĕrn′um, *n.* Iwi umauma.

Stĕ′ve-dōre, *n* Kanaka hao ukana iloko o ka moku, a hoolei ukana nohoi.

Stew, *v.* E kupa ai.

Stew, *n.* Ai i kupa pu ia.

Stew′ard, *n.* 1. Kuene.

2. Luna malama waiwai.

Stew′-păn, *n.* Ipu hao, mea kupa ai.

Stĭck, *n.* Ho laau. *Stick of timber,* pauku laau.

Stick, *v.* 1. E pipili.

2. E hoopili; e pili.

Stĭck′ler, *n.* Kanaka manao nui i na mea liilii ano ole.

Stick′y, *adj.* Pipili.

Stĭff, *adj.* 1. Oolea; paakiki. SYN. rigid.

2. Ikaika. *A stiff breeze,* he makani ikaika. SYN. strong.

Stĭff′en, *v.* E hoo-olea; e hana′ku i oolea.

Stĭff′-nĕcked, *adj.* A-i′ oolea.

Stĭff′ness, *n.* 1. Oolea.

2. *Stiffness of manners,* pahapaha; pahaha.

Stĭ′fle, *v.* E puua; e uumi i ka hanu. SYN. smother; suffocate.

Stĭ′fling, *adj.* Ikiiki. SYN. close.

Stĭg′mä, *n.* He kina′; kumu hoohaumia. SYN. reproach.

Stĭg′ma-tize, *v.* E hoailona ino aku.

Stĭle, *a.* Alapii no ka pa.

Sti-lĕt′to, *n.* Pahi winiwini, mea hou.

Still, *adj.* Malie.

Still, *adv.* 1. A hiki i keia wa. *Still there,* malaila a hiki i keia wa.

2. Aka nae. SYN. yet; nevertheless.

Still, *n.* He mikini puhi wai ona; me na wai e ae.

Still′born, *adj.* Hanau ia ua make.

Stilt, *n.* Kuku′luseo.

Stilt′ed, *adj.* Hookiekie.

Stim′u-lant, *n.* 1. Laau hooikaika kino.

2. Mea hoo-hoihoi ai ka naau.

Stim′u-late, *v.* E hoohoihoi; hoo-eueu.

Stim′u-lus, *n.* Kumu hoolalelale.

Stĭng, *v.* E aki; e o.

Sting, *n.* He mea ooi.

Stin′gi-ness, *n.* Hoii; ano pi.

Stin′gy, *adj.* Pi; aua; hoomakue; puki

Stink, *v.* E pilau; pilopilo.

Stĭnk′ing, *adj.* Pilau.

Stĭnt, *n.* Hana uku pau; hana pauku.

Stĭnt, *v.* 1. E haawi ukupau.

2. E hoohaiki; e aua.

Stĭ′pend, *n.* Uku paa; uku mau. SYN. salary.

Stĭp′u-lāte, *v.* E hooholo no kekahi hana. SYN. bargain.

Stĭp′u-lā′tion, *n.* Ka olelo i hooholo ia ma ka ae like. SYN. condition.

Stir, *v.* 1. E kawili.

2. E hoala. SYN. rouse.

3. E eu; hooeueu.

4. E oni.

5. *Stir around;* *stir your stumps,* e eu ka lemu.

Stir, *n.* He haunaele; uluaoa SYN. commotion.

Stir′rup, *n.* Keehi.

Stir′rup-strāp, *n.* Kaula keehi.

Stĭtch, *v.* E humuhumu; e meu; e hono.

Stĭtch, *n.* 1. Hookahi o ana o ke kuikele.

2. He umii.

Stŏck, *n.* 1. Ke kumu paa o ka hui.

2. Na holoholona i hanai ia.

3. Waiwai iloko o ka hale kuai.

4. *Stock in trade,* waiwai hoopukapuka.

5. Poo laau o ka pu.

6. Kumu.

7. Waihona. *Stock of knowledge,* waihona o ka ike.

Stŏck, *v.* E hoopiha mai; e hoolako mai. *Stock a store,* e hoolako i ka hale kuai.

Stock-āde′, *n.* He pa kaua.

Stŏck′brŏk′er, *n.* Kanaka kuai i na bila waiwai o kela me keia ano.

Stŏck′hŏld′er, *n.* Ona o na mahele waiwai.

Stŏck′ing, *n.* Kakini.

Stŏcks, *n.* Waihona dala o ke aupuni.

2. Na laau e koo ai ka moku i ka wa i kapiliia.

Stock′-still, *adv.* Oni ole; malie loa.

Stō-ic, *n.* Kanaka manaka′ like i na eha me na lealea.

Stŏl′id, *adj.* Hoomaloka loa.

Stóm′ach, *n.* Opu.

Stŏne, *n.* 1. He pohaku.

2. He ana kaumaha, 14 paona.

Stŏne, *v.* E hailuku i ka pohaku; e nou i ka pohaku.

Stŏne′brüise, *n.* Huahua ma ka wawai.

Stŏne′cŭt′ter, *n.* Mea kalai pohaku.

Stŏne′häm′mer, *n.* Hamale kui pohaku.

Stŏne′mā′son, *n.* Kanaka kukulu pohaku.

Stŏne′s′-thrŏw, *n.* Ka hoolei pohaku

Stŏne'-wạll, n. Pa pohaku.
Stŏn-y, adj. 1. Aa; paapu i na pohaku.
2. Paakiki. A stony heart, he naau paakiki.
Stool, n. Keehina wawae; paepae wawae; noho liilii.
Stoŏp, v. E kulou; hanunu; oohu.
Stoŏp-shoŭl'dered, adj. Oohu; hanunu.
Stŏp, v. 1. E papani a paa. SYN. cause to cease flowing.
2. E hooki; e hoopau. SYN. cease.
3. Uoki.
Stŏp'cock, n. Nuku wai.
Stŏp'per, n. Umoki; he popoi.
Stŏr'age, n. 1. Ka hoo-ahu ana; ka malama ana.
2. Uku no ka malama waiwai.
Stŏre, n. Hale kuai; he waihona.
Stŏre'house, n. Hale hoo-ahu waiwai; hale papaa.
Stŏre'keep'er, n. Mea malama hale kuai.
Stŏre'room, n. Keena waiho ukana.
Stŏrm, n. He ino; makani me ka ino.
Stŏrm'y, adj. 1. Ino; inoino. A stormy day, he la ino.
2. Haunaele. A stormy meeting, he halawai hoohaunaele.
Stŏ'ry, n. 1. Kaao. SYN. narrative.
2. Papa oluna o ka hale. Second story, papa elua oluna.
Stŏ'ry-tĕl'ler, n. He kukahekahe.
Stŏut, adj. Puipui; ikaika.
Stŏut'ly, adv. Ikaika. Stoutly deny, hoole ikaika.
Stŏve, n. Kapuahi-hao.
Stŏw, v. E hao. Stow in a trunk, e hao iloko o ka pahu.
Străd'dle, v. E kihelei.
Străg'gler, n. Mea auwana hele ma ke alanui.
Strāight, adj. Pololei.
Strāight'en, v. E hoopololei.
Strāight'ened, adv. Hoohaiki ia; pilikia. Straightened circumstances, pilikia o ka noho'na.
Strāight-fŏr'ward, adj. Pololei; hoopono. SYN. upright.
Strāight'way, adv. Koke. SYN. immediately.
Strāin, v. 1. E hoomaloeloe. SYN. stretch tightly.
2. E kanana.
3. E hai. SYN. sprain.
4. E hooikaika nui. SYN. strain every nerve.
Strāined, p. p. Lio; liolio; lina. SYN. tightly stretched.
Strāin'er, n. Kanana no ka mea wai.
Strāit, n. 1. Kowa.
2. Pilikia. In great straits, pilikia nui.
Strāit, adj. Ololi; haiki; pilikia.
Strāit'en, v. E hoohaiki. In straitened circumstances, haiki loa ka noho'na.
Strāit'-jăck'et, n. Lakeke hoopaa poe pupule.

Strănd, n. 1. Kahakai. SYN. shore.
2. Maawe kaula.
Strănd, v. E ili. SYN. run ashore; ground.
Strănge, adj. Kupanaha; ano e; kamahao.
Strănge'ly, adv. Ano e.
Străn'ger, n. Malihini.
Străng'le, v. 1. E puua. SYN. choke.
2. E umi.
Străn'gu-lā'tion, n. Ka umi ana.
Străp, n. Kaula ili.
Străp'ping, adj. Ikaika. SYN. strong.
Strā'tā, n. Papa lepo o ka honua.
Străt'a-gem, n. Hana hoohalua; hana hoopunihei.
Străt'e-gy, n. Hana hoohalua.
Străt'i-fi-cā'tion, n. Ka waiho papa ana o na mea iloko ka honua.
Străt'i-fy, v. E moe papa; hoomoe papa.
Strạw, n. Opala palaoa.
Strạw'ber-ry, n. Ohelo papa.
Strāy, v. 1. E auwana. SYN. wander.
2. E holoholo wale.
Strēak, n. 1. He onionio.
2. Streak of light, he kukuna malamalama.
3. The first streak of dawn, ka moku ana o ka pawa; ka wehe ana o ke alaula.
Strēam, n. 1. Kahawai.
2. Au. Stream of time, ke au o ka manawa.
3. Mea kahe. A stream of lava, he pele e kahe ana.
Strēam'er, n. Lepa.
Strēam'let, n. Kahawai uuku. SYN. rivulet.
Strēet, n. Alanui kulanakauhale.
Strĕngth, n. Ikaika. SYN. vigor.
Strĕngth'en, v. E hooikaika; e hana a paa.
Strĕn'u-oŭs, adj. Ikaika. Strenuous exertion, hana ikaika.
Strĕn'u-ous-ly, adv. Me ka ikaika.
Strĕss, n. 1. Stress of weather, ka ikaika o ka ino.
2. Stress of voice, ke kalele ana o ka leo.
3. Mana; ikaika. SYN. force.
Strĕtch, v. E hoohola.
2. E kikoo; e o.
3. Stretch out to dry, e kalena.
4. Stretching out, moau.
5. E hoomaloeloe. Stretch a rope, e hoomaloeloe i ke kaula.
Strĕtch'er, n. Manele. SYN. litter.
Strĕw, v. E hoohelelei; e halii.
Strĭck'en, p. p. 1. I komo i ka popilikia.
2. Luuluu. Stricken in years, luuluu i na makahiki.
Strĭct, adj. Hoopololei; hoopono loa.
Strĭct'ly, adv. Me ka pololei loa.
Strĭct'ūre, n. Olelo ku e'; olelo pa'pa'; olelo kaohi.
Strĭde, n. He kikoo moau.
Strĭfe, n. Huahua'; mokuahana; hakaka. SYN. contention.

Strike, v. 1. E kui; e hau; hahau.
  2. Kani. *The clock strikes,* kani ka wati.
  3. E hooki hana, no ka uuku o ka uku.
Strike, n. He hooki hana.
Strik'ing, adj. Kupaianaha; kamahao.
String, n. He kaula liilii.
Strin'gent, adj. Oolea. SYN. severe.
Strip, v. 1. E wehe. SYN. take off.
  2. E maihe. SYN. peel.
  3. E hooneoneo. SYN. make destitute.
Strip, n. He apana loihi; molina.
Stripe, 1. Onionio.
  2. He hili; he paopao.
Strip'ling, n. He keiki kane ui.
Strive, v. 1. E hooikaika.
  2. E hakaka; aumeume.
Stroke, n. 1. He kui; hahau; hili.
  2. He kaha. *Stroke of the pen,* kaha ana o ka peni.
  3. *A good stroke of business,* puka pono ma ka oihana.
  4. *Stroke of the oar,* ke ku ana o ka hoe i ka wai.
  5. *Stroke of sickness,* ka loaa ana o ka mai; ka loohia'na o ka mai.
Stroke, v. E kahi oluolu me ka lima.
Stroke'oar, n. Ka hoe mua o ka waapa; nana e hooponopono i na hoe e ae.
Stroll, v. E holoholo makaikai.
Strong, adj. 1. Ikaika; puipui. SYN. vigorous; robust.
  2. Hauna; hohono; maeaea. SYN. strong smelling.
Strong at-tach'ment, n. Paeauma.
Strong'ly, adv. Ikaika.
Strop, n. He ili hookala pahiumiumi.
Struct'ure, n. Mea i kukuluia.
Strug'gle, v. 1. E hooikaika.
  2. Aumeume; hakaka; paio.
Strug'gle, n. 1. He hooikaika nui.
  2. He hakaka; paio; kaua. *Struggle ineffectually,* e uilani.
Strum'pet, n. Wahine hookamakama. SYN. prostitute.
Strut, v. E hooha'ha; kai-i'.
Stub'bed, adj. Kumukumu.
Stub'ble, n. 1. Na kumukumu.
  2. Opala. SYN. trash.
Stub'born, adj. 1. Paakiki; nuha.
  2. Huakeeo. SYN. stubborn in wickedness.
Stub'born-ness, n. Ka paakiki o ka naau.
Stud, n. 1. Laau ku na ka hale.
  2. Pihe palule.
  3. He poe lio hoolaha.
  4. Lio kea. SYN. stallion.
Stu'dent, n. Mea iini naauao.
Stu'di-o, n. Keena hana kii.
Stu'di-ous, adj. Imi. *A studious boy,* he keiki imi.
Stud'y, v. E imi naauao.
Stud'y, n. 1. Imi naauao.
  2. Keena palapala.
Stuff, n. 1. Waiwai o kela me keia ano.
  2. Opala. SYN. trash.
  3. *Stuff and nonsense,* olelo lapuwale.

Stuff, v. E hoonuu ai. SYN. eat greedily
  2. E kupalu. SYN. fatten.
  3. E hoopiha.
Stuff'ing, n. Mea i hookomoia.
Stul'ti-fy, v. E hoike i ka naaupo; e hana mamuli o ka naaupo.
Stum'ble, v. E okupe; e hina wale.
Stum'bler, n. Mea okupe wale.
Stum'bling-block, n. Mea e hina ai; kumu hoohihia.
Stump, n. Kumu i koe.
Stun, v. E kuli ka pepeiao; e kulikuli.
Stunt, v. E keakea ka ulu ana.
Stunt'ed, adj. A-a'; i-i'i.
Stu'pe-fac'tion, n. Ka maeele ana o ke kino, o ka noonoo paha.
Stu'pe-fy, v. 1. E hoomaeele.
  2. E kaili i ka noonoo.
Stu-pen'dous, adj. Nui weliweli.
Stu'pid, adj. Unea; naaupo; lo'lo'.
Stu-pid'ly, n. Ano unea; kualala.
Stu'por, n. Maeele; unea.
Stur'dy, adj. Ikaika; puipui. SYN. robust.
Stut'ter, v. E olelo u-u'. SYN. stammer.
Stut'ter-er, n. Mea leo u-u'. SYN. stammerer.
Sty, n. 1. Pa puaa.
  2. Uleule maka.
Style, n. Ano. *Style of speaking,* ano o ke kamailio.
Style, v. E kapa'ku. SYN. call.
Styl'ish, adj. Hiehie; hookahakaha.
Sua'sion, *See* Persuasion. *Moral suasion,* ka haawi ana i ka olelo ao.
Suav'i-ty (suav-ity), n. Ano oluolu; akahai.
Sub-al'tern, n. Luna malalo iho.
Sub'di-vide', v. E mahele hou i ka mahele.
Sub'di-vis'ion, v. He mahele o ka mahele.
Sub-due'. v. 1. E hoopio! hoolakalaka.
  2. Kumu manao; kumu.
Sub'ject, adj. Malalo o ka malu; malalo.
Sub'ject, n. 1. He makaainana.
  2. Kumu manao; kumu.
Sub-ject', v. E hoopio; waiho malalo.
Sub-jee'tion, n. Ka noho ana malalo iho. *Subjection to law,* ka noho ana malalo iho o ke kanawai.
Sub-joined', p, p. I pakuiia mahope.
Sub'ju-gate, v. E lawe pio. SYN. subdue.
Sub'ju-ga'tion, n. Ka lawe pio ana.
Sub-let', v. E hoolimalima hou malalo iho o ka hoolimalima mua.
Sub-lime', adj. Nani; kamahao. SYN. grand.
Sub-lim'i-ty, n. Ka nani. SYN. grandeur.
Sub'lu-na-ry, adj. No ka honua nei. SYN. terrestrial.
Sub'ma-rine', adj. Malalo o ke kai.
Sub-merge', v. 1. E komo. SYN. sink.
  2. E hookomo malalo o ka wai.

Sub-mis′sion, *n.* Ka ae ana i ko hai; ka hoolohe.

Sub-mis′sive, *adj.* Akahai; hoolohe.

Sub-mit′, *v.* E ae i ko hai; e hoolohe.

Sub-ôr′di-nāte, *adj.* Malalo iho *Subordinate position*, he kulana malalo iho.

Sub-ôrn′, *v.* E kono i ka hoike wahahee.

Sub′or-nā′tion, *n.* E hookonokono no ka hoohiki wahahee.

Sub-pē′na, } *n.* Palapala kena hoike.
Sub-poē′na, }

Sub-scribe′, *v.* 1. E kakau inoa malalo iho.
2. *Subscribe for a newspaper*, e lawe nupepa.

Sub-scrīb′er, *n.* Mea kakau inoa; mea lawe nupepa.

Sub-scrip′tion, *n.* 1. Dala lawe nupepa.
2. Kakau inoa ana no kekahi mea. *Subscription paper*, palapala noi dala.

Sûb′se-quent, *adj.* Mahope mai. *Subsequent events*, na hana mahope mai.

Sûb′se-quênt-ly, *adv.* Mahope iho.

Sub-sêrv′i-ent, *adj.* Kupono; hoolohe.

Sub-side′, *v.* E emi iho. E paholo.

Sûb′si-dence, *n.* Ka emi ana iho.

Sûb′si-dize, *n. v.* E kokua me ke dala.

Sûb′si-dy, *n.* Uku kokua.

~~Sub-sist′, *v.* E ola. SYN. live.~~

Sub-sist′ence, *n.* Ke ola ana; na lako no ke ola.

Sûb′soil, *n.* Lepo paa malalo iho o ka lepo oluna.

Sûb′stance, *n.* 1. Na lako kino. *A man of substance*, he kanaka lako.
2. I-o. *The substance of the remark*, ka i-o o ka olelo.
3. Mea. *Another substance*, mea e.

Sub-stân′tial, *n.* 1. Koikoi. *A substantial man*, he kanaka koikoi.
2. Paa.

Sub-stân′tial-ly, *adv.* 1. Paa. *Substantially built*, paa ke kukulu ana.
2. I′o. *Substantially the same*, like i′o no.

Sub-stân′ti-āte, *v.* E hooia. SYN. prove; verify.

Sûb′stan-tive, *n.* Haiinoa. SYN. noun.

Sûb′sti-tūte, *n.* Pani hakahaka; hope.

Sûb′sti-tūte, *v.* E pani.

Sub-tênd′, *v.* E kaha aku. SYN. produce.

Sûb′ter-fūge, *n.* Hana epa; hana hoopunipuni.

Sûb′ter-rā′ne-an, *adj.* Maloko o ka honua.

Sûbt′le (sûtl), *adj.* Maalea. SYN. sly.

Sûbt′le-ty (sutl-ty), *n.* Ano maalea; ano epa.

Sub-trâct′, *v.* E unuhi; e hoolawe.

Sub-trâc′tion, *n.* He hoolawe; he unuhi.

Sûb′tra-hend, *n.* Kumu hoolawe.

Sub-ûr′ban, *adj.* Mawaho ae o ke kulanakauhale.

Sûb′urbs, *n.* Ka hocauhuli ana.

Sub-vêrt, *v.* E hookahuli. SYN. overthrow.

Suc-ceed′, *v.* 1. E ko.
2. E noho i hope; e noho i pani.
3. E hahai. *Day succeeds night*, e hahai ana ke ao i ka po.

Suc-cêss′, *n.* Ke ko ana; ke kuonoono. SYN. prosperity.

Suc-cêss′ful, *adj.* 1. Ko; lanakila.
2. Kuonoono. SYN. prosperous.

Suc-cêss′ful-ly, *adv.* Lanakila.

Suc-cês′sion, *n.* 1. Ka hahai ana. *Succession of events* ka hahai ana o kekahi hana i kekahi hana.
2. Hooilina. *Succession to the throne*, ka hooilina ana o ka noho alii.

Suc-cês′sive, *adj.* Kekahi mahope mai o kekahi.

Suc-cês′sor, *n.* He hope mai. *Successor in office*, he hope mai ma ka oihana.

Suc-çinct, *adj.* Pokole; ano nui. SYN. concise.

Suc-çinct′ly, *adv.* Me ka pokole. SYN. concisely; briefly.

Sûc′cor, *v.* E kokua hoopakele.

Sûc′cu-lent, *adj.* Momona. SYN. juicy.

Suc-cûmb′, *v.* 1. E make. *Succumb to sickness*, make i ka mai. SYN. yield.
2. E ae aku mamuli o ke koiia′na.

Sûch, *adj.* 1. O ia ano.
2. Like me.

Sûck, *v.* E omo.

Sûck′er, *n.* He oha′; pohuli.

Sûck′le, *v.* E hanai wai-u′; e omo wai-u′.

Sûck′ling, *n.* Keiki omo waiu.

Sûc′tion, *n.* Ka omo ana.

Sûd′den, *adj.* Emo ole; kuhewa; hikilele.

Sûd′den-ly, *adv.* Emo ole.

Sû′dor-if′ic, *n.* Laau hookahe hou.

Sûds, *n.* Wai sopa.

Sûe, *v.* 1. E hoopii kanawai.
2. E nonoi haahaa.

Sû′et, *n.* Ka aila e hoopuni ana i na puupaa.

Sûf′fer, *v*; 1. E hoomanawanui i ka eha.
2. E ae mamuli o ke koi ana. SYN. permit.

Sûf′fer-ance, *n.* 1. Hoomanawanui.
2. Ka ae ana. SYN. permission.

Sûf′fer-er, *n.* Ka mea i eha; ka mea i poino.

Sûf′fer-ing, *n.* 1. Eha; poino.
2. Ka hoomanawanui ana.

Sûf-fice′, *v.* E lawa.

Suf-fi′cien-cy, *n.* Ka lawa kupono. SYN. competency.

Suf-fi′cient, *adj.* Lawa. SYN. enough.

Sûf′fix, *n.* Mamala pakui mahope o ka huaolelo.

Sûf′fo-cāte, *v.* E kalea; uumi; puua.

Sûf′fo-cā′tion, *n.* Ka paa ana o ka hanu.

Sûf′frage, *n.* Ka pono koho balota.

Suf-fūse′, *v.* 1. E uhi. *Cheeks suffused with blushes,* na papalina i uhi ia i ka ula.
2. Haloiloi. *Eyes suffused with tears,* na maka i haloiloi i na wai maka.

Sug′ar (shoog-ar), *n.* Ko paa.

Sug′ar-cāne, *n.* Ko ulu.

Sug-ar′mill, *n.* He wili ko.

Sug-gēst′, *v.* E hoopuka manao; e kuhikuhi.

Sug-gēs′tion, *n.* Manao kuhikuhi. SYN. hint.

Sug-gēst′ive, *adj.* Hoala manao.

Su′i-cide, *n.* Mea lawe i kona ola iho.

Suit, *n.* 1. Paa. *Suit of clothes,* paa lole komo.
2. Hihia hookolokolo.
3. He imi mare. *To press a suit,* e koi e mare.

Suit, *v.* Ku; kupono.

Suit′a-ble, *adj.* Kupono. SYN. appropriate; fit.

Suite (sweet), *n.* 1. He poe ukali.
2. He mau keena pili pu.

Suit′or, *n.* 1. Mea e noi ana e mare.
2. Mea e hoopii ana ma ke kanawai.

Sŭlks, *n.* Ano nunuha.

Sŭlk′y, *adj.* Nunuha.

Sŭlk′y, *n.* Kaa lio no ka mea hookahi.

Sŭl′len, *adj.* Keemoa; kaki; hookananuha.

Sŭl′len-ly, *adv.* Mumule; nuha.

Sŭl′ly, *v.* E paumaele. SYN. tarnish. E hooemi i ka nani.

Sŭl′phur, *n.* Luaipele; kukaepele. SYN. brimstone.

Sŭl′tan, *n.* Inoa moi no Tureke.

Sŭl-tä′nä, *n.* Inoa moi wahine no Tureke.

Sŭl′trÿ, *adj.* Wela; welawela; koe′haeha.

Sŭm, *n.* Huina pau.
2. Ninau helu.

Sŭm′ma-ri-ly, *adv.* Koke. *Summarily dismissed,* hookuu koke ia; hookuke ia.

Sŭm′ma-ry, *n.* 1. Ka hoouluulu ana.
2. Ka i-o-o ka olelo.

Sŭm′ma-ry, *adj.* Koke; hakalia ole. *Summary punishment,* hoopai koke.

Sŭm′mer, *n.* *v.* Kau wela.

Sŭm′mit, *n.* Ka wekiu; ka piko. SYN. top.

Sŭm′mon, *v.* E kena aku; e kahea.

Sŭm′mons, *n.* Palapala kii; palapala kena.

Sŭmp′tu-oŭs, *adj.* Hiehie; kahikoia a nani.

Sŭn, *n.* La.

Sŭn, *v.* E kaulai i ka la.

Sŭn′beam, *n.* Kukuna o ka La.

Sŭn′burnt, *adj.* Wela i ka La; mala; no′no.

Sŭn′day, *n.* La Sabati. SYN. sabbath.

Sŭn′der, *v.* E oki a kaawale; e hookaawale.

Sŭn′di′al, *n.* Pa kuhikuhi hora mamuli o ke aka o ka La.

Sŭn′dries, *n. pl.* Kela me keia mea liilii.

Sŭn′drÿ, *adj.* Kekahi mau. SYN. several.

Sŭn′light, *n.* Malamalama o ka La.

Sŭn-ny, *adj.* Laelae.

Sŭn′rise, } *n.* Ka puka ana o ka La.
Sŭn′ris-ing, }

Sŭn′set, *n.* Ka na-poo′ ana o ka La.

Sŭn′shine, *n.* Laelae o ka La.

Sŭn′shin-y, *adj.* Laelae. SYN. sunny.

Sŭn′strōke, *n.* Poniuniu ku hewa mai no ka wela o ka La.

Sŭp, *v.* E omo iki. SYN. sip.

Sū′per-a-bŭn′dançe, *n.* Ka oi pakela.

Sū′per-än′nu-āt-ed, *adj.* Kolopupu.

Su-pērb′, *adj.* Maikai loa; hiehie; nani.

Sū′per-cär′go, *n.* Kupakako.

Sū′per-çil′i-oŭs, *adj.* Haakei; haaheo; SYN. haughty.

Sū′per-ēx′çel-lent, *adj.* Oi ka maikai.

Sū′per-fī′çial, *adj.* 1. Papau. *Superficial knowledge,* ike papau.
2. Pupuahulu.

Sū′per-fī′çies, *n.* He ili; he akea. SYN. area.

Sū′per-fīne, *adj.* Oi loa ka maikai.

Sū′per-flū′i-ty, *n.* Mea i oi i ka mea kupono.

Sū-pē′rï-flu-oŭs, *adj.* Waiwai ole; makehewa.

Sū′per-hū′man, *adj.* 1. Weliwell; eehia.
2. Mawaho ae o ke ano kanaka.

Sū-per-in-tēnd′, *v.* E hooponopono.

Sū′per-in-tēnd′ent, *n.* Luna hooponopono.

Su-pē′rï-or, *adj.* Maluna′e; oi ae; kiekie ae.

Su-pē′rï-or, *n.* Mea kiekie ae.

Su-pē′rï-ôr′i-ty, *n.* Ka oi.

Su-pēr′la-tive, *adj.* Oi loa; pookela.

Su-pēr′nal, *adj.* No luna; no ka lani· SYN. celestial.

Sū′per-năt′u-ral, *adj.* Eehia; aole no ka honua nei.

Sū′per-scribe′, *v.* E kakau mawaho o ka palapala.

Sū′per-sēde′, *v.* E noho mai ma ka hakahaka.

Sū′per-sti′tion, *n.* 1. Hoomanakii.
2. Ka manaoio i na lapu, na′kua; na ouli, etc.

Sū′per-sti′tioŭs, *adj.* Maka′u i na lapu, etc.

Sū′per-strŭct′ure, *n.* Ka mea i kukulula maluna o ke kahua.

Sū′per-vise′, *v.* E hooponopono. SYN. oversee.

Sū′per-vis′ion, *n.* Ka hooponopono ana. *Under his supervision,* malalo iho o kana hooponopono.

Sū′per-vis′or, *n.* Luna hooponopono. SYN. overseer.

Su-pine′, *adj.* 1. Kua hanee.
2. Molowa; palaleha.

Sŭp'per, *n.* Aina ahiahi.
Sup-plänt', *v.* E kaili i ko hai pono.
Sŭp'ple (**pl**), *adj.* Alu; loeloe; nape-nape.
Sŭp'ple-ment, *n.* 1. Olelo pakui.
　2. Ka piha ana. *Supplement of an an-gle,* ka piha ana o na huina kupono elua.
Sŭp'ple-mĕnt'a-ry, *adj.* E hoopiha ana; pani hakahaka.
Sŭp'pli-ant }
Sŭp'pli-cant } *n.* Mea noi ana.
Sŭp'pli-cate, *v.* E noi; e pule; e kalo-kalo.
Sŭp-pli-eā'tion, *n.* He nonoi; he pule.
Sup-plỹ', *v.* E hoolako; e hoopiha mai i ka nele.
Sup-plỹ', *n.* Lako; ka piha ana o ka nele.
Sup-pŏrt', *n.* 1. He koo.
　2. He kokua oia.
Sup-pŏrt', *v.* 1. E paepae; e koo. SYN. stay.
　2. E hoolako pono no ka noho ana. SYN. nourish.
　3. E kokua. *Support the motion,* e ko-kua i ka manao.
　4. E hooia. *Support the charge,* e hooia i ke kumu hoopii. SYN. substantiate.
　5. *Support the pain,* e hoomanawanui i ka eha. SYN. bear.
Sup-pŏrt'er, *n.* 1. He koo; makia.
　2. Mea nana e kokua i ke ola; mea malama i ke ola.
Sup-pōse', *v.* 1. E manao wale.
　2. Ina paha. *Suppose it should rain,* ina paha e u-a ana.
Sŭp'po-si'tion, *n.* Ka manao wale. SYN. hypothesis.
Sup-prĕss', *v.* 1. E kinai; e hoopau.
　2. E umi. *Suppress emotion,* e umi i ka iini.
Sup-prĕs'sion, *n.* Ke kinai ana; ka hoopau ana.
Sŭp'pur-āte, *v.* E hookahe palahehee.
Su-prēm'a-çỹ, *n.* Ka mana kiekie.
Su-prēme', *adj.* Mana kiekie; kiekie loa.
Su-prēme' Bē'ing, *n.* Ka Mea Kiekie Loa.
Sur-chärge', *v.* E hoopiha pono ole.
Sŭr'çin-gle, *n.* Kaula apo no waho ae o ka noho lio.
Sŭrd, *n.* He kuaniti i hiki ole ke hoo-maopopo pono ia.
Sure, *adj.* 1. Oiaio loa; maopopo loa. SYN. certain.
　2. Paa loa. SYN. secure.
Sure'ly, *adv.* Oiaio; maopopo. SYN. certainly.
Sure'ty, *n.* 1. Mea hoohiki panai no kekahi.
　2. Waiwai panai.
Sure'ty-ship, *n.* Hoohiki panai.
Sŭrf, *n.* Nalu; kai nalu.
Sŭr'façe, *n.* Ili. *Surface of the sea,* ka ili o ka moana.
Sŭr'feit, *n.* Ka oi pakela o ka ai, ka inu.
Sŭrge, *n.* Ale nui.

Sûrge, *v.* E aleale; ooloku'.
Sûr'geon, *n.* Kauka oki.
Sûr'ger-y, *n.* Oihana lapaau ma ka oki.
Sûr'ly, *adj.* Opukopekope; keu; kee-moa.
Sur-mise', *v.* E hoohuoi. SYN. suspect.
Sur-mount', *v.* E lanakila maluna'e.
Sŭr'nāme, *n.* Inoa ohana.
Sur-pàss', *v.* E kela; e oi imua. SYN. excel; out do.
Sŭr'plus, *n.* Ke keu; ka mea i oi pa-kela.
Sur-prise', *n.* Haohao; kaha'ha'. mea i iki ole ia e mamua.
Sur-pris'ing, *adj.* Kamahao; haohao.
Sur-rĕn'der, *v.* 1. E haawi pio.
　2. E haawi lilo.
Sur-rĕn'der, *n.* Ka haawi pio ana.
　2. Ka haawi lilo ana.
Sŭr'rep-ti'tioŭs, *n.* Malu'; maalea. SYN. underhanded.
Sur-round', *v.* E hoopuni; e poai a puni.
Sur-vey', *v.* 1. E ana aina.
　2. E nana pono. *Survey the landscape,* e nana pono i na hiona o ka aina.
Sur-vey'ing, *n.* Ana aina.
Sur-vey'or, *n.* 1. Mea ana aina.
　2. *Port surveyor,* luna kiai awa.
　3. Luna kiai; luna nana.
Sur-vive', *v.* E ola. *Survive an injury,* e ola mai ka eha.
Sur-viv'or, *n.* Ka mea i koe ke ola.
Sus-çĕp'ti-ble, *adj.* I alakai ia ka noonoo. SYN. impressible.
Sus-pĕct', *v.* E manao hoohuoi.
Sus-pĕnd', *v.* 1. E kaulai. SYN. hang out.
　2. E kaawe; e li. SYN. hang by the neck.
　3. E kapai iki. *Suspend judgment,* e kapai iki ka olelo hooholo.
Sus-pĕnd'ers, *n.* Kaula kaawe.
Sus-pĕnse', *n.* Anoninoni; manao pi-lihua.
Sus-pĕn'sion, *n.* 1. Ke kapai ana.
　2. Ke kaulai ana; kaawe ana.
Sus-pi'çion, *n.* Manao hoohuoi; ma-nao kanalua. SYN. doubt; distrust.
Sus-pi'eioŭs, *adj.* Haohaoia; kanalua ia; hoohuoi. *A suspicious man,* he ka-naka hoohuoi.
Sus-tāin', *v.* 1. E koo. SYN. support.
　2. *Sustain life,* e pono ai ke ola.
Sŭs'te-nançe, *n.* Ai e pono ai ke ola kino.
Sŭt'ler, *n.* Mea kalepa iwaena o na koa.
Sŭt'üre, *n.* 1. Kahi e pili pu ai na iwi-poo.
　2. Ka humuhumu ana o na wahi mo-ku o ka ili.
Swạb, *n.* Welu holoi papa. SYN. mop.
Swàg'ger, *v.* 1. E kikoo moau aku.
　2. E akena wale; e haanou.
Swạl'low, *v.* E ale; e moni.
Swạmp, *n.* Aina pohopoho'
Swạmp, *v.* E komo. *The boat is swamped,*

ua komo ka waapa.

Swamp'y, *adj*   Pohopoho'.

Swap, *v.*   E panai waiwai; e kuapo. SYN. barter.

Sward, *n.*   Aina mauu.

Swarm, *n.*   Huhui. *Swarm of bees*, huhui nalo meli.

Swarth'y, *adj.*   Hauli; hauliuli. *A swarthy complexion*, hauliuli ka ili.

Swāy. *n.*   Ka noho aupuni ana; ka hoomalu ana.

Swāy, *v.*   1. E hoomalu.

2. *Sway to and fro*, e polewa; e luliluli.

Swear, *v.*   E hoohiki.

2. E hoohiki ino i ka inoa o Ke Akua.

Sweār'er, *n.*   Mea hoohiki ino; mea kuamuamu.

Sweār'ing, *n.*   1 He hoohiki. SYN. taking the oath.

2. Olelo kuamuamu. SYN. profanity.

Swĕat, *n.*   Hou.

Swĕat'y, *adj.*   Ma-u' i ka hou.

Sweep, *v.*   1. E pulumi; e kahili.

2. E hoonea. *Pestilence sweeps the land*, ke hoonea nei ka ahulau i ka aina.

3. E nei. *To sweep by*, e nei aku.

Sweep'ings, *n.*   Opala i pulumi ia.

Sweet, *adj.* 1. Ono.

2, Nahenahe; polinahe.

3. Oluolu; akahai.

Sweet'en, *v.* 1. E hookomo i ke ko.

2. *Sweeten life's troubles*, e hooluolu i na pilikia o keia noho ana.

Sweet'heärt, *n.*   He ipo. SYN. lover.

Sweet'ly, *adv.*   Oluolu; nahenahe; unahe.

Sweet'mĕat, *n.*   Na hua ai i hookomoia ke kopaa.

Sweet'ness, *n.*   Ono; akahai.

Sweet-scĕnt'ed, *adj.*   Ala.

Swĕll, *v.*   E pehu; e haanou.

Swĕll, *n.*   1. Ale ha'ha' o ke kai.

2. Kanaka hookahakaha.

Swĕl'ling, *n.*   He puu; he pehu.

Swĕl'ter, *v.*   E maule i ka wela.

Swĕl'ter-ing, *p. p.*   Koehaeha; ikiki.

Swĕrve, *v.*   E aui ae mai ka pololei.

Swift, *adj.*   Mama loa; kiki. SYN. fleet.

Swift'ly, *adv.*   Awiwi loa; mama loa.

Swift'ness, *n.*   Ka awiwi o ka holo; ka mama o ka holo.

Swig, *v.*   E inu a nui.

Swill, *n.*   Ai kawiliia na ka puaa.

Swill, *v.*   E hoonuu inu.

Swim, *v.*   1. E au.

2. E poniuniu. *My head swims*, poniuniu kuu poo.

Swim'mer, *n.*   Mea ike i ke au.

Swim'ming-ly, *adv.*   *To get on swimingly*, e holo pono imua.

Swin'dle, *v.*   E apuka; e pakaha wale. SYN. cheat.

Swin'dler, *n.*   Kanaka apuka. SYN. cheat.

Swine, *n.*   Puaa.

Swine'herd, *n.*   Kahu hanai puaa.

Swing, *n.*   He lelekoali.

Swing, *v.*   E kau iluna; e lele; e lewa; e lewalewa; e lelekoali.

Swin'ish, *adj.*   Like me ka puaa. SYN. hoggish.

Switch, *n.*   1. Laau hili. SYN. whip.

2. Hao alakai no ke alanui hao; mea alakai i na kaa ma kekahi alanui e ae.

3. Owili lauoho.

Switch, *v.*   1. E hili. SYN. whip.

2. E kai i na kaa ahi mai kekahi alanui a i kekahi aku.

Swoōn, *v.*   E maule. SYN. faint.

Swoōp, *v.*   E poi; e popoi.

Sword (sörd), *n.*   Pahi kaua.

Sword-arm (sörd), *n.*   Lima lalau pahi kaua.

Sword'belt, *n.*   Kaei pahi kaua.

Syc'o-phant, *n.*   He hoopilimeaai; he kuapelu.

Syl'la-ble, *n.*   Mamala hua olelo.

Syl'van, *adj.*   No na ulu laau. SYN. rustic.

Sym'bol, *n.*   Aka; ouli; hoailona. SYN. type; emblem.

Sym-bŏl'ie-al, *adj.*   Hoailona.

Sym'bol-ize, *v.*   E hoailona. SYN. represent.

Sym-mĕt'ri-eal, *adj.*   Kohu pono mai mua a hope.

Sym'me-try, *n.*   Ke kulike; ke kohu pono.

Sym'pa-thĕt'ie, *adj.*   Aloha me'nemene.

Sym'pa-thīze, *adj.*   E aloha menemene; e uwe pu.

Sym'pa-thy, *v.*   He aloha menemene.

Sym'pho-ny, *n.* 1. Ke kani like o na leo.

2. Leo mele no na ohe puhi.

Symp'tŏm, *n.*   He ouli. SYN. sign.

2. *Symptom of sickness*, halia

Syn'a-gogue (gŏg), *n.*   Hale halawai o ka poe Iudaio.

Syn'eo-pāte, *v.*   E hoopokole ma ke kapai ana.

Syn'eo-pe, *n.*   Ke kapai ana o kekahi mau hua palapala.

2. He maule.

Syn'od, *n.*   Aha kuka' ekalesia.

Syn'o-nym, *n.*   Hua olelo ano like.

Syn-ŏn'y-moŭs, *adj.*   Like ma ke ano.

Syn-ŏp'sis, *n.*   Ke ano nui; ka i-o o ka olelo. SYN. epitome.

Syn'tax, *n.*   Ke kakau pololei ana i ka olelo.

Sȳph'i-lis, *n.*   Mai kaokao.

Sȳr'inge, *n.*   He hahano.

Sȳs-tem, *n.*   1. Ka hoonohonoho pono ana.

2. *The human system*, ke kino kanaka me na kanawai e hoopono ana.

3. *The solar system*, ka la me kona mau hoku hele me ko lakou mau kanawai hooponopono.

Sȳs'tem-at'ie, *adj.*   Hoonohonoho pono ia.

Sȳs'tĕm-a-tīze, *v.*   E hoonohonoho pono. *Systematize the work*, e hoonohonoho pono i ka hana.

T

Tăb'er-na-cle, *n.* Halelewa.

Ta'ble, *n.* 1. Papa. *Multiplication table,* papa hoonui.
2. *Dining table,* papa aina; papa kaukau.
3. *Writing table,* papa kakau.

Ta'ble, *v.* E waiho ma ka papa. *Table a bill,* e waiho ka bila ma ka papa.

Tăb'leau (tăb'lo), *n.* He hoikeike o ka poe ola me he mau kii la.

Ta'ble-lănd, *n.* Aina papa.

Ta'ble-spoon, *n.* Puna nui.

Tăb'let, *n.* Papa liilii, mea kakau.

Ta'ble-talk, *n.* Ke kamailio ma ka papa aina.

Ta'ble-türn'ing, *n.* Ka hoonaue ia ana o na papaaina e na uhane lapu, wahi a kekahi poe.

Ta-boo', *n.* He kapu.

Tăb'u-lar, *adj.* Papa. *A tabular view,* he hoike papa.

Tăb'ū-lâte, *v.* E hoonohonoho papa.

Tăç'it, *adj.* Ekemu ole. *Tacit consent,* ae ekemu ole.

Tăç'it-ly, *adv.* Me ka ekemu ole.

Tăç'i-turn, *adj.* Ekemu ole; mumule. SYN. silent.

Tăck, *n.* 1. Kui liilii kakia moena.
2. Kaula hoopaa pea.
3. Hoopii moku.

Tăck'le, *n.* 1. Ka likini me na pono e ae o ka moku.
2. *Fishing tackle,* na lako no ka lawai'a.
3. Kaula huki o ka palaka.

Tăck'le, *v.* 1. E hookomo llo i ke kaa.
2. E apo; e lalau lima aku; e hoopaa.

Tăct, *n.* Noeau; naiau.

Tăc'tics, *n.* Ka ike e pili ana i ke kaua.

Tăg, *n.* 1. He hoailona kau mawaho o ka ukana.
2. *Dog tag,* hoailona ilio.

Tăg, *v.* E hahai koke mahope.

Tăil, *n.* 1. *Tail of a fish,* he hiu.
2. *Tail of an animal,* he huelo.
3. *Tail of a cock,* koola; puapua.
4. *Tail of a kite,* kakaiapola.

Tăil, *v.* *Tail on* or *tail after,* e hahai mai mahope.

Tăil'or, *n.* He tela; mea humuhumu lole.

Tăint, *n.* He kina'; he hauna.

Tăint, *n.* E hoohaumia; e hauna. SYN. corrupt.

Tăke, *v.* 1. E lawe; e hopu; e hoopaa.
2. *Take aim,* e hoopololei i ka pu. *To*

take breath, e hanu; e hoomaha. *To take care,* e akahele; e malama. *To take down,* e hoohaahaa. SYN. write down, e kakau iho. *Take down pride,* e hoohaahaa i ka haaheo. *Take down a house,* e wawahi i ka hale. *To take effect as a law,* e lilo i kanawai. *To take effect as medicine,* e naha'. *To take heart,* e hoolana i ka manao. *To take heed,* e noonoo pono. *To take in,* e hoopunihei; e hoopuni. *To take in sail,* e li ka pea. *To take in the meaning,* e hoomaopopo. *To take in hand,* e hoao e hana. *To take leave of,* e haawi i ke aloha hookaawale. *To take notice,* e nana mai. *To take off,* e wehe. *To take on one's self,* e hapai i ke kaumaha. *To take offense,* e huhu. *To take out a stain,* e holoi i ka paele. *To take part with,* e kokua pu. *To take place,* e ko. *To take root,* e hookumu. *To take advantage of,* e apo i ka pomaikai; e hana maalea. *To take the air,* e hele i ka holoholo. *To take to heart,* e hookomo ma ka naau. *To take up,* e hapai ae. *To take up the time,* e hoopiha i ka manawa. *To take up arms,* e hoomakaukau no ke kaua. *To take up time,* e lawe i manawa kupono. *To take a thief,* e hopu i ka aihue. *To take up room,* e hoopiha wale. *To take up a note,* e hookaa i ka bila aie.

Tăke'in, *n.* He hoopuniwale; he halua.

Tăk'ing, *adj.* Onou. SYN. alluring. *A taking way,* he ano onou; hoomalimali.

Tăke'off, *n.* He hana e hoohenehene.

Tāle, *n.* 1. Kaao; moolelo. SYN. story.
2. He heluna. SYN. number; count.

Tāle'beăr-er, *n.* Holoholo olelo.

Tăl'ent, *n.* 1. Talena.
2. Noeau; akamai. SYN. ability.

Tăl'ent-ed, *adj.* Noeau; makaukau SYN. able.

Tāleş'man, *n.* Panihakahaka ma ke jure.

Tạlk, *n.* Kamailio. *Loud talk,* walaau.

Tạlk, *v.* 1. *Talk quietly,* e kamailio. SYN. converse.
2. *Talk altogether,* e hoo-uwauwa; e hauwalaau. SYN. gabble.
3. *Talk foolishly,* hoohauhili; kualauwili.

Tạlk'a-tïve, *adj.* Walaau wale. SYN. loquacious.

Tall, adj. Kiekie. *Tall and slender,* pahio.

Tal'low, n. Aila bipi; aila hipa.

Tal'ly, v. E ku-like. SYN. agree. *Keep tally,* e malama i ka helu.

Tal'ly-man, n. Kanaka malama helu.

Tal'on, n. Ka maiuu o ka manu.

Tam'a-ble, adj. Hike ke hoolakalaka ia.

Tam'a-rind, n. Ka laau wi; hua wi.

Tame, adj. 1. Laka.
2. Hoihoi ole. SYN. dull.

Tame, v. E hoolakalaka.

Tame'ly, adv. *Tamely submit to insult,* e ae molowa aku i ka hoinoia mai.

Tame'ness, n. Ke ano laka.

Tam'per, v. 1. E lalau wale. SYN. meddle.
2. E kipe. SYN. bribe.

Tan, v. 1. E hoo-lu ili.
2. E hauli i ka la.

Tan'gent, n. Kaha pili.

Tan'gi-ble, adj. Ike maka ia. SYN. palpable.

Tan'gle, v. E kahihi; e hihia.

Tank, n. Lua wai nui. SYN. cistern.

Tan'ner, n. Kanaka hoo-lu ili.

Tan'ner-y, n. Hale hoo-lu ili.

Tan'ta-lize, v. E hoala makehewa i ka manaolana; e hooeha maau.

Tan'ta-mount, adj. Like a like. SYN. equivalent.

Tap, v. 1. E kike; e koni.
2. E hou aku i kahe mai.

Tape, n. Lipine.

Ta'per, n. Ihoiho kukui.

Ta'per, v. E hele a winiwini. *Tapering to a point,* lipilipi; miomio.

Tap'root, n. Ka mole o ka mea ulu.

Tar, n. Ta; kepau.
2. Inoa no ke sela.

Tar'di-ly, adv. Me ka lolohi; me ka hakalia; hookaulua.

Tar'di-ness, n. Ka puka hope; ka hoolohi.

Tar'dy, adj. Puka hope; lohi.

Tare, n. 1. Kikania.
2. Ke kaumaha o ka mea hao waiwai; kaumaha i helu ole ia.

Tar'get, n. Papa ki poka.

Tar'iff, n. Papa auhau dute waiwai.

Tar'nish, v. E hoohapala. SYN. sully. e hooemi i ka aiai.

Tar-pau'lin, n. Kapolina.

Tar'ry, v. E kali; e noho; e kakali.

Tart, adj. Awaawa; awahia.

Tart'ly, adv. Me ka awahia; okalakala.

Task, n. 1. Pauku hana; uku pau.
2. Hana; haawina. *School tasks,* na haawina kula.

Task'-mas'ter, n. Luna hooponopono hana.

Taste, v. E hoao; e koni.

Taste, n. 1. Mikioi; maiau.
2. Ka ike o ke alelo ma na mea ai.

Taste'ful, adj. Mikioi; aulii. SYN. tasty.

Tas'ti-ly }
Taste'ful-ly } adv. Me ka aulii.

Taste'less, adj. Hukahukai; ono ole. SYN. insipid.

Tat'ter, n. Mea weluwelu.

Tat'tle, v. E holoholo olelo.

Tat'tler, n. Holoholo clelo. SYN. tale-bearer.

Tat-too', v. 1. Ka hookani pahu o ke ahiahi, no na koa e hoi i ko lakou wahi noho no ka po.

Tat-too', v. 2. E kakauhi; e kakaukaha.

Taunt, v. E loiloi; e nuku. SYN. sneer at.

Taut, adj. Maloeloe; lina.

Tau-tol'o-gy, n. Olelo kuawili wale.

Tav'ern, n. Hale hookipa; hotele.

Tav'ern-keep'er, n. Mea malama hotele.

Taw'dry, adj. Hookahakaha wale.

Taw'ny, adj. Hauli; olenalena.

Tax, n. He auhau.

Tax, v. 1. E auhau.
2. E ahewa. SYN. accuse.

Tax'a-ble, adj. Ku i ka auhau.

Tax-a'tion, n. Ka auhau ana.

Tax'i-der'my, n. Ka hoomakaukau ana i na ili holoholona; me ke kukulu hou ana mehe mau holoholona ola la.

Tea, n. 1. Ti inu.
2. Aina ahiahi.

Tea'can'is-ter, n. Pahu waiho ti.

Teach, n. E ao.

Teach'a-ble, adj. Hoolohe; hiki ke aoia.

Teach'er, n. Kumuao.

Tea'cup, n. Kiaha ti.

Tea'ket-tle, n. Ipu ti.

Team, n. He paa holoholona hoounauna.

Team'ster, n. Mea hoo-a holoholona hoounauna.

Tea'pot, n. Ipu ti.

Tear, n. Kulu wai maka.

Tear, v. E haehae; e hoopohae.

Tear'ful, adj. Haloiloi; maloi.

Tear'less, adj. Waimaka ole.

Tease, v. 1. E ne. SYN. fret.
2. E hanawale; hoonaukiuki. SYN. vex.
2. E kauloloa; noi pinepine; hoohane.

Teas'er, n. 1. He hoohane; mea noi pinepine.
2. Mea hoonaukiuki wale.

Tea'spoon, n. Puna ti.

Teat, n. He u; maka waiu.

Tea'ta'ble, n. Papa aina ahiah

Teeh'nie-al, adj. Pili pono i kekahi ike a hana paha.

Teeh'no-log'ic-al, adj. Pili i na oihana akamai.

Teeh-nol'o-gy, n. Olelo wehewehe no na oihana akamai.

Te-De'um, n. Himeni hoolea.

Te'di-ous, adj. Luhi wale; lolohi. SYN. wearisome.

Te'di-um, n. Luhi; lohi. SYN. weariness; fatigue.

Teem, *v.* E hoohua nui mai. Paapu loa.

Teens, *n. pl.* Na makahiki o ke ola kino mawaena o 12 me 20.

Teeth, *n. pl.* Na niho.

Teeth'ing, *n.* Ka wa i kupu ae na niho.

Tee-to'tal-er, *n.* Mea hoole loa i ka wai ona.

Tĕl'e-gram, *n.* Olelo uwia telegrapa.

Tĕl'e-graph, *n.* He telegarapa.

Te-lĕg'ra-phy, *n.* Oihana telegarapa.

Tĕl'e-phōne, *n.* Mikini kamailio no ke telegarapa.

Tĕl'e-scōpe, *n.* Ohe nui mea nana i na ao o ka lani

Tĕl'e-scōp-ie, *adj.* Telescopic star, he hoku i ike ia me ka telescope wale no.

Tĕll, *v.* E hai; e helu.

Tĕl'ler, *n.* 1. Mea hai. SYN. narrator.
2. Mea helu. SYN. counter.
3. Luna helu dala ma ka baneko.

Tĕll'tāle, *n.* He holoholo olelo.

Te-mĕr'i-ty, *n.* Hooaano. SYN. presumption.

Tĕm'per, *n.* 1. Ke ano o ka naau. *Good temper,* ano oluolu. *Bad temper,* ano huhu wale.
2. Ke degere o ka paakiki o ka metala.

Tĕm'per-a-ment, *n.* Ano. *A nervous terperament,* ano pihoihoi *A sanguine temperament,* ano hoihoi. *A phlegmatic temperament,* ano malie; poonoo. *A bilious temperament,* he ano hikiwawe i ka huhu.

Tĕm'pĕr-ançe, *n.* Ano pakiko.

Tĕm'pĕr-ate, *adj.* Pakiko.

Tĕm'pĕr-a-tūre, *n.* 1. Ka wela me ke anu.
2. *A high temperature,* nui ka wela. *A low temperature,* nui ke anu.

Tĕm'pest, *n.* He ino; makani ino me ka u'a.

Tĕm-pĕst'u-oŭs, *adj.* 1. Ino; inoino. *A tempestuous day,* he la ino.
2. *A tempestuous sea,* kai ooluku'.

Tĕm'ple, *n.* 1. Luakini.
2. Maha poo.

Tĕm'po-ral, *adj.* 1. No keia ao. *Temporal good,* he pomaikai no keia ao.
2. Pili i ka maha poo.

Tĕm'po-ra-ri-ly, *adv.* No ka wa pokole; iki.

Tĕm'po-ra-ry, *adj.* No ka wa pokole; ku i ka wa. SYN. transient; transitory.

Tĕm'po-rize, *v.* E ae no ka wa pokole.

Tĕmpt, *v.* E hoowalewale; e hoao.

Tĕmp-ta'tion, *n.* He hoowalewale; kumu onou.

Tĕmpt'er, *n.* Mea hoowalewale.

Tĕmpt'ing-ly, *adv.* Ma ke ano onou; hoomalimali.

Tĕn, *adj.* Umi.

Tĕn'-a-ble, *adj.* Hiki ke hookupaa ia ke hooku-e ia.

Te-nā'çioŭs, *adj.* 1. Pili; pipili; pilipaa.
2. *Tenacious memory,* ike poina ole.

Te-nāç'i-ty, *n.* Ke ano pili paa.

Tĕn'ant, *n.* 1. Hoa aina; mea hoolimalima hale.
2. Lopa. SYN. serf.

Tĕn'ant-ry, *n.* Na hoa-aina.

Tĕnd, *v.* 1. E kiai; malama; lawelawe.
2. E nee.

Tĕn'den-çy, *n.* 1. Au. *Tendency of time,* ke au o ka manawa.
2. He hilinai. *Tendency to evil,* ka hilinai i ka hewa.

Tĕn'der, *n.* 1. Moku lawelawe no ka moku nui.
2. Kaa lawe wahie me ka wai no ka enikini mahu.
3. *Legal tender,* dala ma ke kanawai.
4. Ka haawi ana. *Tender of service,* ka haawi ana i ke kokua.
5. Palapala koho no kekahi hana, etc.

Tĕn'der, *v.* E haawi. SYN. offer.

Tĕn'der, *adj.* 1. Palupalu; eha koke; nolu.
2. Ahonui. SYN. compassionate.
3. Puloku. SYN. delicate.

Tĕn'der-heärt'ed, *adj.* Ahonui; naau menemene.

Tĕn'der-ly, *adj.* Ahonui; menemene.

Tĕn'der-ness, *n.* 1. Ano eha koke; ano palupalu.
2. Menemene; ahonui.

Tĕn'don, *n.* Olona'.

Tĕn'e-ment, *n.* Hale noho.

Tĕn'et, *n.* Loina. SYN. principle.

Tĕn'fōld, *adj.* Pa-umi.

Tĕn'on, *n.* Ule papa.

Ten'or, *n.* 1. Leo tenora.
2. Ano nui. *The tenor of the remark,* ke ano nui o ka olelo.

Tĕnse, *adj.* Liolio; lina. SYN. taut.

Tĕnse, *n.* He wa. *Present tense,* keia wa. *Past tense,* wa i hala.

Tĕn'sion, *n.* Lio; lina; linalina. SYN. strain.

Tĕnt, *n.* Hale lole; hale lewa.

Tĕnth, *n.* Hapa-umi; ka umi.

To-nŭi'i-ty, *n.* Ano lahilahi; ano winiwini.

Tĕp'id, *adj.* Pumahana.

Tĕrm, *n.* 1. Mahele manawa; wa.
2. He olelo; hua olelo.
3. He mahele o ke kuaniti hoailona helu.

Tĕrm, *v.* E kapa. SYN. designate; call.

Tĕr'ma-gant, *n.* Wahine nuku; wahine pakakeu. SYN. scold; shrew.

Tĕr'mi-na-ble, *aaj.* Hiki ke hoopau ia; kau palena ia

Tĕr'mi-nāte, *v.* 1. E hoopau; hoo'ki.
2. E kau palena.

Tĕr'mi-nā'tion, *n.* Ka pau ana; ka hope loa; ka palena. SYN. end.

Tĕr'mi-nus, *n.* 1. Ke poo me ka pau ana o ke alanui.
2. Palena; mokuna; pea.

Tĕr'raçe, *n.* Honua papa.

Tĕr'ra-pin, *n.* Honu; ea.

Ter-rĕs'tri-al, *adj.* No ka honua

Tĕr′ri-ble, *adj.* Weliweli; eehia. SYN. awful.

Tĕr-rif′ie, *adj.* Weliweli.

Tĕr′ri-fy, *v.* E hooweliweli.

Tĕr′ri-to-ry, *n.* 1. Aina.
2. Panalaau.

Tĕr′ror, *n.* Kumu hooweliweli; weliweli; eehia.

Tĕrse, *adj.* Mikioi; olelo mikioi. SYN. concise. A terse expression.

Tĕst, *n.* 1. Mea hoao. *Test question,* ninau hoao.
2. He ana. SYN. standard.

Tĕst′a-ment, *n.* 1. Kauoha. *New Testament,* Kauoha Hou.
2. Palapala hooilina. SYN. will.

Tĕst′a-mĕnt′a-ry, *adj.* Pili i ka palapala hooilina.

Tes-tā′tor, *n.* Ka mea nona ke kauoha hope.

Tĕs′ter, *n.* Uhi oluna o ka moe.

Tĕs′ta-ele, *n.* Laho; opea.

Tĕs′ti-fy, *v.* E hoike; olelo hoike.

Tĕs′ti-ly, *adv.* Me ka huhu.

Tĕs′ti-mō′ni-al, *n.* 1. Palapala apono.
2. Mea hoike aloha, mahalo, etc.

Tĕs′ti-mo-ny, *n.* Olelo hoike. SYN. witness; evidence.

Tĕs′ty, *adj.* Nanau. SYN. peevish; crabbed.

Tête′a-tête′ (tāt-ä-tāt), *n.* Kamailio hoonanea iwaena o na mea elua.

Tĕth′er, *v.* E hoopaa i ke kaula.

Tĕth′er, *n.* Kaula hoopaa holoholona.

Tĕxt, *n.* 1. Poo olelo; kumumanao.
2. Olelo i pai ia.

Tĕxt′book, *n.* Buke ao.

Tĕx′tile, *adj.* Ulana ia.

Tĕxt′ūre, *n.* 1. Ke ano o ka ulana ana.
2. *Texture of the skin* ke ano o ka ili.

Thănk, *v.* E aloha aku no ka pomaikai i loaa mai.

Thănk′ful, *adj.* Piha i ke aloha. SYN. grateful.

Thănk′ful-ly, *adv.* Me ke aloha.

Thănk′ful-ness, *n.* Ke aloha no ka hoopomaikai ia mai. SYN. gratitude.

Thănk′less, *adj.* Aloha ole. SYN. ungrateful.

Thănks, *n. pl.* Aloha.

Thănks′giv′ing, *n.* Ka hoaloha′loha ana.

Thăt, *pron.* Kela; ia; oia; ua mea la.

Thăt, *conj.* I. *That you may know,* i ike oe.

Thătch, *n.* Mea ulu ako hale.

Thătch, *v.* E ako hale.

Thạw, *n.* Ka hooheehee ana o ka hau.

The, *def. art.* Ka; ke.

Thē′a-ter,⎫ *n.* Hale keaka.
Thē′a-tre,⎭

The-ăt′ri-cal, *adj.* Pili i ke keaka.

The-ăt′ri-cals, *n. pl.* Na hana keaka.

Thĕft, *n.* Aihue ana.

Thēir, *pron.* (dual) Ko laua; (*pl.*) ko lakou.

Thēme, *n.* Kumu olelo; kumumanao.

Them-sĕlves′ *pron.* Lakou iho; laua iho.

Thĕn, *adv.* 1. Ia wa: ia manawa.
2. *Conj.* Alaila.

Thĕnçe, *adv.* Mai laila aku.

Thĕnçe-forth,⎫ *adv.* Mai ia mana-
Thĕnçe-fôr′ward,⎭ wa′ku.

The-ŏd′o-lite, *n.* Panana′ ana aina.

Thē′o-lō′ġi-an, *n.* Mea huli Akua.

Thē′o-lŏġ′ie-al, *adj.* Pili no Ke Akua.

The-ŏl′o-ġy, *n.* Huli Akua.

Thē′o-rem, *n.* Manaohai; nanehai.

Thē′o-rize, *v.* E kukulu i manae.

Thē′o-ry, *n.* Manao i kukulu ia.

Thêre, *adv.* 1. Malaila; ma-o′; i-o′.
2. Aia la!

Thêre′a-bouts′, *adv.* Ma kauwahi malaila.

Thêre-ăft′er, *adv.* Mai ia hope mai.

Thêre-bŷ′, *adv.* Mamuli o ia.

Thêre-for′, *adv.* No ia.

Thêre′fore, *adv.* Nolaila; no ia mea.

Thêre-in′ *adv.* Iloko; maloko; ma ia mea.

Thêre-of′, *adv.* No ia mea. *To give notice thereof,* e kukala no ia mea.

Thêre-ŏn′, *adv.* Maluna iho.

Thêre′up-ŏn′, *adv.* No ia mea; nolaila.

Thêre-with′, *adv.* Me ia mea.

Ther-mŏm′e-ter, *n.* Mea ana wela.

Thē′sis, *n.* Kumu paio; iwiao. SYN. theme.

They, *pron.* Lakou; laua.

Thick, *adj.* 1. Manoanoa.
2. *Thick, as fluid,* kuhu-a′.
3. *Thick, as a cloud or darkness,* panopano.
4. *Thick, as a crowd,* paapu.

Thick′en, *v.* 1. E hana a manoanoa.
2. E paapu. *Dangers thicken,* paapu mai na popilikia.
3. E pouli mai. *The weather thickens,* ke pouli mai nei ka ino.

Thick′et, *n.* Wahi paapu o ka nahele-hele; wahi hihi o na mea ulu.

Thick′ly, *adv.* Paapu.

Thick′ness, *n.* Ka manoanoa.

Thick′sĕt, *adj.* 1. Poupou. SYN. burly.
2. Kanu pili.

Thick′-skinned⎫ *adj.* Kolo o ka noo-
Thick′-skŭlled⎭ noo.

Thief, *n.* He aihue.

Thieve, *v.* E aihue. SYN. steal.

Thiev′ish, *adj*; Aihue.

Thiev′ish-ness, *n.* Ke ano aihue.

Thigh (thi), *n.* U-ha′.

Thills, *n.* Na au o ke kaa lio.

Thim′ble, *n.* Komo humuhumu.

Thin, *adj.* 1. Lahilahi. (*Of fluids.*)
2. *Thin in flesh,* homa; wiwi; hakanele.

Thing, *n.* Mea.

Think, *v.* 1. E manao.
2. E noonoo; poonoo. SYN. reflect.
3. *Think to one's self,* e halalo.

Think′er, *n.* Mea noonoo nui.

Think′ing, *n.* Noonoo; poonoonoo.

Thin'ly, *adv.* 1. Kawalawala. SYN. sparsely.
2. Lahilahi.
Thin'-skinned, *adj.* Huhu wale; huhu koke.
Third, *adj.* Ke kolu; hapa-kolu.
Thirst, *n.* Makewai.
Thirst'y, *adj.* Makewai.
Thir-teen', *adj.* Umikumamakolu.
Thir'ty, *adj.* Kanakolu.
This, *pron.* Keia.
This'tle, *n.* Puakala.
Thith'er, *adv.* I-o'. *Hither and thither,* i-o' a ia nei.
Thith'er-ward, *adv.* I-o' la, i na wahi la.
Thôle'-pin, *n.* Pine hoe waapa.
Thôrn, *n.* Mea oioi; kakalaioa.
Thôrn'y, *adj.* Oioi; wanawana.
Thôr'ough, *adj.* Olahonua; hoomakaulii; paa pono
Thôr'ough-fâre (thŭr'o), *n.* Alanui akea.
Thôr'ough-ly (thŭr'ō-ly), *adj.* Olahonua; paa pono.
Though (thō), *adv.* and *conj.* Ina paha; oiai nae.
Thôught, *n.* Manao; noonoo.
Thôught'ful, *adj.* Noonoo; poonoonoo; mikolelehua.
Thôught'ful-ly (thawt), *adv.* Mikolelehua; noonoo.
Thôught'less, *adj.* Noonoo ole. SYN. heedlessly.
Thôught'less-ness, *n.* Ka noonoo ole. SYN. hedlessness.
Thôu'sand, *adj.* Kausani; tausani.
Thrąll'dôm, *n.* Ka noho ana kauwa kuapaa. SYN. slavery.
Thrash, *v.* E hahau; e hili.
Thrĕad, *n.* He lopi.
2. *Thread of the discourse,* ke kumu noonoo o ka haiao.
Thrĕad, *v.* 1. E hookomo ka lopi ma ka maka o ke kuikele.
2. E hele akahele ma kahi ololi; kahi pilikia.
Thrĕad'bâre, *adj.* Kohu ole no ke kahiko loa.
Thrĕat, *n.* Olelo hooweliweli.
Thrĕat'en, *v.* E hooweliweli.
Thrĕat'en-ing, *adj.* 1. Hooweliweli. *Threatening language,* olelo hooweliweli.
2. E kau weliweli mai ana. *A threatening evil,* popilikia e kau weliweli mai ana.
Three, *aj.* E kolu.
Three'fold, *adj.* Pa-kolu.
Three'scôre, *adj.* Kanaono.
Thrĕsh, *v.* E hahau hua palaoa.
Thrĕsh'ôld, *n.* Paepae puka.
Thrift'y, *adj.* Hoomakaulii; kuonoono.
Thrill, *v.* 1. E kapalili ka houpo.
2. E hoopiha i ka oli; a i ka maka'u paha.
Thrive, *v.* 1. E noho kuonoono.
2. E ulu ae.

Thriv'ing, *adj.* Hoomakaulii; kuonoono. SYN. prosperous. *A thriving business,* he oihana kuonoono.
Thrôat, *n.* Ka puu.
Thrŏb, *v.* E koni; e pana; e kapalili.
Thrône, *n.* Noho alii.
Thrŏng, *n·* Puuluulu kanaka.
Thrŏng, *v;* E kupipi; e akoakoa nui mai.
Thrŏt'tle, *v.* E umi; e puua. SYN. choke.
Through (thrū), *adv.* and *prep.* 1. *Through the garden,* mawaena o ke kihapai.
2. *Through the country,* mai kahi pea a i kekahi pea o ka aina.
3. Pau. *Through eating,* pau ka ai ana.
Through-out', *adv.* Mai o a o.
Thrôw, *v.* E kiola; e hoolei; e nou.
Thrŭst', *v.* E hou; e o.
Thŭmb, *n.* Ka manamana nui o ka lima.
Thŭmp, *v.* E kui.
Thŭn'der, *n.* Hekili.
Thŭn'der-bôlt, *n.* Uila i kui mai.
Thŭn'der-clăp, *n.* He kui hekili.
Thŭn'der-cloud, *n.* He ao nona mai ke hekeli me ka uila.
Thŭn'der-shŏw'er, *n.* Naulu me ke hekili.
Thŭn'der-strŭck, *adj.* Pilihua; puiwa loa.
Thŭrs'day, *n.* Poaha'.
Thŭs, *adv.* Pe; penei.
Thwăck, *v.* E hahau me ka mea nui.
Thwąrt, *v.* E keakea; e hoohoka.
Tick, *n.* 1. Ke koele ana o ka wati.
2. He aie. *To get things on tick,* e komo i ka aie.
3. He uku hipa.
Tick'et, *n.* 1. Balota. SYN. ballot.
2. He pepa uku moku; uku kaa. etc.
Tick'le, *v.* 1. E iniiniki; hoomaneoneo.
2. E hoomalimali; hoolealea.
Tick'lish, *adj.* Maneoneo wale.
Tid'al, *adj.* No ke kai. *Tidal wave,* kai hooee; kai mimiki.
Tide, *n.* Kai. *High tide,* kai nui. *Low tide,* kai maloo. *Ebb tide,* kai emi. *The tide flows,* ke pii nei ke kai.
Tide'wâit'er, *n.* Luna kiai ukana maluna o ka moku, i ku i ke dute.
Tide'wą'ter, *n.* Kai.
Tid'ings, *n.* Na lono; na nuhou. SYN. news.
Ti'dy, *adj.* Aulii; maiau; hiehie. SYN. neat.
Tie, *v.* E nakinaki; hikii; nakii.
Tie, *n.* 1. He nipuu. SYN. knot.
2. *A tie vote,* koho like iwaena o na aoao elua.
3. He pili. *A family tie,* he pili ohana.
Tiĕr, *n.* Lalani. *A tier of boxes,* he lalani pahu.
Tiff, *n.* He wahi nuku iki ma ka olelo.
Ti'ger, *n.* He tiga.

Tight, *adj.* 1. Paa. *Air-tight,* paa, i komo ole ke ea.
2. Ona iki.
3. Oolea.
Tight'en, *v.* E nakii a paa; e huki a maloeloe.
Tile, *n.* He uwinihepa.
Till, *n.* Pahu liilii waiho dala.
Till, *v.* E mahi i ka aina. SYN. cultivate.
Till, *adv.* A hiki i ka manawa. SYN. until.
Till'áġe, *n.* Ka mahi ana i ka aina.
Till'er, *n.* 1. He kanaka mahiai.
2. Ke au o ka hoeuli o ka waapa.
Tim'ber, *n.* Laau kukulu hale, etc.
Time, *n.* 1. Manawa; wa.
2. Keia ao.
Time, *v.* E haawi i manawa; e kakau i ka manawa.
Time'keep'er, } *n.* Mea kuhikuhi ma-
Time'piéçe, } nawa.
Time'ly, *adj.* I ka wa kupono. SYN. opportune.
Time'sêrv'er, *n.* Mea lolelua o ka manao; he hoopilimeaai.
Time'-wôrn, *adj.* Kahiko; lawelawe nui ia. SYN. old.
Tim'id, *adj.* Pihoihoi; hopohopo; puiwa.
Tim-id'i-ty, *n.* Ano pihoihoi; ano puiwa wale.
Tim'id-ly, *adv.* Me ka pihoihoi.
Tim'o-roùs, *adj.* Maka'u wale. SYN. timid.
Tin, *n.* Tini.
Tinçt'ûre, *n.* He wai i miko me kekahi mea e ai.
Tin'der, *ni* Pulupulu ho-a' ahi.
Tin'der-bôx, *n.* Pahu pohaku paea, mea ho-a' ahi.
Tin'ġle, *v.* E kani. *Ears tingle,* kani na pepeiao.
Tink'er, *n.* Kanaka kapili hou i na mea metala.
Tink'er-ing, *n.* Ka oihana o ke *tinker.*
Tin'kle, *n.* E kani ooi.
Tin'man, *n.* Kanaka hana mea tini.
Tint, *n.* He hooluu ili.
Ti'ny, *adj.* Uuku loa.
Tip, *n.* 1. Piko; wekiu.
2. *Tip of the tongue,* lau-alelo.
Tip'ple, *v.* E inu mau i na mea ona.
Tip'pler, *n.* Mea inu mau i na mea ona.
Tip'sy, *adj.* Ona iki.
Fire, *n.* Apo hao no na huila.
Tired, *adj.* Luhi; maloeloe.
Tire'sôme, *adj.* Maluhiluhi.
Tit'bit, *n.* Huna mea ono.
Tithe, *n.* He hapaumi.
Tit'il-lãte, *v.* E hoomaneoneo. SYN. tickle.
Ti'tle, *n.* 1. He inoa hanohano.
2. He poo. *Title of a bill,* ke poo o ka bila.
Ti'tled, *adj.* Haawiia ka inoa hanohano.
Ti'tle-deed, *n.* Palapala alodio.
Ti'tle-pãġe, *n.* Ka aoao poo o ka buke.

Tit'ter } *n.* He aka iki. SYN. gig-
Tit'ter-ing } gle.
Tọ, *prep.* I. *Go to Honolulu,* e hele i Honolulu.
2. Ia. *Give to them,* e haawi ia lakou.
3. Io. *Go to him,* e hele io na la.
Tõad'y, *n.* He hoopilimeaai.
Tõast, *n.* 1. Berena papaa.
2. He inu hoo-mahalo.
Tõast, *v.* 1. E koala.
2. E inu hoo-mahalo.
To-bãç'co, *n.* Baka.
To-bãç'eo-nist, *n.* Mea hana a kuai baka.
To-bãç'eo-pïpe, *n.* Ipu baka.
To-dãy', *n.* Keia la.
Tõd'dle, *v.* E hele ku'ku'.
Tõd'dler, *n.* Keiki liilii akahi no a hele.
Tõe, *n.* Manamana wawae.
To-ġêth'er, *adv.* Pu. *Go together,* e hele pu.
Toil, *v.* E kamau hana.
Toil'et, *n.* Ka aahu me ka hoopono-pono kino.
Toil'sôme, *adj.* Luhi; kaumaha.
To'ken, *n.* He hoailona. SYN. symbol; sign.
Tõl'er-a-ble, *adj.* Aho iki.
Tõl'er-a-bly, *adv.* Aho iki.
Tõl'er-ant, *adj.* Ahonui; laulea. SYN. indulgent.
Tõl'er-ãte, *v.* E ahonui; e hoomanawanui.
Tõl'er-ã-tion, *n.* Ahonui; laulea.
Tõll, *n.* He mahele; he auhau.
Tõll, *v* E hookani i ka bele kanikau.
Tõll'brïdġe, *n.* Alahaka i hoo-uku ia no ka hele ana maluna.
Tõll'gãte, *n.* Puka komo i hoouku ia.
Tõll'gãth'er-er, *n.* Kiai ohi auhau.
Tõm'a-hạwk, *n.* Koi kaua o na inikini.
To-mã'to, *n.* Ohia haole.
Tọmb (tūm), *n.* Ilina; hale kupapau.
Tọmb'stọne, *n.* Pohaku ilina.
To-môr'rõw, *n.* Apo'po'.
Ton (tŭn), *n.* He tona, elua tausani paona.
Tõne, *n.* 1. Ke kani o ka leo.
2. Anuu. *Semi-tone,* anuu-hapa.
Tõngs, *n.* Upa' ahi.
Tõngue (tung), *n.* 1. Alelo; elelo.
2. Olelo. *A foreign tongue,* he olelo haole.
Tõngue'tïed, *n.* 1. Elelo hepa.
2. *Cart-tongue,* ka ihu o ke kaa.
Tõn'ic, *n.* Laau hooikaika kino.
To-night', *n.* I keia po; keia po.
Tọn'naġe (tŭn-ej), *n.* Ka helu o na tona.
Tõo, *adv.* 1. Nohoi. SYN. also.
2. Loa. *Too much,* nui loa.
Tõol, *n.* Mea hana; paahana.
Tõoth, *n.* Niho.
Tõoth'ãehe, *n.* Eha o ka niho; pakoni o ka niho.
Tõoth'less, *adj.* Niho ole.

Tŏŏth'-pick, n. O niho.
Tŏŏth'sŏme, adj. Ono; miko.
Tŏp, n. 1. Ko luna loa; welau; wekiu; piko.
2. He hu.
Tŏ'per, n. Kanaka ona mau.
Tŏp'ie, n. Kumumanao; kumu noonoo.
Tŏp'măst, n. Ke kia oluna.
Tŏp'mŏst, adj. Oluna loa.
To-pŏg'ra-pher, n. Mea kaha kii aina.
To-pŏg'ra-phy, n. Kaha kii aina.
Tŏp'ple, v. E kulanalana; e hiolo mai.
Tŏp'sy-tûr'vy, adj. Huikau; ilalo iluna.
Tôrch, n. Lama; lamaku'.
Tôrch'light, n. Malamalama o ka lamaku.
Tôr'mĕnt, n. 1. Eha nui.
2. Mea hoopilikia nui.
Tor-mĕnt', v. E hoomaau; e hoopilikia; e hana ino.
Tor-mĕnt'or, n. 1. Mea hooehaeha wale.
2 Mea hoonaukiuki.
Tor-nā'do, n. He mumuku; makani ikaika ino. SYN. hurricane.
Tor-pé'do, n. Mikini hoo-pahu'.
Tôr'pid, adj. Hiamoe wale; maeele. SYN. sluggish.
Tôr'por, n. Ano hiamoe wale; ano maeele.
Tôr'rent, n. Wai kahe nui; wai nui.
Tôr'rid, adj. Wela; papaa. Torrid zone, kaei wela.
Tôr'toïse (tis), n. He honu; ea.
Tôr'tu-oŭs, adj. Pakaawili; kuawili.
Tôrt-ûre, n. Eha nui.
Tŏss, v. 1. E kiola; e hoolei.
2. To toss about in bed, e onioni maluna o ka moe.
3. Toss up the nose, auku ka ihu.
Tŏ'tal, adj. Pau loa. Total loss, poino loa. Sum total, huina pau loa
Tŏ'tăl-ly, adv. Loa; pau loa. SYN. wholly.
Tŏte, v. E halihali; e haawe. SYN. carry.
Tŏt'ter, v. E hika'ka'; e kulanalana.
Tŏŭch, v. 1. E paa aku; e pili.
2. E lalau aku.
3. E ku. To touch at a port, e ku ma kekahi awa.
4. E noonoo iki. SYN. to touch on a subject.
Tŏŭch, n. Ka ha'ha' ana; ka pili ana.
Tŏŭch'ing, adj. Manaonao.
Tŏŭch'y, adj. Huhu koke. SYN. irritable.
Tŏŭgh (tūf), adj. Oolea; uaua.
Tŏŭgh'en, v. E hana i oolea; e hoolilo a uaua.
Tŏur, n. He huakai kaapuni. SYN. circuit.
Tŏur'ist, n. Kanaka huakai kaapuni.
Tŏŭr'na-ment, n. Lealea kau lio o ka wa kahiko.
Tŏw, n. 1. Kekahi ano olona'.
2. Hookolo moku.

Tŏw, v. E hookolo moku.
Tŏ'ward (to-ard), To'wards (to-ardz), } prep. I; io, ma.
Tŏw'el, n. Kawele.
Tŏw'er n. Hale pakui.
Tŏw'er-ing, adj. Kiekie loa, me he hale pakui la.
Tŏw-line, Tŏw-rŏpe, } n. Kaula hookolo.
Tŏwn, n. Kulanakauhale; he taona.
Tŏwn-clĕrk', n. Kakauolelo no ke taona.
Tŏwn-eri'er, n. Luna kukala akea.
Tŏwn'house, n. Hale noho ma ke taona.
Tŏwns'fŏlk, n. Na kamaaina o ke taona.
Tŏwns'man, n. Kamaaina o ke taona hookahi.
Tŏwn'-talk', n. Mea i wawa nui ia.
Toy, n. Mea paani no kamalii.
Toy, v. E hoonanea.
Toy'shop, n. Hale kuai mea paani.
Trăçe, n. 1. He meheu. SYN. track, vestige.
2. Kaula huki o ke kaa, a mea e paha.
Trăçe, v. 1. E hahai mamuli o ka meheu.
2. E kahakaha. Trace a line, e kaha i kaha.
Trăck, n. 1. He mehĕu; mooa.
2. Alanui.
Trăck, v. E alualu. SYN. trace.
Trăck'less, adj. Hele ole ia; alanui ole.
Trăct, n. 1. Buke liilii.
2. Aina.
Trăct'a-ble, adj. Lohe; laka, hoolohe. SYN. docile.
Trāde, n. 1. Oihana kalepa.
1. Oihana hana lima.
Trād'er, n. Kanaka kalepa.
Trādeş'man, n. Kanaka kalepa; kanaka hana lima.
Trādeş'ün'ion, n. He hui o na oihana hanalima.
Trāde'wind, n. Moae; kaomi.
Tra-di'tion, n. Olelo mai na kupuna mai.
Tra-di'tion-al, Tra-di'tion-a-ry, } adj. No na kupuna mai; kuuna'.
Tra-dūçe', v. E aki, niania; alapahi. SYN. slander.
Tra-dūç'er, n. Mea niania; kanaka aki. SYN. slanderer.
Trăf'fie, n. Oihana maauauwa'.
Trăf'fick-er, n. Kanaka maauauwa'.
Trăg'e-dy, n. He hana weliweli e make ai.
Trăg'ie, adj. Poino i ka make. SYN. fatal.
Trāil, v. E hookolo; e kauo mahope.
Trāil, n. 1. Meheu. SYN. track.
2. Hu-a'. Trail of a garment, hu-a' aahu.
Trāin, n. 1. He poe ukali. SYN. retinue.
2. He mau kaa i kauoia e ka enikini mahu.

3. Hu-a aahu. SYN. trail.
4. *A train of ideas*, he mau kumu noonoo e pili pu ana.

Train, *v.* 1. E ao. SYN. teach.
2. E hoolakalaka. SYN. break in.
3. E hoo-ulu pono.

Trait, *n.* Ano. SYN. peculiarity.

Trait'or, *n.* He kumakaia.

Trait'or-oŭs, *adj.* Kumakaia.

Tràmp, *n.* 1. He kuewa; aea wale.
2. Mea makaikai wawae.

Tràm'ple, *v.* E hehi.

Trän'quil, *adj.* 1. Lai; malie. SYN. calm.
2. Kuapapa. SYN. quiet.

Trän'quil-ize, *v.* E hoomalielie; e hoo-na'.

Tran-quil'i-ty, *n.* 1. Malie; lai.
2. Maluhia; ka noho kuapapa ana.

Trän'quil-ly, *adv.* Me ka malie.

Trans-àct', *v.* E hana; e hooko'. SYN. perform.

Trans-àc'tion, *n.* Ka hana; ka hooko ana.

Trans-àl'pine, *adj.* Ma kela aoao o na mauna Alepe mai Roma aku.

Tràns'at-làn'tic, *adj.* Mao aku o ka moana Atelanika.

Tran-sceénd', *v.* E kela. SYN. excel; surpass.

Tran-sceénd'ent, *adj.* Kela loa. SYN. surpassing.

Trän-scríbe', *v.* E kakau kope. SYN. copy.

Trän-scríb'er, *n.* Mea kakau kope. SYN. copyist.

Trän'script, *n.* Kope.

Trans-fēr', *v.* 1. E hoolilo.
2. E lawe; e halihali. SYN. convey.

Tràns'fer, *n.* 1. Ka halihali ana mai kauwahi a i kau wahi aku.
2. Ka hoolilo ana ia hai.

Trans-fēr'a-ble, *adj.* 1. Hiki ke hooliloia.
2. Hiki ke halihali ia.

Tràns'fer pä'per, *n.* Pepa i hoomakaukauia no ka pai kope ana.

Trans-fíg'u-rä'tion, *n.* Ka hoopahaohao ana.

Trans-fíg'ūre, *v.* E hoopahaohao.

Trans-fíx', *v.* E hou aku a puka.

Trans-fôrm', *v.* E hoo-ano e; hoo-malule.

Tràns'for-mä'tion, *n.* Hooano e ana.

Trans-fūse', *v.* 1. E ninini mai kela a i keia.
2. E hookahe mai kela a i keia.

Trans-grèss', *v.* 1. E hoohaki kanawai.
2. E kela i ka mea kupono.

Trans-grès'sion, *n.* Haki ana i ke kanawai; hana hewa.

Trans-grès'sor, *n.* Mea hoohaki kanawai; lawehala.

Trän'sient, *adj.* No ka wa pokole.

Trän'sit, *n.* Ka hele ana; ka halihali ana.

Tran-sĭ'tion, *n.* Ka loli ana mai kau wahi a i kau wahi aku.

Trän'si-to-ry, *adj.* Pokole. SYN. transient.

Trans-lāte', *v.* E mahele olelo; e unuhi olelo.

Trans-lā'tion, *n.* Mahele olelo; ka olelo i maheleia.

Trans-lā'tor, *n.* He unuhi olelo; mahele olelo.

Trans-lū'çent, *adj.* Komo ka malamalama, aole nae aiai.

Tráns'mi-grä'tion, *n.* Ka lele ana o ka uhane mai kela a i keia kino.

Trans-mis'si-ble, *adj.* Kupono ke hooili ia.

Trans-mĭt', *v.* E hooili.

Trans-mūte', *v.* E hoomalule.

Trans-pär'ent, *adj.* Aiai; moakaka.

Trans-pire', *v.* 1. E hana ia. SYN. come to pass.
2. E hooakaka. SYN. become known.

Trans-plänt', *v.* E hehu; e kanu ma kahi e.

Tràns'pōrt, *n.* 1. Moku lawe ohua.
2. Ka lilo loa. *A transport of anger*, ka lilo loa i ka huhu.

Trans-pōrt', *v.* 1. E kipaku a i ka aina e.
2. E halihali; e lawe. SYN. convey.

Trans-pōrt'a-ble, *adj.* Hiki ke halihali ia.
2. Ku i ke kipaku. *A transportable crime*, he karaima ku i ke kipakuia.

Tràns'pōr-tä'tion, *n.* Ka halihali ana.

Trans-pōse', *d.* E hoololi ae.

Tràns'po-sĭ'tion, *n.* Ka hoololi ana.

Trans-shĭp', *v.* E hoolei ukana mai kahi moku a i kekahi moku ae.

Trans-vērse', *adj.* Mawaena.

Tràp, *n.* Upiki; pahele.

Tràp'dóor, *n.* Puka pani e paa ana.

Tra-pē'zi-um, *n.* Huina-ha elua aoao like ole.

Tràp'e-zoid, *n.* Huina-ha elua aoao moe like.

Tràp'pings, *n.* Na mea e kahiko ai.

Tràsh, *n.* Opala.

Tràsh'y, *adj.* Opala; i'o ole; waiwai ole.

Tràv'ail, *n.* 1. Hana oolea; hana luhi.
2. Haakokohi.

Tràv'el, *v.* E huakai; e kaahele.

Tràv'el-er, *n.* He mea huakai hele.

Tràv'erse, *v.* E auwana hele.

Tràys, *n.* Pa palahalaha; mea lawe pa.

Trèach'er-oŭs, *adj.* Kumakaia; hoohalua; kipi.

Trèach'er-y, *n.* Ke kumakaia; kipi.

Trèad, *v.* 1. E hehi.
2. *To tread water*, hoopinana.

Trèa'son, *n.* Kipi i ke aupuni.

Trèa'son-a-ble, *adj.* Kipi.

Trèas'ūre, *v.* 1. E hoo-ahu.
2. E hoomanao; e malama loa.

Trèas'ūre, *n.* Waiwai.

Trèas'ur-er, *n.* Puuku dala.

Trèas'ur-y, *n.* He waihona dala.

Trēat, *v.* 1. E hana. *Treat me well,* e hana pono mai ia'u.
2. E lapaau. SYN. to doctor.
3. E wehewehe kumumanao.
4. E hoohoihoi. SYN. to give pleasure.

Trēat, *n.* Mea e hoihoi ai ka naau.

Trēat'ise, *n.* He buke; manao i hakuia.

Trēat'ment, *n.* 1. Ka hana ana. *Good treatment,* hana lokomaikai.
2. Ka lapaau ana.
3. *Treatment of a subject,* ke ano o ka noonoo ana no ke kumumanao.

Trēat'y, *n.* He kuikahi. *Reciprocity treaty,* kuikahi panai like.

Trĕb'ie, *n.* Leo wahine. SYN. soprano

Trĕb'le, *adj.* Pa-kolu. SYN. three-fold'

Tree, *n.* Kumu laau.

Tree, *v.* E hahai a pii i ke kumulaau.

Trĕm'ble, *v.* E haalulu.

Tre-mĕn'doŭs, *adj.* Weliweli ka nui.

Trē'mor, *n.* He haalulu.

Trĕm'u-loŭs, *adj.* Haalulu; kapalili; luliluli.

Trĕnch, *n.* Awaa; auwaha.

Trĕnch'er, *n.* 1. Mea eli auwaha.
2. Pa laau palahalaha; mea lawe ai.

Trĕnd, *n.* Ka huli ana; ka aui ana. *The trend of the coast,* ka huli ana o ke kahakai.

Trep-i-dā'tion, *n.* Kapalili o ka houpo; hopohopo nui.

Trĕs'pass, *v.* E komo hewa.

Trĕs'pass, *n.* 1. Hewa; hala.
2. Komo hewa.

Trĕs'pass-er, *n.* 1. Mea komo hewa.
2. Kanaka hewa.

Trĕss, *n.* Owili lauoho.

Trĕs'tle, *n.* He mea laau paipai. *A trestle bridge,* he alahaka i paipaiia maluna o na koo laau.

Trī'al, *n.* 1. He hoao.
2. He popilikia. *Trials of life,* na popilikia o keia ola.
3. He hookolokolo.

Trī'ang-le, *n.* Huina kolu. *Right-angled triangle,* huina kolu kupono. *Obtuse-angled triangle,* huina kolu peleleu. *Isosceles triangle,* huina-kolu-aoao like-lua.

Tri-ăn'gu-lar, *adj.* Huina kolu.

Tribe, *n.* Mamo; ohana.

Trib'u-lā'tion, *n.* Popilikia.

Tri-bū'nal, *n.* Aha hookolokolo.

Trib'une, *n.* Lunakanawai o Roma i ka wa kahiko.

Trib'u-ta-ry, *n.* Muliwai la'la'; he la'-la'.

Trib'u-ta-ry, *adj.* Auhauia.

Trib'ūte, *n.* Auhau.

Trice, *n.* Manawa ole. SYN. moment.

Trick, *n.* 1. Hana akamai. SYN. juggle; sleight.
2. Hana apiki; hana maalea. SYN. cheat.
3. Ano. SYN. trait.

Trick'ish, *adj.* Maalea; apiki.

Trick'le, *v.* E kulu; e kahe lolohi.

Tri'dent, *n.* He ihe me na manamana ekolu.

Tri-ĕn'ni-al, *adj.* Kela me keia kolu makahiki.

Tri'fle, *n.* Mea liilii.

Tri'fle, *v.* E paani wale.

Tri'fler, *n.* Mea lauwili wale, noonoo ole; he puni lealea.

Tri'fling, *adj.* Mea ole; mea liilii. SYN. trivial. *Of trifling importance,* he mea ole.

Trig'ger, *n.* Ke ki o ka pu.

Trig'o-nŏm'e-try, *n.* Ana huinakolu.

Trill, *n.* Ka haalulu o ka leo ma ke mele.

Tril'lion, *adj.* Teriliona.

Trim, *adj.* Aulii; mikioi; maikai. SYN. neat.

Trim, *v.* 1. E paipai. *Trim a tree,* e paipai i ke kumulaau.
2. E hooponopono. *Trim sail,* e hooponopono i na pea.

Trim'mer, *n.* 1. Mea paipai.
2. Hoopilimeaai.

Trim'ming, *n.* Mea kahiko lole.

Trin'i-ty, *n.* Ke Kahikolu; Ke Akua.

Trink'et, *n.* Mea liilii milimili.

Tri-nō'mi-al, *n.* Kuaniti mahele ekolu.

Trio, *n.* 1. Mele leo ekolu.
2. Ekolu mea.

Trip, *v.* 1. E hele mikioi. SYN. trip along.
2. E okupe. SYN. trip up.
3. E hoohina; e kulai.

Trip, *n.* Huakai makaikai. SYN. excursion.

Tri-pärt'ite, *adj.* Mahele pa-kolu.

Trip'-hăm'mer, *n.* Hamare mikini.

Trip'le, *adj.* Pa-kolu. SYN. three-fold.

Trip'li-eāte, *adj.* Pa-kolu.

Tri'pod, *n.* Laau kukulu panana.

Tri-sĕct', *v.* E oki pa-kolu.

Tri-sĕc'tion, *n.* Ka oki pa-kolu ana.

Tri-sȳl'la-ble, *n.* Hua olelo mamala ekolu.

Trite, *adj.* Kahiko. SYN. old; common. *A trite saying,* he olelo kahiko.

Trit'ū-rāte, *v.* E wili a aeae loa; e kui a aeae. SYN. pulverise.

Tri'umph, *v.* 1. E lanakila.
2. E hauoli nui.

Tri-ŭmph'ant, *adj.* Lanakila.

Tri-ŭm'vi-rate, *n.* Ke aupuni o na 'lii ekolu.

Triv'i-al, *adj.* Mea liilii wale no. SYN. trifling.

Trŏm'bŏne, *n.* Kekahi ano ohe puhi.

Troop, *n.* He puali koa; puali.

Troop'er, *n.* Koa lio.

Trŏ'phy, *n.* Hoailona no ka lanakila.

Trŏp'ie, *n.* Poai. *Tropic of Cancer,* Poai Olu Akau. *Tropic of Capricorn,* Poai Olu Hema.

Trŏp'ie-al, *adj.* No na wahi mahana. *Tropical verdure,* ka uliuli o na wahi mahana.

Trŏt, v. E holokuku; e holo peki. *To pace,* e hoolailai.

Trŏt'ter, n. Lio holo kuku.

Trŏub'le, n. Pilikia.

Trŏub'le-sŏme, adj. 1. Hoopilikia wale.
2. Koe-a'.

Trŏub'lŏŭs, adj. Popilikia. *Troublous times,* na wa popilikia.

Trough (trawf), n. Holowaa hanai holoholona.
2. *The trough of the sea,* ka poli o na ale.

Trŏu'ṣers, n. Paa lole wawae. SYN. pantaloons.

Trŏus'seau (trŭ'-sō), n. Na kahiko mare no ka wahine.

Trŏw'el, n. Mea hamo puna.

Trṳ'an-çy, n. Ka haalele ana i ke kula.

Trṳ'ant, n. Keiki haalele kula.

Truçe, n. Kuikahi ku i ka wa.

Trŭck, n. 1. Kaa liilii halihali ukana.
2. Kela me keia mea liilii kuai.

Trŭçe'u-lent, adj. Lokoino; hihiu. SYN. fierce.

Trŭdge, v. E maalo ae.

Trṳe, adj. Oiaio.

Trṳe'heart'ed, adj. Naau oiaio; kupaa.

Trṳ'iṣm, n. He oiaio maopopo lea. SYN. axiom.

Trṳ'ly, adv. Oiaio; me ka oiaio.

Trŭmp, v. *A trumped up charge,* he hoopii imihala.

Trŭmp'et, n. Pu kani memele.

Trŭmp'et-er, n. Mea hookani pu.

Trŭn'dle, v. E olokaa.

Trŭnk, n. 1. Pahu lole.
2. Ihu o ka elepani.
3. He alanui hao loihi nona na la'la'.
4. Ke kumu o ka laau.

Trŭst, n. 1. Paulele.
2. Hoo-aie'.

Trus-tee', n. Puuku.

Trŭs'ty } adj. Pauleleia.
Trŭst'wor-thy }

Trŭth, n. Oiaio.

Trŭth'ful, adj. Oiaio.

Trȳ, v. E hoao.

Trȳ'ing, aej. Pilikia. *A trying occasion,* he manawa pilikia.

Tŭb, n. He ta-bu.

Tūbe, n. Ohe.

Tū'bu-lar, adj. Me he ohe la; ohe. *A tubular boiler,* he ipu hao piha i na ohe.

Tŭck, n. He pelu ma ka aahu.

Tūes'day, n· Poalua.

Tŭft, n. Eka *Tuft of hair,* eka' lauoho.

Tŭg, n. 1. Moku mahu hookolo moku.

Tŭg, v. 2. E huki ikaika.
2. E hookolo moku.

Tū-ï'tion, n. E ao ana. *Tuition fees,* ka uku no ke ao ana.

Tŭm'ble, v. 1. E kaa. SYN. roll.
2. Tumble down, e hiolo; e hina.
3. E kulai: e hoohina.

Tŭm'bler, n. Kiaha aniani.

Tū'mor, n. Puu; mai pehu.

Tū'mult, n. Haunaele; uluao'a

Tu-mŭlt'u-oŭs, adj. 1. Uluaoa; haunaele.
2. *Tumultuous waves,* na ale kupikipiki-o'.

Tū'mu-lus, adj. He ahua lepo.

Tūne, n. Leo mele.

Tūne, v. E hoomakaukau i na mea kani.

Tŭn'nel, n. 1. Tini ukuhi.
2. He alanui iloko o ka honua.

Tŭr'ban, n. Kaei poo.

Tŭr'bid, adj. Lepo. *Turbid water,* wai lepo.

Tŭr'bu-lent, adj. 1. Hoohaunaele; uluaoa. SYN. noisy.
2. Ooloku. *Turbulent waters,* na ale ooloku'.

Tu-reen', n. Ipu kai.

Tŭrf, n. Puupuu mauu. SYN. sod.

Tŭr'key, n. He palahu'.

Tŭr'moil, n. Wawa; haunaele. SYN. tumult.

Tŭrn v. 1. E huli. *Turn to the right,* e huli i ka pono.
2. E aui. *To turn on hinges,* e olepe.
3. E wili.
4. E awaawa. *The milk has turned,* ua awaawa ka waiu.

Tŭrn, n. 1. Ka huli ana,
2. He wa. *Your turn,* kou wa.

Tŭrn'coat, n. Kanaka loli lua o ka manao.

Tŭrn'er, n. Kanaka wili poepoe.

Tŭrn'ing, 1. Oihana wili poepoe.
2. Ka huli ana; ka aui ana.

Tŭrn'ing-lāthe, n. Mikini wili poepoe.

Tŭrn'key, n. Kahu malama ki o ka hale paahao.

Tŭrn'pike, n. Puka komo no ke alanui i auhauia.

Tŭrn'stile, n. Puka kakaa ma ka pa.

Tŭr'pen-tine, n. Wai hoomaloo pena.

Tŭr'pi-tūde, n. Ano haahaa ino. SYN. baseness.

Tŭr'ret, n. 1. He hale pakui.
2. Paku no ka pu nui o ka moku manuwa.

Tŭr'tle, n. He ea; honu.

Tŭr'tle-dŏve, n. Manu nunu.

Tŭsk, n. Niho nui loloa.

Tŭs'sle, n. He aumeume. SYN. scuffle.

Tū'tor, n. Kumu-ao.

Twăd'dle, n. He walaau wale.

Twāin, adj. Elua.

Twăng, n. Ke kani ana o ka pana; a ukeke paha.

Twĕak, v. E iniki. SYN. pinch.

Tweez'erṣ, n. Upa' umiki.

Twĕlfth, adj. Hapa-umikumamalua.

Twĕlve, adj. Umikumamalua.

Twĕlve'mŏnth, n. Makahiki. SYN. year.

Twĕnty, adj. Iwakalua.

Twiçe, adj. Pa-lua.

Twīg, n. Laalaau.

Twī'light, n. *Morning twilight,* alaula; pawa. *Evening twilight,* liula'. *Morning or evening twilight,* molehulehu.

Twin, *n.* Mahoe.
Twine, *n.* Lopi kuaina.
Twine, *v.* 1. E milo; e hili.
  2. *Twine about (as vines),* e hoohihi.
  3. *Twine the arms,* e puliki.
Twinge, *n.* He umii.
Twink'le, *v.* E imo; e imoimo.
Twirl, *v.* E wili; e kaa.
Twist, *v.* E hilo; hili; milo.
Twit, *v.* E loiloi; e nuku.
Twitch, *v.* E huki ino; e kaili ino. SYN.
  jerk.
Twit'ter, *n.* Ka walaau o ka manu.
Two (too), *adj.* Elua.
Two'-edged, *adj.* Oi elua.
Two'fold, *adj.* Pa-lua.
Type, *n.* 1. Hua kepau.

  2. Hoailona. SYN. emblem.
Ty'phoid (ty'foid), *n.* He fiva nui.
Ty'phoon (ty-foon'), *n.* Makani pu-
  kiki ma ke kai o Kina.
Typ'i-cal, *adj.* Hoailonaia. SYN. em-
  blematic.
Typ'i-fy, *v.* E hoailona.
Ty-pog'ra-pher, *n.* Mea paipalapala.
  SYN. printer.
Ty-pog'ra-phy, *n.* Paipalapala. SYN.
  printing.
Ty-ran'nic-al, *adj.* Hookaumaha wale.
Tyr'an-nize, *v.* E hookaumaha wale.
Tyr'an-ny, *n.* Ka hookaumaha wale.
Ty'rant, *n.* Mea hookaumaha wale.

Ty'ro, *n.* Mea hou wale no ma ka ike.

U

Ubiq'ui-tous, *adj.* Ma na wahi a
  pau. SYN. everywhere.
Ud'der, *n.* Ka u o na holoholona.
Ug'li-ness, *n.* Ino; inoino.
Ug'ly, *adj.* Inoino; pou'hu.
Ul'cer, *n.* Mai puha'; aai.
Ul'cer-ous, *adj.* Aai.
Ul-te'ri-or, *adj.* Hope; mahope.
Ul'ti-mate, *adj.* Hope loa. SYN. final.
Ul'ti-mate-ly, *adv.* Mahope; mahope
  loa. SYN. finally.
Ul'ti-ma'tum, *n.* Olelo hope loa.
Ul'tra, *adj.* Hala loa. SYN. extreme.
Um'brage, *n.* Huhu; ukiuki. SYN.
  offense.
Um-bra'geous, *adj.* Malumalu. SYN.
  shady.
Um-brel'la, *n.* Mamalu; lou'lu.
Um'pire, *n.* Mea nana e hooholo i ka
  pono iwaena o na aoao elua.
Un. He mamala hua olelo e hoike mai-
  ana i ka nele.
Un-a'ble, *adj.* Hiki ole.
Un'ac-cept'a-ble, *adj.* Makemake ole
  ia.
Un'ac-com'plished, *adj.* Hooko ole ia.
Un'ac-count'a-ble, *adj.* Pohihihi; ma-
  opopo ole.
Un'ac-quaint'ed, *adj.* Ike ole.
Un'ad-vis'a-ble, *adj.* Kupono ole.
  SYN. inexpedient.
Un'ad-vis'ed-ly, *adv.* Me ka noonoo
  ole.
Un'af-fect'ed, *adj.* 1. Ano maoli.
  SYN. natural.
  2. Hookamani ole.

Un'al-loyed', *adj.* Makamae. SYN.
  pure.
Un-al'ter-a-ble, *adj.* Loli ole; onipaa.
  SYN. unchangeable.
Un-a'mi-a-ble, *adj.* Kaki; keemoa.
  SYN. cross.
U'na-nim'i-ty, *n.* Lokahi o ka ma-
  nao.
U-nan'i-mous, *adj.* Lokahi.
U-nan'i-mous-ly, *adv.* Me ka lokahi.
Un-an'swer-a-ble, *adj.* Hiki ole ke
  paniia; oiaio.
Un-an'swer-a-bly, *adv.* Hiki ole ke
  hoole ia.
Un'as-sum'ing, *adj.* Akahai; hookie-
  kie ole.
Un'a-vail'ing, *adj.* 1. Makehewa; wai-
  wai ole.
  2. Inea. *Unavailing labor,* hana inea.
  SYN. ineffectual.
Un'a-void-a-ble, *adj.* Hiki ole ke pale
  ia. SYN. inevitable.
Un'a-ware', *adj.* Ike ole; manao ole.
Un'a-wares,' *adv.* Hikilele; manao ole
  ia 'ku. SYN. suddenly.
Un-bal'anced, *adj.* 1. Kaulike ole.
  2. Noonoo kupono ole.
Un'be-com'ing, *adj.* Kupono ole. SYN.
  unsuitable.
Un'be-lief', *n.* Naau hoomaloka. SYN.
  infidelity.
Un'be-liev'er, *n.* He aia'; hoomaloka;
  hoomalau.
Un'be-liev'ing, *adj.* Manaoio ole; hoo-
  maloka.
Un-bend', *v.* 1. E hoo-alualu.
  2. E hoolauna; e launa oluolu.

Un-bĕnd′ing, *adj.* Oolea; paakiki. SYN. inflexible.
Un-bi′ased, *adj.* Ewaewa ole. SYN. unprejudiced.
Un-bĭd′den, *adj.* Kahea ole ia. SYN. uninvited.
Un-bind, *v.* E wehe ae; e wehe i ka nakii.
Un-blĕm′ished, *adj.* Kina′ ole.
Un-blĕst, *adj.* Hoopomaikai ole ia.
Un-blŭsh′ing, *adj.* Honekoa. SYN. impudent.
Un-bŏrn, *adj.* Hanau ole ia.
Un-bo′som, *v.* E hai pau loa.
Un-boŭnd′ed, *adj.* Palena ole.
Un-brŏk′en, *adj.* Wa′hi ole ia. SYN. entire.
Un-bŭck′le, *v.* E wehe i ka pihipihi.
Un-bur′ied, *adj.* 1. Kanu ole ia.
2. Hoolewa ole ia.
Un-bŭr′den, *v.* 1. E kala i ka haawe.
2. E hai pau mai i ke kaumaha o ka naau.
Un-bŭt′ton, *v.* E hemo mai ka pihi.
Un-çeas′ing, *adj.* 1. Pau ole; na ole.
2. Mau. SYN. unending; ceaseless.
Un-çĕr′tain, *adj.* Maopopo ole; kanaluaia. SYN. doubtful.
Un-çĕr′tain-ty, *n.* He kanalua; kulanalana. SYN. doubt.
Un-chánge′a-ble, *adj.* Luli ole; loli ole.
Un-chár′i-ta-ble, *adj.* Aloha ole; laulea ole.
Un-chảste′, *adj.* Maemae ole; haumia. SYN. impure.
Un-christ′ian, *adj.* Ku-e′ i ke ano kristiano.
Un-çiv′il, *adj.* Makoe-a′; kamaniha. SYN. impolite.
Un-çiv′il-ized, *adj.* Naaupo; kuaaina.
Un-çiv′il-ly, *adv.* Makoe-a′. SYN. impolitely; rudely.
Un-cle, *n.* Makuakane ma ka hanauna.
Un-clean′, *adj.* Maemae ole; paele; paumaele.
Un-clean′ness, *n.* Paumaele; haukae.
Un-cloud′ed, *adj.* Alaneo.
Un-clôse′, *v.* E wehe ae.
Un-coil′, *v.* E ko-a′.
Un-cóme′ly, *adj.* Nani ole; pou′hu.
Un-cóm′fort-a-ble, *adj.* Oluolu ole.
Un-cŏm′mon, *adj.* 1. Kakaikahi. SYN. rare.
2. Ano e. SYN. unusual.
Un-cŏm′mon-ly, *adv.* 1. Loa. *Uncommonly bad weather*, he wa ino loa.
Un-com-mu′ni-ca-tive, *adj.* Ekemu ole.
Un-cŏm′pro-mĭs′ing, *adj.* 1. Launa ole; laulea ole.
2. Onipaa. SYN. firm.
Un′con-çĕrn′, *n.* Unea; hoomalau. SYN. indifference.
Un′con-çĕrn′ed-ly, *adv.* Wale. *To look unconcernedly on*, e nana wale aku no.
2. Me ke ala ole mai o ka manao.

Un′-con-dĭ′-tion-al, *adj.* Pau loa; koe ole.
Un-cŏn′quer-a-ble, *adj.* Pio ole. SYN. invincible.
Un-cŏn′sçioŭs, *adj.* Noonoo ole; lilo ka noonoo.
Un-cŏn′sçioŭs-ly, *adv.* Me ka noonoo ole e mamua.
Un-cŏn′sçioŭs-ness, *n.* Lele o ka noonoo; ka noonoo ole.
Un-cŏn′sti-tū′tion-al, *adj.* Ku-e′ i ke kumu kanawai.
Un-cŏn′sti-tū′tion-ăl′i-ty, *n.* Ke ku-e′ ana i ke kumukanawai.
Ŭn′con-trŏl′la-ble, *adj.* 1. Hiki ole ke hoolakalaka ia.
2. Hiki ole ke uumi ia. SYN. ungovernable.
Ŭn′con-vĕrt′ed, *adj.* Hoohuli ole ia.
Un-coŭp′le, *v.* E hookuu.
Un-coŭr′te-oŭs, *adj.* Makoe-a. SYN. uncivil; rude.
Un-coŭth′, *adj.* Hemahema; kaialile. SYN. awkward.
Un-cŏv′er, *v.* E wehe i ka uhi.
Unc′tion, *n.* Ka poni ana.
Un-daunt′ed, *adj.* Wiwo ole; koa. SYN. intrepid.
Un′de-çeive′, *v.* E hoike i ka wahahee.
Un′de-nî′a-ble, *adj.* Hiki ole ke hoole ia; maopopolea. SYN. indisputable.
Un′de-nî′a-bly, *adv.* Maopopolea. SYN. indisputably.
Un′der, *prep.* and *adv.* Malalo iho.
Un′der-bĭd′, *v.* E emi iho ma ke koho ana.
Un′der-brŭsh, *n.* Nahelehele o ka ululaau.
Un′der-clôthes
Un′der-clôth′ing } *n.* Na lole palemai.
Un′der-cŭr′rent, *n.* Ke au o kahi hohonu; ke au ilalo loa.
Un′der-gö′, *v.* E hoomanawanui. *Undergo pain*, e hoomanawanui i ka eha.
Un′der-grăd′u-ăte, *n.* Haumana i puka ole mai ke kula nui.
Un′der-ground, *adj.* Iloko iho o ka honua; malalo iho o ka lepo. SYN. subterranean.
Un′der-grŏwth, *n.* Nahelehele o ka ululaau.
Un′der-hănd, *adv.* Huna′; epa.
Un′der-lie′, *v.* E waiho malalo iho.
Un′der-line′, *v.* E kaha malalo iho.
Un′der-ling, *n.* Mea noho kauwa.
Un′der-mine′, *v.* 1. E eli malalo iho.
2. E hoonawaliwali. *Undermine the health*, e hoonawaliwali i ke ola kino.
Un′der-nêath′, *prep.* Malalo iho.
Un′der-pĭn′ning, *n.* Na koo; na paipai o ka hale.
Un′der-rȧte′, *v.* E koho malalo iho o ka mea kupono.
Un′der-sçore′, *v.* *See* underline.
Ŭn′der-sĕll′, *v.* E kuai emi i ko hai kuai.

Ún'der-sīgned', *adj.* Ka mea nona ka
inoa malalo iho.

Ún'der-stánd', *v.* E hoomaopopo.

Ún'der-stánd'ing, *n.* Ka noonoo.

Ún'der-stráp'per, *n.* *See* underling.

Ún'der-tāke', *v.* E hoao. Syn. attempt.

Ún'der-tāk'er, *n.* Kanaka hoolewa kupapau.

Ún'der-tāk'ing, *n.* He hana; oihana.
Syn. enterprise.

Ún'der-tōne, *n.* He leo haahaa; leo hawanawana.

Ún'der-tōw, *n.* Ka au malalo iho o ka
ilikai, e holo ku-e' i ka au oluna.

Ún'der-vál'ūe, *v.* See underrate.

Ún'der-writ'er, *n.* Kanaka kakau inoa
no ka panai waiwai.

Ún'de-sērv'ing, *adj.* Pono ole.

Ún'de-tēr'mined, *adj.* Hoomaopopo
ole ia.

Ún-dē'vi-ā'ting, *adj.* Pololei loa; aui
ole. Syn. straight.

Ún'di-vid'ed, *adj.* Okoa; mahele ole
ia.

Un-dọ', *v.* 1. E wehe hou ae.
2. E hookahuli i ka mea i hana ia.

Un-dóne', *p. p.* 1. Ko ole ia; waiho wale
ia.
2. Poino.

Un-doubt'ed, *adj.* Akaka lea. Syn.
indubitable.

Un-doubt'ed-ly, *adv.* Pela io no.

Ún-drēss', *v.* E wehe i ke kapa.

Ún'drēss, *n.* Kapa komo wale.

Ún'du-lāte, *v.* 1. E aleale; kapalili;
hulili. Syn. vibrate.
2. *Undulating,* (as ground,) malualua.
Syn. uneven.

Ún'du-la-tō'ry, *adj.* Aleale; kapalili.

Un-dūe', *adj.* Pono ole.

Un-dū'ly, *adv.* Pono ole; loa. Syn. im-
properly. *Unduly excited,* pihoihoi loa.
Unduly influenced, hoohuli pono ole ia
ka manao.

Un-dȳ'ing, *adj.* Make ole; mae ole.

Un-ēarth', *v.* E huai.

Un-ēarth'ly, *adj.* Eehia.

Un-ēas'y, *adj.* Pihoihoi; maha ole.
Syn. restless.

Un-ēnd'ing, *adj.* Mau loa; pau ole.
Syn. everlasting.

Un-ē'qual, *adj.* 1. Like ole.
2. Ewaewa. Syn. unjust.

Un-ē'qual-ly, *adv.* Like ole.

Ún'e-quīv'o-cal, *adj.* Ewaewa ole;
oiaio. Syn. straightforward.

Un-ērr'ing, *adj.* Kuhihewa ole; pololei loa.

Un-ē'ven, *adj.* Malualua; apuupuu;
puaali.

Ún'ex-ām'pled, *adj.* Lua ole.

Ún'ex-çēp'tion-a-ble, *adj.* Kina' ole.

Ún'ex-pēct'ed, *adj.* Hikilele; manao
ole ia mamua. Syn. unlooked for.

Ún'ex-pēct'ed-ly, *adv.* Manao ole ia;
lohe ole ia. *He arrived unexpectedly,*
ku mai oia me ka lohe ole ia; or, me
ka manao ole ia.

Un-fāil'ing, *adj.* Mau; pau ole.

Un-fāir', *adj.* Paewaewa; kapakahi.

Un-fāir'ness, *n.* Ewaewa; kapakahi
o ka hana.

Un-fāith'ful, *adj.* Malama pono ole.

Un-fāsh'ion-a-ble, *adj.* Kuaaina; ku
ole i ka mea mau.

Un-fāst'en, *v.* E wehe.

Un-fāth'om-a-ble, *adj.* Hohonu loa;
lipolipo.

Un-fāv'or-a-ble, *adj.* 1. Kupono ole;
maikai ole. *Unfavorable weather,* wa
kupono ole.
2. Oluolu ole; maliu ole; ku-e.

Un-fāv'or-a-bly, *adv.* Ku-e. *Report
unfavorably,* e hoike kue.

Un-feel'ing, *adj.* Lokoino; naau paakiki; menemene ole. Syn hard-hearted.

Un-feigned', *adj.* Oiaio; hookamani
ole.

Un-fēnced', *adj.* Paa ole i ka pa.

Un-fil'ial, *adj.* Aloha ole i ka makua.

Un-fin'ished, *adj.* Paa ole; ko hapa.
Syn. incomplete.

Un-fit', *adj.* Kupono ole; makaukau
ole.

Un-fōld, *v.* 1. E wehe i ka opi.
2. E hohola; e uhola.

Ún'for-giv'en, *adj.* Huikala ole ia.

Ún'for-giv'ing, *adj.* Hoomauhala.

Un-fōrt'u-nāte, *adj.* Pilikia; poino.

Un-found'ed, *adj.* Kahua ole; oiaio
ole.

Un'fre-quěnt'ed, *adj.* Hele pinepine
ole ia.

Un-fre'quent-ly, *adj.* Kakaikahi; pinepine ole.

Un-friend'ly, *adj.* Launa ole; enemi.

Un-frūit'ful, *adj.* Hua ole; panoa.

Un-fūrl', *v.* E wehe.

Un-fūr'nished, *adj.* 1. Hoolako ole ia;
kulekule.
2. Olohelohe. *An unfurnished room,*
he keena oloheloh.

Un-gāin'ly, *adj.* Hemahema; manuea. Syn. blundering; ungraceful.

Un-gēn'er-oùs, *adj.* Pi; a'ua. Syn.
illiberal.

Un-gōd'ly, *adj.* Aia'; hewa; hoomaloka.

Un-góv'ern-a-ble, *adj.* Hiki ole ke
hoolakalaka ia; hoomalu ole ia.
2. Hiki ole ke uumi ia. *An ungovernable temper,* he huhu i hiki ole ke uumi
ia.

Un-grāçe'ful, *adj.* Mikioi ole; papalale.

Un-grā'çioùs, *adj.* Oluolu ole; lokomaikai ole.

Un-grāte-ful, *adj.* Aloha ole.

Un-hāl'lōwed, *adj.* Hewa. *Unhallowed
pleasures,* na lealea hewa. Syn. unholy;
impure.

Un-hánd'sóme-ly, *adv.* Me ka pololei
ole.

Un-hănd'y, adj. Hemahema ma ka hana; makaukau ole. SYN. awkward.

Un-hăp'py, adj. Oluolu ole; kaumaha.

Un-här'ness, v. E wehe i ka lei o ka lio.

Un-health'y, adj. Omaimai; kupono ole i ke ola kino. SYN. sickly.

Un-hĕard', adj. Lohe ole ia. Unheard of, mea hou; kupaianaha.

Un-hĕs'i-ta-ting, adj. Kanalua ole. Unhesitating obedience, ka hoolohe kanalua ole.

Un-hĕs'i-tā'ting-ly, adv. Me ke kanalua ole.

Un-hĭnge', v. E wehe mai kona ami.

Un-hitch', v. E wehe i ka nikii.

Un-hō'ly, adj. Aia'; hemolele ole.

Un-hoŏk', v. E wehe i ka lou.

Un-hŏrse, v. E kiola mai ka lio.

Un-hûrt', adj. Eha ole; poino ole.

Ū'ni-fôrm, adj. Like; ano like.

Ū'ni-fôrm, n. Lole koa; lole kahiko like.

Ū'ni-fôrm'-i-ty, n. Ke ano like.

Ū-ni'-fôrm-ly, adj. Mau.

Un'ĭm-pēach'a-ble, adj. 1. Hiki ole ke hooleia.

2. Kina' ole. SYN. blameless.

Ŭn'in-tĕl'li-gi-ble, adj.1. Maopopo ole.

2. Namunamu wale ia.

Ŭn-in'ter-est-ed, adj. Molowa ma ka naau.

Un-in'ter-est-ing, adj. Hoohoihoi ole; eleu ole. An uninteresting speech, he haiolelo hoohoihoi ole.

Ūn'ion, n. 1. He hui.

2. Ka hoohui ana.

3. Ke ano lokahi. SYN. unity.

4. The Union, Amerika Huipuia.

Ū-nīque' (ū-neek',) adj. Lua ole; ano e loa.

Ū'ni-son, a. Like; lokahi. Read in unison, e heluhelu like.

2. Pualu.

Ū'nĭt, n. Mea hookahi.

Ū-nite', v. E hoohui; e hookuikui.

U-nit'ed-ly, adv. Alu pu. To work unitedly, e alu pu ma ka hana.

Ū'ni-ty, n. 1. Lokahi.

2. Mea hookahi.

Ū'ni-vêrs'al, adj. Mai o a o; a pau loa.

Ū'ni-vêrs'al-ism, n. Ka manaoio e ola mau loa'na kanaka a pau ma ka lani.

Ū'ni-vêrs'al-ly, adv. Mai o a o.

Ū'ni-verse, n. Na ao a pau.

Ū'ni-vêrs'i-ty, n. Kula nui; kahi i aoia'i na ike a pau.

Un-jŭst', adj. Pono ole; paewaewa; hoopono ole.

Un-kind', adj. Lokomaikai ole; lokoino.

Un-kind'ly, adv. Lokoino.

Un-knŏw'ing-ly, adv. Me ka ike ole; me ka naaupo.

Un-known', adj. Ike ole ia.

Un-lāde', v. E hoolei ukana.

Un-lạw'ful, adj. Ku-e' i ke kanawai. SYN. illegal.

Un-lạw'ful-ly, adv. Me ke kanawai ole.

Un-lēarn', v. E hoopoina.

Un-lēarned', adj. Ike ole; naaupo.

Un-lĕss', conj. Ke ole.

Un-lĕt'tered, adj. Ike ole i ka palapala. SYN. illiterate.

Un-like', adj. Like ole.

Un-like'ly, adj. 1. Aole paha.

2. An unlikely story, he kaao oiaio ole paha. SYN. improbable.

Un-lĭm'it-ed, adj. Palena ole. SYN. boundless.

Un-lōad', v. E hoolei ukana. Unload a ship, e hoolei ka ukana o ka moku.

Un-lŏck', v. E ki a wehe.

Un-love'ly, adj. Maikai ole; aloha ole ia.

Un-lŭck'y, adj. Inea; kuonoono ole.

Un-măn', v. E hoopilihua; hoopaumako. SYN. unnerve.

Un-măn'ly, adj. Ku ole i ka hoo-kanaka.

Un-măn'ner-ly, adj. Kamaniha; pawaa.

Un-mēan'ing, adj. Ano ole.

Un-mêr'çi-ful, adj. Lokoino; makona. SYN. cruel.

Un-mêr'çi-ful-ly, adv. Me ka lokoino.

Ŭn'mis-tāk'a-ble, adj. Maopopolea; akaka lea.

Ŭn-nat'ur-al, adj. 1. Aloha ole. An unnatural parent, he makua aloha ole.

2. Kue i ke ano mau.

Un-nĕç'es-sā'ry, adj. Make hewa; wai-wai ole.

Un-neigh'bor-ly, adj. Launa ole; naa-naa.

Un-nêrve', n. SYN. unman.

Un-nŭm'bered, adj. Helu ole ia; lehulehu wale. SYN. numberless.

Ŭn'ŏb-strŭct'ed, adj. Keakea ole ia. SYN. unhindered.

Ŭn'ob-tru'sive, adj. Akahai. SYN. modest.

Ŭn-ŏs'ten-tā'tioŭs, adj. Hoohiehie ole; akahai.

Un-păck', v. E wehe i ka mea i hoa ia a i haoia paha.

Un-pāl'at-a-ble, adj. 1. Ono ole.

2. Ku ole i ka makemake.

Un-păr'al-lel-ed, adj. Lua ole; like ole.

Un-pär'lia-mĕnt'a-ry, adj. Ku ole i na rula.

Un-pŏp'u-lar, adj. Makemake ole ia e ka lehulehu.

Un-pŏp'ū-lär'i-ty, n. Hoowahawaha ia e ka lehulehu.

Un-prĕç'e-dent-ed, adj. Ike ole ia mamua; mea hou.

Un-prĕj'u-diçed, adj. Hoopono. SYN. just.

Un'pre-tĕnd'ing, adj. Manao akahai.

Un-prĭn'çi-pled, adj. Manao ole i ka pono; ino loa.

Un'prō-dŭc'tive, adj. Hua ole; panoa.

Un-prŏf'it-a-ble, adj. Waiwai ole; makehewa.

Un-prŏf'it-a-bly, *adv.* Makehewa.
Un-prŏm'is-ing, *adj.* Kohu pono ole ana. *Unpromising weather,* wa e kohu pono ole ana.
Un'pro-pi'tioŭs, *adj.* Kue; pono ole. SYN. adverse.
Un-qual'i-fied, *adj.* Makaukau ole; kupono ole.
Un-quĕs'tion-a-ble, *adj.* Oiaio maoli.
Un-quĕs'tion-a-bly, *adv.* Oiaio no. SYN. certainly.
Un-răv'el, *v.* E hoomohala.
Un-rĕas'on-a-ble, *adj.* 1. Ku ole i ka mea pono.
2. Kaulike ole.
Un're-gĕn'er-āte, *adj.* Enemi i Ke Akua.
Un're-lĕnt'ing, *adj.* Menemene ole; hoomauhala loa.
Un're-li'a-ble, *adj.* Hiki ole ke paulele ia.
Un're-mĭt-ting, *adj.* Mau; pau ole. SYN. ceaseless.
Un're-sĕrved', *adj.* Koe ole; huna' ole.
Un're-sĕrv'ed-ly, *adv.* Koe ole; pau loa.
Un-rĕst', *n.* Ka pihoihoi mau; maha ole.
Un-right'eoŭs, *adj.* Hewa; pono ole.
Un-right'eoŭs-ness, *n.* Hewa. SYN. sin.
Un-ripe', *adj.* Oo ole; maka.
Un-ri'valed, *adj.* Lua ole; pookela.
Un-rŏll', *v.* E uhola.
Un-rŏŏf', *v.* E hoohemo i ke kaupoko.
Un-rŭf'fled, *adj.* 1. Lai; malie; malino.
2. Pihoihoi ole. SYN. calm.
Un-ru'ly, *adj.* Hookuli; hoolohe ole.
Un-sad'dle, *v.* E wehe i ka noho lio.
Un-safe', *adj.* Malu ole; pilikia.
Un-săl'a-ble, *adj.* Lilo ole ma ke kuai.
Un-săne'ti-fied, *adj.* Huikala ole ia; hewa.
Un-sat'is-făe'to-ry, *adj.* Kupono ole i ka manao.
Un-să'vo-ry, *adj.* Miko ole.
Un-screw', *v.* 1. E wehe i ka mea i wili ia.
2. E wehe i ke kui nao.
Un-scrŭ'pu-loŭs, *adj.* Manao ole i ka pono; mahiehie. SYN. unprincipled.
Un-sĕal', *v.* E wehe i ka sila.
Un-sĕarch'a-ble, *adj.* Loaa ole ma ka imi. SYN. inscrutable.
Un-sĕa'son-ā-ble, *adj.* Wa kupono ole. SYN. untimely.
Un-sĕat', *v.* E kapai mai ka noho.
Un-sĕa'worth-y, *adj.* Kupono ole ke holo moana.
Un-seem'ly, *adj.* Hilahila; kupono ole.
Un-seen', *adj.* Ike maka ole ia. SYN. invisible.
Un-sĕt'tled, *adj.* 1. Lewa wale; kulekule.
2. Kalewa; pualewa.
Un-shăk'en, *adj.* Oni paa; naue ole.
Un-shēathe', *v.* E unuhi ae; e wehe ae la mai ka wahi'. *He unsheathed his sword,* unuhi ae la oia i kana pahi-kaua.

Uu-sīght'ly, *adj.* Kohu ole i ka ike o ka maka; inoino.
Un-skill'ful, *adj.* Akamai ole. SYN. clumsy.
Un-sŏ'çi-a-ble, *adj.* Naanaa; launa ole.
Ŭn'so-phis'ti-cat-ed, *adj.* Hookamani ole; oiaio; maalea ole.
Un-sŏund', *adj.* 1. Popopo. SYN. decayed.
2. Oiaio ole. SYN. insincere.
3. Paa ole. SYN. defective.
Un-spâr'ing *adj.* Aua ole. *With an unsparing hand,* me ka lima aua ole.
Un-spĕak'a-ble *adj.* Hiki ole ke olelo ia; hiki ole ke hai ia. SYN. unutterable.
Un-spĕak'a-bly, *adv.* Piha; hiki ole ke hai ia. *Unspeakably happy,* hauoli piha. SYN. unutterably.
Un-spŏt'ted, *adj.* Paele ole; maemae.
Un-stā'ble, *adj.* Lauwili wale; loli wale. SYN. inconstant.
Un-stĕad'y, *adj.* Onioni; luliluli.
Un-strŭng', *adj.* 1. Uluhua. *Nerves unstrung,* uluhua ka manao.
2. Alualu.
Ŭn'sŭc-cĕss'ful, *adj.* Hoka; kulea ole; lanakila ole.
Un-sûit'a-ble, *adj.* Kupono ole. SYN. unfit.
Un-tăm'a-ble, *adj.* Hiki ole ke hoolakalaka ia.
Un-thănk'ful, *adj.* Aloha ole. SYN. ungrateful.
Un-think'ing, *adj.* Noonoo ole.
Un-thrift'y, *adj.* SYN. shiftless.
Un-tie', *v.* E wehe i ka nipuu.
Un-til', *prep.* 1. A. *Wait until night,* e kali a po.
2. A hiki. *Until it is time,* a hiki i ka manawa.
Un-time'ly, *adj.* Wa kupono ole. SYN. unseasonable.
Un-tir'ing, *adj.* Luhi ole. *Untiring industry,* makaala luhi ole.
Un'to, *prep.* I; ia. SYN. to.
Un-tōld', *adj.* I hai ole ia. *Untold suffering,* popilikia i hai ole ia.
Un-tō'ward, *adj.* 1. Popilikia. *Untoward events,* na ouli popilikia.
2. Ino; kolohe. *An untoward man,* he kanaka kolohe. SYN. perverse.
Un-trăv'el-ed⎫
Un-trŏd'den⎭ *adj.* Hele ole ia.
Un-trūe', *adj.* Oiaio ole. SYN. false.
Un-trūth', *n.* He wahahee. SYN. falsehood.
Un-trŭth'ful, *adj.* Wahahee.
Un-twist', *v.* E mola.
Un-ūsed', *adj.* 1. Lawelawe ole ia; waiho wale ia.
2. Maa ole. SYN. unaccustomed.
3. Walea ole.
Un-ūs'u-al, *adj.* Hou; ike pinepine ole ia.
Un-văr'nished, *adj.* 1. Pena ole ia i ka vaniki.
2. *Unvarnished truth,* oiaio maoli.

Un-veil′, *v.* E wehe i ka uhi.

Un-war′rant-ed, *adj.* Kauoha ole ia; apono ole ia.

Un-wā′ry, *adj.* Maalea ole; puni wale.

Un-wea′ried, *adj.* Luhi ole; maha ole. SYN. untiring.

Un-wĕll′, *adj.* Omaimai: nawaliwali. SYN. ailing.

Un-whōle′sŏme, *adj.* Kupono ole. *Unwholesome food,* ai kupono ole.

Un-wiĕld′ly, *adj.* Nui kupono ole.

Un-wil′ling, *adj.* Makemake ole; aua.

Un-wil′ling-ly, *adv.* Ahu′ahu′; me ka makemake ole.

Un-wind′, *v.* E wehe i ka mea i wili ia. *Unwind the rope,* e wehe i ka owili kaula.

Un-wise′, *adj.* Naaupo.

Un-wit′ting-ly, *adv.* Me ka ike ole; me ka naaupo. SYN. ignorantly.

Un-wont′ed, *adj.* Maa ole; walea ole.

Un-wor′thi-ly, *adv.* Me ke kupono ole.

Un-wor′thi-ness, *n.* Ano kupono ole.

Un-wor′thy, *adj.* Kupono ole.

Un-writ′ten, *adj.* Kakau ole ia.

Un-yiĕld′ing, *adj.* 1. Paakiki; oolea.
2. Maliu ole.

Un-yōke′, *v.* E wehe i ke auamo; e wehe i ka lei bipi.

Ŭp, *adv.* Iluna; maluna.

Up-brāid′, *v.* E hoohewa.

Up-hēav′al, *n.* Ke kiola ana iluna.

Up-hēave′, *v.* E kiola iluna.

Up-hĭll′, *adj.* 1. Iuka.
2. *Uphill work,* hana inea; hana oolea.

Up-hōld′, *v.* 1. E kokua.
2. E koo. *Uphold the power,* e koo i ka mana.

Up-hōl′ster-er, *n.* Kanaka hana i na lako hale.

Up-hōl′ster-y, *n.* Na lako oloko o ka hale.

Ŭp′land, *n.* 1. Aina kuahiwi; aina o uka.
2. *Upland taro,* kalo o ka aina maloo.

Up-lĭft′, *v.* E hapai iluna.

Up-ŏn′, *prep.* 1. Ma; maluna.
2. 1. *Upon arrival,* i ka hiki ana′aku.

Ŭp′per, *adj.* Maluna. *Upper room,* keena maluna.

Ŭp′per-hānd′, *n.* Ka lanakila; ka mana oi. SYN. ascendency.

Ŭp′per-mōst, *adj.* Maluna loa.

Up-rāise′, *v.* E hoala iluna; e paipai iluna.

Ŭp′right, *adj.* 1. Kupono; kupololei. SYN. perpendicular.
2. Hoopono. SYN. honest.

Ŭp′right-ness, *n.* Kuonoono o ka noho ana; hoopono.

Ŭp′ris-ing, *n.* Ke ala ana mai.

Ŭp′rōar, *n.* He haunaele; uluaoa.

Up-rŏŏt′, *v.* E hehu.

Up-sĕt′, *v.* 1. E hookahuli. SYN. overturn.
2. E hoohanini.

Ŭp′shŏt, *n.* He hopena. SYN. final issue.

Ŭp′stärt, *n.* He mea i lele mai ka ilikole a i ka waiwai nui.

Ŭp′wärd, *adj.* Iluna′e.

Ŭp′wards, *adv.* 1. Keu aku.
2. Iluna′ku.

Ur-bāne′, *adj.* Laulea; oluolu. SYN. polite.

Ur-băn′i-ty, *n.* Ke ano laulea; ano oluolu. SYN. politeness.

Ŭr′chin, *n.* Keiki liilii.

Urġe, *v.* E koi; e kaohi; e kono. SYN. importune.

Ŭr′ġent, *adj.* Koi ana; kaohi ana. *An urgent necessity,* he nele e koi ana.

Ŭ′rin-āte, *v.* E mimi.

Ŭ′rine, *n.* Mimi.

Urn, *n.* He ipu.

Ŭs, *pron. pl.* Kakou; (*dual*) maua; kaua. SYN. you and I.

Ŭs′aġe, *n.* He hana maa; hana walea. SYN. custom.

Ūse, *n.* 1. Waiwai.
2. Ka lawelawe ana.
3. Pomaikai.

Ūse, *v.* E lawelawe; e lawe a e hoohana. SYN. employ.

Ūse′ful, *adj.* 1. Waiwai; makepono.
2. Kokua. *A useful boy,* keiki kokua. SYN. helpful.

Ūse′ful-ly, *adv.* Makepono. *Usefully employed,* e hooikaika makepono.

Ūse′ful-ness, *n.* 1. Ka makepono; ka waiwai.
2. Ke ano kokua.

Ūse′less, *adj.* Makehewa; waiwai ole.

Ūse′less-ly, *adv.* Poho′; makehewa.

Ŭsh′er, *n.* 1. Luna hoonoho i ka poe o ke anaina.
2. He kokua kumu.

Ŭsh′er, *v.* 1. E hookomo; e kai. *Ushered into a room,* kai ia iloko o ke keena.
2. *Usher in the day,* e wehe i ke alaula.

Ū′sū-al, *adj.* Mea mau; mea i maa.

Ū′sū-al-ly, *adv.* He mea mau.

Ū′sū-rer, *n.* Kanaka hoopukapuka dala.

U-sū′ri-oŭs, *adj.* Hoopukapuka ino.

U-sŭrp′, *v.* E kaili hewa; e lawe wale. *Usurp authority,* e lawe wale i ka mana.

U′sur-pā′tion, *v.* Ka lawe hewa ana.

U-sŭrp′er, *n.* Mea i lawe wale i ka pono o hai.

Ū′su-ry, *n.* Hoopukapuka ino i ke dala.

U-tĕn′sil, *n.* Mea hana; mea lawelawe.

U-til′i-ty, *n.* Pomaikai.

Ŭt′most, *adj.* Hope loa; loa.

U-tō′pi-an, *adj.* Makehewa; io ole SYN. useless.

Ŭt′ter, *adj.* Loa. *Utter destitution,* nele loa.

Ŭt′ter, *v.* E ekemu; e hai.

Ŭt′ter-ançe, *n.* Olelo; ka hai ana.

Ŭt′ter-ly, *adv.* Loa. *Utterly miserable,* oki loa.

Ŭt′ter-mōst, *adj.* Loa. *Save to the uttermost,* e hoopakele loa.

Ux-ō′ri-oŭs, *adj.* Pili loa i ka wahine mare.

V

Va'can-çy, *n.* He hakahaka; wahi kaawale.

Va'cant, *adj.* 1. Kaawale; kawaha.
2. *A vacant place,* kahi koo; kahi kaawale.
3. *A vacant expression of countenance,* he helehelena nele i ka hoihoi.

Va'cate, *v.* 1. E waiho kaawale.
2. E waiho aku. *Vacate an office,* e waiho aku i ka oihana.

Va-ca'tion, *n.* Wa hoomaha.

Vac'çi-nate, *v.* E o lima.

Vac'çine vi'rus, *n.* Palaheehee o lima.

Vac'il-late, *v.* E kulanalana; e loli wale. SYN. waver.

Vac'il-la'ting, *adj.* Kulanalana; lauwili.

Va-cu'i-ty } *n.* He hakakaka; kahi kaawale; wahi ole o loko.
Vac'u-um }

Va'de-me'cum, *n.* Mea lawe pu.

Vag'a-bond, *n.* Aea haukae; he hoomalau.

Va'ga-ry, *n.* Noonoo ulu wale; noonoo kupono ole.

Va'gran-çy, *n.* Ka aea wale; noho wale.

Va'grant, *n.* See vagabond.

Vague (vág), *adj.* Powehiwehi. SYN. indefinite.

Vail } *n.* 1. He paku'.
Veil } 2. He uhi maka.

Vain, *adj.* 1. Makehewa, waiwai ole. SYN. useless.
2. Hookiekie; haakei.

Vain-glo'ri-ous, *adj.* Hookiekie; haanui.

Vain'ly, *adv.* Makehewa.

Val'ançe, *n.* Lole paku' no lalo a me luna o ka moe.

Vale, *n.* Awawa.

Val'e-dic-to'ri-an, *n.* Haumana o ke kula nui i haawi i ka haiolelo hope loa.

Val'e-dic'to-ry, *n.* Haiolelo hope loa.

Val'et, *n.* Kauwa lawelawe kino.

Val'iant, *adj.* Koa; aa. SYN. brave.

Val'id, *adj.* Pono; kupono. SYN. good; sufficient. *A valid excuse,* he kumu kupono.

Va-lid'i-ty, *n.* Ka pono; ke kupono. *Validity of a will,* ke kupono o ka palapala hooilina i ke kanawai.

Va-lise', *n.* Pahu ili liilii.

Val'ley, *n.* Kahawai; awawa.

Val'or, *n.* Ano koa. SYN. bravery

Val'or-ous, *adj.* See valiant.

Val'u-a-ble, *adj.* Waiwai.

Val'u-a'tion, *n.* Ka hoonohonoho wai wai.

Val'ue, *n.* Kumu lilo; waiwai.

Val'ue, *v.* 1. E manao. *Value highly,* e manao nui aku. *Value slightly,* e manao liilii aku.
2. E hooholo i ke kumukuai; e hooholo i ka waiwai.

Valve, *n.* He pani.

Van, *n.* 1. Hunalewa.
2. Kaa halihali ukana.

Vane, *n.* Ane makani.

Van'-guard, *n.* Ke kulana mua o ka puali koa ma ka huakai; hunalewa.

Van'ish, *v.* E nalo koke aku. SYN. disappear.

Van'i-ty, *n.* Kilohi; haakei.

Van'quish, *v.* E hooauhee; hoopio. SYN. conquer.

Van'tage-ground, *n.* 1. Ke kulana mua.
2. Ka oi o ka pomaikai.

Va-por, *n.* 1. *Vapor of steam,* mahu.
2. Ohu. SYN. fog.

Va'ri-a-ble, *adj.* Lauwili; loli wale. SYN. changeable.
2. *Variable as wind,* pahili; lauwili.

Va'ri-ançe, *n.* Ano ku-e; mokuahana.

Va'ri-a'tion, *n.* Ka loli ana; aui ana.

Va'ri-e-gat'ed, *n.* Kiokio; ponapona.

Va-ri'e-ty, *n.* Kela me keia ano.

Va'ri-o-loid, *n.* Kekahi ano o ka mai puupuu liilii.

Va'ri-ous, *adj.* Kela me keia.

Var'nish, *n* Vaniki; wai hoohinuhinu.

Var'nish, *v.* E hamo i ka vaniki.

Va'ry, *v.* E loli ae; e hoo-ano e.

Vase, *n.* He ipu loloa. *Vase for flowers,* ipu no na pua.

Vas'sal, *n.* Kauwa kuapaa. SYN. slave.

Vas'sal-age, *n.* Ka noho ana kauwa kuapaa. SYN. slavery.

Vast, *adj.* 1. Nui loa.
2. Palena ole. *The vast universe,* ke ao palena ole.

Vast-ness, *n.* Ka nui loa.

Vat, *n.* He tabu nui.

Vault, *v.* E lele. SYN. jump.

Vault, *n.* He lua. SYN. cellar.

Vaunt, *v.* E kaena wale. SYN. boast.

Veal, *n.* I'o bipi keiki.

Veer, *v.* E aui ae; e huli ae.

Veg'e-ta-ble, *n.* Hua o ka honua; mea ulu. *The vegetable world,* ka mahele o na mea ulu.

Vĕg′e-tāte, v. E ulu wale me he mea kanu la.

Vĕg′e-tā′tion, n. Kela me keia mea ulu.

Vĕ′he-mençe, n. Ikaika nui. SYN. fervor.

Vĕ′he-ment-ly, adv. Me ka ikaika loa.

Vĕ′hi-cle, n. 1. Kela me keia ano kaa.
2. Mea halihali.

Veil (vāle), n. He uhi; uhi no ka maka.

Veil, v. E uhi.

Vein, n. 1. Aa koko.
2. He au metala; a minerala paha maloko o ka honua.

Veined, adj. Paapu i na aa.

Ve-lŏç′i-ty, n. Ka mama; ka wikiwiki.

Vĕl′vet, n. Lole veleveta.

Vĕnd, v. E kuai aku. SYN. sell.

Vĕnd′er⎱ n. Kanaka kuai aku; he ma-
Vĕnd′or⎰   au'auwa'.

Vĕn′due, n. Kuai kudala. SYN. auction.

Ve-neer′, n. Papa lahilahi, mea kapili maluna o ka papa e ae.

Vĕn′er-a-ble, adj. Ku i ka mahaloia.

Vĕn′er-ate, v. E haawi i ka mahalo; e hoomaikai.

Vĕn′er-ā′tion, n. Mahalo; hoomaikai.

Vĕnge′ançe, n. Ka hoopai huhu.

Vĕ′ni-al, adj. Hiki ke kalaia.

Vĕn′om, n. Mea make.

Vĕn′om-oŭs, adj. Awaawa e make ai.

Ve′noŭs, adj. No na aa-koko.

Vĕnt, n. 1. Puka hookahe; kahi e hemo ai.
2. Ka hoopuka ana. To give vent to feelings, e hoopuka manao.

Vĕnt′-hōle, n. Puka hookomo ea.

Vĕn′ti-lāte, v. 1. E hookomo pono i ke ea.
2. E hoolaha; hoo-akea. To ventilate an opinion, e hoolaha manao
3. To ventilate a subject, e hooakea i kekahi mea.

Vĕn′ti-lā′tion, n. Ka hookomo pono ana i ke ea.

Vĕn′ti-lā′tor, n. Mea hookomo i ke ea maikai.

Vĕnt′ure, v. 1. E hoao. SYN. risk.
2. E aa.

Vĕnt′ur-sŏme, adj. Aa; koa; maka'u ole. SYN. bold.

Ve-rā′çioŭs, adj. Oiaio. SYN. truthful.

Ve-răç′i-ty, n. Ano oiaio. SYN. truthfulness.

Ve-răn′dă, n. Lanai hale.

Vĕrb, n. Haina.

Vĕrb′al, adj. Hai waha; olelo waha. SYN. oral.

Vĕrb′al-ly, adv. Waha; me ka waha. SYN. orally

Ver-bā′tim, adv. Like loa ma ka olelo.

Ver-bōse′, adj. Makena olelo.

Ver-bŏs′i-ty, n. Ka nui pono ole o ka olelo.

Vĕr′dan-çy, n. 1. Ke ano uliuli.
2. Ano hou; maa ole.

Vĕr′-dant, n. 1. Uliuli.
2. Hou; maa ole.

Vĕr′dict, n. 1. Olelo hooholo a ke jure.
2. Olelo hooholo.

Vĕrd′ure, n. Ka uliuli o na mea ulu.

Vĕrge, v. E hookokoke aku.

Vĕrge, n. Ke kae; ka lihi.

Vĕr-i-fi-cā′tion, n. Ka hooia ana. SYN. confirmation.

Vĕr′i-fӯ, v. E hooia; e hooiaio. SYN. confirm.

Vĕr′i-ly, adv. He oiaio. SYN. truly.

Vĕr′i-ta-ble, adj. Oiaio maoli. SYN. true.

Vĕr′i-ty, n. Ke ano oiaio.

Ver-mie′u-lar, adj. Me he enuhe la.

Vĕr′mi-fūge, n. Laau hoo-naha no na mea ola iloko o ka opu.

Ver-mil′ion, n. He hooluu ulaula.

Vĕr′min, n. Mea kolo liilii.

Ver-năc′u-lar, adj. Maoli. SYN. native.

Vĕr′nal, adj. No ke kau kupulau.

Vĕr′sa-tile, adj. Makaukau ma na mea he nui.

Vĕr′sa-til′i-ty, n. Ke ano makaukau ma kela me keia mea.

Vĕrse, n. 1. Pauku himeni.
2. Pauku olelo.

Vĕrsed, adj. Makaukau; akamai.

Vĕr′si-fi-cā′tion, n. Haku mele.

Vĕr′sion, n. Ke ano o ka olelo.

Vĕr′te-brā, n. Pauku iwi o ka iwi kuamoo.

Vĕr′tex, n. 1. Ka piko; ka wekiu.
2. Kiko hui o ka huina.

Vĕr′ti-cal, adj. Kupono. SYN. perpendicular.

Vĕr′ti-go, n. Nenewa; poniuniu.

Vĕr′y, adv. Loa. Very great, nui loa.

Vĕs′per, adj. Ahiahi. Vesper bell, bele pule ahiahi.

Vĕs′pers, n. Halawai haipule ahiahi.

Vĕs′sel, n. 1. Moku.
2. Ipu; apu.

Vĕst, n. Puliki.

Vĕst′ed, adj. Pili paa. Vested rights, pono pili paa.

Vĕs′ti-būle, n. Ipuka.

Vĕs′tige, n. He meheu; lihi iki. SYN. trace.

Vĕs′try, n. 1. Keena halawai no na luna ekalesia.
2. Aha luna ekalesia.

Vĕst′ure, n. Lole komo; aahu. SYN. raiment.

Vĕt′er-an, n. 1. Koa kahiko.
2. Mea i maa; mea i walea.

Vĕt′er-i-na-ry, adj. Pili i ka lapaau holoholona.

Ve′to, v. E hoole. To veto a bill, e hoole i ka bila.

Vĕx, v. E hoonaukiuki; hoouluhua. SYN. tease.

Vex-ā′tion, n. Mea luhi wale; mea hoopilikia.

Vex-a'tioŭs, *adj.* Luhi wale; hoo-ulu-
hua.
Via, *adv.* Ma o. SYN. by way of. *Via
Honolulu,* ma o Honolulu la.
Vi'a-duct, *n.* He alahaka no ke ala-
nui hao.
Vi'al, *n.* Omole liilii.
Vi'ands, *n.* Kela me keia mea ai. SYN.
victuals.
Vi'brāte, *v.* 1. E lewa; e mahiki. SYN.
oscillate.
2. E hulili.
Vi-brā'tion, *n.* 1. Ka mahiki ana.
2. Ka hulili ana. *Vibrations of light,*
hulili o na kukuna malamalama.
Vi'bra-to-ry, *adv.* Mahikihiki.
Vi-cā'ri-oŭs, *adj.* Panai; panihaka-
haka.
Viçe, *n.* 1. Hewa; hala; ino.
2. He uma.
Viçe, *prep.* Ma ka hakahaka.
Viçe-con'sul, *n.* He hope kanikele.
Viçe'prĕs'i-dent, *n.* Hope peresidena.
Viçe-roy', *n.* Hope moi.
Vi-çin'i-ty, *n.* Kahi kokoke. SYN.
neighborhood.
Vi'çioŭs, *adj.* 1. Puni i ka ino; hau-
mia.
2. Ino; huhu. *A vicious horse,* he lio
huhu.
Vi-çis/si-tūde, *n.* Luli; loli. SYN.
change. *Vicissitudes of life,* na loli ana
o keia ola.
Vic'tim, *n.* 1. He pio.
2. Mea hoopunihei ia.
Vic'tim-ize, *v.* E hoopunihei.
Vic'tor, *n.* Ka mea i lanakila. SYN.
conqueror.
Vic-to'ri-oŭs, *adj.* Lanakila. SYN.
triumphant.
Vic'tory, *n.* Ka lanakila. SYN. triumph.
Vict'u-al, *v.* E hoolako i ka ai.
Vict'uals (vit-lz), *n.* Na mea ai.
Vie, *v.* E hooikaika i like.
View, *v.* E nana.
View, *n.* Ka nanaina.
Vig'il, *n.* Ke kiai i ka po.
Vig'i-lançe, *n.* Ke ano makaala; kuoo.
Vig'i-länt, *adj.* Kuoo; kiai; makaala.
Vig'or, *n.* Ikaika. SYN. strength.
Vig'or-oŭs, *adj.* 1. Ikaika; makaala.
SYN. strong; energetic.
2. *Vigorous in growth,* koii; *slow in
growth,* ko-i'.
Vile, *adj.* Haukae; paumaele; pelapela.
Vile'ness, *n.* He paumaele; he haukea.
Vil'i-fi-er, *n.* He hakuepa; kanaka
niania. SYN. traducer.
Vil'i-fŷ, *v.* E olelo ino; hakuepa.
Vil'la, *n.* Hale noho ma kuaaina no ka
poe koikoi.
Vil'lage, *n.* He kau-hale.
Vil'la-ger, *n.* Kamaaina o kauhale.
Vil'lain, *n.* Kanaka lilo loa i ka hewa.
SYN. scoundrel.
Vil'lain-oŭs, *adj.* Hewa loa; ino loa.
Vil'lain-y, *n.* Hana keekee loa.

Vin'di-cāte, *v.* E hoapono. SYN. justify
Vin'di-cā'tion, *n.* Ka hoapono ana.
Vin'di-cā'tor, *n.* Ka mea e hoapono
ana.
Vin-dic'tive, *adj.* Hoomauhala. SYN.
revengeful.
Vin-dic'tive-ness, *n.* He hoomauhala.
Vine, *n.* 1. Laau hihi.
2. *Grape vine,* kumu waina.
Vin'e-gar, *n.* Vinika.
Vine'yard, *n.* Mala waina.
Vint'age, *n.* 1. Na hua o ka mala
waina.
2. Wa ohi hua o ka mala waina.
Vint'a-ger, *n.* Mea ohi hua waina.
Vi'o-lāte, *v.* 1. E lima ikaika aku; e
pue.
2. E hana ku-e aku; e haki. *Violate
his promise,* e haki i kana olelo ae.
Vi'o-lā'tion, *n.* 1. Ka pue ana. SYN.
rape.
2. Ka hoohaki ana. SYN. non-ob-
servance.
Vi'o-lā'tor, *n.* 1. Kanaka pue wahine.
2. Mea hoohaki.
Vi'o-lençe, *n.* 1. Ka hao wale; lima
ikaika.
2. Ikaika o ka ino. *Violence of the
storm,* ka ikaika o ka ino.
Vi'o-lent, *adj.* 1. Ino. *A violent wind,*
makani ino.
2. *A violent man,* he kanaka hikiwawe
i ka huhu.
Vi'o-lin, *n.* He pila; violina.
Vi'per, *n.* Nahesa niho awa.
Vi-rā'go, *n.* Wahine nuku wale; wahine mahaoi.
Vir'gin, *n.* Wahine puupaa.
Vir-gin'i-ty, *n.* Ka noho ana wahine
puupaa.
Vi'rile, *adj.* Ano kane.
Vir'tu-al-ly, *adj.* Aneane; mehe mea
la.
Vir'tūe, *n.* 1. Pono.
2. Mana. SYN. power.
Vir'tu-oŭs, *adj.* Pono; noho pololei.
Vir'u-lent, *adj.* 1. Awahia loa. *A viru-
lent poison,* he laau make, laau awahia.
2. Manao enemi loa. SYN. malignant.
Vi'rus, *n.* Palaheehee.
Vis'age, *n.* Helehelena. SYN. counte-
nance.
Vis-a-vis (vīz'a-vē'), *n.* He alo he alo;
mea imua o ke alo.
Vis'çe-ra, *n.* Na naau.
Vis'çid, *adj.* Pipili. SYN. sticky.
Vise, *n.* He uma. SYN. vice.
Vis'i-ble, *adj.* Ike maka ia. SYN. ap-
parent.
Vis'i-bly, *adv.* I ka ike o ka maka.
Vis'ion, *n.* 1. Ka ike o ka maka. SYN.
eyesight.
2. He hihio.
Vis'ion-a-ry, *adj.* Hihio wale.
Vis'it, *v.* 1. E launa. *Visit persons,* e
launa me keahi poe.
2. E makaikai. *Visit places,* e makai-
kai ma na kauwahi.

Vis'it-ā'tion, *n.* 1. Ka launa ana; ka hele ana e ike.
2. Ke kau ana mai. *Visitation of Divine Providence,* ke kau ana mai o ka lima o Ke Akua.

Vis'it-or, *n.* He hoalauna; he makaikai.

Vis'ta, *n.* 1. He nanaina iwaena o ke alanui, na ululaau, na awawa paha.
2. *Down the vista of ages,* i ke kuamoo o na au i hala.

Vis'u-al, *adj.* No na maka.

Vi'tal, *adj.* 1. Kupono i ke ola.
2. *A vital necessity,* he mea e pono loa ai.
3. *Of vital importance,* waiwai pono; ano nui.

Vi-tāl'i-ty, *n.* 1. Ka ikaika o ke ola.
2. Ano eueu; lalelale.
3. *Small vitality,* ano nawaliwali.

Vi'tals, *n. pl.* Na lala o ke kino e pili loa ana i ke ola.

Vi'ti-ate, *v.* 1. E hoolilo i mea ole. *Vitiate a bargain,* e hoolilo ka ae-like i mea ole.

Vit're-oŭs, *adj.* Me he aniani la.

Vit'ri-fy, *v.* E hoolilo i aniani.

Vi-tŭ'per-āte, *v.* E olelo nuku; olelo aki.

Vi-tŭ'per-ā'-tion, *n.* Olelo nuku; olelo aki.

Vi-tŭ'per-a-tĭve, *adj.* Nuku wale; aki.

Vi-vā'çioŭs, *adj.* Hoihoi; lalelale. SYN. animated.

Vi-vāç'i-ty, *n.* Ke ano hoihoi; ano lalelale.

Viv'id, *adj.* 1. Moakaka.
2. Olinolino; hulali.

Viv'id-ly, *adv.* 1. Me ka moakaka.
2. Me ka hulili.

Vix'en, *n.* He wahine nuku wale. SYN. scold.

Viz'ier (Vĭz-zier'), *n.* Luna kiekie o ke aupuni o Tureke.

Vō-cāb'u-la-ry, *n.* Buke unuhi olelo.

Vō'cal, *adj.* Pili i ka leo. *Vocal music,* leo pa-ko-li.

Vō'cal-ĭst, *n.* Mea akamai i ka pa-ko-li.

Vo-cā'tion, *n.* Oihana. SYN. calling; business.

Vo-çif'er-ā'tion, *n.* Hauwalaau; wawa nui.

Vo-çif'er-oŭs, *adj.* Walaau nui; wawa.

Voiçe, *n.* Leo.

Voiçe'less, *adj.* Leo ole.

Void, *adj.* 1. Ole loa. *Null and void,* l'lo i mea ole.
2. Akea; kaawale. *A void place,* wahi kaawale.

Vōl'a-tile, *adj.* 1. Pau koke; puehu wale.
2. Puni lealea. SYN. gay.
3. Loli wale. SYN. changeable.

Vol-cā'no, *n.* 1. Mauna pele; luapele.
2. Ahiaihonua (old).

Vo-li'tion, *n.* Ka makemake; ka manao. SYN. will.

Vŏl'ley, *n.* 1. Ke kani like o na pu.
2. *A volley of words,* ka nui mai o na hua olelo.

Vŏl'u-bil'i-ty, *n.* Ka makaukau ma ka olelo.

Vŏl'u-ble, *adj.* Makaukau ma ka olelo; palolo.

Vŏl'ume, *n.* 1. He buke.
2. *Volume of smoke,* he punohu uahi.
3. *Volume of water,* mahele o ka wai.

Vo-lŭ'mi-noŭs, *adj.* 1. Nui wale o na buke. *A voluminous author,* he mea i kakau buke he nui wale.
2. Kakau nui. *A voluminous correspondence,* he kakau nui i na palapala.

Vŏl'un-ta-ri-ly, *adv.* Mamuli o ka makemake.

Vŏl'un-ta-ry, *adj.* No ka makemake mai.

Vŏl'un-teer', *n.* Mea e kokua ana mamuli o kona makemake.

Vŏl'un-teer', *v.* 1. E kokua mamuli o ka makemake.
2. E kokua wale.

Vo-lŭpt'u-a-ry, *n.* Mea puni lealea.

Vo-lŭpt'ū-oŭs, *adj.* Kuko nui ia.

Vŏm'it, *v.* E luai.

Vo-rā'çioŭs, *adj.* Hoonuu; pakela ai.

Vo-rāç'i-ty, *n.* Hoonuu ai.

Vŏr'tex, *n.* Mimilo; lua mimilo. SYN. whirlpool.

Vō'ta-ry, *n.* Mea lilo loa i kekahi hana. *A votary of science,* mea lilo loa i ke akeakamai. *A votary of pleasure,* mea lilo loa i ka lealea.

Vōte, *v.* E koho; e balota.

Vōte, *n.* He koho; he balota. SYN. ballot.

Vōt'er, *n.* Mea koho balota.

Vō'tive, *adj.* Hoolaaia. *A votive offering,* he mohai i hoolaa ia.

Vouch, *v.* E olelo hoohiki.

Vouch'er, *n.* Palapala hoike no na lilo.

Vouch-sāfe', *v.* E oluolu e pane mai.

Vow, *v.* E hoohiki imua o Ke Akua.

Vow'el, *n.* Huapalapala leo-kahi.

Vŏy'age, *n.* 1. He holo moana.
2. He holo ma kela me keia mahele wai.
3. He holo ma ka baluna.

Vŏy'a-ger, *n.* Mea holo maluna o ke kai; maluna o ka wai.

Vŭl'gar, *adj.* 1. Kuaaina.
2. Haahaa; pelapela.

Vul-gār'i-ty, *n.* Ano haumia; ano pelapela.

Vŭl'ner-a-ble, *adj.* Hiki ke hooehaia.

Vŭlt'ūre, *n.* Vuletura; manu ai mea pilau.

W

Wab′ble, *v.* E onioni; e naue.

Wad, *n.* Umoki pu.

Wade, *v.* E hele iloko o ka wai.

Wa′fer, *n.* 1. Wepa, mea hoopaa palapala.
2. He papaa berena liilii.

Waft, *v.* 1. E peahi; e ani.
2. E halihali.

Wag, *n.* Kanaka hooakaaka.

Wag, *v.* E onioni; e luliluli.

Wage, *v.* *Wage war,* e hoouka kaua.

Wa′ger, *v.* E pili waiwai. SYN. bet.

Wa′ges, *n.* Uku hana.

Wag′ger-y, *n.* Ano hooakaaka; olelo hooakaaka.

Wag′on, *n.* Kaa lio.

Wag′on-er, *n.* Mea hookele kaa.

Wail, *n.* Leo kaniuhu′; uwe; leo pihe′

Waist, *n.* Ka puhaka.

Waist′band, *n.* Kaei puhaka.

Waist′coat, *n.* Puliki. SYN. vest.

Wait, *v.* 1. E kali; e kakali.
2. E lawelawe. *To wait on the table,* e lawelawe ma ka papa aina.

Wait′er, *n.* 1. Mea lawelawe ma ka papa aina; he kuene.
2. He pa palahalaha mea lawe ai.

Wait′ing-maid, *n.* Wahine lawelawe.

Wait′ress, *n.* Kuene wahine.

Waive, *v.* E haalele; e waiho. SYN. relinquish.

Wake, *v.* E ala mai.

Wake, *n.* Ka aweawe kai o ka moku.

Wake′ful, *adj.* Hiaa; makaala.

Wa′ken, *v.* E hoo-ala mai ka hiamoe.

Walk, *v.* 1. E hele wawae.
2. *Walk stealthily,* e amio.

Walk, *n.* Ka hele malie ana ma ka wawae.
2. He ala mawaena o ke kihapai.
3. He holoholo.

Walk′er, *n.* Mea hele wawae.

Wall, *n.* 1. Pa. *Stone wall,* pa-pohaku.
2. Paia. *Wall of a house,* ka paia o ka hale.

Wal′let, *n.* He aa; he eke.

Wall′-eyed, *adj.* Makapaa. *A wall-eyed horse,* he lio makapaa.

Wal′lop, *v.* E hahau ikaika.

Wal′low, *v.* 1. E kaa ma ka lepo.
2. *Wallow in sin,* e lu iloko o ka hewa; e kaa iloko o ka nenelu.

Wall′-pa′per, *n.* Pepa kapili no ke keena.

Wam′pum, *n.* Lei lehu o na Inikini, oia ko lakou dala.

Wan, *adj.* Hakeakea. SYN. pale.

Wand, *n.* He kookoo loihi;

Wan′der, *v.* E auwana; e kuewa.

Wan′der-er, *n.* He mea auwana wale; he aea; he kuea.

Wane, *v.* E emi iho. *The moon wanes,* ke emi nei ka mahina.

Want, *n.* 1. He nele; he ilihune.
2. Ka makemake.

Wan′ton, *adj.* 1. Uhauha wale.
2. Makaleho.

Wan′ton-ly, *adv.* Uhauha wale. *Destroy wantonly,* e luku wale; e hoopoino wale.

War, *n.* Kaua.

War′ble, *v.* E memele me he manu la.

War′bler, *n.* Manu memele.

War′-cry, *n.* Leo hoo′ho kaua.

Ward, *n.* 1. Keiki hanai.
2. He apana maloko o ke kulanakauhale. SYN. precinct.
2. Keena o ka hale mai.

Ward′en} *n.* Kahu malama: luna kiai.
Ward′er}

Ward′robe, *n.* 1. Wahi e malama lole.
2. He ahu lole komo.

Ward′room, *n.* Keena hookipa no na luna moku manuwa′.

Ware′house, *n.* Hale hoo-ahu waiwai.

Wares, *n. pl.* Na waiwai kuai. SYN. goods.

War′fare, *n.* Oihana kaua; ke kaua.

War′-horse, *n.* Lio holo kaua.

Wa′ri-ly, *adv.* Me ka noonoo akahele.

War′like, *adj.* Puni kaua; koa.

Warm, *adj.* 1. Mahana; pu-mahana.
2. Hoihoi. SYN. ardent.

Warmth, *n.* Ka mahana; ka pu-mahana; ke ano hoihoi.

Warn, *v.* 1. E ao. SYN. admonish; caution.
2. E kukala. SYN. give notice.

Warn′ing, *n.* 1. Olelo ao. SYN. admonition.
2. Olelo kukala. SYN. notice.

War′-of′fice, *n.* Keena oihana kaua.

Warp, *n.* 1. Kaula hookolo moku.
2. Maawe loloa.

Warp, *v.* E aapu; e anapa; na′pana′pa.

War′rant, *n.* 1. Palapala haawi mana.
2. *Warrant of arrest,* palapala hopu. *Search warrant,* palapala imi.

War′rant, *v.* E hoike me ka maopopo.

Warr'rant-a-ble, *adj.* Kupono; aponoia. Syn. justifiable.

War'ran-ty, *n.* He palapala hoopaa. Syn. guarantee.

War'ri-or, *n.* He koa. Syn. soldier.

Wart, *n.* He ilikona.

War'-whoop, *n.* Hoo'ho kaua a na Inikini.

War'-worn, *adj.* Maa i ke kaua.

Wa'ry, *adj.* 1. Noonoo akahele. Syn. cautious.
   2. Kuoo; makaala i na pilikia.

Wash, *v.* 1. E holoi.
   2. *Wash the shore,* e popoi ana ma ka-hakai.
   3. *Rains wash away,* lilo i ka u-'a.

Wash'-board, *n.* 1. Papa holoi lole.
   2. Papa pale e pili ana i ka papa hele.

Wash'er, *n.* He apo metala, mea nao.

Wash'er-wo-man, *n.* Wahine holoi lole. Syn. laundress.

Wash'ing, *n.* Na lole holoi.

Wasp, *n.* Nalo aki; nalo paka.

Waste, *v.* E mauna wale; hoomauna-una; euhauha.

Waste'ful, *adj.* Maunauna; uhauha. Syn. prodigal.

Waste'ful-ness, *n.* Ka uhauha wale.

Watch, *n.* 1. He wati liilii; wati pakeke.
   2. Poe kiai.
   3. Wa kiai.

Watch, *v.* E kiai; e kuoo.

Watch'er, *n.* He kiai.

Watch'ful, *adj.* Makaala; kuoo; kiai. Syn. vigilant.

Watch'man, *n.* Kiai-po; kiai.

Watch'tow'er, *n.* Hale kiai.

Watch'word, *n.* Hua olelo huna' no ka poe kiai. Syn. password; countersign.

Wa'ter, *n.* Wai.

Wa'ter, *v.* E hookahe wai; e ka wai.

Wa'ter-col'ors, *n.* Na hooluu i kawili ia me ka wai.

Wa'ter-course, *n.* Kahawai; auwai.

Wa'ter-cress, *n.* Leikoa.

Wa'ter-cure, *n.* Lapaau me ka wai.

Wa'ter-fall, *n.* Wai-lele; wai paihi'. Syn. cascade.

Wa'ter-fowl, *n.* Manu o ka wai.

Wa'ter-ing-place, *n.* 1. Wahi hoohainu i ka wai.
   2. Wahi e akoakoa ai o kanaka e inu i ka wai o ia wahi.

Wa'ter-lev'el, *n.* Ili-wai.

Wa'ter-mark, *n.* He kaha kahi i hiki ai o ka wai. *High water mark,* kaha o ka wai nui. *Low water mark,* kaha o ka wai emi.

Wa'ter-mel'on, *n.* Ipu ai maka; ipu haole.

Wa'ter-pail, *n.* Bakeke wai.

Wa'ter-pitch'er, *n.* Pika wai.

Wa'ter-pot, *n.* Bakeke ninini wai.

Wa'ter-pow'er, *n.* Ka ikaika o ka wai ma ke kaa ana i na huila.

Wa'ter-priv'i-lege, } *n.* Ke kuleana
Wa'ter-right, } ma ka wai o kahawai.

Wa'ter-proof, *adj.* Paa i komo ole ka wai.

Wa'ter-rate, *n.* Auhau no ka wai.

Wa'ter-shed, *n.* He aina kiekie ma na aoao o kekahi muliwai, e hookahe ana i kona wai a iloko o ka muliwai. *The water shed of the Mississippi,* ka aina i hookahe ia kona wai a iloko o ka muliwai Misisipi.

Wa'ter-soaked, *adj.* Komo loa ia i ka wai.

Wa'ter-spout, *n.* Wai-pui-lani.

Wa'ter-tight, *adj.* Paa i komo ole ka wai.

Wa'ter-wheel, *n.* Huila kaa i ka wai.

Wa'ter-works, *n.* Oihana hoolako wai.

Wa'ter-y, *adj.* 1. Loliloli.
   2. *Watery eyed,* makakole.

Waul, *v.* E owao e like me ka popoki.

Wave, *n.* 1. Ale.
   2. *Wave of the hand,* peahi lima.

Wa'ver, *v.* E luli wale; e kulanalana. Syn. vacillate.

Wax, *n.* Pilali nalo meli.

Wax, *v.* E mahuahua ae. *Wax and wane,* e mahuahua'e alaila emi mai.

Wax'work, *n.* Na mea i hana ia me ka pilali.

Way, *n.* 1. Ano.
   2. Ala; alanui. Syn. path.

Way'bill, *n.* Papa inoa o na ohua; na ee moku.

Way'far-er, *n.* Mea hele malihini. Syn. traveller.

Way-lay, *v.* E powa ma ke alanui; e hoohalua.

Way'ward, *adj.* Hookuli; paakiki. Syn. perverse.

Way'ward-ness, *n.* Ke ano paakiki; hookuli. Syn. perversity.

Way'worn, *adj.* Luhi ma ke alanui.

We, *pron. pl.* Makou; (*dual*), maua.

Weak, *adj.* Palupalu; nawaliwali.

Weak'en, *v.* E hoonawaliwali; e hooemi i ka ikaika.

Weak'ness, *n.* 1. Ano palupalu; ano nawaliwali.
   2. Ikaika ole.

Weak'ling, *n.* Mea ikaika ole; mea palupalu.

Weal, *n.* Kuonoono; kuapapa nui. Syn. prosperity.

Wealth, *n.* 1. Waiwai. Syn. riches.
   2. He lako. Syn. affluence.
   3. *Wealth of affection,* ka nui o ke aloha.

Wealth'y, *adj.* Waiwai; koikoi. Syn. rich.

Wean, *v.* 1. E ukuhi i ka waiu. *A weaned child,* he keiki ukuhiia.
   2. E hoohuli. Syn. alienate.

Weap'on, *n.* Mea pale i ka ino; mea kaua; mea hakaka.

Wear, *v.* 1. E aahu; e komo; e kahiko.
   2. E hookaumaha; hooluhi.
   3. *To wear away,* e emi iho ka ikaika. *To wear out clothes,* e komo lole a pau ko lakou pono. *To wear out one's patience,* e hoopaupauaho.

Wēa-ri-ly, *adv.* Me ka luhi.

Wēa'ri-ness, *n.* Luhi; maluhiluhi. SYN. fatigue.

Wēa'ri-sŏme, *adj.* Maluhiluhi. SYN. fatiguing.

Wēa'ry, *adj.* Maluhiluhi; maloeloe; luhi. SYN. tired.

Wĕath'er, *n.* Wa. *Good weather,* wa maikai.

Wĕath'er, *v.* E lanakila; *Weather the gale,* e lanakila maluna o ka ino.

Wĕath-er-cŏck, *v.* Anemakani. SYN. vane.

Wĕath'er-gāge, *n.* 1. Aoao manai. 2. Ka aoao lanakila.

Wĕath'er-wiṣe, *adj.* Akamai ma ke kuhikuhi ana i ke ano o ka la.

Weave, *v.* E ulana.

Wēav'er, *n.* Mea nana e u.ana.

Wĕb, *n.* 1. Mea i ulanaia. 2. *Spider's web,* he punawelewele. SYN. cobweb.

Wĕb'-foŏt'ed, *adj.* Wawae koloa.

Wĕd, *v.* 1. E mare. SYN. marry. 2. E pili.

Wĕd'ding, *n.* He mare. SYN. marriage.

Wĕdge, *n.* He unu.

Wĕd'lŏck, *n.* Mare. SYN. marriage.

Wĕd'neṣ-day (Wĕnṣ'day), *n.* Poakolu.

~~**Wee,** *adj.* Uuku loa.~~

Weed, *n.* Nahelehele.

Weed, *v.* E olaulau; e waele.

Weed'y, *adj.* Nahelehele.

Week, *n.* Hebedoma.

Week'-dāy, *n.* La noa.

Week'ly, *adj.* and *adv.* Kela me keia hebedoma.

Ween, *v.* E manao. SYN. think.

Weep, *v.* E hookahe wai maka; e uwe'; e haloiloi.

Wee'vil, *n.* Mu ai palaoa.

Weigh (way), *v.* 1. E kaupaona. 2. E poonoo. SYN. consider. 3. *Weigh anchor,* e huki i ka heleuma.

Weight (wāte), *n.* 1. He kaumaha. 2. Po-ka' kaupaona.

Weight'y, *adj.* Kaumaha; koikoi. SYN. heavy.

Weird, *adj.* Eehia; ano lapu. SYN. supernatural.

Wĕl'eŏme, *n.* Kipa aloha.

Wĕld, *v.* E hookui pu i na mea metala.

Wĕl'fāre, *n.* Pomaikai; kuonoono o ka noho'na. SYN. prosperity.

Wĕl'kin, *n.* Ke aouli; na lani. *Make the welkin ring,* e hoo'ho a i na lani.

Wĕll, *n.* Lua wai; lua.

Wĕll, *v.* E puai mai.

Wĕll, *adj.* Mai ole; ola pono.

Wĕll, *adv.* 1. Pono; me ka pololei. 2. Ae. *Well, and what did he say?* Ae, a heaha kana i olelo?

Wĕll'-be'ing, *n. See* welfare.

Wĕll'-brĕd, *adj.* Ao pono ia; mikioi.

Wĕll'-in-fŏrmed', *adj.* Noeau. SYN. intelligent.

Wĕll'-in-tĕnd'ed, *adj.* Manao maikai ia.

Wĕll'-knŏwn, *adj.* Ike pono ia; ike akea ia; kaulana.

Wĕll'-mĕan'ing, *adj.* Manao maikai.

Wĕll'-mĕant, *adj.* SYN. well-intentioned.

Wĕll'-nīgh, *adv.* Aneane; kokoke.

Wĕll'-rĕad, *adj.* Makaukau ma na buke.

Wĕll'-pro-pōr'tioned, *adj.* Hua-ke'.

Wĕll'-spĕnt, *adj.* 1. Hoohala pono ia. *A well-spent day,* he la i hoohala pono ia. 2. *Well-spent money,* dala i hoolilo makepono ia.

Wĕll'-spring, *n.* Puna wai. SYN. fountain.

Wĕll'-wish'er, *n.* Hoa'loha. SYN. friend.

Wĕl'ter, *v.* E kaa. SYN. wallow.

Wĕst, *n.* Ke komohana.

Wĕst'er-ly, *adj.* Mai ke komohana; i ke komohana.

Wĕst'ern, *adj.* Komohana.

Wĕst'ward, *adv.* I ke komohana aku.

Wĕt, *adj.* 1. Pulu; kawau. 2. *Wet with perspiration,* ka'wakawau'.

Wĕth'er, *n.* Hipa kane i poa ia.

Wĕt'-nūrse, *n.* Makua wahine hanai.

~~**Whāle,** *n.* He kohola'.~~

Whāle'bŏne, *n.* Iwi kohola'.

Whāle'ship, *n.* Moku o kohola'.

Whạrf, *n.* He uapo.

Whạrf'age, *n.* 1. Wahi ma ka uapo. 2. Uku no ka uapo.

Whạrf'in-ger, *n.* Luna kiai uapo.

Whạt, *pron.* 1. Heaha. 2. Ka mea.

Whạt, *interj.* Kai! *What a bore!* kai ka luhi!

Whạt-ev'er, } *pron.* Kela me keia.
Whạt'so-ev'er, }

Whēat, *n.* Hua palaoa.

Wheed'le, *v.* E hoomalimali. SYN. coax; flatter.

Wheel, *n.* Huila; pokakaa.

Wheel, *v.* E kaa.

Wheel'bär-rŏw, *n.* Kaa-huila-kahi.

Wheel'wright, *n.* Mea hana huila.

Wheeze, *v.* E hanou.

Whĕlp, *n.* Keiki holoholona. SYN. cub.

Whĕn, *adj.* 1. I ka wa. 2. Ina hea.

Whĕnçe, *adv.* Mai kahi; mai hea.

Whĕn-ĕv'er, } *adv.* I ka wa; ai a.
Whĕn-so-ĕv'er, } *adv.* *Whenever you like,* ai a makemake oe.

Whĕre, *adv.* Ma kahi; mahea; ai mahea.

Whĕre'a-bouts', *adv.* 1. Mahea la. 2. Wahi noho. *His whereabouts,* kona wahi noho.

Whĕre-aṣ', *adv.* Oiai; no ka mea. SYN. since.

Whĕre-bȳ', *adv.* Mamuli o ia mea.

Whêre'fôre, adv. 1. Nolaila. SYN. therefore.

2. No ke aha la. SYN. why.

Whêre-in', adv. 1. Ma ka mea hea la.

2. Kahi. *Wherein he trusted,* kahi ana i paulele ai.

Whêre-ôf', adv. Ka mea. *Whereof he spake,* ka mea ana i olelo ai.

Whêre-ôn', } adv. No ia mea.
Whêre-up-on', }

Whêr-êv'er, } adv. Ma kahi. *Wher-*
Whêre'so-êv'er, } *ever you go,* ma kahi au e hele ai.

Whêre'with-al', adv. Me ke aha la.

Whêt, v. 1. E hookala. SYN. sharpen.

2. E hoala; hoo-eueu. SYN. excite.

Whêth'er, pron. 1. *Whether of the two,* owai o laua.

2. Ina paha. *Whether you like it or not,* ina paha makemake oe ina aole paha.

Whêt'stône, n. Pohaku hookala; hoa'-na.

Whey, n. Ka wai o ka waiu awaawa.

Which-êv'er, pron. Kela paha; keia paha. *Whichever you like,* kela paha, keia paha, ai i kou makemake.

Whiff, n. 1. Punohu. *Whiff of smoke,* punohu uahi.

2. *Whiff of wind,* he wahi puhi makani.

While, n. Wa; manawa.

While, v. E hoohala manawa; hoonanea.

While, } adv. Oiai; i ka wa; i. SYN. as.
Whilst, }

Whim, n. He manao i ulu wale mai.

Whim'per, v. E uwe. SYN. cry.

Whim'si-cal, adj. I'-o ole.

Whine, n. 1. Leo uwe o ka ilio.

2. Leo ohumuhumu.

Whin'ney, v. E i'hihi'. SYN. neigh.

Whip, n. 1. Laau hahau; laau hili.

2. Luna akoakoa i na hoa o ka ahaolelo o Beritania no ke koho ana.

Whip, v. E hili; e hahau.

Whip'ple-tree, } n. Laau hoopaa i ke
Whif'fle-tree, } kaula huki o ke kaa a oo-palau paha.

Whip'stôck, n. Au o ka laau hili. SYN. whip handle.

Whîr, n. Leo kamumu. SYN. whiz.

Whirl, v. E wili; e kaa; kakaa; niniu.

Whirl'wind, n. Puahiohio; makani pukiki.

Whirl'pôol, n. Mimilo.

Whisk, v. E kahili.

Whisk'er, n. Umiumi ma ka papalina.

Whis'key, } n. Wai ona; kulu.
Whis'ky, }

Whis'per, v. E hawanawana.

Whist'le, v. 1. E pio; e hookiokio.

2. *Whistle as wind,* e hu.

Whit, n. Lihi iki.

White, adj. Keokeo; kea.

White-liv'ered, adj. 1. Hakeakea. SYN. pale.

2. Maka'u wale. SYN. cowardly.

Whit'en, v. E hana a keokeo.

White'ness, n. Keokeo.

White'wash, n. Wai puna, mea hamo.

White'wash, v. E palaina; e hamo puna.

Whith'er, adv. 1. I hea? *Whither away,* i hea aku nei.

2. Ma kahi. *Whither I go,* ma kahi au e hele ai.

Whith'er-so-êv'er, adv. Ma kahi; ma kauwahi. *Whithersoever the pilot listeth,* ma kahi a ka pailaka e makemake ai.

Whit'ing, n. Poho aeae.

Whit'tle, v. E kolikoli me ka pahi.

Whiz, v. E oeoe; me he pokala i kona lele ana.

Whô (hū), pron. 1. Ka mea.

2. Owai?

Whô-êv'er, pron. Ka poe; ka mea.

Whôle, adj. 1. Okoa. *A whole number,* he helu okoa.

2. Pau loa. *Take the whole,* e lawe pau loa.

3. Ola. *The whole need not a physician,* aole no ka poe ola ke kahuna lapaau.

Whôle'sāle, n. Kuai nui.

Whôle'sāle, adj. Nui loa. *Wholesale destruction,* luku nui loa.

Whôle-sóme, adj. 1. Kupono i ai; ono.

2. Kupono. *Wholesome advice,* olelo ao kupono.

Whôl'ly, adv. Loa. *Wholly given to study,* lilo loa i ka imi naauao.

Whôop, n. Hoo'ho hoohenehene.

Whôop'ing-cough (hôop'ing-kawf), n. Kunu kalea.

Whôre, n. Wahine hookamakama.

Whôse, pron. Ka mea nana; nawai? ka wai?

Whô-sō, } pron. Ka mea; ka poe.
Whô'sō-êv'er, }

Why, adv. No ke aha.

Wick, n. Uwiki.

Wick'ed, adj. Hewa; ino. SYN. sinful.

Wick'ed-ness, n. Hewa; ino. SYN. iniquity.

Wick'et, n. Puka komo haiki.

Wide, adj. Laula'; akea. SYN. broad; extensive.

Wide'ly, adv. Akea. SYN. extensively. *Widely known,* ike akea ia.

Wid'en, v. E hoo-akea; e hoopalahalaha.

Wid'ôw, n. Wahine kane make.

Wid'ôw-er, n. Kane wahine make.

Wid'ôw-hôod, n. Ka noho ana he wahine kane make.

Width, n. Ka laula'; ke akea.

Wield, v. 1. E lawe. *Wield the power,* e lawe i ka mana.

2. E lalau. *Wield a club,* e lalau i ka newa.

Wield'y, adj. Hiki ke hooponoponoia. SYN. manageable.

Wife, n. Wahine mare.

Wife'ly, adj. Pili i ka wahine mare.

Wig, n. He uhi lauoho no ke poo.

Wig'gle, v. E laumilo. SYN. squirm.

Wig'wam, *n.* Hale lewa o na Inikini.

Wild, *adj.* 1. Hihiu; ahiu; laka ole.
2. *Wild country,* aina i noho oleia e kanaka.
3. *Wild honey,* meli i loaa wale.

Wil'der-ness, *n.* Wao-akua; waona-hele.

Wild'ly, *adv.* 1. Ano hihiu.
2. Me ka noonoo ole. SYN. heedlessly.

Wild'ness, *n.* 1. Ke ano hihiu.
2. Ke ano wao-akua.

Wile, *n.* Hana hoohalua; hana maalea.

Will, *n.* 1. Ka makemake; ka mana e koho kekahi nona iho.
2. Kauoha; palapala hooilina.
3. Manao.

Wil'ful, *adj.* Nunuha; paakiki. SYN. stubborn.

Wil'ling, *adj.* Makemake; oluolu; ano ae aku.

Wil'ling-ly, *adv.* Me ka manao oluolu; me ka ae o ka manao.

Wilt, *v.* E mae; luhe'; e mimino; lo'ha.

Wi'ly, *adj.* Maalea.

Win, *v.* 1. *Win at cards,* e eo.
2. E puka.
3. *Win a wife,* e loaa i wahine mare.

Wince, *v.* Eeke. SYN. shrink.

Wind, *n.* Makani. *Against the wind,* manai. *To raise the wind,* e loaa i ke dala. *To get wind,* e lohe; e laha. *The story got wind,* ua laha ka olelo.

Wind, *v.* 1. E wili; e owili.
2. E hoa.

Wind'bound, *adj.* Holo ole no ka makani ino.

Wind'fall, *n.* Hua haule wale mai ke kumu laau.
2. Pomaikai kau wale mai.

Wind'ing-sheet, *n.* Lole kupapau.

Wind'lass, *n.* Pokakaa huki heleuma, me na mea kaumaha e ae.

Wind'mill, *n.* Wili makani.

Win'dow, *n.* Puka makani.

Win'dow-blind, *n.* Olepelepe no ka puka makani.

Win'dow-frame, *n.* Lapauila o ka puka makani; kikihi puka makani.

Win'dow-sash, *n.* Na aniani o ka puka makani.

Win'dow-shade, *n.* He uhi no ka puka makani.

Win'dow-shut'ter, *n.* Pani puka makani.

Win'dow-sill, *n.* Paepae o ka puka makani.

Wind'pipe, *n.* Kani a-i'.

Wind'ward, *n.* Manai.

Wind'y, *adj.* Makani. *A windy day,* he la makani.

Wine, *n.* Waina.

Wine'-bib'ber, *n.* Mea hoonuu waina.

Wine'-cask, *n.* Pahu hoopaa waina.

Wine'-glass, *n.* Kiaha inu waina.

Wine'-vault, *n.* Keena lua, wahi waiho waina.

Wing, *n.* 1. Eheu; pekekeu. SYN. pinion.
2. Hale i pakuiia i kekahi hale.
3. He mahele o ka puali koa. *Right wing,* ka puali ma ka akau.

Wing, *v.* E lele.

Wink, *v.* E imo; awihi.

Win'ner, *n.* Mea e puka ana; ka mea i eo.

Win'ning, *adj.* Oluolu.

Win'now, *v.* E peahi i ka opala.

Win'ter, *n.* Kau hooilo.

Win'ter, *v.* E noho a hala ke kau hooilo.

Win'ter-quar'ters, *n.* Wahi e noho ai no ka hooilo.

Win'try weath'er. Wa anu.

Wipe, *v.* E kawele a maloo; e holoi.

Wip'er, *n.* Mea kawele; mea holoi.

Wire, *n.* Uwea.

Wire'-pull'er, *n.* Mea hookonokono malu'; mea kokua malu. SYN. intriguer.

Wir'y, *adj.* Mehe uwea la; uau'a; oolea.

Wis'dom, *n.* Naauao; noeau; noonoo. SYN. sagacity.

Wise, *adj.* Naauao; noeau. SYN. sagacious.

Wise'a-cre, *n.* Mea e akena wale ana i kana ike.

Wise'ly, *adv.* Me ka naauao. SYN. sagaciously.

Wish, *v.* E makemake; e ake. SYN. desire.

Wisp, *n.* Pu-a uuku o ka mauu maloo.

Wist'ful, *adj.* Ake nui. SYN. desirous.

Wist'ful-ly, *adv.* Me ka iini nui.

Wit, *n.* 1. Olelo akamai; olelo noeau. SYN. humor.
2. Noonoo; akamai. SYN. ingenuity. *At his wit's end,* lilo ka noonoo.

Witch, *n.* He kupua; wahine kilokilo.

Witch'craft, *n.* Hana kilokilo; anaana.

With, *prep.* Me; pu.

With-draw', *v.* 1. E lawe hou. *Withdraw a motion,* e lawe hou i ka manao.
2. E haalele. *Withdrawal from the company,* e haalele i ka hui.

With'er, *v.* E luhe'; e loha. SYN. wilt.

With-hold', *v.* E aua.

With-in', *prep.* Iloko; maloko.

With-out', *adv.* 1. Mawaho.
2. Me ole. *Without assistance,* me ke kokua ole.

With-stand', *v.* E keakea; e ku-e'; e hoo-ke'.

Wit'less, *adj.* Noonoo ole; nele ka noonoo.

Wit'ness, *n.* Mea ike maka; he hoike.

Wit'ness, *v.* 1. E ike maka.
2. E hoike.

Wit'ti-cism, *n.* Olelo hoomakeaka.

Wit'ti-ly, *adv.* Me ke akamai.

Wit'ty, *adj.* Hoomakeaka.

Wiz'zard, *n.* He kilokilo. SYN. magician.

Woe, *n.* He popilikia nui kaumaha nui.

Wŏe'bē-gŏne', *adj.* Kupaka; pioloke; luuluu.

Wŏe'ful, *adj.* Kaumaha; walohia.

Wŏlf, *n.* Ilio-hae.

Wŏlf'ish, *adj.* Mehe ilio-hae la.

Wŏm'an, *n.* Wahine.

Wŏm'an-hŏŏd, *n.* Ke kulana wahine.

Wŏm'an-ish, *adj.* Mehe wahine la.

Wŏm'an-ly, *adj.* Kupono no ka wahine.

Wŏmb, *n.* Ka puao; ka opu.

Wŏn'der, *n.* Mea kupaianaha; mea kamahao.

Wŏn'der, *v.* E haohao.

Wŏn'der-ful, { *adj.* Kupaianaha; ka-
Wŏn'droŭs, } mahao.

Wŏn'der-ful-ly, } *adv.* Me ke kama-
Wŏn'droŭs-ly, { hao; kupaianaha.

Wŏnt, *v.* E hoomaamaa; e walea.

Wŏnt'ed, *adj.* Maa mau; walea.

Wŏŏ, *v.* E imi ma ka mare. SYN. court.

2. E koi oluolu.

Wŏŏd, *n.* Laau.
Wahie. SYN. firewood.
3. *Drift wood*, piha-a'.

Wŏŏd'cut, *n.* Kii i kahakahaia ma ka laau.

Wŏŏd'ed, *a.* Uhiia i na ulu-laau.

Wŏŏd'en, *adj.* Laau. *Wooden house*, hale laau.

Wŏŏd'house, *n.* Hale waiho wahie.

Wŏŏd'land, *n.* Aina ulu-laau.

Wŏŏd'man, *n.* Kanaka kua laau; mea oki wahie.

Wŏŏds, *n.* Ululaau.

Wŏŏ'er, *n.* Kanaka imi wahine mare.

Wŏŏf, *n.* Maawe pokopoko.

Wŏŏl, *n.* Hulu; hulu hipa.

Wŏŏl'en, *adj.* Huluhulu.

Wŏŏl'ly, *adj.* Piipii. *Wooly hair*, hulu piipii.

Wŏrd, *n.* Olelo; hua-olelo.
2. *The Word*, ka Logou.

Wŏrd'ing, *n.* Ke ano o ke pai ana; ka-kau ana.
2. Na hua-olelo i kakauia.

Wŏrd'y, *adj.* Paapu na olelo. SYN. verbose.

Wŏrk, *n.* Hana.
2. Haua i hoikeia ma ka buke; he buke.

Wŏrk, *v.* E hana.
2. E awaawa mai.

Wŏrk'er, *n.* Mea hooikaika hana.

Wŏrk'house, *n.* Hale oihana.

Wŏrk'ing, *n.* Ke ko ana. *The working of the law*, ke ko ana o ke kanawai.

Wŏrk'man, *n.* Kanaka akamai i ka hana.

Wŏrk'man-like, *n.* Ano akamai o ka hana.

Wŏrk'man-ship, *n.* Ke ano o ka hana.

Wŏrks, *n.* 1. Hale oihana.
2. Na buke.

Wŏrk'shŏp, *n.* Hale oihana.

Wŏrld, *n.* Ao. *This world*, keia ao. *The world*, ka Honua Nei. *The next world*, kela ao. *All worlds*, na ao a pau.

Wŏrld'li-ness, *n.* Ka iini nui no ko keia ao.

Wŏrld'ly, *adj.* No keia ao. *Worldly minded*, manao nui i ko keia ao.

Wŏrm, *n.* Enuhe. *Army worm*, peelua. *Worm of corruption*, ilo. *Cloth eating worm*, hu'hu.

Wŏrm'-ēat'en, *adj.* Hu'hu; huhu'-hu.

Wŏrm'y, *adj.* 1. Kakani. *Wormy potatoe*, uala kakani.
2. Iloilo.

Wŏrn'-out, *adj.* 1. Maluhiluhi. SYN. tired.
2. Apu'lu. SYN. useless.

Wŏr'ri-sŏme, *adj.* Uwe mau; na ole.

Wŏr'ry, *n.* Pihoihoi o ka naau.

Wŏrse, *adj.* 1. Ino oi aku.
2. Nui mai o ka mai.

Wŏr'ship, *n.* E hoomana.

Wŏr'ship'er, *n.* Mea e hoomana ana.

Wŏrst, *adj.* Ino loa.

Wŏrth, *adj.* 1. Ka waiwai io o kekahi mea.
2. *Moral worth*, pono maoli.

Wŏr'thi-ly, *adv.* Kupono.

Wŏrth'less, *adj.* Waiwai ole; pono ole; lapuwale. *A worthless fellow*, he mea lapuwale.

Wŏr'thy, *adj.* Pono; kupono.

Wŏr'thy, *n.* Kanaka kaulana no kona pono.

Wound (wŏŏnd or wŏwnd), *n.* Eha; palapu'.

Wŏund, *v.* E hoo-eha.

Wŏv'en, *p. p.* Ulanaia.

Wrăn'gle, *v.* E hoopaapaa.

Wrăp, *v.* 1. He uhi.
2. Kihei.
3. Mea opiopi.

Wrăp'per, *n.* 1. Mea opiopi; kipola.
2. *A morning wrapper*, he holoku no ke kakahiaka.

Wrăth, *n*; He inaina; huhu weliweli.

Wrăth'ful } *adj.* Inaina loa.
Wrăth'y }

Wrēak, *v.* E hooko i ka hoopai.

Wrēath, *n.* Lei. SYN. garland. *Wreath for the neck*, wehi.

Wrēathe, *v.* E kau i ka lei; e hoo-lei.

Wrĕck, *n.* 1. Moku poino.
2. Kela me keia mea i hoopoinoia. *The wreck of a man*, kanaka poino loa.

Wrĕck, *v.* E ili a naha'; e poino loa.

Wrĕck'er, *n.* Mea hoopakele waiwai pcino o ka moku.

Wrĕnch, *n.* Hao wili.

Wrĕnch, *v.* 1. E kaili ino mai ka lima.
2. E okupe. SYN. sprain.

Wrĕst, *v.* E kaili ino.

Wrĕst'le, *v.* E hakookoo.

Wrĕst'ler, *n.* Mea hakookoo.

Wrĕst'ling, *n.* Hakookoo.

Wrĕtch, *n.* Kanaka ino.

Wrĕtch'ed, *adj.* 1. Kaumaha; luuluu. SYN. miserable.
2. Inoino. *A wretched reader*, mea heluhelu inoino.

3. Makehewa. *A wretched business*, he hana makehewa.
4. Paumaele. *A wretched sinner*, he kanaka paumaele.

Wrĕtch′ed-ness, *n.*   1.   Ka nele loa. SYN. squalor; misery.
2. Inoino; poino o ka noho ana.

Wrĭg′gle, *v.* E pakaawili. SYN. squirm.

Wring, *v.* E uwi′. *Wring dry*, e uwi a maloo.

Wring′er, *n.* Mikini uwi lole.

Wrĭnk′le, *n.* Minomino.

Wrĭnk′led, *adj.* Pukapuka.

Wrist, *n.* Ka pu-lima.

Wrist′band, *n.* Lihi no ka lima lole.

Writ, *n.* Palapala o ke kanawai.
2. *Holy Writ*, Palapala Hemolele.

Write, *v.* E kakau lima; e kakau.

Wrīt′er, *n.* Mea kakau; mea haku manao.

Writhe, *v.* E kupaka; e laumilo.

Writ′ing, *n.* He palapala.
2. Ka mea i kakauia.

Writ′ing-bŏŏk, *n.* Buke kakau lima.

Writ′ing-dĕsk, *n.* Pahu kakau palapala.

Writ′ing-mäs′ter, *n.* Kumu ao ka-kaulima.

Writ′ing-pā′per, *n.* Kalana.

Writ′ing-schōōl, *n.* Kula kakau lima.

Writ′ten, *adj.* Kakaulima ia; kakauia.

Wrŏng, *adj.* Hewa; pono ole.

Wrŏng′ful, *adj.* Pono ole; ewaewa.

Wrŏng′hĕad-ed, *adj.* Noonoo hewa.

Wrôught, *adj.* Kuiia. *Wrought iron*, hao kuiia.

Wrȳ, *adj.* Nukee′.

X

Xē′bee (zē-bek), *n.* He moku liilii kiakolu e holo ana ma ke Kaiwaenahonua.

Xȳ′lo-grăph (zi′lo-graf), *n.* Kii i kahakaha ia ma ka laau.

Xȳ-lŏg′ra-pher (zī-lŏg′ra-fer), *n.* Mea kahakaha kii ma ka laau.

Xȳ-lŏg′ra-phy (zī-lŏg′ra-fy), *n.* Oihana kahakaha kii ma ka laau.

X′mas, *n.* SYN. Christmas. La hanau o Iesu.

Y

Yacht (yot), *n.* Moku hooholo lealea.

Yacht′ing, (yot′ing), *n.* Hooholo lealea.

Yäm, *n.* He uhi.

Yän′kee, *n.* Kamaaina o Nu Enelani.
2. *The Yankee Nation*, ka Lahui o Amerika Hui.

Yärd, *n.*   1.   He iwilei; i-a′.
2. Pa. *House yard*, pa-hale.

Yärd′stick, *n.* He laau ana iwilei.

Yärn, *n.* Lopi huluhulu mea kui kakini, ete.
2. Kaao o na luina moku.

Yạw, *v.* E aui ae mai ka holo pololei.

Yạwn, *v.* E hamama waha no ka makahiamoe. SYN. gape.
2. *A yawning abyss*, he mawae e waiho hamama ana.

Yē, *pron.* Oukon. SYN. you.

Yēar, *n.* Makahiki.

Yēar′ling, *n.* Makahiki hookahi, o na holoholona.

Yēar′ly, *adv.* Kela me keia makahiki.

Yēarn, *v.* E iini. SYN. long for.
2. Mokumokuahua.

Yēarn′ing, *n.* Iini o ka naau. SYN. longing.

Yēast, *n.* Hu berena.

Yĕlk, } *n.* Ka olenalena o ka hua moa.
Yŏlk, }

Yĕll, v. E uwa′; e hooho.

Yĕl′lōw, adj. Melemele; olenalena.

Yĕlp, v. E aoaoa.

Yĕs, adv. Ae; u; e.

Yĕs′ter-day, n. Inehinei.

Yĕs′ter-night, n. Ka po nei. SYN. last night.

Yĕt, adv. 1. Aka nae. SYN. nevertheless.
2. *Not yet,* aole i keia wa. *Remaining yet,* ke waiho nei; ke koe nei a hiki i keia wa.

Yĭeld, v. 1. E hoohua mai.
2. E ae mamuli o ka makemake.

Yĭeld, n. Hua loaa.

Yōke, n. Lei bipi; auamo.

Yōke, v. E kau i ka lei bipi.

Yōke-fĕl′low, n. Hoa hana. SYN. associate; fellow laborer.

Yŏn′der, adv. I o′; mao′.

Yōre, adv. Wa kahiko.

You, pron. *Sing,* oe. *Dual,* olua. *Pl.,* oukou.

Young, adj. Opiopio; hou; ui.
2. *Young fruit,* hua maka; oo ole.
3. *Young animals,* holoholona opiopio.
4. *Young children,* keiki hou; keiki opiopio.
5. *Young persons,* poe u′i.

Young′er, adj. Mahope mai; muli mai, hou ae.

Young′ster, n. Keiki kane opio.

Your, pron. *Sing,* kou; kau. *Pl.,* ko oukou; ka oukou.

Yoursĕlf′, pron. Oe iho no. *For yourself,* nou iho.

Youth, n. He ui; he opio.
2. Ka wa ui; ka wa opiopio.

Youth′ful, adj. Ui; opio; hou. *Superlatively fine looking,* kilakila.

Youth′ful-ness, n. Ano ui; ano opio.

Z

Zēal, n. Manao ikaika.

Zēal′ous, adj. Ikaika ma ka manao. SYN. earnest.

Zēal′ous-ly, adv. Me ka ikaika o ka manao.

Zē′nith, n. Lolopua.

Zĕph′yr (zĕf′er), n. He onini makani.

Zē′rŏ, n. He ole. SYN. naught; cipher.

Zĕst, n. Hoihoi; makemake nui.

Zĭg′zăg, adj. Io′ ia nei; keekee; kikeekee.

Zĭne, n. Kepau keokeo.

Zō′di-ac, n. 1. Ke ala hele o ka La.
2. He umikumamalua huhui hoku e waiho ana ma ke ala hele o ka La.

Zōne, n. He kaei. SYN. belt. *Torrid Zone,* Kaei Wela. *North Temperate Zone,* Kaei Olu Akau. *South Frigid Zone,* Kaei Anu Hema.

Zō′o-lŏg′i-cal, adj. Pili i ke ano o na holoholona.

Zo-ŏl′o-ġist, n. Kanaka imi no ke ano o na holoholona.

Zo-ŏl′o-ġy, n. Ka ike e pili ana i ke ano o na holoholona.

TABLE

— OF —

ABBREVIATIONS IN COMMON USE

A

@. or a. (*Ad.*) **To or at.** I, ma, no.

A. B. C. F. M. American Board of Commisssoners for Foreign Missions. Ka Papa Misionari ma Bosetona.

Abp. Archbishop. Bihopa nui.

Acc., or Act., or a/c. **Account.** Helu.

A. D. (*Anno Domini.*) **In the year of our Lord.** Ma ka makahiki o ko kakou Haku.

Ad lib. (*Ad libitum.*) **At pleasure.** Ai i ka makemake.

Adm. Admiral. Adimarala.

Admr. Administrator. Luna hooponopono waiwai.

Admx. Administratrix. Luna wahine hooponopono waiwai.

Æ. or Æt. (*Ætatis.*) **Of age; aged.** Helu o na makahiki.

Agt. Agent. Egena; Agena.

Ala. Alabama.

A. M. 1. (*Artium Magister.*) **Master of Arts.** Hoa o na oihana naauao. 2. (*Ante Meridiem.*) **Before Noon.** Mamua o ke awakea.

Amer. American. No Amerika.

Am't. Amount. Ka huina.

Anon. Anonymous. Inoa ole.

Ans. Answer. Haina.

Apr. April. Aperila.

Ark. Arkansas, (*Ar'kan-sąw.*)

Ass't. Assistant. Kokoolua; kokua.

A. U. C. (*Ab Urbe Condita.*) **In the year from the building of Rome.** Mai ka makahiki aku o ke kukuluia'na o Roma.

Aug. August. Augate.

Av. Avenue. Ala hele.

B

B. Born. Hanauia.

B. A. 1. **British America.** Amerika Beritania. 2. **Bachelor of Arts.** Haumana o ka Naauao.

Bbl. Barrel. Barela.

B. C. Before Christ. Mamua o Kristo.

Bd. Board, Bond. Papa, Bona.

Bd. of Ed. Board of Education. Papa Hoonaauao.

Bd. of Im. Board of Immigration. Papa Hoopae Lima Hana.

Benj. Benjamin. Beniamina.

Bp. Bishop. Bihopa.

Br., Bro. Brother. Hoahanau.

Brig. Gen. Brigadier General.

Brit. Britain, British. Beritania.

C

Cal. California.

Capt. Captain. Kapena.

C. E. Civil Engineer. Mea ana aina.

Cent. (*Centum.*) **A hundred.**

C. H. 1. **Court House.** Hale Hookolokolo. 2. **Custom House.** Hale Dute.

Ch., Chapt. Chapter. Mokuna.

Chron. Chronicles.

C. J. Chief Justice. Lunakanawai Kiekie.

C. M. Common Meter.

Co. 1. **Company.** Hui. 2. **County.** Mokuna Aina.

C. O. D. Cash (or Collect) on Delivery. E uku i ka loaa'na ma ka lima.

Col. 1. **Colonel.** Kenela. 2. **Colossians.** Kolose.

Conn. or Ct. Connecticut.

Const. 1. **Constitution.** Kumukanawai. 2. **Constable.** Makai; Kaiko.

Cor. Corinthians. Korineto.

Cor. Sec. Corresponding Secretary. Kakau Olelo no ke kakau palapala.

Cos. Cosine.

Cr. Credit, Creditor. Hooaie; nana e hooaie.

Crim. Con. Criminal Conversation, Adultery. Moekolohe.

Ct. Cent, Court, Connecticut. Keneta; Ahahookolokolo.

Cts. Cents. Na keneta.

Cwt. (*Centum* and *Weight.*) **A hundred weight.** Na paona he haneri.

D

D. C. 1. **District of Columbia.**
2. (*Da Capo.*) **Again; from the beginning.** Hoi hou; mai ka hoomaka'na.
D. C. L. **Doctor of Civil Law.** Poonoo ma ke kanawai kiwila.
D. D. **Doctor of Divinity.** Poonoo ma ka Hoike Akua.
Dea. **Deacon.** Diakono.
Dec. **December.** Dekemaba
Dft., Deft. **Defendant.** Aoao pale.
Del. 1. **Delaware, Delegate.** Elele.
2. (*Delineavit.*) **He—or She—drew it.** Nana i kaha; pakuiia i ka inoa o ka mea nana i kaha.
Dep't. **Department.** Keena Oihana, oihana.
Deut. **Deuteronomy.** Kanawaielua.
Dict. **Dictionary.** Buke Unuhi Olelo.
Do. (*Ditto.*) **The same.** Ia mea hookahi no.
Dols. **Dollars.** Na dala.
Doz. **Dozen.** Kakini, 12.
Dr. 1. **Debtor.** Mea aie.
2. **Doctor.** Kauka.
3. **Dram.** Mahele inu.

E

E. **East.** Hikina.
Eccles. **Ecclesiastes.** Kekahuna.
Ed. **Editor, Edition.** Luna hooponopono nupepa: helu o na nupepa i hoopukaia.
E. E. **Errors excepted.** Koe na hewa.
e. g. (*exempli gratia.*) **For example.** I nane; e laa.
E. Lon. **East Longitude.** Lonitu Hikina.
Eng. **England, English.** Enelani; Beritania.
Esq. **Esquire.**
et al. (*et alii.*) **And others.** Me ka poe e ae. **And so forth.** A pela'ku. **And the like.** A me ia like.
et seq. (*et sequentes, et sequentia.*) **And the following.** A me keia iho.
Ex. 1. **Example.** E nane.
2. **Exodus.** Pukaana.
Exec., Exr. **Executor.** Luna hooko palapala hooilina.

F

Fahr. **Fahrenheit.** Kekahi o na mea ana wela.
Feb. **February.** Feberuari.
Fec. (*Fecit.*) **He — or She — did it.** Nana ia i hana.
Flor. **Florida.**
Fr. **France, French.** Farani.
F. R. G. S. **Fellow of the Royal Geographical Society.** Hoa o ka Ahahui Imi Hoikehonua.
Fri. **Friday.** Poalima.

Ft. 1. **Foot, feet.** Kapuai.
2. **Fort.** Papu.
Fur. **Furlong.** Setadia.

G

Ga. **Georgia.**
Gal. 1. **Gallon.** Galani.
2. **Galatians.** Galatia.
G. B. **Great Britain.** Beritania.
Gen. 1. **General.** Kenela or Generala.
2. **Genesis.** Kinohi.
Gent. **Gentleman.** Keonimana.
Geo. **George.** Keoki.
Geog. **Geography.** Hoikehonua.
Gov. **Governor.** Kiaaina.
Gr. 1. **Grain.** Huna.
2. **Gross.** 12 kakini.
3. **Greek.** Helene.

H

H., h. **Hour, hours.** Hora.
H. B. M. **Her Britannic Majesty.** Ka Mea kiekie ka Moi Wahine o Beritania.
H. H. M. **His Hawaiian Majesty.** Ka Mea kiekie, ka Moi o ko Hawaii Aupuni.
Hebr. **Hebrew, Hebrews.**
Hhd. **Hogshead.** Poo.
Hdkf. **Handkerchief.** Hainaka.
H. I. M. **His — or Her — Imperial Highness.** Ke 'Lii.
H. M. S. **His—or Her Majesty's—Steamer, Ship or Service.** Ka Mokuahi, ka Moku, ka Oihana o ka Moi.
Hon. **Honorable.** Mea Hanohano; Honolulu.
H. R. H. **His—or Her—Royal Highness.** Ka Mea kiekie, Ke 'Lii.
Hund. **Hundred.**

I

Ia. **Indiana.**
Ib. **Ibid. In the same place.** Ma ia wahi hookahi no.
Id. (*Idem.*) **The same.** Ia mea no.
I. e. (*Id est.*) **That is.** Oia hoi.
I. H. S. (*Jesus Hominum Salvator.*) **Jesus Savior of Men.** Iesu ka Hoola o Kanaka.
Ill. **Illinois.**
In. **Inch, inches.** Iniha.
Ind. **Indiana.**
Incog. (*Incognito.*) **Unknown.** Ikeoleia.
Int. **Interest.** Uku panee.
Inst. **Instant.** A no, keia mahina.
Ins. Gen. **Inspector General.** Luna Nui.
I. O. O. F. **Independent Order of Odd Fellows.**
I. O. U. **I Owe you.** Aie wau ia oe.
Is., Isa. **Isaiah.** Isaia.
Is., Isl. **Island.** Mokupuni.
It., Ital. **Italian, italic.** Italia.

J

J. Judge. Lunakanawai.
Jan. January. Ianuari.
Jno. John. Ioane.
Jos. Joseph. Iosepa.
Josh. Joshua. Iosua.
J. P. Justice of the Peace. Lunakanawai Hoomalu.
Jr., Jun. Junior. Opio.

K

Kan. Kansas.
Ken. Kentucky.
Knt., Kt. Knight. Naita.
Ky. Kentucky.

L

lb., ℔. (*Libra.*) **A pound, in weight.** Hookahi paona kaumaha.
L., l., £. A pound Sterling. Hookahi paona dala.
La. Louisiana.
Lat. 1. Latin. Latina.
   2. Latitude. Latitu.
Ld. Lord, lady.
Lea. League. Ekolu mile.
Lev. Leviticus. Kanawai.
L. I. Long Island.
Lieut., Lt. Lieutenant. Lutanela.
L. L. D. (*Legum Doctor.*) **Doctor of Laws.**
Lon., Long. Longitude. Lonitu.
Lou., La. Louisiana.
L. S. (*Locus Sigilli.*) **Place of the Seal.** Wahi o ke Sila.

M

M., m. Mile, Monsieur.
Mag. Magazine.
Maj. Major. Mekia.
Maj. Gen. Major General.
Mar. March. Maraki.
Mass. Ms. Massachusetts.
Matt. Matthew. Mataio.
M. C. Member of Congress. Lunamakaainana.
Md. Maryland.
M. D. Doctor of Medicine. Kauka lapaau.
Mdlle., Mlle. Mademoiselle. Wahine ui, mare ole.
Me. Maine.
M. E. Methodist Episcopal.
Mem. Memorandum. Mea hoomanao.
Messrs. Gentleman, Sirs. Ano kakau leta.
Mich. Michigan.
Min., min. Minute, minutes. Minute.
Miss. Mississippi.
Mme. Madame. Wahine i mare.
Mo., mo. Month. Mahina.
Mon. Monday, Monede. Poakahi.
Mons. Monsieur, Sir.
Mos. Months. Na mahina

M. P. Member of Parliament. Lala o ka Ahaolelo o Beritania.
Mr. Master, Mister.
Mrs. Mistress, Misses. Wahine mare.
Ms. Manuscript. Pepa i kakaulima ia.
Mss. Manuscripts. Na pepa i kakaulima ia.
Mt., Mts. Mountain, Mountains. Mauna.

N

N. North. Akau.
N., or n. Noun. Haiinoa; neuter.
N. A. North America. Amerika Akau.
Naut. Nautical. No ka moana.
N. B. 1. (*Nota Bene.*) **Note well, or take notice.** E noonoo pono.
   2. New Brunswick.
N. C. North Carolina.
N. E. New England, North-East. Hikina-Akau.
Neb. Nebraska.
Nem. Con. (*Nemine Contradiscente.*) **No one contradicting, unanimously.** Me ka lokahi.
Neut. Neuter.
N. F. Newfoundland.
N. H. New Hampshire.
N. J. New Jersey.
No. (*Numero.*) **Number.** Helu.
Nos. Numbers. Na helu.
Nov. November. Novemaba.
N. P. Notary Public. Luna Hooia palapala.
N. T. New Testament. Kauoha Hou.
N. W. North-West. Komohana Akau.
N. Y. New York.

O

O. Ohio.
Obt., Obdt. Obedient.
Oct. October.
Or. Oregon.
O. S. Old Style. Mamua iho o 1752.
O. T. Old Testament. Kauoha Kahiko.
Oz. Ounce, ounces. Auneki

P

P., p. Page. Aoao
Pa. Pennsylvania.
Pd. Paid. Hookaaia; ukuia.
Penn. Pennsylvania.
Per. an. (*Per annum.*) **By the year.** Ma ka makahiki.
Per. Cent. or per. ct. (*Per centum.*) **By the hundred.** Ma ka haneri.
Phila. Philadelphia.
Plff. Plaintiff. Ka mea—or aoao—hoopii.
P. M. 1. Post Master. Luna leta. (*Post Meridiem.*)
   2. Afternoon. Auina la.

P. M. G. Post Master General. Luna Leta Nui.
P. O. Post Office. Hale Leta.
pp. Pages. Na aoao.
Pres. President. Peresidena.
Prof. Professor. Kumu Ao.
Pro. tem. (*Pro tempore.*) **For the time being.** No ia manawa.
Prov. Proverbs. Na Olelo Ao o Solomona.
Prox. (*Proximo.*) **Next Month.** Keia mahina ae.
P. S. (*Post Scriptum.*) **Postscript.** Kakau hope.
Ps. Psalms. Na Halelu.

Q

Q. Question. Ninau.
Q. C. Queen's Counsel. Loio kiekie ma Beritania.
Q. E. D. (*Quod Erat Demonstrandum.*) **Which was to be demonstrated.** Ka mea e wehewehe ia'na.
Q. M. G. Quarter Master General. Luna Nui no na lako koa.
Qt., qt. Quart, Quantity. Kuata; kuaniti.
q. v. (*Quod vide.*) **Which see.** E nana ia mea.
Qy. Query. Ninau.

R

R. A. Royal Academy, Royal Academician.
Rec'd. Received. Loaa mai.
Rec'pt. Receipt. Palapala hookaa.
Rec. Sec. Recording Secretary. Kakauolelo o ka moolelo.
Regt. Regiment. Regimana koa.
Rep. 1. Representative. Lunamakaainana.
2. Republic. Aupuni makaainana.
3. Report. Olelo hoike.
Rev., Rev'd. Reverend. Inoa kapa kahunapule.
R. I. Rhode Island.
R. N. Royal Navy. Aumoku o ke Aupuni.
Rob't. Robert. Lopaka.
Rom. Roman, Romans. Roma.
Rom. Cath. Roman Catholic. Hoomana Katolika.
R. R. 1. Railroad. Alanui hao.
2. Right Reverend.
R. S. V. P. Answer, if you please. E oluolu oe e pane mai.
Rt. Hon. Right Honorable Ka Mea Hanohano.

S

S. 1. South. Hema.
2. Sunday. Sabati.
3. Saturday. Poaono
4. Sign. Hoailona.

S. A. South America. Amerika Hema.
Sam., Sam'l. Samuel. Samuela.
Sat. Saturday. Satude, Poaono.
Sc., sc. (*Scilicet.*) **To wit, namely.** Oia hoi.
Sch. (*Scholium.*) **A note.** Olelo hoakaka.
Sch., Schr. Schooner. Moku kialua.
Sci. Science. Ike.
Script. Scripture. Palapala Hemolele.
Sculp. Sculpture. Kalai kii.
S. E. South-East. Hikina-Hema.
Sec. 1. Secretary. Kakauolelo.
2. Second. Kekona.
3. Section. Apana.
Sen. Senate, Senator, Senior.
Sep., Sept. September. Sepetemaba.
Seq. (*Sequentes.*) **The following.** Keia mea ae.
Serv., Serv't. Servant. Kauwa.
Sh., sh. Shilling. Silina.
Sing., sing. Singular. Mea hookahi.
S. Lat. South Latitude. Latitu Hema.
S. M. Short Meter.
Soc. Society. Hui.
S. of Sol. Songs of Solomon. Na Mele o Solomona.
Sq. Square. Huina-ha-like.
Sq. ft. Square feet. Kapuai kuea.
Sq. in. Square inches. Iniha kuea.
Sq. yds. Square yards. Iwilei kuea.
S. S. Sunday School. Kula Sabati.
St. Saint. Street. Alanui. **Strait.** Kowa.
Sup't. Superintendent. Luna hooponopono.
Surg. Surgeon, Surgery.
Surv. Gen. Surveyor General. Luna Nui o ka Ana Aina.
S. W. South-West. Komohana-Hema.
Syn. syn. Synonym, Synonymous. Like me.
Synop. Synopsis. Wehewehe.

T

T., t. 1. Town. Taona. **Territory.**
2. Ton. Tona.
Ten., Tenn. Tennessee.
Tex. Texas.
Th., Thur. Thursday. Poaha.
Theol. Theology. Hoike Akua.
Theol. Sem. Theological Seminary, Kula Kahunapule.
Thess. Thessalonians. Tesalonia.
Topog. Topography.
Tr. 1. Translation. Unuhi.
2. Transpose. Hoololi.
3. Treasurer. Puuku dala.
4. Trustee. Kahu malama.
Trans. Transactions. Na oihana.
2. Translator. Mea unuhi.
Trav. Travels. Huakai hele.
Tu., Tues. Tuesday. Poalua.

U

U. C. Upper Canada.

Ult. (*Ultimo.*) **Last, last month.** Ka mahina i hala iho nei.

U. S. United States. America Hui.

U. S. A. United States of America.

U. S. M. United States Mail. Eke Leta o America Hui.

U. S. N. United States Navy. Aumoku o America Hui.

U. S. S. United States Ship or Steamer. Moku manuwa o America Hui.

U. T. Utah Territory. Panalaau o Uta.

V

V., v. Verb. Haina. (*Vide.*) **See.** E nana.

Vs., vs. (*Versus.*) **Against.** Ku-e'.

V. a. Verb Active.

Va. Virginia.

Ver. Vermont, verse. Pauku.

Vice Pres. Vice President. Hope-Peresidena.

Vid. (*Vide.*) **See.** E nana.

Viz. Namely. To wit. Oia hoi o.

Vol. Volume. Buke.

Vols. Volumes. Na buke.

V. R. (*Victoria Regina.*) **Queen Victoria.** Vitoria; ka Moi wahine o Beritania.

V. t. Verb transitive.

W

W. 1. West. Komohana.
   2. Wednesday. Poakolu.

Wed. Wednesday.

Whf. Wharf. Uapo moku.

Wk., wk. Week. Hebedoma.

W. I. West India. Inia Komohana.

W. Lon. West Longitude.

Wm. William. Wilama, Wiliama.

W. T. Washington Territory. Panalaau o Wasinetona.

wt. weight. Pauna kaumaha.

W. Va. West Virginia.

X

X. Christ. Kristo.

Xmas. Christmas. Karikimaka.

Y

Yr. Year. Makahiki.

Yd. Yard. Iwilei.

Yds. Yards. Na iwilei.

Y. M. C. A. Young Men's Christian Association. Ahahui Kristiano o ka poe ui.

Yrs. Yours. Nau.

VOCABULARY OF COMMON
ENGLISH CHRISTIAN NAMES

— AND THEIR —

Hawaiian Equivalents.

I. NAMES OF MEN.

A

A-a-ron, (Är'un), Aarona. Kiekie; hiehie.
A'bel, Abela. Hanu: mahani.
A-bi'jah, Aoaia. O Ke Akua ka Makua.
Ab'ner, Abenera. Makua o ka Malamalama.
A'bra-ham, Aberehama. Makua o ka lehulehu.
Ad-am, Adamu. Lepo ulaula.
Al'bert, Alapaki. Kaulana; alohilohi.
Al'ex-än'der, Alekanadero. Ke koa o ka'naka.
Al'fred, Alapai. Kakaolelo naauao.
A'mos, Amosa. Ikaika; koa.
An'drew, Aneru or Anelu. Hookanaka.
An'tho-ny, Akoni. Makamae.
Är'chi-bald, Aki. Koa maoli.
Är'thur, Aka. Hanohano.
A'sa, Aka. Kauka; kahuna lapaau.
Aus'tin, Ausetina. No Augusetina.
Au-gŭs'tus, Auguseto. Kiekie; alii.

B

Bald'win, Balauina. Hoa wiwo ole.
Bär'na-bas, Barenaba.
Bar-thŏl'o-mew, Baretolomeo. Keiki koa.
Bĕn'ja-min, Beniamina. Keiki o ka lima akau.

C

Cæ'sar, Kaisaro. Huluhulu; maka uliuli.
Cä'leb, Kalepa. He ilio.
Cäl'vin, Kalawina. Ohule.

Ce'cil, Kikila or Kekila. Maka po̅wehiwehi.
Ce'phas, Kepa. Pohaku.
Chärles, Kale. Manao koa.
Chris'tian, Kristiano.
Clau'di-us } Kalaudio. Oopa.
Claude }
Clĕm'ent, Kelemenete. Ahonui.
Cor-në'li-us, Korenelio.
Cy'rus, Kuro. Ka La.

D

Dän, Dana. Lunakanawai.
Dän'i-el, Daniela. Lunakanawai lani.
Da-ri'us, Dario. Mea hoopakele.
Dä'vid, Davida. Punahele.

E

Ĕd'gar, Eka or Ega.
Ĕd'mund, Ekemana, or, Ailuene. Koa malama waiwai.
Ĕd'ward, Aikue', or Ailuene. Kahu malama waiwai.
Ĕd'win, Ewini, or Edewini. Mea hoiliili waiwai.
Ē'li, Eli. Keiki hanai.
E-li'ab, Eliaba. Ke Akua kona makua.
E-li'as, Elisai. Ke Akua ko'u Akua.
Eli'jah, Elia.
E'noch, Enoka. Laa.
E'phra-im, Eparaima. Hua nui.
Eu-gene, Eugene. Alii.
Ez'ra, Ezera or Ekela. Kokua.

F

Fĕr'di-nand, Ferdinana. Koa.
Fran'cis, Farani. Hookuuia; kuokoa.
Fränk, Farani.
Frĕd'er-ic, } Pele. Alii o ka maluhia.
Frĕd'er-ick, }

G

Gā'bri-el, Gaberiela. Kanaka o ke Akua.
George, Keoki. Konohiki; kanaka mahiai.
Gĕr'ald, Gerala. Ikaika me ka ihe.
Gĕr'shom, Kelekoma. Kuewa.
Gĭd'e-on, Gideona. Mea luku.
Gil'bert, Kilipaki. Kaulana.

H

Hăr'old, Hare or **Harola.** Alihikaua.
Hĕn'ry, Heneri, or **Hale.** Poo o ka ohana.
Hĕr'bert, Haba. Ka nani o ka puali koa.
Hĕr'man, Hama. He koa.
Hez-e-ki'ah, Hezekia. Ka ikaika o Iehova.
Hi'ram, Hairama. Pookela o ka hanohano.
Ho-rā'tio, } **Horaka,** or **Horesa.**
Hŏr-ace, }
Ho-sē'a, Hosea. Ke ola.
Hūgh, } **Ugo.** Uhane; naau.
Hū'go, }

I

I'saac, Isaaka or **Aikake.**
I-sā'i-ah, Isaia. Hoola o Iehova.
Ĭş'ra-el, Iseraela. Koa o Iehova.

J

Jā'cob, Jakobo or **Jakoba.** Kailii i ko hai pono.
James, Jacobo or **Kimo.**
Jā'phet, Iapeta. Hooakea ana.
Jā'red, Iared or **Kere.** Kuauhau.
Jĕr'e-mi'ah, Ieremia. Hookiakiaia e Jehova.
Jĕs'se, Ieke or, **Iese.** Waiwai; lako.
Jŏb, Ioba. Hoomaauia.
Jō'el, Ioela. O Iehova no Ke Akua.
Jō'nah } **Iona.** Manu nunu.
Jō'nas }
Jŏn'a-than, Ionatana. Makana o Iehova.
Jō'seph, Iosepa. E hookui hou mai.
Jŏsh'u-a, Iosua. Ke Akua o ke Ola.
Jō'tham, Iokama. Pono o Ke Akua.
Jū'dah, Iuda. Mahaloia.
Ju'li-an } **Iule** or, **Iulio.** Lauoho palupalu.
Ju'li-us }

L

Lạw'rençe, Lowene. Kau lei ia.
Lĕm'u-el, Lemuela. Na Ke Akua i hana.
Lĕon'ard, Leonara. Koa, mehe liona la.
Lē'o-pōld, Leopolo. Aa no ka lehulehu.
Lē'vi, Levi. Pilipaa.

Lew'is } **Lui.** Koa wiwo ole.
Loū'is }
Lōr'rin, Lolena.
Lŏt, Lota. Kapa uhi.
Lūke, Luka. Malamalama.
Lū'ther, Lutera. Koa kaulana.

M

Ma-năs'seh, Manase. Poinawale.
Măn'u-el, Manuela.
Măr'cus, } **Mareko.** He hamale.
Mărk, }
Măr'tin, Makini. Koa.
Măt'thew, Mataio. Makana o Jehova.
Măx'i-mil'i-an, Makimilio.
Mi'cah, Maika, or **Mika.** Owai i like me Jehova.
Mō'şeş, Mose, or **Mcke.** Laweia no loko mai o ka wai.

N

Nā'than, Natana. He makana.
Na-thăn'a-el, } **Nataniela.** Ka makana o ke Akua.
Na-thăn'i-el, }
Nich'o-las, Nikolo. Lanakila o ka lahui.
Nō'ah, Noa. Maha.
Nō-el, Noela. Hanauia ma ka la karikimaka.

O

Ō'ba-dī'ah, Obadia. Kauwao ka Haku.
O'bed, Obeda. Hooko ana mamuli o ke Akua.
Ŏl'i-ver, Oliva. Kumu oliva.
Ŏs'car, Oka. Koa lelelele.
Ow'en, Owena. Koa opio.

P

Pạul, Paulo. Liilii.
Pē'ter, Petero. He pohaku.
Phil'ip, Pilipo. Makee lio.
Phin'e-as, Pinihasa. Waha keleawe.

R

Rălph, Rala.
Răph'a-el, Rapaela. Ka hoola ana mai a Ke Akua mai.
Reụ'ben, Reubena. Aia hoi! he keiki kane.
Rich'ard, Likeke. Mana; koikoi.
Rob'ert, Lopaka. Alohilohi ka nani.
Rŏg'er, Lokeke. Kaulana me ka ihe.
Rū'fus, Lupe. Ehu, lauoho ehu.

S

Săm'son, } **Samesona,** hauoli nui.
Sămp'son, }
Săm'u-el, Samuela. Noi ia; Noialoha.
Sạul, Saulo. Noi ia.
Se-rē'no, Sereno. Lai; malie.

Sĕth, Seta. Hookohoia.

Si'las, Sila. Noho ma ka ululaau.

Sĭm'e-on,) Simeona, Simona. Hoo-
Si'mon,) lohe pono ia.

Sŏl'o-mon, Solomonạ. Malu; kuapapa.

Stë'phen, Setepano. He lei alii.

T

Thăd'de-us, Tadaio. Ka mea naauao.

Thĕ'o-dōre, Teo, or Teodore. Makana o ke Akua.

Ti'tus, Tito.

W

Wạl-ter, Wala. E hoomalu ana i ka
puali.

William, Wilama or Uilama. Pa-
kaua.

II. NAMES OF WOMEN.

A

Ăb'i-gail, Abegaila. Ka hauoli o kuu
makuakane.

Ăd'a-line,) Adalina. Aliiwahine.
Ăd'e-line,)

Alice) Alika or Alisa. Alii wahine.
Alicia)

Al-mi'ra, Alamira. Kiekie.

Al-thē-ā, Alatea. Mea hoola.

A-mē-li-ā, Amelia. Makaala; hoihoi.

Ā-my, Ema. Halialia.

Ăn'na,)
Ăn'ne, > Ana, Ane. Onaona; puloku.
Ănn,)

Ăr-a-bĕl'lā, Arabela. Wahine no
Arabia.

Ạu-gŭs'ta, Auguseta. Alii.

B

Băr'ba-ra, Babara. Ano e; haole.

Bĕr'tha, Beke. Mikiala.

C

Căr'o-līne, Kalolina, or Karolaina;
wahine koa.

Căth'a-rine, Katalina, or Kakarina.
Makamae.

Çe-çil'i-ā, Kikilia, or Kekila.

Çhär'lotte, Kaloka. Naau koa.

Chris'ti-än-ā,) Kirikina. No Kristo.
Chris-ti'na,)

Clär'ā,) Kalara. Alohilohi.
Cla-ris'sā,)

Çō-rā. Kora. Kaikamahine; wahine ui.

Çor-nē'li-ā, Korenelia.

D

Dĕb'o-rah, Debora. Nalo meli.

Dē'li-ā, Delia.

Dī-än'ā, Diana, or Kina. Akua wahine.

Di'nah, Kina. Hookolokoloia.

Dō'rā, Dora. Ka makana o Ke Akua.

Dŏr'cas, Doreka. He dia.

Dŏr'o-thē'a,) Doreka. Ka makana o
Dor'o-thỹ,) Ke Akua.

E

Ē'dith, Edi. Hauoli; makana makamae.

Él'e-a-nor, Elianora. Malamalama.

E-lĭs'a-beth, Elisabeta. Hoomana i
Ke Akua.

E-li'za, Elisa. Hoolaa ia na Ke Akua.

Ĕl'la, Ela. Malamalama.

Ĕl'len, Elena.

El-vi'rā, Elevira. Keokeo.

Ĕm'e-līne,) Emelina. Hoihoi;
Ĕm'me-line,) miki.

Ĕm'i-ly, Emelia, or Emalia. Makaala.

Ĕm'ma, Ema. Miki.

Ĕs'ther, Eseta, or Esetera. Pomaikai.

Ĕth'el, Etela. Hanohano.

Eu'niçe, Eunika. Lanakila hauoli.

E-va, Ewa. Ola.

E-vän'ge-line, Euanelia. Lawe ana
i ka olelo maikai.

Ẹv'e-li'na,) Ewalina. Like me Ewa.
Ĕv'e-line,)

F

Făn'ny,) Fani. Hookuu ia.
Frän'çes,)

Fi-dĕl'i-ā, Fidelia. Kupaa.

Flō'ra, Felora. Na pua.

Flŏr'ençe, Felorena. Omeomeo.

H

Hän′nah, }
An-na,   } Hana. Puloku.

Här′ri-et, Hariaka. Ke poo wahine o ka ohana.

Hĕl′en,   }
Hel-ē′na, } Helena. Malamalama.

Hĕn′ri-ĕt′ta, Henerieta. No Heneri.

Hĕs′ter, Eseta.

I

I′da, Ida. Me he Akua la.

I-re′ne, Irene. Lai; malu.

Ĭṣ-a-bel,   } Isabela. Ano like me
Ĭṣ-a-bel′là, } Elisabeta.

J

Jāne, Kina. Ano like me *John*.

Jēan-nĕtte′, Kina. Ano like me Jane.

Jō′se-phine, Kepina. E pakui hou mai.

Jŭl′i-à, Iulia.

Jūli-an-a, Iuliana.

Ju-li-ĕtte′, }
Ju-li-ĕt, } Iulia.

L

Lau′ra, Lala.

Lē′o-nō′ra, Leonora.

Lil′i-an, }
Lil′ly, } Lilia. Pua lilia.
Lil-y,   }

Lō′is, Loika. Maikai.

Lou-ĭ′sà, }
Lou-ĭṣe′, } Luika.

Lu-çin′da, }
Lŭ′çy,   } Luki.

Lўd-i-à, Lidia, or Lilia.

M

Mā′bel, Mabela. Punahele.

Mäd′e-line, Madelina.

Mär′ga-ret, Makaleka. He momi.

Ma-ri′à, Maraea. Hoku o ke kai.

Mä′ri-on, Mariana. Farani no *Mary*.

Mär′tha, Mareka. Ke poo o ka ohana.

Mä′ry, Mere, or Maria. Hoku o ke kai.

Māy, Mahina o Mei, or *Mary*.

Mĭ′ri-am, Miriama. Ano like me *Mere*.

N

Nän′çy, Ane. Aulii.

Ṇō′rah, Nora. Malamalama.

Ŏl′ive,   }
O-lĭv′i-à, } Olivia. He oliva.

P

Pau-lĭ′na, }
Pau-line, } Paulina. Uuku.

Phē′be, }
Phœ′be, } Poipe′. Makamae; hulili.

Pŏl′ly, Poli. Like me Mere.

Pris-çil′la, Perisila. Kahiko iki.

R

Rā′chel, Rahela, or Lahela. Hipa keiki.

Re-bĕc′ca, } Lepeka, or Rebeka,
Re-bĕk′ah, } Onaona; puloku.

Rhō′da, Roda. Pua rose.

Rōse, Rose. Pua rose.

Rŏ′sa-bĕl′la, Rosabela. Pua rose nani.

Ro-sa-liē′. Pua rosa mohala.

Ruth, Luka, or Ruta. Nani.

S

Sā′rà,   } Sarai, or Sara. Alii wa-
Sä′rah, } hine.

Se-li′na, Selina. Mahina.

So-phi′à, Sopia. Naauao.

Sū′ṣan, Suke, or Suse. He lilia.

Su-ṣän′nà, Susana. Lilia.

T

Täb′i-thà, Kapika. He dia.

V

Vic-tō′ri-à, Vitoria. Lanakila.

CHRONOLOGICAL TABLE

— OF —

EVENTS IN HAWAIIAN HISTORY.

PREPARED BY
ABRAHAM FORNANDER.

Every people, possessed of some civilization, attempts to preserve a record of its past, whether that record be handed down orally or by some sort of writing. With the Hawaiians, as with their Polynesian congeners everywhere, such records were passed down orally from father to child, or from master to disciple, within the pro fessional circle of those to whom immemorial usage had consigned the preservation of them. But history, or a record of the past, would become unintelligible and rank confusion unless set forth, or arranged, upon some system of Chronology. Some peoples counted time by the number of generations from some common ancestor; some counted by the length of reign of each successive king or chief; some counted eacn individual year within a, by them, generally adopted era. The Hawaiians counted by generations of their principal Chiefs or Kings. They started from WAKEA as a common ancestor of all the Chiefs on all the islands of the Hawaiian group; but for convenience or clearness sake, time was counted by either of the reigning families on the four principal islands—Kauai, Oahu, Maui, or Hawaii. Thus an event worthy of being preserved on the national records, was said to have occurred "in the time of" (*i ke au o*), such and such a prominent chief of this or that island; and, in order to ascertain the when, generations were counted, either down from WAKEA, or, more generally up (back) from the then present generation. Thus Hawaiian chronology was not very exact, it must be admitted, but to a people who depended entirely upon the faithful memory of their Bards and Priests, it was sufficiently approximate to bring order and sequence in their unwritten records of the past. To us, of a later and more developed civilization, the exactitude of dates is the very essence of history, or at least one of its most necessary elements, but an approximation to truth satisfied the ancient Hawaiian. In my work, "*An Account of the Polynesian Race; its Origin and Migrations,*" vol. i, p. 166, I have approximately fixed the period of WAKEA at about 190 A. D., and the length of a generation, for the purposes of historical compilation at thirty years   Counting fifteen generations after WAKEA we arrive at NANA-ULU, in whose time the Hawaiian group was undoubtedly occupied by the Hawaiian branch of the Polynesian Race, say 500 A. D. Continuing on the Genealogical line of NANA-ULU, as the safest and most correct, we arrive after fifteen more generations, or 450 years, at the period of MAWEKE, say 1030 A. D., when that remarkable intermigratory movement between the Southern and Northern Polynesian groups, of which their legends and chants give so ample evidence, had already commenced. From MAWEKE down, therefore, Hawaiian chronology may be computed from any of the leading genealogies, counting MAWEKE as No. 29, PAUMAKUA as No. 30, and PILIKAEAEA as No. 31 from WAKEA.

Thus, to take a few genealogies out of many we get the following approximate chronological lists, viz:

HAWAII.

No.		A. D.
31.	Pilikaeaea	1090
32.	Kukohau	1120
33.	Kaniuhi	1150
34.	Kanipahu	1180
35.	Kalapana	1210
36.	Kahaimoelea	1240
37.	Kalaunuiohua	1270
38.	Kuaiwa	1300
39.	Kahoukapu	1330
40.	Kauholanuimahu	1360
41.	Kiha nui lulu moku	1390
42.	Liloa	1420
43.	Umi a Liloa	1450
44.	Kealiiokaloa	1480
45.	Kukailani	1510
46.	Kaikilani, (w)	1540
47.	Keakealanikane	1570
48.	Keakamahana, (w)	1600
49.	Keakealani, (w)	1630
50.	Kalanikauleleiaiwi, (w)	1660
51.	Keawepoepoe	1690
52.	Kameeiamoku	1720
53.	Kepookalani	1750
54.	Aikanaka	1780
55.	Keohokalole, (w)	1810
56.	Kalakaua, born	1836

OAHU.

No.		A. D.
29.	Maweke	1030
30.	Mulielealii	1060
31.	Moikeha	1090
32.	Hookamalii	1120
33.	Kahai	1150
34.	Kuolono	1180
35.	Maela, (w) and Lauli a Laa	1210
36.	Laulihewa	1240
37.	Kahuoi	1270
38.	Pua a Kahuoi	1300
39.	Kukaaliaililani	1330
40.	Mailikukahi	1360
41.	Kalona iki	13.0
42.	Piliwale	1420
43.	Kukaniloko, (w)	1450
44.	Kalaimanuia, (w)	1480
45.	Kaihikapu a Manuia	1510
46.	Kakuhihewa	1540
47.	Kaihikapu a Kakuhihewa	1570
48.	Kahoowahaokalani	1000
49.	Kauakahi a Kahoowaha	1630
50.	Kualii	1600
51.	Peleioholani	1690
52.	Kumahana	1720
53.	Kaneoneo	1750
54.	Kapuaamohu, (w)	1774
55.	Kinoike, (w)	1804
56.	Kapiolani, (w) born.	1834

MAUI.

No.		A. D.
30.	Paumakua	1060
31.	Haho	1090
32.	Palena	1120
33.	Hanalaa	1150
34.	Mauiloa	1180
35.	Alo	1210
36.	Kuhimana	1240
37.	Kamaloohua	1270
38.	Loe	1300
39.	Kaulahea I	1330
40.	Kakae	1360
41.	Kahekili I	1390
42.	Kawaokaohele	1420
43.	Piilani	1450
44.	Kiha a Piilani	1480
45.	Kamalalawalu	1510
46.	Kauhi a Kama	1540
47.	Kalanikaumakaowakea	1570
48.	Lonohonuakini	1600
49.	Kaakaualani (w)	1630
50.	Mopua	1660
51.	Kalahuimoku II	1690
52.	Kahikikala (w)	1720
53.	Kalokuokamaile	1750
54.	Kaohelelani (w)	1780
55.	Laanui	1800
56.	E. Kekaaniau (w)	1834

OAHU.

No.		A. D.
30.	Paumakua	1060
31.	Kumakaha	1030
32.	Luahiwa	1120
33.	Ahukai	1150
34.	Laa mai Kahiki	1180

KAUAI.

No.		A. D.
35.	Ahukini a Laa	1210
36.	Kamahano	1240
37.	Luanu.u	1270
38.	Kukona	1300
39.	Manokalanipoo	1330
40.	Kaumakamano	1360
41.	Kehakuakane	13.0
42.	Kuwalupaukamoku	1420
43.	Kahakumakapaweo	1450
44.	Kalanikukuma	1480
45.	Ilihiwalani	1510
46.	Kauhi a Hiwa	1540
47.	Kawelomahamahaia	1570
48.	Kawelomakualua	1600
49.	Kawelo Peekoa	1630
50.	Kau a Kaweloaikanaka (w)	1660
51.	Kukalanihoouluae	1690
52.	Kaiakea	1720
53.	Kekuelike-nui	1750
54.	Kaena Ku Kalili	1780
55.	Alanakaku Pionao (w)	1824
56.	C. Kaonohiulaokalani (w)	1840

1527—*November.* Arrival of shipwrecked Spaniards at Keei, S. Kona, Hawaii, in the time of *Kealiiokaloa.* Probably survivors from one of the three vessels under the command of Don Alvaso de Saavedra, bound from New Spain, to the Molucca Islands.

1555—The Hawaiian Islands discovered by Juan de Gaytan, on a voyage from New Spain to the Moluccas. The islands were called in Spanish, "Los Majos."

1736—*November. Kekaulike,* King of Maui, died and was succeeded by his son, *Kamehameha-nui.*

" —*November. Kamehameha I,* afterwards the famous consolidator of the Hawaiian group under one government, was born at Kokoike, N. Kohala, Hawaii.

1737—Early in the year the battle at Kawela, Molokai, between *Alapai-nui,* King of Hawaii, and *Kapiiohokalani,* King of Oahu, in which the latter was defeated and slain.

" —After the battle of Kawela *Alapai-nui* invaded Oahu, but towards the end of the summer concluded peace with *Peleioholani,* then King of Oahu, at Naone-a-Laa, in Kaneohe, Koolaupoko, Oahu.

" —Rebellion on Maui by *Kauhiaimoku-a-Kama,* against his brother *Kamehameha-nui.*

1738—Battle of Keawawa (between Black Rock and Lahaina), between *Alapai-nui* and *Kamehameha-nui* on the one side, and *Peleioholani* and *Kauhiaimoku-a-Kama* on the other side. *Kauhiaimoku* was killed. *Kamehameha-nui* assumed the government of Maui and *Alapai-nui* returned to Hawaii.

1752—*Keoua Kalanikupua-paikalani-nui,* the father of *Kamehameha I,* and nephew of *Alapai-nui,* died at Piopio, Hilo.

" —Revolt of *Kalaniopuu,* son of *Kalaninui-amamao* against *Alapai-nui.*

1754—*Alapai-nui* died at Kikiakoi, S. Kohala, Hawaii.

" —Battle (between Keei and Honaunau, S. Kona, Hawaii), between *Keaweopala,* the son and successor of *Alapai-nui* and *Kalaniopuu. Keaweopala* was defeated and killed and *Kalaniopuu* assumed the sovereignty of Hawaii.

1759—*Kalaniopuu* invades Maui and occupies the districts of Hana and Kipahulu.

1765—*Kamehameha-nui,* King of Maui, died and was succeeded by his brother *Kahekili.*

1768—*Kaahumanu,* daughter of *Keeaumokupapaiaaheahe* and *Namahana,* was born at Kauwiki, Hana, Maui.

1770—*Peleioholani,* King of Oahu, died.

1773—*Kumahana,* son and successor of *Peleioholani,* deposed from the sovereignty of Oahu and *Kahahana* elected King in his place.

1775—War renewed between Hawaii and Maui. *Kalaniopuu* was defeated at the battle called "Kalaehohoa" and at "Kalae-a-Kailio," in Kaupo.

1776—Battle called "Ahulau ka piipii i Kakanilua" fought near Waikapu sand hills, Maui, between *Kalaniopuu* and *Kahekili. Kalaniopuu's* famous regiment *Alapa,* comprising 800 picked men of the Hawaiian nobility, annihilated with the exception of two.

1777—*Kalaniopuu* again invades Maui. Repulsed at Lahaina, he invades Lanai; successful at Lanai, he invades Hamakualoa, Maui; defeated there, he retreats to Koolau, Maui.

1778—*January 18.* Capt. J. Cook, in command of H. B. M. ships "Resolution" and "Discovery," sights the islands of Oahu and Kauai.

" —*January 20.* Cook landed at Waimea, Kauai.

" —*January 29.* Cook anchored off west point of Niihau.

" —*February 2.* Cook leaves Niihau and proceeds to the N. W. coast of America and Behring's Straits.

" —*November 26.* On his return from the North, Cook sights Maui. On *November 30,* Cook being off Wailua, Koolau, Maui, *Kalaniopuu, Kamehameha,* and other chiefs came on board of Cook's ships.

1779—*January 17.* Cook anchored at Kealakeakua Bay, Kona, Hawaii.

" —*January 24. Kalaniopuu* returns to Kealakeakua from Maui.

" —*February 4.* Cook leaves Kealakeakua Bay, but returned on February 11th, to repair damages sustained in a gale of wind on the 8th.

" —*February 14.* Capt. Cook killed in an affray with the natives at Kealakeakua.

1781—*Kahekili* reconquers the East Maui districts and the fort at Kauwiki, at Hana. This was called the war of "Kaumupikao."

1782—*January. Kalaniopuu*, King of Hawaii, died at Kailikii, in Waioahukini, Kau, Hawaii.

" —*July.* Battle of "Mokuohai," between *Kamehameha I* and *Kiwalao*, son and successor of *Kalaniopuu. Kiwalao* slain.

1783—*January. Kahekili* invades Oahu; conquers *Kahahana* in the battle at Kaheiki and assumes the sovereignty of Oahu.

" —War between *Kamehameha I* and *Keawemauhili*, of Hilo, at Puaaloa, near Panaewa. *Kamehameha I* defeated and retreats to Laupahoehoe. The war called "Kauaawa."

1784—*Kekuhaupio*, the famous warrior chief of Keei, died at Napoopoo, Kona, Hawaii.

1785—*Kahahana* betrayed by his brother-in-law, *Kekuamanoha*, and killed.

" —The conspiracy and revolt against *Kahekili*, on Oahu, called "Waipio-Kimopo," suppressed.

" —War between *Kamehameha I* and *Keawemauhili* and *Keoua Kuahuula*, of Kau. Desultory fighting; no result. *Kamehameha I* returns to Kohala. This war was called "Hapun."

1785—*Kamehameha I* sends his brother *Kalanimalokuloku - Keliimaikai* to retake the districts of Hana and Kipahulu, on Maui. At the battle of Maulili, in Kipahulu, the Hawaiian expedition was defeated and driven out of the island.

" —The first foreign vessels since Capt. Cook's death, arrive at the Hawaiian Islands. On *May 26th*, the "King George" and "Queen Charlotte" from London, under Capts. Portlock and Dixon, touched at Kealakeakua Bay.

" —*May 28.* La Perouse, commanding a French exploring expedition, anchored near Lahaina, Maui.

1787—*August.* Capt. Meares, in the English ship "Nootka," and Capt. Douglas in the "Iphigenia" arrived at the Hawaiian islands. *Kaiana-a-Ahuula* goes with Capt. Meares from Kauai to China.

1788—*Kaiana-a-Ahuula* returns in the "Iphigenia" from Canton, China, to Kauai, and

1789—*January*, arrives at Kealakeakua, Hawaii, and is received by *Kamehameha I.*

17:0—*February.* Massacre of natives at Olowalu, Maui, by American ship "Eleanor," Capt. Metcalf.

1790—*March 17.* The "Fair America," tender to the ship "Eleanor" was cut off at Kaupulehu, N. Kona, Hawaii, by *Kameeiamoku*, and all the crew was killed except Isaac Davis, an Englishman.

" —*March 17.* John Young, an Englishman, boatswain of the ship "Eleanor," was kidnapped by order of *Kamehameha I*, and detained.

" —In the summer months *Kamehameha I* invades Maui, lands at Hana; proceeds through the Koolau District to Hamakualoa, and between Halehaku and Kokomo a battle was fought against the Maui forces. *Kamehameha I* victorious.

" —Battle of "Iao" or "Kepaniwai" fought between *Kamehameha I* and *Kalanikupule*, the son of *Kahekili. Kalani-kupule* beaten and fled to Oahu.

" —*Kalola*, widow of *Kalaniopuu* and mother of *Kiwalao*, died at Kalamaula, Molokai.

" —*Keoua Kuahuula* invades Hilo. The battle of Alae is fought, in which *Keawemauhili* is slain. *Keoua* carries the war into Hamakua and Waimea. *Kamehameha I* returns from Molokai, and the battles at Paauhau and at Koapapa, in Hamakua were fought between *Kamehameha* and *Keoua*, the latter retreating to Hilo, and *Kamehameha* stopping to recruit at Waipio.

" —*November.* Great eruption from the crater of Kilauea. A portion of *Keoua's* army passing by destroyed by showers of heated sand and cinders.

1791—Battle of "Ke-pu-waha-ula-ula" or "Kawai" fought by the combined forces of *Kahekili* and his brother *Kaeo*, king of Kauai, against *Kamehameha I*, at the Pali-Hulaana, near Waimanu, Hamakua, Hawaii. It was a sea-fight. *Kamehameha I* victorious.

1791—The Heiau of Puukohola, at Kawaihae, built by order of *Kamehameha I.*

" —*Keoua Kuahuula* treacherously killed at Kawaihae Bay by *Keeaumoku papaiaaheahe*, latter part of the year. *Kamehameha I* supreme on Hawaii.

1792—*March 3.* Capt. Vancouver, with H. B. M. ships "Discovery" and "Chatham," arrives at Kealakeakua bay.

1792—*May 11.* Massacre of Lieutenant Hergest and McGooch of the English store-ship "Dœdalus," by the natives at Waimea, Oahu.

1793—*February 13*—Second visit of Capt. Vancouver. Anchors at Kawaihae and lands the first bull and cow on Hawaii.

1794—*January 9* Third visit of Capt. Vancouver.

" —*July. Kahekili* dies at Ulukou, Waikiki, Oahu.

" —English vessels "Jackal" and "Prince Leboo" first to enter the harbor of Honolulu.

1795—*January 1.* Captain Brown of the "Jackal" and Capt. Gardner of the "Prince Leboo" with most of their crews massacred by *Kalanikupule* and his chiefs in Honolulu harbor.

" —*April and May.* Invasion of Oahu, by *Kamehameha I.* Battle of Nuuanu; defeat and death of *Kalanikupule.* All the islands subject to *Kamehameha* except Kauai and Niihau.

" —Latter Part. *Kamehameha I,* starts with his fleet to invade Kauai. Encountered a gale of wind in the channel, many canoes lost, returns to Oahu. The expedition called "Ieiewaho."

1796—Rebellion of *Namakeha* in Hamakua, Hawaii, *Kamehameha* goes to Hawaii in August, battle of Kaipalaoa in Hilo. *Namakeha* killed.

1797—*Liholiho* afterwards *Kamehameha II,* is born to *Kamehameha* and his wife *Keopuolani.*

1801—The fleet of canoes called "Peleleu," built by *Kamehameha I,* muster at Kawaihae, and

1802—*Kamehameha* goes with said fleet to Lahaina.

" —*Kameeiamoku,* father of *Hoapilikane* and of *Kepookalani,* dies at Lahaina.

1803—*January 23.* The first horse landed in Honolulu from a Boston ship.

" —*Kamehameha I* goes to Oahu to prepare again for the invasion of of Kauai.

1804—The pestilence, or plague, called "Ahulau" and "Okuu" is raging over the islands. *Keeaumoku-papaiaaheahe* dies this year.

1809—*Kaumualii,* King of Kauai, goes to Oahu and negotiates with *Kamehameha I* for the cession of Kauai at the death of *Kaumualii.*

1810—Isaac Davis died.

1812—*Kamehameha I* returns to Hawaii. The voyage is called "Kaniaukani."

1813—*Kauikeaouli,* afterwards *Kamehameha III,* was born on *August 11th,* to *Kamehameha I* and *Keopuolani.* The day of his birth, however, was in after years conventionally fixed for *March 17th,* but the above date is the testimony of his nurse *Emilia Keaweamahi,* wife of *Kaikeoewa,* Governor of Kauai. *Kauikeaouli* was born at Keauhou, N. Kona, Hawaii.

1815—*Nahienaena* (the Princess) born to *Kamehameha I* and *Keopuolani.*

" —Russians, under a Doctor Scheffer, build the redoubts at Hanalei, and the fort at Waimea, Kauai.

1816—The Russians leave Kauai. Building of the fort at Honolulu commenced by *Kalaimoku.*

" —*Pauli Kaoleioku,* first-born son of *Kamehameha I,* died in Honolulu, aged about 60 years.

" —*November 21.* Capt. Kohzebue, in the Russian corvette "Rurik," arrived at Kealekeakua, Hawaii; proceeds to Oahu and is the first man-of-war that entered the harbor of Honolulu and exchanged salutes with the battery there. The "Rurik" left Honolulu *December 14th.*

" —The present Hawaiian flag adopted as the national flag.

1819—*May 8. Kamehameha I* died at Kailua, Kona, Hawaii. His son *Liholiho* succeeded him as *Kamehameha II.*

" —During the balance of this year the Kapu in regard to eating was frequently and openly broken by *Liholiho, Kaahumanu, Keopuolani,* and most of the highest chiefs. In *October* the abolition of the Kapu, the "Ainoa," was formally proclaimed from Hawaii to Kauai.

1819—*August.* French Corvette "l'Uranie" Capt. Freycinct arrives at Kawaihae, Hawaii, *Kalaimoku* and *Boki* baptised by the ship's chaplain.

" —In *November* Revolt of *Kekuaokalani,* son of *Keliimaikai,* and cousin of *Liholiho,* in defense of the Kapu. Insurrection in Hamakua; *Liholiho's* troops defeated by the insurgents.

1820—*January.* Battle at Kuamoo, N. Kona, Hawaii, between the forces of *Liholiho* and *Kekuaokalani.* The latter defeated, and he and his wife *Manono* killed.

1820—General destruction and burning of Heiaus and Idols.

" —*March 30.* American Brig "Thaddeus," Capt. Hunnewell, from Boston, arrives at Hawaii, and on April 5th anchors at Kailua, Kona, having on board the first missionaries of the A. B C. F. M. This first party consisted of Rev. Asa Thurston and Rev. Hiram Bingham, ordained Missionaries, with their wives; Dan'l. Chamberlain, Tho. Holmes, Sam'l Whitney, Samuel Ruggles, Elisha Loomis and four Hawaiians, Honolii, Hopu and Kanui who had received some education at Cornwall Institute, and George Humehume, the son of *Kaumualii* the King of Kauai.

" —First Whaleship "Mary" Capt. Allen, enters Honolulu harbor.

" —*December.* *Liholiho* visits Maui.

1821—*February 4.* *Liholiho* visits Oahu.

" —*July 21.* *Liholiho* starts from Honolulu in an open boat and arrives at Kauai on the 22d. Conference with *Kaumualii*, who is brought as a *quasi* State prisoner to Honolulu, and *Keeaumoku-opio* appointed as Governor of Kauai.

" —*Kaahumanu* takes *Kaumualii* and his son *Keliiahonui* as husbands in October.

First Christian meeting house erected in Honolulu *Aug. 25th.*

1822—*January 7.* The first printed sheet in Hawaiian, was struck off at the American Mission, Honolulu.

" —*May 1.* Captain Kent presents to *Liholiho* in the name of H. B. Majesty a schooner, "Prince Regent," of 70 tons, fully armed and equipped.

"—*July 4.* First celebration of American Independence held in Honolulu. Acting Consul J. S. Jones, presiding.

" —*August 11.* First Christian marriage celebrated in the islands between two natives.

" —*August 13.* *Kaumualii* and *Kaahumanu* visit Kauai and returned in December.

" —*December.* First Christian burial of a native.

1823—*February.* Law proclaimed for public observance of the Sabbath.

" —*April 4.* Rev. Mr. Ellis arrives from Tahiti.

" —*April 26.* *Liholiho's* festival in commemoration of the death of *Kamehameha I.*

1823—*May.* *Hoapilikane* appointed Governor of Maui.

" —*September 16.* *Keopuolani*, widow of *Kamehameha I*, died at Lahaina and was buried there. She was born probably in 1778.

" —*October 19.* *Hoapilikane* is married by Rev. W. Richards to *Kaheiheimalie*, generally known as *Hoapiliwahine.* another widow of *Kamehameha I* and sister of *Kaahumanu.*

" —*November 27.* *Liholiho* and his Queen *Kamehamalu*, with their suite, leave Honolulu on board of the English ship "L'Aigle," Capt. Starbuck, bound to England.

1824—*March 23.* *Keeaumoku-opio* (generally known as George Cox), Governor of Kauai, died.

" —*May 22.* *Liholiho* and suite land at Portsmouth, England.

" —*May 26.* *Kaumualii*, ex-king of Kauai, died in Honolulu and was buried at Lahaina.

" —*July 8.* *Kamehamalu*, *Liholiho's* wife, dies in London of the measles.

" —*July 13.* *Liholiho*, *Kamehameha II*, dies in London of the measles.

" —*August 8.* George Humehume, son of *Kaumualii*, raises a revolt on Kauai and attacks the Fort at Waimea.

" —*September.* Battle at Wahiawa, Kauai. The insurgents defeated. *Kiaimakani* killed, *Humehume* taken prisoner and rebellion extinguished.

" —Fort at Lahaina built.

" —*Kapiolani* descends into the crater of Kilauea and defies the heathen Goddess *Pele.*

1825—*April 16.* Richard Charlton, English Consul, arrives at Honolulu.

" —*May 4.* English frigate "Blonde," Lord Byron, Captain, arrives at Lahaina with the corpses and coffins of *Liholiho* and *Kamehamalu.* Arrived at Honolulu on the 6.

" —*June 6.* *Kauikeaouli* is publicly proclaimed king, as *Kamehameha III*, in succession to his brother *Liholiho.* *Kaahumanu* is declared Regent during the Minority. The Chiefs' lands declared inalienable in their families.

" —*October.* The crew of the British whale ship "Daniel," Captain Buckle, attack the house of Rev. Mr. Richards, in Lahaina, but are repulsed.

1826—The U. S. schooner "Dolphin," Lieut. John Percival, commander, arrived at Honolulu.

" —*February 26.* The crew of the "Dolphin" attack the houses of *Kalaimoku* and Rev. Mr. Bingham, but are repulsed.

" —*April.* *Kahalaia* son of *Kalaimamahu,* and nephew of *Kamehameha I,* died.

" —*September 27.* The church at Kailua, Kona, Hawaii, finished and dedicated.

" —*October.* The U. S. ship "Peacock," Capt. ap Catesby Jones, arrives at Honolulu.

1827—*February 8.* *Kalaimoku,* son of *Kekuamanoha* and *Kanakahukilani,* (*w*), died at Kailua, Kona, Hawaii, and *Boki,* his brother, appointed Governor of Oahu, and guardian of the young King.

" —*July 7.* The ship "Comet," Captain Plaisard, from Bordeaux, arrives at Honolulu with the first Catholic Missionaries, Rev'd Messrs. Bachelot and Short.

" —*July 14.* First Catholic Mass celebrated in Honolulu.

" —*October.* Marriage of *Kinau,* daughter of *Kamehameha I,* and *Kaheiheimalie,* with *M. Kekuanaoa.*

1828—*September 14.* Cornerstone of Wainee church, in Lahaina, laid.

1829—*December 2.* Governor *Boki* and his company, in the brig "Kamehameha" and schooner ":Becket," leave Honolulu for a voyage to the South Pacific.

" —*Namahana Kekuai Piia,* sister of *Kaahumanu,* and wife of *Laanui,* died.

1830—*March.* *Kaahumanu* makes circuit of Oahu; also, during the year, circuit of Maui and Hawaii.

" —*August 3.* The schooner "Becket" returns to Honolulu from the South Pacific expedition and reports the brig "Kamehameha" lost and *Boki* dead.

" —Disturbances in Honolulu by the party of *Liliha,* widow of *Boki,* and daughter of *Hoapilikane.* *Kuakini,* brother of *Kaahumanu,* appointed Governor of Oahu; order restored.

1831—*September.* The Lahainaluna High School opened.

" *December 24.* The Catholic priests sent out of the country on board the brig "Waverly," by order of *Kaahumanu* and landed at San Pedro, California.

1831—*December 29.* *Naihe,* son of *Keawe-a-Heulu,* died, and *Kuakini* appointed Governor of Hawaii.

1832—*Kaahumanu* makes her second circuit of Maui and Hawaii.

" —*June 5.* *Kaahumanu* died. *Kinau* succeeds her as Premier ("Kuhina-nui.")

" —*August.* U. S. frigate "Potomac," Commodore Downes, arrives at Honolulu.

" —*September.* The disorderly conduct of *Kaomi* commences.

1833—*March.* *Kauikeaouli,* *Kamehameha III* assumes the Government. Revocation of most of the laws imposed by *Kaahumanu.*

" —The Bethel Church built at Honolulu.

" —*Kaomi* died.

1834—*February 14.* First newspaper printed in Hawaiian at *Lahainaluna,* called the "Lama Hawaii."

" —*June.* *Kamanele,* daughter of *Kuakini,* died.

" —The newspaper "Kumu Hawaii" commenced at Honolulu.

1835—First Hawaiian Almanac printed.

" —*Nahienaena,* sister of the king, married to *Leleiohoku,* son of *Kalaimoku.*

" —*December 16.* John Young dies in Honolulu.

1836—*September 30*—Robert Walsh, Catholic Priest, lands at Honolulu.

" —The newspaper (English) "Sandwich Island Gazette" commenced, Honolulu.

" —*December 30.* *Nahienaena* died at Lahaina.

1837—*April 17.* Bachelot and Short return to Honolulu on the brigantine "Clementine."

" —*May 20.*—Mr. Dudoit, owner of the "Clementine," hauls down her flag and surrenders the vessel to the Hawaiian Government under protest.

" —*July 7.* English surveying ship "Sulphur," Capt. Belcher, and on July 10, French frigate "Venus," Capt. dus Petit Thouars, arrive at Honolulu.

" —*November 2.* Mr. L. Maigret, Catholic Pro-Vicar, arrived at Honolulu in the ship "Europa."

" —*Nov. 7.* Extraordinary Tidal-wave sweeping the coasts of the Hawaiian group.

" —*November 23.*—Messrs. Maigret and Bachelot, Catholic Priests, leave Honolulu by order of Government.

1837—*Aikanaka*, son of *Keohohiwa* (w), and *Kipookalani*, and grandson of *Keawe-a-Heulu*, died.

" —The streets in Honolulu, as now existing, laid out.

1838—J. C. Jones, American Consul at Honolulu, superseded, and P. A. Brinsmade appointed in his place.

1839--*April 4. Kinau*, daughter of *Kamehameha I*, and *Kaheiheimalie*, wife of Governor *Kekuanaoa* and Premier of the kingdom, dies. The next day the King appoints his cousin *Kekauluohi* as Premier (Kuhina Nui).

" —*April 10. Kaikioewa*, Governor of Kauai, dies.

" —*May 10.* Hawaiian Bible, first edition, finished printing at the Mission Press.

" —*June 17.*—The King, in Council, issues orders from Lahaina that no more punishments should be inflicted on Catholics for religious differences.

" —*July 10.* French frigate "Artemise," Capt. La Place, arrived at Honolulu.

" —*July 14. Kekauluohi* and *Kekuanaoa* sign the treaty with Capt. La Place and pay $20,000 to France.

" —*August 25. Liliha*, widow of Governor *Boki* and daughter of *Hoapilikane*, died.

1840—*January. Hoapilikane*, Governor of Maui, son of *Kameeiamoku*, dies.

" —*May.* Mr. Maigret returns to Honolulu.

" —The Royal School for Chiefs in Honolulu commenced under Mr. and Mrs. Cooke.

-Kawaiahao Church, Honolulu, commenced.

" —*August 3.* Mr. Bingham and family return to the United States of America.

" --*August 6.* Corner stone of Roman Catholic Church in Honolulu laid.

" --*September.* Arrival of the U. S. Exploring Expedition under Commodore Wilkes.

" —*October 8.* First written Constitution granted by *Kamehameha III.*

" —*October 20. Kamanawa* and accomplice publicly executed for crime; the murder of *Kamanawa's* wife *Kamokuiki.*

1841—*May. Kapiolani* wife of *Naihe*, and daughter of *Keawemauhili*, dies.

" —The School at Punahou commenced.

1842—*January. Kahieheimalie Hoapiliwahine*, sister of *Kaahumanu* and mother of *Kinau* and *Kekauluohi*, died.

" —*July 8. Haalilio* and Mr. Richards as Commissioners, sail for the United States and Europe to secure the recognition of Hawaiian Independence.

" —*July.* Doctor G. P. Judd takes service under the Hawaiian Government and is appointed to fill the place of Mr. Richards.

" —*September.* Mr. Charlton, English Consul, goes to England via Mazatlan and is there removed from office. Before leaving, Charlton appointed Mr. Alexander Simpson as the Consul, whom the King declined to receive.

" —*December 19.* The United States acknowledge the Independence of the Hawaiian Kingdom.

1843—*January 18.* First number of the "Friend" printed.

" —*January 20.* Eruption on Mauna Loa Hawaii.

" —*February 10.* H. B. M. Ship "Carysfort," Lord George Paulet, Capt. arrived at Honolulu.

" —*February 17.* Lord George Paulet makes his demands on the Hawaiian Government.

" —*February 25.* The King under pressure from Lord Geo. Paulet and the English Consul, Mr. Simpson, cedes the islands provisionally to Great Britain and the English flag is hoisted on the Fort in Honolulu.

" —*March 14.* Mr. Simpson leaves with dispatches from Lord Geo. Paulet for England, and J. F. B. Marshall on behalf of the King, leaves in the same vessel.

" —*July 6.* U. S. S. "Constellation", Commodore Kearney, arrives at Honolulu.

" —*July 26.* H. B. M. Ship "Dublin" Rear-Admiral Thomas, arrives at Honolulu.

" —*July 31.* Admiral Thomas restores the sovereignty of the islands to the King; Hawaiian flag re-hoisted and saluted.

" —*August 25.* Gen'l Wm. Miller appointed English Consul General at Hawaiian Islands.

" —*November 28.* The independence of the Hawaiian Kingdom recognized jointly by England and France.

" —The Masonic Order established in Honolulu.

1844—First silk (197 pounds) exported from these islands. Raised on Kauai by Ch. Titcomb.

" —*July 6.* The U. S. Government formally recognizes the independence of Hawaiian Islands.

" —*July.* The newspaper "Polynesian" established in Honolulu.

" —*December 3.* Haalilio, one of the Hawaiian Commissioners to England and France, dies on his passage home.

1845—*March 23.* Mr. Richards returns to Honolulu with the remains of Haalilio.

" —*May 20.* The first Legislative Assembly, under the Constitution of 1840, opened by the King in Honolulu.

" —*June 7.* Kekauluohi, the Premier (Kuhina-nui), dies.

" —*June.* John Young, son of John Young, Sr. and *Kaoanaeha,* appointed Premier.

" —First Coffee (248 pounds) exported from Honolulu.

1846—*February 11.* Commissioners appointed to settle land-claims.

" —Oahn Temperance Society formed. J. F. B. Marshall, first President.

" —*March 26.* French frigate "Virginie," Admiral Hamelin, arrives at Honolulu and restores the $20,000 exacted by Capt. La Place in 1839. The French Consul General, Mr. Perrin, arrived in the frigate.

" —*March 26.* Treaty with France negotiated.

" —*March 26.* Treaty with England negotiated.

" —*June 9.* U. S. frigate "Congress," Commodore Stockton, arrives at Honolulu with the U. S. Commissioner A. Ten Eyck as successor of Mr. Brown, recalled.

" —*October 29.* The Danish frigate "Galathea" Capt. Steen Bille, negotiates the treaty between Denmark and Hawaii.

" —*December 10.* Excelsior Lodge I. O. O. F. instituted in Honolulu.

1847—*June 2.* Keahikuni Kekauonohi, wife of *L.* Haalelea and daughter of *Kahoanokukinau* and *Kahakuhakoi* w. and grand daughter of *Kamehameha I,* died in Honolulu.

" —*September 11.* The first theatre in Honolulu, the "Tespian," opened, corner of Maunakea and King streets.

" —*November.* Mr. Richards, Minister of Public Instruction, died.

1848—*January 8.* Treaty with Hamburg negotiated.

" —*February 1.* The French Consul, E. Dillon, arived in the French ship "Sarcelle."

" —*June 17.* Royal Hawaiian Theatre opened, corner of Hotel and Alakea streets.

" —The Measles raging through the islands. Commenced in the fall of 1847.

" —*W. P. Leleiohoku,* Governor of Hawaii, son of *Kalaimoku* and *Kuwahine,* (w), died.

" —Gold discovered in California, and in *August* the first party of Hawaiians, native and foreigners, started for the gold diggings.

1849—Beef first exported from the islands by Mr. French—158 barrels.

" —Admiral Tromelin, of the French frigate "Poursuivante," lands his forces and seizes the fort in Honolulu and the King's yacht "Kamehameha."

" —G. P. Judd, Minister of Interior, sent to United States, England and France on a diplomatic mission. He is accompanied by the Princes *Lot* and *Alexander.*

" —*December 20.* Treaty with the United States negotiated.

1850—Return of G. P. Judd and the Hawaiian Princes.

" —*June 8.* W. C. Parke appointed Marshal of Hawaiian Islands.

" —*December.* Rowe's "Olympian Circus," the first of the kind, arrived at Honolulu.

" —*December 20.* Honolulu Post-office established.

1851—*January 11.* Election of Representatives.

" —*June.* Court-house in Honolulu built, now Hackfeld & Co.'s store.

" —*July 10.* Treaty with England negotiated.

" —*August 7.* Treaty with Bremen negotiated.

" —*December.* Sailor riot in Honolulu.

1852—*January 25.* The first consignment of Chinese coolies arrive from Hongkong.

" —*February 10.* Eruption of Mauna-Loa, Hawaii, flow of lava reaching within seven miles of Hilo.

" —*June 7.* "Stranger's Friend Society" organized in Honolulu.

" —*July 1.* Treaty with Sweden and Norway negotiated.

" —*December 6.* Hawaiian Constitution granted by *Kamehameha III,* and proclaimed.

1852—*December 17.* First Hawaiian Cavalry organized in Honolulu.

" —Fungus first exported.

1853—*March.* Beginning of Small-pox epidemic, which swept over all the islands of the group and only abated in October.

" —*April 28.* Arrival of Mormon missionaries.

" *September 12.* Variety Theater opened in Honolulu.

" —Resignation of Dr. G. P. Judd from the Administration ; E. H. Allen appointed in his place.

" —*November 14.* Arrival of steamer "S. H. Wheeler", afterwards named the "Akamai," from San Francisco; enrolled in the coasting trade.

" —*December 20.* First regular Census of Hawaiian Islands taken.

1854—*June 1.* Fort at Lahaina demolished by order of Government.

" —*June 1.* Honolulu Steam Flouring Mill Co. started.

" —*October 14.* Steamer "Sea-Bird" arrives from San Francisco and is enrolled in the coasting trade.

" —*October 24.* Steamer "West Point" arrived from San Francisco and is enrolled in the coasting trade under name of "Kalama."

" —*December 15.* *Kauikeaouli Kamehameha III* died, and *Alexander Liholiho,* nephew of the late King proclaimed as *Kamehameha IV.*

1855—*January 10.* Funeral of *Kamehameha III.*

" —*June 13.* A *Paki,* son of *Kalanihelemailuna,* and grandson of *Kamehameha Nui,* King of Maui, dies in Honolulu.

" —*July 7.* Varieties Theatre in King street, Honolulu, burnt down.

1855—*August.* Rev. H. R. Hitchcock died at Kaluaaha, Molokai, aged 55 years.

1856—*June 19.* *Kamehameha IV* married Emma Rooke.

" —*June 22.* Mormons arrived en route for San Francisco.

1857—The Fort at Honolulu was demolished.

" —*Konia,* widow of *A. Paki,* died.

" —*May 29.* *Victoria Kamamalu* was appointed Premier.

* —*July 18.* John Young (*Keoni Ana*), the Premier, died.

1857—*David Malo,* the celebrated Hawaiian historian, died, and was buried on the summit of Mt. Ball, back of the Lahainaluna Seminary.

1858—*May 20.* The Prince of Hawaii was born.

1859—*April 20.* J. *Piikoi* died.

" —*July.* The Civil Code of the Kingdom was promulgated.

" —*July 23*—The Post Office Department was established.

" —*Sept. 9.* W. P. *Kinau,* son of *Leleiohoku* and *R Keelikolani,* died.

1860—*February.* The Custom House building was begun.

" —*July 17.* The corner stone of the Queen's Hospital was laid.

" —*August 29.* *Lot Kamehameha* visited San Francisco.

1860—*Sept. 5.* The steamer "Kilauea" arrived, to run between the islands.

" —*Sept. 23.* Rev. R. Armstrong, D. D. President of the Board of Education, died.

1862—*April.* The island of Palmyra became a dependency of the Hawaiian Kingdom.

" —*August 27.* The Prince of Hawaii died.

" —The Lahainaluna Seminary building was destroyed by fire.

" —*October 11.* Bishop Stayley and the Church of England Mission arrived.

1863—*November 30.* *Kamehameha IV* died, aged 29 years, and *Lot Kamehameha* succeeded to the throne, as *Kamehameha V.*

1864—*July 7.* The Constitutional Convention, called by *Kamehameha V,* convened, to frame a new Constitution.

" —*August 3.* The King dissolved the Constitutional Convention.

" —*August 20.* The King proclaimed a new Constitution.

" —*Levi Haalelea* died.

1865—*May 6.* *Queen Emma* left Honolulu on board of H. B. M. S. "Clio," for a visit to England.

" —*October 19.* R. C. Wyllie, Minister of Foreign Affairs, died aged 67 years.

" —*November 30.* The remains of the Kings were transferred from their old tomb to the Royal Mausoleum.

1866—*May 29.* H. R. H. *Victoria Kamamalu,* Premier of the Kingdom, and heir apparent to the throne, died.

1866—*October 22.* *Queen Emma* returned to Honolulu from her visit to England.

1867—*March 5.* The corner stone of the Pro-Cathedral of the English Church was laid.

1868—*April 2.* Great earthquake at Kau, followed by a burst of mud from a mountain side and a tidal wave which, together, caused great destruction of life and property.
— Great earthquake felt severely all over Hawaii.
" — Lava flow at Kahuku.
" — *October 19. Kaona,* the false prophet, incited an insurrection at Kona.
" — *November 24.* H. H. M. *Kekuanaoa,* Governor of Oahu, and father of *Kamehameha IV* and *V,* died, aged 75 years.

1869—*July 21.* The Duke of Edinburgh arrived at Honolulu.

" — *August 2.* The lighthouse in the harbor of Honolulu was lighted for the first time.

1870—*April 4.* Jubilee of the American Mission to the Hawaiian Islands.
" — *April 19.* The "Wongawonga," first China steamer, arrived from Sydney.
" — *September 20. Queen Kalama,* widow of *Kamehameha III,* died, aged 53 years.

1871—*March 18.* The new Post-office was opened for business.
" — *September 14.* Thirty-three whaleships were abandoned in the ice, in the Arctic.

1872—*March 1.* The Hawaiian Hotel was opened to the public.
" — *March 20.* The corner-stone of the new Government House (*Aliiolani Hale*) was laid.
" — *Kamehameha V* died, aged 43 years.

1873—H. R. H. *W. C. Lunalilo* was elected King by the Legislature.

1873—*January 9th.* The King took the oath to support the Constitution in the Kawaiahao church.
" — *July 12.* G. P. Judd, M. D. died, aged 70 years.
" — *September 7.* The great mutiny at the Barracks occurred.

1874—*February 3.* H. M. *Lunalilo* died, aged 39 years.

" — *February 12. David Kalakaua* was chosen King by the Legislature.

" — A great riot in Honolulu, during which the Court House and Legislative Hall were sacked by the mob, and several members of Legislature were fatally injured.

1874—*February 13.* The King, *Kalakaua,* took the oath to support the Constitution.

" — *February 14.* H. R. H. *W. P. Leleiohoku,* was proclaimed heir-apparent to the throne.

" — *Nov. 17.* The King departed for San Francisco, on a visit to the United States, on board the U. S. S. "Benicia."

" — *December 8.* The Transit of Venus was observed at Honolulu.

1875—*February 15.* His Majesty *Kalakaua* returned to his Kingdom on board of U. S. S. "Pensacola."

" — *October 16.* H. R. H. *Kaiulani* was born.

" — *Nov. 23.* The remains of King *Lunalilo* were placed in the Royal Mausoleum expressly constructed to receive them in the Kawaiahao church yard.

1876—*February.* The Government sent forward an exhibit to the Philadelphia Centennial Exhibition.

" — *Aug. 15.* The Reciprocity Treaty was ratified.

1877—*May 10.* A great tidal disturbance at Hilo occurred, which lasted all day, and did great damage along the shore.

" — *July 23.* The first telegraph and telephone line was constructed on Maui, connecting Haiku with Lahaina.

" — *Dec. 24.* A destructive fire occurred on the esplanade, Honolulu.

1878—*March 13.* H. H. C. *Kanaina,* father of King *Lunalilo,* died.

" — The inter-island steamer "Likelike" arrived at Honolulu.

" — *Sept. 8.* W. L. *Moehonua,* former Minister of Interior, died.

1879—The Kahului railroad, reaching from Kahului to Paia, was opened.

" — The first Steam Fire Engine was imported.

" — *December 31.* The corner-stone of the Palace was laid.

1880—The first Artesian well was bored in Honolulu.

" — The system of telephonic communication was established in Honolulu.

1881—*January 2.* The Chinese Church building was dedicated.

" — *January 20.* King *Kalakaua* set out on his journey around the world.

" — *April 9.* The Corner-stone of the "Lunalilo Home" was laid.

1881—Small Pox spread on Oahu ; 789 cases and 289 deaths.

" —*June.* Jubilee exercises were held at Lahainaluna, in commemoration of the 50th Anniversary of the establishment of the Seminary.

" —*October 29.* King *Kalakaua* returned from his journey around the world.

" —*November.* Great lava flow which reached Halai Hill, Hilo before it stopped.

1882—*January 1.* Postage stamps for the Postal Union were first issued in Honolulu.

" —*December 1.* Rev. Titus Coan, for many years Pastor of the Haili Church, Hilo, died.

1883—*January 1.* The Marine Railway was opened for business.

" —*February 12.* The Coronation of King *Kalakaua* took place.

" —*April 21.* The Y. M. C. A. building was dedicated.

" —*May 24.* H. R. H. *Ruth Keelikolani,* formerly Governess of Hawaii, died, aged 65 years.

" *October.* The O. S. S. "Alameda" arrived on her first voyage between San Francisco and Honolulu.

" —*November 1.* The inter-island steamer "Kinau" arrived.

" —*December 16.*—The first instalment of "Kalakaua" currency arrived.

1884—*January 1.* Postal notes were issued.

" —*March.* Foundation laid of the Hall of Records (Kapuiwa Hale).

" —*June 13.* Portuguese immigrants (917) arrived at Honolulu.

" —*August 11.* Rev. W. P. Alexander, for many years Principal of the Lahainaluna Seminary, died at Oakland, Cal.

" —*October 4.* Rev. D. B. Lyman, founder of the Hilo Boys' Boarding School, died at Hilo.

1884—*October 16.* Princess *Pauahi,* Hon. Mrs. C. R. Bishop, died.

1885—*February 5.* The foundations of the new Police Station (Kalakaua Hale), were laid.

" —*April 25.* Queen Emma, widow of *Kamelameha IV,* died.

" —*November 10.* P. *Kanoa,* formerly Governor of Kauai, died.

1886—*April 18.* Great fire in Honolulu, which destroyed a million and a half of property.

" —*July 10.* Postal Savings Bank was established.

" —*September 21.* Ocean Island became a dependency of the Hawaiian Kingdom.

" —*October.* Rev. L. Lyons, for 54 years missionary at Waimea, Hawaii, died, aged 79 years.

" —*Nov. 15.* The Jubilee Anniversary of King *Kalakaua's* birth was celebrated.

1887—*January 16–20.* Severe earthquakes occurred in the district of Kau.

" —*February 2.* H. R. H. *Miriam Likelike* (Mrs. Cleghorn) died, aged 36.

" —*April 12.* Queen *Kapiolani* set out on her visit to England.

" —*June 30.* A great political mass meeting was held in Honolulu.

" —*July 7.* The new Constitution was promulgated.

" —*September 13.* General elections to the first Legislature under the New Constitution were held.

" —*October 20.* Supplementary convention between the United States of America and His Majesty the King of the Hawaiian Islands, to limit the duration of the convention respecting Commercial Reciprocity concluded January 30th, 1875, ratified by the King, and November 9, proclaimed by President Cleveland.

" —*November 3.* The first Legislative Assembly under the new Constitution meets at Honolulu.

COMMON PHRASES

—— FROM ——

THE GREEK, THE LATIN, AND MODERN LANGUAGES,

RENDERED INTO HAWAIIAN.

NOTE.—L. LATIN, FR. FRENCH, IT. ITALIAN.

A

A la Française, Fr. *After the French mode,* mamuli o ke ano Farani.

A la mode, Fr. *In fashion,* e like me ke ano mau.

A priore, L. *From the cause to the effect,* mai ke kumu a i kona hoopena.

A vinculo matrimonii, L. *From the tie of marriage,* mai ka berita mare.

Ab initio, L. *From the beginning,* mai ka hookumu ana.

Ad infinitum, L. *To infinity,* i ka mau a mau loa aku.

Ad interim, L. *In the meanwhile,* ia wa no.

Ad libitum, L. *At pleasure,* ai i ka makemake.

Ad nauseam, L. *To disgust,* a i ke poluea.

Allons, Fr. *Let us go,* ina kakou.

Alma mater, L. *A cherishing mother,* he makuahine hanai.

Alter ego, L. *Another self,* ko'u lua.

Amende honorable, Fr. *A satisfactory apology,* olelo hoolaulea i aponoia.

Au fait, Fr. *Skillful; well instructed,* akamai.

Au revoir, Fr. *Adieu until we meet again,* aloha a hui hou kaua (or kakou).

B

Beau monde, Fr. *The gay world,* ka poe puni lealea.

Bête noir, Fr. *A bugbear,* mea eehia.

Billet doûx, Fr. *A love letter,* he palapala i ka ipo.

Bona fide, L. *In good faith,* me ka manao pono.

Bon jour, Fr. *Good day,* aloha hookaawale.

Bon soir, Fr. *Good enening,* aloha o ke ahiahi.

Brusque, Fr. *Rude; blunt,* kamaniha.

C

Cacoëthes scribendi, L. *An itch for scribbling,* ake e haku manao.

Cæteris paribus, L. *Other things being equal,* ke like na mea e ae.

Casus belli, L. *A cause for war,* he kumu no ke kaua.

Chef-d'œuvre, Fr. *A masterpiece,* he hana i pookela.

Comme il faut, Fr. *As it should be,* ka pono maoli no ia.

Con amore, L. *With love; earnestly,* me ka manao hoihoi.

Cui bono ? L. *For whose benefit ?* no ka pono owai la ?

Cum grano salis, L. *With a grain of salt; with some allowance,* me ka haohao o ka manao.

D

De jure, L. *By right,* mamuli o ka pono paa.

De mortuis, nil nisi bonum, L. *Say nothing but good of the dead,* e hai i na mea maikai wale no no ka poe i make;

De novo, L. *Anew.* Hou.

De Profundis, L. *Out of the depths,* mailoko o ka popilikia lipolipo.

Dei gratia, L. *By the grace of God,* ma ka lokomaikai o Ke Akua.

Demi-monde, Fr. *Abandoned women,* na wahine hookamakama.

Denouement, Fr. *Catastrophe* ka haule mai ana o ka poino.

Deo volente, L. *God willing;* ke oluolu o Ke Akua.

Dernier ressort, Fr. *A last resource,* he kokua hope loa.

Dies iræ, L. *Day of wrath,* la hoopai.

Dieu et mon droit, Fr. *God and my right,* Ke Akua a me ko'u pono paa.

Dolce far niente, It. *Sweet idleness,* luana wale; hiolani.

Dominus vobiscum, L. *The Lord be with you,* Ka Haku pu me oe.

Douceur, Fr. *A bribe,* he kipe'.
Dramatis personæ, L. *Persons represented in the drama,* ka poe i hoikeia ma ke kike' keaka.
Dulce et decorum est pro patria mori, L. *It is sweet and honorable to die for one's country,* he nani a he hanohano ke lilo ke ola no ka one-hanau.
Dum vivimus, vivamus, L. *Let us live while we live,* e eu a e hoihoi i ko kakou wa ola.

E

Eau de vie, Fr. *Water of life; brandy,* barani.
Elite, Fr. *A select body of persons,* he poe hanohano.
Employe', Fr. *One who is employed,* mea i hoolimalimaia e hana; he paahana.
En passant, Fr. *By the way,* a eia keia.
En route, Fr. *On the way,* ma ke alanui; ke hele mai nei.
Ennui, Fr. *Weariness; disgust,* molowa ka manao.
Ensemble, Fr. *The whole,* ka huina pau.
Entente cordiale, Fr. *Evidevces of good will,* ka lokahi o ka manao.
Entre nous, Fr. *Between ourselves,* iwaena o kaua wale no.
Entree, Fr. 1. *Entry,* ke komo ana.
2. *First course at table,* ka ai i kau mua ia ma ka papa aina.
Entrepôt, Fr. 1. *A bonded warehouse,* he hale hooahu no na waiwai i bona ia.
2. *A free port,* he awa ku moku i auhau ole ia na moku.
E pluribus unum, L. *One composed of many,* lokahi o ka lehulehu; *or* hookahi, ka huina o ka lehulehu.
Ergo, L. *Therefore,* nolaila.
Esprit de corps, Fr. *The animating spirit of a collective body,* ka manao hoihoi like o ka hui, a papa paha.
Esto perpetua, L. *Let it be perpetual,* e mau loa'ku no ia mea.
Et id genus omni, L. *And everything of the sort,* a me na mea a pau o ia ano.
Eureka, Gr. *I have found it,* ua loaa ia'u.
Ex officio, L. *By virtue of his office,* mamuli o ka mana o kana oihana.
Ex parte, L. *On one side only,* ma kahi aoao wale no; paewaewa.
Ex post facto, L. *After the deed is done,* mahope o ke ko ana.
Excelsior, L. *Higher,* iluna'e.
Exuent omnes, L. *All go out,* pau i ka hele iwaho.
Expose', Fr. *An exposition,* he wehewehe.

F

Faux pas, Fr. *A false step,* he hana kuhihewa.
Festina lente, L. *Make haste slowly,* e hoohikiwawe me ke akahele nae.
Fete champetre, Fr. *A rural festival,* he anaina hoolealea ma kuaaina.

Flagrante delicto, L. *In commission of the crime,* i ke ko ana o ke karaima.
Fusillade, Fr. *A simultaneous discharge of firearms,* ke kani like o na pu kipoohiwi.

G

Garçon, Fr. *A boy,* or *waiter,* he kiekikane, he kuene.
Gens d'armes, Fr. *Armed police,* na makai i hoolakoia me na mea kaua.

H

Hic jacet, L. *Here lies,* ke moe nei maanei.
Hic labor, hoc opus est, L. *This is labor, this is work,* he luhi keia, he hana keia.
Hoc age, L. *Do this,* e hooko i keia.
Honi soit qui mal y pense, Fr. *Evil be to him who thinks evil.* E poi mai ka ino i ka mea i manao ino.
Hors de combat, Fr. *Out of condition to fight,* hiki ole ke hakaka.
Humanum est errare, L. *To err is human,* ku i ke ano kanaka ke lalau.

I

Id est, L. *That is,* oia hoi.
In articulo mortis, L. *At the point of death,* i ka ipuka o ka make.
In esse, L. *In being,* ke waiho nei.
In extremis, L. *At the point of death.*
In flagrante delicto, L. *Taken in the act,* hopuia oiai e hooko ana.
In loco, L. *In the proper place,* ma kahi kupono.
In loco parentis, L. *In the place of a parent,* ma kahi o ka makua.
In medias res, L. *Into the midst of things,* mawaena konu o na hana.
In memoriam, L. *In memory,* mea hoomanaonao.
In perpetuum, L. *Forever,* mau a mau loa'ku.
In posse, L. *In possible existence,* e hiki ana paha.
In propria persona, L. *In person,* kino.
In puris naturalibus, L. *Quite naked,* kohana, olohelohe.
In re, L. *In the matter of,* no ka hihia.
In situ, L. *In its original situation,* ma kona wahi i kinohou.
In statu quo, L. *In the former state,* ma ke kulana mua.
In toto, L. *Entirely; wholly,* a pau loa.
In transitu, L. *On the passage,* I ka nee ana.
In vino veritas, L. *There is truth in wine,* komo ka waina puka mai ka oiaio.

L

Labor omnia vincit, L. *Labor conquers everything,* lanakila loa ka hooikaika.

Lapsus linguæ, L. *A slip of the tongue,* ha lalau o ke alelo.

Lapsus pennæ, L. *A slip of the pen,* he lalau o ka peni.

Lex non scripta, L. *The unwritten law,* ke kanawai i kakau ole ia.

Locum tenens, L. *A substitute; a proxy,* he hope; he panihakahaka.

Lusus naturæ, L. *A freak of nature,* he mea ano e loa.

M

Magnum opus, L. *A great work,* he hana nui.

Maitre, d'hotel, Fr. *A house steward,* he kuene nui.

Mal a propos, Fr. *Ill timed,* ku ole no ia wa.

Malum in se, L. *Bad in itself,* ino iloko iho ona.

Mêlée, Fr. *A riot,* he haunaele; uluaoa.

Memento mori, L. *Remember death,* e hoomanao i ka make.

Memorabilia, L. *Things to be remembered,* na huna mea hoomanao.

Mens sana in sano corpore, L. *A sound mind in a sound body,* he noonoo makaukau iloko o ke kino ikaika.

Meum et tuum, L. *Mine and thine,* ko'u a me kau.

Mirabile dictu, L. *Wonderful to be told,* kupaianaka ke haiia'ku.

Mittimus, L. *We send,* ke hoouna nei makou. He palapala hoopaa i ka lawehala ma ka hale paahao.

Modus operandi, L. *Manner of operation,* ke ano o ka hana.

Multum in parvo, L. *Much in little,* ka mahuahua o ka mea iki.

N

Ne plus ultra, L. *Nothing further,* i ka hopena loa; aole mea i koe.

Nemine contra discente, L. *No one speaking against,* aole mea i kamailio kue.

Nil desperandum, L. *Never despair,* mai paupauaho; mai make ka manao.

N importe, Fr. *It matters not; never mind,* he mea ole ia.

Nolens volens, L. *Whether he will or not,* ke ae oia a ke ae ole paha.

Noli me tangere, L. *Don't touch me* mai lalau mai ia'u.

Nolle prosequi, L. *To be unwilling to proceed,* e hoole ana e hoopii (ma ka aoao o ke aupuni).

Nom de plume, Fr. *A pen name,* he inoa kapakapa no ke kakau.

Non compos mentis, L. *Not sound in mind,* lalau ma ka noonoo.

Non est inventus, L. *He cannot be found,* ua nalowale loa.

Non sequitur, L. *It does not follow,* aole no laila.

Nota bene, L. *Mark well,* e noonoo pono.

Nous verrons, Fr. *We shall see,* e ike ana kakou.

Nunc aut nunquam, L. *Now or never,* aole loa ke ole a no.

O

Obiit, L. *He,* or *she, died.* Ua make oia.

Omnia vincit labor, L. *Labor conquers everything.* Lanakila loa ka hooikaika.

On dit, Fr. *Flying rumor,* lono wale ia.

Onus probandi, L. *The burden of proving,* ka haawe o ka hooiaio ana.

Otium cum dignitate, L. *Dignified leisure,* hiehie a kuapapa ka noho'na; or kuapapa a kuonoono.

P

Par example, Fr. *For example,* e nane; e laa.

Par excellence, Fr. *By way of eminence,* Pookela, kilohana.

Pari passu, L. *With equal pace,* me ka hehi like.

Par nobile fratrum, L. *A noble pair of brothers; two just alike,* he paa hoahanau nani; na kokoolua like.

Parole d'honneur, Fr. *Word of honor,* olelo paa oiaio.

Particeps criminis, L. *An accomplice,* he kokoolua ma ka hewa.

Parvenu, Fr. *An upstart.* (See Dict. *upstart.*)

Paterfamilias, L. *The father of a family,* ka makuakane o ka ohana.

Pater patriæ, L. *Father of his country,* ka makua o kona aupuni, or ka makua o kona lahui.

Peccavi, L. *I have sinned,* ua hewa wau.

Penchant, Fr. *Inclination; liking,* ka hilinai o ka manao; ke koho o ka manao.

Per contra, L. *Contrariwise,* ma ka aoao ku-e'.

Per se, L. *By itself considered,* i noonoo kaawale ia.

Personnel, Fr. *Body of persons employed in some public service,* ka papa (or kulana) o ka poe e lawelawe ana kekahi hana akea.

Poco a poco, It. *Little by little,* ma ka liiiii.

Poeta nascitur, non fit, L. *The poet is born, not made,* ua hanauia he haku mele, aole i aoia.

Pons asinorum, L. *Bridge of asses,* ke alahaka no na kekake; oia ka manaohai o ke Anahonua e pili ana no na aoao ekolu o ka huina-kolu-kupono.

Post mortem, L. *After death,* mahope o ka make.

Prima facie, L. *On the first view,* i kino hou o ka nana'na.

Principia, non homines, L. *Principles, not men,* na mole o ka pono, aole na kanaka.

Pro bono publico, L. *For the public good,* no ka pono o ka lahui.

Pro et con, L. *For and against,* he ko-kua a he ku-e'.

Pro rata, L. *In proportion,* ma ke kau-like.

Q

Quantum sufficit, L. *A sufficient quantity,* he nui kupono.

Quid pro quo, L. *One thing for another,* kela no keia.

Qui transtulit, sustinet, L. *He who transplants will sustain,* na ka mea i hehu e koo.

Qui vive? Fr. *Who goes there? On the alert,* e anehe.

Quod erat demonstrandum. *Which was to be demonstrated.* ka mea e we-hewehe ia'na.

R

Regnant populi, L. *The people rule,* e noho aupuni ana ka lahui.

Requiescat in pace, L. *May he rest in peace,* e maha oia me ka maluhia.

Resurgam, L. *I shall rise again,* e ala hou ana wau.

Revenous a nos moutons, Fr. *Let us return to our sheep;* that is, *let us return to our subject,* e hoihou kakou i ko kakou mau hipa; oia hoi, e hoi hou kakou i ko kakou kumu manao.

Ruse de guerre, Fr. *A stratagem of war,* he pahele o ke kaua.

S

Salus populi suprema est lex, L. *The welfare of the people is the Supreme Law.* o ka pomaikai o ka lahui ka makia ia o na kanawai.

Sanctum Sanctorum, L. *The holy of holies,* wahi hemolele loa.

Sans ceremonie, Fr. *Without ceremony,* me ka hookahakaha ole.

Sans peur et sans reproche, Fr. *Without fear and without reproach,* he wiwo ole a he makamae.

Savoir faire, Fr. *Ability,* makaukau.

Secundem artem, L. *According to rule,* mamuli o ka loina.

Semper felix, L. *Always fortunate,* po-maikai mau.

Semper fidelis, L. *Always faithful,* ku-paa mau.

Semper idem, L. *Always the same,* oia mau.

Semper paratus, L. *Always ready,* lo-lii mau.

Sic itur ad astra, L. *Such is the way to immortality,* oia ke ala i ke ola mau loa.

Sic transit gloria mundi, L. *So passes away the world's glory,* pela e mahani aku ai ka nani o keia ao.

Sicut patribus, sit Deus nobis, L. *God be with us, as he was with our fathers,* o Ke Akua pu me kakou, me ia i noho pu me ko kakou poe kupuna.

Similia similibus curantur, L. *Like cures like,* na ka like e hoola i kona like.

Sine die, L. *Without appointing a day,* me ke koho ole i ka la.

Sine qua non, L. *An indispensible condition,* he mea hiki ole ke hoole ia.

Soi-dissant, Fr. *Self styled,* kapaia iaia iho.

Stet, L *Let it stand,* pela iho.

Suaviter in modo, fortiter in re, L. *Gentle in manners, but resolute in deed,* me ke ano akahai e onipaa ke hooko.

Sub judice, L. *Under consideration,* ke noonoo ia nei.

Sub rosâ, L. *Under the rose; privately,* malu'.

Sui generis, L. *Of its own kind,* o kona like maoli iho no.

Summum bonum, L. *The chief good,* ka pookela o ka pomaikai.

Suum cuique, L. *Let each have his own,* e lawe kela me keia i kona iho.

T

Tempora mutantur, et nos muta-mur in illis, L. *Times are changed and we change with them,* huli ke au o ka manawa, a huli pu hoi kakou.

Tempus fugit, L. *Time flies,* ke mahani aku nei ka manawa.

Terra firma, L. *The solid earth,* ka hon-ua paa.

Terra incognita, L. *An unknown country,* he aina i ike ole ia.

Tout ensemble, Fr. *The whole taken together,* ka huina nui okoa.

U

Uitima ratio regum, L. *The last resort of Kings—war,* ke koo hope loa o na'lii —ke kaua.

Ultima Thule, L. *The utmost limit,* ka palena hope loa.

Utile dulci, L. *The useful with the pleasant,* ka waiwai me ka nani.

V

Vade mecum, L. *Go with me; a constant companion;* he hoa pili mau; hoa hele mau.

Vale, L. *Farewell,* me oe ke aloha; me oukou (or oe) ka pomaikai.

Veni, vidi, vici, L. *I came, I saw, I conquered,* hiki aku wau, ike aku wau, lanakila aku wau.

Verbatim et literatim, L. *Word for word, and letter for letter,* like na huao-lelo, like hoi na hua palapala.

Vi et armis, L. *By main force,* mamuli o ka lima ikaika; me ka lima kakauha.

Vincit omnia veritas, L. *Truth conquers all things.* Lanakila loa ka oiaio.

Viva voce, L. *With the voice,* me ka leo.

Vox populi, vox Dei. L *The voice of the people is the voice of God,* ka leo o ka lahui ka leo ia o Ke Akua.